News Clippings from Fillmore, Utah

1864 - 1900

Compiled from the Deseret News (Utah), Evening Dispatch (Utah), Millard County Progress (Utah), Provo Daily Enquirer (Utah), Richfield Reaper, (Utah), Salt Lake Herald (Utah), Salt Lake Mining Review (Utah), Salt Lake Times (Utah), Salt Lake Tribune (Utah), Territorial Enquirer (Utah), The Union (Utah), Union Vedette (Utah), Utah Enquirer, Wasatch Wave, (Utah) Washington County News (Utah) & contributions from other regional papers.

Often while working on family history (genealogy) I wonder about more than is listed on the pedigree sheets and am so grateful for their sacrifices and love for the generations to follow.

Some of the names include: Alves, Appleman, Atkinson, Bartholomew ,Beaugard, Bishop, Black, Bowley,Brenton, Brynum, Callister, Closs, Collier, Crane, Croft, Davis, Douglas, Faust, Frampton, George, Goulder, Greenway, Greenwood, Hanson, Henry, Hensley, Holbrook, Hook, Huntsman, Jensen, Jacobson, Judson, Kelly, King, Knox, Lambert, Liddle, Lyman, Mace, Manning, Marquadson, Maycock, McBride, McMicken, Melville, Merrill, NIchols, Nowell, Noyes, Olsen, Owen, Partridge, Payne, Penrose, Potter, Ray, Reese, Robinson, Robison, Roof, Rose, Sherman, Speed, Starley, Squires, Swallow, Talbot, Trimple, Tyler, Webb, Williams and many, many more.

Some of the articles are easier to read than others, please consider that they are 100 years or more old.

ISBN-13: 978-1533243522

ISBN-10: 1533243522

ARRIVAL & DEPARTURE OF MAILS

FROM

SALT LAKE CITY POST OFFICE.

DEPARTURES.

Eastern Mails.

For all places East of Salt Lake City, closes at 8 A. M. each day.

Western Mails.

For all places West of Salt Lake City, closes at 6 P.M. each day.

Northern Mails.

For Bannack City, East Idaho, on Mondays at 7.30 A. M.

For all settlements in Northern Utah and Soda Springs Idaho, on Mondays and Tuesdays at 7 30 A. M.

Southern Mails.

For all settlements in Southern Utah, including the Cotton country, all settlements in San Pete county, for Alpine City and Cedar Valley, on Tuesdays at 6 30 A. M.

For Fillmore City, and all settlements between Salt Lake City and Fillmore, on Mondays and Thursdays, at 6 30 A. M.

ARRIVALS.

Eastern Mails.

Arrive at Salt Lake City each day—P. M.

Western Mails.

Arrive at Salt Lake City each day—A M.

Northern Mails.

From Bannack City, East Idaho, on Saturdays 4 P. M.

From all settlements in Northern Utah and Soda Springs, Idaho Territory on Wednesdays and Saturdays at 4 P. M.

Southern Mails.

From all settlements in Southern Utah, in including the Cotton country, and all settlements in San Pete County, on Wednesdays, 5 P. M.

From Fillmore City, and all settlements between Fillmore and Salt Lake City, on Wednesdays and Saturdays, 5 P. M.

From Alpine City and Cedar Valley, on Fridays, 5 P. M.

Another phase of the Abduction case.

The abduction and seduction case, to which we referred a few days since, and which has excited considerable interest in the community, has assumed another phase. The party arrested—one C. M. White—and who was bound over by Justice Miner in the sum of $1,000 to appear before the next Grand Jury, was on Friday last taken before Chief Justice Titus on a writ of *habeas corpus*. Mr. Miner, who appeared against the prisoner, objected to the Judge investigating the case, beyond an inquiry into the legality of the papers. Judge Titus overruled the objection, and cited the Utah statute, to show that he was bound to inquire into the merits of the whole question, and the matter then came up *de novo*, all the witnesses being re-examined. Judge Titus decided that while the evidence disclosed improprieties on both sides, no criminal offence under the statute had been committed, and discharged the prisoner from custody. Such was the substance of the decision, although the Judge had a good deal more to say. He commented severely on the conduct of all parties engaged in this business, and gave the young lady some wholesome fatherly advice.

the circumstances disclosed, it was competent for the Court, while dismissing the *criminal* action, to have bound him over to keep the peace and refrain from further interference with the lady. Before rendering the decision, Judge Titus called out the Attorneys, and it is understood, this or a similar view was suggested, with the *addenda* that if White would pay the lady's expenses back to the train she had so injudiciously left, the holding him to bonds to keep the peace would be unnecessary. With this understanding the decision was rendered. Should the defendant fail to comply with this just suggestion, the Court can re-arrest and hold him to trial as we have suggested. We take this occasion to commend the course of the Chief Justice as one eminently sound in law, while his forcible remarks and strictures gave evidence that to the extent of his power, innocence and virtue will be protected against designing men, whether pretended or real friends. It is to be hoped that the young lady will take warning from this experience and not lend a willing ear to the protestations of friendship which strangers may for their own purposes whisper beguilingly to her. She has evidently escaped a snare which might have ruined her for life.

He also required that the defendant should pay her expenses from the time she left her friends near this city, and also her stage fare to Fillmore, where she might rejoin the train which she had left, under the inducements held out to her by White.

As there has been a good deal said about this decision, we propose to notice it more at length. The statute under which White has been arrested and committed to prison, reads as follows:

SECTION 19. If any person take or entice away any unmarried female from her father, mother, *guardian*, or other person having the *legal* charge of her person * * * he shall, upon conviction, etc., etc.

It is a well understood and wise rule of law, that criminal statutes must be strictly construed. The prosecuting witness herself ended the case when she testified that she was 21 years of age, had left her father's roof without his consent, had no guardian, and was in law and fact entitled to go when, where and with whom she pleased. The Judge so ruled, and under the law and his oath he was bound to discharge the prisoner. But there was another phase in this matter. White, although he had been guilty of no crime, had been guilty of improprieties and actions which gave the Court jurisdiction over his person. Under

We are told, that notwithstanding the manifestly righteous decision of the highest judicial officer in the Territory, it is still proposed to press the matter further and present an indictment against White. What may be the real and ultimate object of this course, it is unnecessary for us to say. The only result of it, however, will be to keep the young lady in this community for a month or two, and until her traveling friends have got beyond reach. Then indeed, will she be left a stranger in a strange land, and compelled to accept charities and gratuities from whoever they may be tendered.

A CUSTOM MORE HONORED IN THE BREACH THAN IN THE OBSERVANCE.

There are some of the institutions of Mormondom which excite our unqualified admiration, albeit like many others of the ungodly world outside, we are unable fully to appreciate all their inherent virtues. For instance, it must be eminently conducive to placidity of mind and equanimity of temper to have somebody else do one's thinking for him—to have some heavenly impressed being consider and dictate what we shall sell our wheat and barley for—to tell us whether we shall let our produce lie and rot rather than sell to "Uncle Abraham's minions" or the ungodly Gentiles—or through apostles, bishops and teachers instruct us just how many potatoes we shall cook for dinner. Then again it must be a state of supreme felicity tending to a delightfully indifferent lassitude (no pun, we vow) to be from time to time informed that our temporal happiness and eternal salvation require us to indulge in connubial joy of another wife. Still like many another poor mortal, there are times when we are entirely too obtuse exactly to "see it" in that light.

But we intended to say a word about another "institution" which seems to be in vogue here. Every now and then, once or twice a year, we hear of what are termed "drives" in the various parts of the Territory. At these times energetic and fleet vaqueros ride over the country and collect all the horses and cattle which roam the hills and valleys in the vicinity of the "drive." The farmers and others interested, assemble at the appointed rendezvous and select out their stock for branding or other disposition. Now, thus far, even our obtuse intellect can see some good in all this. But, when we are credibly informed that all the unclaimed (branded or not) stock is at once taken possession of by the "Trustee in Trust," marked with the Church brand and driven to other parts of the Territory, to enure to the benefit of the said Church, it does strike us that the institututton. yclept "drive" is liable to very great abuse and individual wrong. For instance, if a chap happens in some of the abstruse rites of the Church while ascending from the lower to the higher flights of the mysteries of the Temple—if, at such a time a Saint should break his leg, or albeit his neck, and be unable to attend the "drive," away goes his live stock, "his cattle, his horse and his ass." Or, If again. in Scriptural language. one has "married a wife" (a not unlikely event in this land of many mothers-in-law) "and cannot come," the Church forsooth, gobbles up his ox or his pony, and he has little recourse.

: Now we have heard a good many complaints about the way in which these 'drives" are conducted, and thought we sympathized with the poor folks who were thus bereft by this peculiar tithing arrangement of their property, but not until the thing comes home to us, do we fully feel the whole beauty of the thing. So long as the Saints themselves allow their cattle to be thus impounded for the benefit of the Church, it is to us very much like the tithing business, none of our particular concern, but when our own stock is thus bodily carried off and branded with the Church mark, under authority of a custom, whose heavenly character we do not fully appreciate, we think it is time most mildly but persistently to suggest, that this thing won't do. We are informed that at one of these recent drives two fine horses belonging to officers at Camp Douglas, and duly branded with their private marks, were thus gobbled up, the Church brand stuck on to them, and report says, hurried off

to Fillmore with other alleged Church property, similarly obtained, we suppose. We remember hearing Billy Birch, the famous California Minstrel, once complaining (on the stage) that he had been arrested, tried, convicted and sent to the Penitentiary, "just for walking off with a little piece of rope," and subsequently adding, as a matter of very little importance, "that there was a mule attached to the other end." A corporation (which the Church claims to be) has been defined to be "a thing without a body to be kicked, or a soul to be damned," but, we opine, there is enough personality about some of its chief men or lowly stewards, to be prevented from taking other people's property, even though they claim to do it by virtue of a custom of the Church of Jesus Christ of Latter Day Saints on earth, or by order of a council of most holy men.

Territorial Enquirer
April 27, 1886

"THE FILLMORE HOMICIDE."

Another Version of the Killing, Corroborated by Forty-Seven of Fillmore's Citizens.

Editor Enquirer:

In your issue of March 26th appears an article headed "The Fillmore Homicide," which contains statements that we, as citizens of this place, desire to correct.

The man Speed was not "a low, vicious character, despised by all respectable classes in the community in which he had lived;" on the contrary, he was an honest, industrious, unoffending man. He worked for different men in this community from time to time and gained upon their confidence and esteem as he became better known.

The "abominable practice," of which he is accused, we defy anyone to prove, nor was it heard of by us until after the murder.

The unmerciful beating spoken of consisted of slapping the boy two or three times on the side of the head. The wounding and bleeding must have been all in his feelings, as not a scratch was visible upon the boy at the time nor subsequently by those who saw him. According to the testimony of the dying man, as well as that given before the coroner's jury, Mr. McBride came towards the man Speed, revolver in hand; refused to hear Speed's version of the difficulty; struck at him with his revolver (which he fired at the same time) the pistol striking Speed on the side of the head, whereupon he took hold of McBride to save himself. McBride then fired two shots in succession, so near as to set the clothes of the murdered man on fire. One shot entered near the heart, the other near the right nipple. If Mr. McBride went about his business until called for, as you state, it was just then his business to run off and hide, nor was he found and arrested until about six hours after, when every avenue of escape was guarded.

We look upon the whole affair as a brutal murder, and view with contempt, and brand as despicable in the last degree, the effort of your informer (whoever he or they may be) to traduce the character of an innocent man who has been cruelly murdered, in order to shield the culprit from the hand of the law he has outraged.

It is due to the public that this be as widely circulated, by means of your paper, as was given the article to which this is a reply.

We subscribe ourselves for equal justice to all through the law.

[SIGNED.]

John W. Jackson,	John Bourne,
George Greenway,	W. B. Warner,
Almon Robison,	N. B. Baldwin,
H. Roof,	John McNield,
Ben Stewart,	John Anderson,
Wm. Speakman,	Ann Carling,
Tim Scottern,	J. A. Tyler,
C. Hansen,	Hans Peterson,
W. E. Robison,	Geo. O. Veill,
E. Bartholomew,	Daniel Rolph,
John Nichols,	Jesse Millgate,
J. L. Robison,	J. McMahon, Coroner
Edward Maycock,	Nelson Beauregard,
J. H. Holbrook,	Alex Melville,
A. V. Robison,	Dan Melville,
P. B. Stewart,	W. J. Gouter,
Theodore Rogers,	H. Mace, Jr.
Alex Foote,	William Jackson,
Thomas Turner,	H. H. Noyes,
Thomas Davies,	G. A. Sheil,
John Kelly,	Wesley Dame,
Milo Warner,	Geo. H. Davies,
James Rowley,	A. V. Robison,
	A. Lowder.

FILLMORE, April 10, 1886.

I know O. H. Speed. He was industrious, sober; had good habits. Never heard him use any bad language. Was quiet and peaceably disposed. Accusation made by McBride boy I am confident is untrue. I have never heard him so charged before. Has been in my employ three months and was intimately acquainted with him during the time.
(Signed)   J. H. MACE.

O. H. Speed worked for me two years and three months and never lost a day. Was a good, honest, industrious hard working man. Never knew him to be quarrelsome. Never heard the accusation made against him by McBride boy, before. Was not addicted to bad language.
. (Signed)   JOHN McNEILL.

DEPOSITION OF JOHN W. JACKSON.

McBride boy spoke to "Doc" from among a crowd of boys and said to him, "Doc" you would make a good sheep herder; then gave the reason as before published. Speed then slapped him on the side of the head two or three times, could not tell exactly. Did not see any blood upon the boy. Do not think he was hurt much as he was not struck hard. When the boy told his father, R. A. McBride, he said,—"I'll see about this" then went to "Doc" and said—"what have you been doing to my boy. "Doc" made answer" wait a moment and I will tell you." McBride then struck him on the side of the head with his pistol, at the same time firing it off. Speed then clinched his assailant and was shot twice, one ball entering the right breast, the other under left arm. Both men then fell partly down Speed underneath. McBride then got up and in answer to some remark that he had shot Speed and would have to suffer for it said,—Yes I have killed him and will kill any man who slaps my boy. Never heard before of Speed being accused of what the McBride boy charged him with.
(Signed)   JOHN W. JACKSON.

Salt Lake Herald
July 14, 1870

NOTICE —On and after Friday, July 15th, an express and letter mail will be forwarded from the office of Wells, Fargo & Co., via southern stage line, to Pioche (Meadow Valley mines), Provo, Nephi, Fillmore, Beaver, Cedar, St. George and intermediate points in southern Utah.

Leaving Salt Lake City every Friday at 8 a. m.; arriving at Pioche on Monday at 4 p. m.

Returning, leave Pioche every Wednesday at 8 a. m., arriving at Salt Lake City on Saturday at 4 p. m.
THEO. F. TRACY, AGT.

Salt Lake Herald
August 26, 1870

WHO IS TO BLAME?—Mr. Hammer, of the post office, gave us yesterday ocular demonstration of an act of mail delinquency which deserves the strongest and most severe censure. On the 16th inst. two mail sacks were despatched from this city tagged Fillmore and Toquerville, containing letters, paper packages and periodicals. On Wednesday night the same two sacks were received back by the post office here, with their contents in a most dilapidated condition. They bore the appearance of having been soaked for a few days in some creek. The wrappers were torn, soiled and had marks of frequent handling. Who is the delinquent in this matter? Who opened the sacks and handled the contents? Who caused the soaking to which they were subjected? Why did not the mail carrier deliver them at Fillmore and Toquerville, to which places they were tagged? Did the mail carrier pass them into the hands of any postmaster south with the tags torn off? And if so, why did not that postmaster re-tag them and forward them to their destination? It is to be hoped an investigation into the matter will not cease until these questions are satisfactorily answered. There has been an outrage committed in the affair on the post office department and the public, and it is due to both that the matter be sifted to the bottom.

Salt Lake Herald
September 1, 1870

PRESIDENT YOUNG'S MOVEMENTS.—By Deseret Telegraph line we learn that President Young and party held meeting at Scipio, Millard county, on Tuesday evening, at which the speakers were Elders Nephi Pratt, R. T. Burton and B. Young, Jr. The company left Scipio yesterday morning at 5.30 for Fillmore, which was reached at 1 p.m. Meeting was held there at 4 o'clock yesterday afternoon.

Salt Lake Herald
November 16, 1870

SOUTHERN STAGE LINE.—This line which now runs daily stages from this city to Fillmore, and on alternate days to Meadow Valley, the Star District and St. George, offers excellent facilities for travelling between the mines of this region and those of the Panaca country, as well as between this city and the various settlements south to St. George. Mr. White has lately largely increased the stock on the line. The coaches are comfortable, the animals lively, the drivers careful, and good accommodations can be obtained along the route.

SAVE A JOURNEY.—We understand from General Maxwell, Register of the land office of this Territory, that he, or some one for him, will make a trip south to enable the people living upon the lands lately surveyed to file their pre-emptions and make homestead entries. He will visit Fillmore and the various towns and settlements south to St. George, including those named in the notice of surveys published in yesterday's HERALD. This will be a very great accommodation to the people of that region, and an opportunity of which they should avail themselves to obtain titles for their lands. We need not bespeak for the Register that hospitable reception he is sure to receive; and his visit will save a tedious journey to those who would otherwise have to come to this city to make their entries.

HOTEL ARRIVALS.

Friday, December 2.

SALT LAKE HOUSE.

C M Brown, C P R R, Ogden; A S Gould and wife, city; J Campbell, C P R R; Wm Auman, U S A; A R McLain, city; S L Robinson; T W Wiswell, South Pass; M C Farwell, Carthage, Mo; John Boyd, South Pass; E M Wilson, Corinne.

TOWNSEND HOUSE.

A Sternfeld and lady, Boston; H R Bishop and two ladies, New York; G H Adams and wife, Cheyenne; J B Girard, U S A; Thos Rhodes, Akron, O; Russell Benedict, and Wm P Mallory, Chicago; Almon Robson and wife, Fillmore.

OMAHA HOUSE.

Board $2.00 per day. Free Omnibus from Railroad Depot.

Thursday, December 1.

C. A. Semler, Bingham; T A Cunningham, Little Cottonwood; G W Graham, City; Wm Sheuff, Nevada; Thos Ellis and Robert Ellis, Utah Mines; Jno J McNamee, City; J P Bradford and James Wilson, Colorado; Wm Rose, Jno Dearden, A D Baker and A Plummer, Nevada; Wm Hamlin, Pioche; S L McGuire, Sam Buck, Dan Dixon, Smith Dixon and H Hudson, Bingham; Mr Robb, U P R R; W J Ribelin, Little Cottonwood; S B Moore and M G Cughman, City; Jno Hogan, Bingham Canon.

CO-OPERATIVE ORGANIZATIONS.— A letter from Hons. T. Callister and F. M. Lyman, Millard county, to Hon. W. Woodruff, President of the Parent Society for the improvement of stock, &c.; on the subject of co-operative herding and other matters connected therewith, was read at the meeting on Monday night, from which we summarize as follows:

On the 13th of November, 1869, an association was organized at Fillmore for the improvement and raising of sheep. This society has been eminently successful, by moving the sheep, beforetime kept near the settlements and poorly cared for, to high, mountain ranges not previously pastured; and by keeping them in two herds—one of ewes and the other of wethers—under competent men, instead of in twenty herds badly looked after by children. The sheep have improved in wool, quality and healthy appearance most encouragingly. A dividend of thirty-seven and a half per cent. was declared on the capital stock of $16,000, at the end of the first six months.

On March 26th, another company was organized for raising and improving neat stock. A suitable herd-ground was selected, responsible herdsmen hired, and at the end of five months a dividend of twenty per cent. was declared on the capital stock of $28,000. This company uses one brand; and entrusts the sale of stock to one man, under the direction of the Board of Directors, who keep informed as to the price of stock and hold their marketable animals to it.

Improvements continue in progress at the herd ground; and the intention is to excel in dairy produce. A wise policy is being pursued for the improvement of stock, the preservation of ranges contiguous to settlements, and for increasing the property of the stockholders.

Five settlements out of six have Co-operative Mercantile Institutions in successful operation; and three of the settlements have organized for co-operative farming during the ensuing season.

This is a most encouraging record of the progress of co-operation in Millard county; and other counties that have not branched out so successfully nor to the same extent, may be benefitted by giving the practice adopted there a careful consideration.

FILLMORE.—"What's the news from Fillmore?" was a query we asked yesterday; and the reply was brief: "None; all is peace, quietness and prosperity." Good for the place, that; and the great public can look elsewhere for the news.

Salt Lake Herald
May 4, 1871

First District Court.

Judge Strickland's Charge to the Grand Jury.

HE "GOES FOR" THE SALT LAKE "HERALD."

All about the Man in the Moon Paying Jurors' Fees.

[By Deseret Telegraph Line.]

Provo, May 3.—The U. S. District Court for the 1st Judicial District, met yesterday morning, as per adjournment, Hon. O. F. Strickland presiding. The venires for grand and petit juries were returned by Deputy Marshal Paul. The names of the jurors were called, twenty-one grand and fifteen traverse jurors answering. The traverse jury was discharged till 10 a. m. to-day; whereupon the Court, after appointing William J. Hawley foreman of the grand jury said:

"I wish to say a few words in relation to the pay of jurors. The government has hitherto paid on their part, and it has been the practice for the Territory to pay on their part, until recently. The press of this country has made some wrong assertions in relation to the object of these courts, in that the courts had decided that the U. S. Marshal should receive funds to pay jurors for United States and Territorial business, and that he was the only lawful officer for this purpose.

This is not so. This question has never been before the courts and it has not been so decided. The papers put this before the people in a wrong light; and lately there was a piece in the Salt Lake HERALD, headed 'another attempt at outrage,' and referred to my going to Washington to endeavor to procure means through Congress, to run these courts in opposition to the people. These are not the facts. I have been to Washington to endeavor to raise money to pay jurors, and made an unsuccessful trip. I went for money to pay jurors who have served the people and should have their pay. It was for this purpose they have served the courts, as men and good citizens, and their services are very essential among the people. This Court has been respected, and with your help it shall continue to be.

In your deliberations you will consider offenses against the United States, for which you will be paid, and should I detain you a few days on Territorial business, it may be without pay; but I would advise you on receiving your certificate from the clerk, to put your accounts together and employ an attorney to collect your pay for you. I want you to have your pay, and do not care whether the Government, Territory or the man in the moon pays you, so that you get it. And we shall do all in our power to pay you. It is true that Judge McKean discharged his jury, not wishing to keep men from their work without pay; but these newspaper reports are not true.

Your first duties will be to investigate into matters pertaining to the United States, such as violation of the common laws, post office laws, &c. You will have the assistance of the United States Attorney, after which you will direct your attention to Territorial matters, such as murder, arson, robbery, &c., and I will call your attention to a case reported, wherein two men were arrested in Juab county, and while in custody attempted to escape and were followed and killed. I am informed these are not the facts. You will inquire into this; also a case of castration somewhere in Fillmore or other part of the district. Some of the citizens have made me acquainted with matters that I will call your attention to.

While east I had a personal interview with President Grant, and in speaking about this people he expressed the kindest feelings towards them. In the conversation he said you should be protected in your duties as jurors, he did not care if you were Mormons. We have no prejudice against Mormons, and this feeling is dying out among the masses of the people of the United States, and is only held to by a few crazy persons; but sensible men feel that Mormonism had rights as much so as other isms. I am glad to see this. There is no reason why one denomination should be held to account and others not. We desire to give every man his rights and protection, and to punish the unruly only. We desire to make our courts respected on their merits.

The clerk will now administer the oath, and you will retire to deliberate. You will appoint one of your number as clerk, and will meet and adjourn from time to time, as your duties may require.

The clerk administered the oath to the foreman, afterwards to the jury, and they retired to the jury room.

The Judge said: "We will now attend to the naturalization of aliens. If there are any present who desire their naturalization papers they will please come forward." Some fifty arose and twenty-three were admitted.

At 12 m. Court adjourned till 2 p.m. At 2 p. m. the Court resumed its session, and admitted some forty or fifty aliens. It then adjourned till 10 a.m. to-day.

SECOND DISPATCH.

Provo, 3, evening.—The grand jury was in session this morning but not this afternoon. The Judge stopped naturalizing to again lecture on the compensation of jurors. The jury is not yet charged on Territorial business. The Judge complained that he could not learn that jurors had been paid, or that the taxes which are duly paid had been properly appropriated. He did not know whether the jurors before the court could be paid without Congressional legislation, but hoped to be able to pay them by December. He said there is a quarrel between the Court and the Territory as to who shall pay court expenses; admitted that the law provides for the county courts to pay jurors; and read the law, but could not learn whether jurors had been paid.

The facts in this district are, that Utah county did pay all the fees of the jury for the entire district, until Judge Strickland, while on the bench a year ago, said it was unfair that one county alone should pay these expenses, and suggested a division of the expenses among the counties of the district; since which time Utah county has only paid when the cases originated in Utah county.

The Judge might have learned these facts if he had breathed a wish to learn the truth of the matter.

Salt Lake Tribune
May 17, 1871

SOLDIERS MAY BE REMOVED.—There is a rumor that the soldiers at Camp Rawlins are to be sent farther South, perhaps to Beaver county. We are not positive that Provo does not require a military post, but we are certain that soldiers are required in the southern part of the Territory. There should be at least one regiment sent south of Fillmore. We will refer to this subject again, and give such information as we are in possession of pertaining to the South and its needs in this respect.

Salt Lake Herald
May 30, 1871

POW-WOW.—That big Indian pow-wow is to be held on the east bank of Bear river, just south-east of Corinne, so soon as the "high joints" are assembled. There have already arrived chiefs and delegations, with their wives and families, from the White Knives of the Humboldt and Goose creek; Bannacks from Fort Hall; the broken bands of Bannacks and Shoshones from Soda Springs and Cache Valley. Wash-a-kie, with his band, now en route, camped last night at Bear Lake. Representatives from the Utes of the Uintah reservation; Shib-er-ech's, from Green river; Pah-vants from Fillmore, and Gosha-utes from Skull Valley and Tooele, are also expected to be present.

Little Soldier, now in town, who is the big "high joint" of the camp meeting, is very anxious that the delegates from the south should put in an appearance as soon as possible, and requests us, through the HERALD, to ask the whites in our southern settlements to notify the Indians of this fact.

We understand that there is considerable dissatisfaction among our red friends at the manner in which the government has neglected them in not carrying out treaty stipulations and leaving them without proper officers, there being no superintendent or regularly appointed agents in the Territory at the present time, except Mr. Critchlow, at the Uintah reservation.

Pleasure parties from the east, who never saw the noble red man in his native grandeur, can have an excellent chance to see the elephant in all his pristine glory on the banks of Bear river in a few days. Couldn't the railroads get up excursions specially for this purpose? We think it would pay. Where is Peter Cooper, Vincent Colyer, and the Indian peace commissioners? They should certainly have a delegate at this important convention of the Great Basin red men. Due notice of the day for the opening of the session will be given through the columns of the HERALD.

Salt Lake Herald
June 23, 1871

A SCANDALOUS PROCEEDING.—The following dispatch was received by Deseret Telegraph last evening:

Fillmore, 22. — Yesterday, while John Nicholls was crossing the valley east of Holden, in charge of the co-operative ewe herd of this county, consisting of 3,000 ewes and 1,800 lambs, a reckless band of men and boys on horseback forcibly took the herd and scattered it in three directions, driving them some five miles. The damage to the ewes and lambs is not yet ascertained, but is serious. Immediate steps will be taken to bring the offenders to justice. The herdsman considers William Probert, of Holden, was the leader of this outrage.

MILLARD COUNTY MAIL MATTERS.

FILLMORE, August 21, 1871.

Editors Herald:

It is becoming customary when any just cause of complaint arises on the part of the public, to ventilate it through the medium of your valuable paper, which, so far as I am able to form a just estimate, is always prepared to vindicate the right regardless of consequences. Every cause should have a proper hearing, but they don't always get it.

We have had very good reason for complaint against our postmaster here, but as things are now more satisfactory, it is not my purpose to animadvert upon those who may have endeavored to exculpate conduct the most insulting to a peaceably disposed community, who would not come in contact with it only from necessity to obtain their mail matter.

What I wish to draw attention to, is not the distribution of the mail, as matters now stand, but the carrying part. Your paper has several times spoken commendatory of the southern mail contractors and stage proprietors. It is understood that we have a daily mail, I wish this corrected. Government pays for a daily mail, and no doubt supposes it to be carried. Let me explain: The stage arrives every alterne's day, and a pony fills in the balance of the time. The conseqence is, a considerable portion of the mail, *i. e.*, the papers and the most bulky part, is left till the next day for the stage to bring, so that it amounts to a tri-weekly. It is consequently a drawback on subscribers to dailies, and an annoyance to every one interested in getting the news.

If this is according to contract it certainly does not meet the expectation of the people. It is no particular improvement on the "tri-weekly" arrangement of the days of "L. I.," when the mail carrier went up one week and *tried* to get back the next.

I trust you will give place to these few words from one who is

INTERESTED.

COMPLAINT WAS made through this paper, some little time ago, from Fillmore, Millard county, that the daily mail to that point was not properly nor fully carried every day. Col. Wickizer informs us that the matter has been attended to, and our subscribers there may expect to receive their copies of the HERALD regularly.

Salt Lake Herald
September 8, 1871

HOTEL ARRIVALS.

TOWNSEND HOUSE.
SEPT. 7.

A Bradley, Pittsburg; A M Wrenloss, England; A Ralston, G W Brown, Lockport, N Y; S R Brown, A Eilers, New York; H A Palmer and family, Oakland; M Watson, Jas Mooshall, Pittsburg, Pa; Mr and Mrs A W Stowe, Savannah, Ga; E Doggett.

SALT LAKE HOUSE.

H Newcomb, Boston; C G McGhee, Miss; J Jamie, M M Jamie, Rock Springs; S R Brown, New York; P A Ramee, Yokohama, Japan; S W Hyde, China; D W Fisher, H B Campbell, F H Hill, Big Cottonwood; Wm Bordee, Chicago; John Baker, Idaho; Wm Botsford, Bingham; Thos Jennings, Big Cottonwood; Geo W Crowley, Bingham; Henry Trumburn, San Fran; E P Johnson, Corinne; E B Garrett, Texas; M Webb Fillmore; H F McCarty, F St John, Cleveland, Ohio; S P Rancis, St Louis.

AMERICAN HOTEL.

Samuel E Rodgers, wife and son, Omaha; J M Russell and wife, Provo City.

Salt Lake Herald
October 3, 1871

Bishop Wm. Budge and Joseph R. Rich, Esq., from Rich county; Bishop Edward Partridge, of Fillmore, and Hon. Silas S. Smith, from Paragoonah, are among the earliest arrivals from a distance to attend the semi-annual conference.

SEMI-ANNUAL CONFERENCE.

SATURDAY, Oct. 7, 10 a.m.

Conference called to order by Prest. Geo. A. Smith.

Singing by the Tabernacle choir; prayer by Elder Joseph F. Smith. Tabernacle choir sang "Come all ye Saints, &c."

ELDER ISAAC GROO said the Latter-day Saints were a peculiar people, with peculiar institutions, and living in a peculiar country, but the people of God had been always deemed peculiar; and in support of this he cited numerous Biblical illustrations, referring among other instances, to Noah's building the ark and preaching the coming of the flood, and Abraham going to offer his son as a sacrifice. The plan of salvation was the same in the days of Jesus as it is now, but only in the Territory of Utah can the gospel now be found in its fullness; and no people in the world have so much reason to be thankful for blessings received. He urged the congregation to be faithful and prayerful, holding that everything that had been done to stop the progress of the work of God had only helped to advance it.

Hymn by Professor Fishburne's choir.

ELDER D. McKENZIE spoke next and dwelt on plural marriage, reasoning that it was scriptural and approbated by the Almighty. Once he was escorting Governor Shaffer to his hotel, and they met President Young who was introduced to the Governor. Afterwards the Governor remarked that the President was a very healthy and well preserved man, when the speaker answered that he lived so as to be healthy, for he was temperate in all his habits, and not licentious as

reported. Continuing on, the speaker referred to the Cullom bill, and said had it passed it would have had the effect of driving him into polygamy, as it would have done with all half-hearted Mormons; and the present course taken by parties here, if persisted in, would have a similar result. He dwelt on the law of adultery and its being given to a polygamic people, referring to the strictness with which it was enforced where polygamy was practiced, as recorded in the scriptures. Speaking of leading citizens being araigned before prejudiced courts and packed juries, he said, "we respect the law and trust in God," and prayed "Father forgive them, they know not what they do!"

Hymn by Professor Fishburne's choir.

BISHOP E. F. SHEETS made the law of tithing the subject of his remarks, and said the temple now being erected must be built by tithing. Two temples had been built by the Saints; one had been destroyed and the other passed into the hands of their enemies. Another temple had to be built; and it was the duty of the Saints to meet their tithing obligations, that there might be means for its erection. The speaker dwelt at some length on the doctrine of baptism for the dead; and testified to the truth of the gospel which he had embraced.

Anthem by the Tabernacle choir.

Benediction by Elder B. Young, Junr.

Adjourned till 2 p.m.

2 P.M.

Hymn by the Tabernacle choir. Elder Geo. Q. Cannon prayed. Choir sang an anthem.

The church authorities were then presented to the congregation by Elder Geo. Q. Cannon, for re-election, and were sustained by unanimous votes.

Fishburne's choir sang the anthem "Behold He that keepeth Israel."

ELDER GEO. Q. CANNON then presented the names of the following elders to the Conference, selected to go on missions to the Eastern States. The Conference sustained, by vote, the selection:

From Salt Lake City.—Wm. H. Miles.

From Farmington.—Thomas Stead, John Wood, Truman Leonard, Henry Moon, John S. Gleason, Charles Boin, Allan Burk, E. T. Clark, Daniel A. Miller.

From Ogden.—Israel Canfield, G. Rufus Stewart, Clinton Wilson, John R. Pool, Warren G. Child, Thomas Bingham, Jonathan Campbell, Dudley Chase, Jonathan Browning, B. C. Crichelow, P. Green Taylor, William Ellmer, Nathan Porter.

From Willard City.—Robert Henderson, Charles Harding, Omer Call, George J. Marsh, John Ousterhouse.

From North Willow Creek.—Chas. Hubbard.

From Tooele City.—Thomas Lee, Orson P. Bates., Robert McKendrick, David H. J. Caldwell, John J. Childs.

From Grantsville.—Alma H. Hale, Wm. C. Martindale, Edward Hunter, Benj. F. Barrus, Cyrus Bates, Samuel W. Woolley.

From Provo.—William A. Follet, Edson Whipple, James Bean, Jr., Robert T. Thomas, Sen., Wm. Haws, Orin Glazier, Joshua Davis.

From Springville.—Jacob Houtz, Sen., Wm. H. Kelsey, G. D. Wood.

From Spanish Fork.—Charles A. Davis, William H. Gay.

From Fillmore. — Gabriel Huntzman.

From Kanosh.—Collins Hakes.

From Holden.—Walter Stevens.

BISHOP ABRAHAM HATCH referred to the time the Saints were driven from Nauvoo, and compared it with the present. Then as now they were the most peaceable, orderly, law-abiding people in the world. In the town where he resided at present there was but one lawyer, and he was so poor he could not buy a law book, and had been compelled to run a mill; for there had not been a law suit in the town for the past three years. Now that lawyer is an honest miller. The speaker also referred to polygamy, maintaining the consistency and correctness of this article of their faith.

BISHOP A. O. SMOOT bore a strong testimony to the truth of the work in which he was a participant, and held that they had the immutable promise of God that it should never be overcome. The devil was doing his utmost to destroy the work, and chose agents who would serve him; but he and they would fail. The speaker hoped the Saints would continue to increase in faith, build school houses, promote education, encourage literature and science, and progress in good works.

ELDER W. C. STAINES reviewed the success which had attended the immigration of the Saints from Europe. Sensible people, business men and others, he said, desired to leave the Mormons and their religion alone, including polygamy; and only a portion of the religious sects approved the course of the officials here. He had just returned from traveling extensively in the east, while there in charge of emigration business, and this was the result of his observations and knowledge of public sentiment with regard to Utah matters. Polygamy, he said, was as much a part of the faith of the Latter-day Saints as baptism for the remission of sins; and when they appealed from the decision of courts with regard to it, they would not appeal to the world but to One above. After touching on the growth of the city and Territory, and the disadvantages under which they had grown; he said that God was satisfied with the course of the church leaders; and prayed that His blessing and Spirit might be with them and the people.

The Tabernacle choir sang the anthem, "Sing ye Jehovah's name."

Benediction by President George A. Smith.

Conference adjourned till 10 a.m. this morning.

Salt Lake Herald
October 15, 1871

[By Deseret Telegraph Line.]

AN ITEM FOR COL. WICKIZER.

Fillmore, 14.—There is something wrong with our mail communication. We have had no HERALD nor *Evening News* since Saturday, Oct. 7th. Three were due up to last evening. The coach and pony arrive every day alternately, but fail to bring the right mail. One letter last evening was the total mail for Fillmore. There were also two registered letters that should have been taken out at Nephi, for Sanpete county. Our HERALD and *Evening News* are very irregular.

C. MERRELL.

Salt Lake Herald
October 17, 1871

More of the Fillmore Mail.

Fillmore, 16.—We have received two *Evening News* for the last week, Monday's and Wednesday's; three are yet due. The mail arrived last night at 11 o'clock without papers or letters for Fillmore. No HERALD received for several days.

CLARENCE MERRILL.

Salt Lake Herald
November 26, 1871

Fillmore, 25th, 7:50 p.m. — The roads are in splendid condition and lined with teams hauling grain and produce to Pioche and other mining camps. A heavy wind is blowing from the south-west, with strong indications of a snow storm.

Salt Lake Herald
December 29, 1871

HOTEL ARRIVALS.

DEC. 28.

TOWNSEND HOUSE.

S A Raymond, San Fran; Theo L Couch, Sac; E Daggett, New Haven, Conn; F E Sargeant, East canon; John N Bell, Chicago; J W Schoonmaker, San Fran; E Ashley Smith, wife and family, Lockport, N Y; C L Morehouse, Cleveland, O.

SALT LAKE HOUSE.

N Armstrong, Ophir; Wm H Court, Unionville; Jona Barrett, Pittsburg; Fred Bosh, Ma; Leonard Martin, St Louis; S L Matheny, Fillmore; Eliza B Smith, Ill; George E Huntington, North Mo R R.

Salt Lake Herald
February 11, 1872

ELECTION RETURNS.—The county clerk of Tooele county furnishes the following election returns from that county, for the delegates to the constitutional convention. Six precincts had made returns to him, showing a vote of 670, divided as follows: Tooele, 260; Grantsville, 241; Stockton, 20; Johnson, 44; Vernon, 35; Mill, 70. Of the candidates, John Rowberry, R. Warburton, Edward Hunter, John Franks and G. W. Bryan received 670 votes each; G. Burridge, 645; and Dr. Stewart, 435.

The returns from Millard county also reached us last night, through the courtesy of hon. Thomas Callister. The vote cast in the county was 774, all for the convention, and unanimously sustaining the nominees, and was thus divided: Fillmore, 224; Holden, 113, Kanosh, 180; Meadows, 85; Scipio, 98; Oak creek, 74.

Salt Lake Herald
February 14, 1872

THE TRAINS.—The following telegrams were received over the Deseret line.

OGDEN, 13, 10:30 a.m.

Fillmore, the station at and near which all the trains are, is between Creston and Separation, instead of between Creston and Washakie as reported last night; and they are not expected to reach Creston to-day. The road is blocked as far west as Piedmont, and coal trains from Evanstown are unable to get through.

6 p.m.—The U. P. trains are still between Separation and Creston. The weather has been somewhat milder to-day.

The following was subsequently received over the Western Union line:

Carbon, 14, 3:30, p.m.—Bitter creek reports that no trains have passed there yet, and says they are still near Separation. Some passengers to-day walked to Washakie, and an engine and car are going down after them now.

Salt Lake Herald
February 15, 1872

THE TRAINS ON THE U. P. R. R.

[By Deseret Telegraph Line.]

Ogden, 14, 5.30 p. m.—The following has been received here:

Creston, 14.—Five trains are about half a mile east of here. There is about thirty hours' work to do before they can arrive. The passengers are all well, with plenty of food and fuel, and are in good spirits. The work trains from the west are within five miles of this station. We expect all the trains will pass here in thirty or thirty-five hours. Prospects are very flattering.

Green River, Feb. 14, 9:50, p.m.—We left the blockaded westward bound trains at Fillmore, at 6 o'clock, p.m., on the 12th inst., and walked with five others to Creston, ten miles, a perilous trip. We left Creston next morning and walked to Washakie, fourteen miles, arriving at 7 p.m. We encountered six miles of heavy snow drift between Fillmore and Washakie. Left Washakie on a special train at 11 p.m., arrived here at 4 a.m.; and leave to-night on a special.

The health of the passengers is good, and they are well provided, and all attention and every effort is being made for their comfort within the power of the railroad company. Salt Lake passengers are all well.

B. M. DuRELL,
JNO. E. COWLES.

[By W. U. Telegraph.]

Salt Lake Herald
May 12, 1872

THE CROPS SOUTH.—Dr. Taggart, U. S. assessor of internal revenue, got back yesterday evening from a trip south as far as Fillmore, and informs us that the crops along the line of his travel look splendid. The prosperous prospects of Utah were never better than at the present time, and with "good peace" prevailing, whether Utah continue a Territory or become a State, it will make a long stride forward in material prosperity during the present year.

Salt Lake Herald
August 7, 1872

COUNTRY RETURNS.—Below we give election returns received by telegraph. It is refreshing to know the Tooele dispatch was prepaid. We don't mean to insinuate anything.

Fillmore, 6.—Returns of votes cast for the People's ticket in this county, as far as ascertained, are as follows: Fillmore, 153; Holden, 125; Scipio, 113; three precincts not heard from.

Ogden, 6.—The following is the result of the election held in Weber county yesterday, for delegate to congress: Geo. Q. Cannon, 1,193 votes; Geo. R. Maxwell, 12 votes.

Tooele, 6.—Election in Tooele, so far as returns are made, delegate to congress, Geo. Q. Cannon, 690; Geo. R. Maxwell, 165. Commissioners to locate university lands, John Van Cott, L. S. Hills, J. Rowberry, 753; representative, J. Rowberry, 756; select-man, sheriff, superintendent of schools, and treasurer, no opposition, Four precincts not heard from.

R. WARBURTON,
County Clerk.

Salt Lake Herald
October 4, 1872

Yesterday we had the gratification of meeting Hon. F. M. Lyman, of Fillmore, Millard county, in town to attend the Fair and general Conference. He is hearty and healthy, and feeling excellently.

Salt Lake Herald
November 21, 1872

[By Deseret Telegraph.]

FRIGHTFUL ACCIDENT AT BULLIONVILLE.

Bullionville, Nev., Nov. 20.—A terrible accident occurred here at 4:20 this morning. F. Wagner, in the employ of the Magnet mill company, while repairing and adjusting the belt connected with the principal shafting, was drawn in and frightfully mangled. Mr. Wagner belongs to Fillmore, Utah, where he has a wife and child.

Salt Lake Tribune
November 25, 1872

Fillmore,

Which, by the way, was once the capital of the great Territory of Utah. This town is distant from Nephi sixty-three miles and is the County seat of Millard County. At this town I lay over one day in order to see the sights, and throw myself out, for it is an established fact that the temperature down this way is terribly frigid about this time in the year, consequently I advise everybody coming this way to bring plenty of blankets or buffalo robes. The population of this town as reported to me by our mutual friend Mr. John Kelly, is 1,000. The stage station at this town is kept by Mr. N. W. Bartholomew, who always gives the traveller a "square meal," gotten up in the latest approved style. I noticed in this town an indication of opposition to priestly rule, which appears remarkable, and goes a long way in convincing me that the anomalous power held over these people for years is on its last legs. An opposition beef market is run in this town by Mr. John Aloes, who informed me that "free trade" was "panning out" splendidly, for all those in opposition to Zions's co-operative arrangement. On leaving the above named town I took passage on the "jerky" that is run by Gilmno & Salisbury to connect this place with their main line to Pioche. This town,

Salt Lake Herald
December 4, 1872

WEATHER REPORT.—By Deseret telegraph we have the following territorial weather reports for yesterday:

Alta.—Very warm, scarcely any snow whatever.

Paris.—Very pleasant, no snow of consequence. Roads getting dry.

Logan.—Mild and pleasant. Very clear. No snow.

Nephi.—Pleasant. Quite warm.

Provo.—Very pleasant.

Pioche.—Clear and very pleasant.

Toker.—Fine. No clouds.

Beaver.—Clear and very pleasant.

Star.—Delightful. Clear and fine.

Fillmore.—Little hazy. Quite warm and pleasant.

Payson.—Fine and pleasant. Roads good.

Silver.—Warm and pleasant. Like midsummer. No snow.

Salt Lake Herald
February 4, 1873

THE STORM.

The following weather items were received by Deseret telegraph last evening, February 3:

Brigham — It has been storming most of the day; the snow is fifteen inches deep; there are appearances of clearing up and being cold.

Alta—Cloudy; not snowing now; no road broken; about one foot of new snow; total depth at least twelve feet.

Payson—Clear and cold.

Scipio—Snow about four or five inches deep; cloudy; wind blowing from south.

Fillmore—Had six inches of snow; it is clearing up now; quite cold.

Beaver—Cloudy; about four or five inches of snow; looks like more.

St. George—Cloudy and cool; occasional showers of rain since night before last.

Salt Lake Herald
April 23, 1873

THINGS LESS MORAL THAN MYSTERIOUS.

SCIPIO, MILLARD CO., U. T.,
April 20, 1873.

Editors Herald:

We have been in daily expectation of seeing an article in the HERALD, or some other good paper, on the all absorbing topic—"The civilization and moral improvement of the people of Utah."

Our reason for such expectation is that we have been favored with the presence of two reformers, (lady? and gentleman?), for the past few days. The gentleman arrived here per mail coach one morning and the lady per mail coach the next. The gentleman has been moving quietly around, doubtless simply taking items, whilst the lady has been visiting around oraculously descanting on the evils of polygamy.

The two are living here together, as man and wife, and the lady speaks very kindly of her husband(?) From the time of arrival of the lady, and a paragraph in your paper concerning a fracas in your city between two "soiled doves," wherein a champagne bottle was used freely and a few other trifles, also the advent of another lady this morning per coach, who seems, by inquiry, to be much interested in the whereabouts of the first two, we have wondered, could there be any connection with your paragraph and the above parties?

There has been talk of prosecuting attorneys, lascivious conduct, houses of assignation, etc.; but we have the fear of opinions, writs of habeas corpus and the like, before our eyes, and forbear.

Yours, etc.,
OBSERVER.

Later: Things did look for a little while this morning as though Utah might be minus a regenerator. Lady No. 2 admitted that she and No. 1 were the principals in the fracas referred to, she also hired a horse and an escort to take her to Fillmore; before starting, she proceeded to interview the gentleman and No. 1, but they declined to be interviewed, but were represented by deputy, and it's said money changed hands to settle. No. 2 was well armed, and that, in connection with sundry and divers threats, produced a stampede, and the way No. 1 and her partner dodged around haystack and fence was lively to say the least.

No. 2 and her chivalrous escort departed south, the lady remarking the "end was not yet." O.

Salt Lake Tribune
June 7, 1873

Departure of A. B. O'Dougherty.

Mr. A. B. O'Dougherty departs on this morning's stage for Fillmore and Salt Lake on important business. He may visit the Kanarra coal mines before he returns. John O'Dougherty, Mr. A. B.'s brother, is operating very extensively in the Sevier country, and we have heard it intimated that the latter's trip is connected with important local enterprises about to be inaugurated.

Salt Lake Tribune
June 16, 1873

UTAH SOUTHERN RAILROAD.

We are informed that the recent visit of railroad magnates culminated in an arrangement between the directors of the Lake Shore and Michigan Southern Railroad, and the directors of the Utah Southern, by which this important road will be pushed as far as Fillmore the present season.

If this news be true, and we have every reason to believe it is, there will be busy times this summer, and our Southern mining districts will rapidly rise in importance. Miners in Sevier and Star districts should take fresh courage from this information and develop their mines as fast as possible.

Salt Lake Tribune
June 20, 1873

Returned from Beaver.

We had a call yesterday from the Rev. Mr. Peirce of this city, who has just returned from a preaching tour of about five hundred miles, chiefly by stage, through Southern Utah. On Sunday, June 1, Mr. Peirce preached at Provo. The Methodists here have a beautiful church nearly completed. Sunday, June 8, Mr. Peirce preached at Beaver. By the courtesy of Bishop Murdock the Mormon meeting house was opened to Mr. Peirce at two p.m. of the above day. A large audience was present. Arrangements were made to have a Methodist school started at Beaver about the 1st of September, also for a Methodist preacher to take up his residence at Beaver in August. Mr. P. also held meetings at Fillmore, Wednesday evening, June 11. A large audience was present. Also in Payson, Friday evening, June 13, when between three and four hundred were present. Mr. Peirce favorably mentions the courtesy of Bishop Murdock, of Beaver, Bishops Callister and Partridge of Fillmore, and Bishop Tanner of Payson, through whom the meeting-houses of these places respectively were opened for Methodist services.

Salt Lake Tribune
August 15, 1873

The Experience of a Correspondent with the Powell Expedition.

A correspondent of the New York Times with the Powell Exploring Expedition, gives a history of his experience in Southern Utah. He says: "In Juab Valley, at Stewart's Ranch, we delayed a day to ascend Mount Nebo, the highest mountain of either Utah or Nevada. It is one of the Wasatch Range, and 12,000 feet high. Starting from Stewart's about four o'clock in the afternoon, we drove to the base of the mountains, about five miles. Then, with our blankets and rations upon our backs, we climbed till dark. We camped by a little spring, lighted a fire, and, after a supper of coffee and bread and chicken roasted in the coals, we retired to our blankets. The night was cold and we slept little. Early in the morning we renewed the ascent, and at 12.20 we stood upon the highest peak. Part of the ascent was difficult, and not without danger, perhaps for often we had to go where a misstep might be instant death. We were repaid for our toil by a glorious mountain view, extending from the Rocky Mountain summits in Colorado, to the mountains of Nevada, and from Salt Lake on the north, almost to the Grand Canyon on the south. We descended with much greater ease and rapidity, reaching the base of the mountain before dark, and proceeded five miles on our way to Fillmore, stopping for the night at Willow Creek, or Mona.

This is a rough country. As for the dwellings, very rarely can more than one bed be found in a house, and, for that matter, oftener than otherwise there is no room for more. If a man has more wives than one he manages to provide a room and bed for each. The children, young and old, sleep out of doors in summer. What they do in winter, is more than I can imagine. The "dwellers in Zion" do not seem to have even Ginx's knack for tucking away a round dozen of dirty babies. Sometimes there is a little bed in the yard near the door, or on the front porch, if there happen to be one. Sometimes it is an affair of dog-kennel architecture, placed near the wood-pile, or in some corner, into and out of which a big boy or a half grown girl may crawl, sleeping like a spaniel. We have found our most luxurious couches under a hay-stack. But such good fortune has not fallen to us often. We go to bed early, sleep soundly, get up with the sun, and have no headaches from bad ventilation.

Salt Lake Tribune
October 17, 1873

HELD FOR POSTAGE.

James Starley, Fillmore, Utah;
Mrs A P Waller, Salem, Oregon;
Mrs B Wren, Melbourne, Australia;
Postmaster, Granite, Utah;
Robert Chile, Deer Lodge, Montana;
Mrs Lydia West, Ogden, Utah;
& J Lyman, Clousdale, Nevada.

J. M. MOORE, Postmaster.

Salt Lake Herald
October 22, 1873

Like the more northern settlements money is scarce and business is consequently dull in Beaver, Parowan and Fillmore.

Salt Lake Tribune
January 4, 1874

PUBLIC SALE.

IN THE FIRST DISTRICT COURT, [...] Judicial District for the Territory [of] Utah, George Bodenburg and [Samuel] Kahn, partners under the firm name and [style of] Bodenburg & Kahn, complainants, [vs. Roy] H. McBride, Jack Oilmer and [Henry New-]bury, defendants.—Master's sale in chancery.

In pursuance of a decree in the above [enti-]tled cause to me directed by the First [Judicial] District Court of Utah Territory, [on the] 9th day of January, A. D. 1874, I [will offer] to public sale at the north outside door of [the] Court House, in Provo city, U. T., between the hours of 11 o'clock a. m. and 3 [o'clock p.] m., on Monday, the 15th day of March, [A. D.] 1874, the following described property, [to-]wit:

"That certain piece of property known [as] the 'National Hotel,' situated on [ ] in the city of Fillmore, Millard count[y, U.] T., the said building being built of brick [ ] in size about forty-five feet by thirty-[six to-]gether with all right, title, interest [and] of said Roy H. McBride to a [certain] land whereon said building [stands and] all the store houses and out houses [ ] and appurtenances thereto belonging.

The foregoing described property [to be] sold to secure the payment of a [certain debt] given by Roy H. McBride to Bodenburg [&] Kahn, and dated March 14, A. D. 18[72, in] the sum of thirty four hundred and [fifty-four] dollars and ninety-five cents ($3454.[95] [cur-]rency, together with accrued interest [thereon] and costs of suit. Terms of sale made [cur-]rency.

C. W. EMERSON,
Master in Chancery.

Provo City, U. T., Jan. 3, 1874.
jan21-44t

Salt Lake Herald
January 6, 1874

Fillmore Improvement Society.

Fillmore, Dec. 31st, 1873.

Editors Herald:

On Monday, the 15th inst., a Mutual Improvement Society was organized in this place. Our regular meetings are to be held once a week, and in addition a course of public lectures will be delivered weekly during the winter, the first of which will be delivered by C. Anderson on the evening of January 8th, subject, "The Origin of Man."

The officers are as follows: E. M. Webb, president; T. C. Callister, vice-president; E. P. Marquardson, secretary; W. E. Robison, treasurer; T. E. King, editor.

At our last meeting the following resolution was unanimously adopted:
Resolved, That the Secretary send a report of our organization to the Salt Lake HERALD and *Deseret News.*

The young people of Fillmore are wide awake, and do not intend to be left behind in the march of intellect.

E. P. MARQUARDSON,
Secretary.

Salt Lake Herald
January 21, 1874

(By Telegraph.)

MAN LOST IN THE SNOW.

He Leaves the Pioche Stage Near Fillmore and Wanders Off.

Fillmore, Jan. 20.

A man named Connell, who left Pioche last Tuesday by coach for Salt Lake, got out of the coach about three o'clock yesterday morning, six or seven miles west of Fillmore, to walk, for the purpose of warming himself, and has not been heard of since. Two men were out searching all yesterday, till eleven o'clock at night. They tracked him through the snow many miles. He seems to have taken nearly every point of the compass, and at one time came nearly into town. They left his track four miles north of here last night. A number of citizens are going to-day to take up the search where they left off. It is the general conviction that the cold caused him to become delirious. He is forty or forty-five years old, and has been in the boot and shoe trade at Pioche; had recently sold out and was going east.

Salt Lake Herald
February 4, 1874

Found.

From the Pioche *Record* of the 30th ultimo, we learn that James Connolly, an account of whose loss in a snow storm near Fillmore, appeared in the HERALD some days since, was found and taken to Fillmore. His feet and hands were badly frozen, and he was suffering from a deranged mind. It is feared he cannot recover.

DARK DAYS OF MORMONISM.

"The Jew Abraham" Presents the Poisoned Chalice to the Lips of His Tormentors.

Mr. Adolphe Rasin, in his address in the M. E. Church on Friday evening gave his personal experiences as a former member of the Mormon Church and was listened to with the closest interest. He was induced to become a disciple of the Prophet Brigham through the preaching of Parley P. Pratt, in Valparaiso, in 1852. The following year he left South America to gather with the Saints in Zion, and on arriving in Salt Lake, went into business as a merchant. He seems to have been a useful convert, for his contributions to the Church the first year of his membership, exceeded one thousand dollars. He took up his abode with the Apostle Pratt, and shortly after his arrival here, married a young lady sixteen years old, whom he also took to Pratt's house. Things went pleasantly for a time, till the Mormon propagandist began to cast longing eyes upon the Israelite's wife, and she not approving his suit, one day he made

A RUDE ATTEMPT UPON HER VIRTUE.

This rather affected the speaker's confidence in the divine origin of Mormonism, and he ventured to intimate to his host his entire disapproval of such free and easy proceedings. The Mormon preacher made light of his disciple's qualms, and proposed an exchange of the latter's wife for one of his own. "I had long followed the exchange of merchandise for a living," the speaker remarked, "but the article of wife I had never regarded as

A MERCHANTABLE COMMODITY."

He now thought the Kingdom of Zion a good place to get out of, and the following year he started with a company of emigrants for California. Arrived in Fillmore, the company fell in with Lee and Peterson, of Mountain Meadows notoriety, and some searching questions addressed by the first named to the speaker as to the arms and provisions of the party, led him to believe that an attack was designed. An attack was made the next night by a party of Danites disguised as Indians. The emigrants lost

TWO WOMEN AND AN INFANT

by their fire, and succeeded in driving the brigands off and killing two or three of their number. He returned shortly after with some goods, among which was a keg of brandy bought for his own use. Finding the teamsters were making free use of the liquor, he poured it out, for which offense he was arrested and prosecuted by Judge Stout.

He described at length his repeated attempts to leave the Territory and the impediments that were thrown in his way. In 1855 he was again arrested in Fillmore, on a charge of killing Indians, but the jury disagreed in consequence of one of them named Bear, having a sympathy, which Jedediah Grant deprecated, for those killed by judicial process, preferring the more pious method of saving the souls of transgressors by Blood Atonement.

The speaker gave full and interesting details of his ultimate escape from Utah, in company with Secretary A. W. Babbitt, W. S. Godbe and one Appleby. The death of Babbitt seems to have been designed, and towards the close of the following year, he was assassinated between Fort Kearny and Cottonwood by two men whose names are known. During these dark days of Mormonism, he mentioned the case of a married pair—the man a tailor and the woman a music teacher. This latter was employed to teach music in Brigham's family, and she not being favorably impressed with the royal seraglio, spoke of the inmates as a strutting rooster surrounded by a bevy of hens. For this license she was denounced by Bishop Woolley, who furiously demanded what right this woman had to mix with the family affairs of the Lord's anointed. The pair were cut off from the Church, and were quietly "used up" while on their way to California.

Mr. Rasin made a prolonged stay in the East, and during his absence, his wife was married polygamously to a man named Frothingham, who now lives in Beaver, by Squire Wells. He has fared roughly at the hands of the Church. Despoiled of his property, of which he owns considerable in this city, his wife and child taken from him, and his life placed in danger. He returned to this city a month or two ago, and is one of the many thousands in this Territory who are now watching the progress of the McKee bill in Congress, with absorbing interest, in order that he may have justice done to a murderous and debased Priesthood, who have robbed him of all that renders life desirable.

Cattle Starving.

A gentleman who keeps a stock herd at Cedar Springs, Millard county, arrived in this city from that place yesterday. He brings the report that it has been snowing there almost continually for the last two weeks, and when he left the snow was then three feet deep on the level. The feed was all covered up and cattle were perishing from hunger and cold every day. The snow is so deep that it is impossible to drive the stock to another range, and there is no hay in the vicinity. One man has lost several head of cattle, and unless there is an immediate change in the weather hundreds more cannot live. The snow is quite deep at several points between here and Fillmore.

PUBLIC SALE.

IN THE FIRST DISTRICT COURT, First Judicial District for the Territory of Utah. George Bodenburg and Samuel Kahn, partners under the firm name and style of Bodenburg & Kahn, complainants, vs. Roy H. McBride, Jack Gilmer and Monroe Salisbury, defendants.—Masters sale in chancery.

In pursuance of a decree in the above-entitled cause to me directed by the First Judicial District Court of Utah Territory, dated the 9th day of January, A. D. 1874, I will expose to public sale at the north outside door of the Court House, in Provo city, U. T., between the hours of 11 o'clock a. m. and 3 o'clock p. m., on Monday, the 16th day of March, A. D. 1874, the following described property, to wit:

"That certain piece of property known as the 'National Hotel,' situated on Main street, in the city of Fillmore, Millard county, U. T., the said building being built of brick, and is also about forty-five feet by thirty-three, together with all right, title, interest and claim of said Roy H. McBride, in and to the lot of land whereon said building is crooted, and all the store houses and out houses, privileges and appurtenances thereto belonging."

The foregoing described property will be sold to secure the payment of a mortgage given by Roy H. McBride to Bodenburg & Kahn, and dated March 14, A. D. 1867, for the sum of thirty-four hundred and fourteen dollars and ninety-five cents ($3414 95) currency, together with accrued interest thereon and costs of suit. Terms of sale, cash in currency.

C. W. EMERSON,
Master in Chancery.

Provo City, U. T., Jan. 9, 1874.
jan21-til

BURNED TO DEATH.

Fillmore News.

FILLMORE, March 8, 1874.

Editors Herald:

A resident of this city—Mrs. Joseph Judson, aged about sixty-four—was fatally burned at ten o'clock, yesterday morning. It is supposed she was doing her house work when, getting too near the fire, the flames caught her clothes. She was alone at the time. She ran out of the house, screaming for help. Her daughter was the first person who saw her and ran to her assistance, but was too late. Her clothes were all burned off, and her flesh charred. She expired at half-past six o'clock this morning. She has a son living at Salt Lake City.

We have had a severe winter, seventeen feet of snow having fallen on the level, causing the roads to be very heavy since thawing has commenced. A large number of stock on our range have perished. The snow has mostly disappeared, and we have hopes of better weather, though slush and mud are now the order.

The health of the people has generally been good during the winter, though many are now troubled with colds.

C. MERRILL.

President Young's Party.

The following programme of the journeyings, meetings, etc., of President Young's party, on its return from St. George, we take from last evening's *News:*

Leave St. George on Monday, April 6th, hold meeting at Belleyue at 4 p. m., and stay there all night.

Tuesday, 7th.—To Kanarra, and hold meeting at 2 p. m.

Wednesday, 8th.—To Cedar City, and hold meetings at 11 a. m. and 3 p. m.

Thursday, 9th.—To Parowan, and hold meeting at 2 p. m.; tarry there Friday and hold meetings at 10 a. m. and 2 p. m.

Saturday, 11th.—To Beaver, hold meeting at 6:30 p. m.; tarry over Sunday, 12th, and have meetings at 10 a. m. and 2 p. m.

Monday, 13th.—To Cove Creek.

Tuesday, 14th.—To Fillmore, hold meeting at Kanosh at 12 m. on the way.

Wednesday, 15th.—Tarry at Fillmore, and hold meetings at 10 a. m. and 2 p. m.

Thursday, 16th.—To Scipio, hold meeting at 12 m. on the way at Cedar Springs, and Scipio at 6:30 p. m.

Friday, 17th.—To Nephi.

Saturday and Sunday, 18th and 19th.—Hold meetings each day at 10 a. m. and 2 p. m.

Monday, 20th.—To Provo.

OLD EUCHRE IN FILLMORE.

The Profit Exhibits Him to the Saints in Wooden Shoes.

No Ruffs for the Ladies, and no Bread for the Gentiles.

Correspondence Tribune.]

FILLMORE, April 16, '74.

The inhabitants of Fillmore were started out of their prosy, kind of life Tuesday evening by the appearance among them of "the Prophet," with a few of his satellites. The people began to gather in little groups on the corners to discuss the probable result of the efforts that were to be made on the morrow to "Enochize" the people and bring them into the "united order." There was considerable difference of opinion expressed in the street, but when the vote was taken to see who would go into the "Order," and they were in the State House under the eye of the "Prophet," Mormon-like, they nearly all voted as he wished them.

THE PROFIT WANTS WOODEN SHOES.

Brother Brigham wou'd have worn a pair of wooden shoes, but there was none to be got in St. George. He told the people that when any of them who did not belong to the "united order" spoke to him, he wanted them to understand that they were talking to a man who was as high above them as the sun is above this earth. The sisters who join the "Order" are to

WEAR NO RUFFLES,

except those of their own manufacture, and they must quit trafficking with "our enemies." The "Enochites" are all to wear wooden shoes, to stop the expense of sending East and West for a poor article made by the Gentiles to sell. Some of our merchants would do well to order a few car loads of these shoes right off. The people who do not join are to apostatize and go to hell. "The car has started, has got over the rim of the basin into the great basin of America, and those who do not get aboard must get out of the way."

STARVING GENTILES OUT.

One of the speakers, (I think it was George A.) said that the grain raised by the people was to be stored away in bins, and when the grain famine stalked through the land of the Gentiles, they would have to come to Zion to get bread; then the people would appoint an agent to go East and buy up the "centre stake of Zion," in Jackson county, and the Gentiles will become the servants of the faithful, and be their "hewers of wood and carriers of water," the same as our jack-Mormons now are.

FOOL NONSENSE.

How long can such nonsense be stuffed into the people? They seem to forget that America is a free country, and that American citizens cannot be bought and sold as slaves; but the time will soon come when a great many of them will open their eyes and see the cloven foot, and then how they will regret the time that they signed away their possessions to the Lord's big thief.　　　　AMERICAN.

Sad Case of Bereavement.

We commiserate with Mr. Benj. Judson, in his affliction. Yesterday he had to bury his mother-in-law, who died of inflammation of the bowels; on New Year's day he buried his wife, who died from premature childbirth; about that time he received tidings of his mother being burned to death at Fillmore; and in the latter part of last year his child died of dropsy on the brain. Such a combination of bereavements we seldom hear of, and Mr. Judson, well known as the *Deseret News* engine driver, will, we are assured, have the sympathy of his many friends, in this, his last, at present, trouble.

In the trip to this city Mr. Clawson found the mail facilities and accommodation much better than has been represented. Mr. Hugh White, the new proprietor of the Southern mail line, is making a great change. New coaches are being put on the road, which hereafter will go direct from Fillmore to Beaver via Cove Creek; which will shorten the distance very considerably; and Mr. White will send passengers through in two and a half days from the end of the track. The people have great faith in Southern Utah, notwithstanding its vast beds of sand. The elements of progress is there, and they are being utilized by the people. Our sympathies are with "our Dixie."

Salt Lake Herald
July 14, 1874

Southern Stage Line.

Our enterprising friend, Mr. Hugh White, has taken possession of his recent purchase, the Southern stage line, and announces in this issue of the HERALD that stages will leave the terminus of the Utah Southern railroad daily, for Pioche, passing through Springville, Payson, Salt Creek, Fillmore, Beaver and Star and San Francisco Districts, making the trip to Pioche in fifty-five hours. Tri-weekly stages also run from Payson to the Tintics; from Salt Creek to the coal fields and all points in Sanpete County, and from Beaver to Parowan, Cedar and St. George. We understand Mr. White is restocking the road and will shortly put a number of new coaches on the line. Negotiations are also pending for securing the contract for carrying the Arizona mails via St. George and Hardyville, and within ninety days Mr. White expects to have a daily line of coaches running direct to Prescott. By this arrangement, the Arizona mails will reach their destination several days earlier than at present, besides the principal part of the passengers and express matter will go by this route, and we doubt not a brisk freight business will be carried on between Utah and Arizona. We wish friend Hugh success, and say to the travelling public that by placing themselves in his care all that can be done for their comfort and convenience will be accomplished.

Salt Lake Herald
August 14, 1874

PERSONAL.

Judge Partridge of Fillmore is in town looking well and hearty.

Salt Lake Herald
September 4, 1874

HOTEL ARRIVALS.

September 3.

TOWNSEND HOUSE.

G Rossiter, T H Major, M L Hass, San Francisco; L S Perry, S B Davis, D S M Bean, M S Brown and wife, Miss Brown, Chicago; H A Walker and wife, Boston; L W Johnston and wife, Miss Johnston, H B Todd, New York; T H Low, Galena Smelter; J Hutchins, Cleveland; W J Fordney, Lancaster, Pa.; H J Whitman, St Louis; G Baillie, England, J Pearson, Nottingham, England; E Watts and wife, Springfield, Ill.; E C Wessells, Nevada.

WALKER HOUSE.

W F Blackwell, W A Stephens, New York; W A Mitchell, Pierce Evans, San Francisco; W H Redemeyer, St Louis; A Schmolv, Germania Works; L L Warren and wife, Master O J Warren, Louisville, Ky.; E Schoenberg, Bingham; E R Burdick, Fillmore.

Salt Lake Tribune
September 5, 1874

FINANCE & TRADE.

MONETARY.

Corrected Daily by the Salt Lake City National Bank.

NEW YORK.

Gold opened at 109⅛.   Closed at 109½.

SALT LAKE.

Gold buying at 108.   Selling at 110.

SAN FRANCISCO STOCK MARKET

September 4, 1874.

Forenoon Report.

1815 Ophir 23 23½ b30 22½ 22½ b5 24½ 22½ s10 22½ b5 22½ 22½
410 C & C 22 21½ 21½
410 B & B 31 s1b5 33½ 33½
500 Savage, 80 b30 b4 60 b30 60½
60 Chollar, 66 66½
80 H & N, 41½ 41 41½
490 O Point, 69 70 b20 70½ 69½ s9
800 Jacket, 81 80½ 81 81½ 81½ 82
8105 Imperial, 9½ 9½ 9 b30 9½ 9½ 10 b15 10 10 b30 7½
8120 Empire Mill 10 10¾ 10½ 10½ s10 10½ 10½ b5
655 Kentuck, 15½ 16 16½ 16 15½ 10 b10
215 Alpha 13½ 14 13½
406 Belcher 72 71½ 71½
805 Confidence, 16 16½ 16½
145 Con Va, 7¾
623 Sierra Nevada 4½ 4½
20 Exchequer 73
170 Seg Belcher 100 103 20 b20 100 100
720 Overman, 45 46 45½ 46½ 45 45½ 45½ 45½
300 Justice 10½ 10½ 10½ b30
401 Buckeye 2½ 2½ 3
815 Julia, 3½ 3½ 3
255 Caledonia, 21½
161 Knicker 5½ 5½ b30
400 Ohio 1½ 1½
60 Bacon 2½
125 Bullion, 8½ 9
195 Baltic 7¼ 7½
1400 R Island 4½ 4½
50 Dardanelles 13½
100 New York 2½
185 Flat 7½
100 Tyler, 65c
170 Eclipse 7½

80 S Hill 7½
76 California 38½ 38½
150 Utah 8½
220 Dayton 5½
800 Nevada 1½
90 Franklin, 2½ 2½
1710 Woodville, 8 7½ 7½ b5 7½ 8 b30 8
100 N Overman 87½
800 S Cloud 1½
710 Senator 1
60 American Con 5
60 Pacific 6c
50 C Point Ravine 90c
100 Kossuth, 87½ 75c
100 Leo, 1½ 1½ 1½ b5 1½
60 Andes 90c

Afternoon Report.

70 Valley 5½ 5½
680 Eureka Con 11 10½ 11½ b30
20 Pioche, 7
170 Flag 2½
90 Belmont 9½ 9½ b30 9½ 9½ b16 9½ b30
700 Charlot Mill 10½ b30
50 G Charlot 7½
35 N Belmont 2½
100 Mahogany, 5
100 M Belmont 2½ 2½
100 O Hill 1½
100 Eldorado South 1½ 1½ 1½
25 Ku Klux 3
100 Cherry Creek, 1½
300 Eldorado North, 1½ 1½
20 Mammoth 20c
75 Empire Idaho 1½
165 Fillmore, 1½ 1½
280 Empire Mill 10½ 10½ b30 10½ 10½ 10½ s30 80
100 S Cloud, 1
50 Bellevue 25c
15 Justice, 16
400 Confidence 16 17 b5 11½
410 Savage, 59 68 59½ b4 59½
175 Imperial 10 9½ 9½ 9½
60 Seg Belcher 104 104 s10 101 103½ s10
250 Ophir 22½ 22½ 22½ 22½
450 Alpha, 14 14½ b9 1½
285 California 39 39½ 39 40
100 Con Va, 8 b5 8d
350 Jacket 82½ s10 82½ 82 b5 81 83½ b30 83½ b30 83½ 83 83 b30 84
130 O Point 66½ 70 70 70 70 b5
180 B & B 33½ 33 33½ b30
800 Belcher 71½ 71½ 71
695 Overman, 43½ 44½ 44 44½ 45 b30 44½
90 Baltic, 7½ 7½
100 Con Va, 8 b5 83
110 Chollar 57 58½
175 Woodville, 8 8½ 8½ b30 8½ 8½ b4 8½

IST OF LETTERS.

dvertised November 20th, 1874—which if
called for within thirty days will be
to the Dead Letter Office. Persons
ling for any of the following will please
Advertised.

LADIES' LIST.

A

derson B.

B

rey A, Broden A M, Betirman A M,
colm C, Burrows E, Brathol F, Est-
F L, Buckle J G, Barton H, Brandle T,
me M, Horoton M T, Bassett M, Bloget
Booth S J, Broqu C S, Brown L, Brown

C

immings L, Cross M Crouch N, Clougg
L, Crabtree M A, Clayton P, Chapman
Cable A, Cole Mrs, Chapman O, Claff S,
m E, Cowley A Cummins E E, Condie
, Clayton L

D

nuson L, DeBooth M L, Dick M G
lleg J F, Davis B, Davis L D, Davis M
ris E,

E

lliott J,

F

nsom O, Fisher F, Fowler H, Farrer J
urnam M M, Farnam M J, Finot D,

G

llan Mrs, Green E, Gale G H, Garner
Graven M.

H

athcote H, Hunter C, Harper E, Heag-
S, Howe M A, Hawks M A, Hansen M,
hos S E, Hardman R, Heywood E.

J

mes N, Jones J, Jenson C, Johnson E,
son B M,

K

lstrom W, Kessell M A,

L

renson E, Lewis E E, Libby Mrs,
Loe Larson T, Lingstrom L,

M

ay J, Milder C M, Miller G W, Miller M
ping M E,

N

rhtman O, Newton V D, Nathon M.

O

llar S, Oatland H, Oldham A,

P

erson M, Pratt S H, Pratt S N, Poter
E,

R

gers M, Eisely M, Roy F, Robson E,
F, Rodwell E J, Rigley H,

S

rley Miss, Sproul A, Slack E, Shaw L,
L, Skidmore M F, Smith M A, Smart

T

bot C T, Taylor H, Tatem M.

W

bster A D, Webb A E, White A. Walk-
B, Walcott E G, Wilson E A, Wheatly
hitney H, Wardrop M, Williams L.

Y

ung C, Young S.

GENTLEMEN'S LIST

A

on A, Arnold A 2, Allen L M, Ander-
, Alderston B K, Aarther G, Axsetton
Alexander R, Almire T J,

B

tty John, Barney Alex, Bashton John,
Jas, Brand George, Belonger L,
L, Daly D N, Bernat H, Bartlett H,
George Burgess H Byroll Edward,
E J, Barnes C, Bunting Chas, Pen-
H, Backwater J, Ball J D, Bryne J,
J, Brett J, Barnes J D, Bland J,
L 2, Bailey W, Battle W, Broum-
W, Enslow R, Barnes R, Bostwist O
um N, Bacon L W, Brown D O,
L A,

C

p A A, Canady A N B, Capes D, Car-
D, Counell D, Coves D, Caellion Geo,
E, Cruthen E D, Clayborne B, Cal-
, Crowell J, Chandler G, Chissolet E,
M, Campbell H, Carlson M, Cook S
ambers M D, Crane R W, Clark T A,
r W T,

D

glas J, Durke J, Duffenbacher W 2,
B,

E

worth B M, Emery H B, Eddey H M,
J F, Ernes J E,

F

lbory A T, Falt A, Fiveryear A,
m O, Fryer J, Fulce R J, Fuller R,
S 2, Fletcher S

... C, Gilmer J, Giles J B, Gillott J,
N D, Gardner B, Gear Wm.

H

ry A, Hindrads G G, Hall C W, Han-
Hook L 2, Hazel T B, Hubbard F,
ook G S, Hiel J, Haninson J, Hale J,
H J P, Hall M S, Hansen N, Hotchy
albot O, Harrison S J, Hungard J,
rd S, Highley Wm, Horn B, Hall T
ano Jy Bros, Hartley W B, Hill Wm.

I

b J.

J

ison & Taylor, Jackson W T, Judd T
son N M, Johnson G G, Johnson Wm

K

mead K 2, Kinney J F, Kinney J,
T.

L

per Dr, Longstraw A, Lunt Dan.
H, Lollin John 2, Lauraine J A.
B, Larson L, Lind J F, Langford
Lyon N H.

M

er A J, Merrill B G, Mind A L,
al E, Miller H E, Meredon J, Ma-
John, Mills J G, Miller J, Morris J O
A, Mathews N V, Maglan S, Monsly
s V K, Miller W H, Mills V R, Mc-
W B, McClery W Montague W A.

N

son A.

O

doyo Wm, Olson J, Openshaw J W,
H 2, Orchard Mr.

P

ian L, Fry S, Parsons T, Perkins W
engale B F, Payson A T, Pendleton
llips A J, Peabody D G, Parker D,
C, Perkins F, Pitts E, Pottet J, Pet-
M, Parr J, Paul J, 2, Peterson F,
se, Palmer J G.

Q

en's Montgomery. 5.

R

ck J G, Rapoll J, Robertson, John,
a R, Robinson Wm, Rogers & Donoh-
nfield A S, Rastall Mr; Runlow, O,
D K, Riley F, Reed P, Rhinsoern L,
s G F.

S

rd G, Shillingford B, Sandberg A
yer C, Skow G J, Sprague E A, Simp-
l, Snow F D, Stone F E, Stoneburg H
G, Seville G F, Simmons J, Sprague
rt J A, Stanberg M S, Shaw J G, Shel-
J, Sears T H, Scott Wm, Sant Art,
J, Sant J F.

T

mpson Chris, Treadwell G A, Thomp-
hn, Tillet James, Taplin J O, Toot J,
br J, Thompson J, Tucker S, Taylor
2, Toftgard O.

U

W H, 5, Ullett A.

V

dyke J.

W

on A, Wall A, Warm F, Wallcott E
ither G S, White G, Willson H, Whit-
H, Wortz J M, Wright James,
rd S, Waldin R A, Wicst T, Walcot
llams W T, William John, William

HELD FOR POSTAGE.

Brinhall, Spanish Fork.
orecroft, Green Creek Canyon.
een, West Jordan.
bbson, Rush Valley.
Harley, Stockton City.
A M McIntosh, Verginnia City, U,
andberg, Logan City.
Lynch, Tooele.
Kagoll, Omaha.
terson, Logan City.
oreman, Eureka, Nev.
Jones, Bingham Canyon.
Pratt, Fillmore City.
Jones, Fort Shaw, Montana.

Salt Lake Tribune
November 22, 1874

DESECRATION.

How Barbarism sits Enthroned in the Capitol at Fillmore.

The Government of the United States has at various times appropriated money to the extent of $60,000, for the purpose of erecting a Territorial Capitol at Fillmore, when that place was the seat of government in Utah. With this money the Territory built an edifice of some pretensions for the use of the Legislative Assembly and other public offices; but only a comparative trifle of the appropriation was expended in the work. Later, the seat of government was removed to this city where it has remained up to the present time, and is likely to be here for generations to come. The capitol at Fillmore was then gobbled by the Church and the bishops of Millard county, and is now used in various ways, but mostly for "religious" purposes, as the term is understood among the Mormons. In the chambers once dedicated to sorghum statesmanship, are to-day the tithing office, meeting house, and a dancing room in which the Saints and "celestial" mates trip their fantastic fetlocks, the divertisement being always sandwiched between the opening prayer of some libertine and the closing benediction of a hoary headed debauchee. From a gentleman who recently visited the place, we have a description of the mottoes painted on the walls of the sacred hurdy-gurdy room in this structure built at the expense of the American people. Over the "platform" where the stake fiddler draws the tanned bowels of grimalken across the equine capillaries is an inscription, "The Kingdom of God or Nothing!" and on one side the sticking phrase, "Polygamy forever." Opposite this is to be seen, in smoky characters, "Brigham the sword of the Lord," and in another place, "Vengeance for the Prophet Joseph Smith." "Many smaller mottoes are plastered over the walls, such as "The Seed of Israel," "Tithing the pass-port to Salvation," "We marry for Heaven," "Brigham is our Redeemer," "Hell for the Gentile," "The Government of God alone to be maintained." These are a few of the ornaments of the priests who have appropriated to their own barbarous use the property of all the citizens of Utah. Let us make the inquiry: Is it not the duty of the United States Marshal to have those infernal mottoes scraped off, and the building restored to the people?

Salt Lake Tribune
November 28, 1874

MARRIED.

BOWLY—LYMAN—At the residence of Mrs. Pricilla Lyman, Fillmore, on Saturday, Nov. 21, 1874, by Judge Partridge, Zuriah Bowly to Lorenzo S. Lyman, both of Fillmore.

BUTERBAUGH — BABCOCK — At the Townsend House, in this city, on Thanksgiving day, November 26th, inst., by Chief Justice McKean, Mr. George Buterbaugh to Miss Alice Babcock, both of Corinne.

RIDEOUT—TAYLOR—In this city, on Thanksgiving day, November 26th, inst., by Chief Justice McKean, Mr. Everett N. Rideout to Miss Mary Taylor, both of this city.

[Special to The Tribune.]

Royalty on Its Travels.

FILLMORE, Feb. 16.—The royal party arrived at Cove Creek yesterday at 2.10 p.m., where we remained all night, the guests of Brother Hinckley. A testimony meeting was held in the evening, which was a very enjoyable affair. The spirit of the late B.Y. appeared in our midst and said, "Not long since, when the Saints were discouraged and cast down by the persecutions of the ungodly, the Lord did give to me a revelation, that before the carrot crop should be gathered to the garner, he would raise up from the midst of our enemies a friend and champion. The record of George Seizer shows that my prophecy was fulfilled. So also did I prophesy in St. George this winter that a mightier than Seizer should soon arise from the ranks of the unfaithful. He has arisen."

The communication of the materialized spirit was received with great approval, President Geo. A. Smith being moved to tears.

I stopped at Kanosh long enough to instruct the Indians more fully in the Blood Atonement degree, and to give them their orders as to their future conduct in case Brother Allapico should fail to keep up Brother John D. Lee's spirits.

A revelation was read from B. Y., stating that on no account was he (J. D.) to be allowed to turn State's evidence. Brothers Spicer and Seizer are authorized to promise him anything, even to calling out the Nauvoo Legion and taking him from the scaffold, if necessary; but in case he doubts our power, then must he be taken from the post and blood-atoned.

Arrived at Fillmore at 3:30 p.m. Were not the guests of Apostle Amasa Lyman. Will probably reach Buttermilk Fort and perhaps Round Valley to-morrow; the day after will proceed to Levan, that Danite stronghold, and may, perhaps reach Nephi. In case we do, will be the guests of Bishop Foote, of Sevier bridge and Aiken brothers notoriety, and the next day will reach the end of the track, where we will be met by the Nauvoo Legion, together with a large and enthusiastic band of jacks, who came here to make money. A grand distribution of Axtell grease will then take place. This grease is warranted to be far superior to Hucks & Lambert's—I know whereof I affirm, as I have used both. GREASED LIGHTNING.

SALT LAKE CITY TO PIOCHE.

Table of Distances by Rail and Stage.

By Rail, ...75 miles
" Stage, ...232 "

307 miles

We give below, for the benefit of traveling public, the distances between the several stage stations on this route. We believe the railroad will steadily move southward, thereby, from time to time, shortening the stage transit:

		Miles
Salt Lake City	to York, rail,	75
York	" Nephi, stage,	10½
Nephi	" Chicken Creek	13
Chicken Creek	" Sevier	12
Sevier Bridge	" Scipio	10
Scipio	" Holden	14
Holden	" Fillmore	9
Fillmore	" Corn Creek	12
*Corn Creek	" Twin Peaks	11
Twin Peaks	" Antelope	12
Antelope	" Riverside	12
Riverside	" Shauntie	14
Shauntie	" Blue Mount'n	18
Blue Mountain	" Sulphur	14
Sulphur	" Cottonwood	18
Cottonwood	" Hanson's	13
Hanson's	" Rose Valley	18
Rose Valley	" Pioche	15

Total miles, 307

*Corn Creek is the point where this route turns southwest to Pioche. The main road to Beaver and St. George, with stage connections, keeps the general course of our great valley.

Salt Lake Herald
August 14, 1875

PERSONAL.

F. B. Gillmore, representing the Omaha distillers and liquor dealers, Iler & Co., is in the city.

Bishop Callister, of Fillmore, arrived in the city last evening.

Salt Lake Herald
September 5, 1875

PERSONAL.

Bishop Callister, of Fillmore, is in town.

Salt Lake Tribune
September 29, 1875

The Lamanites in Council.

An ambassadorial party of the Lord's Battle-axes, consisting of the second chief of the Navajoes, with four attendants, sons of lesser chiefs, left Beaver a few days ago to hold an audience with Brigham Young. Bishop Murdock furnished transportation for the party to Fillmore, the Bishop of Fillmore sent them to Round Valley (Scipio), the Bishop of Scipio forwarded the redskins to Nephi, and at Nephi they were sent to York, the end of the Southern Railroad track. One Dimick Huntington took charge of them on the cars, and was very solicitous to get them through to Provo—where Brigham was staying—without attracting the attention of outsiders. The party were kept in the baggage car, and were closely watched. Arrived at Provo, Dimick Huntington directed the man in charge of the Indians to take them to "President" Young, and he enjoined him to impress upon their minds the fact that these free rides and meals by the way, were furnished by the Mormons. Shortly we shall hear of some more villany cooked up by these high contracting parties.

ELEVATIONS ABOVE THE SEA.

How High is This for the Towns, Cities and Lakes of Utah.

The following table, showing the elevations of Utah towns, cities and lakes, is compiled from Government reports:

Cities, etc.	Elevation in feet	Cities, etc.	Elevation in feet
Am. Fork	4,536	Lehi	4,584
Beaver	5,927	Logan	4,567
Blue C'k, RR	4,360	Lucin, RR	4,400
Bonneville, RR	4,310	Matlin, RR	4,521
Bennington	5,790	Mill Spring	5,504
Bovine	4,547	Montpelier	5,793
Bingham City	4,226	Monument Pt	
Buckhorn Sp'g.	5,648	RR	4,290
Bear Lake	5,931	Mt Pleasant	5,875
Laidy (Mt)	11,730	Mount Nebo	11,992
Leckler (Mt)	9,716	Mt Tahkwano	13,500
Camp Douglas	4,891	Nephi	4,938
Camp Floyd	4,803	Ogden, RR	4,323
Castle Rock, RR	6,282	Oak Creek	5,188
Cedar City	5,718	Paragoonah	6,522
Centreville	4,233	Parowan	5,990
Circleville	5,634	Payson	4,551
Copenhagen	4,949	Fremont'y RR	4,913
Corinne, RR	4,194	Provo RR	4,363
Cottonwood	4,300	Peak (Dawe's)	13,300
Deseret City	4,612	Peak (Lone)	10,713
Devil's Gate, RR	4,815	Peak (Hay-	
Draper	4,521	dens)	11,500
Echo, RR	5,507	Richmond	4,641
Ephraim	5,533	Roxel, RR	4,531
Evanston, RR	6,870	St. Mary's	6,200
Fairfield	4,866	St. George	
Farmington	4,296	Salt Lake	4,210
Faust Station	5,296	Salt Lake City	4,320
Fillmore	5,125	Sevier Lake	4,630
Fish Springs	4,249	Sessions	4,163
Fort Crittenden	4,861	Silver City	6,300
Franklin	4,552	Smithfield	4,610
Gunnison	5,144	Terrace, RR	4,150
Hanging Rock	5,975	Uintah, RR	4,531
Hebron	5,474	Wasatch, RR	6,870
Hyde Park	4,553	Wanship	6,200
Iron City	6,400	Weber, RR	5,096
Kanara	5,449	Wellsville	4,568
Kelton, RR	4,569	Willard City	4,350
Lake	4,233	Willow Springs	4,441

Salt Lake Tribune
January 22, 1876

RAILROADS.

I see by the latest accounts that a strong movement is on foot to extend the Utah Southern Railroad to Southern California. God speed the day, for the want of it is now seriously felt by everybody. The roads between Fillmore and the end of the track have been almost impassable, and freight for this camp has been over three weeks in coming here, which same is rough on ye honest miners and business men.

I will venture to say, however, that more work has been performed on roads leading into and through these districts by the Gentle miners than has been done by the Territory on their public roads since Brigham Young has been the head chief and director of all Territorial laws and appropriations.

Salt Lake Herald
January 22, 1876

The Storm.

The snow storm which set in about midnight on Thursday, was one of the heaviest that has occurred in this valley for years. Yesterday morning the snow, on the level, was thirteen inches in depth. The storm, we learn by telegraph, was pretty general throughout the territory. The Deseret line reported the depth of snow at different points, as follows: Paris, 18 inches; Logan, 20 in.; Brigham city, 12 in.; Ogden, 6 in.; Alta, 14 feet; Bingham, 5 in.; American Fork, 5 in.; Provo, 5 in.; Nephi, 12 in.; Manti, 8 in.; Fillmore, 5 in.; Beaver, 5 in.; Hebron, 2 inches and still snowing.

Salt Lake Herald
April 14, 1876

Utah Post Roads.

The annual post road bill, as finally passed through congress, establishes the following routes as post roads in this territory: From Richfield, Sevier county, to Cove Creek. From Fillmore to Deseret, Millard county. From Glenwood to Circleville, Piute county, via Koosharem, Grass Valley. From Manti to Mayfield, San Pete county.

Salt Lake Herald
June 1, 1876

The Weather.

In Salt Lake, on Tuesday, a cold windstorm was succeeded by a drizzling rain, which increased to a heavy shower in the evening, turning to snow towards morning. Several inches of snow fell, but laid on the ground only a short time. Yesterday the atmosphere was cold and raw.

Following is a report of the weather in various parts of the territory on Wednesday:

American Fork—Cloudy.

Payson—Cloudy; looks like rain again.

Fountain Green—Cloudy and cold.

Spring city—Cloudy; looks like storm; quite cold.

Ephraim—Cold and cloudy; snowed a little yesterday afternoon.

Manti—It has been storming; quite cold.

Monroe—Pleasant. It has been storming and cold all yesterday and last night.

Fillmore—Cloudy and cool, with a little rain last night.

Cedar city—Cold north wind; slight sprinkling of snow this morning.

Hebron—Warm and pleasant to-day; very cold and windy yesterday.

Toquerville—A little windy, but clear; rather cool, very heavy wind all night.

St. George—Pleasant, thermometer 77.

Wood's Cross—Sun shining; pleasant.

Logan—It rained some last night; still cloudy and windy, but trying to clear up.

Franklin—Very cold, and has been raining all day.

Salt Lake Herald
August 14, 1876

PERSONAL.

F. B. Gillmore, representing the Omaha distillers and liquor dealers, Iler & Co., is in the city.

Bishop Callister, of Fillmore, arrived in the city last evening.

Salt Lake Herald
October 20, 1876

Fillmore — Considerable rain fell yesterday; mild with few clouds to-day.

Salt Lake Herald
November 9, 1876

MILLARD COUNTY.

Fillmore, 8.—Fillmore city polled 204 votes—193 for Geo. Q. Cannon and eleven for R. N. Baskin. There are but few precincts in the county. The vote will be nearly solid for Cannon, the people's candidate.

Salt Lake Herald
December 17, 1876

Brigham Young Academy, Provo.

The academical year of the institution commenced August 20th, with Professor K. G. Maeser as principal, Professor M. H. Hardy for the intermediate department, and Miss Teenie Smoot for the primary, with seventy-eight students, which number has increased since to 143 at present, from nearly all the towns and settlements of Utah county, some from Sanpete and even Fillmore. The difficulty with many desirous to attend has been the expenses for boarding, which the directors are making efforts to obviate by various arrangements, until the organization of a boarding house connected with the institution will have been effected.

The greater majority of the students in the grammar department have already advanced sufficiently as to necessitate the organization of an academical department for next term, which has been done thus far only for the higher arithmetical studies, which have been conducted by Professor Booth.

The normal department has been attended by eleven students, but we understand that the county court of Utah has made arrangements to have twenty-six normal students put through a normal training in the institution.

The teachers of the district schools of Utah county meet twice a month at the academy building for a normal class, taught by Professor Maeser, for the purpose of getting the common schools of the county upon a more uniform basis. A characteristic feature of the academy are the theological classes, attended by all the students of the academy.

All appearances show the academy to be a rising institution which is destined to make its mark in the educational interests of our territory. President Young, in founding this institution, has certainly done something which reflects the highest credit upon him as a benefactor of the people.

Salt Lake Herald
December 20, 1876

A Card to the Public.

The Provo Manufacturing Company intend to shut down their manufacturing department on the 23d inst. for the holiday season, and probably for some little time after, to make some needed repairs, etc.

The Company have on hand a large and well-assorted stock of seasonable goods, which they are offering at low figures for CASH and all kinds of MARKETABLE PRODUCE.

Now is the time to obtain your supplies of nice, warm winter clothing for yourselves and families.

The Company are paying the HIGHEST MARKET PRICE FOR WOOL, IN CASH OR CLOTH, and intend to continue to do so, and trust that the Wool Growers will favor us with their patronage, as we guarantee best prices and fair dealings. For reference as to our mode of doing business we refer by permission to the following Wool Growers:

John Bennion & Sons, West Jordan.
Saml. Bennion & Sons, " "
E. M. Weiler, Salt Lake City.
Herriman Co-op. Sheep Company.
James Jordan, Tooele.
W. C. Rydalch, Grantsville.
H. E. Booth,
Tooele Co-op. Sheep Comp'y, Tooele.
Philip De La Mar, Tooele.
H. E. Miller, Farmington.
Anson Call, Bountiful.
C. J. Arthur, Cedar, Iron Co.
F. Webster, " "
Parowan Co-op."
U. Roucher, Pine Valley, Kane Co.
Fillmore Co-op., Millard Co.
W. H. Chipman & Bro., Am'n Fork.
Wm. Clark, Lehi.
Wm. Winn, "
And may others.

Remember, IF YOU DO NOT WANT GOODS, YOU CAN GET YOUR MONEY; also, that we calculate to stay here and you will always know where to find us.

Address: JAMES DUNN,
d20   Sup't.

Salt Lake Tribune
February 7, 1877

Death of Amasa Lyman.

By a private dispatch to a gentleman in this city, we learn that Amasa Lyman died at his residence in Fillmore on Sunday morning, at 11 o'clock. Elder Lyman was extensively known throughout Utah, having been for many years one of the Twelve Apostles of the Mormon Church. Although ostracised by Brigham Young, and by him handed over to the buffetings of satan for apostasy, he was yet admired by thousands of Mormons, because in their estimation he was an honest man.

Elder Lyman, from the time Brigham assumed the leadership of the Church, was at war with this arch impostor for his corrupt and wicked practices; but as is the case with the whole Mormon people to-day, he believed the principles of his faith were correct, and that the Prophet's corruption did not effect them. This, of course, was unconscious apostasy, and when Brigham Young, through the mediumship of the school of the prophets, robbed his followers who had labored for him on the Union Pacific Railroad, and then farther sought to outrage them by reducing the wages of laboring men in Utah, contrary alike to the laws of political economy and justice, Elder Lyman, in common with Messrs. Godbe, Lawrence and other patriotic men, rebelled against the tyranny and oppression of Brigham, for which he was excommunicated from the Church.

Elder Lyman was of a religio-philosophical turn of mind, and after being handed over to the buffeting of Satan, he studied God with much more satisfaction to himself than he could when bound down by the iron priesthood. After his connection with the Church ceased, and the excitement of that epoch of apostasy died away, he settled down to a quiet life of study and research at his home in Fillmore.

The reasons which led him to this course, aside from his inclinations in that direction, after ceasing to be a Mormon, were probably his polygamous relations, which had entailed too many responsibilities to an innocent progeny to permit of his making a vigorous war upon that social system in which they were born. Otherwise it is more than probable that he would have contributed not a little from his heart and mind to uproot this Latter-day ism and dethrone the impostor at its head.

Whatever may be said of him, it is doubtful if anything can be raked up against his memory except his polygamy. He was naturally too honest a man to be a follower of Brigham Young.

At the time of his death he was about sixty-four years of age.

Salt Lake Herald
April 8, 1877

Missionaries.

(Special Telegram.)

St. George, 7.—At the conference this forenoon the following named persons were called to go on missions:

TO EUROPE.

Alex. F. McDonald, sen., St. George.
Alex. F. McDonald, jun., "
David Milne, "
Daniel D. McArthur, "
Wm. H. Branch, jr., "
Edwin D. Woolley, jr., "
Erastus W. McIntire, "
Aaron McDonald, "
John Steel, Toquerville.
Mahona Steele, Panguitch.
George Kirkham, Lehi.
Thomas Lockyer, Logan.
Joseph E. Cowley, "
Franklin S. Richards, Ogden
Warren B. Smith, American Fork.
R. Cleghorn, Salt Lake City.
Aurelius Miner, "
Edward Partridge, Fillmore.

TO ARIZONA.

Neils Joseph Rosebury, Richfield.
Henry Job Smith, Salt Lake city.
Philip De La Mere, Tooele city.
A. H. Patterson, Pondtown or Payson
L. Curtis and Sons, " "
William Ballard, " "
Marlin Plumb, " "
John Plumb, " "
Parley Sabins, " "
Libeus T. Coons, " "
George Patten, jr., " "
George Killian, " "
Daniel Thomas, " "
William Hall, " "
John Syms, " "

TO THE UNITED STATES.

John Alger, St. George.
John D. L. Pearce, "
— Page, Washington.
Joseph Nobles, Springville.

This afternoon the following were also called as missionaries, but the countries to which they are to go were not designated:

Walter J. Winsor, Kanab.
Elijah Potter, "
Frederick Hamblin, "
Charles Riggs, "
Lawrence C. Mariger, "
John Esger, "
David K. Udall, "
Levi Stewart, "
David Johnson, Johnson.
Almon W. Johnson, "
W. J. Powell, Joseph City.
Hans Golbranson, "
George B. Gardner, Virgen City.
Jefferson C. Wright, "
Wm. Esger, Hillsdale.
John Averett, Washington,
John W. Freeman, "
—Nicholls, "
Wyllys D. Fuller, Harrisburg.
Revilo Fuller, "
Alfred Randall, "
George Earl.

James Dean, St. George.
Calvin Kelsey, "
Frederick Judd, "
Brigham Hall, "
Commodore P. Liston, "
Samuel L. Adams, "
W. J. Carter, "
Moses Curtis and sons, Payson.
Jacob Scharron, "
Joseph Bull, jr., Salt Lake.
O. H. Riggs, "
Robert Sloan, "
William Burton, "
Royal B. Sagers, "
Harry Emery, "
Samuel Peterson, "
A. Franzen, "
G. P. Mortensen, "
Joseph W. Taylor, "
Mosiah L. Hancock, jr., Alma.
— Angell, Leeds.
Robert G. Barrett, North Ogden.
James Montgomery, "
Eugene Campbell, "
Edward W. Wade, "
Peter Graves, Ephraim.
Fred. A. Miller, Lynne.
John Hubbard, Willard city.
M. W. Dalton, "
Robert Lake, Kiowa Nation.
Henry Flamm, Logan.
A. Fredrickson

Jacob Naef, Providence.
Jacob Miller, "
Daniel Jacobs, St. Charles.
Peter Graff, Draperville.
Niels Madsen, jr., Brigham City.
F. F. Hintz, Cottonwood.
B. P. Wulfenstein, Price City.
Edward Hemsley, Mill Creek.
Job Hemsley, " "

No changes were made in the general church authorities.

Salt Lake Herald
April 24, 1877

New Postal Routes.

The following new Pacific coast routes, on all of which service is to be weekly, have been established and proposals for contracts for carrying the mails have been issued, to run from the 1st day of next September to June 30th, 1878: Idaho—Rock Creek via Marsh Basin to Kelton, Utah; Idaho city to Banner; Eagle Rock via Burch Creek to Junction; Montana—Old agency via Fort Maginnis to new agency; Buttes city to Boulder valley, tri-weekly; Fort Shaw via Bird's Creek to Camp Baker.

Utah—Deseret to Fillmore; Eureka to Homansville, tri-weekly; Manti to Mayfield; Glenwood via Koosharen to Circleville.

Salt Lake Herald
May 18, 1877

Killed by Frost.

More than half of the fruit crop of Fillmore has been destroyed by frost. There has been considerable loss of fruit from the same agency all over the territory.

Salt Lake Herald
June 23, 1877

Mail Lettings.

The following mail routes have been let in Utah:

Glenwood to Centerville, C. W. Powell, $870; Fillmore to Deseret, Alex. Melville, $340; Manti to Mayfield, J. L. Peacock, $195.

The route from Rock creek *via* Goose creek, Marsh basin and Caspia, Idaho, to Kelton, Utah, was not let. All bids were suspended awaiting the result of efforts to make arrangements with the contractor on the route to Dalles to embrace these settlements by a slight increase in the length of the present service.

All the other routes in the territory advertised April 10th will not be relet, although numerous bids have been received. Some of them may, however, be advertised next spring, if the development of the country in the meantime seems to justify them.

Salt Lake Herald
December 20, 1877

Postoffices.

A postoffice has been established at Petersburgh, Millard county, Utah, with Richard Holton as postmaster. The following postmasters for this territory have been appointed: Joshua R. Clark, Grantsville, Tooele county; James H. Wells, Joseph, Sevier county; Andrew Henry, Fillmore, Millard county.

Salt Lake Herald
September 28, 1878

Wheat.

A gentlemen, who has just returned from a trip through the south, says the quantity of wheat raised this year in that section is simply immense. The country is flooded and the price is so low that it can be purchased for 50c per bushel and under. Oats, however, are not so plentiful and command a proportionately larger price. He says that money is by no means as scarce as represented, and that in the neighborhood of Fillmore, where there is considerable dealing in cattle, gold is very plentiful.

Salt Lake Tribune
November 14, 1878

Another Old Fogy.

ED. TRIBUNE It would seem from present indications that some of "this people" at last are resolved to live up to their privileges so called. Of late years there have been but few in Fillmore ambitious of patriarchal homes, if the limited number who have entered the polygamic order may be considered any criterion. Foremost, however, in the revival of the "twin relic," amongst us is Christian Anderson, a Scandinavian by birth, and a recently elected Justice of the Peace, who a few weeks ago took another lady love to his manly bosom, and apparently liking the situation, has just gone to Salt Lake City to repeat the offense. Such zeal in the violation of the law can hardly be commended in one who has sworn to support it.

OBSERVER

FILLMORE, Nov 12, 1878.

Salt Lake Herald
November 21, 1878

Horse Thieves.

The rumor that a number of horse thieves had been captured south of this city on Tuesday night, does not seem to have had any foundation. However, a couple of horse thieves were arrested a few days since, and lodged in the Fillmore jail, where they await the arrival of an escort to bring them to this city for confinement. Their names are Tommy Reed and Chas. Gifford. The former is said to be of Park city and was arrested for appropriating to himself a horse belonging to General R. T. Burton, of this city. Gifford, if he prove to be the right man, is arrested for first stealing a saddle and bridle from a man in Bingham, and pursuing a systematic course, next took the horse. Marshal Shaughnessy will send a deputy after them, and bring them here for safe keeping.

Salt Lake Herald
December 3, 1878

Horse Thieves.

The horse thieves, Charles Gifford and Thomas Reed, brought up from Fillmore on Saturday, by Sheriff Huntsman, charged with horse stealing, had an examination before Commissioner Sprague yesterday. The preliminary examination elicited such facts as warranted the commissioner in binding them over in $500 each to await the action of the grand jury. Being unable to secure bondsmen, they were committed to custody.

Salt Lake Herald
April 6, 1879

Mt. Baldy and Dodge Districts.

The excitement that was occasioned by the reported discovery of mineral between Holden, Millard county, and Oak Creek, and of which mention was made in the HERALD some weeks ago, is said to have died out somewhat. An expert is reported to have examined the claims and reported that there was no mineral in the rock. Samples have been sent to this city to be assayed, but with what result we have not yet learned. The district was named Dodge district. Work has been suspended in it for the present, at least, and undoubtedly for good should the assay prove unfavorable.

A gentleman writing from Holden says that he recently met an acquaintance who lives near the newly discovered mines of Mt. Baldy, opposite Richfield, Sevier county, from whom he learned that the name of the person who made the first discovery in that region is Heber Gillings. It is said that surface assays gave $1,200 in gold and about $6 in silver to the ton, and a second assay gave $3,000 in gold per ton. The vein is reported to have been traced for six miles.

A number of persons have taken up claims in a district some thirty miles southeast of Holden, which are supposed to contain tin. The gentleman writing had a talk with one of the persons who have laid out claims. It seems that he was herding out on the desert about a year ago when he first discovered the ore, and not being in a position to develop it at the time, kept quiet about it until a short time ago when he took legal possession of it. The claim was recorded at Fillmore, and the location being thus brought out, considerable of a fever of excitement has ensued, and a large number of persons in that locality have now taken up claims. Some of the ore from these claims will be assayed in Salt Lake within a few days, when the spirits of the prospectors will be either raised or correspondingly depressed. It is to be hoped that the assay will prove favorable, as a few tin mines would greatly enhance the wealth of the territory in a short time.

Salt Lake Herald
July 26, 1879

Captured.

By correspondence we learn that Sheriff Huntsman, of Millard County has arrested the parties that committed the highway robbery between Fillmore and Scipio, on the 14th inst. The parties were taken to Fillmore and examined, one of them pleading guilty, and the other waiving examination, and both were bound over to await the action of the grand jury of the First district. Their names are William Morgan, and the other calls himself Frank Jones, but is known to none other than the old stage robber, J. H. McKinney. They say they have just served ten years in the California penitentiary for robbing Wells, Fargo & Co., of $8,000. Since the highway robbery in Millard County, Sheriff Huntsman has been steadily on their trail, and succeeded in capturing them at Richfield, Sevier County, on the 22d. Sheriff Huntsman says he will make it warm for the highwaymen and thieves around his quarters if he has but the support of the people.

Salt Lake Herald
November 25, 1879

Demise.

Mr. William Lambert, who had his arm badly hurt with a threshing machine at Deseret five weeks ago, died from the effects at Fillmore, November 12th, 1879. He was aged 32 years, 1 month and 6 days, and he leaves a wife and four children, and a large circle of friends to mourn his loss.

Nevada papers please copy.

Salt Lake Herald
January 10, 1880

The Lost Found.

Last August a couple of men named Wm. Morgan and James H. McKinney broke from the jail at Fillmore, were they were held on larceny charges. Their whereabouts was not known until lately, when it was ascertained that they had made their way through to Arizona and figured conspicuously in robbing a coach at Prescott. Morgan was arrested and sentenced to the penitentiary for life, while McKinney was killed. The sheriff tracked him up and when he tried to make the arrest, McKinney resisted, and the result was that he became a cold corpus. McKinney is now in the best place he ever found since his birth. He came here from California, having just finished serving out a ten years' sentence in the penitentiary at San Quentin. He had not been in the territory six months before he had stolen 600 head of cattle, horses and sheep, and was arrested under five indictments, but got off with one year in the penitentiary. When released he went south and fell in with Morgan, and they were arrested on a charge of larceny and awaiting trial when they made their escape from the Fillmore jail. Morgan had been previously arrested on a chage of rape and released on bonds. He was then arrested on the second charge, and before his bondsmen could get released he cleared out. He has a wife in this territory. To all general purposes he is now as dead as McKinney. He claims that he was led astray by McKinney.

Salt Lake Herald
February 22, 1880

HOTEL ARRIVALS.

February 21, 1880.

WHITE HOUSE.

C Speed, Fillmore; S J Delavan, J D Crawford, St Louis; E W Davis, Lake Point; H M May, J Williams, Mrs Coakley, Mrs Mount, Wm Carter, Bingham; E W Cummings, Sandy; W Anderton, Richfield.

UTAH NAMES.

It has been suggested, and the idea is a good one, that something be published and thus placed on record of the county and town nomenclature of Utah. There are twenty-three counties in the territory, and while the reasons for attaching certain names to most of them are apparent and well known, why the special names were given to others, and what significance there is in them, are conundrums even to the residents of the counties themselves. Box Elder, Cache, Juab, Sanpete and Tooele are instances that illustrate. We undertake to say that comparatively few people in these counties can say why the names above were given to those geographical sections. Kane was named in honor of General Thomas L. Kane, Millard in honor of President Millard Fillmore, Rich in honor of General C. C. Rich, Washington in honor of "the father of his country," and Emery in honor of our late governor. There is fitness in the name of Iron County; Davis and Morgan were doubtless named for men, but who and why? The reasons for naming Salt Lake, Summit and Wasatch are apparent in the geography of the respective counties. Besides the peculiar nomenclature of the counties there are between 300 and 400 cities, towns, villages, settlements and cross-roads in the territory, each with its particular name, and some of them with remarkably queer names. There must have been special reasons for the selection of each of these titles, and it would be interesting and hereafter prove useful to know just why the names were applied. Honeyville, Cub Hill, Panguitch, Pinto, Levan, Pahreah, Kanab, Kamas, Annabella, Wallsburgh, Uintah, Pettyville and Loa, are some of the many strange names of Utah towns and postoffices. Whose inventive genius has been taxed to fix these appellations, and what circumstance, event or other thing gave occasion for the poetic, historical, and romantic christenings? If those who have knowledge as to how these names were called into existence, and why they were applied to particular cities, towns or counties, will communicate the facts to the HERALD, we will cheerfully publish the stories, which cannot be otherwise than entertaining and instructive.

CENSUS ENUMERATORS.

A Complete List of the Appointments So far Made, with Precincts, Etc.

A list of the appointments of census enumerators made up to the present time, is given below, together with the counties and precincts in which they will operate. Secretary A. L. Thomas desires that those appointed will immediately send their postoffice addresses to the supervisor, in order that he may be enabled to communicate with them:

BEAVER COUNTY.

First District—A. A. Putnam. Beaver, Greenville and Adamsville Precincts.

Second District—Edward Keae's. Star and Minersville Precincts.

Third District—James R. Lindsay. Grampion Precinct.

BOX ELDER COUNTY.

First District————— Box Elder Precinct.

Second District—James J. Chandler. Willard and Mantua Precincts.

Third District—Wm. H. Anderson. Portage, Plymouth, Bear River, Malad, Deweyville and Call's Fort Precincts.

Fourth District—S. H. Cave. Curlew, Promontory, Kelton, Rush Valley, Grove Creek and Terrace Precincts.

CACHE COUNTY.

First District—Edw. N. Rowland. Logan Precinct.

Second District—Aaron DeWitt. Logan Precinct.

Third District—Henry McBride. Hyrum, Wellsville and Paradise Precincts.

Fourth District—Mark Fletcher. Millville, Providence, Mendon and Peterson Precincts.

Fifth District—Wm. H. Miles. Smithfield, Benson and Hyde Park Precincts.

Sixth District—John H. Barker. Newton, Clarkston, Trenton, Richmond and Lewiston Precincts.

DAVIS COUNTY.

First District—Charles E. Pearson. Bountiful Precinct.

Second District—Walter Walker. Centreville and Farmington Precincts and Antelope Island.

Third District—H. W. Haight. Kaysville, South Weber and Hooper Precincts.

EMERY COUNTY.

First District—————— All of County west of Green River.

Second District—L. W. Bartlett. All of County east of Green River.

IRON COUNTY.

First District—Wm. O. Mitchell. Escalante and Cannonsville Precincts.

Second District—M. M. Steele. Hillsdale and Panguitch Precincts.

Third District—Daniel Page. Parowan, Paragoonah and Summit Precincts and Little Salt Lake Valley.

Fourth District—Robt. W. Heyborne. All of western portion of County not included in other districts and Cedar City Precinct.

JUAB COUNTY.

First District—A. S. Kendal. Mono Precinct.

Second District—J. F. Hartley. Nephi Precinct.

Third District—A. S. Kendall. Levan Precinct.

Fourth District—Patrick Cusick. Tintie Precinct.

KANE COUNTY.

First District—Lewis W. Stout. Kanarra and Harmony Precincts.

Second District—Dr. John Steele. Bellevue, Toquerville, Virgen City, Duncan's Retreat, Grafton, Rockville, Shunesberg and Springdale Precincts.

Third District—Elmer W. Johnson. Kanab, Johnson, Pahreah, Mount Carmel, Orderville and Glendale Precincts.

MILLARD COUNTY.

First District—John Kelly. Fillmore and Holden Precincts.

Second District—D. S. Dana. Oak City, Leamington and Sciple Precincts.

Third District—Edward Partridge. Deseret and Lakeville Precincts.

Fourth District—George Finlinson. Meadow and Kanosh Precincts.

MORGAN COUNTY.

First District—Hugh L. Pennington. All that portion of the county south of the Weber River.

Second District—John S. Barrett. All that portion of the county north of the Weber River.

SUMMIT COUNTY.

First District—W. O. Young. Ben-netorville, Echo, Upton and Wasatch, and all east to Uintah County.

Second District—John Boyden. Coal-ville and Hoytsville Precincts.

Third District—George B. Leonard. Wanship, Rockport, Peos and Kamas Precincts.

Fourth District—Robert W. Davis. Park City and Parley's Park Precincts.

UINTAH COUNTY.

One District—William Ashton. All of county.

WASATCH COUNTY.

First District—T. H. Giles. Heber Precinct.

Second District—David Van Wagoner. Midway Precinct.

Third District—Richard Camp. Charleston and Wallsburgh Precincts.

WASHINGTON COUNTY.

First District—Daniel H. McAlister. Commencing at southern boundary of county and extending northeast and west, to include all of St. George, Washington, Santa Clara, Price City, and all on the Rio Virgen River to the Mary Cotton Farm.

Second District—W. P. Poole. That portion of county north from Washington and east of Pine Valley mountains, not included in First District, embracing Harrisburg, Leeds, St. Louis, Babylon, Stormont and Silver Reef.

Third District—F. L. Cushing. All on the Santa Clara River north of Three Mile Piace, embracing Dameron Valley, Gunlock and settlements west of Pine Valley mountains, i.e., Pine Valley, Grass Valley, Hamblin, Pinto, Iron Works and Hebron.

Appointments for Salt Lake, San Juan, Tooele, Utah and Weber Counties to be announced hereafter.

PIUTE COUNTY.

First District—Charles Morrell. Circleville and Marysvale Precincts.

Second District—John H. Wright. Greenwich and Fremont Precincts.

RICH COUNTY.

First District—Wm. P. Nebeker.

Second District—C. Bevans.

SANPETE COUNTY.

First District—A. J. P. Benuman. Thistle, Fairview and Mount Pleasant Precincts.

Second District—Reese Llewellyn. Fountain Green, Moroni and Freedom Precincts.

Third District—Emil Konnecke. Ephraim Precinct.

Fourth District—Janie Peacock. Petty and Manti Precincts.

Fifth District—George Scott. Wales, Chester and Spring City Precincts.

Sixth District—Edward Reid. Fayette, Gunnison and Mayfield Precincts.

SEVIER COUNTY.

First District—G. W. Bean. Salina, Redmond, Willow Bend, Vermillion, Richfield and Central precincts, including Gooseberry Valley.

Second and Third Districts—Edward Payne. Glenwood, Burrville, Annabella, Monroe, Elsinore, and Joseph Precincts, including Grass Valley.

Salt Lake Herald
June 18, 1880

A SCHOOL TRIP.

To-day, Dr. J. R. Park, principal of the University of Deseret, accompanied by Prof. M. H. Hardy, county superintendent of schools in Utah County, will start on an extended tour through the southern part of the territory. The gentlemen go at the instance of the territorial superintendent of schools, and will examine school matters throughly. The trip is in no sense a pleasure one, and will be devoted wholly to the object in view, and will therefore not only necessitate visiting the districts, but will require the giving of advice to teachers and trustees, where such advice is desired and needed. The trip will certainly be one of benefit to the school interests of the southern part of the territory, and we commend Dr. Park and his companion to the care of the good citizens of the south.

Here is the programme adopted and the settlements given below will be visited on the dates stated, as near as can be estimated now, though there may be some deviations:

June 21—Provo to Santaquin, Utah County.

June 22—Santaquin to Nephi, Juab County.

June 23—Nephi to Scipio, Millard County.

June 24—Scipio to Fillmore, Millard County.

June 25—Fillmore to Cove, Millard County.

June 26—Cove to Beaver, Beaver County.

June 27—Beaver to Parowan, Iron County.

June 28—Parowan to Cedar, Iron County.

June 29—Cedar to Harmony, Kane County.

June 30—Harmony to Hamlin, Washington County.

July 1—Hamlin to Pine Valley, Washington County.

July 2—Pine Valley to St. George, Washington County.

July 3 and 4—In St. George.

July 5—St. George to Washington and return.

July 6—In Leeds.

July 7—Leeds to Toquerville, Kane County.

July 8—Toquerville to Rockville, Kane County.

July 9—Rockville to Zion and Springdale, Kane County.

July 10—Springdale to Virgen, Kane County.

July 11—Virgen to Windsor Castle, Kane County.

July 12—Windsor to Kanab, Kane County.

July 13 and 14—In Kanab, where they will rest for four or five days.

July 28—Kanab to Orderville, Kane County.

July 29—Orderville to Panguitch, Iron County.

July 31—Panguitch to Kingston, Piute County.

August 1—Kingston to Greenwich, Piute County.

August 2—Greenwich to Koosharen, Fish Lake, and back to Burrville, Sevier County.

Salt Lake Herald
September 26, 1880

MOUNT BALDY.

The Country of Blanket Veins— Mountains of Ore.

MARYSVALE, UTAH,
September 23, 1880.

Editors Herald:

In regard to the mines of Mount Baldy, they are still here, and the interest is still increasing among miners. In regard to blanket veins, a *lead*-ville is the only term that can be applied to the mine owned by Charley Converse, George M. Scott and our jovial Mr. Lighter, and there is no doubt that they have a claim worth owning. They have opened the ore body for some 300 feet, and the more they try to define it the more they are lost in a mountain of ore, for a mountain it is. There are other claims on the same reef that are opening in a similar manner. The Independence is another of the same kind, owned by Mr. Goodridge. The ore body is about 700 feet in length and 200 feet in width on the surface. The Mountain Lion is another of the same kind, also showing a blanket vein that nearly covers fifteen acres on the St. John Peak, and is one of John Ferris' big claims. He only has about fifty locations in the Mount Baldy range, amounting to about 75,000 feet. John understands the mountains, and owns them pretty much all himself.

Some of the ore from Bullion is now running up to 240 ounces.

In the Beecher Mine is shown a fine body of ore in the main shaft, which is now down 125 feet.

The Fillmore Mine is improving every foot, as the work is being pushed ahead.

The two districts, the Ohio and the Mount Baldy, are on the same mineral belt, and the ores are in comparison the same.

Professor J. S. Newberry, M.E., of the School of Mines of Columbia College, and Mr. John Sharp, jr., recently visited the mines of both districts, having John Ferris for a guide. After going through the mines they went back to Salt Lake City highly pleased with the prospects of a big camp.

From a recent publication in the *Tribune* it would seem that the Mormons have lived in this country, and that they once took some interest in the mines here in former days. The writer in the *Tribune* may think that capitalists would not buy a mine from Mormons. The article is written in a spirit of anathemas, and will have no weight with intelligent minds and business men. The mines are here, and citizens of the United States that own good mining claims and comply with the laws of the government can sell them, whether Mormons or Gentiles. Uncle Sam does not make any difference. We congratulate the *nom de plume* writer in the *Tribune* as a *flat* for trying to incite a Mormon and Gentile difference to Uncle Sam. It is too late in the evening for anything of the kind among business circles.

RAM'S HEAD.

Salt Lake Herald
October 19, 1880

HOTEL ARRIVALS.

October 18, 1880.

VALLEY HOUSE.

M Cushman, Tintic; J C Chipman, Am Fork; J Day, H R Clinton, S Hays, H Van Legat, C W Heidel, W S Brown, Bingham; T Kely, Wood River; J Alnes, Fillmore; N C Scow, Helena, M T; E W Larne, Virginia City; P I Nickols, H Graham. J Anderson, Park City; E J Fullmer, Fort Hall; J Brown, R Sherwood, Stockton; R Gardner, W Dall, G Bird, Coalville; A Wyman and wife, P L Wheeler and wife, C Norris and wife, O Shattuck, Miss B Wallace, S Speck, J P Howe, Wyman Comedy Company; J B Worthington, Idaho; W Hudson, Grantsville; W Beasby, Evanston; P D Hamlin, Mifflintown, Pa; H H Hamlin, Monticell. Ind; H J Haven and wife, Howell, Mrs M Whittock, C Coleman and wife. St Johns, Mich; J A Loftus, Bingham; M Collins, Beaver; M Masters, Alta; J Tifield, Springville; C Brown, C P Joseph, R A Neven, Ogden; L Hatch, Colorado; J Rogers, W B Sessions, Park City; G L Hall, Wood River; G F Russell, H Haven, Omaha; C W Ward and wife, Marshalltown, Iowa.

Salt Lake Herald
November 30, 1880

HOTEL ARRIVALS.

WHITE HOUSE

P Henson, J W Russell, South Cottonwood; D Gallofent, Challis; C W Kitchen, jr, Ogden; W Maycock, Fillmore; A Tatro, J Dwyer, Pioche; G E Tyler, J C Whaler, O R Allen, Park City; A Hoolin, J Orr, N Scribner, Rush Valley; R H Hills, Tintic; S Avery, R Green, Granger; F M Lanford, H C Booley, Park. J Heber, J F Blatner, Wood River, T W Bates, Chicago; S Hays, J Gibbons, J G Wilder, Miss Simpson, H D Jones, A Ledders, A Bemis, Bingham; A D Williams, Bullion; D P Cussians, Nevada; A T Mathews, F Coblentz, San Francisco.

Rape Fiend Captured.

Some time ago we published an item stating it had come to light that a fellow named Roy Parrish, about 25 years of age, had committed rape on the persons of two little girls, aged respectively 6 and 8, who were the children of a gentleman at Springville, Utah County, with whom he resided. The beastly crime was discovered by the children talking among themselves, the conversation being overheard by the parents, which aroused their suspicions. An examination proved that the suspicions were well founded, and a warrant was issued for the arrest of Parrish.

Somehow he got wind of the affair, and left, having considerable start of the officers. His whereabouts were unknown, but Sheriff Turner, of Utah County, strongly suspected that he would be liable to turn up in the vicinity of Fillmore, as he was known to have relatives there. Therefore, a watch was instituted, and on Friday evening or Saturday morning, Sheriff Turner received a dispatch from Fillmore informing him of the capture of the fiend Parrish. Mr. Turner immediately started south to get him, and he will probably be in jail at Provo by tomorrow night.

HOTEL ARRIVALS.

VALLEY HOUSE.

F Burns, R G Owen, New York; J O'Brien, Chicago; W Willie, Cache Valley; W Watson, Alta; N P Nielson, Miss Jackson, Blackfoot; J B Stoddard, Wellsville; P C Olson and wife, Weber; E Roach, W Noland, Capt Z Wilson, Bingham; J Berriman, Michigan; W H Bishop, Fillmore; J Bull, W Garvin, J R Worthington, Nevada; D Whitney, Minneapolis; Mrs J Riley, C Thornley, H Tay, Miss G Earnest, Ogden; H Gale, Indianapolis; T Chap'n, Holyoke, Mass; J Tellie, Indiana; Z Johnson, Marsh Basin; Miss J Gaka, Denver; E Gillett, Richmond, Va; E Sullivan, Coalville.

HOTEL ARRIVALS.

WHITE HOUSE.

B Bennett, Holden; O V Robinson, L Holbrook, Fillmore; T H Ewan, H E Tyson, Park City; J H Vane, Springville; Mrs Case and family, Alta; R C Whitney, J W Russell, Big Cottonwood; H Kaiser, G Johnson, W Sutton, J Black, Bingham; J H Graham, Marysvale; E W Thompson, Beaver; H Seeley, Payson; G Johnson, Circle Valley.

Salt Lake Herald
February 10, 1881

HOTEL ARRIVALS.

February 9, 1881.
WHITE HOUSE.

M Detjens, Rock Island; J Lambert, Kamas; A M Durkee, Marysvale; A M Forbs, Coalville; A E Bryan, Silver Reef; E Rotch, Alta; J D Wines, Lehi; L Holbrook, Fillmore; J Vergo, Kokama; M Drew, J Burns, Stockton; F Lawrence, Park City.

Salt Lake Herald
April 13, 1881

HOTEL ARRIVALS.

WHITE HOUSE.

J Mayfield, H Todter, J Collins, P Redmond, W Watson, Frisco; M G Cushman, Tintic; H Barnett, J McCann, Bingham; T H B Jones, Sandy; H C Sock, Park City; M A Acelmeyer, O Stanley, Silver Reef; R Baird, Wyoming; W T Shafer, Evanston; D B Nye, E C Killie, San Francisco; W Maycock, Fillmore, Utah; S Horn, J Johnson, Sanpete; W H Wright, Laramie; G Ryman, Cincinnati; C A Rond, Warm Springs; A J Moore, A Lee, Park City.

Salt Lake Herald
April 26, 1881

HOTEL ARRIVALS.

WHITE HOUSE.

A J White, J Brady, Park City; J J Freyer, J Duffey, Ogden; C C Rhoades, E M Allison, G Sweeting, Coalville; R T Turner, Douglas; W Reynolds, Warship; J Hatch, Heber; J Oaks, Tintic; J Alues, Fillmore; B C Berry, England; R J Joy, Australia; A Mason, New York; A J Moore, H R Lane, Park City; N B Smitg, Ogden; W Miller and family, J Fall, W S Brown, Bingham; M M Cahoon, T Romney, D Hunt, South Cottonwood; G W Leonard and family, Springville, C Forsch n, Sandy.

Salt Lake Herald
April 30, 1881

HOTEL ARRIVALS

WALKER HOUSE.

Mrs C A Porter, C D Porter, Colorado; F G Brown, F W Bacon, New York; J A Stevens, Ogden; A H Wilson, W D Wrighter, Omaha; D Ward, jr., Mr and Mrs D Ward, Sheffield, Eng; P E Conner, Stockton; Col Royal, U S A; W Phillips and wife, Taunton; O F Griffin, A Varnberg, G F Grant, San Francisco; E Parrish, A Bruner, Philadelphia; W Benedict, Germania; E F Hooker, DesMoines; J C Bennett, Lynn, Mass; J G Gardner, Boston.

Salt Lake Herald
May 7, 1881

HOTEL ARRIVALS

VALLEY HOUSE.

W C Larsen and wife, Montana; P Snider, Idaho; W S Hebboer, Arizona; W V Anderson, San Francisco; C R Leroy, Omaha; P Barry, A Marched, gden; W P Payne, Fillmore; L D Parson, Laramie; M E Young B Mahan, Park City; H Ruth, Bingham; S Kent, Silver Reef; E F Fanham.

Salt Lake Herald
May 22, 1881

HOTEL ARRIVALS

WHITE HOUSE.

G Bogarel, Keeneville, N Y; J W Bently, Taylorsville; A J Critchfield, Tooele; J Broughton, Stockton; C P Beebee, Bingham; C Davis, Ft Douglas; J Schwartz, Silver Reef; S F Bingham, G Thompson and wife, Park City; J Alves, Fillmore; J N Gifford, F W Noble, J F Campbell, Detroit; J Gerba, Tintic; G M Snow, Idaho; G W Roberts, Omaha; S D Lewis, S D Pardy, Warsaw, N Y.

Salt Lake Herald
June 3,1881

HOTEL ARRIVALS

WHITE HOUSE.

J Barron, Stockton; T W Packard, Deadwood; T W Bates, Park City; T Brough, London; W L Robinson, W H Dyer, I Venard, Bingham; L Holbrook, Fillmore; J H Hancock, Tintic; Geo Atkin, Tooele City; Chas R son, San Francico ; S B Kingsbury, Constantine, Mich.

Salt Lake Herald
June 5, 1881

HOTEL ARRIVALS

WHITE HOUSE.

J Barron, John Byrne, Stockton; R Maker, Ogden; C E Young, Evanston, Wyo; P S Kirby, McWales Dramatic Company; J S Black, Fillmore; Joseph Lietz, Denver; L B S Miller, T H Condeman, F Hunter, Philadelphia; C S Little, Carson City, Col; D McGuinness, Bingham.

Salt Lake Herald
June 8, 1881

HOTEL ARRIVALS.

WHITE HOUSE.

J N Powers; Sparks Troupe; A Saunder, Pleasant Grove; J H Varnes, Denver; C H Wood, San Francisco; J Alves, J G Squires, Fillmore; A Morrinso, San Francisco; M B Dodds, Tooele City; T W Packard, Deadwood; C H Wood, San Jose; G Walker, Cincinnati; W Musser, Washington; Mrs Simons, Park City.

Salt Lake Herald
June 28, 1881

HOTEL ARRIVALS.

WHITE HOUSE

J A Vane and wife, Miss Bissell, Springville; G F Watkins, Fort Douglas; J u Kelly, Stockton: A Clauseer, E Anderson, Meadow Lake; W Holladay, W Bates, F H Meyers, M Frasker and family, Park City; A V Field, San Francisco; H Thompson, Cariboo, T Venard, Bingham; D Rathbone, San Bernardino; M Schroder, W Wagner, D McCartney, Pittsburg; A C Scott, W S Hedger, R M Rogers, jr, Colorado Springs; J Bourgard, P M Heaston, W J Strickley, Bingham; F M Langford, J H Larsen, Park City; E W Hanson, Provo; J Alves, J Squires, Fillmore; J Sampson and wife, T Odgers, Nevada; S C Gilliland, Omaha.

Salt Lake Herald
January 24, 1882

HOTEL ARRIVALS.

WHITE HOUSE.

Alk. Oates Opera Company; T Nugent and family, Mrs T Lewis, E Oaks, Sandy; G H Parker, Ward, Nev; C G Terry, E E Brim, R L Scannell, Bellevue, Idaho; J Lee, Grantsville; A A Fairchild, N McLean, Ophir; I W Brown, Provo; C R Pettet, Spanish Fork; W D Rollins, Centreville; T F Hurler, New York; B Wright, Cottonwood; E G Demmick, Nephi; A T Alexander and wife, J W Henry and wife, Fillmore; F H Dyer, P Phelan, A Lodders, E A Gunnison, Bingham; M Bruneau, Tooele.

Salt Lake Herald
March 9, 1882

HOTEL ARRIVALS.

VALLEY HOUSE.

Charles Marshall and wife, Philadelphia; Wm Adams, Park City; W W Kennedy, wife and children, W J Grose, wife and child, J Rouse, wife and child, Terrace; John Williams, R Williams, Ogden; N Hubbell, Arizona; John Berdall, Logan; John Mann, Sandy; B Thomkinson, John Hardy, Fillmore; T Lorrimer, Chicago; S J Allen, Fillmore; H Huttemeyer, San Francisco; G Kroft, F Schickler, John Starr, L Thomas, C Rhodes, Denver.

Salt Lake Herald
April 5, 1882

HOTEL ARRIVALS.

WHITE HOUSE.

A E Draper, M H Taylor, Sanpete; G W Hickerson, J C Worth, Kanosh; R H McBride, Fillmore; A B Holbrook, Omaha; J Metcalf, Gunnison; J P Bush, Milford; H C Jacobs, New York; W G S Brodish and wife, Park City; S Kennicott, J B Francis, Grove, Ill; J W Brown, Provo; A Uebel, Horn Silver; R M Morrill, S L Adams, W H Buckner, E E Smith, C N Sinclair, St George; N Benardon, Ogden; E G Dimmiek, Nephi; C Halifax, Park City.

Salt Lake Herald
April 6, 1882

HOTEL ARRIVALS.

VALLEY HOUSE.

F A Hoagland, Silver Reef; J B Taylor, Wollscote, Eng; A Luman, Rock Springs; E M Yocum, E B Northrup, Silver Reef; J Mynderse, Nephi; Geo Croft and wife, Fillmore; L D Bunce, Manti; J Ashworth, Beaver; S King; E Wood, Fillmore; J Reynolds, Pioche; H Palmer, Michigan; E Raker, E Effinger, D Farmer, Clear Creek; J D Reese, A H Dunning, A M Sager, Sanpete; C Hifford, J R Blanchett, wife and two children, Franks, Logan; D Newell, Butte; D F Kreler, Park City; A Randolph, Nevada; J N Hendricks, Richmond; J Ratcliffe, J Stoddard and wife, Grantsville; J Lavin, J Maughan, Wm Rose, J Johnson, Bingham.

Salt Lake Herald
May 4, 1882

HOTEL ARRIVALS.

VALLEY HOUSE.

C S Hefferson, Dubuque, Iowa; D W Stoddard, J Brown, Wellsville; S Day, Central City; Peter Franklin, Frisco; T A Haynes, H Jensen, Fillmore; J E Frederick, Shelbyville, Mo; S A Losergan, Chicago; J S Thomas, J Thomas, Alex. M. Supper D and E R Anton Young Silver Ree.

Salt Lake Herald
May 7, 1882

HOTEL ARRIVALS.

VALLEY HOUSE.

C Petersen, Manti; F J Berryessa, P D McClanahan, C P R R; A M Pringle, G Tucker. W G Mowers, Bingham; W T Owen, Fillmore; E W Ormsby, Scipio; J Brooks. Beaver; L W Wheeler and wife, W G Wilson, H Ferrer, C Shelton S S Dummitt, Ogden; J F Hope and wife, New York; O W Hathaway, Virginia, Nev; S D Osburn; Stockton, Cal; D McMahon, E S Benton, San Francisco.

Salt Lake Herald
June 11, 1882

LIST OF AGENTS.

The following gentlemen are authorised to canvass for the SALT LAKE DAILY, SEMI WEEKLY and WEEKLY HERALD; also to receive payment and receipt for the same:

M. Muir	Bountiful, Woods Cross and Centreville
W. W. Barnett	Spring Lake and Santaquin
H. A. Lewis	Georgetown, Bear Lake Co.
Wm. Hulme	Bloomington, Bear Lake
W. A. Stewart	Inverury, Sevier County
John Hertin	Rockport and Wansnip
Alex. Graham	Lemington, Millard Co
H. Tuft	Monroe, Sevier County
Jos. Lapish	Salina, Sevier County
Thos. Wallace	Ogden and Weber Co
O. F. Lyons	Summit County
E. Henriod	American Fork
A. Leslie	Fountain Green
N. A. Rolph	Mount Pleasant
James B. Wallis	Paris, Idaho
B. W. Driggs, Jr	Pleasant Grove
E. E. Cowdell	Beaver County
Wm. Monteith	Tooele County
Coop. Store	Spanish Fork
W. L. Watkins	Brigham City
D. G. Brian	Piute County
Thomas Crawley	Juab County
J. S. Moffat	Meadowville
Jos. T. Ellis	Spring City
J. P. Wakefield	Huntington
S. R. Jewkes	Castle Dale
John Batty	Toquerville
J. K. Clark	Grantsville
James Bullock	Providence
Wm. Mendenhall	Springville
J. E. Johnson	Silver Reef
John Pymm	St. George
John Duncan	Heber City
C. T. Mills	Hoytsville
B. W. Bayborne	Cedar City
John Morgan	Mill Creek
Jos. H McCracken	Smithfield
Jos. Morgan	Wellsville
John G. M. Barnes	Kaysville
A. V. Robinson	Fillmore
S. Williams	Ephraim
John Boyden	Coalville
B. Peirce, Jr	Paradise
H. P. Miller	Richfield
F. Yates	Millville
Jasper Lemmon	Mendon
S. Francis	Morgan
John Swain	Fayette
T. Greener	Kanosh
S. Marsh	Payson
Wm. Probert, San	Holden
Charles O. Shaw	Hyrum
John S. Black	Deseret
Wm. Probert	Scipio
Charles Foote	Nephi
John W. Shepherd	Levan
William Burbeck	Provo
J. T. Hammond	Logan
George Scott	Manti
John Woodhouse	Leh

Salt Lake Herald
July 4, 1882

HOTEL ARRIVALS.

VALLEY HOUSE.

A S Pennoyer, agent J K Emmett; O
T Clark, South Star; T Service, Ogden;
G C Kidder, W H Knox, M Geary, J
Hosmer, Park City; C Finell, H Ruthi
and wife, W E Terhune, N and H Ross,
Bingham; C J Linquist, Logan; J Terry,
Mines; E Reeves, Kankakee, Ills; J J
and A McMicken, Fillmore; G W Hays,
Silver Reef; S Ball and wife, Wellsville;
A James, Rochester, N Y; J Spittigue,
O Lane, Evanston; P M Smith, Park
City; J Duke, Ophir; P Mahnken and
wife, M Mayers, Silver Reef; T M
Jacobs, New Jersey; E Davis, Colum-
bus, O; Miss E F Johnson, Logan; P W
Kerr, T J Young, New York; T J Sulli-
van and wife, Cincinnati; T Orn, Bing-
ham; M Stevenson, Cheyenne; W Forst
and family, C McPherson, Alta City.

Salt Lake Herald
July 8, 1882

HOTEL ARRIVALS.

WHITE HOUSE.

J H Vane, Provo; P Gillespie, A Lee,
Tooele; T J Brandon, Centreville; J A
Thomas, G Hammer, O Wallin, Lehi;
H D Connor, W P Parker, Milwaukee;
R O Bouton, Iowa City; N S Little,
Parksville; H P Redfield, Dubuque; F
Goetz, Chicago; J A Roddan, Mitchel-
ville; J Alves, Fillmore.

Salt Lake Herald
July 21, 1882

HOTEL ARRIVALS.

WHITE HOUSE.

A Eldridge, Centerville; J Johnson,
Coalville; T S Merchant, J Atkins, San
Francisco; B Bachman, J Vane, Provo;
O Mullett, F Dwyer, Bingham; H M
Barrett, Silver City; G Osborne, Ogden;
J Grant, Wyoming; L Bittern, Missouri;
G Hamlin, Ward; N C Springer and
wife, Miss H Springer, Park City; J
Meyer, Butte; A J Nixon, Omaha; P
Hemisan, Fillmore; W G Cushman, S
W Miller, Tintic; W M Hatfield, Spring-
ville; R Hampton, Cincinnatti.

Salt Lake Herald
August 3, 1882

HOTEL ARRIVALS.

WHITE HOUSE.

T D Brown, Chichago; G Aiken, Geo Scott, Tooele; G Pierce, Nevada; M M Johnson, W Foster, Denver; T J Brandon, Centreville; J N Erickson, R Whittaker, Cottonwood; H McInnly, O G Snow, G W Coomley, Bingham; D D Welch, Price; F Coblentz, San Francisco; Miss J Smith, E Stott, Ogden; E T George, Nev dr; J W Sweyea, Walla Wall; Mrs Norton, J H Vane, Provo; M L Powers, American Fork; J Alves, Fillmore; D Drystale, Idaho; R M Pierce, O Cowley, Wood River.

Salt Lake Herald
September 8, 1882

HOTEL ARRIVALS.

September 7, 1882.

WHITE HOUSE.

A Voyce, S Lock, Soda Springs Id; M Bruneau, Tooele; P Grill, D Owen, D R Hancock, S Larsen, Ogden; Pearce, Wm Pearce, Denver; H Tattersall, Pleasant Valley; S P Paterson, City; W J Strickley, Brooklyn, N Y; R M Keoney, D S Camp, Lancaster Pa; R S Edmunds, R J Beck, Walla Walla; S Stone, Austin, Nev; S Levi, Park City; Mrs S Morton, Canada; E Wooley, Grantsville; S Kimball, T Fell, Leavenworth, Kansas; A H Dyer, Butte, M T; S James, St Paul; A E Powell, Am Fork; S Brew, Spring City; O Blackwell, Denver, Col; L Wagner, Midway; J Johns, Alta City; A Brown, Garfield Landing; E Haydon, P Tate, South Cottonwood; B Trozona, Alta City; S Ryan, H Thomas, J Clark, Bingham; S Holderman, Morris, Ill; O Searle, Joliet, Ill; Mrs G H Hubert, Provo; F Cirkhorn, Denver, Col; Mrs Slater and children, City; Mrs West, Ogden; John Prelstley, Park City; G Houldeman, Payson; A Glispie, San Jose; T Cushing, C Cowell, Fort Douglas; J S Smith, Fort Ephram; P Hensley, S Manning, Fillmore; T Taylor, Juab; O Hall, Beaver; E Haywood, American Fork; F Stephens, Butte; S Piercy, S Bennett, Ogden.

Salt Lake Herald
September 15, 1882

HOTEL ARRIVALS.

WHITE HOUSE.

F P Horry and wife, S H Ensine, Salem, Oregon; H Williams, Springville; S Hall, Rock Creek; P Campbell, J L Thomas, Evanston; D Mulloon, Provo; T Shepard, Alta City; D Marshall, S D Russell, Butte City; G Kinghorn, S P Hewlett, Bear Lake; J Jones, Sawtooth; Miss S Atkin, Miss B Conklin, Payson; G D Frost, Fayette; D White, Oxford, Idaho; G Dickinson, Pioche; J Levy, City; R H Hill, Tintic; E D Clast, Idaho; F D Brown, Chicago; D Hills, Boston; H Morris, Bingham; I Griffin, Alta; H Williams, City; B Shurtliff, W Corrall, Provo; E F Canfield, Ogden; S Spfye and wife, St Charles, Ohio; S G Fisher and family, Crystle, Idaho; J Alves, Fillmore; G W Crowley, Bingham; C Stunne, F Schultz, Cleaveland; S P Blink, South Cottonwood; R Claabey, Butte; P Jensen, S Lewis, Mount Pleasant; D A Segmiller, G P Pierce, Boston; S Bigler, Lehi; J Phillips, Park City; E B Burnett, Logan; R T Duglas, South Cottonwood; A Alexander, American Fork; H S Conner, B Snydam, Paris, Idaho; M Powers, A T Walker, Tintic; Wm Butcher, Dick Ivy, Bingham; S Finch, J S Jack, City; S Pickett, Payson; C Chewings, South Australia; M Ragall, M Mathias, New York; Mrs Schofield, Iowa.

Salt Lake Herald
October 5, 1882

HOTEL ARRIVALS.

VALLEY HOUSE.

George Mason, Springville; James Sodore, Fort Douglas; H Gardner, Cottonwood; Samuel Ecoff, Sandy; A Abbott and wife, J D Merville and wife, Frisco; R M Nowell, Fillmore; W H Clark, Richfield; W D Pace, Washington, U T; P T Farnsworth, Beaver; J Tuckett and wife, Springville; Levi Curtis and wife, L Johnson, Isabella Johnson, Charles Curtis, Henry Redda, Spanish Fork; E L Burgoyne, Miss E Cederden, Mrs Reese, Bear Lake; L C Davis and wife, Denver; Miss E Eckersell, Evan Lewis, Chicago; W Stevenson, Echo; John Stanger and wife, James Stanger and wife, Weber; G W Spicer, wife and child, Miss Etta Vorhees, Mrs E Jones, Manti; John Cazair, Nephi; N Madsen, R Ingalls and wife, Mount Pleasant; T P Cooper, Beaver; J P Hennissey, New York; Geo Ewer, wife and son, Evanstyn; J B Stodkard, W H Malgham, Wellsville.

Salt Lake Herald
October 13, 1882

HOTEL ARRIVALS.

Salt Lake Herald
October 18, 1882

HOTEL ARRIVALS.

WHITE HOUSE.

K Haley, Buffalo; G Taylor, Tintic; W
Ainscough, Cherry Creek; E M James,
Muldove; I Janes, G F Bower, P Brad-
ford, Spanish Fork; G Walter, Ogden;
B Schurtleff, Provo; I A McKay, St
Louis; J Currad, Montana; J Kelly,
Park City; F Barrett, Chicago; Mrs
Cheroquin, M Arnett, Bingham; I Alves
Fillmere; Mt Wermbach, San Francisco;
A Egge, Rock Island; F Daly, Cotton-
wood; J Beaurgardred wife, A Leddars,
Bingham; I Brinkhurst, Juab; M Bil-
lingsly, Frisco; R R Thomas, Homans-
ville; H L Driver, Bingham; N McCarty
Ogden; O VonTrott, Butte City; T Car-
ter, Denver

Salt Lake Herald
October 22, 1882

ELECTION JUDGES.

The Final Appointments by the Commissioners,

Following are the names of the election judges appointed by the Commission, and not heretofore published:

ELECTION JUDGES.

Schofield, Emery County—Robert
McKelvey, Robert O Burkhardt, Lafayette Granger

Quincy precinct, Tooele County—Benjamin F Jenkins, Charles F Hansen,
James P Kilpatrick

Poll No. 2, Leeds precinct, Washington County—Thomas P Gillespie, Richard Kemwill, Henry Seiventopp

GARFIELD COUNTY.

Panguitch precinct—
Escalante precinct—Josiah Barker
Cannonville precinct—John H Hatch
Hillsdale precinct—R C Pinney

HOTEL ARRIVALS.

WHITE HOUSE.

John Gillespie, Tooele; Charles West, Chicago; F Fishel, Park City; R R Connell, Ogden; Chas Weltner, Ft Douglas; Harry J Curran, Cheyenne; Herrman Michky, Blackfoot; J Bourgard, Bingham; D Williams. city; L Chase, Nephi; I Jensen, Fish Creek; I McHendry, Idaho; John Johnson, Stockton; G W Smith, Ogden; John D Borip, Ft Thornburgh; Wm Bailey, Arimo; D Buckley, Bingham Canyon; Frank Peach, Fort Douglas; D Driscol, Philipsburg, Chas Galagher, George Winsor, Wood River; H L Fisher, Butte City; T R Simmons, John A Lawrence, Park City; Ed H Patter, Ogden; J C Crissman, Kelton; Wm Samsion and wife, Springville; John Closs, Fillmore; L Vestergard, Ogden; G A Wilcox, Franklyn; St Bays, Bullion, Idaho; T I Cahill, Sanpete Co; Ehoe White, Sawtooth; Chas Dixon, Jno Lloyd, Park City; L D Bunce, Springville; E A Gunsen, Bingham.

'RAH!

For Hon. John T. Caine.

A Heavy Vote all Round.

With Sweeping Majorities for the People's Candidate.

Special Returns to the "Herald" From all Parts of the Territory.

The enterprise of the HERALD in arranging for special dispatches from all parts of the Territory where a telegraph office was in the vicinity, has enabled this journal to lay before its readers, this morning, comparatively complete returns of the vote in this Territory on Tuesday. According to the estimate of the HERALD, about three-fourths the total vote is reported, though less than half the precincts have reported. It will be fully a week before all the returns are in, some of the precincts being out of the way. The indications now are that Hon. John T. Caine will receive about 20,000 votes, and P. T. VanZile about 5,000, or four to one for the People's nominee. The election, while awakening a great deal of interest, passed off without any disturbance or without much complaint. In this city and in Logan, it is charged that some Liberals who were watching the interests of their party at the polls were guilty of an act which was base in itself, and could do no good to their cause or candidate. It is alleged that they offered People voters envelopes, in which were secreted Liberal tickets. The consequence would be that the ballot would have to be thrown out, and the majority of the People's candidate would be reduced in proportion to the number of stuffed envelopes they could foist upon innocent voters.

Beaver County was considered close, and there was some hope among the Liberals that they would outvote their opponents, but the table below shows how badly they were astray and the appended special dispatch can afford no consolation.

Beaver County gives Caine nearly 300 majority. Frisco, with a total registration of 262, polls only 103 votes; the falling off being a Liberal loss. We have gained considerably and decimated the opposition. Congratulations all around.

No definite information was received from Spanish Fork in Utah County; but a gentleman sends word that the election passed off smoothly, there being but one challenge. Up to 2 p.m 355 votes had been polled, the proportion being about 30 to 1 in favor of the People's nominee.

We give here the result of the vote at some eighty precincts, which was secured by special dispatch:

BEAVER COUNTY.

Precinct.	Caine.	VanZile.
Milford,	79	26
Frisco,	9	94
Carbonate,	—	33
Grampion,	—	27
Beaver,	—	70
Minersville,	88	8
Adamsville,	41	2
Greenville,	49	4
	329	261

BOX ELDER.

Precinct.	Caine.	VanZile.
Box Elder,	369	14
Promontory,	15	3
Corinne,	—	74
Terrace,	1	7
Bear River,	77	—
Kelton,	6	15
	450	140

CACHE COUNTY.

Precinct.	Caine.	VanZile.
Millville,	79	—
Logan,	617	48
Providence,	80	1
Paradise,	116	—
Smithfield,	238	8
	1130	57

DAVIS COUNTY.

Precinct.	Caine.	VanZile.
Kaysville	284	20
West Bountiful	50	—
Totals	334	20

EMERY COUNTY.

Precinct.	Caine.	VanZile.
Scofield	13	10

IRON COUNTY.

Precinct.	Caine.	VanZile.
Cedar	157	—
Parowan	157	20
Total	314	20

JUAB COUNTY.

Precinct.	Caine.	VanZile.
Nephi	398	8
Tintic	2	60
Juab	84	5
Total	484	73

KANE COUNTY.

Precinct.	Caine.	VanZile.
Toquerville	64	—
Orderville	44	—
Mt. Carmel	27	—
Glendale	51	—
	186	

MILLARD COUNTY.

Precinct.	Caine.	VanZile.
Leamington	36	1
Fillmore	127	27
Deseret	81	1
	244	29

MORGAN COUNTY.

Precinct.	Caine.	VanZile.
Morgan	110	12
Canyon Creek	89	2
Milton	41	9
Croydon	38	8
Peterson	35	5
	312	36

HOTEL ARRIVALS.

Salt Lake Herald
November 12, 1822

"What Fools," Etc.

One week ago last night was what might be termed the culmination of the campaign in Salt Lake City, and the big guns were fired preparatory to counting the captured hosts on Tuesday. True on Monday night good work was got in at Ogden and other places, but all conversions and calculations were made on or before a week ago to-day.

It is certainly edifying to look over the professions of love made by the leading speakers of the Liberals to the voters in their own settlements, some admissions which the loving ones are now ashamed of, but it is also very amusing to remember with what high hopes every member of the little band was filled and how crestfallen they must feel at viewing the contrasts. They all knew that it needed but the ventilation of Liberal ideas to transform a large majority of the members of the People's party into rabid malcontents and active workers among those who were opposed to the people. Reference to the returns will show how these self-made champions of their rights miserably failed, and their Bombastes Furioso march was nothing more than the sound of tinkling cymbals.

"In Bountiful something near 500 people attended the rally, and everybody felt pleased and satisfied. It was the largest and most enthusiastic ever held in Davis county." So said the reporter. The returns show that West, East and South Bountiful gave John T. Caine 326 votes, and P. T. Van Zile 29 votes.

At Scipio, Kanosh and Fillmore, Bane and McBride and reported as having "by their burning words of eloquence allayed any prejudice that might exist against the Liberal party." The vote was J. T. Caine 306, P. T. Van Zile 43.

At "Ephraim about 400 people were present. Sanpete will one day be the banner Liberal county. The people feel as if they had a 'new revelation.'" The vote was J. T. Caine, 247, P. T. VanZile, 11.

At Brigham city "the court house was well filled, and the speakers won the hearts of the people who heard them;" they turned out for J. T. Caine 300, for P. T. VanZile 14.

At Coalville "the schoolhouse was packed. Judge VanZile had the crowd with him, quiet and attentive, and often applauding." On November 7th they applauded J. T. Caine with 197 votes, P. T. VanZile with 26 votes.

At Lehi "about 150 persons were present, who listened to the Liberal speakers attentively, and the audience seemed to be well impressed with what was said." The people said 324 votes for their candidate and 18 for the other man.

And so we might enumerate *ad infinitum*. But the folly of the pretenders is made manifest, and, as the returns come rolling in the reformers feel smaller every day, by the comparisons. They sadly overshot the mark in the measure of their own abilities and the credulity of the people they sought to allure.

Salt Lake Herald
November 18, 1882

HOTEL ARRIVALS.

VALLEY HOUSE.

G J Puhek, New York; H Maend, J Dunn, F Bare, Butte; J H Robertson, Salina; W H Knox, F S Dresser, H Collins, Park City; H D Douglas, A J Page, Leadville; A Dennis, Eureka; G Dunne, Illinois; A J Rohde, Nevada; G M Webster, West Jordan; F E Browne, San Francisco; J Kelly, Fillmore; J Taylor, Utah, W F Purver, Harrisburg, Pa; V F Taylor, Baltimore; H Smith, Omaha; M Dolan, A W Woodbury, H P Wheeler, Montana.

Salt Lake Herald
November 30, 1882

HOTEL ARRIVALS.

WHITE HOUSE.

T George, Green River; C Weaver, Soda Springs; R Green, Cottonwood; C A Vanderhoop, Grantsville; C F Harvey, Kansas; J O Carkwyk, D R G Ry; Jos Mason, Liverpool; Jas Donelson, Butte; E I' Buffington, Green Castle, Mo; A Higham, Virgin Creek; D B Holmes and wife, Mrs Sands, St Louis; R Thompson, Park City; A V Robinson, Fillmore; J G Keeney, Springville; W S Willis, Jas Clyde, Miss Mary Clyde, Miss Mary Campbell, Weber City; R E Brien, Ophir; Jos Saberger; S D Edwards, Challis; Mrs Chereguin, Geo Mullctd, D Clays, Bingham; N Coils, Jho Royle, Neil Romer, Alta; H Slyckherr, South Cottonwood; Ed Gleason, Tintic; M Foley, Bingham; Fr Shester, Helena.

Salt Lake Herald
December 14, 1882

HOTEL ARRIVALS.

WHITE HOUSE.

B Fowler, Park City; G L Collidan, Tuscarora; P W Ousley, Cala; H M Tanner and wife, Wm Gyde, Ogden; R D Mansfield, Big Cottonwood; M Cushmore, Cedar Creek; J Ford, C W Watson, W G Summers, Bingham; N L Darling, Missoula, M T; Miss Southworth, Farmington; G Englehard, Morgan Smelter; R C Whitney, Big Cottonwood; M Evans, Lehi Junction; A W Thompson, D A Despain, Granite; Jenson, Sandy; T A Cramer, City; Bruce Griffin, Bingham; J W O'Conn, Park City, G H Steed and wife, Farmington; Mrs Wilson, Provo; J Alma Fillmore; P Smith, Provo; C W Gr no, Bingham; J H Wilson, Juab; D'Courcy, Stockton.

Salt Lake Herald
December 15, 1882

HOTEL ARRIVALS.

VALLEY HOUSE.

G E Wallace, Ogden; Peter Morahan, Cheyenne; S P Hancock, J Sweeney, Draper; Pat Mulloy, Idaho; Thomas Bailey, Silver Reef; J Halfen, Kendale Station; P J Snyder, E R Holmes, Omaha; S J Courtney, Ill; A Dean, Alta; T O Ellis, Tuscon; J D Ellet, Fillmore; M Brown, Ogden; H J Murdock, Bingham; H J Brown, Ogden.

Salt Lake Herald
January 4, 1883

HOTEL ARRIVALS.

VALLEY HOUSE.

H Harris, Beaver; P Johnson, Ogden; D Davis, Miss Gregory, Franklin, Idaho; J B Champion, Miss Champion, Park City; Jos Payne, Joe Henery, Green River; E S Larson, F Smith, Logan; M Hegarty, Park City; C Snyder, H Smith, Fillmore; W Gunnell, Stephen Nye, Idaho; M O Bailey, Omaha; Wm McLaughlin, Toana, Nev; D Stoddard, Wellsville; L Johnson, Miss L Matson, Miss H S5nford, Springville; E Blewett, Jas Geach, Chas Geach, Tintic.

Salt Lake Herald
February 8, 1883

HOTEL ARRIVALS.

VALLEY HOUSE.

C S Nelson, Battle Creek; S A Hendricks, J E Williamson, Richmond; L Cain, F King, Carson Nev; Mrs Manvick, A E Lewis, Elko; T Fagan, Nevada; H H Woodman, Catawba; A C Campbell, Missouri; A Lumman, Rock Springs; J E Williams, city; J Salby, N Y; J J Micken, Fillmore; J Barry, H J Millar, Eagle Rock; W Hogan, Stockton; W McHarvey and wife, Evanston.

Salt Lake Herald
February 28, 1883

HOTEL ARRIVALS.

WHITE HOUSE.

W C ad, Lander; T B Lee, Tooele; H H Schweitzer and brother, San Francisco; S Davis Rush Lake; A J ff W Vtley, Tintic; J Hatch, Heber; T Powell and wife, S Powell Lehi; S and H Liler, Pleasant Valley; D McInu s Bingham; C M Sickler J C Morrill Alta; J M Worth, Fort Bridger; J George, Fillmore; J A Smith, Pleasant Valley Junction; G W Kingsley, Tintic; S F Gare, Ogden.

Salt Lake Herald
March 13, 1883

HOTEL ARRIVALS.

WHITE HOUSE.

E J Ward, Pleasant Grove; Bernard Edwards, D M Litts, Wm Willson, Jos Johnson, A M Vale, S E Fitch, Ogden; W Dobbie, Morgan Williams; Dr G Haes, Ed R Adkin, Jos R Bush, Robert Edwards, J Williams E H Ferguson, J Stanley, H Christy, city; R K Green, G R Green, A J Erskins, Park City; Wm Wiley jr, Colorado Springs, E Ranch, G Mullett, Thos Winn, Chas Rossi, W H Goldsworth, Thos Price, Al Gauchah, Bingham; J B Williams, Fillmore; Tom Ferguson, Marysvale; M J Brockway, Wood River, Wm Hooper, West Jordan; Ficholo Fox, Chicago; Wm Nieschwatz, Grand Junction, Col; Frank Pierce, Uintah Agency, Utah; John Poolen, John Wordsworth, Tintic.

Salt Lake Herald
March 25, 1883

A Singular Find.

The *News* of last evening learns from Dr. J. D. M. Crockwell, who is located at Clear Lake, Millard County, that while his son William, a lad of about 10 years of age, was hunting stock in that locality last Wednesday, he discovered a portion of the remains of a man lying upon the ground. When the boy returned home and reported to his father, the latter with the lad and Mr. Peter Woolsey, proceeded to the spot where the bones lay. With them were portions of a snuff colored fustian box coat, with side pockets. None of the other clothing could be identified so far as color was concerned. There were also found near the spot a silver watch, brass chain and $400 in money. Dr. Crockwell at once sent a messenger to Fillmore, to notify the coroner.

Salt Lake Herald
March 30, 1883

HOTEL ARRIVALS.

WHITE HOUSE.

J Walsh, Fish Creek; E Otella, J J
Beauregard Edward Cook, W S Hussey,
Bingham; F Fischel, C E Preves, A A
Huber, H Manuel, Park City; H Doug-
lass; S R Worthington, Deep Creek; A P
Cook, N Sampson, S A Tatman, N A A
Collins, American Fork; H A Schubert,
Sandy; E Wilcox, Provo; N Parry, Park
City; Caleb Hunt, Echo; W Williams, J
R O Cariston, and son, Evanston; A T
Quince, Cheyenne; John A Alvers, Mrs
Bartholomew, Fillmore; J P Languishe,
Harold Forster, Wm Cullington and
wife, Miss K Bube, Mionie Maddern Co;
E Wheeler, Butte; J C Chaven, Harry
Haynes and wife, South Cottonwood; R
Prideane, Bingham; P D Ao per, Rich-
field; J Smith, Payson.

Salt Lake Herald
April 3, 1883

HOTEL ARRIVALS.

WHITE HOUSE.

Edward Plant, Warren Will, J S
McBoller, C W Thompson, H Gerun,
Brigham; H Grune, F Grune, Lehi; C H
Creek, Park City; J Q Knowlten, S A
Kemrer, J C Flood, A M Cameron, J
Stanley, Grantsville; H Lyons, San
Francisco; W Hickman, Park City;
C W Beidel, H R Rogers, Bingham;
Peter Poulaski, Chicago; H Stephens, H
Comming, Piedmont; E J Jackmann,
Tintic; C J Mielsen, Big Cottonwood;
H Behman, Park City, J L Young,
J Jones, M Crawford, Alta; Forrest
Green, Lehi; Harry Rich, Frank Rose,
Frank Colfax, New York; Wm Sturte-
vant, D R McCarady, J McPaerson,
D R G R R; Geo Metzler, Des Moines;
W D Brandt, Austin Bemis, Frank
Bemis, Bingham; Jos Vana, Spanish
Fork; D McInnes, Bingham; B Norton,
Cottonwood; J B Eastman, Bingham;
E F Sherman, Fillmore; J J Hill, Tin-
tic; Miss McHadden, Payson; Dr John
Biggs, Provo.

The Weather.

The following telegraphic summary shows the condition of the weather throughout the Territory on Wednesday:

Moroni—Slight fall of snow last night; snowing at intervals to-day.

Richfield—Stormed a little during the night; still cloudy.

Mount Pleasant—Been snowing all day—looks like more; very cold.

Fairview—Cold and snowing at intervals.

Manti—Very cold and snowing a little at intervals.

Deseret—Clearing up; pleasant.

Ogden—Cloudy ;looks like it would storm shortly.

Fillmore—Snowed two inches last night; thawing fast; clouds not yet dispersed.

Springville—Cool and cloudy; looks like more rain.

Frisco—Cloudy; looks like more storm; quite cool.

Monroe—Rained last night; still cloudy, with cold wind.

Juab—Cloudy; looks like storm.

Glenwood—Cold wind blowing, cloudy; looks like storm.

Corinne—Raining; rained most of last night.

Brigham City—Snowing but calm; thermometer 40.

Logan—Very cloudy; snowing quite fast.

Payson—Rained last night; still raining.

Pleasant Grove—Rained all night; clearing up now.

St. George—Windy last two days; very pleasant to-day.

Silver Reef—Clear and pleasant.

Beaver—Slight snow last evening; pleasant to-day.

Cedar City—Fine morning; slight snow storm last evening.

Hebron—Calm and cloudy; sun shining at intervals.

HOTEL ARRIVALS.

May 4, 1883.

CLIFT HOUSE.

E Pratt, Wood River; M A Gordon, Bellevue, Ida; John Manuel, Snake Valley; J T Hallaway, Tintic; M M Silveria, Silver Reef; James O Liddle, Fillmore; T R Sandberg, Pleasant Grove; William Carroll, Provo.

DEPUTY REGISTRARS.

Following is a list of the deputy registration officers for the registration commencing on Monday, June 4, and ending on Saturday, June 9, 1883. The list is complete as to all precincts, except those in Uintah County, for which appointments have been forwarded, and doubtless accepted by the appointees, though Secretary Thomas has not yet received official notification of the fact:

MILLARD COUNTY.

John Nield, Meadow precinct.

Alvin L. Robinson, Fillmore precinct.

Nicholas Paul, Holden precinct.

George Monroe, Scipio precinct.

George Morrison, Leamington precinct.

George Finlinson, Oak Creek precinct.

William A. Ray, Deseret precinct.

MORGAN COUNTY.

Eli Kilbourn, Canyon Creek precinct.

A. F. Poulson, Milton precinct.

Thomas Walker, Croydon precinct.

A. D. Shurtliff, Morgan precinct.

John Green, Peterson precinct.

Terrific Hail Storm.

FILLMORE, UTAH, June 15, '83.

(Special to the HERALD.)

Editors Herald:

A mysterious, rumbling noise from the west announced the approach of a terrific hail storm, which lasted about fifteen minutes. Hailstones of an immense size and quantity descended with a force that stripped trees of their tender foliage, cut down fields of grain and all manner of vegetation, broke window panes, and generally effecting damage that cannot be estimated. The ground was spread with a mantle of three inches of hailstones

Death of Mrs. Faust.

A brief item in Tuesday's issue of the HERALD was the first intimation that many had of the serious illness of the wife of Dr. H. J. Faust. As will be seen by notice elsewhere death occurred early yesterday afternoon. This sad event deprives a happy family of a loving wife and affectionate mother, and takes from earth a noble woman, for Mrs. Faust was the wife, mother and woman in the best senses of the terms. Her life, which has been suddenly cut off in its prime, was a remarkable one, and she the true heroine. Dark shadows and bright sunshine have alternated frequently during her comparatively brief sojourn in this world, but whether shrouded by one or basking in the other she was ever the same good and grand woman, bearing her sufferings with a courage and cheerfulness that did honor to her sex, and enjoying life best when those about her were happy. She was a pioneer, a child of the frontier; and a noble specimen of the woman of the broad west. While yet an infant her mother and father died, victims to the early persecutions and drivings of the Mormons. The homeless orphan was adopted into the family of Peter Robinson, and with them came to Utah the second year after the settlement of this city. Fate seemed to have ordered that she pass her life on the borders of civilization. The Robinsons went to Fillmore, then a mere outport or way station on the emigrant road to Southern California. Here it was that she met and married Dr. Faust. Her next pioneering was to accompany her husband on the Overland-stage line, she being the first woman to travel on the trans-continental coach out of Salt Lake. For long years she braved the dangers of Indians and outlaws on the western borders of the territory and when perils were most threatening she appeared bravest, cheering and encouraging those about her. Sunshine came with financial prosperity, when she proved that though surrounded by anything but the refining influences of civilization she had not neglected the cultivation of her mind, for it was demonstrated that she could shine among people who had been blessed all their lives by elegant and refining associations. For long years she has been virtually an invalid, suffering at times severely, but with fortitude and without complaining. None but her family and most intimate friends knew how much she encouraging those about her. Sunshine came with financial prosperity, when she proved that though surrounded by anything but the refining influences of civilization she had not neglected the cultivation of her mind, for it was demonstrated that she could shine among people who had been blessed all their lives by elegant and refining associations. For long years she has been virtually an invalid, suffering at times severely, but with fortitude and without complaining. None but her family and most intimate friends knew how much she endured from physical ailments. A sketch of her remarkable life would read like highly drawn romance, and in it all there could be nothing found that would not mark her as the true woman. To her family—husband, two sons and two daughters—her death will be irreparable; but they may be assured of such comfort and consolation in their deep grief as can come from the consciousness that hundreds will unite with them in sorrow and mourning for the dear departed. The funeral services will be conducted in the Fourteenth Ward Assembly Rooms on Thursday at 3 o'clock p.m.

Salt Lake Herald
June 23, 1883

GENERAL ELECTION, AUGUST, 1883.

List of officers to be elected for Millard County on August 6, furnished by Mr. Anderson, County Clerk.

FOR UNEXPIRED TERMS.

Probate Judge.
One Selectman.
County Clerk.
Assessor and Collector.
Sheriff.
Coroner.
Prosecuting Attorney.
Surveyor.
Justice of the Peace and Constables for Fillmore, Meadow Creek, Kanosh, Holden, Oak Creek, Scipio, Deseret, Leamington.

FOR FULL TERMS.

One Selectman.
County Superintendent of District Schools.
Justice of the Peace for Fillmore Precinct.

THE SOUTH.

Bright Crop Prospects—A Spirit in Progress—Mineral Discoveries, etc.

HOLDEN, MILLARD COUNTY,
June 16th, 1883.

Editors Herald:

Thinking a word from Millard County might interest some of your readers, I drop down in this Elysium of the south where a decade since I sojourned for several months.

Holden is certainly the oasis of Millard County, and its inhabitants among the most unsophisticated in the Territory. My observations and dealings prove them to be firm in their convictions, honorable in their dealings, and noted as a community, and comparatively rich in this world's goods. A few years since this place was considered over-stocked with half a dozen families. Last evening I sat down with a couple of friends, who counted over sixty thriving families. Yesterday I visited the day school, it being the gala day, after one year's tuition by Mr. Oscar Burglund, a graduate from the B. Y. Academy at Provo. The exercises were of a very interesting nature, the most pleasing feature of which was to see the love and confidence that existed between the children and their teacher, and to hear the eulogy from all sides upon this young man, who certainly appears to possess, in an eminent degree, the qualifications for a successful teacher. The report showed that the second quarter he had one hundred scholars, and the third ninety-nine. In fact, every house in this vicinity appears to have a full quorum of Utah's best crop, although very few of the citizens appear to have broken the law of '62, or any other law; and a trip through these country towns and villages would or ought to convince the small-family advocates that no law framed by man can stay the coming power of these healthy, strong, virtuous and exceedingly numerous people.

Holden is certainly not very enthusiastic about building its meeting house, for the brick was burned for that building when I was here ten years since; but it is thought by some that they will be cool enough to handle the coming fall. The crop prospect is very good, although a somewhat limited area was planted through fear of a scarcity of water, which has proved to be abundant.

Scipio has, as usual, a good harvest prospect. They are preparing for quite a building boom in that fertile valley. The Co-operative Mercantile Institution under the successful management of Bishop Yates has matured plans and is letting contracts for quite a large building. President Thompson and several others are busy in the same line.

I also observed a new store building in course of erection in Fillmore.

At Meadow and Kanosh the crop prospects never before were so good. At Meadow the area is the largest ever sown, and my informant, himself an extensive farmer, told me that he thought Bishop Bennett would be put to his wits' end to know where to store the tithing grain. To a man up a tree, this anxiety appears strange, but all good Mormons evidently believe in paying there tithing as correctly as any other debts. At Kanosh the crops are very forward and looking splendid. Bishop Kimball has gone somewhat exclusively into the dry wheat farming, and seem to take a pride in coaching his friends down to the farm and insisting upon their footing it right into the finest stand of wheat we ever saw attempted to be raised in Utah without irrigation. The season has certainly been very propitious, and the bishop has certainly good cause for the satisfaction he takes at his venture.

Bishop Black, of Deseret, informs me that their crop prospects, although rather backward, are very good. Their new dam is a perfect success, which gives the inhabitants confidence. Deseret is one of those places whose permanency and success depend upon a good damming.

The people last week appear to have had a very pleasing visit from F. M. Lyman, the Millard County apostle as he is claimed. They certainly repose great confidence in this gentleman, and consider him a safe counselor.

I hear of some mineral prospects of a bright nature hereabouts, which I shall probably refer to hereafter.

WHY NOT.

Salt Lake Herald
August 7, 1883

HOTEL ARRIVALS.

VALLEY HOUSE.

H Sloan, Butte; J R Liddle, Alabama; James Powell, Alonzo Nest, George H J P McFarlane, A Remo, F McCulloh John Kambitsch, Emil Piel, Denver; T J Hart, Cheyenne, John Piazzi, M E Greenwalt, J Greenwalt, H N Smith, Kate Smith, Adelena Smith, Mrs K T Beverly, Pittsburg, Pa; D E Bartruff and Harrisburg; W Stephenson, B Antonio, L Antonio, Sacramento; W Mitchell, Joseph Andrews, Silver Reef; James Shannon, James Keller, Stephens Point, Wis; F M Ludington, F Hyslop, Omaha; J W Baldie, wife and daughter, Mich; P Barox and wife; J Callahan, Ohio; D C Reed, G W Cropper, M Beauregard, W W Davis, Fillmore; T W Stewart, wife and daughter, Idaho; J P Clark, M J Holland, St Louis; E Shanks, C Anderson, Deseret; John Stoddard Aspen.

Salt Lake Herald
September 26, 1883

HOTEL ARRIVALS.

September 25, 1883.

CLIFT HOUSE.

J W Johnson; Idaho; S G Monroe, Osceola, N v; Mrs A Swain, Cleveland, O; F W Riddle, Tuscarora, Nev; S O Snyder, W J Kinsey, H A Olney; Denver; A Mapberry, T C Devlin, Bingham; W P Payne, J H Grimm, T Hook, Fillmore City; Frank Roader and family, U & N; Smith Eltenge; Park City.

NEW METROPOLITAN HOTEL.

F Hedges, Sandy; C A Smith, Clear Creek; B Rivers and wife, Leavenworth, Kan; J E Whiting and wife, I E Stoddard, Miss M Lewis, Miss N Wekrell, J Maginnis, B F Ringgold, Mr and Mrs Tearl and child, J Parnee, J M Sibevon, W E Morse, C Stanley, Mrs Phillips, New York; H Sommers, Denver, J Tait, Park City.

Salt Lake Herald
October 5, 1883

PERSONAL.

Bishop Lunt, of Cedar City, is here.

J. V. Robinson, Esq., of Fillmore, is paying a visit to Salt Lake.

Commissions.

Since the last report the following commissions were issued by Acting Governor Thomas:

Millard county.—C. P. Beauregard, justice of the peace, Filmore precinct; C. C. Beauregard, constable, Fillmore precinct.

HOTEL ARRIVALS.

CONTINENTAL HOTEL.

E Charomah, Nevada city; J C Russell, Washington; G Lavaguinc, West Jordan; A T Wright Ogden, P Porter Park city; D C Kane and wife, Chicago; W G Ryland and wife, Chicago; W P Buckhurst, Walter Buckhurst, Melbourne Jas W Thompson and wife. J W Farrer, Ogden; Frank Newell, Psovo; J Sontag C L Stevenson, San Francisco; E W Davis, F C Bleachy, H C McBurney, Umatila Agency; H T Allen Danver; W H King, Fillmore; J A Shepley, Am Fork; J H Samson, wife and daughter Chicago; Carey M Mason, Denver; Dr W H Olsten, Provo; M Flavin, Cincinnat'; Joseph Tucker, Cleer creek; W M Ferry, Ed P Ferry, D C McLaughlin, Park city; Fred Turner, Logan; O T Richmond, L W Shurtliff, Ogden; W N Dugenbury, Provo; M W Merrill, Richmond; M C Jenes, Miss Mary Ridges, W L Webster and wife, Franklin, Id.

HOTEL ARRIVALS.

VALLEY HOUSE.

J Stradford, John Castleberg, R S Field, Illinois; Geo C Parkinson and wife, Franklin; P Burton, Echo; P R James, M J Carroll, Dubuque; Miss C Peterson, R B Moore, John D Howe, J J Worenhimer, Denver; L J Harris, E J Dillinger. Botany, N. Y.; S M Stone, Chicago; J W Galvin, W H Branch, Portsmouth; J D Reese, Fillmore; M A Burgess, Omaha; M A Taylor and wife, Sanpete; D J Post, Hillsdale; J T Shipley, H D Burgess, Honolulu; John Lawrence, Bullion; Thomas E Davis, Chache; W J Vallean, Barrie, Ont; Geo C Prentice, San Francisco; Mrs Ollie Silver and child, Ogden; Miss A Bohn, Tooele; J A Jenniss, G A Spencer, Palisade, N J Wallace, Carson, Nev; Ed R Adkins, Leavenworth; D H Peery, Ogden; M B Bates, G Dyer, Steubenville; J B Foot.

Salt Lake Herald
October 16, 1883

Serious Injury.

John Warren Henry, of Fillmore was seriously hurt on Sunday while discriminating between two herds of cattle. A furious bovine came in contact with his horse, throwing him violently against the ground, injuring his spine. He also sustained internal injuries which it was thought would prove fatal. The poor man was not expected to live last night, but was still alive at 4 p.m. to-day, but death might ensue at any time.   D.

PLEASANT GROVE, Oct. 15th, 1883.

Salt Lake Herald
October 30, 1883

Commissions.

Acting-Governor Thomas has issued commissions since the last report as follows:

Millard county—E. L. Lyman, constable, Oak Creek precinct; Hyrum Mace, probate judge; J. C. Metcham, constable, Leamington precinct; L. R. Crocker, justice of the peace, Deseret precinct; George Finlinson, justice of the peace, Oak Creek precinct; C. Overson, justice, Leamington precinct; W. H. King, justice, Fillmore precinct.

MILLARD COUNTY.

Good Reports from the South--The Tin Mines.

HOLDEN, Millard County,
November 2, 1883.

Editors Herald:

Kindly grant us a small portion of your valuable space, in the which to say a few things concerning our little county, for, while we are aware we do not occupy a position among the foremost, we are vain enough to suppose there are some of your readers who will be sufficiently interested in our welfare to desire to know what we are doing and what more we hope to do for the weal of our fair Territory. In the first place we can say that generally speaking the county has enjoyed the most prosperous season for cereals and fruit—excepting the peach crop, which unfortunately was destroyed totally by the spring frosts, that it has known for years. Of course the low price of grain is somewhat of a drawback, but in this, as "misery loves company," we are glad to find we are not alone, our sister counties being in similar circumstances. The grain crop is estimated at 100,000 bushels, 47,000 of which was raised in Scipio, better known as Round Valley. The lowest estimate of the apple crop gives it as 40,000 bushels for the county.

The general health has been and is most excellent, and with the desire to improve and build up the animate, has come also one to do likewise with the inanimate, as the number of buildings of both public and private nature will testify. In Deseret our well known and respected citizen, Bishop J S. Black, is erecting an elegant brick residence, in which he is combining art with use. The bricks of which it is constructed are the first made in Deseret. His brother William Black, is also having a fine home put up for him of brick made and shipped from Provo. The Cooperative store of Scipio, which is under the efficient management of Bishop Yates, is building more commodious, convenient and desirable quarters on the corner adjoining the site of the present one. It will be completed and ready for occupancy, it is thought, by Christmas at the latest. The brick of which it is built is very similar to what is known in your city as the "Groesbeck," and is made right in their own little burg. Report has it that early in the spring a new school-house will be another addition to the improvements of the town

As regards our own beloved town, we are trying to keep abreast with our neighbors in all things. Our new meeting house, the plans of which have been drawn for some time, is being rapidly pushed towards completion. Mr. C. Rawlinson has charge of the carpenter department, while Mr. N. Paul presides over the stone work, our genial friend, William Probert, formerly of Scipio, being the general drummer and pusher of the structure. All of these gentlemen are hard to beat in their several lines. When completed, if we may be allowed to judge from the present appearance of the building, as well as the designs as explained to us, we consider our place of worship will be second to none of the kind in even your beautiful metropolis. Everything which tends to form the structure is of home product, including the rock foundation, brick walls and stone facings. The stone which is to be used in the door step, window sills and lintels is a very curious composition, and is thought by Mr. Paul to contain traces of marble. It is brought from a quarry some ten miles distant. The outside dimensions of the main building are 65 feet long by 35 feet wide, with a ceiling inside of 20 feet. In the rear of the main building there is to be a vestry twelve feet square, with an upper room the same size for special meetings. The roof is to be ornamented with a steeple in which will be a clock and bell. The style of the architecture is the old gothic. It is thought the people will be able to use the building for worship early next Spring. Our school, of which Mr. Oscar B. Berglund is superintendent, is well attended and under his tuition the scholars are making rapid and healthy progress. Since his advent to our town, some two years ago, by his genial manners and thorough discipline of the young, he has so endeared himself to the people as to make them look forward with regret to the time when he will possibly leave them for climes better adapted to his ambitions. He is a graduate of Provo Academy, that institution towards which hundreds of our youth will ever turn with feelings of delight and gratitude. We are in hopes to be able at a very early date to give our children more cheerful and appropriate quarters for their pursuit of knowledge.

In Fillmore, there is at present considerable excitement over the discovery in the adjacent hills of large bodies of ore containing a metal which has every appearance and property of tin when smelted and which the locaters persist in believing to be tin notwithstanding some of the assayers in your city declare it iron. The metal when smelted can be used as tin in brazing and soldering. It will cut with a knife exactly like tin. Experiments show that horse shoes and other iron articles, such as frying pans, etc., can be coated with it similar to the general form of tinning. Eastern assayers give returns as 47 per cent. tin. In the early part of the week, a meeting of the citizens was held, organizing a mining district. Should the hopes of the locators be realized, a most valuable discovery will have been made, over which not only the Territory but the nation will have cause for gratulations, and our county will assume an enviable position in the ranks of the mineral producing portions of our glorious country.

The sulphur mines at Cove Fort are already working a considerable force and are affording labor as woodhaulers to some of our settlers. Thus far developments are very satisfactory. Should present indications continue of our mineral products, we are looking forward with pleasurable anticipations to the introduction of the Denver & Rio Grande narrow guage to our settlements.

Kanosh, Meadow, Oak Creek and the other towns are all in a prosperous condition and lending valuable aid towards the county's progress.

The Ruby Lafayette Comedy company, under the management of J. P. Curran, have been "doing" the county and meeting with good success. They give an exhibition far above the general run of traveling companies. They have made many friends and speak very highly of the kind treatment received on their trip.

The improvement associations have commenced again for the season, and anticipate pleasurable and instructive times.

CONCERNED.

Salt Lake Herald
November 16, 1883

Fillmore Tin.

From Mr. G. Huntsman, of Fillmore, who arrived in Salt Lake yesterday, we learn that there is not a little interest being taken thereabout as well as here in the supposed tin mine discovery. The location is about three and a half miles southeast of Fillmore, near a place bearing the euphonious and suggestive title of "Hell Hole." It is claimed that some specimens have yielded eighty per cent. of tin, while others produce a white metal which may be tin or something more valuable. The find was first made nineteen years ago, but the discoverer was called away, and it not being a good time for such ventures, it has lain idle through all the intervening time. It is said to be a bold and well-defined vein, traceable for ten miles, and the probabilities are that if it holds out anywhere near what present indications point to, there will be considerable interest manifested in it during the coming year. It is tolerably certain that the half has not yet been told of the resources of Southern Utah, and when substantial developments take place there will be gained another conspicuous and enduring step in the material progress of the Territory.

Mr. G. Huntsman, a prominent business man of Fillmore, is in the city. He says the prospects for his town were never so bright as now.

Salt Lake Herald
November 21, 1883

Mr. G. Huntsman, of Fillmore, leaves for his home to-day.

Salt Lake Herald
November 23, 1883

Mr. Dan Olsen, the pioneer musician of Utah, passed through Salt Lake from the East on his way to Fillmore on Wednesday.

Salt Lake Herald
November 27, 1883

Commissions.

The following commissions have been issued by Acting-Governor Thomas:

Millard county—Joseph Holbrook, sheriff; W. H. King, county clerk; T. C. Callister, superintendent of district schools; Joshua Greenwood, justice, Fillmore city; T. C. Callister, assessor and collector.

Salt Lake Herald
November 29, 1883

HOTEL ARRIVALS.

WHITE HOUSE.

C Dodon, Cottonwood; T Gibbons, Sandwich Islands; O W Lowell, Tintic; G L Hyde, Spring City; F B Pierpont, Fossil; P H Lashbrook, W A Sparks, Bingham; W Margan and family, Cache Valley, D Lambert, J P Lambert; A McCornick, Kansas; J Welch, Park City; T D Stone, S Moore, Ohio, J Dordon, J Morriss, T Williams, L Huey, Ogden; W J Rowline, Fillmore; G H Ceysor, Sanpete; O W Royce, Butte; S F Haines, Norriston; E Hoakofsky, San Francisco; J Chipman, Spanish Fork; H Feltache, Ogden; J Wrathall, Grantsville; W Hatfield, Springville; Mrs Eummins and daughter, Sandy; M Mc Beaver, Bingham; O M Kerry, Montezuma; M O'Rourk, Chicago.

Trained Horses.

THE HERALD recently contained an account of the remarkable success attending Mr. George Bartholomew's efforts in the direction of narrowing the gap separating the human and equine families, his results seeming to foreshadow Robert Bonner's prediction that horses would yet be able to talk. The latter individual is too enthusiastic on the subject, while others are not enthusiastic enough, as anyone will say who recognizes what actual results Bartholomew is achieving. He was visited by our townsman, Mr. P. Margetts, while recently in the East, and a reliable endorsement of all that is claimed as to the wonderful results of systematic horse training can be obtained from the latter gentleman. He has recently received a set of photographs of the horses referred to in various attitudes and groups, all the positions exhibiting the very perfection of animal training, the horses being as well disciplined as a company of soldiers. Mr. Bartholomew was once a resident of Fillmore, in this Territory, and was always noted for his skill in subduing and educating horses.

A Mail Complaint.

FILLMORE, January 7, 1884.

Editors Herald:

Well knowing your desire for fair play and improvement, we would crave your attention to a matter which for some time past has been the cause of great grievance and annoyance to the citizens of Millard county. In the spring of 1883 the officials at Washington were kind enough to grant our petition for a daily mail, and we thought indeed we were blessed; but, through mismanagement somewhere, our daily mail is more often tri-weekly; that is to say mail which should reach us the same day as posted in Salt Lake is sometimes two and often three days in arriving, so that those of us who subscribe to your valuable paper never get Saturday's issue of the SEMI-WEEKLY till the following Monday evening, whereas we should have it Saturday evening; and those who live at the end of the mail route should have it Sunmorning, instead of Tuesday morning as at present. We do not desire to appear as grumblers, but think this could and should be remedied. It is the same with letters as well as papers, and we who have dealings with your merchants in Salt Lake often find great inconvenience in consequence. We think if the mail was met at Juab at the time of its arrival there and brought straight through, in place of laying over till 7 o'clock the following day and Saturday's mail waiting till Monday, this could be remedied. Can you suggest anything to help us in the matter? If so, you will confer a great favor upon your subscribers and the general public. SUFFERERS.

MILLARD MATTERS.

Evidences of Development and Progress in the South.

HOLDEN, Jan. 7, 1884.

Editors Herald:

Since our last communication to you in November, 1883, quite a few pleasant changes have occurred in our county; that is so far as the progress and development of the county is concerned. The holiday season just closed has been one of excellent enjoyment, and great pains were taken to make it memorable in the hearts of our good people. In our little burg on Christmas the Relief Society gave a public dinner, and in the evening a party to the inhabitants.

In Scipio on New Year's Day, one of those happy events of which we all love so well to hear—the union of two happy hearts—took place, Bishop Yates being the uniter and Miss Adelaide Matthews, daughter of Mr. James Matthews, and Mr. Andreas Peterson, the parties united. The ceremony took place in the afternoon at 3, at the residence of the bride's parents, and of course the usual congratulations were extended the happy couple. The assembly were regaled with the accustomed feast, etc., till 7 o'clock, when all adjourned to the schoolhouse, where the gay and festive dance was indulged in till the "wee sma' hours," everybody having a grand time. I understand several similar affairs will soon be participated in by others of our county. I mention these matters to show you "city chaps" you are not the only ones who are striving to make this world happier and better.

The building boom continues and is spreading. Our neighbor town, Deseret, has commenced the construction of a new meeting-house, 50 feet wide by 70 feet long, outside, the foundation of which is already laid, and the people are determined nothing in the county, of the kind, will outstrip it in neatness and comfort. Our meeting-house, mentioned in my last letter, is already roofed and the good people hope to be able to meet in it before the summer is over. Much credit is due our energetic citizens for their liberal donations of both means and muscle in pushing this building ahead as they have done, all the labor being performed by local hands. We attribute this in a great measure to the union that exists among us, and we feel we have reason to be proud of it. When we have completed the meeting house it is our intention to erect a new school house, if the means of the people will possibly admit of it. We understand the neighboring "villa" of Fillmore has caught some of our enterprising spirit and intends starting a new place of worship early in the spring. Building is one of the surest indications of progress, so long as good judgment is used in its pursuit, and as we think we are using that judgment, we feel our county is progressing on a safe basis. For some time past, we are aware, the people of Millard County have been thought as lacking in enterprise, and perhaps the opinion was justly formed, but quite a damper was thrown on our energies by the giving out of our range, thus clogging our then greatest industry and means of support. Of late more attention has been paid to sheep raising, which we regard as the coming industry of the county. More attention is given to quality than quantity, quite a number of the best bred animals having been lately imported. We are also striving to improve our horseflesh, and we think some of our stock will compare favorably with any in the Territory; at least, we would like to see another fair in Salt Lake at which we could compete for some of the prizes in this line. Of course, we are aware that we can improve in many particulars, which we hope to do, not the least of which is the building of a new and improved mill at Scipio, styled by us the granary of the county.

Education is progressing and the desire for learning is certainly increasing, as the attendance of our Sunday and day schools, as well as improvement associations will testify. It is not an uncommon thing to see married couples attending our day schools, which shews they feel they are never too old to learn. The general health of the county is excellent. Weather exceedingly fine for this season of the year. While there is not much snow in the valleys the mountains are pretty well supplied, which is certainly a cause of rejoicing. Everywhere one goes in the county he notices the improvement among the youth. Both male and female are striving to acquaint themselves with those principles and form those habits which will make them truly useful in the world. This we are very glad to see, it being certainly another indication of

PROGRESS.

Salt Lake Herald
January 29, 1884

BAGGED.

James H. Dunlap Bagged near Dakova Creek.

Wednesday night last a young man named James H. Dunlap, who had been living on S. Milner's farm between Springville and Provo, left Provo to go to the farm to look after Milner's stock. About noon, the day following, George Milner went to the farm and discovered a couple of guns, several blankets, a fine new saddle, and a horse—all belonging to Colorado parties to be missing. The case was reported to Sheriff John Turner, at Provo. Thomas Schofield, deputy sheriff of Juab county, was at Mr. Turner's house at the time, and he learned the description. As he was going south he agreed to look for him in that direction. Sheriff Turner telegraphed to a number of points south, and the following morning he went north to Salt Lake by the Utah Central.

That afternoon he received a dispatch from E. Taylor, at Juab, stating that the horse-thief had just passed and that shots had been exchanged, but the thief had gone. It was then too late for Sheriff Turner to leave Salt Lake, and telegraphed Mr. Taylor to put a good man on the trail. Mr. Taylor and Mr. Jennings and three others subsequently discovered the horse, saddle, and one gun and spurs, and followed him that night. The next morning Messrs. T. and J. tracked him through the Washboard valley to the Sevier bridge. He then left the road, and traced him to the top of a hill to Round valley, when he left the road and camped for the night. He was trailed through Round valley into Northwest Oak Creek mountains, and thence into Millard county, near Whisky creek, and some eight miles further on found his camp, and beyond this about five miles they came in sight of him. Upon seeing them he went into the grove. They surrounded him. Upon discovering that he was surrounded he stacked his arms and surrendered, being brought to Juab on the early train Monday morning.

He told Mr. Schofield he was going to the depot to give himself up. He claimed that the shooting at Mr. Taylor was merely to frighten Mr. Taylor and that he had no intention whatever of doing him any bodily harm.

Sheriff Turner, on arriving at Juab, went on the direct road to Fillmore, and when he learned of the arrest returned to Juab and took Dunlap to the Provo jail, Sheriff Schofield having turned him over.

Sheriff Turner is desirous of returning thanks to parties in different parts of the south, who rendered him every assistance in their power.

HOUSE OF REPRESENTATIVES.

THIRTY-SEVENTH DAY.

Salt Lake, Feb. 19th, 1884.

House met at 2 p.m

Journal of Monday read and approved.

A communication from the Territorial auditor was read, transmitting bills for action of the House. These bills are such as were paid Z. Snow, legal services, J R Wilkins, moving safe, and requisitions, the total being $553.95. Referred to committee on claims and public accounts.

Mr. Anderson presented the petition of Louis Straunsburgh, asking change of name to Louis Strassburgh. Referred to committee on judiciary.

Mr. Hatch submitted the report of the committee on judiciary, to whom was referred various petitions and bills, recommending H. F. No. 40 to be rejected, amendments to C. F. No. 19, etc., H. F. No. 40 provides for prohibiting the herding of sheep in the neighborhood of cities and towns. Report of committee adopted and H. F. No. 40 was rejected.

C. F. No. 19, a bill to regulate the keeping and herding of sheep, was taken up and read, the amendments recommended adopted, and placed on file for its second reading

Mr. Hatch, of the same committee, also submitted a report, recommending that H. F. No. 29, a bill concerning occupying claimants of lands, recommending its rejection. Report adopted and H. F. No. 29 rejected.

Same submitted report of same, recommending the rejection of H. F. No. 35, a bill to punish persons entering railroad cars on certain occasions, recommending that it do not pass. Report adopted and H. F. No. 35 rejected.

Same submitted report of same, recommending the rejection of H. F. No. 35, a bill to punish persons entering railroad cars on certain occasions, recommending that it do not pass. Report adopted and H. F. No. 35 rejected.

Same submitted report of the same on H. F. No. 42, a bill to prevent children under certain ages from entering saloons, recommending the rejection of the bill. This report brought on an interesting discussion, and the bill was read for information of members. The report of the committee was adopted and H. F. No. 42 was rejected.

Mr. Thurman submitted the report of the committee on fish and game, recommending certain amendments to H. F. No. 37. A bill to provide for the election of a board of fish commissioners and to prescribe their duties. Report adopted and the bill placed on file for second reading.

Mr. Brinton submitted a report of the committee on H. F. No. 24, recommending certain amendments and the passage of the bill. Report and amendments adopted and bill ordered printed and placed on file for second reading.

Mr. Francis submitted a report of the committee on claims and public accounts, relative to the bill of Mr. Spence for $5, recommending the payment of the same. Report adopted and the committee on appropriations instructed to include said bill in their general bill.

A report from the Territorial Auditor was read, relative to commissioners to examine accounts of courts, and also relative to mileage of witnesses and jurors between Park City and Salt Lake, and asking an increase of salary. Referred to committee on judiciary.

Also from the same, as Recorder of Marks and Brands, relative to marks and brands of stock for use of pound keepers, asking an appropriation for such purposes. Referred to committee on agriculture.

Mr. Brinton submitted the report of the committee on agriculture relative to H. F. No. 27, a bill defining the duties of pound keepers, recommending that the bill do not pass. Report adopted and H. F. No 27 rejected.

Mr. Thurber submitted the report of the committee on fish and game relative to C. F. No. 12, a bill for the protection of game and fish, reporting certain amendments and moved the passage of the bill. Report adopted and bill placed on file for second reading.

Mr. Boyden introduced H. F. No. 48, a bill providing for the health and safety of persons employed in coal mines. Read twice by its title and referred to the committee on mines and mining.

Mr. Robinson introduced H. F. No. 49, a bill to amend the charter of Fillmore City. Read twice by its title and referred to the committee on municipal corporations and towns.

C. F. No. 19, a bill to regulate the keeping of sheep, was taken up on its second reading and amended, after which a motion prevailed to take it up on its third reading, subject to amendment. A motion to recommit it to the committee on judiciary was lost. On passage of the bill the vote stood, ayes 12, noes 4.

H. F. No. 37, a bill to provide for the election of a Board of Fish Commissioners and to prescribe the duties thereof, was taken up on its second reading, read by title and placed on file and ordered printed.

H. F. 24, a bill to amend an act for the disposal of estrays, was read by title on second reading and placed on file.

C. F. No. 12, a bill for the protection of fish and game, passed second reading.

H. F. No. 20, a bill regulating the branding, herding and care of stock.

Mr. Cummings moved to strike out the enacting clause because, as he claimed, it was special legislation in favor of a special class of citizens. The motion to strike out was lost. Mr. Boyden moved to refer the bill to the committee on agriculture.

Mr. Hatch moved to have 15 copies of probate and civil procedure bills printed for distribution. Carried.

At 4 45 o'clock, adjourned till 1 p.m. February 20th.

UTAH LEGISLATURE.

Twenty-Sixth Session.

COUNCIL.

FORTY-FOURTH DAY.

Salt Lake, Feb. 26, '84.

Council met at 10 a.m., President Cluff in the chair.

H. F. No. 50, providing "for the purchase of 200 copies of a new and revised sectional and topographical map of Utah Territory, on a scale of six miles to the inch, and appropriating $1,500 for the same. Read the first time by title, and referred to the committee on education.

H. F. No. 54, a bill making an appropriation for furnishing and completing the insane asylum, of $51,697.43. Read the first time and referred to the committee on asylum for the insane.

H. F. No. 52, authorizing Provo School District No. 1, in Utah Territory, to issue bonds to the amount $15,000, for the purpose of completing a schoolhouse, passed to its second reading, and was referred to the committee on education.

On motion, the rules were suspended and C. F. No. 33, a bill concerning voters and office-holders, and regulating elections, was taken up on its third reading. The measure was read by title, amended and passed.

C. F. No. 37, providing for private roads, applying particularly to persons whose lands are surrounded, without right of way, by the lands of others, and facilitating the procuring of such private road, was read, amended and passed to its third reading.

H. F. No. 43, a bill to amend an act incorporating Salt Lake City, was taken up on its third reading, amended and passed.

H. F. No. 37, providing for the election of a board of fish commissioners, and prescribing the duties thereof, was read the second time.

C. F. No. 38, a substitute for C. F. No. 22, to appropriate $10,000 to aid in sinking artesian wells in certain desert lands in the Territory, was brought up. On the question of adopting the substitute there was considerable diversity of opinion.

Mr. Woolley was not favorable to the bonus system advocated, it would make exploration more a matter of private speculation; and besides, if adopted, should be confined to certain parts of the Territory.

Mr. Barton said the idea of appropriating money for sinking artesian wells was about as reasonable as giving money for sinking mines. As every one knew, the latter were always worked by private companies.

President Cluff having temporarily vacated the chair, said the object was very praiseworthy and one to which money could be very advantageously appropriated. There were over 2,000 square miles of desert lands in the south of Utah, equal to 1,280,000 acres, and if one-half of this could be reclaimed it would open up for settlement a vast country that would sustain almost double the present population of Utah. Thousands of dollars were given for road-making and he thought something ought to be done for this equally important matter—sinking artesian wells.

Mr. Grover differed from Mr. Barton's assertion of non-legislative aid to miners. He thought the government had afforded very material aid to them. What was principally wanted, however, in reference to the subject under discussion was that a start should be given to the enterprise. He certainly thought some encouragement should be given to the sinking of these wells.

Mr. Page agreed that the sinking of artesian wells should be encouraged. He thought, however, the parties owning the lands received all the benefit, should be willing to run the risks. It was necessary to demonstrate whether artesian water could be obtained, for up to the present it had not been accomplished here. They had not penetrated deep enough for the purpose. So far as roads were concerned he considered the public were mainly interested; in regard to artesian wells it appeared to him it was private individuals who were concerned.

Mr. F. S. Richards was of the opinion that the Territory would receive considerable benefit from the sinking of artesian wells. It was a public matter; for the sinking of wells and procuring of water where required would facilitate settlement and produce through taxes increased wealth to the Territory. He differed from both bills in the means suggested to gain the end, the best method in reference to premiums would be to advance money as the work progressed. He thought the subject a very legitimate one, and therefore would move that the two bills be referred to a special committee for further consideration. This was agreed to.

Council took a recess until 2 p.m.

2 p.m.

Council met pursuant to agreement, President Cluff in the chair. Roll call. All present but two, Taylor and Hammond, who came in subsequently.

Prayer by the chaplain.

The minutes of yesterday's session were read, and after one or two unimportant changes were adopted.

The chair appointed as a special committee to consider C. F. No. 22 and 38, Messrs. F. S. Richards, Barton, Grover, Woolley and Page.

C. F. 12, reported back from the House with amendments, was taken up. (The bill is in relation to fish and game). The amendments were concurred in.

C. F. 1, amending the charter of Kaysville City, was read the third time. An amendment reported by the committee was adopted, and the bill passed.

C. F. 26, in relation to the pedigrees of stock, was taken up on its third reading, read by its title and passed.

H. F. 33, in relation to the pay of jurors, was read the third time by its title and passed.

C. F. 13, providing for the preservation of domestic animals, was taken up, read the third time and voted on, 6 ayes, 4 nays and 1 absent. There not being a majority of the whole body in favor, the bill was defeated.

C. F. 10, amending Section 1, Chapter XIII, Laws of 1882, was taken up and laid over.

H. F. 37 was taken up on its third reading, under suspension of the rules. (The bill provides for a board of fish commissioners.) After amendment the bill passed.

Mr. Grover, from the committee on municipal corporations reported in relation to the amendment to the Payson City charter, presenting a bill for that purpose. The rules were suspended and the bill was read the first and second times and laid on the table.

Consideration of C. F. 10 was resumed; some changes were made and the bill passed.

Adjourned till 2 p.m. on Wednesday, February 27th.

HOUSE OF REPRESENTATIVES.

FORTY-FOURTH DAY.

Salt Lake, Feb. 26, 1884.

House met at 2 p.m.

Minutes of Monday read and approved.

Message from the Council read, giving notice of concurrence in amendments of H. F. 34, incorporating Park City.

Also passage of H. F. 45, amending charter of Salt Lake City, with amendment in enacting clause and title. The House concurred.

Also passage of C. F. 33, a bill prescribing qualifications for electors and office holders, e'c. Read first time, second by title, ordered printed and referred to committee on elections.

A communication from the Auditor relative to discrepancy in reports was read. He accounts for the surplus by making the showing of warrants issued as early as 1873. Referred to committee on ways and means.

A communication from the treasurer relative to payment of warrants and discrepancy in reports was read and referred to same committee

Mr. Farnsworth presented the petition of James Fahr and others, with documents, asking the Legislature to restrain the auditor from bringing suit against them for delinquent taxes. Referred to committee on judiciary.

Mr. Young presented the petition of members of the county court of Salt Lake, relative to revenue and taxation in said county and various matters pertaining to licenses, keeping the roads and bridges in repair, disbursement of funds, etc. Referred to committee on ways and means.

Mr. Houston presented the petition of George Dodge and seventy-five others for a change in county line between Iron and Garfield counties, by removing said line six miles west. Referred to committee on counties.

Mr. Thurman, of committee on municipal corporations and towns, relative to several bills and petitions. Report adopted and bills placed on file. These petitions and bills refer to Ephraim, Spanish Fork and Fillmore cities.

Mr. Francis, for committee on claims and public accounts, recommended an appropriation to clerk of Third District Court to pay the bill. Referred.

Mr. Hatch, for committee on judiciary, reported amendments to C. F. 23. Report and amendments adopted

Mr. Snow, for committee on manfactures and commerce, reported relative to sugar, recommending printing 15,000 copies of the report of Arthur Stayner, for distribution. Report adopted.

Mr. Thurman, for committee on corporations and towns, submitted H. F. No. 55, a bill incorporating Ephraim City. General file.

Mr. Stanford introduced H. F. No. 56, a bill relative to barb wire fences. Referred to committee on agriculture.

The concurrent resolution relative to authorizing the Auditor to procure two canceling stamps was taken up and passed.

H. F. No. 55, a bill amending the charter of Ephraim, passed its second reading. Rules suspended, bill read third time and passed.

H. F. No. 15, a bill to authorize the incorporation of companies for the construction of union railroad stations and depots, etc., passed its second reading.

H. F. No. 4, a bill authorizing limited partnership, passed its third reading and was passed.

H. F. No. 53, a bill to amend the city charter of Spanish Fork city, was read the third time and passed.

H. F. No. 49, a bill to amend the charter of Fillmore, was made a special order for next Friday.

C. F. No. 17, a bill to extend the powers of incorporated cities, read third time and passed.

C. F. No. 16, a bill authorizing county courts to grant licenses read, third time and passed, 19 ayes, 3 noes.

Mr. Cummings offered a resolution providing for two sessions per day, commencing on Thursday the 28th. Adopted.

At 4.20 adjourned till 2 p.m. Wednesday.

UTAH LEGISLATURE.

Twenty-Sixth Session.

COUNCIL.

FORTY SEVENTH DAY.

Friday, Feb. 29.

Council met at 10 a. m., President Cluff in the chair.

Minutes of previous session were read and approved.

Mr. F. S. Richards presented a report from the committee on judiciary in reference to H. F. No. 28, without amendment, and recommending its passage. Accepted, and bill tabled to come up in its order.

Mr. Barton introduced C. F. No. 51, a bill providing for the organization and regulation of telephone companies. Read first and second times by title and referred to the committee on private corporations.

Mr. Hammond submitted C. F. No. 52, making provision for disincorporating irrigation districts. Read the first and second times by title and referred to the committee on irrigation.

C. F. No. 45, amending section 213 of the Compiled Laws of Utah, taken up on its second reading, the rules having been suspended, was read the third time by title and passed.

C. F. No. 44, amending the charter of Logan City, providing for the licensing or prohibiting of the manufacture or sale of intoxicating liquors, licensing hotels and restaurants, billiard and pool tables, etc. The measure was read the second time and, the rules having been suspended, was read the third time by title and passed.

H. F. No. 53, amending the charter of Spanish Fork City, was taken up on its third reading. The bill gives the municipal authorities of said city power to impound and sell horses, cattle, sheep, swine, etc., to enforce the payment of taxes, and refers to water rights, the location of railroad tracks, etc. Read the third time and passed.

H. F. No. 58, amending section 5, chapter 28, of the session laws of 1882, was read the third time and passed.

Mr. Tuttle presented a petition from E. A. Merriam, praying for reimbursement in the sum of $50 for services rendered. Read and referred to the committee on claims and public accounts.

Mr. Grover, by deputy, asked leave of absence on account of sickness. The chair appointed Mr. Page to represent the absentee on the joint committee of conference on C. F. No. 11.

Mr. F. S. Richards presented a report from the committee on judiciary, referring to C. F. No. 50 amended. It provides for the qualifying of county, precinct and road district officers. Being taken up on its third reading, the amendments were concurred in, and the bill was read the third time and passed.

Council took a recess until 3 p. m.

3 p.m.

The Council resumed its session.

A communication was received from the House announcing the passage, with amendments, of the Park City charter, said amendments having been made at the instance of the Governor, the bill being forwarded to the Council for its action. The amendments were read and concurred in. Under suspension of the rules the bill was read the first, second and third time by its title and passed, 10 ayes, 1 absent.

A communication was received from the House announcing its passage of the bill providing for probate procedure; also the bill in relation to voters and officers.

Mr. Taylor, from the committee on claims, etc., reported in relation to the petition of William Reeves, ex-assessor of Davis county, for relief, recommending that the relief be granted. Report adopted.

Mr. F. S. Richards, from the judiciary committee, reported on the bill in relation to limited partnerships, that an amendment had been made, recommending its passage. Laid on the table.

Mr. Page, from the committee on highways, reported in relation to the petition of certain citizens of Iron county, praying for an appropriation to make a wagon road, recommending that the petition be not allowed. Adopted.

Mr. Woolley presented a report from the special joint committee on university lands. It states the conclusions of the committee to be that the Legislature has authority to dispose of such lands, and presenting a bill to that end. Read the first time. The bill creates the University of Utah, and authorizes the University of Deseret to transfer its property to the former; provides for officers and trustees, and prescribes their duties; makes the Governor an ex officio member of the board; prescribes the modes and branches of education; defines the departments, etc.; provides that no religious tenets shall be recognized or made a qualification for admission to the University, nor shall any special religious exercises be enforced. It was referred to the committee on education, and ordered printed.

The bill to provide for assignments, etc., was read the first and second time by its title, and referred to the committee on judiciary.

H. F. 4, authorizing limited partnerships, was taken up on its second reading. An amendment by the committee was adopted. Read by its title.

Mr. F. S. Richards moved that H. F. 48 be read the first and second time by its title and made the special order for Monday next at 2 p.m. (It is the probate procedure bill.) The motion was carried.

The Chief Clerk proceeded to read the bill, which is a very long one (fifty printed pages), and instancing the changes made in the bill by the House.

Adjourned.

HOUSE OF REPRESENTATIVES.

Salt Lake, Feb. 29.

House met at 10 a. m. Journal of Thursday read and approved.

Mr. Clark, from committee on enrollment, reported H. F. No. 20, H. F. No. 5, H. F. No. 3, having been engrossed and forwarded to the Governor.

H. F. 48, relating to procedure of probate courts in settlement of estates and guardianship, special order for this hour was taken up, as special order, amended and passed, 19 ayes, 2 noes.

A message from the Council was read giving notice of passage of H. F. 55 amending the city charter of Ephraim with amendments. House concurred and amendments and bill ordered enrolled.

Communication from his Excellency Governor Murray, returning H. F. 36, chartering Park City, recommending certain amendments. Referred to committee on municipal corporations and towns.

Message from the Council read, giving notice of concurrence in resolution ordering printing of report of directors of Asylum for Insane.

Message from the Council read, giving notice of passage of C. F. 47, in relation to mortgages of personal property. Read twice, ordered printed and referred to the committee on judiciary.

Mr. Morgan presented the petition of Alderman Spiers, for remuneration in Territorial cases. Referred to committee on claims and public accounts.

Mr. Boyden presented a petition of the probate judge of Summit County, relative to expending money for bridges. Referred to the committee on highways.

Mr. Brinton from the committee on agriculture reported favorably relative to C. F. 26, general file. Same on H. F. 6, relative to pedigree of stock, reported adversely. Adopted and bill rejected.

Mr. Thurman submitted H. F. 61, incorporating Park City. Read twice by title and referred to committee on municipal corporations and towns.

Mr. Francis submitted H. F. 62, for the support of paupers. Read the first time and referred to committee on judiciary.

Mr. Boyden submitted H. F. 63, to prevent importation of, selling or running at large, animals infested with infectious diseases. Referred to committee on judiciary.

At 12 o'clock recess till 2 p.m.

2 p.m.

C. F. 33, prescribing qualifications for electors and office holders, providing for registration of voters and regulating the manner of conducting elections, passed on a vote of 19 ayes, 1 no.

Mr. Thurman, from the committee on municipal corporations and towns, reported back H. F. 36, incorporating Park City, recommending its passage with the amendments asked by the Governor. Report adopted, and the bill passed as amended.

Mr. Stanford presented the petition of merchants of Salt Lake City for a drummer's tax, with a bill providing for such tax or license. Referred to the committee on judiciary.

H. F. 22, encouraging mining, brought up for passage as per special order. Rejected, 6 ayes, 15 nays.

H. F. 49, amending the act incorporating Fillmore City, passed its third reading and was passed unanimously.

C. F. 21, to regulate practice of medicine and selling of medicines, passed second reading.

Mr. Clark, from the committee on enrollment, reported H. F. 50, 55 and 7 enrolled and forwarded to the Governor.

H. F. 20, regulating the branding, herding and and care of stock, on third reading and passed; 13 ayes, 6 noes.

Message from Council giving notice of passage of C. F. 44, 45 and 50, also H. F. 33 and 58.

C. F. 44, amending act incorporating Logan City. Under suspension of rules read three times and passed.

C. F. 45, amending Section 213 Compiled Laws, relating to county treasurers. Rules suspended, read three times, amended and passed unanimously.

C. F. 50, providing for the qualifying of county, precinct and road officers. Read twice and referred to committee on judiciary.

Message from Council read giving notice of concurrence in H. F. 36, incorporating Park City. Referred for enrollment.

C. F. 26, providing for the recording of pedigrees of stock, read third time and passed.

Mr. Thurman, from the committee on municipal corporations and towns, reported favorably relative to C. F. 1, 8, 57, amending charters of cities; also on petition from citizens of Lehi for city charter.

C. F. 1, amending act incorporating Kaysville, read third time and passed.

C. F. 8, amending act incorporating Richmond City, read third time and passed.

H. F. 57, amending an act incorporating Wellsville City, was read the third time, amended and passed.

H. F. 64, granting to Lehi City certain powers, was read three times and passed.

H. F. 65, granting to American Fork City certain powers, was read three times and passed.

A message from the Governor was read, giving notice of his approval of the bill changing the name of John M. Nevenhurst; also

from the same, objecting to the bill relative to the payment of jurors.

At 4.55, adjourned till 10 a.m., Saturday, March 1st.

UTAH LEGISLATURE.

Twenty-Sixth Session.
COUNCIL.
FIFTIETH DAY.
March 3d, 1884.

Council met pursuant to adjournment from Saturday, President Cluff in the Chair.

Roll called, and after prayer by the Chaplain the minutes of Saturday's session were read and approved.

Mr. Woolley presented a petition from citizens of Washington Co., asking an appropriation of $3,008 to complete the wagon road from Washington to St. George. Referred to committee on highways.

A communication was received from the House announcing that it had adopted C. R. 6, for a joint memorial to Congress, and appointed its committee. The President appointed Messrs. Taylor, Grant, Hammond, F. S. Richards and Woolley for the Council.

The special order for the day, H. F. 43, the probate procedure bill, was taken up on its third reading. A number of amendments were made and agreed to. The reading and amendments were not concluded till 3.25, when, on motion of Mr. H. J. Richards, the bill was read the third time.

Before proceeding far, a message was received from the Governor, announcing his approval of C. F. 12, for the protection of fish and game, and C. F. 12, extending the powers of incorporated cities.

The reading of the bill was proceeded with, and after the dreary proceeding had been engaged in some minutes, Mr. Hammond came to the rescue, moving that further reading be dispensed with and the bill pass. Carried.

Mr. H. J. Richards announced that the committee on highways decided to reconsider the petition of citizens of Iron County for a wagon road, and moved reconsideration. Carried, and the matter was recommitted.

On motion of Mr. Woolley, adjourned till Tuesday, March 4th, at 2 p.m.

Prayer by the Chaplain.

HOUSE OF REPRESENTATIVES.
FIFTIETH DAY.
Salt Lake, March 3d, 1884.

House met at 10 a.m. Quorum present.

Journal of Saturday was read, amended and approved.

Mr. Cummings was excused for the day, to do committee work.

Mr. Hatch asked for the return of H. F. 29, a rejected bill to the committee on judiciary, and was informed it was not the property of the House.

A resolution from the Council was relative appointing a joint committee on a memorial to Congress, asking a committee of disinterested persons to investigate the charges against the people. The House concurred in the resolution, thirteen voting for and six against it.

H. F. 15, authorizing incorporation of union depots, etc., came up as the special order. Mr. Creer moved to recommit to the committee on judiciary; so ordered.

Mr. Hatch moved to reconsider the action of the House rejecting H. F. 29, concerning occupying claimants. Lost.

H. F. 41, for the formation of and granting powers to private corporations, called for second reading.

Mr. Creer moved to make it the special order for 2 p.m. to-morrow. Carried.

At 10 40 recess taken till 2 p.m.

AFTERNOON SESSION.

2 p.m.

House called to order.

The Speaker announced Messrs. Morgan, Stanford, Thurman, Boyden, Clark, Howell and Farnsworth as members of joint committee to memorialize Congress.

Communication from the Governor giving notice of having signed H. F. 36, incorporating Park City; H. F. 55, incorporating Ephraim, and H. F. 58, amending section 5, chapter 18, Laws of 1880, and having placed the same in the hands of Secretary Thomas.

Message from the Council giving notice of passage of C. F. 37, and concurrence in C. F. 56, relative to possessory action in public lands, and H. F. 57, relating to roads.

C. F. 57, providing for private roads, read twice by title and referred to the committee on highways.

The committee on mines and mining reported favorably relative to H. F. 43.

Mr. Hatch, from the committee on judiciary, reported favorably on petitions for change of names, and submitted bill for same.

Mr. Hatch, from the committee on judiciary, reported back H. F. 63 and 64 without amendments. General file.

Same, reported favorably relative to petition in relation to fumes of smelters, submitting bill for same.

Mr. Morgan, from the committee on education, reported relative to a communication from the Governor in relation to furnishing statistics, saying they had performed said duty.

The same reported favorably on the petition of citizens of Fillmore, relative to memorializing Congress about a deaf and blind school. Adopted.

Mr. Hatch, from the committee on claims, reported favorably on bills for clerks for certain committees. Report adopted.

Mr. Hatch, from the judiciary committee, introduced H. F. 69, changing the names of Hedquist Stransberg and Hans Olson. Read first time, second by title. Rules suspended and bill passed.

The same submitted H. F. 70, regulating the building of and operating smelters. Under suspension of rules passed to third reading and ordered printed.

Mr. Thurman introduced H. F. 71, providing for the payment of jurors. Read first time, second by title; rules suspended; read third time and passed unanimously.

Mr. Thurman introduced H. F. 72, relating to contracts and promises. Read twice by title and referred to committee on judiciary.

H. F. 62, for the support of paupers, read second time. General file. Ordered printed.

H. F. 66, amending an act relative to inn and hotel keepers, read third time and passed.

Mr. Creer, from the committee on private corporations, submitted bill of Snow for clerk services of said committee. Adopted.

Mr. Thurman offered a resolution providing that no bill shall be introduced after March 19, without the consent of two-thirds of the members present, except such bills as may be introduced by committees to whom subject matter had been committed. Adopted.

Message from the Council read, giving notice of passage, with amendments, of H. F. 43, relative to probate procedure. All the Council amendments were concurred in and the bill was referred for enrollment.

Adjourned at 4.10 o'clock till 10 a m. Tuesday, March 4.

UTAH LEGISLATURE.

Twenty-Sixth Session.

COUNCIL.

FIFTY-THIRD DAY.

March 6, 1884, 2 p. m.

Council met pursuant to adjournment.

Roll called; quorum present.

Prayer by the Chaplain.

The minutes of yesterday's session were read and approved.

A communication was received from the House announcing the passage of C. F. 41 and 42.

The House amendments to C F. 41 were concurred in.

Mr. F. S. Richards presented a petition from the collector of Weber county, asking relief in the sum of $45.99. Committee on claims.

Mr. Richards reported H. F. 71, for jurors' fees, with an amendment. Table.

Mr. Grant reported 100 copies of C F. 00 printed.

Mr. Woolley reported a substitute bill for C. F. 40, recommending its passage. Adopted.

Mr. Page reported back H. R. 28, with one amendment, recommending its adoption. Adopted.

Mr. Grover reported back H. F. 20, with two amendments, recommending its passage. Table.

Mr. Grover reported back H. F. 64 amended, recommending its passage. Table.

Mr. Grover reported H. F. 65 amended, recommending its passage; also H. F. 53 without amendment. Table.

Mr. F. S. Richards reported back the bill in relation to assignments, recommending its passage. Table.

Mr. Hammond, from the education committee, reported adversely on H. F. 30, presenting a substitute. Adopted.

H. R. 28, in relation to the introduction of bills, was taken up and rejected.

C. F. 61, in relation to mining, was adopted in lieu of C. F. 49, rejected.

C. F. 62, amending several sections of the Compiled Laws, was tabled, to come up in its order.

H. F 71 was taken up and passed.

A communication was received from the House, announcing the passage of several bills.

H. F. 48 was referred to committee on mines and mining

H. F. 77, amending Salt Lake charter, was referred to committee on municipal corporations.

H. F. 73 was referred to the committee on counties.

H. F. 34, amending Lehi charter was taken up (Mr. Woolley in the chair), and passed.

Mr. Grant presented C. F. 63, in relation to fire insurance companies. Committee on private corporations.

H. F. 70 was taken up and recommitted.

The bill amending the charter of Spanish Fork passed.

The bill granting certain powers to American Fork passed.

At 4.30 p.m. the Council adjourned till Friday at 2 p.m.

HOUSE OF REPRESENTATIVES.

FIFTY-THIRD DAY.

March 6, 1884.

House met at 2 p.m., quorum present.

Journal of Wednesday read and approved.

A message was received from the Council giving notice of the passage of H. F. 49, relative to Spanish Fork City, without amendment; also H. F. 56, for the protection of keepers of inns, hotels and boarding houses; also the rejection of memorial relative to government building at Fillmore City; also the passage of C. F. 51, to provide for the organization of telephone companies. Read twice and referred to committee on private corporations.

H. F. 60, relative to civil procedure, was made the special order for 2 p.m. to-morrow.

H. F. 48, for the protection of persons employed in coal mines, put on its passage and passed.

Mr. Dusenberry presented the petition of Miram Janner, director of the penitentiary, for services in 1876 7, amounting to $100. Referred to committee on claims and public accounts.

Mr. Hatch, from the committee on judiciary, reported amendments to H. F. 58, amending sections 445 and 648, compiled laws. Report adopted.

Same from same, relative to H. F. 47, in relation to mortgages. Reported same back without recommendation. General file.

Mr. Hatch, from committee on counties, reported relative to petition on change of line between Iron and Garfield Counties, submitting a bill for such a change. Report adopted.

Mr. Anderson, from the committee on highways, reported favorably on the petition for an appropriation of $2,000 to expend on a road through Spanish Fork canyon. Adopted.

H. F. 76, amending an act changing the line between the counties of Iron and Garfield. Read first time.

Mr. Clark introduced H. F. 77, amending an act incorporating Salt Lake City. Read first time; second by title; rules suspended; read third time and passed.

H. F. 76, relative to boundary line between Iron and Garfield counties, read second time, rules suspended and passed, 19 ayes, 1 no.

H. F. 76, regulating the building and operating of smelters in the Territory of Utah, passed, 16 ayes, 5 noes.

H. F. 62, providing for the support of paupers, read third time, passed, 13 ayes, 9 noes.

H. F. 56, for the protection of animals from injury by the use of barbed wire in construction of fences, read third time and passed, 15 ayes, 6 noes.

H. F. 63, to prevent the importation, selling or running at large of domestic animals affected with infectious or contagious diseases, read third time and passed.

H. F. 75, relative to water rights, made the special order for Saturday.

C. F. 47, relative to mortgages of personal property, read third time and rejected, 9 ayes, 13 noes.

Mr. Creer presented the claim of A. C. Emerson for $329.40, services as clerk of First District Court in certain cases. Referred to committee on claims and public accounts.

At 4:40 adjourned till 2 p. m., Friday, March 7th.

Salt Lake Herald
March 20, 1884

Death of Myron Hawley.

News has been received of the death in Fillmore, Millard County, on Wednesday morning, of C. Myron Hawley, a lawyer of Beaver, and well known in this city, where he formerly resided. Deceased was a son of ex-Associate Justice Hawley, of this Territory, whose residence since he left Utah, several years ago, has been in Chicago. Judge Hawley is at present in Florida, whither he went some time since, in search of health. The deceased will be buried at Fillmore, but it is thought the remains will be removed to Chicago by the father.

WHITE HOUSE.

W H Caroll, Pleasant Valley; W M Lean, Soda Springs; F Lappert, Italy; H Riper, W H Burns, Butte; W Riley, Lehi; S Truscott, Alta; J Bowden, Tintic; C Laney and wife, Michigan; J Johnson, Spring City; S B Worthington, Grantsville; K B Wilcox, Leadville; G. Pink, st Louis, J H Aluman, Ogden; J D Reese, Fillmore; C C Fox, J McNulty, Ogden; G Peabody, Park City; J Roblins, Provo.

Salt Lake Herald
April 5, 1884

Bishop Thomas Smith, Judge Robinson and W. H. King, of Fillmore, were among the visitors yesterday.

Salt Lake Herald
April 25, 1884

DEPUTY REGISTRARS.

The Latest Commissions Issued by the Secretary.

Secretary Thomas, of the Utah Commission, has forwarded commissions as deputy registrars to the following named persons:

MILLARD COUNTY.

John Nield, Meadow.
George Chesley, Konosh.
Alvin L. Robinson, Fillmore.
Nicholas Paul, Holden.
George Monroe, Scipio.
George Finlinson, Oak Creek.
George Morrison, Leamington.
Wm. A. Ray, Deseret.

MILLARD COUNTY.

A Run Through It, With Notes on the Towns.

The Business—Hopeful Out-look.

(Special Correspondence.)

FILLMORE, MILLARD
COUNTY, UTAH,
April 24, '84.

Having completed my travels in Millard County I am prepared to furnish you with a few items, a number of the people expressing a desire to have their county represented in the columns of the popular paper.

Many of your readers are aware that Millard County is one of the largest in the Territory; but are they cognizant of the fact that it is the least populated, considering size, age and advantages, and that it is the poorest in natural resources? But let us not look upon this county in such an unfavorable light. Before the railroad was extended through the county travel was very heavy; a ready market was the farmer's least trouble and on the whole times were lively. Soon after the completion of the railroad the whole county was seriously affected; the sudden collapse in trade and traffic followed and the winter of our discontent is with us. It is to be hoped the dawn of a brighter day is near.

After leaving Juab, the first town of importance on the line of the railroad is Deseret. For many miles north and south of Deseret a few ranches, farms and section houses are about all that greet the traveler. Deseret, I believe, is more scattered than any place in Utah. It is Deseret a long while before you get there and the same after you leave. But for all that it is destined to become a place of considerable importance. Even at this time it has the best commercial facilities of any place in Millard county. Tanning is the principal industry of the inhabitants

—and a very fair market for the farm products is found in Eastern Nevada and on the line of the Utah Central railway. The soil in this vicinity, although variable, is well adapted to raising grain and hay, and live stock appear to do well. A dam in the Sevier river, above the town, will cause an abundance of water to be had for this season's irrigation. The Deseret Store, kept J. S. Black, supplies the people with all the necessaries; as do also Mr A. Ray and W. V. Black & Co., who carry a full line of general merchandise. Mr. E. Webb provides for the wants of the weary traveler. A good grist mill will soon be in operation here, and is expected to be kept busy this season. A new meeting-house is in course of erection, which is calculated to be as neat, substantial and commodious as any in the county.

The journey from here to Kanab is a tedious one. The only place of note on the road is Clear Lake, about fifteen miles southeast of Deseret. The fish-raising industry at this place, although in its infancy, is sure to prove a success, if rightly managed. A fine ranch adjoins the place and everything seems to be well adapted; our old-time friend, Dr. Crockwell is at this place.

Kanosh is the farthest south in the county, of any settlement of promise. Stock-raising and farming are the main industries and seem to flourish. The sheep-raising industry in this county is fast becoming an important one. One mark of enterprise is the breeding and importing of blooded merino rams, Scotch collie dogs, Berkshire pigs, game and fowl, by Charles Crane, Esq. A. Nadauld & Co., William Hunter and the Kanosh Co-op. keep a full line of general merchandise, produce, hides, wool and farming machinery are their specialties. The people here seem hopeful of the next season bringing better times.

At Meadow, the next place towards Fillmore, nothing unusual is transpiring, except that a large brick meeting-house is being built.

Fillmore, the county seat, and also the only incorporated city, is the largest and most important place in Millard County. It is nicely located, and having good irrigating facilities and water power unsurpassed, is bound at some future day to become one of the most prosperous cities of Southern Utah. All kinds of general merchandise are supplied to the people by the Fillmore Co-op. James King

John Kelly and G. Huntsman & Co. All the preliminaries are arranged for building a large meeting house, and it is to be hoped that this much needed building will be pushed ahead without any delay. Mr. Joshua Greenwood has charge of the district high school, and under his able management it has proved a success; as also has the mission school taught by Miss M. E. Campbell.

Fillmore is the proud possessor of a young man who will soon be shining among the literary stars of Utah's intellectual circles. He is very studious and an accomplished speaker. It will be remembered that Fillmore was formerly the capital of Utah, and it was about that time that the "State house" was built by a joint appropriation of Congress and the Territorial Legislature. Since the Legislative assembly abandoned it for law making purposes, in 1856, it has been of little or no use to anybody, except that occasionally a few meet'ngs and dramat'c perfor ma ce are held there. The building, however, is now occupied by the Presbyterian mission school. To obtain a title to the property, either by lease or purchase, was the object of some of Fillmore's ambitious citizens, but in this they were unsuccessful. The matter was referred and can only be decided by an act of Congress, and the decision is anxiously looked for.

It was expected the last Legislature would memorialize Congress to appropriate the statehouse and the grounds for educational purposes for the Territory. A bill to create a school for the deaf, dumb and blind was presented to the Legislative Assembly, but I believe it was not passed. The building is a large and substantial rock structure, and with a few improvements would be well adapted for such purposes, or even for a normal school.

Millard County, and even the southern part of Utah recognize the necessity of having better school and teachers superior to the ones we now have. Accomplished teachers and better school facilities are wanted, and it is a pity that two years will probably elapse before anything favorable to these objects in this locality may be looked for.

A quiet little place is Holden, about ten miles north of Fillmore. Improvements are continually going on. The most important is the building of a new meeting house. The fact of so many church edifices in course of erection speaks well for the enterprise and liberality of the people of this county. The Holden Co-op. and C. Wood are dealers in general merchandise, etc., in this place.

A pleasant ride over the mountain and Scipio is soon reached, the northern settlement of the county. Farming is carried on here to a great extent and a rich yield of grain is looked for this season. Robison & Co., successors to Roberts & Co., do an extensive general merchandising business. The Co-op's new building is about ready for occupancy, the former quarters being too cramped for the largely increasing trade. Accommodations are found at Wm. Robins hotel.

It may not be out of place to mention something in regard to mail matters, which of late have been very irregular and have caused much dissatisfaction. From the investigations made it would appear that the postmasters of the several places and the mail carriers are not at fault; the majority would rather place the blame on the railway mail service. It is to be hoped the matter will be remedied at once.

A visit to the several schools laid bare the fact that much better educational facilities are needed in this part of the country, although great interest seems to be manifested and a progressive tendency is apparent. Some little prospecting is going on in the mountains and future developments are expected to bring forth something rich in mining interests. Already the Detroit Mining district is showing up something of a very promising character.

Many natural curiosities exist in this country. A description of some of them will be given next time.

The stock and sheep raising industries are the important ones in this county and nearly every effort is manifested to properly develop these industries. The ranges look well and an abundance of feed is expected; in short the horses, cattle and sheep are thriving. The stockbuyers bring considerable cash into the country and exchange for the cattle which bring good prices. The farming industry looks exceedingly promising for the coming season.

Never was there more snow in the mountains at this time of the year, and several reservoirs have been constructed to keep the surplus water till needed. Many acres of land heretofore valueless will be made to produce an abundance.

All the indications in Millard County point favorably to a bountiful harvest and a good market for all the products—in brief a prosperous season is expected.

XTIAN.

HOTEL ARRIVALS.

ay 14, 1884.

WHITE HOUSE.

J B Miredith, Kaysville; W P Maycock, T Ashishurst, Fillmore; J N Van Noy, Beaver Canyon; S S Childs, R E Williams, Ogden; A J Esaoman, Mount Pleasant; F Graves, Frisco; C C Hoyt, L A Gardner, P Comstock, Eureka; J Powell, F Birch, Ophir; P Ferguson, Missoula, MT; T E Jamison, S Clark, A Dyer, D N Swan, Bingham, C Dillon, Chicago; J Carleton, Denver; S L Taft, Leadville; W Hyde, Ogden; B Sloan, Park City; H Haynes, Murray; F Sowang, Bonanza City, Idaho.

Salt Lake Herald
May 24, 1884

HOTEL ARRIVALS.

WHITE HOUSE.

S C Lowe, Salt Lake & Western Ry; Geo Warburton, Stockton; Joe Gerry, Martin Curtin, Durango, Colo; D Duncan, Stockton; Ewan Arthur, Orlando McGee, St John; Geo Higsay, Charles Beam, A Hanson, John Duttan, P V Junction; L Taft, Leadville; John Bushnell, Leadville; P Wyman, Lu Plumaer, P V Junction, Elman Taylor and wife, Juab; Geo Williams, Fillmore; I H Dickmann, San Francisco; Andus Schmidb, Cainna, Mex; H L Jackman and wife, Juab.

Salt Lake Herald
July 11, 1884

HOTEL ARRIVALS.

CLIFT HOUSE.

Mrs Barthalomy, Fillmore; Dr Silas Re. Boston; J Farmer, Ogden; H E traig, Chicago; Thos Lyons, Frisco; J H Wood and F D Johnson, San Francisco; H L Sud worth, Provo; E R Bartlett, P V Junction; C N sinnor, Denver; W T Coal, Geo Crford, Evanston.

Salt Lake Herald
July 12, 1884

HOTEL ARRIVALS.

July 11, 1884.

WHITE HOUSE.

E Huntsman, Fillmore; W Burnes, E Mackay, Ohio; Mrs D H Chase, Schuyler, Neb; M Don, Nephi; W T Ourel, Tacoma, Nev; John Mack, W Donnelly, M Madden, J Dorsey, Frisco; J R Watson, Nevada; J Turner, Heber City; J G Ruse, Newport, W T; Horace H Kimball, Iowa; J More, C More Baxion, M T; H E Brdy, Ridder's Station M T; J R Cohn, Missoula, M T; T M Bacon, Roseburg, Or; J E Cox, Ashland, Or; G R Thorne, Port Costa, o'; E L Ruse, M Jones, A Walker, T D Clark, S Davis, T Davis, R M Wiley, Southern Pacific railroad, California; L Alexander, Virginia; J Anderson, Ganhausen; Mrs C Hutchinson, Sioa City; J McCullough, Altoona, Pa; M Seeley, Mt Pleasant; Miss L Hilbman, Park City; G Attion, Tooele; H A Whitney, Springfield, O; Mrs Brisco', Bingham; W T Whittemore, Chicago; J P Treboon, Silver Reef.

THE TABERNACLE.

Adjournment of the Semi-Annual Conference.

THE LIST OF MISSIONARIES.

President Taylor again Addresses the People—The Subjects Preached Upon.

Monday, Oct. 7th, 10 a. m.

The Choir sang:

O say what is truth! 'Tis the fairest gem
That the riches of worlds can produce.

Prayer by President John D. T. McAllister.

The Choir sang:

Praise to the Man who communed with Jehovah,
Jesus anointed that Prophet and Seer.

PRESIDENT GEORGE Q. CANNON read the names of missionaries in addition to those called yesterday, the vote to sustain the brethren selected being unanimous.

Following is the full list of missionaries who have been called since the April Conference, 1884, and now in their fields of labor, and whose names are now submitted:

GREAT BRITAIN.

Reuben Carter, Sr., Fountain Green.
Robert Marshall, Toquerville.
Heber Sutton Goddard, Thirteenth Ward.
Joseph Spendlove, Littleton.

SCANDINAVIA.

Hans Christensen, Richfield.

UNITED STATES.

Samuel Witwer, Santa Clara.
Richard Rawle Fry, Morgan.
John Zimmerman, Lehi.

SOUTHERN STATES.

Samuel Chandler Parkinson, Franklin.

NEW ZEALAND.

William Gardner, Pine Valley.

HINDOOSTAN.

William Willes, Twentieth Ward.
Milson K. Pratt, Sixteenth Ward.
Henry F. McCune, Nephi.
George Booth, Calcutta.

Names of Missionaries, October 6th, 1884:

GREAT BRITAIN.

George Armond, Bloomington.
Peter Winward, Payson.
Thomas Butterfield, Herriman.
Joseph H. S. Bodell, Herriman.
Jesse B. Martin, Jr., Scipio.
William Horsley, Brigham.
George Gidney, Brigham.
George H. Powers, Hooper.
L. L. Hatch, Franklin.
John Rowley, Nephi.
William Rex, Randolph.
Thomas Slight, Paris.
Robert W. Sloan, Eighteenth Ward.

SWISS AND GERMAN MISSION.

Gustave Henriod, Nephi.
Godfrey G. Fuhriman, Providence.
Conrad Fairclouse, Paris.
John Kunz, Jr., Bern.
David Kunz, Bern.
Arnold Henry Schulthess, First Ward.

SCANDINAVIA.

Jeppa Jeppson, Brigham.
Niels Hansen, Manti.
Rasmus Borquist, Tenth Ward.
S. A. Wannberg, Twentieth Ward.
Christian Nielsen Lundsteen, Levan.
Matts S. Mattson, St. Charles.
Thomas C. Petersen, Ovid.
Niels C. Christensen, Levan.
Christian Christiansen, Levan.
Thomas K. Shroder, Nephi.
Mads Peter Madsen, Ephraim.
Andrew C. Anderson, Richmond.
Christian Anderson, Ogden.
Nephi Anderson, Peterson.
Johan Peter Mortensen, Eighth Ward.
August K. Anderson, Grantsville.
Chas. J. Stromberg, Grantsville.
Peter M. Anderson, Grantsville.
John Alfred Eliason, Grantsville.
Anders Gustaf Sandberg, Grantsville.
Erasmus P. Margnerdson, Elsinore.
N. P. Peterson, Pleasant Grove.
Carl G. Anderson, Nineteenth Ward.
John J. Johnsen, Logan.
Andras Olsen, Gunnison.
Lars Poolson, Smithfield.
Peter W. Pett'son, Smithfield.

UNITED STATES.

John D. Chase, Nephi.
Joseph Shipley, American Fork.

SOUTHERN STATES.

Wm. P. Camp, Samaria.
Thomas E. Harper, Call's Fort.
James W. Quayle, Logan.
Richard Thorne, Three-Mile Creek, Box Elder Co.
William M. Daines, Hyde Park.
W. M. Webster, Franklin.
Wm. H. Gibbs, West Portage.
Elisha D. Clapp, Chester.
Frederick Rich Lyman, Oak Creek.

NEW ZEALAND.

George S. Taylor, Fourteenth Ward.
James A. Slater, Slaterville.
Edwin L. Davis, South Cottonwood.
Ezra F. Richards, Farmington.
Franklin Hill, Fayette.
William C. Mellor, Fayette.

SANDWICH ISLANDS.

Robert B. T. Taylor, Sixteenth Ward.
Hyrum S. Harris, Provo.
Enoch Farr, Ogden.
Alberto J. Merrill, Smithfield.

MEXICO.

Isaac S. Stewart, Draper.
Alvin Vickry Robison, Fillmore.

PRESIDENT JOHN TAYLOR then spoke in relation to the accusations made against the Latter-day Saints by their traducers, to the effect that they are immoral and corrupt. He stated that he would not dwell upon the crimes of the accusers of the Saints if we were not on the defensive, but they made it imperative that they should be exposed. At the President's request, President George Q. Cannon read the criminal statistics of Utah, taken from the official records, showing that over ten times the amount of crime is committed in the Territory proportionately by non-Mormons than by people professing to be Mormons. He continued to speak for some time upon the corruptions, chicanery and perfidy practiced upon

the Latter-day Saints by designing schemers. He asserted that great numbers of honorable people despised these outrageous doings as much as we do.

President Cannon, at the request of the speaker, then read statistics from papers published by notable eastern authorities, showing the horribly immoral condition of society in the New England States.

Resuming, President Taylor said these people described by the statements read are those who are so horrified at the immoral situation in Utah, and from these come our would-be reformers. He was gratified that men could be found who are ready to denounce such abominable practices. His purpose in having those statements read in relation to infanticide and other crimes was two-fold. One was to exhibit the true character of those who perpetrated them, and the other was to warn the Saints against such characters, some of whom were endeavoring to insinuate themselves into the society and houses of the people here. No such persons could have any lot or place among the Saints, and on no consideration could they be permitted to enjoy the privileges of the gospel. He warned the officers of the church against giving recommends to adulterers, murderers, or either men or women who are guilty of the unnatural crimes which had been defined in the extracts which had been presented. He directed that those guilty of such practices be cut off the church, and requested that all who favored this view should say aye. The response was loud and unanimous. President Taylor then spoke at some length upon the temporal affairs of the Saints. He gave an interesting review of the experiences of the Saints in this connection in the past. There had been a depression of late in monetary affairs, and improvements in the shape of new buildings had not been so numerous recently as some time ago. He described a visit by himself and associates in the Priesthood to what are now known as the Bannock and Oneida Stakes, where the land and other facilities are good and settlements are growing up. More people are wanted to help develop those portions of the country, and a similar situation exists in the south. Those who are out of employment are wanted to go to such places, where there is plenty of room. There are room and opportunities for all kinds of mechanics, especially in the building lines, as well as other branches of business in Bannock and other outlying Stakes, and those who had no work in the older settled parts should make their way to the more sparsely populated portions of the country. The speaker had advised, in the newly formed settlements, that when the people build houses, they should construct them according to a comely and intelligent plan, that beautiful homes may be reared. Those who wished to adopt this advice about going into the country should call upon Bishop Preston, that the method of getting to those places may be decided upon. The speaker then asked President Ricks of Bannock and President Hendricks of Oneida Stake as to whether they could employ a number of new settlers acquainted with the various branches of industry. These gentlemen responded in the affirmative. President Taylor next touched upon the situation of Z. C. M. I., which was established for the purpose of furthering the interests of co-operation in mercantile and manufacturing directions. It is in a solid and flourishing condition, notwithstanding the general stringency of the times. There is not a better or safer institution in this Territory. There are a number of Mormon and non-Mormon stores and Z. C. M. I. does more in relation to home manufactures than all these put together. The speaker then read a concise statement in regard to what the institution had done in that line. He also stated that arrangements had been made to conduct the industry of manufacturing clothing, and for the furtherance of this branch it had agreed with the Provo woolen factory for the purchase of its entire product of cloth. President Taylor expressed regret at the carelessness that had been exhibited by many people indebted to the Perpetual Emigration Fund. Four years ago $800,000 of the amount due that fund had been forgiven to those owing it. About the same amount as that named still remained upon the books, and since then but $25,000 of that sum had been refunded by individuals obligated. This was a lamentable showing, and if the law of God were applied to those who had been so negligent in relation to paying their just debts, and thus robbed the poor of their rights, some of them would have to be severed from the church.

APOSTLE HEBER J. GRANT hoped that he might enjoy a portion of the same spirit which had prompted the utterances of all the speakers at the Conference. He could well understand that to live our religion requires a constant exertion on our part. In brief the whole of this religion is to live lives of righteousness. Many believed that if they are barely able to hold a standing in the Church they are still living their religion. The fallacy of such an idea—that simple faith or belief without works was sufficient, was briefly touched upon; and the speaker declared it his belief that no person who does nothing toward building the houses of God had a right to enter these houses and take a part in the blessings and privileges therein conferred. Referring to our position in the world, he said, honest, upright men not of us recognize the merits of the Saints and their honesty of dealing, while it is only by those who are not themselves above reproach that the calumnies against us are set in circulation. He regretted the growing tendency among the saints to run into debt and urged farmers in the purchase of machinery to use more wisdom, and the people generally to adopt a more healthy method of financiering. Sufficient instruction had been given at this conference to enable the Saints, if they would observe it, to make a great improvement on their past record, and he prayed that they might be enabled to do so.

APOSTLE JOHN W. TAYLOR had been reminded on hearing the remarks and statements of President Taylor, of the admonition of the Savior to those who could discern the signs of the sky but were not able to discern the signs of the times. John the Revelator had been moved to cry out concerning the judgments that would come upon the earth, and it was to escape these and to fulfil many other predictions of the ancient prophets, that the saints had gathered out of all nations. He prayed that our strongest desire, now that we are gathered here, might be to remain firm, and devote all our strength to the building up and establishment of the kingdom of God upon the earth.

Conference adjourned till April, 1885, in the Large Tabernacle.

The choir sang:

Where the voice of friendship's heard,
Sounding like a sweet-toned bird.

Benediction by Patriarch John Smith.

JOHN NICHOLSON,
Clerk of Conference.

Salt Lake Herald
November 7, 1884

W. H. KING, of Fillmore, has returned from Logan, and will spend a few days in the city.

THE TOTAL COUNT.

Nineteen Thousand Majority for John T. Caine.

RANCID'S SUSPENSE IS OVER.

The Full Vote of Every Precinct in the Territory for Both Candidates.

At 10 o'clock yesterday morning the board appointed to canvass the returns of the recent election for Delegate to Congress, met in the rooms of the Utah Commission and proceeded to their work. A HERALD reporter called in during the afternoon and found the gentlemen comprising the board immersed in additions, the very sight of which made one giddy. The count was finished early last evening, and the following figures were obtained. Hon. John T. Caine's majority, it will be seen, is but a few votes short of 19,000. Hon. (that was to have been) Rancid Smith is understood to have grown quite haggard from the protracted suspense, but he may now congratulate himself on the long agony being concluded:

Beaver County.

Precincts	Caine.	Smith.
Adamsville	87	
Beaver	220	32
Grampian, 1st Poll	2	52
Grampian, 2d Poll	1	17
Greenville	49	
Star	16	20
Minersville, 1st Poll	79	12
Minersville, 2d Poll	3	14
Totals	473	154

Box Elder County.

Precincts	Caine.	Smith.
Bear River	64	
Box Elder	298	6
Calls Fort	67	
Curlew	22	1
Deweyville	53	4
Grass Creek	34	
Malad (Corinne)		57
Mantua	66	
Park Valley	74	
Plymouth	17	1
Portage	45	
Promontory	4	3
Terrace	8	49
Willard	115	2
Totals		

Morgan County.

Precincts	Caine.	Smith.
Canyon Creek	86	
Croyden	38	6
Milton	31	4
Morgan	86	2
Peterson	23	
Totals	274	12

Piute County.

Precincts	Caine.	Smith.	Blank.
Circle Valley	53	9	
Bullion	3	16	
Fremont	64		1
Deer Trail	8	2	
Koosharen	63	1	*
Wilmot	10	0	
Thurber	52		
Totals	212	34	1

Rich County.

Precincts	Caine.	Smith.
Garden City	32	
Meadowville	16	
Laketown	49	
Randolph	50	
Woodruff	40	1
Totals	187	1

Salt Lake County.

Precinct	Caine.	Smith.	Horne.
Salt Lake City			
First, Poll 1	278	38	
" " 2	279	44	
Second, " 1	194	72	1
" " 2	272	68	
Third, " 1	340	39	
" " 2	815	6	
Fourth, "	434	28	
Fifth, " 1	282	70	
" " 2	160	32	
Big Cottonwood	105	3	
Bluff Dale	15		
Bingham	3	48	
Butler	27		
Draper	111	1	
East Mill Creek	68	3	
Farmers	48	3	
Fort Herriman	27	9	
Riverton	40		
Granger	89	2	
Brighton	21	4	
Granite	22	1	
Hunter	10	1	
Little Cottonwood	1	28	
Mill Creek	100		
Mountain Dell	11		
North Point	22	2	
Pleasant Green	34		
Sandy	91	21	
South Cottonwood	140	39	
South Jordan	55		
North Jordan	72	3	
West Jordan	185		
Union	68	8	
Sugar House	91	17	
Silver		9	
Totals	4,326	613	1

	Caine.	Smith.	
Spanish Fork	438	9	2
Spring Lake	15		
Lakeview	34		
Springville	332	29	
Provo Bench	31	1	
Thistle	18		
P. V. Junction	4	14	
Totals	3160	127	2

Wasatch County.

Precincts	Caine.	Smith.	Hatch.
Charleston	48		
Heber	238	1	1
Midway	115		
Wallsburgh	68	1	
Totals	469	2	1

Washington County.

Precincts	Caine.	Smith.
Duncan's Retreat	15	
Hebron	18	
Grafton	23	
Gunlock	13	
Leeds, 1st Poll	26	2
Leeds, 2d Poll		
New Harmony	29	
Pine Valley	50	
Price	27	
Pinto	37	
Rockville	89	
St. George	166	3
Santa Clara	36	
Silver Reef	10	45
Shonesburgh	15	
Springdale	12	
Toquerville	54	
Virgen City	52	
Washington	66	
Totals	670	50

Weber County.

Precincts	Caine.	Smith.
Eden	40	2
Harrisville	90	1
Hooper	161	18
Huntsville	140	11
Lynne	70	16
Marriot	38	1
Ogden, 1st Poll	345	195
Ogden, 2d Poll	294	138
Ogden, 3d Poll	392	112
Plain City	125	36
North Ogden	124	4
Riverdale	70	1
Slaterville	54	38
Uintah	25	2
West Weber	101	
Wilson	30	18
Pleasant View	62	
Totals	2218	599

Total vote for Caine	21,190
Total vote for Smith	2,294
Caine's majority	18,906

Cache County.

Precincts.	Caine.	Smith.
Benson	94	2
Clarkston	46	
Hyde Park	86	
Hyrum	201	
Lewiston	103	2
Logan	512	6
Mendon	116	
Millville	81	
Paradise	104	
Providence	81	
Peterboro	10	
Newton	30	
Richmond	131	2
Coveville	93	
Smithfield	198	4
Trenton	29	3
Wellsville	177	4
Totals	1,850	28

Davis County.

Precincts.	Caine.	Smith.
Centreville	79	7
East Centreville	173	12
Farmington	144	11
Kaysville	230	16
South Kaysville	79	
South Hooper	55	12
South Weber	85	6
West Weber	60	
Totals	874	64

Emery County.

Precincts.	Caine.	Smith.
Castle Dale	51	
Ferron	68	
Huntington	92	
Moab	98	2
Price	54	3
Orangeville	70	2
Scofield	24	16
Muddy	15	
Totals	382	23

Garfield County.

Precincts.	Caine.	Smith.
Cannonville	24	
Escalante	62	
Hillsdale	15	
Coyote (No election)		
Panguitch	99	
Total	190	

Iron County.

Precincts.	Caine.	Smith.
Cedar	141	
Kanarra	37	
Paragoonah	53	
Parowan	115	7
Summit	21	5
Totals	339	12

Juab County.

Precincts	Caine.	Smith.
Levan	66	
Nephi	396	7
Mona	65	
Tintic	6	25
Totals	500	32

Kane County.

Precincts.	Caine.	Smith.	Biggs
Glendale	36		
Johnson	18		
Kanab	10		1
Upper Kanab	48		
Orderville	29		
Mount Carmel	22		
Pareah	10	2	
Totals	104	2	1

Millard County.

Precincts.	Caine.	Smith.
Deseret	54	8
Fillmore	43	
Holden	82	
Kanosh	54	3
Leamington	25	
Meadow	40	
Oak Creek	33	
Scipio	87	9
Burbank	No election.	
Total	408	22

San Juan County.

No returns.

Sanpete County.

Precincts.	Caine	Smith	Christiansen	Stott.	Johnson.
Ephraim	253	4			
Chester	29				
Fairview	170	1			
Fayette	84				
Gunnison	111		2		
Manti	229	1		4	
Moroni	157	4		4	
Mount Pleasant	220	23			
Mayfield	64				
Fountain Green	118				
Petty	45				
Spring City	129	1			1
Thistle	16	1			
Winter Quarters	16	1			
Wales	48	1			
Totals	1655	48	2	4	1

Sevier County.

Precincts.	Caine.	Smith.
Annabella	53	2
Burrville	43	1
Central	56	
Elsinore	80	3
Glenwood	68	1
Gooseberry	18	3
Monroe	86	9
Redmond	45	
Richfield	90	15
Joseph	58	7
Salina	46	11
Vermillion	18	3
Willow Bend	46	
Totals	628	82

Summit County.

Precincts.	Caine.	Smith.	J. Pack, Jr.
Echo	25	21	
Coalville	199	7	
Grass Creek	28		
Hennefer	53	4	
Hoytsville	64	5	
Kamas	78	4	1
Park City, 1 P	23	155	
Park City, 2 P	3	19	
Park City, 3 P	1	8	
Peoa	61		
Parley's Park	13	5	
Rockport	22	3	
Upton	44		
Wanship	45	10	
Totals	668	254	1

Tooele County.

Precincts.	Caine.	Smith.
Batesville	22	
Clover	19	
St. John	38	
Deep Creek	No returns.	
Grantsville	128	5
Lakeview	28	
Mill	31	
Ophir	1	17
Stockton	6	27
Vernon	28	
Tooele	164	18
Totals	486	65

Uintah County.

Precincts.	Caine.	Smith.	Johnson.
Ashley	89	9	4
Brown's Park	No returns.		
Totals	89	9	4

Utah County.

Precincts.	Caine.	Smith.	Butts.
Alpine	79		
American Fork	255		
Benjamin	41	11	
Cedar Fort	24	3	
Fairfield	15	11	
Goshen	85	3	
Lehi	305	7	
Payson	301	8	
Pleasant Grove	244	8	
Provo	687	19	
Salem	102		
Santaquin	129		

Salt Lake Herald
January 9, 1885

Dr. Pike was called suddenly to Fillmore on Wednesday, to attend to a man named Huntsman, who is said to have been shot in the head; further particulars were not obtainable.

Salt Lake Herald
January 10, 1885

THE FILLMORE SHOOTING.

W. H. King Reported to have Killed Young Huntsman.

Further particulars have been received in this city, of the shooting at Fillmore, and though none of them are definite, they give more details, than any other reports have yet done. According to what was heard by a gentleman up from the south on Thursday evening, a party of young men went out to shoot rabbits, taking a double team and a wagon; the whole party were driving along when Mr. King announced that he was about to fire, and asked those in front of him to "duck their heads;" he delayed somewhat in taking aim, and young Huntsman imagining that he had decided not to shoot, raised his head, just in time to receive the charge in his skull. One rumor had it that he was still alive, and another states that he died on Thursday. Mr. King is a prominent young man in the south, and holds a prominent civil office in Millard county; he is represented as being nearly distracted with grief at the unfortunate occurrence.

AN UNTIMELY DEATH.

Complete Details of the Fillmore Accident.

MR. KING FULLY EXONERATED.

Another Casualty to Swell the Long List of Accidents from the Handling of Firearms.

FILLMORE, Millard Co., Utah,
January 10th, 1885.

To the Editor of THE HERALD.

In justice to all parties concerned, and to prevent any misunderstanding, the following facts are submitted concerning the dreadful accident which deprived one of our young men, Mr. Joseph Alonzo Huntsman, of his life.

Early on Wednesday last, the 7th inst., six young men, viz: Joseph Alonzo Huntsman, D. P. Callister, Wesley W. Dame, Charles Mace, Wm. H. King and Jacob Hawley, with team proceeded to the Cedar Mountain to shoot rabbits. They had been out several hours, and concluding it time to return, were all in the wagon except W. W. Dame, who had taken passage in another wagon, and were driving towards home when a rabbit was observed some little distance away to the left of the wagon, upon which Huntsman exclaimed, "Shoot it!" Thereupon, W. H. King and Jacob Hawley, who occupied the rear seat, rose to their feet and raised their guns to fire. Upon rising, W. H. King said: "I will shoot." Simultaneously with the firing of the guns by the aforesaid, Huntsman, the deceased, raised to the level of the guns, inclining his body to the left, and the charge from the gun held by W. H. King struck the side of his head near to the centre, literally blowing off a portion of the skull, leaving the brain exposed, and fragments of the scalp were subsequently found as far as twenty-two yards from the place where the accident happened. This move on the part of Huntsman was unexpected, from the fact that he and another or two having rifles, were to shoot such game as should be too far for the shot guns, such arrangements having been thoroughly understood.

The accident occurred early in the afternoon, and two hours later the unfortunate young man was brought home to his grief-stricken family unconscious; yet not quite dead. Hopes were entertained by some that his life might yet be saved. Accordingly, Dr. Pike, of Provo, was telephoned to immediately, who took the evening train for Juab, and was there met by team and conveyed to Scipio, where horses were changed and at 12 o'clock at night continued his journey. Arriving at Holden, he was met by a dispatch to the effect that his services were not needed, as the young man had died at 8.30 p. m.

As soon after life had become extinct as a jury could be empaneled, a coroner's inquest was held over the remains, and the following is a transcript of the verdict of the jury:

"We, the jury empaneled and sworn, examined into the cause of the death of Joseph Alonzo Huntsman, before us there lying dead, do find and present: that the deceased came to his death by the accidental discharge of a gun in the hands of William H. King, on January 7th, 1885, in the County of Millard, Territory of Utah, and furthermore, we find that no censure or blame is attached to the aforesaid Wm. H. King.

JOSEPH J. McMICKEN,
J. DANIEL OLSON,
GEORGE CROFT,

Attest: J. GREENWOOD,
Ex-officio Coroner,
Justice of the Peace."

On Friday, at 12.30, the funeral services were held in the Fillmore meeting house, the room being packed to its utmost capacity. Several elders made remarks calculated to enlarge the heart, lift up the drooping spirits and comfort with hope the sorrowing relatives and friends. Previous to the funeral, the wife, parents, brothers, sisters and other relatives had signed the following resolution, which was read by Bishop Smith to the meeting and adopted by unanimous vote:

Resolution of Exoneration of Brother W. H. King.

FILLMORE, January 9th, 1885.

Whereas, our much respected brother and esteemed friend, W. H. King, was the one whose hands held the fated gun, the discharge of which deprived our deceased husband, brother and son, Joseph Alonzo Huntsman, of his life; and,

Whereas, we appreciate the deep sorrow and constant regret occasioned the said brother, W. H. King, because of the said unfortunate accident; Therefore, we, the undersigned, upon this public occasion, wish to offer the following:

Resolved, That brother W. H. King is entirely blameless in this most unfortunate affair. Such being the case, we continue to extend to him the same feelings of respect and friendship we have heretofore entertained towards him, and in our bereavement do not forget to extend to him our heartfelt sympathy at the deep distress experienced him by this accident.

(Signed,) Ella Huntsman, wife; Gabriel Huntsman, father; Eunice Huntsman, mother; Gabriel E. Huntsman, brother; Orson H. Huntsman, brother; Eunice Mary Huntsman, sister; Heber Huntsman, brother; Lafayette Huntsman, brother; Ida Huntsman, sister; Chandler Holbrook, grandfather; Eunice Holbrook, grandmother; O. C. Holbrook, uncle; J. H. Holbrook, brother-in-law; W. A. Ray, brother-in-law; Joseph E. Ray, brother-in-law.

A large concourse of people in twenty-six vehicles followed the remains to the grave, and amid the tears and sobs of many people, the last sad rites were performed, which consigned a good loving man to his last resting place.

Joseph Alonzo Huntsman was born January 15th, 1862, in Fillmore, Utah. He was the third son of Gabriel and Eunice E. Huntsman. After attaining to his majority he seemed desirous of improving himself morally and intellectually, and latterly was studying with a view to becoming a useful member of society. He frequently expressed a wish that he might soon be called on a mission, as by such labors his qualifications for usefulness might be increased. He was a kind and tender husband, and possessed many qualities of heart and brain that endeared him to hosts of friends. He leaves a large circle of friends

diate relatives, deceased left a wife of
tender years and in delicate health, to
mourn his loss. It is to be hoped that
He who is a husband to the widow and a
father to the fatherless will pour the
balm of healing into her wounded and
bleeding heart.

It is but just and proper, in concluding this article, to set forth the generous, prompt and noble parts enacted by
men of all classes and conditions, irre-
spective of party, sect or creed, during
the terrible hours of trial which dis-
qualified the family of the deceased from
acting in their own behalf. Telegrams
were sent; teams promptly forwarded
for the physician, and driven without
regard to horseflesh; outsiders flew like
the hurricane to other settlements
north, to arrange proper changes of
horses to carry the physician with all
speed to the scene of trouble. Funeral
arrangements in all their details were
thoughtfully considered, planned and
carried into effect. In short, all things
were done that good, earnest, thought-
ful men and women could devise to alleviate the sorrow of the living and lov-
ingly put to rest the dead.

Respectfully,

NEPHI PRATT,
C. ANDERSON.

Salt Lake Herald
January 16, 1885

SOUTHERN SPORTS.

Horse Racing and Other Pastimes in Millard County.

KANOSH, MILLARD CO., Jan. 12th, 1885.

[Correspondence of THE HERALD.]

During the last month the sports of
this county have been looking for fun
as the result to two races arranged to
come off on the 9th. Mr. Wise Cropper,
of Deseret, backing Mr. Orson Huntsman, of Fillmore, to run 40 yards against
Mr. C. W. Watts, of Kanosh, for $250.
The same parties also made a horse race,
Mr. Cropper backing Charley Webb's
bay colt "Switch Tail," and Watts backing Mr. W. Cummings' brown horse,
"Dick."

Owing to the dreadful calamity in the
Huntsman family, the foot race was declared off, and the stakes transferred to
the horse race, which made the stakes
for that event $500, the distance half a
mile. This event came off on the 10th,
and brown "Dick" won the stakes.

A second race also came off between
Mr. Lucil Hinckley's "Bluch" and Mr.
G. Robinson's, of Deseret, colt "Blizzard." The Blizzard was too keen for
Bluch and again the Kanosh boy scoop-
ed in the ducats. Then races were run
at the Sink below Fillmore, to accommodate the Deseretes. The Kanosh
wing arrived home yesterday while the
citizens generally were attending meeting. They showed as happy as a main of
triumphant roosters. Among the trophies
were a buggy, a rifle, a band of horses,
and cattle yet to come. We, in common
with most of our citizens, wished it had
been otherwise, and we here enter our
gentle protest against Deseret and Fillmore, for seducing our youth (at a time
when our bishop is sick) from their
usual peaceful, pastoral pursuits and
imitating innocence into the question-
able science of horse racing.

But if Tibbetts or Wright should be
meandering in the south and are speedy
enough, they could compel us in self
defense to permit them to leave hereabouts with a band of horses large
enough to induce the energetic H. J. F.
to come amongst us to organize.

TWO-FORTY.

Arrest of a "Suspect."

For some time there has been a demand for one Reed. He has been wanted
by the officials of Colorado, and Sheriff
Salee, of Chaffee County, has had a good
long hunt for the fugitive from justice,
going recently to California on a rumor
that his man had been arrested there;
but that trip was a fruitless one. A
couple of days ago, Mr. Charles H.
Glover, of Fillmore, apprehended an individual answering Reed's description,
and telegraphed the sheriff of Chaffee
County to that effect. The Colorado
official replied, asking Mr. Glover to hold
the "suspect" until the necessary requisition arrived from the east. If the man
held at Fillmore proves to be the Reed
wanted, the Utah capturer will no doubt
be properly rewarded.

Salt Lake Herald
January 18, 1885

G. HUNTSMAN, of Fillmore, father to
the unfortunate youth who recently
lost his life in an accident, is in Salt
Lake.

Salt Lake Herald
February 24, 1885

APOSTLE H. J. GRANT has returned from his visit to the conferences in the southern counties. The roads are something terrific, he says, himself and companion being compelled to abandon an empty buggy in "Mud Lake," between Fillmore and Deseret, and betake themselves to the horses.

Salt Lake Herald
March 1, 1885

HOTEL ARRIVALS.

WHITE HOUSE.

J. McCarthy, Leadville, Colo.; J. George, Fillmore; L. R. Tyson, U. P. Railroad; J. Fishell, Tooele; E. C. Briarley, Hailey; J. Bash, Bingham; Miss Heaston, Bingham; D. N. Ewan, Bingham; C. M. Frisbie, P. V. Junction; F. Ferris, P. V. Junction; Miss E. Thomas, P. V. Junction; J. Holter, Bingham; T. Allen, Bingham; C. Truscott, Bingham; T. McMahon, Denver; T. J. Thomas, New York; H. Brown, city; T. Carwick, Evanston; M. M. Beaver, Bingham; E. H. Test, Rochester, N. Y.; S. S. Bamberger, San Francisco.

Salt Lake Herald
March 10, 1885

W. H. KING, of Fillmore, has been in Salt Lake several days, but expects to return home to-day.

Salt Lake Herald
March 11, 1885

A PLUCKY COMMUNITY.

Deseret Undismayed by its Washouts— Bishop Preston's Generosity.

DESERET, Millard Co., March 9, 1885.

To the Editor of THE HERALD:

After an absence of nearly six months, (being detained in Fillmore through a severe sickness) I arrived home last week. The people generally enjoy good health, but grain for seed and bread is very scarce, owing to our heavy losses last summer of all. It has cost over $30,000 to repair the dam and the break around it and we probably lost 30,000 or 40,000 bushels of grain for want of water besides a heavy percentage of our income. Last week we took preliminary steps for organizing a Joint Stock Canal Company for the purpose of taking the water from the river without a dam. We have made a survey and find it can be done at a reasonable cost and it will bring under cultivation much new and very fertile land. Through the kindness of Bishop Preston, who has loaned our citizens 1,500 bushels of grain, we shall be able to put in a heavy crop for those who we not able to obtain seed, will thus be supplied.

We are not discouraged, as we expect to make a complete success, for our settlement continues to grow and peace prevails. Wishing THE HERALD much success, I remain, yours truly,

J. S. BLACK.

Salt Lake Herald
March 18, 1885

HOTEL ARRIVALS.

WHITE HOUSE.

T. Orchard, P. McCaffee, Ogden; W. Dutton, M. Gibbons, D. N. Swan, S. W. Burrows, J. G. Brager, Bingham; A. M. Holt, J. H. Russell, J. McClary, Rush Valley; T. J. Startgee, Omaha; Fritz Rittick, Alta; J. A. Flange, Glendive; John Smith, Park City; E. J. Gragon, California; Miss Emma Knox, Fillmore; J. P. Doolan, City; J. McLaughlin, St. Patrick.

Salt Lake Herald
April 1, 1885

Bishop Smith, of Fillmore, is among the visitors to the metropolis.

Salt Lake Herald
April 10, 1885

A party of C. P. officials came in from San Francisco yesterday morning, over the D. & R. G. Colonel C. F. Crocker, son of the second vice-president of the C. P., J. A. Fillmore, general superintendent of the road and Hon. L. W. Sanderson, attorney. They went to Ogden in the afternoon, after viewing this city in its spring beauty.

Salt Lake Herald
April 16, 1885

Thos. Callister, the well-known citizen of Fillmore, is among the visitors to Salt Lake.

COUNTY REGISTRARS.

List of the New Officers Appointed by the Commissioners.

The following named gentlemen have been appointed County Registrars by the Commissioners, and their certificates were forwarded yesterday. These offices, since the recent ruling, are apt to be less eagerly desired than before, and the new appointees will be apt to make all their moves with extreme caution. A circular for their information is now in course of preparation:

Beaver County—James McGarry, Milford.

Box Elder County—D. D. Ryan, Corinne.

Cache County—C. C. Goodwin, Logan.

Davis County—Hector W. Haight, Farmington.

Emery County — S. J. Harkness, Scofield.

Garfield County—John M. Dunning, Panguitch.

Iron County — Daniel Page, Parowan.

Juab County—Edward Booth, Nephi.

Kane County—John Stewart, Kanab.

Millard County—John Kelley, Fillmore.

Morgan County—A. D. Shurtliff, Morgan.

Piute County—James A. Stark, Marysvale.

Rich County—Wesley K. Walton, Randolph.

Salt Lake County—Thomas C. Bailey, Salt Lake.

San Juan County—Charles Walton, Bluff City.

Sanpete County—A. J. F. Beaumann, Mount Pleasant.

Sevier County—S. F. Mount, Salina.

Summit County—Wilson I. Snyder, Park City.

Tooele County—David B. Stover, Stockton.

Uintah County—Isaac Burton, Ashley.

Utah County—A. G. Sutherland, Provo.

Wasatch County — John Duncan, Heber City.

Washington County—Jas. N. Louder, Silver Reef.

Weber County—L. B. Stevens, Ogden.

HOTEL ARRIVALS.

May 6, 1885.

WHITE HOUSE.

James Hoatson, J. W. Mulford, Evanston; John Hurmane, Bingham; Amos Feustermaker, Box Elder Ranch; Jas Brown, John Kelley, Bingham; A. J. McCullough, Ohio; Peter Welte, Silver Reef; John Anderson and family, Manti, T. C. Walch, Bingham; John McIntire, A. McFarlane, Jr., William Clark, John Bryson, W. T. Williams, Mill Creek; James D. Rowe, Ed. J. Rowe, George Polland, Evanston; Wm. Cooper and wife, West Jordan; M. M. Beaver, Bingham; J. W. Henry Fillmore; J. O. Hooper, Ogden; J. Davis, Peter Kreller, A. Bisens, Park City.

Salt Lake Herald
May 9, 1885

HOTEL ARRIVAL.

May 8th, 1885.

WHITE HOUSE.

James Hoatson, J. M. Mulford, Evanston; Edwin Stewart, Bloomington, Ill.; James McFleny, Duncan McInnes, Sen., E. Hill, E. Brumaghine, Bingham; T. S. Schenck, Park City; D. A. Sanders, Osceola; M. Taylor, Sanpete; Jas. Doyle, Penitentiary; G. R. Huntsman, Fillmore City; Albert Peters, Cincinnati; John Jones, Spanish Fork; B. Bachman, Provo; J. Manning, Chicago; J. M. McGinn, Sacramento; Dave Musselman, Bingham; J. W. Browning, Nelson McCarty, C. W. Middleton, Ogden; J. Marks, J. C. Rud, San Francisco.

Salt Lake Herald
May 13, 1885

HOTEL ARRIVAL.

May 12th, 1885.

WHITE HOUSE.

F. M. Smith, Detroit; M. Sacks, Cincinnati, J. H. Youngblood, A. Bustch, Douglass; J. W. Sayers, Bingham; Harry Haynes, Murray; J. D. Reese, Fillmore; H. Thompson, Joseph Lee, Bingham; George McKenzie, L. N. Wood, Springville; J. C. Treynon, Frisco; Chas. Bently, Jerry K. Sullivan, Eureka, Utah; Rasmus Christenson, Deseret; John Butler, Bingham; J. E. Larkins, Ogden; J. C. Varner, Oxford; J. Gallagher, Ogden; Jas. Ratcliffe, Ogden; John Egan, D. & R. G.; J. O. Hooper, Ogden; J. Johnson, John Barrett, Bath; Wm. Benney, John Taylor, Alta.

Salt Lake Herald
July 4, 1885

THE COMING ELECTION.

The Judges Appointed by the Utah Commission.

List of the names of Judges of election appointed by the Utah Commission to serve at the ensuing election to be held in the Territory of Utah, August 3d, 1885:

MILLARD COUNTY.

Burbank—Wm. Atkinson, Charles Rowland, Brigham Young.

Fillmore—A. C. Robison, E. Bartholomew, James A. Melville.

Holden—Joseph S. Gyles, Thomas Evans, Enoch Dodge.

Scipio—Samuel Rowley, Hans Marquarson, Peter Meilson.

Oak Creek — Maxwell Webb, Ole Jacobson, Simms Walker.

Learington—Judge Wilson, Christian Overson, Lewis Stout.

Deseret—Edward Webb, Thomas W. Copper, Willard Rogers.

Meadow — Joseph Adams, John Stredder, Abraham Greenhalgh.

Kanosh—Peter Robison, George Crane, Richard Hatton.

Note—The first named person in each precinct is the presiding judge.

Salt Lake Herald
December 4, 1885

W. H. King of Fillmore, Utah, is a guest at the Valley House, having returned from St. Louis last night.

Salt Lake Herald
January 1, 1886

After Horse Thieves.

Sheriff McBride came in from Tooele yesterday *en route* for Fillmore where he goes to bring back two hore thieves who recently took a number of animals from Grantsvi'le, and while speeding on their way southward gathered up a band of fifteen horses *en route*. They were captured and detained by the sheriff at Deseret.

Salt Lake Herald
January 10, 1886

THE LEGISLATORS.

McLaughlin Not to be Disturbed.

THE GATHERING OF THE CLANS.

An Organization To-morrow – The Governor's Message — Arrivals— Hon. Ward E. Pack's Views

To-morrow at 2 o'clock p.m. the City Hall chambers will be filled once more with the representatives of the people who will organize for work, and plunge at once into the task of law making. Whether the Governor's message will be read to-morrow or not depends upon the time which it takes the legislators to agree upon their officers. There are all sorts of rumors afloat as to probable speakers, presidents, clerks, chaplains, etc., but it is too soon as yet to speculate with any certainty on the names. Following is the list of the members to whom certificates of election have been issued:

COUNCIL.

Cache and Rich Counties—James T. Hammond.

Box Elder and Weber Counties— Lewis W. Shurtliff.

Wasatch, Uintah, Summit and Morgan Counties—Samuel Francis.

Salt Lake, Davis and Tooe'e Counties—James Sharp, Joseph Barton, John W. Taylor, Elias A. Smith.

Sanpete, Sevier and Emery Counties —L. S. Tuttle.

Utah and Juab Counties—Joel Grover, Jonathan S. Page.

Millard, Beaver, Iron, Piute and Garfield Counties—Robert W. Heybourne.

Washington, Kane and San Juan Counties—Martin Slack.

HOUSE OF REPRESENTATIVES.

Cache and Rich Co inties Representative District—Joseph Howell, Joseph Kimball.

Box Elder County—R. H. Batr.

Weber County—Joseph A. West, Edwin Stratford.

Wasatch and Uintah Counties— Abram Hatch.

Summit County—D. C. McLaughlin.

Morgan, Salt Lake and Davis Counties —John Clark, Wm. W. Riter, Don Carlos Youn , John Q. Cannon, Orson A. Woolley, J. R. Stuart.

Tooele County—Charles L. Anderson.

Utah and Juab Counties—Samuel R. Thurman, Wm. Creer, Thomas J. McCullough, W. C. A. Smoot, Jr.

Sanpete, Sevier and Emery Counties —A. H. Lund, A. D. Thurber.

Millard County—William H. King.

Beaver and Piute Counties—P. T. Farnsworth.

Iron, San Juan and Garfield Counties— John C. Houston.

Washington and Kane Counties—Jno. Rider.

On the street, yesterday and last evening, were noticed the bronzed faces of several country members, who came in early to look over the field. Among those encountered were Messrs. Howell and Hammond, of Cache; Messrs. Francis and Stuart, of Morgan; Mr. Kimball, of Rich; Mr. Barton, from Kaysville, and Mr. King, from Fillmore.

AT THE TABERNACLE.

Divine Worship on Sunday Afternoon Last.

PLAN OF THE PERFECT GOSPEL

Elders G. G. Bywater, J. T. Hammond and W. H. King and Apostle H. J. Grant the Speakers.

Sunday afternoon services in the Tabernacle were commenced with the choir singing the hymn:

O my Father, thou that dwellest
In the high and glorious place!
When shall I regain thy presence,
And again behold thy face?

Elder George G. Bywater offered the opening prayer and the choir sang another hymn:

A poor wayfaring man of grief
Hath often crossed me on the way,
Who sued so humbly for relief
That I could never answer nay.

The Sacrament was then administered by the priesthood of the Fifth Ward.

ELDER J. T. HAMMOND, of Logan, addressed the congregation, saying: In looking around and making comparisons, we notice the contrast between the religion of the Latter-day Saints, inasmuch that it is much more practical than other faiths, for it requires its members to obey every law of God. The constant fear is that the Saints are liable to be entrapped with the cares of the world and forget the objects and aims of their religion. It would be well for each person, at the close of every day, to review their acts of that day, and see wherein they had come short of doing right, and determine to do better next day. Our probation in this life is for a definite purpose. Some persons seemingly have no definite object in their lives, and seem to be automatons. The Latter-day Saints have in view their own salvation and the welfare of all men for which to labor continually.

BISHOP JOS. KIMBALL, of Meadowville, said: I realise that we are living in an important age of the world's history. If we will live the lives of Saints, and humble ourselves before the Lord, keeping His commandments, He will remove the clouds that now hang over us. I am satisfied that He will not do so, and hope and pray that He will not stay our trials and persecutions until we do humble ourselves entirely before Him. The blessings of God will continue to be with us if we will live deserving of them.

ELDER W. H. KING, of Fillmore, said: I feel grateful unto God for the blessing and privilege of meeting on the Sabbath to partake of the Sacrament, and above all do I feel glad that I have received the true gospel of Jesus Christ. I feel proud of being a Latter-day Saint, and hope to live worthy of the honor. We claim to have the same plan of the gospel as taught by the Savior, Jesus Christ. We are not necessarily antagonistic to other religious faiths. We claim to have a more perfect plan, a higher faith, a living truth, the gospel of Jesus Christ. The Christian sects have made similar claims, and men have followed them, but have failed to find the living truths of God. We claim not only to have the form, but the true life of the gospel principles. A tree is known by its fruits, and we ask the world to so judge us. If we cannot demonstrate what we say to be true, then is the world justified in refusing to believe us. There are many candid-minded men, who are willing to admit, if the Bible is true, that our position cannot be assailed. Whatever was true in the meridian of time, when Christ was on earth, must be true now; truth cannot change. The code of laws which constituted the gospel then, are the same now. We believe in revelation, knowing that it is impossible for men of their own wisdom to know God. We believe that to know God is life eternal. No one can truly say, "I know that my Redeemer liveth," unless they obtain that knowledge by revelation. Revelation is the foundation of the gospel of Jesus Christ. We not only believe this, but believe in the principles of faith, repentence and baptism by immersion, and the gift of the Holy Ghost by the laying on of hands. We believe these not to be mere ordinances of admission into the church, but they are life-giving principles, leading to eternal life. If you repudiate any principle of the gospel, you make it imperfect, and it will result only in an imperfect salvation. The Latter-day Saints accept and believe in a perfect gospel, a plan comprising apostles, prophets, evangelists, pastors and teachers and its officers. Whenever God has visited His displeasure upon any people, He has deprived them of these officers. The gospel in its ancient purity was revealed unto the prophet Joseph Smith, and we offer it unto the world assuring them that it will bring unto them all the gifts and blessings of the true and everlasting gospel. But why do the Latter-day Saints incite the opposition of the world? We can only answer in the words of our Savior, that it is because men are lovers of evil rather than of good, and prefer darkness to light. Error has crept among the nations and endangered their social position. Crime and iniquity are increasing, and history will repeat itself, for the same cause will always produce the same results. The conflicting opinions and forms of faith of the Christian world cannot be productive of good. God reveals the gospel, but will not compel men to believe it, and to those who refuse it the results are inevitable. The advocates of truth—not only of religion, but of the truths of art, science and literature, have always met with opposition and persecution. The Latter-day Saints dare to stand true to their convictions, they will not be cowards to the truth. God desires a tried and chosen people,

and every effort will be made to have us deny our faith in God. The Saints must be tried in the fire of the furnace of persecution. I pray that all of us may be true and faithful to the covenants we have made, and endure unto the end.

APOSTLE HYRUM J. GRANT said—It is very pleasing to hear the testimonies of the elders, and gratifying to know they are in consonance with our own. I am not surprised at the opposition of the world, because I know that we have the truth. If we were like unto the world, then would they cease to dislike us. A person who has the consolation within themselves to know that they are honest, virtuous, and living aright before God, cares not for the opinion of

experiencing is in fulfillment of the prophecies of the prophets, and further testimonies that we have the truth. The principles of our religion will benefit and ennoble mankind. No objection can be sustained to any of its doctrines, as being derogatory of virtue and purity. The Latter-day Saints are being deprived of every right that can be taken from them. I am gratified that the laws are being enforced in such a manner and by such representatives of humanity. Why, the Edmunds law offers an inducement for men to be dishonest, and those who maintain being honest men to their wives and children, are subjects for prison. I am glad that such opportunities occur to enable us to find out who are true and firm to their faith. I pray that God may continue to bless all those that remain faithful to the truth.

The choir sang the anthem "Sweet is thy Mercy," with solo by Mrs. Nellie Druce-Pugsley.

Elder George Goddard pronounced the benediction.

Salt Lake Herald
January 26, 1886

PERSONAL.

W. C. Rydalch of Grantsville, was in town on Monday.

Thomas C. Callister, of Fillmore, was a visitor at the House yesterday.

George Stringfellow has returned from the Ogden conference. He reports a number of missionaries called to the Southern States.

Salt Lake Herald
January 29, 1886

Mr. T. C. Callister, who is up from Fillmore, has sustained a heavy blow in the loss of his little 2-year old son. He left him well and hearty several days ago, but was yesterday apprized of his death by telegram. He returns home this morning.

Salt Lake Herald
February 21, 1886

A NEW BUSINESS VENTURE.

The Liddle Agricultural and Cattle Company Organized.

Articles of incorporation of the Liddle Agricultural and Cattle Company were filed with County Clerk Cutler yesterday. The object of the association is the purchasing, herding, selling and bartering of cattle in Utah Territory and at any other points they may see fit, and to acquire such such lands as may be necessary to maintain said cattle.

The capital stock is placed at $50,000, which is divided into 500 shares of $100 each. The following stock has been subscribed and is held by the parties named:

	SHARES.
J. C. Liddle, Fillmore	90
Donald S. Liddle, Fillmore	90
Jos. R. Walker, Salt Lake	90
S. O. L. Potter, Salt Lake	50
David F. Walker, Salt Lake	90
Matthew H. Walker, Salt Lake	90

The directors of the company are: James C. Liddle, Donald S. Liddle, S. O. L. Potter, Jos. R. Walker, M. H. Walker and David F. Walker. Joseph R. Walker is named for president; David F. Walker, vice-president; Matthew H. Walker, treasurer.

The existence of the corporation is placed at twenty years, unless sooner dissolved according to law.

A Fruit and Vegetable Cannery.

Mr. Gabriel Huntsman of Fillmore has been in Provo for a couple of days conferring with a few of our prominent citizens in relation to the establishment here of a fruit cannery. Several influential gentlemen in Salt Lake are reported to be greatly in favor of an enterprise of this kind and announced their intention of becoming directly interested in it. The idea of establishing the factory at this point was first suggested in Salt Lake; hence, Mr. Huntsman's presence here at present. We are glad to find that the few citizens of Provo who have been consulted on the matter are warmly favoring the project. Two meetings have already been held, when the subject was thoroughly discussed. At the second meeting, held last night in the Court House, a committee of three gentlemen were appointed to visit and confer with several Salt Lake gentlemen and ascertain to what extent their co-operation can be depended on in the pursuit of the fruit canning industry if the citizens of Provo should lead out in the matter. The committee consists of Mayor Dusenberry, Jacob Gates and S. S. Jones.

Mr. Huntsman informed the meetings that he had secured recently in California on excellent terms the entire apparatus and fixtures essential in the erection of a factory, which he was prepared to turn over at cost to a regularly organized company, and would himself retain as stock in the company at least one-half of the amount the machinery cost him. He made this purchase some few weeks since with the view of erecting the factory at his home in Fillmore, but has, since doing so, become convinced that the products, in the shape of certain fruits and vegetables, of the district he lives in would be totally insufficient for the requirements of such a factory. Provo is in the centre of a very extensive fruit and vegetable growing country, is accessible to the markets, and possesses other facilities that are necessary to the permanent success of such an enterprise. These facts are recognized not only by him but many Salt Lake gentlemen who understand and appreciate the advantages such an establishment would be to the Territory at large.

We sincerely hope that our citizens will themselves recognize the advantages that an industry of this kind in their midst will afford, and give it that encouragement and practical support necessary to secure its establishment in Provo city.

A PERILOUS POSITION.

Left on the Range With a Broken Leg.

Chas. A. Mace, the son of Hyrum Mace, was out riding on the range about six miles west of Fillmore, a few days ago, when his horse stumbled and fell upon him, breaking his right leg in three places between the foot and knee. The animal arose and immediately started for home, and left his rider helpless and alone. The accident occurred at about 2 o'clock p.m. on Friday, and the riderless horse was found about 2 o'clock Saturday morning. The alarm was soon given to the citizens, by the ringing of the town bell, and sixteen able-bodied men, with horses and lanterns, at once endeavored to find some trace of the lost gentleman. The horse was taken and his foot placed in the supposed track, which exactly fitted. They traced them with great anxiety and speed, knowing that the young man was without an overcoat, and the night was very cold. During the search, a brother of the lost man was dispatched to Holden, ten miles north of this place, thinking he might possibly be there. On his way he heard a voice from a distance and answered it at once; he traced the sound for a short distance, and there he found his brother sitting against a cedar tree in the position that he had spent the night. He succeeded in getting him on his horse, thinking he could get him home, but soon found that he was unable to ride horseback, therefore he was obliged to leave his brother and endeavor to find the party that was following the horse's tracks, which he soon found. The party was supplied with a team and carriage, and soon conveyed the lost child to his aged parents in Fillmore, where he received a hearty welcome, after suffering fifteen hours. Doctor J. S. Giles was summoned from Holden, who soon came and fixed the broken leg.

The young man is very courageous, and is doing as well as could be expected, under such circumstances.

Mary E. Warner, the wife of Orange Warner, deceased, died at the residence of Joseph Kay, her son in-law, March 13, 1886. Aged 64 years. Funeral on the 14th, at 2 p.m.

The health of the people is generally good. Weather is very changeable and the roads are very bad, so says the traveler. Times are very dull, but we trust that a bright future will soon dawn.   G. HUNTSMAN.

Fillmore, March 13th, 1886

ANOTHER TRAGEDY.

A Fatal Shooting Affray at Fillmore.

The following dispatch was received yesterday:

FILLMORE, Utah, March 18.—About 7 o'clock last night, Oliver Speed, when going home from work, was accosted by little John McBride, who made the remark, "Doc, you would make a good sheep herder." He also made use of some very obscene and disgusting remarks, reflecting upon Mr. Speed, when the latter became exasperated and slapped the boy in the face. The lad ran and told his father, F. A. McBride, who was near at hand and came out. He asked Speed why he had slapped the boy. Speed began explaining, when McBride stepped up to him and struck him by the side of the head with his revolver, at the same time firing it off. The men then clinched, and McBride fired two more shots, both taking effect, one in Speed's right breast, under the left arm. Speed fell to the ground and McBride was pulled off him by bystanders. The wounded man was carried to his father-in-law's house near by. Dr. J. S. Giles was summoned who examined the wounds and pronounced them mortal. His diagnosis proved correct, as the man died at 10 o'clock. The dying man's deposition was taken by Dr. Giles, and it concurs with the above statement. McBride was allowed to escape, but during the night he gave himself up.

WE HAVE received from our Fillmore correspondent a corroboration of the particulars of the recent killing of Oliver Speed, an account of which we have already published. McBride's examination has been postponed until the 29th inst.

In the First District.

R. C. Kirkwood and Nicholas H. Groesbeck pleaded not guilty to indictments for unlawful cohabitation, and William Duncan to that of assault.

Two counts were brought against W. M. Bromley in the one indictment for unlawful cohabitation. Defendant was examined and the jury brought in a verdict then and there. Sentence fixed for April 12th.

The People vs. C. F. Dixon—appeal; demurrer to complaint and motion; to dismiss cause taken under advisement.

Reuben A. McBride, for the murder of Oliver H. Speed at Fillmore, was to-day arraigned on a charge of murder in the first degree and given time to plead.

The people vs. Archibald Oldrod and Andrew Anderson; murder in the second degree; trial in progress.

John S. Jewkes was admitted to citizenship.

The grand jury adjourned to-day, subject to the call of the foreman it is supposed.

PROVO, March 23, 1886.

Territorial Enquirer
April 27, 1886

In another column of to-day's Enquirer will be seen a communication signed by a number of the citizens of Fillmore, purporting to be a truthful account of the alleged murder of O. H. Speed by Reuben A. McBride at that place.

The account which appeared in our issue of March 26th was obtained from parties who claimed to be con versant with all the facts connected with the deplorable occurrence. We avoided publishing the entire account given us for reasons stated by us at the time. However, inasmuch as the reference made to the deceased is so emphatically denounced, and that too by so many of those who knew him, and not wishing to injure the good name of any man, living or dead, much less to shield the guilty, we readily and cheerfully give the communication the circulation asked, trusting and believing, at the same time, that "equal justice through the law" will be meted out.

Salt Lake Herald
May 13, 1886

Hon. W. H. King is up from Fillmore on a brief visit. He looks bronzed and hearty as a cowboy.

A MODEL DEPUTY.

Bert Ether Playing the Role of Impostor.

"Bert" Ether, who it will be remembered played an important part for the prosecution in the Tintic lynching cases and was rewarded for the services he rendered, and because the fellow was afraid, so we were informed, to go back to Tintic lest some of those muscular sons of Erin should get after him, by a commission as deputy U. S. Marshal, has evidently been cutting some of his characteristic capers down in Millard county. The *News* contains the following information on the subject in a letter from A. M. Buchanan and dated at Holden, May 9th:

A little over a week since a thing, it is called a deputy marshal, came to Holden to make an arrest and in justice to the community in general and Sister Johnson, of Holden, in particular, it would be well to make public the following explanation. Albert Ether, a U. S. deputy, came to Sister Johnson's on the evening of the 28th ult. and sought accommodation for himself and his horse for the night. He mentioned as his acquaintances in Holden the Kenny boys, with whom he became a little familiar while they were employed in Tintic. He inquired about them and others. On the morning of the 29th he went to the home of Mr. Stringham to make an arrest of some one he seemed to think was staying there. Seemingly he did not find the party whom he wanted, as he said to a young lady relative of Bro. Stringham, who was visiting his family, "I think you are the person I want," to which he received the cool reply, "I hope you will continue to *think* so." Apparently he had no confidence in his "thinking," as he made no arrests. On returning to Sister Johnson's he remarked, "I have made a trip down here to no purpose." However, in the meantime he paid a visit to a bitter anti-"Mormon" by the name of James Hiki, of whom it is said he could be in the "Pen" for libel were he to get his deserts, and after leaving Hiki, he went and arrested Sister Louise Ashby Badger. Now, the next thing for them to do was to screen the informer from the contempt that naturally arises in the minds of honorable people for that class, so to this end an apostate by the name of Nichols Paul began to circulate that it was Sister Johnson who gave the names of all who were liable under the Edmunds law to the deputy. The apostate's statement obtained to a considerable degree, when it was learned that Ether had with him what purported to be a document dated at Springville, Utah County, and the name of Bishop Packard recommending Ether as a member of the Church in good standing. Ether showed the "*recommend*" to Mr. Jos. S. Giles, of Holden, and to Judge Thos. C. Callister, of Fillmore, saying, "when I show this to any good Mormon I can get all the information I desire." However, this "recommend" was not shown nor spoken of to Sister Johnson, to which fact a lady who resides with her and who heard all that was said by the deputies bears testimony. But the "recommend," according to Brothers Callister and Giles, was made on one of the forms regularly used by the Bishops; as to the genuineness of Bishop Packard's endorsement, these brethren could not state, being unacquainted with his autograph. The name on the recommend was not Ether but that of Stringam. Ether is light complexioned, without beard or moustache, appears to be about twenty-one years of age, and in my opinion is a sneak or he would never seek to injure a venerable lady of sixty-eight years by circulating lies to save the informers.

A. M. BUCHANAN,

Salt Lake Herald
June 29, 1886

MORE ELECTION JUDGES.

Garfield and Millard Counties Provided For.

The Utah Commission yesterday made the following appointments of Judges of Election. The first-named in each three is the presiding judge:

GARFIELD COUNTY.

Benjamin Cameron, George Underwood and Hyrum Pratt, Panguitch.

George H. Wilson, Jos. D. Wilson and James F. Johnson, Hillsdale.

William Lewman, William J. Henderson and Joshua Jones, Cannonville.

William Alvey, Edwin Twitchell and Lewis Duel, Escalante.

J. C. Jones, C. L. King and S. W. Collings, Coyote.

MILLARD COUNTY.

George C. Velle, Edwin Bartholomew and James A. Melville, Fillmore.

Wm. A. Ray, Edward Webb and Marcellus Welb, Deseret.

George Chesley, Peter Robinson and George Crane, Kanosh.

Joseph Adams, Abraham Greenhalgh and John Nield, Meadow.

Nicholas Paul, Enoch Dodge and A. S. Harmon, Holden.

P. C. Nielson, Samuel Rowley and Orville Thompson, Scipio.

George Finlinson, Ole Jacobson and Henry Roper, Oak Creek.

John Wilson, John Strange and Christian Oveson, Leamington.

Charles Rowland, Dan Samison and Brigham Young, Snake Creek.

Salt Lake Herald
July 22, 1886

The Millard County Convention.

A county convention of the People's party of Millard County was held at Fillmore City, July 17th, 1886.

A temporary organization was effected by the election of Wm. H. King as chairman and J. L. Robison secretary. Upon motion, a committee of three, on credentials, consisting of P. D. Lyman, C. Anderson and Wm. Black, was appointed by the chairman.

During the committee's absence speeches were made by George Crane and others, explanatory of the platform of the People's party, the wants of the county and the men required for positions of trust among the people.

The committee reported nineteen delegates entitled to seats in the convention.

After the report of the committee had been accepted, the temporary organization was made permanent, and the convention proceeded to select officers to be voted for at the forthcoming August election.

For Probate Judge, T. C. Callister.
For Selectman, George Crain.
For County Clerk, J. L. Robison.
For Assessor and Collector, Wm. H. King.
For Sheriff, George Nixon.
For Surveyor, J. S. Giles.
For Coroner, James McMahon.

Wm. H. King, J. L. Robison and James A. Melville were chosen as members of the County Central Committee for the ensuing year. Representatives of the People's party for each precinct were elected, and the convention adjourned to eat ice cream at the expense of the chairman and secretary.

Utah Enquirer
October 19, 1886

Personal.

Hon. W. H. King of Fillmore has been in Provo for two or three days past. Last evening he passed an examination for admission to the bar as an attorney. The talented young gentleman intends leaving in a day or two for Ann Arbor, Michigan, to enter upon a few month's studies.

A. G. Sutherland, Jr., and B. W. Driggs,

Salt Lake Herald
August 20, 1886

HEAVY RAIN.

Destructive Downpour at Fillmore, Millard County.

The rainstorm of Wednesday seems to have been of greater extent than is usual in this region, and the fall appears to have been varied, being light in some places and drenching in others. At Fillmore, a perfect flood followed the storm, and considerable damage ensued, as will be seen from the following dispatch received from there yesterday:

A heavy rainfall, followed by a terrible flood, has taken all dams and bridges from across the stream and inundated several acres of garden with mud and water, from two inches to two feet in depth. One house, with all its contents, was carried away in the flood. The inmates barely escaped. Several men are in the canyon but as yet are not heard from. The loss at present is not known, but will aggregate several hundred dollars.

ADMONITION.

Elder B. H. Roberts' Discourse on Sunday.

SOUND ADVICE TO THE PEOPLE.

The Purification of the Church Talked Of—"This is the Way, Walk Ye In It"

The services at the Tabernacle on Sunday afternoon were begun by the singing by the choir of the hymn commencing:

O Thou, at whose supreme command
The hosts of darkness fly,
Upheld by whose eternal hand,
The Saints can dare or die.

Prayer by Bishop Watson.
Singing of the hymn:

Praise to the man who communed with Jehovah, etc.

Elder B. H. Roberts said it is now nearly 1900 years since an event occurred which marked a new era in the world's history. A man of peculiar bearing made his appearance among the Jews, one who preferred to dwell in the desert, out in the wilderness; his teachings were peculiar, not after the manner of men's learning, but as he was moved upon by the Holy Spirit; and although uncouth and uneducated, he attracted attention, and people left cities, hamlets and villages to hear him.

The burden of his remarks was that people should repent, for the kingdom of heaven was at hand. The people of that day had been anticipating the arrival of the Messiah, and from his teachings they wondered if he were not the Deliverer, and on their inquiring, he told them he was not; he was only preparing the way for one who would baptize with fire and with the spirit. Jesus, of Nazareth, subsequently went to John the Baptist, requesting baptism, but John said he needed to be baptized of Him. John baptized the Savior, and when the spirit rested on Him, John knew He was the Messiah. Passing over the life of Jesus, the speaker remarked that after His resurrection he was with His disciples for forty days; but what He taught them is not recorded. On one occasion He called them together and told them they should, according to the promise of John, be baptized with the spirit. After the ascension the apostles received the baptism of the Holy Ghost, and conducted themselves so as to call forth criticism from the rabbis and people, who said they were drunken with new wine. The recital of this portion of the history of the time of Jesus was to show that the promise made through or by an authorized servant of God was strictly fulfilled. The Apostle Peter preached a gospel sermon, which so struck the people that they cried, as with one voice: "Men and brethren, what shall we do?" The gospel being the same in all ages of the world, the reply to that question would have equal force upon people of to-day with those of eighteen centuries ago. Who was Peter? A humble fisherman, picked up by the Savior, on the shore of Galilee; an unlettered, honest man; he was with Jesus throughout his public ministry and was ready in the defense of his Master at the Garden of Gethsemane; his experience was varied but sincere in his followings of the savior, and he was thoroughly qualified to answer the question asked, which he did by saying:

Repent, and be baptized every one of you, in the name of Jesus Christ, for the remission of sins, and ye shall receive the gift of the Holy Ghost. For the promise is to you, and to your children, and to all that are afar off, even as many as the Lord our God shall call.

That promise was for the whole human race; it was not confined to the Jews, or their children, or their children's children, in Judea, but all "those that are afar off." The Holy Ghost was only promised to those that would yield obedience, however Jesus when He departed, said He would send His apostles the Comforter, whom the world could not receive. Elder Roberts reviewed several instances of faith in Jesus Christ, exercised by those who had obeyed the Lord, in which miracles had been performed. It seems that according to Peter's promise, all in the present day are entitled to receive the gift of the Holy Ghost. The speaker here read from the writings of St. John, concerning the Comforter, which should teach men all things. Another important office which it performs is to bring to the remembrance things of the past when they were of need to the individual. The spirit would guide into all truth; it would show the possessor things that are to come. The Latterday saints would bear him out in saying it was this spirit, in this day of their trials that was comforting their hearts. Those who did not understand the Mormons or their faith, saw the nation and people arrayed against the little handful of people in Utah, and they wondered at the calmness of the latter. The world say the serenity of the Mormons is the result of priestcraft, induced by the cunning of their leaders. But they are mistaken. It is the silent influence of the Spirit of God in their midst, which is whispering to them the things that are to come, and saying, that after the clouds will come the sunshine. The philosophy of the gospel was briefly referred to by the speaker. The gospel is pure and holy, and those associated with it must, necessarily, be also pure and holy. The requirement of those before baptism was to repent. The Spirit of God dwells not in an unholy temple. The ordinance of baptism was to cleanse their tabernacles for a reception of the gift of the Holy Ghost. If after this purification, men again defile themselves, God, it is said, will destroy them. It becomes them, therefore, that they remain pure. God does not look upon sin with any degree of allowance. The events which occurred during the later years of Moses' ministry among the children of Israel, and the promises made them which should be fulfilled on the other side of Jordan, if they persevered and were faithful, were recited. That people were to be superior in every respect. Every blessing that the heart could desire, or the mind conceive, was promised them if they continued in their righteousness; and on the contrary curses were pronounced if they yielded to the tempter, fell from grace and sinned by disregarding the commandments of God. Those sayings were literally fulfilled in the history of the Israelites, and the fulness of God's wrath came upon them. When Jesus was sent among them He was persecuted until His crucifixion on Calvary. The fate of the nations of olden times was certain destruction, for their share in opposing the work of God and in harrassing and persecuting His people. Then several instances were cited in eloquent terms. The wrath and curses of God had been poured out upon them, according to promise.

He here called the attention of the Latter-day Saints to and read from the Book of Doctrine and Covenants, Section 103, a revelation given in the year 1834:

But verily I say unto you that I have decreed a decree which my people shall realize, inasmuch as they harken from this very hour, unto the counsel which I, the Lord their God, shall give unto them.

Behold they shall, for I have decreed it, begin to prevail against mine enemies from this very hour.

And by hearkening to observe all the words which I, the Lord their God, shall speak unto them, they shall never cease to prevail until the kingdoms of the world are subdued under my feet, and the earth is given unto the saints to possess it for ever and ever.

But inasmuch as they keep not my commandments, and harken not to observe all my words, the kingdoms of the world shall prevail against them.

For they were set to be a light unto the world, and to be the saviors of men;

And inasmuch as they are not the saviors of men, they are as salt that has lost its savor, and is thenceforth good for nothing but to be cast out and trodden under feet of men.

The same conditions are placed upon the Latter-day Saints as were placed upon the children of Israel. They should prevail against their enemies if they kept his commandments. That revelation was given in 1834, and since then, according to the degree the Saints had observed the word of the Lord, so had they grown and prospered; and to the degree they had failed and are failing to keep God's law, their enemies had prevailed and will prevail against them. Not until they had put away their iniquities could they expect to prevail against their enemies. No one who had received the Holy Ghost, the speaker cared not how profoundly learned, or how rich in this world's goods, or how near he stood to the authorities or the church, if he transgresses and violates his covenant, can retain that spirit and when it is withdrawn amen to the power and influence of that man.

ELDER ROBERTS spoke of his visit and interview with David Whitmer one of the three witnesses to the Book of Mormon, and the testimony of the latter in respect to the divine authenticity of the Book of Mormon. How was it that one who had seen such great visions and occupying so exalted a position could come so low as to become an absolute outcast? Was this case not a proof that there was nothing could save one who transgressed the laws of God, no matter how many revelations

he had? The experience of others in the days of Joseph, who also had become moral wrecks, was referred to. If men become unrighteous they lose caste and influence. This is the fate of all, for God's spirit will not dwell in an unholy temple. God will only deliver you. Latter-day Saints on condition that you will obey his laws and keep his commandments. It would be folly to contemplate force to throw off the opposition arranged against them; the odds were too great. The only hope of the Saints was in the observance of God's laws and commands. The only friend you have is God, and you had better keep on speaking terms with him. Your strength is in your righteousness. In strong terms he urged repentance among the Latter-day Saints. If the priesthood could not uncover the iniquities of the people, then will the deputy marshals and courts and their aids find them out. And this would continue until they were purified. He said they had not so far sinned but they could repent, and be forgiven. Men in high positions might fall, but there fall would not affect the truth.

In conclusion he exhorted all to live in communion with the spirit, which would say to them, "This is the way, walk ye in it," and blessed all Israel.

Singing of an anthem, with tenor solo by Mr. Alfred Nilssen.

Benediction by Elder W. H. King, of Fillmore.

Salt Lake Herald
October 23, 1886

Salt Lake Herald
October 23, 1886

MARRIED.

HINCKLEY-KING—On the 20th inst. at Logan, Ira N. Hinckley, Jr. (son of President L. N. Hinckley of Millard Stake) and Miss Lillian King, both of Fillmore City.

Territorial Enquirer
August 24, 1886

Terrific Flood at Fillmore.

Dr. Pike handed us this morning a letter from G. Huntsman, Fillmore, giving the particulars of a very destructive flood that has lately occurred at that place. The gentleman states that he has lived in Fillmore since 1854 and he has never before seen anything of the kind that would compare with it in point of destruction of property and the general terror incident upon such an occasion.

The flood appears to have been caused by a sudden swelling of the north fork of what is known as Chalk Creek. The water of that stream, says Mr. Huntsman, swelled suddenly to a depth of over fifteen feet, sweeping everything before it in its course. Every bridge and dam throughout the whole length of the stream was torn away and the material together with great quantities of driftwood and other floating debris was carried down with the current. The yards,

sheds and fences of the lower part of Fillmore were totally demolished. One dwelling house shared the same fate; the inmates barely escaping with their lives. A woman with several young children was hemmed in by the flood and while endeavoring to reach a place of safety with one of them in her arms was knocked flat by a mass of drift, but Mr. A. Greenwood coming to the rescue brought her safely to land. No lives were lost but the destruction of property is very great. Wherever the water overflowed it has left a heavy deposit of mud and sand from the mountains.

RELIGIOUS.

Elder W. H. King's Discourse on Sunday Afternoon.

MORMONISM A PHENOMENON.

Religious Truths are Dear to Human Hearts, and Men Will Make Sacrifices for Them.

On Sunday afternoon last the services at the Tabernacle were begun by the choir singing the hymn commencing.

O Jesus! the giver of all we enjoy,
our lives to thy honor we wis ; to employ,
With praises unceasing we'll sing of thy
    name,
Thy goodness increasing, thy love we'll pro-
    claim

Prayer by Elder George Romney.

Singing of the hymn

How great the wied m and the love;
Thai fill'd the co iris on high,
And sent the Savior fr..m above
To suffer, bleed and die!

ELDER W. H. KING, of Fillmore, in addressing the congregation, remarked that the elder who had just prayed had thanked God that the gospel had been restored. A phenomenon was presented in the assembling together of over 200,000 in the valleys of the mountains, observing the doctrines of that gospel. There is a great deal of fanaticism exhibited by the enemies of the Mormon people. The angel seen by John, the Revelator, had flown through the midst of heaven, having the everlasting gospel, and God had established his kingdom on earth. The Saints believed that God had revealed the principles to Joseph Smith, which were designed for the salvation of humanity. Mormonism is not a fantasm; it was not devised by man, but by God. The Saints differed from the world because their religious convictions were different. There must be something peculiar in Mormonism, there must be a powerful factor, in bringing people from the countries of the Old World, inducing them to leave their homes and kindred; rearing temples, educational institutions, and making the desert blossom as the rose. It was Mormonism that had demonstrated that a nation would be established by the people, and that God would be glorified. The Saints believed that the same principles taught in Jesus' day were being taught by them now. They were revealed to Joseph Smith, who received the Book of Mormon, which contained a record of the people who once inhabited this continent. That book was translated by the aid of the Spirit of God. Ancient history was fraught with references to the present day and what should transpire. The mission of the children of Israel was not filled, but was cut off according to prediction. The prophet Daniel saw the downfall of the Israelites. Other prophets saw and referred to the restoration of the gospel in the dispensation of the fulness of time. If that restoration had not taken place, when, the speaker asked, would it? The sects of to-day claimed that the time for revelation was past, while the Latter-day Saints claimed and proclaimed that revelations were as necessary now as formerly and were being daily given; they bore testimony to the divinity of the Book of Mormon, which had been attested by several witnesses.

The speaker briefly sketched the history of the Church of Jesus Christ of Latter-day Saints. The Prophet Joseph Smith's origin as the founder of Mormonism was looked at, and his first work in seeking for knowledge among the schisms of his day was mentioned. He went unto the Almighty, and in sincerity asked Him which of the various sects was correct. The Lord and Jesus appeared to him, and revealed to him the plan of salvation. John the Baptist conferred upon him the priesthood of Adam, which should reign upon the earth for ever. By virtue of this power and authority Joseph Smith could baptize, lay on hands, bestow blessings, etc. The work spread throughout the Eastern States, until from 1830 to the present time the Saints had grown to be a great and prosperous people. What are the tenets of the Latter-day Saints? Elder King briefly stated them, as they are published as the Articles of Faith of the church. As soon as Joseph Smith proclaimed that God had revealed Himself from the heavens, the hatred and ire of the world were aroused against him, as were those of the Jews in olden times raised against the Savior and His disciples. The persecutions of anything put forth as divine was and ever would prevail. The present day Saints, Elder King was sorry to remark, did not improve upon the experiences of the past. There had been a galaxy of opposition to Mormonism since its introduction; since the promulgation of its principles there has been 10,000 calumnies to oppose them. The truth was mighty and would prevail; no matter how trampled upon, how trodden in the dust, it would rise again and shine with renewed splendor. Religious truths, more than any other are dear to the human heart, and men will make unusual sacrifices for them. The ancients were burned at the stake and suffered death in various forms for their sake. The human heart is the same to-day. Therefore, why should the world be so eager to overcome and suppress them, if not peaceably, then forcibly? The efforts of the enemies of the Saint a had hitherto been unsuccessful. What was there to arouse the enmity of the world against the Latter-day Saints? The prophet Joseph taught them that the gospel in its purity had been revealed, and he went forth proclaiming its principles. He taught the world that God was a personal Being; that faith in the personality of God was a grand principle; that there was a vicarious power in the ordinance of baptism; that power was conferred by the laying on of hands; that in order to be entitled to the gift of the Holy Ghost it was necessary to obey the laws of the gospel; that the gifts and blessings, and ordinances and powers once enjoyed by the people of God were to be enjoyed by the people in this generation; that the channel of communication between fallen humanity and heaven was open and ever would be so long as the people lived according to the commandments and laws of God; that every man and woman and child of the proper age was entitled to revelation, to enable them to determine truth from error. This was something different from the world. The divines of the world deemed and preached that revelation was no longer necessary. Joseph Smith furthermore proclaimed the principle of gathering, the doctrine of work for the dead. Mormonism, in its progress has evolved no other principles than those he promulgated; what was revealed unto him is the corpus of the church to-day. What was there in them to excite the animosity of the world against him? What was there to arouse the opposition of those of the days of the Savior against Jesus? The same query might be asked of every reformer. The cry has ever gone forth: "Let us suppress them." History teaches us that out of every one thousand nine hundred and ninety-nine had been wrong and but one right. Was it right for individuals or nations to array themselves against a people because they believed differently from them? He could not see anything in what they taught to call forth such unrelenting persecution. Mormonism was not born of fanaticism; it is true; it came from God, and was not generated by any other power. The similarity of the teachings of the Latter-day Saints and those of Jesus was very marked, Elder King said. The former day Saints warned the people and called on them to repent, for the kingdom of heaven was at hand; so do the Latter-day Saints. The work of Jesus in his day, was the organizing of His church, and the setting of it in order; as long as His disciples and those who lived after Him, adhered to that organization they were blessed; but when they listened to the Romans, the great apostasy followed, until the candlestick, or light, of the priesthood was taken from them. The question might be asked: Why was not the gospel revealed before? God moved slowly but surely in the perfection of his plans for the restoration of the gospel. The hand of God could be seen in the records of history in the discovery of America, and the establishment of the gospel, on the 6th of April, 1830. From that day until the present, the Saints had increased in numbers and influence. They attributed its progress to the aid of God given to the leaders. They believe that only in God is their reliance and hope.

Elder King said there ought to be a respect for a people who were sincere. So long as the belief of a people did not interfere with other people's rights it should not be molested. They claimed the right to worship God according to the dictates of their conscience. If God was at the head the work would live and thrive; if of man, it certainly would fall. The principle of religious liberty he stoutly advocated. He trusted that in these mountains there would be raised up a class of people who would establish and maintain righteousness in the earth; when true men would occupy the stations which were by right theirs; when the kingdoms of the earth would become the kingdoms of our Lord and His Christ.

The choir sang an anthem and Elder George F. Gibbs pronounced the benediction.

LAST WEEK Sheriff Baldwin went to Fillmore and there arrested a fellow named Brig Tompkinson, on a charge of having assaulted and badly cut with a knife, one Peter Sorenson at the sulphur mines, in this county. Tompkinson was brought to Beaver, arriving here late Saturday night, and was at once taken before Justice Fennemore for examination. Something was defective in the charge for after hearing the evidence, the J. P. discharged the prisoner, but had him immediately rearrested for ordinary assault, to which charge Tompkinson plead guilty and was fined $75, which he paid. It is said that Sorenson will carry the marks of his antagonist's knife on his visage as long as he lives.

THE TOTAL TALLY!

Nearly 17,000 Majority for John T. Caine.

W. M. FERRY RESTS AT EASE.

He Downs Smith by 596—The Full Vote by Precincts of all Counties Reporting.

Yesterday the board appointed to canvass the returns of the recent election for Delegate to Congress, met at the rooms of the Utah Commission, and immediately proceeded to work. The board consisted of Secretary Thomas, Messrs. H. S. Krigbaum, of Corinne; V. L. Halliday, of Provo; C. R. Barratt and L. S. Hills. Delegate Caine was also present, but Mr. Ferry, doubtless confident of the result, did not appear. The count was finished late in the afternoon, and the following figures obtained. Mr. Caine's majority, it will be perceived, is 16,795, a falling off as compared with that of two years ago, while Mr. Ferry has earned the proud distinction of having "pulled" 596 more votes than did Mr. Smith, of Ogden (and revered memory), two years ago. The prominent nominees which we have included under the head of "scattering" were E. H. Murray, 3; R. N. Baskin, 3; A. L. Thomas, 11; General Jackson, 1, while W. H. Dickson received somewhere about 30, and a few solitary stragglers make up the total vote cast:

Beaver County.

PRECINCT.	CAINE.	FERRY.
Adamsville	43	0
Beaver	227	24
Grampion	1	24
Greenville	43	0
Minersville	88	4
Star, Poll 1	16	22
Star, Poll 2	0	24
Total	439	127

Box Elder County.

PRECINCT.	CAINE.	FERRY.
Bear River City	87	0
Box Elder	284	10
Calls Fort	87	0
Curlew	15	0
Deweyville	17	3
Malad	1	61
Mantua	65	0
Park Valley	28	0
Plymouth	12	0
Portage	41	0
Terrace	0	50
Willard	45	0
Promontory	No returns.	
Kelton	No returns.	
Grouse Creek	No returns.	
Total	682	130

Cache County.

PRECINCT.	CAINE.	FERRY.
Benton	21	2
Clarkston	45	0
Coveville	31	0
Hyde Park	88	0
Hyrum	198	2
Lewiston	115	1
Logan	366	1
Mendon	95	1
Millville	75	0
Newton	40	0
Paradise	112	0
Peterborough	5	0
Providence	80	4
Richmond	185	4
Smithfield	144	0
Trenton	23	2
Wellsville	290	5
Total	1,795	25
Scattering—9.		

Davis County.

PRECINCT.	CAINE.	FERRY.
Centreville	80	7
East Bountiful	130	6
Farmington	147	4
Kaysville	229	7
South Bountiful	86	0
South Hooper	56	11
South Weber	39	9
West Bountiful	45	0
Total	792	44

Emery County.

PRECINCT.	CAINE.	FERRY.
Blake	6	11
Castle Dale	44	0
Ferron	40	0
Huntington	113	0
Lawrence	24	0
Moab	16	9
Molen	28	0
Muddy	16	0
Orangeville	67	0
Price	22	0
Scofield	26	19
Wellington	9	2
Total	433	41
Scattering—1.		

Garfield County.

PRECINCT.	CAINE.	FERRY.
Cannon	12	2
Hillsdale	15	0
Panguitch	86	0
Escalante	No Returns.	
Cannonville	No Returns.	
Total	113	2

Iron County.

PRECINCT.	CAINE.	FERRY.
Cedar City	140	0
Kanarra	38	0
Paragoonah	56	0
Parowan	127	7
Summit	21	1
Total	376	8

Juab County.

PRECINCT.	CAINE.	FERRY.
Levan, Poll 1	64	5
" " 2	87	0
Mona	59	0
Nephi	329	17
Tintic, Poll 1 (Eureka)	2	60
" 2 (Silver City)	0	17
Total	501	92

Kane County.

PRECINCT.	CAINE.	FERRY.
Glendale	90	0
Johnson	19	0
Kanab	35	0
Mount Carmel	17	0
Orderville	36	0
Upper Kanab	13	0
Paria	No returns	
Total	234	0
Scattering—2		

Millard County.

PRECINCT.	CAINE.	FERRY.
Burbank	No returns	
Deseret	91	5
Fillmore	129	11
Holden	73	7
Kanosh	84	1
Leamington	23	2
Meadow Creek	56	0
Oak Creek	43	6
Scipio	131	7
Total	637	38

Morgan County.

PRECINCTS.	CAINE.	FERRY.
Canyon Creek	40	4
Croydon	29	8
Milton	30	0
Morgan City	75	2
Peterson	50	4
Total	244	18

Piute County.

PRECINCTS.	CAINE.	FERRY.
Bullion, Poll No. 1	1	5
Circle Valley	43	0
Bullion No. 2 (Deer Trail)	8	1
Fremont	49	0
Koosharen	37	0
Thurber	52	0
Wilmot	8	7
Caineville	No returns	
Graves Valley	No returns	
Burgess	No returns	
Total	196	17
Scattering—3		

San Juan County.

No returns.

Sanpete County.

PRECINCT.	CAINE.	FERRY.
Chester	31	7
Ephraim	244	28
Fairview	134	2
Fayette	52	0
Fountain Green	118	0
Gunnison	109	21
Manti	224	14
Mayfield	72	0
Moroni	137	4
Mount Pleasant	215	27
Spring City	130	3
Sterling	56	0
Thistle	18	1
Wales	37	0
Winter Quarters	3	5
Total	1,665	122
Scattering—5		

Sevier County.

PRECINCT.	CAINE.	FERRY.
Annabella	43	0
Burrville	18	1
Central	30	1
Elsinore	56	0
Glenwood	72	1
Gooseberry	10	2
Joseph	47	2
Monroe	80	20
Redmond	56	1
Richfield	84	14
Salina	64	17
Vermillion	29	1
Willow Bend	58	1
Total	637	62

Summit County.

PRECINCT.	CAINE.	FERRY.
Coalville, Poll 1	113	10
" 2	43	0
Echo, Poll 1	14	12
" 2	5	2
Grass Creek	37	4
Hennefer	37	5
Hoytsville	67	6
Kamas	77	
Park City (6 polls)	19	395
Parley's Park	18	4
Peoa	64	5
Rockport	33	2
Upton	35	7
Wanship	35	7
Woodland	40	1
Total	647	674
Scattering—2		

Tooele County.

PRECINCT.	CAINE.	FERRY.
Batesville	26	0
Clover	23	0
Grantsville	139	2
Lake View	36	0
Mill	22	0
Ophir	0	27
St. John's	42	0
Stockton	6	46
Tooele	178	11
Vernon, no returns		
Deep Creek, no returns		
Total	472	86
Scattering—4		

Rich County.

PRECINCTS.	CAINE.	FERRY.
Garden City	20	0
Laketown	58	0
Meadowville	15	0
Randolph	32	0
Woodruff	39	5
Total	164	5

Salt Lake County.

PRECINCTS.	CAINE.	FERRY.
Salt Lake City—		
First Precinct, Poll 1	234	20
First Precinct, Poll 2	226	31
Second Precinct, Poll 1	346	130
Second Precinct, Poll 2	191	61
Third Precinct, Poll 1	205	3
Third Precinct, Poll 2	259	4
Fourth Precinct	413	42
Fifth Precinct, Poll 1	264	74
Fifth Precinct, Poll 2	189	62
Big Cottonwood	107	4
Bingham	1	45
Bluffdale	33	0
Brighton	39	2
Butler	24	0
Draper	148	1
Saw Mill Creek	17	8
Farmers	46	0
Fort Herriman	28	0
Granger	87	2
Granite	27	0
Hunter	17	0
Little Cottonwood	1	31
Mill Creek	144	10
Mountain Dell	12	4
North Jordan	74	
North Point	38	0
Pleasant Green	45	0
Riverton	88	27
Sandy		2
Silver	2	
South Cottonwood	211	20
South Jordan	48	0
Sugar House	42	0
Union	61	0
West Jordan	142	0
Total	3,962	619

Uintah County.

PRECINCTS.	CAINE.	FERRY.
Ashley	75	2
Brown's Park	No returns	
River Dale	15	0
Total	90	2
Scattering—3		

Utah County.

PRECINCTS.	CAINE.	FERRY.
Alpine	65	6
American Fork	162	7
Benjamin	29	9
Cedar Fort	40	3
Fairfield	13	3
Goshen	73	2
Lake View	44	0
Lehi	230	7
Payson	335	20
Pleasant Grove	221	10
F. V. Junction	4	11
Provo	299	41
Provo Bench	25	6
Salem	64	5
Santaquin	150	0
Spanish Fork, Poll 1	245	16
" 2	55	3
Spring Lake	20	0
Springville	320	20
Thistle	4	0
Total	2,506	204

Wasatch County.

PRECINCTS.	CAINE.	FERRY.
Charleston	56	2
Heber	116	3
Midway	86	0
Wallsburg	50	0
Total	304	5

Washington County.

PRECINCTS.	CAINE.	FERRY.
Duncan's Retreat	39	0
Grafton	17	0
Gunlock	14	0
New Harmony	27	0
Hebron	21	0
Leeds	36	1
Pine Valley	44	0
Pinto	31	0
Price	15	0
Rockville	34	0
St. George	192	0
Santa Clara	39	0
Schoenburg	17	0
Silver Reef	4	49
Springdale	15	0
Toquerville	32	0
Virgin City	56	0
Washington	68	0
Hamblin	23	0
Total	678	50

Weber County.

PRECINCTS.	CAINE.	FERRY.
Eden	69	5
Harrisville	106	2
Hooper	182	6
Huntsville	165	11
Lynne	56	6
Marriott	41	7
North Ogden	124	7
Ogden, Poll 1	393	97
Ogden, Poll 2	307	137
Ogden, Poll 3	236	91
Plain City	138	56
Pleasant View	76	0
River Dale	64	4
Slaterville	64	38
Uintah	29	4
West Weber	97	2
Wilson	97	24
Total	2,142	464
Scattering—27.		

The Total Vote

For Caine	19,605
For Ferry	2,810
Scattering	68
Grand Total	22,483
Caine's majority	16,795

Salt Lake Herald
February 1, 1887

Bishop Kimball Arrested.

The following special telegram was received last evening, and will be read with some surprise by the gentleman's friends throughout the Territory:

FILLMORE, Utah, Jan. 31, 6.20 p.m.
Special to THE HERALD.

Advices from Kanosh, this county, state that Bishop Abram A. Kimball was arrested there this morning, for unlawful cohabitation. It was not learned what had been done with him.

Salt Lake Herald
March 17, 1887

THE UTAH MINE

...old by the Mormon Church to Californians.

Under the above heading the San Francisco *Chronicle* of Monday last has the following, concerning the sale of the celebrated property mentioned below. It is learned from local sources that the sale is genuine, and that the purchasers have secured a valuable piece of property goes without saying. "Articles of incorporation were filed in the county clerk's office on Saturday of the Bullion-Beck and California Mining Company to operate in Utah Territory, with the following well-known residents of this city as incorporators and trustees: ex-Governor George C. Perkins, of ...

...-Governor George C. Perkins, of Goodall, Perkins & Co.; Jerome A. Fillmore, General Superintendent Central and Southern Pacific system of railroads; General William H. Brown, late United States Surveyor-General; Cornelius O'Connor, with J. C. Floyd, and Alexander Badiam, President of Bankers and Merchants' Insurance Company. Upon inquiry it was learned that the company has purchased the Bullion-Beck mine in the Tintic mining district, about a hundred miles south of Salt Lake City. This mine has for many years belonged to the Mormon Church, but the recently enacted laws of Congress to suppress polygamy and crush the power of the church, have compelled them to dispose of all their property, and the above syndicate has purchased the Utah mine."—San Francisco *Chronicle*.

Salt Lake Herald
April 12, 1887

DEPUTY REGISTRARS.

The Counties Provided for by the Utah Commission.

The Utah Commission appointed the following deputy registrars yesterday:

WEBER COUNTY.

Plain City—Thomas Stocker.
North Ogden—B. J. Webb.
Marriott—John Allen.
Slaterville—Charles Webb.
Wilson—William Sewell.
West Weber—Samuel F. Jenkins.
Hooper—John Everett.
Uintah—M. C. Daniels.
Huntsville—Edward Sewell.
Pleasant View—Temple Short.
Harrisville—T. W. Hurd.
Lynne—A. J. Stone
Riverdale—George Ritter.
Ogden—Philip Rank, William Farrell,
John W. Ramey.
Eden—George A. Worden.

EMERY COUNTY.

Castle Dale—J. W. Seeley.
Huntington and Laurence — J. F. Wakefield.
Price—B. H. Young.
Green River—J. T. Farrer.
Moab—C. J. Borsen.
Orangeville—J. K. Reid.
Ferron—M. Molen.
Molen—J. D. Killpack.
Muddy—John Lewis.
Wellington—R. B. Thompson.
Schofield—S. J. Harkness.

SAN JUAN COUNTY.

Bluff Precinct—Peter Allen.
McElmo—Joseph Dougherty.
Buena—Joseph Fielder.

MORGAN COUNTY.

Morgan—C. A. Smith.
Croyden—Thomas Walker.
Peterson—Edwin Williams.
Canyon Creek—William Killbourne.
Milton—John Thurston.

UINTAH COUNTY.

Brown's Park, Arthur Briggs.
Riverdale—Heber Orser.
Ashley—C. B. Brooks.

MILLARD COUNTY.

Fillmore—John Reily.
Holden—Nicholas Paul.
Scipio—George Monroe.
Oak City—George Finlinson.
Leamington—William Bean.
Deseret—William A. Ray.
Kanosh—George B. Chesley.
Meadow—John Streider.
Snake Valley—Charles Rowland.

WASATCH COUNTY.

Heber (No. 1)—Robert Lindsay.
" " (No. 2)—William Aird.
Wallsburg—D. C. Wray.
Charleston—John W. Kinney.
Midway—William Buys.
In addition to these W. T. Stewart was appointed register for Kane County, vice J. R. Stewart declined, and James McGarry for Beaver County.

Salt Lake Herald
April 23, 1887

First District Court.

The following business was transacted in the First District Court at Provo yesterday:

The case of the United States vs. Isaac Bullock was continued until Tuesday next.

The long calendar of criminal cases is at an end, and some civil matters are set up for the balance of the term, which ends next week.

Fillmore City vs. Gabriel Huntsman; set for Friday week next.

Hart Preston, William Meakin and George Meakin were arraigned and plead guilty. A fine was imposed of $25 each.

Reuben T. Miller vs. H. R. Watrous; injunction; set for Wednesday next to dissolve injunction.

Messrs. S. R. Thurman and J. E. Booth made arguments this afternoon for a new trial in the case of Joseph Clark.

Salt Lake Herald
June 26, 1887

MILLARD COUNTY'S SOLID DUET

FILLMORE, June 25th.

Special to THE HERALD

The two delegates elected by the mass convention held here to-day are George Crane and Joshua Greenwood.

Salt Lake Herald
July 6, 1887

New Money Order Offices.

WASHINGTON, July 5.—Three hundred and fifty new money order offices were established to-day by the Postmaster-General. The following are among them:

In Arizona—Morenci.

In California — Brooklyn Station, Oakland, Escondido, Lugoma, Mayfield, Michigan Bluff, New Hall, San Jacinto, South Pass.

In Colorado— Akron, Brighton, Lamar, Littleton, Meeker, New Windsor Portland, Rock Vale.

In Idaho—Grangeville, Montpelier, Gurray.

In Montana—Anaconda, Big Timber, Cook, Gorham, Granite, Lewiston.

In New Mexico—Chloride, Magdalena.

In Oregon—Gardiner, Newport, Toledo, Vale.

In Utah—Fillmore, Price.

In Washington Territory—Endicott, New Dungenes.

In Wyoming—Buffalo, Lusk.

One hundred and ninety additional postal note offices also established to-day.

Salt Lake Herald
July 7, 1887

Hon. W. H. KING, of Fillmore, who for the past seven months and a half has been studying law at the Michigan University, Ann Arbor, returned home Tuesday evening, having graduated with honors in the law course. He was in the convention yesterday, greeting old Legislative friends.

Salt Lake Herald
July 12, 1887

DEVASTATION AT FILLMORE.

FILLMORE, Utah, July 11.—Last evening, a flood again devastated Fillmore and the surrounding country. The greatest damage was done in the mountains east of this place. Three saw mills with logs and lumber, aggregating thousands of feet, were swept entirely away. Half a large sheep head was lost, the herders narrowly escaping with their lives. The damage done will materially affect the whole country.

W. H. KING'S NOMINATION.

He Will Fill His Old Seat in the House.

To the Editor of THE HERALD.

As politics is at present the all absorbing question in our Territory, I send you a report of the proceedings of the convention of Representative District No. 19, which met in this city.

Agreeable to previous arrangements, on the 19th inst., the delegation, consisting of fifteen, arrived from Juab at an early hour, and in accordance with the time arranged by the Territorial Central committee, the convention was called to order by Hon. W. H. King who nominated Hon. Alma Hague, of Juab County, chairman of the convention, which nomination was carried unanimously. Alma Greenwood, of Millard, was elected secretary. A committee on credentials having been appointed by the chair, reported that thirty delegates were entitled to seats in the convention.

William H. King, of Fillmore, was unanimously nominated as representative to the Legislature from District No. 19.

Ten delegates were elected to represent Millard and Juab Counties in the Council District No. 7, to be held at Nephi, Juab County, July 12th, at 12 m. Convention adjourned without day. A spirit of unity and good feeling prevailed throughout; immediately following the adjournment of the convention, the Juab delegation turned their faces homeward.

ALMA GREENWOOD,
Secretary of Convention.

THE NEXT LEGISLATURE.

The Thirty-six Solons Who Will Assemble Next Winter.

THE HERALD gives the following list of gentlemen who will make up the next Legislature of Utah, which convenes in this city on the first Monday in January, 1888:

COUNCIL.

John E. Carlisle, Logan; C. F. Olsen, Hyrum; L. W. Shurtliff, Ogden; John M. Young, Salt Lake City; Thomas Marshall, Salt Lake City; Elias A. Smith, Salt Lake City; Richard Howe, South Cottonwood; A. O. Smoot, Jr., Provo; J. P. Wimmer, Huntington; William A. C. Bryan, Nephi; Luther T. Tuttle, Manti; E. G. Woolley, St. George.

HOUSE.

Elias S. Kimball, Meadowville; Joseph Howell, Wellsville; Ricy H. Jones, Brigham City; Charles C. Richards, Ogden; Nathaniel Montgomery, North Ogden; Thomas F. Roueche, Kaysville; D. C. McLaughlin, Park City; C. E. Allen, Bingham; William W. Riter, Salt Lake City; John Clark, Salt Lake City; James H. Moyle, Salt Lake City; E. D. Hoge, Salt Lake City; George M. Spencer, Taylorsville; Levi P. Helm, Mill Creek; William Creer, Spanish Fork; S. R. Thurman, Provo; Lyman S. Wood, Springville; Abram Hatch, Heber City; William H. King, Fillmore; A. H. Lund, Mount Pleasant; William H. Seegmiller, Richfield; P. T. Farnsworth, Beaver; R. W. Heybourne, Cedar City; William F. Stewart, Kanab.

Our Next Body of Law-Makers.

The next Legislature of Utah, which will convene in Salt Lake City, on the first Monday of next January, will be composed of the following gentlemen:

COUNCIL.

John E. Carlisle, Logan; C. F. Olsen, Hyrum; L. W. Shurtliff, Ogden; John M. Young, Salt Lake City; Thomas Marshall, Salt Lake City; Elias A. Smith, Salt Lake City; Richard Howe, South Cottonwood; A. O. Smoot, Jr., Provo; J. P. Wimmer, Huntington; Wm. A. C. Bryan, Nephi; Luther T. Tuttle, Manti; E. G. Woolley, St. George.

HOUSE.

Elias S. Kimball, Meadowville; Joseph Howell, Wellsville; Rich. H. Jones, Brigham City; Charles C. Richards, Ogden; Nathaniel Montgomery, North Ogden; Thomas F. Roueche, Kaysville; D. C. McLaughlin, Park City; C. E. Allen, Bingham; William W. Riter, Salt Lake City; John Clark, Salt Lake City; James H. Moyle, Salt Lake City. E. D. Hoge, Salt Lake City; George M. Spencer, Taylorsville; Levi P. Heim, Mill Creek; William Creer, Spanish Fork; S. R. Thurman, Provo; Lyman S. Wood, Springville; Abram Hatch, Heber City; William H. King, Fillmore; A. H. Lund, Mount Pleasant; William H. Seegmiller, Richfield; P. T. Farnsworth, Beaver; R. W. Heybourne, Cedar City; William F. Stewart, Kanab.

IN SOUTHERN CLIMES.

Milford Struck by an Irish Boom.

AN INTERVIEW WITH CALTON.

The Slayer of Mike Cullen—His Version of the Matter—General News Notes.

Correspondence of THE HERALD.

Three weeks ago, having wearied of the monotonous routine duties connected with the morning newspaper business, I resolved upon an out for recuperation and recreation, and so, boarding one of the Old Pioneer railway coaches started of in the direction of the southern terminus of that road. After an all-night ride I landed at Milford, where friends met me with a conveyance to take me and mine to Minersville, thirteen or fourteen miles distant. Milford appeared to have been recently,

STRUCK BY AN IRISH BOOM,

the places of business being closed up and deserted, and the mill erected by Mr. A. G. Campbell at a great outlay standing idle. Nearly everybody about the place wore a "wonder-what-they'll-do-next" expression, and those who didn't were, Micawber-like, waiting for something to turn up. The few who were still clinging to the ruins had hopes of a revival, but could not tell for their lives, in what shape they looked for it to come. The day I arrived there Mr. Campbell also got in from the north, and immediately set about organizing his forces for a move to the new El Dorado of fabulous wealth he has found in the southwestern corner of Nevada, near the California line, and known as the Calico district. He started with his force the next day.

Minersville, another of those towns which thrived and blossomed while the mines in that neighborhood were being profitably worked, is also dull and almost lifeless, in consequence of the practical shutting down of the properties in the Bradshaw district, and what little business is being done there is so small as to dishearten everybody. And to add to the discouraging state of affairs, the rabbits have been playing havoc with the grain, potato and hay crops, reducing the yields very materially. The pests are in swarms, thousands upon thousands of them, and mow down all in their track. Louis Lessing, who rented his hotel there to Mr. Thomas Jones, has resumed charge of it and will continue to cater to the wanderers who may call on him. Mr. Dupaix, though removed from the centre of the town, does a good general merchandizing business; but latterly he has been investing in some milling property, about two miles away, which will prove a fortune in the near future.

After a rest of a couple of days, I went over to Beaver. Here I found the wave of depression had struck the capital also, but not quite to so marked a degree as the two places before named. There was considerable doing here and a "court boom" was looked forward to next week, which would at least "take off the curse" of dull times. Next Monday the session of the Second District Court will begin, at which the trial of Calton, the killer of Cullen, will take place.

Through the kindness of Sheriff Baldwin I had a brief

INTERVIEW WITH THE MURDERER.

His name is Andy Calton; he is 37 years old; was born in the town of Louise, Finland; stands about 5 feet 8¾; weighs about 150 pounds; he has an open countenance, with a slight cast in his right eye, and when conversing appears to be careless as to the outcome of the forthcoming trial, and supplements his sentences with a semi-idiotic grin. Being asked as to what his plea would be, he replied self-defense, and gave as his ground that before he shot Cullen the latter struck him on the side of the head, knocking him over the dashboard of the conveyance in which they were riding, grabbed him by the throat and began choking him. And, moreover, the aggravation was intensified, Calton said, by Cullen's declaring, in a braggadocio manner, "I'm a brother of Matt Cullen and I'm going to kill you, you s— of a b—." The prisoner admitted he was pretty drunk and said Cullen and a third party—one Tibberty—were also intoxicated. The shooting, he stated, was all done "in no time"—on the impulse of the moment—and after it was all over he felt sorry. Asked as to how many shots he fired, he did not know, but thought three or four. The statement heretofore published to the effect that he drove back into Milford and said: "Here he is; I have killed the s— of a b—," he denied, and said he drove back and gave himself up. Sheriff Baldwin, who arrested him, says this is not so, that he did not surrender himself. From the manner in which the prisoner conversed, I should judge that he was too muddled to know exactly what he did after the tragedy.

Last Monday, Isaac Riddle, brief mention of whose arrest was published in THE HERALD, appeared before District Clerk Barraclough, waived examination and was held in $1,500 bonds. The indictment upon which he was arrested was found about three years ago. Deputies Thompson and Sargent made the arrest on Coyote Creek, between Sevier and Grass Valley.

Probate Judge Frank Clayton, busies himself in his idle moments with various enterprises, and while I was at Beaver he was experimenting on a drive well on the premises of Hon. P. T. Farnsworth, but the cobble formation appeared to bother him considerably.

George Hales, of the Utonian, last Monday packed up press, type and material to take to Richfield, where he in conjunction with the veteran printer, W. M. Cowley, will issue a weekly paper, devoted to the interests of that section.

A company of old residents, among them Messrs. McDonough and Si Rogerson, were on the point of leaving for Fremont's Pass, south from Beaver, intending

TO BUILD RESERVOIRS,

sink wells and otherwise secure water for some of the richest farming and grazing lands out of doors. The party have taken up 640 acres under the desert land act and will locate a townsite on their domain.

One of the leading enterprises of this county is sheep raising, and the recent heavy sales of wool have somewhat revived trade in the city. There are in the hills, mountains and valleys to the east of Beaver, somewhere in the neighborhood of 50,000 sheep, 17,000 of which are being herded in three different flocks by Lyman A. Shepherd, for the Beaver Sheep Herd Association. In this connection, I learned that the woolen factory is not doing as well as its friends would like. It is in a semi-quiescent state, despite the large clip, because the wool has been sold for cash and shipped out of the Territory, and, as a consequence, the supply for the factory is reduced to very meagre proportions.

Early frosts killed all the fruit south of Fillmore and north of the Black Ridge, so that that source of revenue has been cut off for this year at least.

It was stated that the Utonian would have a libel suit on its hands ere long, preferred by Commissioner Smith, concerning whose social life the paper published a letter not long ago.

The district school opened on Monday last, with a fair attendance, under Mr. William Johnson and wife. The latter is better known in literary circles as "Ruby Lamont."

RAILROADS AND EXTENSIONS

are being talked about by nearly everybody, and if one were to believe but one-half the projects and stories related, he would, in his mind's eye, see a perfect network of railways tapping every town of note between Juab and St. George, and touching the boundaries of all the mining districts in the south country. One statement, which was given with every assurance of correctness, was that an offer had been made by Godbe and Hampton, or the Pioche Consolidated Company, of 130 tons of ore daily, if the railroad company would extend the line to that district, and bets have been made that work would begin on the extension within thirty days. Pioche is booming: a stage now makes e. o. d. connections between there and Milford. Another railroad story has it that the D. & R. G. is holding all the passes through the mountains south of Juab: that it has three or four men in the Salina Pass, and the same number in Clear Creek Canyon, and has expended thousands of dollars on the most difficult portions of both, in order to hold them against any other railroad.

The depression of Horn Silver stock is having a deadening effect on the mining industry generally in that portion of Southern Utah.

THE CITIZENS OF BEAVER

have petitioned the County Court to organize in accordance with the act in relation to irrigation companies, as an irrigating district comprising the entire county. The company, when organized, will construct reservoirs, canals, ditches, flumes, locks, waste weirs, and all appurtenances belonging thereto, for the purpose of supplying water on hitherto arid lands. The friends of the projectors will wish them success.

I have briefly mentioned a few of the leading items I picked up in a day or two's sojourn at the headquarters of the Second Judicial District, and have lengthened this epistle out beyond the limits I originally intended, but I have several other matters of interest to the people of Beaver which I must defer for another communication.

J. E. E.

Territorial Enquirer
September 16, 1887

The Jurors.

Deputy Redfield has kindly furnished us with the following list of grand and petit jurors who have been subpœnaed to serve at the next term of the First District Court which convenes in this city on Monday next. Others have been subpœnaed by Deputy Dykes, but their names have not yet been reported:

GRAND JURORS:

R. Gilchrist and R. Norman of Lehi; Wm. Sterrit of Pleasant Grove; W. K. Henry of Provo Bench; Richard Brereton and Henry Chappell of Provo; H. Menary of Springville; Wm. H. Taylor of Salem; Wm. McBeth and R. Kennison of Payson; W. A. Star of Mona; Geo. O. Bean of Nephi; H. Kearnes of Gunnison; H. McKinna of Redmond; J. T. Leonard of Salina; L. Cuddeback and S. S. Milne of Glenwood; Jas H. McCarty of Monroe; E. Bartholomew of Fillmore.

PETIT JURORS:

Israel Evans, Jr., and D. J. Thurman of Nephi; A. K. Thornton, American Fork; Robert Jones, Alpine; J. M. Ballenger, A. Ellis and John Richin, Pleasant Grove; J. Henningsen, Salem; O. H. Harper, Payson; James Mendenhall of Mona; Geo. Howard, John Kirgan and John Cooper, of Nephi; Geo. Larsen, Levan; Gus M. Clark, Wm. Scott and M. P. Laursen of Dover; Wm. Robbins, R. Christensen, Henderson Lee and Wm. Martin, of Gunnison; A. Ivie and C. A. Ivie of Salina; Niels Anderson and M. Christensen, of Richfield; Walter Jones, Monroe; Samuel Rowley, Scipio; and John M. Brown, of Charleston.

Commissions Issued.

The following commissions were issued by Governor West yesterday:

A. E. Keeler, justice of the peace, Park City, Summit County.

John Brunton, justice of the peace, Bingham, Salt Lake County.

John C. Duncan, justice of the peace, Ferron, Emery County.

E. W. McIntire, justice of the peace, Price, Emery County.

J. T. Farrer, justice of the peace, Blake, Emery County.

William Wood, Sr., justice of the peace, Minersville, Beaver County.

Swen Nielsen, justice of the peace, Fairview, Sanpete County.

William D. Funk, justice of the peace, Petty, Sanpete County.

Lauritz Larsen, justice of the peace, Mount Pleasant, Sanpete County.

John Jackson, justice of the peace, Fillmore, Millard County, Utah.

John T. Ashman, justice of the peace, Fillmore, Millard County, Utah.

Joshua Greenwood, justice of the peace, Fillmore, Sanpete County.

William Archibald, justice of the peace, Parley's Park Precinct, Summit County.

Charles E. Miller, justice of the peace, Riverton, Salt Lake County.

John S. Boyer, justice of the peace, Springville, Utah County.

J. D. Alphin, justice of the peace, Panguitch, Garfield County.

THE SOUTH INTERESTED.

The Railway Meeting at Provo on Wednesday.

At about 4 o'clock yesterday afternoon we noticed Will Smoot putting up some posters calling a mass meeting of citizens to assemble in the rooms of the Chamber of Commerce at 8 p.m. At the appointed hour there was quite a large audience present, composed of prominent business men, among whom we noticed Mayor Dusenberry, W. C. A. Smoot, George Sutherland, F. H. Simmons, S. S. Jones, Peter Stubbs, D. P. Felt, W. H. Brown, E. W. Snow, Judge Dusenberry, A. D. Holdaway and many other residents of Provo, with quite a representation from other settlements as far south as Fillmore. The meeting was called to order by the president, W. H. Dusenberry, who stated the object of the meeting and said a telephone message received from the Chamber of Commerce, of Salt Lake City, would be read by the secretary. The substance of the message was that a meeting would be held in Salt Lake City, and suggesting that the Chambers of Commerce in Provo and Ogden hold meetings at the same time, to protest against the unjust discrimination of the Union Pacific Railroad against Utah, and to adopt some united measure to correct the wrong complained of.

W. C. A. Smoot introduced a resolution expressing the sense of the meeting and providing for the appointment of a committee of five in addition to the standing committee to confer and cooperate with the Salt Lake and Ogden Chambers of Commerce. S. S. Jones, George Sutherland, W. C. A. Smoot, Mr. Andrews, of Nephi, and Mr. Huntsman, of Fillmore, spoke in favor of the resolution. Secretary Sutherland read the resolution again, and upon request he also read a resolution that had been introduced by Governor West and adopted by the Salt Lake Chamber of Commerce last Monday night. The question being called, was put to vote, and the resolution introduced by W. C. A. Smoot unanimously adopted. S. S. Jones, W. R. H. Paxman, A. D. Holdaway, W. C. A. Smoot and Professor A. A. Noon were appointed said committee.

Some other business of a local nature was disposed of, and the meeting adjourned until Friday night.   B.

Provo, September 29th.

SOUTHERN SCENES.

The Beauty and Grandeur Near Parowan.

THAT CITY'S EARLY HISTORY.

The Labors of the Hardy Pioneers—Panguitch and Its Lake—General News Notes

PAROWAN, Iron County, Utah,
October 26th, 1887.

To the Editor of THE HERALD.

Parowan was settled by a company of Mormons, mainly selected in Salt Lake by the late President George A. Smith, and conducted by him from there to this place, arriving here January 13th, 1851, the company consisting of about 120 souls. Parowan has not increased in population as many other places in the Territory have since that time, but it is claimed and established in fact that she has been the mother of Southern Utah, furnishing the pioneers that settled Cedar City, Harmony, Tokerville, Harrisburg, Washington, the "Clara Peach Orchard," and the first "Cotton Farm" settlement near the present site of St. George, St. Juan, and also the first settlers of Beaver.

BEES AND HONEY.

One of the best paying of Parowan's industries is the production of honey and bee culture. I am reliably informed that there are not less than a thousand stand of bees here, and during the past season fully fifty tons of honey has been taken, besides the usual number of additional swarms; one widow having produced what will realize her some $500.

Over $1,000 has been expended in the experiment of flowing wells, which after going through some eight streams of surface water in sinking 150 feet, further boring was discontinued, for want of means or lack of energy nd faith.

It is beyond question that if the citizens of this valley will only go ahead with "dry farming," and make a success of the well boring experiment, Parowan will yet become the city that its founder, George A., has so often predicted it would be. I am reliably informed that over 20,000 bushels of grain has been raised and already threshed here this season, and at Paragoonah, or Red Creek, four miles north of here, some 15,000 bushels was raised and threshed. There are two Mormon schools, and one Presbyterian now running, with a daily attendance of near 300, and another Mormon school will be commenced in a few weeks.

The ridge or elevation on which the city is located, has evidently at some time been washed out of the canyon, half a mile southeast of here, and consists of a coarse red sandstone formation, well adapted for fruit and all kinds of garden vegetables. Eight miles northwest of the town is the "Little Salt Lake," some ten miles long by one to two miles wide, the outlet to which is the "Gap," containing numerous Indian hieroglyphics, and opening into the Minersville Desert. The valley is one of the most beautiful in the Territory, being about thirty-five miles long by ten to twelve wide, and the beauties of Parowan Canyon have never yet been done justice in the papers; many of them being capped by flat and round boulders, as though chiseled and put there by the hand of some skilled mason. The sublime grandeur of "Alum Cave," compares with anything in the American Fork, or the Cottonwoods; the blood red cliffs from 2,000 to 3,000 feet high, perpendicular and overhanging, circling a pine grove of about 100 acres with an opening barely admitting the entrance of a wagon, is worthy the pencil of your Ottinger or Lambourne. The quantity and quality of Parowan's saw timber has been justly celebrated since its settlement, as some 10,000 feet of the "picked clear" was hauled from here to Salt Lake, 250 miles, and worked in the Tabernacle organ, when built, and all the lumber in the State House at Fillmore was furnished from here.

The County Court House is a neat, convenient structure, its inside accommodations having been arranged and copied from the Beaver Court House.

The meeting house is a substantial gray sandstone, and a good fac-simile of the people here, being a good deal better looking (and in fact) internally, than externally; but this has no reference to the feminine portion, particularly the marriageable ones, of which quorum there is said to be sixty eligible and not half that number of the young men matrimonially inclined. Another problem for Tucker.

The Young Ladies' Mutual Improvement Association, so far as organization, attendance, punctuality and exercises, are concerned, is said to rank with the best in Utah;

Panguitch Lake is reached by a fair wagon road in about fifteen miles, the road from the Bowery being worked over the Indian trail to the lake three years ago, at a cost of less than $700.

During the first ten years of its settlement an incredible amount of labor was performed by the pioneers in fencing fields, town lots, building houses, saw mills, grist mills, meeting houses and making canyon roads, and up to this time the raising of fruit was regarded as impossible, but immediately after President Young's visit here, where he spent his birthday in 1860, he so earnestly entreated the people to give it their attention that almost every city lot was soon stocked with a good variety, mainly coming from the Robinson Nurseries, at Fillmore. From the date of its settlement the growth of the city as to population and area has been greatly retarded by the limited amount of water coming from its Centre Creek. To-day it contains near 1,300 people, and in the three farming fields, under good fence, are 1,800 acres, comprising 500 acres of lucern. The possibility of "dry farming" was attempted some five years ago, and some Kaysville dry land seed wheat being obtained, the experiment resulted in seventeen bushels to the acre for eight acres. It has increased every year since, and this year some ten acres of corn, without irrigation, resulted in a good yield per acre, and of a good quality. The fruit crop has been good for many years past, with the exception of the present, when a severe frost last June almost entirely destroyed everything in blossom.

and the young mens', together with their reading rooms, is quite commendable. Sunday schools are well attended, so that, summing up, the people here, may be said to be as moral, peaceable, industrious and law-abiding (save a few unlawful cohabitators) as any village of its size on earth, as I haven't heard an oath uttered, nor seen a man with a pipe or cigar in his mouth for the past three days, and there is not a saloon, billiard table, nor a drop of spirits, Dixie wine or otherwise, sold or to be had in town; and this community are over nine-tenths Mormons, and they don't want any "Tribune civilization."

There are 40,000 sheep owned in this county, and the clip has been good throughout the county. More than the average.

I find from the postmaster that your SEMI-WEEKLY is liberally subscribed for here, and if cash wasn't so scarce the patronage would be increased.

As Parowan has long been reputed the healthiest settlement in Utah, to obtain correct statistics on this point, I called upon the sexton for the proof, and after his assuring me that the record was full and correct, I found on his book the record of 415 deaths since January, 1851. Of this number 110 were from 10 years to 89—quite a number over 70, showing 305 under 10 years Additional to the 415, one was exhumed and taken east, and two interred outside the limits, named Johnson and Kimmell.

The above figures include the mortality of Red Creek and Parowan. For the past twenty-five years the population has averaged from 800 to 100, so I need not say the ⁿlth of the people at present is good. Yours, R.

Territorial Enquirer
November 25, 1887

FAIR OR FALSE?

A Statement of Facts That Lead Us to Think the Latter.

A person has been in Provo several days representing himself as a capitalist largely interested in a Denver cannery and the Pueblo Pickling Company, of Pueblo, Colorado. He has passed around his card among our business men, on which his name is made to appear as a proprietor in these pickling works. A number of citizens have been induced by him to meet and consider the question of establishing a tomato cannery. While thus interesting our citizens, he has solicited and obtained from several of our merchants orders for quantities of vinegar to be shipped from his (?) works in Pueblo.

Yesterday two of our leading merchants received instructions by letter from Messrs. Miller & Clock, the *real* proprietors of the works referred to, stating that the self-styled representative and proprietor had no authority to so represent himself, that he was not in their employ, nor had any authority from them to solicit orders from Provo business men, and that they preferred not having any business transacted by him on their account. It is remembered by two merchants in particular that this fraudulent representative endeavored, when taking their orders, to secure a promise of immediate payment for the goods when they arrived.

The question therefore resolves itself into this: Did the bogus proprietor think that the Pueblo firm would ship on his order, and he have an opportunity to collect the money on the arrival of the goods? The conduct of the individual is at least suggestive.

Is it not strange that we should jump at any gnat that happens to alight in our way? Men coming from the East or West, whose antecedents we know nothing about, thoroughly gull us with such tempting inducements as this bogus capitalist has attempted to do. We have had more tangible inducements offered to us in this same line before to-day. Mr. Huntsman, of Fillmore, has the whole plant necessary for the conducting of a cannery. He made the proposition two years ago that if the people would help him get the machinery from Fillmore and start it, that he would come here and open a cannery. Nothing was done. But this fraudulent representative comes along, and says, "Gentlemen, I cannot put any stock in this, as my capital is all tied up in my vinegar works at Pueblo, and in my cannery at Denver, but will run it for you."

Now, the question for the business men of Provo to consider is this: Why cannot we, with all the facilities around us, commence and successfully conduct a cannery ourselves, without trusting our capital and means into the hands of a transient, about whom we know nothing?

MILLARD STAKE ACADEMY.

The Report of Principal Alma Greenwood.

Following is the report of Alma Greenwood, principal of the Millard Stake Academy, at the close of the first term of the third academic year:

PRINCIPAL'S REPORT.

First term, third academic year, of Millard Stake Academy, commencing September 19th, ending November 24th, 1887:

To the Honorable Board of Trustees—Gentlemen: The first term of the third academic year closes to-day, and shows the following statistics:

DEPARTMENTS.

	Students Registered.	Left.
Preparatory	46	2
Advanced	32	1
Total	78	3

DEPARTMENTS.

	Students Registered.	Left.
Preparatory	46	2
Advanced	32	1
Total	78	3

PREPARATORY DEPARTMENT,

in charge of Joshua Greenwood, has been conducted according to the following statistics:

Classes	Students.	Weekly Recitations.
Theology	47	4
Arithmetic, B	19	3
Arithmetic, C	38	5
Grammar and Com. B	14	5
Grammar, C	27	5
Spelling	78	5
Geography, A	50	5
Geography, B	28	5
Physiology	25	5
United States History	19	4
Primary History	21	4
Penmanship	47	5
Totals	13	62

One teacher, assisted by advanced students.

ADVANCED DEPARTMENT,

in charge of Alma Greenwood, has been conducted agreeable to the following statistics:

Classes.	Students.	Weekly Recitations.
Theology	29	4
Penmanship	32	5
Elocution	13	5
Algebra	6	5
Arithmetic	19	5
Grammar	28	5
Orthography	40	5
Astronomy	9	5
Physiology	10	2
Composition	21	2
Bookkeeping	20	1
Ancient History	7	4
Totals	12	53

One teacher.

DOMESTIC ORGANIZATIONS

reports the students tabulated as follows: From Fillmore, 43; Meadow, 7; Kanosh, 2; Deseret, 7; Lemmington, 1; Scipio, 9; Holden, 5; Garfield County, 2; Utah County, 1; Salt Lake County, 1. Total, 78.

Students from other wards have been distributed in fourteen boarding houses. They have been visited by representatives of the principal. Reports of said visits have been made in the domestic meetings held once in two weeks. And judging from the nature of these reports and from personal observations, the students have been comfortably located and they have conformed their lives in accordance with the restrictions of the Academy.

THEOLOGICAL ORGANIZATION.

The record of this organization exhibits the following: Seventies, 2; elders, 2; priests, 1; teachers, 4; deacons, 17; members, 50; non-members, 2. Total, 78. The labor of this very important feature of our Academy are as follows: Priesthood meeting for the hearing of recitation reports which set forth the general standing and advancement of all the students in theology and for brief lectures by the students on the various degrees of the priesthood have been held weekly. General repetitions in theology are held on Mondays; also a grand theological exercise, consisting of a variety programme on Wednesday. The various meetings have been presided over by male students and the minutes taken principally by female students, and a record of said minutes is kept by a student appointed by the principal. Thus far, in the presentation of the principles of the gospel to the students of the academy, much of the Holy Spirit has been realized and has tended to bring forth much gospel truth, especially in the advanced department. Science and religion have been made to harmonize to the removal of infidelity and unbelief. The devotional exercises, consisting of singing by the academy choir, ably conducted by Mrs. Josephine Greenwood, and prayer, principally by one of the students, has contributed much to the interest and spiritual benefits of the institution.

As yet, our Polysophical Society has not been resumed.

CLOSING REMARKS.

As our institution becomes more firmly established by age and experience, its influence in discipline and government becomes more marked. With some exceptions, the students have caused the teachers but little difficulty in the government and manipulation of the exercises. On the whole, the intellectual and religious advancement of the students in attendance during the term has been of such a character as to win for themselves praise and commendation and meet the hearty approval and satisfaction of the teachers. This advancement is made conspicuous by its influence for the refinement and improvement of our young people.

The furniture, borrowed by the academy, is very limited, and of such a construction as to limit the comfort and convenience of those who attend. With the exceptions of two blackboards and a Lamanitish cranium, we have no utensils in the way of maps, globes, charts and apparatus for making demonstrations and explanations, which deficiency works a hardship to the teachers, and retards the advancement of the students. In view of these necessities, your earnest and immediate consideration of the matter is respectfully solicited. Notwithstanding the fact that the teachers have for a number of months past labored with but little financial remuneration, we entertain faith and encouragement for the future prosperity and success of our noble academy, on which may the benign influence of God rest, and stimulate the Saints of Millard Stake to an undivided support of the same, is the sincere invocation of

ALMA GREENWOOD,
Principal.

FILLMORE, November 25, 1887.

Salt Lake Herald
January 3, 1888

TO CONVENE NEXT MONDAY.

The Solons Who Will Assemble in the Legislative Halls

Preparations for the coming session of the Legislature are already noticeable in and around the City Hall. The solons will meet on Monday next, at 10 a. m., and for the first time in the history of Utah, there will be five non-Mormon members—John M. Young, E. D. Hoge, C. E. Allen, D. C. McLaughlin, and Thomas Marshall. Of these, only Mr. McLaughlin has before served in the capacity of legislator. Following is the roll:

First District—John E. Carlisle, Logan, Cache County.

COUNCIL.

First District—John E. Carlisle, Logan, Cache County.

Second District—C. F. Olsen, Hyrum, Cache County.

Third District—L. W. Shurtliff, Ogden, Weber County.

Fourth District—John M. Young, Salt Lake City, Salt Lake County.

Fifth District—Thomas Marshall, Salt Lake City, Salt Lake County.

Sixth District—Elias A. Smith, Salt Lake City, Salt Lake County.

Seventh District—Richard Howe, South Cottonwood, Salt Lake County.

Eighth District—A. O. Smoot, Jr., Provo, Utah County.

Ninth District—J. P. Wimmer, Huntington, Emery County.

Tenth District—William A. C. Bryan, Nephi, Juab County.

Eleventh District—Luther T. Tuttle, Manti, Sanpete County.

Twelfth District—E. G. Woolley, St. George, Washington County.

HOUSE OF REPRESENTATIVES.

First District — Elias S. Kimball, Meadowville Rich County.

Second District — Joseph Howell, Wellsville, Cache County.

Third District—Ricy H. Jones, Brigham City, Box Elder County.

Fourth District—Charles C. Richards, Ogden, Weber County.

Fifth District—Nathaniel Montgomery, North Ogden, Weber County.

Sixth District—Thomas F. Roueche, Kaysville, Davis County.

Seventh District—D. C. McLaughlin, Park City, Summit County.

Eighth District—C. E. Allen, Juab County.

Ninth District—W. W. Riter, Salt Lake City, Salt Lake County.

Tenth District—John Clark, Salt Lake City, Salt Lake County.

Eleventh District—James H. Moyle, Salt Lake City, Salt Lake County.

Twelfth District—E. D. Hoge, Salt Lake City, Salt Lake County.

Thirteenth District—George M. Spencer, Taylorsville, Salt Lake County.

Fourteenth District—Levi P. Helm, Mill Creek, Salt Lake County.

Fifteenth District—William Creer, Spanish Fork, Utah County.

Sixteenth District—Samuel R. Thurman, Provo, Utah County.

Seventeenth District, Lyman S. Wood, Spring Ville, Utah County.

Eighteenth District—Abram Hatch, Heber City, Wasatch County.

Nineteenth District—William H. King, Filmore, Millard County.

Twentieth District—A. H. Lund, Mount Pleasant, Sanpete County.

Twenty-first District—William H. Seegmiller, Richfield, Sevier County.

Twenty second District—Philo T. Farnsworth, Beaver, Beaver County.

Twenty-third District—Robert W. Heybourne, Cedar City, Iron County.

Twenty-fourth District—William F. Stewart, Kanab, Kane County.

Complimentary Benefit.

The following correspondence is self-explanatory:

SALT LAKE CITY, January 18, 1888.

To John S. Lindsay, Esq.:

Dear Sir—Realizing that in the establishment of the drama in Utah, you have played a conspicuous part, and worked, and by your best endeavors helped to create a taste for the Thespian art in our midst, which now stands second to none on the continent, we, whose names are hereunto attached, desire to express to you, in a substantial manner, our appreciation of your services in the cause of art, your merits as a devotee to that cause, and our desire to have such commendation recognized in a fitting and appropriate manner.

We, therefore, as a tender of our best wishes to the histrionic art, and to you, its able exponent, who have, under varying and trying circumstances, advanced its standard and upheld its cause, at times when to do so was unprofitable but hopeful, and having a certain sense of local pride in presenting you as an exemplar of the growth and firm foundation of that art in our growing Territory, as a resident thereof, hereby tender you a complimentary benefit, to take place at such time and place, and under such circumstances as may best accord with your pleasure and convenience.

Signed,

CALEB W. WEST, Salt Lake City.
F. ARMSTRONG, "
ANGUS M. CANNON, "
ED. W. TULLIDGE, "
GEO. M. OTTINGER, "
ARTHUR L THOMAS, "
JAMES JACK, "
H. B. CLAWSON, "
GEO. D. PYPER, "
W. C. HALL, "
ROBT. CLEGHORN, "
S. C. EWING, "
JAMES SHARP, "
GEORGE A. MEEARS, "
JOHN NICHOLSON, "
A. C. BRIXEN, "
C. C. GOODWIN, "
ISADOR MORRIS, "
BYRON GROO, "
C. R. BARRATT, "
H. G. McMILLAN, "
J. M. BENEDICT, "
CHAS. AUER, "
J. H. MOYLE, "
P. H. LANNAN, "
W. W. RITER, "
O. F. WHITNEY, "
HEBER M. WELLS, "
ELIAS A. SMITH, "
N. W. OSBORNE, "
L. W. SHURTLIFF, Ogden.
S. R. RICHARDS, "
F. J. CANNON, "
S. R. THURMAN, Provo.
WM. H. KING, Fillmore.
A. HATCH, Heber City.
And many others.

SALT LAKE CITY January 20, 1888.

To Governor West, Mayor Armstrong, Manager Clawson, Editors Goodwin, Nicholson and Groo, President Cannon, Col. Osborne and others:

Gentlemen—The receipt of your kind communication tendering me a complimentary benefit is hereby acknowledged. In reply, permit me to assure you that I appreciate the friendly feeling which prompted and prevades it, also the flattering tribute you accord me as a "devotee" of the dramatic art. I accept with cordial thanks your kind proffer, and name Tuesday evening, February 1st, as the most opportune time for the benefit.

Yours respectfully.
JOHN S. LINDSAY.

THE FOLLOWING members of the Legislature returned this morning, and may be found at the old quarters at the Valley House: Hon. A. O. Smoot and S. N. Thurman, of Provo; W. H. King, of Fillmore; L. S. Wood, of Springville; William Creer, of Mill Creek; H. N. Montgomery, of Ogden.

Millard Matters.

Who knows? Millard county may have a boom sooner than the moss backs anticipate.

There is no boom here, but a boom of climate, and that is of a kind so excellent as to be unsurpassed.

In the eyes of Legislators. Millard county is the same as Chicago appeared to a Bostonian a few years ago—'Too far from everywhere to amount to much."

The wool men of this section join their brethren in entering an emphatic protest against putting wool upon the free list; all Mr Pul has said to the contrary notwithstanding.

The query hereabouts is "when will work be commenced upon the railroad extension," and the answer each time monotonously comes—" Don't know." Every one is, however, hopeful.

There is reasonable hope that the valuable mineral deposits in Deseret Mining District will soon produce something more than talk. One number has been completed by the Al o M n ng and Smelting Company and another is being erected by the "Baker Smelting Company."

A number of "finds" of more or less importance have excited the mining fraternity of late, and it seems one recently made a short distance south East of Kanosh is valuable. One shipment of ore has already been made and it is rumored that gratifying returns have been received.

There appears good reason for supposing the prediction that Deseret will be the granary of Utah will be realized. A magnificent canal has been completed through which the water for irrigation purposes will be conveyed the coming season. The good people of Deseret have labored against almost overwhelming odds and deserve to succeed.

Millard county has not yet ceased to congratulate itself and Governor West that the "District Division Bill" introduced by the hon member from Nephi, met a deserved fate. We have no ill will against the little Chicago" or as an old gentleman in Wellington dryly remarked, 'little chick I go," but feel confident the only one benefited would be the hamlet above mentioned.

The third term of the Millard Stake Academy closed on the 16th inst In the evening there was a very pleasant social given at the residence of Professor Alma Greenwood. The students and a few invited guests had a most enjoyable time in testing the quality of the good cheer sumptuously provided and in listening to an impromptu programme of songs, readings, and recitations.

Millard county has not yet been struck by any real estate boom, but she longeth with an exceeding desire, and hopeth and expecteth inasmuch as her acres lying out doors are superfluously numerous. "Superfluous" is used for the benefit of adjoining counties. Should any of our neighbors in the future desire a part of our broad domain, made valuable by the passing of a railroad, reference of the matter to a Legislative committee will without doubt give them the coveted ground.

J. L. R.

Fillmore, March 21st, 1888.

Salt Lake Herald
March 30, 1888

First District Court.

The jury returned a verdict of not guilty in the case of the soldiers, Young and Poll, grand larceny.

They also returned a verdict of not guilty in the case of Samuel Singleton, grand larceny.

Henry W. Kemp, John B. Kemp and John Sanfield were admitted to citizensnip

Wi'l'am J. Lewis was arraigned for unlawful cohabitation and took until Friday to enter his plea.

Charles Allred and Joseph Justeson pleaded guilty to the Nephi Bank assault ase, and were sentenced as follows: Charles Allred to five years and Joseph Justeson four years, and the sentence in the larceny of wool was postponed until after the expiration of these sentences.

Thomas Collins, a colored soldier, is on trial for his life, for murdering Frank Washington, last October, at Fort Duchesne.

March 29.—The case was concluded, and the jury retired this afternoon with it.

The following civil cases were set:

April 5th—C. P. Flanders vs. Charles Patten.

April 6th—Frederick Petterson vs. Joseph Weightman.

April 7th—Heber and Susana Giles vs. Anna B. Edford.

April 9th—Horace Holt vs. Indiana Live Stock Company.

April 10th—Omer Call, et al., vs. Joel Grover, et al.

April 11th—Silas Reed vs. George Pearson, et al.

April 11th—Fillmore Co-op. vs Mary L. C. Holt.

April 12th—D. M. McMurphy vs. A. Marks, et al.

April 13th—Ole J. Jacobsen vs. Henry Beal, et al.

April 13th—Gould & Austin vs. James Chipman.

D. S. Dana, et al., vs. H. W. Lawrence was continued for the term.

The cases of W. M. Ormand vs. Frank Argyle and Abegg vs. Ormand are set for to-morrow. The Court will go away to-morrow for a week, to attend Supreme Court. *

Provo, March 28, 1888.

Salt Lake Herald
April 12, 1888

A Pleasant Event.

Mr. Dan Olsen, who will be remembered by old residents as a member of the Pioneer Quadrille Band, which used to play in Social Hall in years gone by, came up from Fillmore on a visit, a few days ago, and John Paul conceived the idea of having a social party in his honor. The event came off at Mr. Paul's residence last night, and among those present were Joshua Midgley and wife, John Thomas and wife, Mr. Jacob West, of Logan. Mrs. O. H. Riggs, Mrs. H. Barrett, Mr. and Mrs. H. Groves, Mr. and Mrs. George T. Bourne, Jr., William Calder, Oscar Bourne. Miss Abbie Dewey, Mr. and Mrs. W. W. Calder, Dr. H. J. Faust, Miss Belle Bourne, Dr. Benedict and wife, James Bourne, John Maberry, William Foster, H. D. Barber and several others. The evening was very pleasantly spent in vocal and instrumental music, dancing, and an elegant repast, gotten by Mrs. Paul. All present enjoyed themselves thoroughly until an early hour this morning, when the party broke up.

Utah Enquirer
April 24, 1888

PROVO CANNERY.

The Necessary Machinery to be Purchased and Buildings Erected.

At the directors' meeting of the Provo Canning company, held in S. S. Jones' office last night, the specifications and plans of the building to be constructed were read and accepted and the secretary instructed to publish notice for receiving bids. Mr. A. A. Noon was elected temporary superintendent of the works.

On motion of W. R. Pike, the secretary was authorized to close bargain and obtain deed for location from P. L. M. & B. company for the sum of $600.

Mr. Reed Smoot stated that he had examined the boiler at the Salt Lake B. & M. company, and found it in good condition. The price asked for it was $475 on cars at Salt Lake.

Mr. Noon said that Mr. Huntsman, of Fillmore, had a complete outfit for cannery purposes and would like to dispose of the same. Mr. Huntsman offered to pay the expenses of Mr. Noon to go and examine it, and see if it would answer the purpose of the cannery.

On motion of Mr. Reed Smoot A. A. Noon was instructed to go and see if the boiler was large enough, and look through the machinery and report at next meeting.

A proposition was read from Mr. John Devey, offering to lay a 30-horse power steel boiler on cars at Provo for $515.

The meeting then adjourned *sine die.*

Salt Lake Herald
May 1, 1888

It is remarked by a country exchange that "Hon. W. H. King, of Fillmore, will make a permanent removal from Millard County to Salt Lake City, in July. The ostensible object of Mr. K's removal being to study and practice law in the metropolis."

Salt Lake Herald
May 20, 1888

W. E. Maycock, was in Ogden Friday night, he having just returned from Fillmore, after a most agreeable visit to that part of Millard County.

Utah Enquirer
May 29, 1888

B. Y. ACADEMY GRADUATES.

NORMAL GRADUATES.

1. Oscar Vance, Alpine.
2. Nephi Savage, Payson,
3. Newton Noyes, Fillmore.
4. Alma Huish, Payson.
5. John Foote, Provo.
6. Jennet Findlay, Panacca, Nev.
7. Celestia Nash, Alpine.
8. Samuel Cornwall, Mill Creek.
9. Mattie Nelson, Goshen.

SPECIAL GRADUATES.

John Foote, Provo, in Rhetoric 91, Physics 90, General Chemistry 90.

Hyrum Anderson, Lehi, in Rhetoric 90, Physics 92, Domestic Science 94, General Chemistry 91, General Geology 90.

Celestia Nash, Alpine, in Rhetoric 90, Domestic Science 92.

Oscar Vance, Alpine, in Physics 91, Domestic Science 93.

John F. Noyes, Fillmore, in Physics 90.

Caleb Tanner, Provo, in Bookkeeping 91, General Chemistry 90.

Grace Tanner, Provo, in Domestic Science 90.

Joseph McGregor, Parowan, in Bookkeeping 94, Physiology and Hygiene 90.

Agnes Lewis, Spanish Fork, in Domestic Science 90.

John Swensen, Pleasant Grove, in Physiology and Hygiene 92.

Lottie Woolley, Tooele, in Domestic Science 90.

Mary E. Taylor, Payson, in Domestic Science 90.

Nettie Bagley, Big Cottonwood, in Domestic Science 90.

Samuel A. King, Fillmore, in Domestic Science 90.

Jedediah Taylor, Payson, in Domestic Science 91.

John G. Lind, Park City, in Bookkeeping 95, Physiology and Hygiene 90, General Chemistry 93.

Newton Noyes, Fillmore, in Physics 91.

James Rawlings, Draper, in Physiology and Hygiene 91.

Axel Nielson, Provo, Physiology and Hygiene 93.

Alexander Hedquist, Provo, in Bookkeeping 92.

Jos. A. West, Snowflake, Arizona, in Bookkeeping 93.

Salt Lake Herald
June 3, 1888

TERRITORIAL TOPICS.

An Interesting Gust from Park City.

THE EVENTS OF A WEEK.

A Breezy Budget from Thrifty Fillmore—Manti Matters—Kaysville Kinks—Provo Points.

Fillmore Facts.

BRONCHO breaking is the order of the day. Dry, very windy, and dusty.

IT is calculated that there will be more small grain raised here than ever before.

THE farmer gazes upon the growing grain with an assurance of high reward for his labors.

Storm all around, with occasional showers; hope it will be pouring in torrents before many hours.

FRUIT prospects are good. Few complain of the frost having killed much of the fruit in the southeast part of the town.

BUSINESS would appear to be good, the Co-op. having declared a dividend of 25 per cent. which has not occurred since 1880.

You talk about Hinglish gardens, but take a walk to Maycock's lot and you will see a regular good old, Hinglish style vegetable garden.

ON account of business being very dull, many of the male portion of the settlement have to go away, some sheep-shearing, logging, mining, etc.

THE lumber trade is in full going order, three steam mills running every day, and the fourth is nearly completed, all within ten miles distance of the city.

MR. ALFRED SMURTHWAITE, your traveling agent, was here trying to stimulate the minds of the people and add new subscribers to the list, which no doubt was done.

WE are sorry to say that Bishop A.A. Kimball, of Kanosh, was unable to attend conference on account of sickness. He has not been able to get around for upwards of two years, but we hope for his speedy recovery.

MR. HUNTSMAN has taken his Fruit Canning Factory to Provo. This action speaks badly for Fillmore, and the country. It is very evident that the people of Millard have not given the gentleman much encouragement in that enterprise.

THE peaceful, slumbering community was last night disturbed by the cry of "Fire, fire," and looking in the direction of the north, could be seen the fierce and wicked flames piercing toward the horizon. It was the lumber mill of Lyman Brothers, which was totally destroyed, the damage being $2,000.

THE boom is not confined to Salt Lake but it reaches as far south as Fillmore, Woolley, Lund & Judd having, established an agency for the sale of farming implements, etc. John Y. Ashman is the appointed rustling agent, and his beaming countenance cannot fail to draw customers. John is confident of success.

WHAT might have resulted in a great loss by fire took place at the sulphur works owned by Dickert & Myers, last Monday night. It seem that a few men were working in the refining department, and by some means not known, the sulphur took fire, causing the refining department to be almost totally burned down, by the efforts of the men the fire was extinguished, very little damage being done.

FILLMORE, May 29.

Salt Lake Herald
June 5, 1888

JUDGES OF ELECTION.

Appointments for Emery, Kane and Sevier Counties.

The following judges of election have been appointed by the Utah Commission:

EMERY COUNTY.

BLAKE—Robert Hatrick, James Gummage, N. D. Higgins.

CASTLE DALE—John W. Kofford, George Kofford, Orange Seely.

MOLEN — Samuel Caldwell, Joseph Swasy, Seth Wareham.

HUNTINGTON—H. S. Loveless, J. E. Johnson, Thomas Wakefield.

LAWRENCE—B. L. Reynolds, Holley Tuffs, P. C. Burch.

MUDDY — Jacob Minchy, Rasmus Johnson, Heber C. Petty.

FERRON — Thomas Market, H. M. Fugate, J. C. Duncan.

MOAB—L. B. Bartlett, G. H. Wade, W. A. Pierce.

ORANGEVILLE—Frank Carroll, Joseph Boulden, W. L. Stilson.

PRICE—J. H. O'Brien, S. C. Mann, L. M. Olsen.

WELLINGTON—L. Benton, E. Jones, Arthur Barney.

SCOFIELD—A. H. Earll, D. W. Holdaway, J. A. Ingalls.

KANE COUNTY.

GLENDALE—B. L. Seathead, John S. Carpenter, Joseph Hopkins.

JOHNSON—Robert Laws, Hyrum Shumway, Jermon Buchanan.

KANAB—John Rider, C. H. Oliphant, John Findlay.

MT. CARMEL—Robert Moncur, Haskel S. Jolley, G. W. Hicks.

ORDERVILLE—C. W. Carroll, Isaac V. Carling, Richard Norwood.

PAHREAH—James A. Stewart, G. M. Bybee, J. W. Mangum.

UPPER KANAB—H. K. Roundy, George Johnson, J. W. Seaman.

SEVIER COUNTY.

REDMOND—Henry McKenna, Charles Herbert, A. C. Anderson.

SALINA—W. H. Rex, J. T. Leonard, Joseph Lapish.

GOOSEBERRY—J. W. Holden, A. J. Russell, Abe Casto.

BURRVILLE—W. H. Shack, C. C. Burr, Edgar Fillmore.

WILLOW BEND—John Larsen, J. C. Larsen, William Harding.

VERMILLIAN—Orson Cuddeback, M. Keighn, P. Dastrap.

GLENWOOD — C. Fairbank, John Crosier, John Kirkman.

RICHFIELD—August Neilson, Mads Christensen, J. A. Hellstrom.

ANNABELLA—L. Thompson, Phillip K. Gouchat. M. A. Abbott.

ELSINORA—Andreas Bertelsen, R. W. Herring. W. Smith.

CENTRAL—Andrew Nelson, J. R. Horten, R. Neilson.

JOSEPH—R. A. Bridges, A. K. Warenski, William M. Carter.

MONROE—Andros Bertelson Jr., Walter Jones, Alvin Hunt

Salt Lake Herald
June 17, 1888

Notes From Fillmore.

THE weather is very windy and dusty.

OUR prospects for crops are No. 1, and th people are f eling good.

MELVILLE and Greenwood have started east with about 1,600 head of sheep, all in first-class condition. They expect to dispose of them in Kansas City.

YORKSHIRE.

FILLMORE, June 13, 1888.

Salt Lake Herald
June 19, 1888

Hon. W. H. KING came up from Fillmore to attend to some legal business yesterday. He goes to Strawberry on cattle business.

Salt Lake Herald
July 1, 1888

Notes from Fillmore.

HOTTER and hotter.

CROPS are looking well.

LUCERN hauling is all the go.

FRUIT is getting ripe, and there are no worms in the apples here this year.

A SAD accident happened here. A young man, John M. Jackson by name, of this place, while mowing, went to pull on the lever to raise the knives; at the same time the machine struck a rock, and threw him from the seat to the ground. The team did not stop, and consequently he had his thumb and part of his hand cut off. Some of our citizens went to his aid and sewed the thumb back on to the hand. The people got up a subscription and sent him to St. Mary's Hospital, Salt Lake City, for treatment.

YORKSHIRE.

FILLMORE June 25th, 1888.

Before the U. S. Commissioner.

James Hanson, of Spanish Fork, was before U. S. Commissioner Hills on Friday last, charged with unlawful cohabitation. There were ten witnesses present, four of whom were Mr. Hanson's alleged wives. The evidence was deemed insufficient to hold defendant, and he was discharged.

On the same day E. B. Hawkins, of Benjamin, was before the Commissioner on the usual charge. Defendant waived examination and was bound over to the next grand jury in the sum of $800.

Yesterday Charles Frampton, of Fillmore, was examined on the charge of unlawful cohabitation, which developed into his commital for adultery, and he was bound over in the sum of $1,000.

Herbert Bate was taken before the Commissioner yesterday afternoon, charged with unlawful cohabitation. His two alleged wives were present and testified, resulting in the dismissal of the first charge and his being bound over in the sum of $500 on a charge of fornication.

Hon. W. H. King, of Fillmore, came in to Provo in the "nick of time" to assist in ratifying.

SUNDAY SERVICES.

The Final Triumph of "Mormonism."

ELDERS GEO. H. BRIMHALL AND
WM. H. KING SPEAK.

The Latter's Remarks on the Outcome of the Kingdom of God.

The usual Sabbath services of the Church of Jesus Christ of Latter-day Saints were held in the meeting-house on Sunday afternoon, at 2 o'clock. Elder Isaac Bullock, presiding.

The choir sang:

Sweet is the work, my God, my King,
To praise Thy name, give thanks and
    sing.

Prayer was offered by Elder S. S. Jones.

Choir sang:

How sweet communion is on earth,
With those who've realized the birth.

The sacrament was administered by the Bishopric of the First Ward.

ELDER GEORGE H. BRIMHALL believed he was a living testimony of the truth of the promises of the Lord in attempting to spiritually feed a multitude. Our Lord and Savior gave a beautiful object lesson on that subject at one time. It was at a period when the multitude were hungry, and it was proposed by the Savior that they have something to eat. His disciples were astonished at the Savior making such a proposition, as they were far from any place of refreshment, But Jesus asked them, "What have ye?" The answer came. "Five loaves and two little fishes." Christ demanded them to be brought to Him. It was done, He blessed the food, and ordered it distributed among the multitude. After everybody had partaken of it, there were twelve basketsful left of the fragments. Here we see a beautiful illustration of the power of God, and I say that I am a living testimony of the truth of the Gospel

in the multitude being fed. I believe that everything that now exists upon the earth, invention and discovery included, are attributable to revelation. When Joseph Smith announced to the world that the Garden of Eden was upon the American continent, the fact was scoffed at by the learned. Some, and, in fact, mostly all, believed it to be located in Asia Minor—the old world. But since discoveries have been made, and science has been more fully developed, it has become a conceded fact that the Garden of Eden was located on this continent. Another poof. You will recollect that when the Book of Mormon was first given to the world, ridicule was hurled at the assertions therein, regarding the existence of horses and cows, and other animals, in bygone ages upon this continent. But since the fossil remains of such animals have been found on the Pacific shores and other places, a change has come over the world, and they see differently. It is like two men writing a history. They do not see alike, they do not have the same ideas. A man cannot view the beauties of a rose while laying under its branches. He must stand erect if he desires to behold it in its glory. We all see differently; consequently we cannot measure things from our own individual standpoint. I believe that the day will come when the prophecy will be fulfilled wherein it says: Saints will be put to death, while those who do so will think they are doing God's service. The speaker then graphically portrayed the rise and destruction of Nauvoo, the exodus of the Saints, another visit of Thomas L. Kane there, and the record he made of that visit. We are serving a God who is leading us on to prosperity; who has not failed us during the past fifty years. I am not ashamed to acknowledge the hand of the Lord in His dealings with His people. He has not forsaken Israel. But He has poured out His blessings upon us; He has increased our streams; He has made more fertile our fields of grain; He has given us freedom and liberty; He has multiplied His blessings upon us; and for these reasons, and for many others, I am willing to acknowledge the hand of God.

ELDER W. H. KING, of Fillmore, next addressed the congregation. He said: I am requested to occupy a few moments of your time this afternoon. This is a position I do not solicit; but nevertheless I feel like endeavoring to give a reason for the hope that is within me, as all Latter-day Saints should be able to do. The immortal principles of truth, advocated by Jesus, have been restored in this day, and God demands at our hands that we live up to them, and do all we possibly can to spread them among the nations. These principles are calculated to redeem the human family,—to raise them from mortality to immortality. With such glorious principles in our possession, what kind of men should we be? We find that infidelity is spreading through the land;—that the world is not growing better but is growing worse. What then can accomplish the unity of the children of God? Christianity has not done it; Mohammedanism has been a failure in bringing about these happy results, the silvery oratory of Robert Ingersoll has not accomplished it. What then, I ask you, will bring this much desired object about? Only in the revelation of God, given in our day, can we look for a solution of this query. And upon the Latterday Saints devolves the duty of heralding to the world the principles of salvation and of preparing the way for the second coming of Christ. If it was necessary in the days of Jesus for a precursor to prepare the way before Him, is it not more necessary that such a thing should take place in this day? The Latter-day Saints are the precursors of the Messiah in this the dispensation of the fullness of times. They are raising the warning voice, calling upon the people to repent, for the day of God's judgment is nigh. Revelation is not a thing of the past; the heavens are not as sealed brass over us, God is the same yesterday, to-day and forever; and revelation is as vital a principle of redemption to-day as it ever was. Knowing all this, what position should we occupy in the earth? Have we the Gospel of the Son of God at heart? Do we have the desire to do good, and redeem the world from its error and iniquity? If we have not, better will it be for us to go to our Father and ask for His spirit, that we might have the power of our callings resting upon us. We are told that the work of God will go onward; that man can do nothing against us, but for us, that the kingdom of God is established for the last time; that "the law shall go forth from Zion, and the word of the Lord from Jerusalem." These are some of the prophecies that have been made to us; that should stimulate us to renewed diligence, and that should cause us to lift up our warning voices to the nations of the earth; that should make us examine ourselves, and realize what condition we are placing ourselves in. Mormonism embraces all that is good, and combines, not only the salvation of the living, but the redemption of the dead. There should be no drones in the hive of Zion. The honey is to be gathered, and we are called to participate in this labor. If we do our duty faithfully, the more of the Spirit of the Lord will we have. We need have no apprehension of the outcome of God's work. Truth cannot be destroyed; though crushed to earth it will surely rise again. There may be times when the storm clouds hover around us; when the sun is enshrouded in a pall of blackness; when there would seem to be no power in heaven or earth to rescue the people from their seeming imminent danger. But, Mormonism is destined to triumph, while the wicked and the ungodly will meet destruction by the judgments of God. We should do right; consecrating all we have to the service of God, and seeking eternal lives.

The choir sang the hymn:

Zion stands with hills surrounded,
  Zion, kept by power divine.

Benediction was pronounced by President Jacob Gates.

Salt Lake Herald
August 5, 1888

THE DEPUTY marshals in the southern part of the Territory, have been quite active of late. The following persons have been arrested within the past few days on the charge of unlawful cohabitation: Henry Neheker, Thomas Ross and Sidney Carter, of Sevier County; C. B. Beauregard and William Beeston, of Fillmore, Millard County; J. C. Anderson, of Koosharem Piute County; and B. H. Watts, of Millard County. The latter was first arrested a couple of weeks ago, and made his escape from the deputies. He afterward came in and gave himself up.

Salt Lake Herald
September 19, 1888

First District Court.

David Williams vs. David J. Williams & Co., defendant's demurrer confessed; seven days given to file an amended complaint.

Angeline Taylor vs. Hyrum J. Taylor; order overruling demurrer; twenty days given in which to file answer.

W. D. Myers vs. C. M. Boley; order dismissing cause at plaintiff's cost.

The People of the Territory of Utah vs. Otto Hudson and Cornelius Sorenson; order entered dismissing appeal.

United States vs. J. P. R. Johnson; plea of not guilty withdrawn; plea of guilty entered; October 9th set for passing sentence.

United States vs. Elijah Burns; defendant arraigned; took statutory time to plead.

United States vs. Charles Hawkins; defendant arraigned; entered a plea of guilty; October 9th set for sentence.

The People of the Territory of Utah vs. Bub Fillmore; order dismissing appeal.

Andrew Lindsay, late of Scotland, now of Wasatch County, admitted as a citizen.

Ottemine Frandsen vs. Lars Frandsen; order entered overruling demurrer.

Chris. C. Christensen vs. Peter C. Burrison et al.; order entered dismissing case at plaintiff's cost.

Provo, September 18, 1888.

Utah Enquirer
October 18, 1888

Personal.

We had a pleasant call yesterday, from J. S. Giles, of Holden.

We received a call on Thursday from Wm. Probert of Holden.

Hon. W. N. King of Fillmore is busy in court, and will remain here for the rest of the term.

Judge Heppler, County Clerk Hellstrom and others from Richfield were in attendance before the grand jury on Wednesday. The jury have had under investigation allegations of official malfeasance on the part of the Assessor and Collector of Sevier county.

Territorial Auditor Clayton came in from Salt Lake yesterday to appear before the grand jury, it is supposed for the purpose of giving testimony in connection with the alleged official malfeasance of the Sevier county collector.

Salt Lake Herald
November 14, 1888

Fillmore Co-operative Institution vs. Mary L. C. Holt; in this cause, on motion of W. H. King, counsel for plaintiff, it was ordered that the United States Marshal have one William Beaston, a witness for plaintiff, in this court on November 16th at plaintiff's expense.

People vs. Ed Jones; rape; sentence and hearing of motion for a new trial set for March 2d, 1889.

Salt Lake Herald
November 17, 1888

The First District Court.

AT PROVO.

Fillmore Co-op. Mercantile Institution vs. Mary L. C. Holt; trial by jury; verdict in favor of the plaintiff; damages assessed at $372.30.

C. H. Blomsterberg vs. Wilhelmina Blomsterberg; divorce; trial by the court; still in progress.

Salt Lake Herald
December 28, 1888

CHRISTIAN P. BEAUREGARD, of Fillmore, was released from the Penitentiary yesterday, after having served a term of ninety days for unlawful cohabitation. Bishop A. A. Kimball, of Kanosh, who received a Christmas present from Mr. Cleveland in the shape of a pardon, was released yesterday. He was sentenced a short time ago to a term of eight months for unlawful cohabitation, and was pardoned on account of his ill-health.

Salt Lake Herald
January 5, 1889

THE SUICIDE AT RICHFIELD.

A Correspondent Sheds Some Further Light.

George Crane, of Fillmore, writes THE HERALD as follows: "In the communication from Richfield, headed 'That Suicide,' there are some inaccuracies which I desire to correct, and with your permission add a word or two of information to the deceased's many friends who read your paper:

His name was L. C. Nield, not 'Niels.' He was not 'district school teacher at Meadow, Millard County'; he was the principal of Richfield district school and secretary to the Sunday school superintendency of the Sevier Stake of Zion. He was born at Oldham, Lancashire, England, November 3, 1864; his parents' names are Joseph Merrick and Jane Standing Nield, now residing at Meadow, Millard County. He also had three married sisters, all of whom regarded Charley with the utmost affection, for nature seemed to have cast him in that mould whose quiet, studious disposition excited the respect of all. By his own untiring industry he was enabled to graduate at the Brigham Young Academy with high honors. And he was one in whom education had not destroyed the most filial regard for humble parentage. I might mention men whose names are "household words" in Utah, who have expressed a patronizing regard for the good qualities of young Nield. I will say that the probate judge, prosecuting attorney and others in this county, have made affidavit to the effect that from years of knowledge of this young man, he could not have performed this dreadful act in other than an unsound state of mind.

The truth is, he had made preparations to be married during the Christmas holidays, and the writer has read letters written by him within a few days of the fearful tragedy, breathing a spirit of joyous anticipation. But, alas, 'tis the old, old story; the winged cherub had mockingly dipped his arrow in gall, and its sudden flight had pierced his reason, as suddenly developing latent hereditary insanity, and transforming a gentle, loving boy into a strong and nerveless maniac. That the deceased was held in high esteem in Sevier County, was attested by Mr. Hayes, the principal of the Richfield Academy, also Mr. Hagge, the district school teacher at Elsinore. These gentlemen accompanied the body to Meadow.

I do not write in defense of the dreadful crime of self-murder, but at the wish of "hearts bowed down" and as an advocate of facts, without flattery, even at the tomb.

Utah Enquirer
January 25, 1889

Writing from Fillmore under date of
January 19th, Mr. J. E. Hickman, principal of the Millard Stake Academy,
says: "We opened the present term on
the 7th of this month, with ninety-six
students, and are expecting more in a
few days. In order to get through with
all classes, some recitations have to be
held from 8 a. m. without intermission,
excepting changing classes, until 4:30
p. m. Snow is about ten inches deep,
and still snowing. People enjoy good
spirits and there is no sickness. There
have been but three deaths in the last
four months."

Salt Lake Herald
February 9, 1889

WILLIAM BEESTON, of Fillmore, was
released from the Penitentiary yesterday, having served his four months'
sentence and an additional thirty days
in lieu of the fine imposed.

Salt Lake Herald
April 11, 1889

Fillmore city vs. Gabriel Huntsman; suit dismissed, costs to be paid by plaintiff.

Salt Lake Herald
April 14, 1889

IN THE SIGNAL OFFICE.

Sergeant Fitzmaurice on the Pacific Slope Rainfall.

The observer, having called the attention of the chief signal officer to the criticisms on the "rainfall of the Pacific slope and the western states and territories" recently published, has been enformed by the signal office that the following explanation can be made in order to avoid any erroneous conclusions that may arise in the minds of those who may examine the paper. The stations of the signal service being too far apart to give anything like an adequate idea of the amount of rainfall throughout the country, the signal office must rely to a great extent on reports furnished by voluntary observers, co-operating with though not belonging to the service, and while the signal office is entirely responsible for the preparation of this publication, except as to typographical and clerical errors arising from copying and computing, still, it must be borne in mind that this publication is almost entirely the summarization of the reports of these observers, for the accuracy of which the signal office cannot vouch, the records being taken as submitted by the observers. A careful examination of the paper will render these facts apparent. Little is known of the rainfall in the region of Fillmore and Mount Carmel. The records are published as made and may be erroneous.

The chief signal officer would be glad to receive supplementary data or other information tending to establish the correctness or incorrectness of the published record.

A number of typographical errors have been discovered in the work, the most noteworthy being one giving the maximum annual rainfall at Salt Lake city as 38.20 in 1886, which should be 38.20 in 1876.

P. H. FITZMAURICE,
Sergt. Signal Corps.

Salt Lake Herald
May 3, 1889

DEPUTY registration officers have been appointed by the Utah commissioner as follows: Louis Hyams vice E. R. Kneass, for the Fifth precinct, Salt Lake city; John C. Kelly vice John Kelly, for Fillmore precinct, Millard county; Abraham Fawson vice Amos Fenstermake, for Grantsville precinct, Tooele county; Lorenzo Snow, Jr., for Box Elder precinct, Box Elder county.

Salt Lake Herald
May 16, 1889

REPORTS from all parts of the Territory over the Deseret Telegraph company's lines stated that at noon yesterday rain was falling all the way from Cache valley in the north to Fillmore in the south and the prospects were favorable for the storm's extending to the southern boundary. These heavy spring rains have been of more value to the Territory than anything that could have happened.

Utah Enquirer
June 7, 1889

Personal.

W. H. Liter of P. V. Junction was seen on the streets to-day.

President H. H. Cluff is in Salt Lake.

We had a pleasant call from Prof J. E. Hickman, Principal of the Fillmore Stake Academy, on Wednesday.

Mr. J. L. Davis, editor of the Pueblo *Daily Press*, left Provo for Pueblo on Wednesday.

Salt Lake Herald
June 8, 1889

Other Business.

The only other business before the Supreme court yesterday was the case of Fillmore city vs. Gabriel Huntsman, which was argued and submitted.

Salt Lake Herald
June 9, 1889

FILLMORE CITY VS. HUNTSMAN.

An opinion was also delivered in this case. The plaintiff secured an injunction forbidding the defendant from constructing a ditch so close to the one owned by the city of Fillmore as to endanger its safety; and also restraining the defendant from obstructing travel on the streets. The action of the court below in granting an injunction was appealed from. The opinion is given given below.

Appeal from the Provo decision of the First district.

The findings of fact in this case by the trial court are well sustained by the proof.

The decree is in accordance with the law, with the following modifications: The defendant will be allowed to construct and maintain his dam and ditch if and when he shall, by the construction of walls, poles and supports, keep and hold the lower wall of the Fillmore city ditch in a good and safe condition, so as to avoid its damage by reason of the existence of his ditch below it. This condition of things he must continue to maintain as well as construct. To this extent the injunction is modified. The injunction as to the streets of the town is so modified as to allow the defendant to flow his water in his ditch provided he do no damage to said streets by the water. The cause is remanded to the court below, where a decree will be entered in conformity to this opinion.

REPORT

Of the Closing Term of the Millard Stake Academy.

To the Hon. Board:

GENTLEMEN:—For the third time I am able to present the labors of the students for your consideration. As heretofore we have had two departments; viz:Preparatory and Advanced. The Preparatory consisted of fourth and fifth reader grades. The Advanced included the intermediate, academic and normal grades. In the Preparatory department, classes have been carried on according to the following programme: Theology, grammar, arithmetic, reading, geography, hygiene, penmanship, orthography and ladies work. The Advanced has been as follows: Theology, grammar, arithmetic, elocution, geography, physiology, penmanship, orthography, bookkeeping. Latin, algebra, normal theory, and ladies work. Following recitations were held daily: Theology A and B; arithmetic A, B, C, D, E and F; grammar A, B, and C; fourth and fifth readers and elocution, elementary, standard and physical geography; hygiene; physiology; penmanship classes A B and C; orthography A and B; bookkeeping A, B and C; algrebra; normal theory and ladies work. In order that this extensive programme could be gone through with six of the normals had to each teach a class daily, which would make a total number of classes daily, 33; 165 weekly; or a total of 1650 recitations a term. Aside from these classes, special recitations have been held nearly every evening for the benefit of students desirous of further information on subjects then at hand. As before, Miss Lawisch has had charge of the preparatory and ladies' department. I have had charge of Intermediate, Academic and Normal students. There have been theological quorums held every Monday evening. We have held no priesthood meetings this term as there were only four or five who held the priesthood. But faculty meetings were held weekly, at which teachers and normal students teaching classes met and considered matters for the good of the Academy and where the necessary instructions to Normals acting as teachers was given. The last hour every Wednesday afternoon was devoted to the students, during which time, they gave addresses on theology from the Bible and Book of Mormon, essays, songs, recitations, readings and asking of theological questions. Although we had but few students yet they took a great interest in their studies and theological meetings.

We had no domestic department as there were only ten domestic students and I took it upon myself to visit all of them and also most of the students, from Fillmore.

I feel to thank the normals that have taught classes this term, as they have tried and succeeded in making their classes interesting.

Thanks are due to Brother O. W. Andelin and Nellie Hinkley for the pains they have taken in the choir and singing class. I feel grateful to all members of the choir for their good singing.

Students have been tabulated as follows: Lemington, 2; Deseret, 3; Meadow Creek, 1; Kanosh, 3; Sanpete County, 1; Utah County 1, and Fillmore, 39; making a total of 49 students this term.

There have been 120 students registered during the present year. But we closed up to-day with 29 students. Although comparatively few, yet this number is more than three times greater than we began with. I can not just now call up any circumstance that has been of a very serious nature during the whole year, for, which I feel very thankful. The earnest labors of students have been greatly appreciated by the teachers. I had the occasion during the term to make the remark that almost any student could start into school, but it took a hero to remain to the end. I am happy to say we have so many heroes to close up with to-day. We gratefully acknowledge two presents, given to the Academy, by Elder Powell and Bishop Callister.

In conclusion I will say that God has made His hand manifest in this Academy during the whole year and my earnest prayer is that He may ever bless this institution and all that pertains to it, and the people of this county that they will ever be ready to aid this institution, that it may become a beacon light of this western country.

J. E. HICKMAN, Principal.

The Injunction Modified.

In the case of Fillmore City vs. Gabriel Huntsman, Judge Judd read the following brief opinion in the Territorial Supreme Court Saturday last, against the defendant in regard to the construction and maintainance of his water ditch and dams:

The findings of fact in this case by the trial Court are well sustained by the proof. The decree is in accordance with the law, with the following modifications: The defendant will be allowed to construct and maintain his dam and ditch when he shall by the construction of wall, props and supports keep and hold the town wall of the Millville city ditch in as good and safe condition so as to avoid its damage by reason of the existence of his ditch below it. This condition of things he must continue to maintain, as well as construct. To this extent the injunction is modified. The injunction as to the streets of the town is so modified as to allow the defendant to flow his water in his ditch provided he do no damage to said streets by the water. The case is remanded to the Court below where a decree will be entered in conformity to this opinion.

Salt Lake Herald
June 18, 1889

BENJAMIN PERKINS, of Rabbit valley; Andrew Anderson, Grass valley; John T. Covington, Orderville; Cornelius McRevy, Washington; James H. Langford, Circle valley; Carl Olsen, Mayfield; Soren Jacobsen, Bountiful, and Charles Frampton, of Fillmore, were all released from the penitentiary yesterday.

Salt Lake Herald
June 26, 1889

HON. WILL KING, late of Fillmore, now of Provo, was encountered on the street yesterday and asked who he thought would fill the Fillmore seat in the next legislature. He said it was as yet a question, but he thought Mr. Melville's chances were good. Asked as to politics in Provo and Utah county, and whether he would be a candidate from there, Mr. King was somewhat evasive, stating that he didn't know that he had resided there long enough to be eligible. He didn't think there was much life in the local Democratic party and wouldn't be surprised to see Sam Thurman sent up to the council or house from that section.

Salt Lake Herald
June 30, 1889

THE coming week will be a lively one throughout the territory in a political sense, as will be seen by the various calls published in THE HERALD, with primaries, conventions, etc. Some of the outlying districts have already held their conventions. At Nephi, on the 26th, J. A. Melville, of Fillmore, was nominated for representative to the legislature from the Nineteenth district. The following special dispatch to THE HERALD explains itself: "Toquerville, Utah, June 29.—The delegates of the Twenty-fourth representative district and Twelfth council district met here to-day and nominated William T. Stewart, of Kane county, to the house of representatives, and Robert C. Lund, of St. George, Washington county, councilor to the twenty-ninth legislative assembly of Utah."

Salt Lake Herald
August 22, 1889

THE OFFICIAL COUNT.

Result of the Labors of the Canvassing Board.

FROM ALL THE COUNTIES.

The Total Vote from the Precincts of Nineteen Counties—Five More to Hear From.

The canvassing board for the recent territorial election has been at work for several days on the returns from the various counties. The result of their labors shows the total vote of the various precincts as given below:

BEAVER COUNTY.

Adamsville	17
Beaver	137
Greenville	98
Grampton	17
Minersville	45
Star	15
	277

BOX ELDER COUNTY.

Box Elder	194
Bear River	43
Call's Fort	49
Curlew	13
Deweyville	36
Grouse Creek	15
Malad	54
Mantua	55
Kelton	6
Park Valley	15
Plymouth	24
Promontory	14
Portage	34
Terrace	18
Willard	75
	358

CACHE COUNTY.

Benson	16
Clarkston	25
Coveville	30
Hyde Park	42
Hyrum	107
Logan	700
Lewiston	38
Millville	50
Mendon	39
Paradise	69
Peterboro	11
Providence	45
Richmond	67
Smithfield	88
Trenton	36
Wellsville	55
Newton	30
	1,080

GARFIELD COUNTY.

312

Cannonville	21
Escalante	55
Hillsdale	13
Panguitch	61
Coyote	15
	175

IRON COUNTY.

Cedar	69
Kanarra	22
Paragoonah	33
Parowan	75
Summit	9
	218

JUAB COUNTY.

Levan	33
Mona	39
Nephi	292
Juab	23
Eureka	212
Silver City	29
Mammoth Poll	65
	729

KANE COUNTY.

Glendale	36
Johnson	6
Kanab	40
Mt. Carmel	21
Orderville	24
Pahreah—(No returns)	
Upper Kanab	22
Georgetown	7
	156

DAVIS COUNTY.

1,080

Centerville	49
Bountiful	97
Farmington	72
Kaysville	73
South	63
South Hooper	26
South Weber	27
West Weber	33
Layton	60
Syracuse	18
	518

EMERY COUNTY.

Blake	20
Castle Dale	11
Cleveland	21
Ferron	30
Huntington	18
Lawrence	3
Moab	9
Molen	18
Muddy	25
Orangeville	43
Price	44
Schofield	60
Wellington	10
	312

MILLARD COUNTY.

156

Oasis	21
Deseret	44
Fillmore	73
Holden	42
Kanosh	41
Leamington	17
Meadow	18
Oak Creek	16
Scipio	57
Smithville—(No returns)	
Burbank	18
	347

MORGAN COUNTY.

Cañon Creek	47
Croyden	19
Milton	58
Morgan	77
Peterson	21
	192

PIUTE COUNTY.

Beaver Creek	13
Bullion	16
Burgess	5
Circle Valley	95
Deer Trail	7
Fremont	25
Graves Valley	6
Kane	10
Koosharem	28
Teasdale	13
Pleasant Creek	11
Wilmot	4
Junction	28
Lou	36
	218

SALT LAKE COUNTY.

139

Salt Lake City—		
First Precinct, Poll 1	427	
First Precinct, Poll 2	374	
Second Precinct, Poll 1	725	
Second Precinct, Poll 2	504	
Third Precinct, Poll 1	385	
Third Precinct, Poll 2	348	
Fourth Precinct, Poll 1	554	
Fifth Precinct, Poll 1	479	
Fifth Precinct, Poll 2	352	4,148
Big Cottonwood		72
Butler		33
Brighton		58
Bluff Dale		18
East Mill Creek		38
Farmer's		43
Granite		25
Granger		48
Hunter		27
Little Cottonwood		43
Mill Creek		181
Mountain Dell		12
North Point		19
North Jordan		69
Pleasant Green		43
Riverton		34
South Cottonwood		215
Silver		5
Sugar House		81
Sandy		124
South Jordan		47
West Jordan		139
Fort Herriman		18
Union		73
Bingham		162
Draper		115
		5,860

SANPETE COUNTY.

5,860

Chester	18
Ephraim	156
Fayette	33
Fountain Green	71
Fairview	96
Gunnison	102
Mayfield	59
Manti	142
Moroni	95
Mt. Pleasant	177
Petty	34
Spring	90
Thistle	9
Wales	38

Winter Quarters	4
Wilburn	18
	1,102

SAN JUAN.

Bluff	11
Montecello	10
McElmo—(No returns)	
Buena—(No returns)	
	21

SEVIER COUNTY.	
Annabella	21
Burrville	22
Central	21
Elsinore	42
Gooseberry	15
Glenwood	53
Joseph	43
Monroe	68
Redmond	36
Salina	76
Vermillion	28
Willow Bend	25
Richfield	122
	522

SUMMIT COUNTY.	
Coalville	177
Echo	33
Grass Creek	8
Hennefer	47
Camas	65
Peoa	41
Park City	818
Hoytsville	57
Rockport	21
Upton	32
Woodland	33
Wanship	41
Parley's Park	31
	1,365

TOOELE COUNTY.	
Batesville	14
Clover	16
Deep Creek	28
Grantsville	102
Mill	29
Lake View	24
Ophir	35
St. John	15
Stockton	47
Tooele	143
Vernon	20
Quincy	4
	489

UINTAH COUNTY.	
Mountain Dell	21
Ashley	79
Brown's Park—(No returns)	
Riverdale	40
Vernal	88
	278

UTAH COUNTY.	
American Fork	181
Benjamin	51
Cedar Fort	17
Fairfield	43
Goshen	55
Lehi	209
Lake Shore	42
Lake View	61
Payson	206
Pleasant Grove	328
Provo Bench	33
P. V. Junction	16
Provo	489
Spanish Fork	255
Santaquin	94
Springville	313
Salem	64
Spring Lake	11
Thistle	13
Alpine	61
	2,546

WASATCH COUNTY.	
Charleston	48
Heber	163
Midway	51
Wallsburg	25
	287

Utah Enquirer
September 20, 1889

Mr. Edward T. Olson, on his return to Ogden from his former home, Fillmore, stopped off at "The Garden City" to-day. Mr. Olson is a very popular young gentleman. As a B Flat cornetist he has no superior in Utah. Professionally he is the boss telegraph operator in the territory, having been engaged in railroad offices for many years. Mr. Olson has a very exalted view of our beautiful city, and thinks somewhat of locating in the place. He will certainly find a cordial welcome to the social and musical circles of Provo.

Mr. Wm. Grimsdell, late foreman of

THE DUTRIE TRIAL.

The Evidence Coming In Thick and Fast.

GRIM AND GHASTLY DETAILS.

What a Shotgun will Do When Properly Charged with Buckshot—Other Proceedings of the Court.

Following is the continuation of Preston's testimony in the Dutrie case, which was broken into by the departure of the mail on Monday evening:

About Dutrie had told the witness that if he touched the water he would kill him.

Cross-examination by Mr. Dickson—First learned of Treffles Dutrie's patent on part of the land he fenced after the killing. Commenced cutting hay on Dutrie's land about the 17th of July. On the 18th started hauling hay. Had hauled one load when the Dutrie boys cut the fence and came in to haul hay. No remarks passed between them. Both parties had guns. Wife of Preston was along with him to hold his gun while he loaded hay. Saw the Dutries going off about dark that evening. Had no understanding that they were to be at the cabin that night. Did not know of Noakes being outside of his house until awakened by his wife. Noakes came in and it was proposed that they go down and get the horses.

The testimony of the witness at the examination before the justice was read to contradict him here. The impeachment of the witness was the object of Mr. Dickson's cross-examination throughout.

Witness said he took his pistol from custom. Noakes was about twenty-five yards ahead when witness stopped to spread the quilt. Noakes was not so far from the cabin. Shots came from the east side of the cabin. Noakes had rubber overshoes.

Eliza A. Preston—Was in the field with my husband hauling hay. Hiram Carter and her husband were there. Saw Dutrie boys getting into the field. They were at the gate and armed. Alex came into the field, and soon after drew his gun on witness, and said: "You'd better get out of there." Witness hurried down in the field where her husband and Carter were. Preston hauled two loads of hay and the Dutries three that day. Noakes had nothing to do with the land. Defendants worked on the house that day. About sundown the work ceased. My husband and the boy that was sleeping in the tent near by were the only men there. Thomas Noakes came to our house that night about 11 o'clock. He spoke to the boy Carter. I awoke my husband and told him Tom was there. He was let in and got a drink of water. Tom said he understood the Frenchmen had cut the fence, and was afraid his horses would get out. He said he would go and sleep down in the trail to keep his horses back. Noakes had overshoes on that night. He had left his boots at our place because they were worn out and full of holes. He had sent for new boots, and they came Sunday, after he was killed. In about five minutes I heard quite a volley of shots and my husband came back. We then bundled up our things and left the house. After we got out I heard a single shot. We went over to Smith's ranch. It was moonlight, but clouds would sometimes hide its face. We met two Indians on the way, named Tintin and Nimrod. Their camp was not far away. They went with us part of the way. We talked about the shooting. We didn't go back to our own place again for nine months.

Cross-examined by Mr. Dickson—The Indians we met had two pistols and a gun. There was a spring near our house, and Noakes knew where it was. His only business seemed to be to get a drink of water and to say that he was going to sleep in the field near the trail. My husband said, "Wait a minute and I will go with you. Noakes went in the tent and got a quilt. On the 19th my husband took a rifle down in the field with him. My husband was loading in one part of the field and the Dutries in another. He (my husband) took a pistol with him down in the field. I don't know whether Noakes was armed or not. I didn't see my husband take a pistol, but heard him say he had one. The rifle was in the house that night.

Mr. Bachman, the clerk of the court—I have a pistol that I got from Mr. Earl. It is in the same condition now as when I got it. The weapon was submitted in evidence.

Mr. George Bishop testified—I reside in Snake valley, Millard county. On the night of the 20th of July, 1888, I met an Indian, who first told me of the shooting. This was before I saw my daughter. I went to look for the body. I called to Dutrie. He replied to come along and without arms. I said I wanted to find the body of Noakes. He said if I went to look for the body they would shoot me too. They, all three of defendants, were armed. They kept me there. About one hour after sunrise I said I am going to hunt Noakes. I found him near the cabin lying on his back. His clothes were unbuttoned and there was a single bullet shot near his heart. A six shooter was lying by him. He had thirteen buck shot in his bowels. His right leg was shot all to pieces, just above the knee. That wound was done with shot. I gave the pistol to Mr. Earl. There was no empty shell in the pistol. I said then, "Tom Noakes never shot." Trif Dutrie said, "No, he never shot." Right away after that, Alex said, "My God, he was close to me when I shot him." Triffy said, "Keep still." I found a pistol, a quilt and a hat not far away. That pistol was also loaded all around. I saw blood on the body. I examined the body at the inquest. The buckshot wounds were sloping down. So was the bullet wound.

Mr. Dickson said he would cross-examine this witness in the morning, and at 5:30 the jury took a walk and Richard Brampton, a son of Bavaria, came forward and applied for citizenship. His honor greeted him with a smile and a word of cheer, and quizzed him gently as to his knowledge of our country and its ways. They were ruled by an Emperor where he came from, and so were we here, he said. He now lived in Lehi, which is in Provo county, he thought. He was told to go home and learn something.

The court adjourned.

This morning, October 1, court was opened with the usual "Hear ye! Hear ye!" at 9:30 o'clock. After the reading of the journal, John W. Jackson was arraigned for adultery, and was allowed till 2 o'clock to plead. Josiah F. Gibbs, arraigned on the same charge, was allowed the same time.

Peter Wimmer, who lives in Iron county, through his attorney, Mr. King, asked for a continuance till next term, as his wife was very ill.

The Dutrie murder case was taken up, and Mr. Bishop continued—Triffy Dutrie asked me if there wasn't an empty shell in the pistol. I saw no evidences of a struggle where the body lay.

Cross-examined by Mr. Dickson—I found an empty shell in the pistol some time afterward. Witness had never shot a pistol or gun in his life, and when he was handed the deadly weapon, which was still loaded, he handled it in a manner to make all cringe. The defendants, when I went to the cabin, were prepared, apparently, to attack anybody who came. Witness said at one time offered to fight Alex Dutrie for $25. Was at one time a detective in England, some twenty years ago.

This witness was followed for an hour.

This witness was followed for an hour.

Albert Earl testified—I was at home till 12 o'clock, the night of the 20th of July, 1888, when I was awakened by Preston. Just before daylight, went down to the cabin. Bishop came out and met us. The defendants were all there. I looked in the cabin after daylight. There was no floor except enough to make their bed upon. The day was breaking when we reached the cabin. About two hours after going there, I saw the body of Noakes. During that time we were all near the cabin. The defendants were all armed. I said I had heard of the shooting, and came up to look for the body. Put me said when other parties came we might look for the body. He made no threats to me. Triffy said he had a right there and would maintain his rights if he had to fight for them. There was but little conversation there about the killing. We found the body near the house lying on the back, straight out. The body had a pair of overalls and a shirt and vest on. His pants and overalls were unbuttoned and his hands were lying across his abdomen. His pistol was lying by his left side. It was clean. The belt was lying straight out from the body on either side. His hands, face and clothes in front were covered with dust. There were tracks about the body. They were boot tracks evidently. The track from the body toward the cabin. There were also tracks below the body, toward the trail. When we went to look for the body Triffy said it wasn't necessary to look for it. It was there. I examined the wounds. Witness' description of the wounds didn't differ from the previous witness. Bishop picked up the pistol and handed it to me. I gave it to the clerk of this court. It wasn't changed while I had it. I heard some of the parties there when we found the body say: "No, he (deceased) didn't shoot."

To Mr. Dickson: The buckshot in the body were all close together. I saw no blood on or around the body. When we put the body in the wagon the blood poured out of the back. I saw no tracks there as if made by overshoes such as deceased had on.

Bishop was recalled for further cross-examination, and some of his testimony in the last trial was read to him, and he was asked to reconcile it with what he had to-day testified to.

James Preston—I live in Snake valley, near the scene of the trouble. Before the shooting, in June, I think, I heard Treffy Dutrie say in the presence of Alex, that he had advice in the matter, and said he meant to kill both of them and would use shot gun law. I didn't testify to this in the former trial, because you shut me off. Alex said, "I am sorry I didn't kill the other one when I had him up the creek." I told my brother, but didn't tell him the exact language the Dutries used.

Alonzo Lyman, of Fillmore, testified—I am engaged in stock business. I know the defendants. I was present at a conversation at Dutrie's ranch before the shooting, when Alex said he had laid in the brush waiting for Preston to come in sight, that he might blow him up. I was working for the Dutrie boys at that time.

At 1:15, when court opened, Robert Edward pleaded not guilty to the crime of grand larceny.

The Dutrie trial being resumed, the land office receipt of filing the declaratory statement on the land in dispute was given in evidence. A party bearing the economic name of Wise Cooper, testified. I know Thos. Noakes. I saw the body after the death. Was one of the jurors at the inquest. Deceased was shot in the left breast near the heart. The shot ranged downwards. Have had some experience with firearms. Buckshot are fired from shot-guns, if they chamber they will be delivered close together, otherwise, not. If you have a good gun twenty-five yards distant, the shot will hold together.

Cross-examined—The shot in the leg were all near together. A good shot-gun at twenty-five yards will scatter over a space of a foot.

This case was broken into and John W. Jackson was arraigned for adultery. He pleaded guilty and stood for sentence. He married his second wife six years ago. He expected to live within the law. He was given ten months and costs.

Josiah F. Gibbs, for the same charge pleaded guilty, and will be sentenced the 10th inst.

On motion of Mr. Varian an indictment for unlawful cohabitation against J. W. Jackson was dismissed.

Again resuming the Dutric trial, R. A. Bridges, a farmer and stock-raiser from Sevier county, was called—Knew Noakes in his lifetime. One of his ankles was injured. He was knock-kneed and pigeon-toed. He was a straight man.

D. C. Reed, from Deseret, was in the Snake valley country at the time of the killing. I was on the coroner's jury. I was at Alex. Dutric's cabin, and saw Patnode there. He said Preston ran from the house down on the flat. He was near the trail when he started to run.

Mr. Earl was recalled, and said to Mr. Dickson that the shot in the knee was on the front and toward one side.

Mrs. Carter was next called—On the 21st of July, 1888, the defendant called at our camp for dinner. There was a conversation about the killing. Defendant said to my husband, "Well, Joe, we've got your partner." I asked Dutric where they were going to bury him. He said, "I don't care, so long as they don't bury him on my land," and Patnode said, "Burn the s— of a b—; that is good enough for him."

The grand jury came into court at 2:20, with an armfull of papers. The foreman reported that two of their number were sick in bed and could not be present.

In the case of C. C. Curtis and Romorel, the jury had ignored the charge.

The United States vs. H. O. Hansen was ignored; also the People against Christian A. Madsen.

Mr. F. C. Jensen, one of the sick men, was excused and R. H. Dodd was sworn in to fill the panel.

The following cases were ignored: The People vs. George Houtz et al., John Devereau, Henry Kelbow and others. United States vs. Hans O. Hansen, Albert Singleton and Christian A. Madsen. They reported having found four United States and one territorial indictment.

In the Dutric case Mr. Reed was recalled—Was in presence of Patnode and he gave me an account of the shooting. He showed us the place of the shooting. He said Noakes was ahead and come up and Preston was behind. He said he was looking out of the window for Preston. He said if Preston hadn't run they would have gotten him. Patnode said Noakes called for water after he was down and said: "Take me down on the meadow and don't let me die here." This was a day or two after the killing. I may have made some mistake in my testimony. Mr. Dickson used the testing of this witness at the previous trial against him with telling effect, as he did with all the witnesses when they varied an an iota from their testimony at that time.

Cropper recalled—I heard Patnode say, "Preston ran like a s—of a b— or I'd have got him too." He said Preston was behind the bushes near by.

With this testimony the prosecution rested. It is understood the court will adjourn for the week after this case to allow its officers to attend the fair and conference(?).

Real Estate Transfers.

The following real estate transfers have been made during the last few days:

To Read Smoot, the property on Centre street known as the "Church lots." Price paid, $3,000. It is the intention of Mr. Smoot to lay the sidewalks around this property with asphalt, and next season to erect a three-story brick business block on it.

To R. H. Dodd, the James Smith property on Centre Street.

To V. L. Halliday, the Buckley store on Centre Street,

To Cid Southworth, the Glenfield property on Centre Street, west of Hines' drug store, and a portion of that opposite the EXQUIRER office. Price, $7,000.

To Mr. Holbrook, of Salt Lake city, the Excelsior Hotel. Price, $10,000.

To J. L. Robinson of Fillmore, the George Sutherland residence on Centre street. Price $3,600.

Thad Flemming, vacant lot, $1,300.

Provo Co-op. to a company (consisting of S. R. Thurman, L. Holbrook, V. L. Halliday and J. F. Gates) the price of now vacant land east of the East Co-op., 56x75, for $7000.

Territorial Supreme Court.

The session of the Territorial Supreme Court was set for 2 o'clock this afternoon, but it was 2:35 when the four judges came in.

The minutes of the last session were read.

Judge Zane announced the appointment, as United States Commissioners, of E. C. Valle, of Fillmore, Millard County, and David L. Hills, of Uintah County.

Ex-Governor West and Messrs. Barton and Zipf were admitted to the bar.

In the case of Alex. Toponce vs. the Corinne M. C. & S. Co., a motion for an extension of time was submitted by defendants and appellants, and argued. The time asked for was granted.

Mr. Varian asked that, in the case of Pardon Dodds, convicted of manslaughter and liberated under a suspension of sentence by Judge Judd, the Supreme Court ordered Judge Blackburn to pass sentence, or failing to do so, to show cause on the first day of the January term why judgment had not been passed. Mr Varian's request was granted.

P. L. Williams submitted a communication from Receiver Dyer, asking instruction in regard to leasing a coal mine in which the Church held a half interest.

Court adjourned till Dec. 16, at 2 p.m.

The Supreme Court.

The Supreme court had a brief session yesterday, when the following business was transacted.

Judge Zane announced the appointment, as United States commissioners, of E. C. Vaile, of Fillmore, Millard county, and David L. Hills, of Uintah county.

Ex-Governor West and Messrs. Barton and Zipf were admitted to the bar.

In the case of Alex. Toponce vs. the Corinne M. C. & S. Co., a motion for an extension of time was submitted by the defendants and appellants, and argued. The time asked for was granted.

Mr. Varian asked that, in the case of Pardon Dodds, convicted of manslaughter and liberated under a suspension of sentence by Judge Judd, the Supreme court order Judge Blackburn to pass sentence, or failing to do so, to show cause on the first day of the January term why judgment had not been passed. Mr. Varian's request was granted.

P. L. Williams submitted a communication from Receiver Dyer, asking instruction in regard to leasing a coal mine in which the church owned a half interest.

Court adjourned till December 16, at 2 p. m.

Millard Stake Conference.

The quarterly conference of this Stake was held at Fillmore, Nov. 24th and 25th. Present, Apostles F. M. Lyman and Abraham H. Cannon, of the local authorities, President Ira N. Hinckly, and most of the High Council. The attendance was large, and much valuable instruction was given by the speakers. Apostles F. M. Lyman and A. H. Cannon addressed the conference on the subjects of charity, and the education of our children in all stages—physically, mental, morally and religiously, and tithing, and the order of the Priesthood. The regular Priesthood meeting, was held on Sunday evening, with a good attendance. The general and local authorities were presented and unanimously sustained. The reports of the Bishops of the various wards showed a spirit of improvement among the people.

After the meeting on Monday afternoon, Apostles Lyman and Cannon, in company with the Stake presidency and others, went to Meadow Ward and assembled with the Saints.

On Tuesday morning, at 10 o'clock, meeting convened at Kanosh Ward, for the purpose of electing a Bishop, which was done by unanimous consent. Brother Jesse Hopkinson was the choice of the people.

At 2 o'clock a meeting was called of all the members of the ward. Brother Jesse Hopkinson was sustained as Bishop and Brother C. P. Christiansen as First and James Gardner as Second Counselor.

At 4 o'clock we left for Fillmore, and at 2 o'clock on Wednesday held a meeting at Deseret, when Vorgie Kelly was presented as First Counselor to Bishop Jos. S. Black. Brother Kelly was unanimously sustained.

Some important questions were answered by Apostle F. M. Lyman upon the duties and callings of Presidents of Stakes, High Councilors, Bishops and other officers of the Priesthood.

Meeting adjourned at 4 p.m.

C. ANDERSON,
Stake Clerk.

FILLMORE FACTS.

The weather king has been raging wildly down here for several weeks. Hills and valleys are covered with an abundance of snow. Sleighing is splendid; better than it has been for years, and the young people are taking advantage of it. The farmers smile at the prospects of plenty of water.

The holidays have been a season of unalloyed pleasure, participated in by the young and old. The Home Dramatic club, organized this winter, appeared before the public in "Time and the Hour" and "Damon and Pythias," and were greeted with full houses, the latter especially being a great success. Miss Eva Olsen as Hermion, and Mr. J. A. Melville as Damon, in the scene where Damon bids his wife and child farewell, was admirably executed.

The Millard Stake academy, after a two weeks' vacation, is running again. Students from far and near and flocking in, numbering 150 at present and more are expected.

Our community is enjoying good health, as a whole. There are only a few cases of sore throat reported. Two small children succumbed to this disease last week.

Over the frosty covering of the earth could be heard the merry jingle of the wedding bells. Several of our young people have agreed to travel the road of life jointly. We wish them success and happiness on their journey.

It has been rumored that we are to have a railroad down this way and collections for this purpose have been started. We will hail the iron horse with joy. Some of the young people are anxiously waiting for its appearance, as they say the road to matrimony (Manti) will be traveled more easily.

The CHRISTMAS HERALD has been greatly appreciated by all its recipients. The choice and select reading matter it contained was perused with pleasure. We hope and wish for THE HERALD's success in future years as in the past.

X. Y. Z.

Fillmore Findings.

During the past few weeks Fillmore and the surrounding country have received more snow than at any previous season, and the farmers smile, seeing in their mind's eye the heaped granaries that next harvest will bring, and stock men, though lamenting the loss of their cattle, etc., live in hopes of retrieving the ranges the long drouth has driven them from. The present prospects are that our desert will yet blossom as the rose.

For some time there has been a dark cloud of trouble hanging over Fillmore which has caused a number of the people to mourn the loss of their children, who have been carried away by a disease resembling diphtheria but not so fatal. The destroyer has been partially checked in his disastrous work, and the people rejoice in the mercy of their God, for a silver lining is now seen to the dreaded cloud.

The M. S. Academy has never before seen such a prosperous season, and the 150 students who have come from four counties and two territories and one state, to attend the academy are zealous in their endeavors to store their minds with useful knowledge. The academy is working a reformation among the young in this part of the vineyard and improving society in general.

The Polysophical society (an appendage to the academy) is made interesting and beneficial by lectures given by those who are able to handle their subjects intelligently.

In the darkest hour of our affliction, the students and teachers of the academy fasted and prayed in behalf of the afflicted and much good was accomplished.

The pleasant weather makes the boys' muscles feel vigorous, and athletic sports takes the place of indoor amusements.

Our mutual county conference assembled here Saturday and Sunday and the reports of the presidents of the various associations are that everything is in a prosperous condition.

A. H.

FILLMORE, February 6, 1890.

TERRITORIAL TOPICS.

The Recent Municipal Election Held at Kaysville.

A DREAD DISEASE AT FILLMORE.

Some Social Events—Theatrical Entertainments—The Millard Stake Academy—Heber Happenings.

The snow has almost entirely disappeared. The warm rays of the sun reminds one very much of spring.

The sugar famine is materially felt here, our merchants not being able to supply the demand.

Dr. Hodges, dentist of Salt Lake city, has been staying here for the last few days.

Prof. Alexander, phrenologist, was here last week, and delivered a series of lectures. He also examined the craniums of a large number of our citizens, and we are pleased to say we have material for making lawyers, doctors and congressmen in abundance.

The ball given at the academy on Thursday eve was a brilliant affair and reflects credit on the committee—O. C. Bennett, F. L. Sheffield, C. Boynton, Minnie Barns and Allie Evans.

The butcher boys are putting up a large amount of ice. The ice this season is a little inferior, it being composed too largely of snow.

Barnes & Layton have made arrangements to have the result of the Salt Lake city election wired to them at different intervals during Monday which will be posted on the bulletin of the saloon.

The social party given by Miss Annie Wade, at the home of her parents last evening, was one of the crowning events of the season. The evening was spent in feasting, games, music, singing, etc., and the young people enjoyed themselves hugely. The donkey game caused a great amount of fun. The whole was a most enjoyable event.

Yesterday was the last day of the second term at the academy. In the morning a very interesting programme was rendered and listened to by quite a number of the parents and friends of the students, who were gratified to see the marked progress being made in that institution of learning.

The municipal election last Monday passed off very quietly. Promptly at one hour after sunrise the judges took their seats and waited for their men. After a weary wait of two hours, in which the political aspect of Salt Lake and other places was freely discussed, the first straggling voter put in an appearance, cast his vote and left. Toward noon it became apparent that certain parties were laboring very hard for the defeat of John Ellison for councilor, and the scratching of tickets that day was unprecedented in our city. Fred Burton was the person that was put up against him and the count showed Fred had a majority of five votes. The rest of the ticket was elected without opposition.

The Johnson Brothers dramatic company appeared here on Monday and Tuesday evenings. On Monday evening they presented the "Creole" to one of the most enthusiastic audiences ever seen here and on Tuesday evening they presented "Better Than Gold" to a much larger, and very appreciative audience. Mr. Aaron Johnson as the Yankee in Cuba was a decided success, and the rest of the company are deserving of great praise for the able manner in which they rendered their parts. The recitations delivered by Moses Johnson and Ella Cluff at the close of the play were also well rendered, and the applause at their close showed how thoroughly they had been enjoyed. The general verdict is, the Johnson Brothers company is the best all round company that ever catered to a Kaysville audience. This is the first time they have appeared here, but we ask them to come again and often, and we will show them by our patronage our appreciation of them.

KAYSVILLE, Feb. 8, 1890.

THE COURT CULLINGS.

What Was Transacted In the District Court.

THE GRAND JURY EMPANELED.

The Settings of United States Criminal Cases — Probate Points — Other Matter.

The examination of grand jurors was in progress when we went to press yesterday afternoon. Soren Sorensen was excused, he being uncertain as to his father's naturalization. J. G. Douglass was also excused, the question of his residence being somewhat mixed.

There were two jurors lacking, and the court ordered four additional names to be drawn from the box, returnable at 9:30 this morning.

The names of the petit jurors were then called. Twenty-nine answered and took their seats. On the Court asking those who wished to be excused to stand up, at least half the number arose. Most of them were permitted to go.

The following names of additional jurors were then drawn from the box:

Philip Beesley, Andrew Robinson, John W. Moore, Sidney Coray, Chas. Samuelson, John Waldermar, Wm. Morgan, John Y. Mason, J. D. Page, D. W. Holdaway, Wm. Bullar, Don C. Robbins, Jas. Clawson, Chas. Covert, Peter Thygersen, Chas. Hamilton, Wm. Young.

The jurors present were severally examined.

John Cook was excused as his opinion on the Edmunds-Tucker law was not as it should be.

The balance of the petit jurors were accepted.

W. G. Williams and Thos. Price natives of Great Britian were not Mormons and did not believe in polygamy. They were admitted to citizenship.

The court was adjourned by the crier until 9:20 oclock Tuesday morning.

Court opened this morning at 9:30 a. m. John J. H. Watson admitted to citizenship. M. W. Molen and Niels Neilson summoned as petit jurors were excused. The grand jury was then completed and stood as follows:

John P. Crosier, Foreman; E. J. Hall, Geo. McLellan, H. A. Clark, Jos. Francom, J. R. Goodwin, C. H. Spink, R. A. Hills, Jr., C. J. Jensen, Jos. Guppee, W. B. Hughes, Moroni Vorhees, John S. Thomas and Alonzo A. Cahoon.

Judge Blackburn then addressed a very moderate charge to the jury which retired and began its labors for the term.

The case of Pleasant Grove vs. John Whitaker, dismissed.

In the case of M. Schwartz vs. Hatel Bros. et al., demurrer withdrawn and forty days allowed to file answer.

A number of cases were called for setting which the prosecution were not prepared to go to trial with this term. Among them was John C. Graham for unlawful cohabitation. This case has been in the courts for a number of years and Mr. King urged in behalf of the defense that it should be brought to trial. Prosecuting attorney Evans stated that the plural wife was on the underground and as long as the defendant was trying to defeat the laws of the United States he would be in favor of holding him over for a hundred years if necessary. No setting of these were made. They will stand over awaiting the pleasure of the prosecuting attorney.

The cases United States vs. the following defendants were passed for the term: William R. May u. c.; F. W. Christensen, misdemeanor; George Gee, u. c.; John C. Graham, u. c.; John D. Page, misdemeanor; E. W. Fox, misdemeanor; Caspar Christensen, misdemeanor; J. L. Peacock, misdemeanor; Nicholas S. Groesback, adultery; William Racker, adultery; S Bradford, u. c.; Levi S. Dunham, adultery.

UNITED STATES CRIMINAL SETTINGS.

The cases of the United States vs. the following defendants were set as follows:

Mads Jorgensen, u. c.; February 20;

Mads Jorgensen, u. c.; February 20; Samuel Linton, u. c. February 20; Geo. Stagg, u. c. April 5; William Sampson, adultery, Feb. 25; Peter Okleberry, adultery, Feb. 21; Peter Wimmer, adultery, Feb. 18; Carl C. A. Christensen, u. c. Feb. 25; W. A. Stewart, u. c. Feb. 28; James Alexander, adultery, Feb. 25.

TERRITORIAL CRIMINAL CALENDAR.

The following settings were made in the cases of the People vs. the following defendants:

Chas. C. Curtis et al., grand larceny, Feb. 19; Anna Marks, assault with a deadly weapon, March 6; Geo. W. Hancock et al., murder, March 17; James Chadwick, grand larceny, Feb. 24; James Chadwick et al (2d case) Feb. 24; James A. Aitkin, arson, March 7.

Cases on appeal were set as follows: Solomon Angell, et al, March 7; Earnest Bullock, March 8; John Bennett, March 8; Anna Marks, March 6; Niels Nielsen, March 10; Geo. Jagers, March 10, and Valentine Acord, Jr., March 10.

Fillmore city vs. Gabriel Huntsman, passed for the term.

American Fork city vs. David H. Kelley, dismissed.

Pleasant Grove vs. John Whittaker, et al; March 10.

Pleasant Grove vs. John Whittaker, stricken from the docket.

Pleasant Grove vs Edith Whittaker, March 10.

Alpine city vs Chester Paddock, March 11.

Mount Pleasant vs. J. B. Hunter, March 11. (two cases.)

Mount Pleasant vs. Bent Rolfson, March 11.

Spanish Fork vs. Aaron Lundquist, March 12.

Richfield vs. William Clark, March 12.

Pleasant Grove vs. Joshua Holman, March 10.

Provo City vs. R. S. Hines, March 13.

Provo City vs J. H. McEwan, March 13.

Springville city vs. Davin Fordonski, March 13.

LAW AND MOTION CALENDAR.

Isaac L Lyons vs. Thomas Davis, passed.

N. Swartz vs. Hatch Bros. et al, demurrer to complaint withdrawn and twenty days allowed to answer.

Kate McNiel vs. B. W. Driggs Jr. et al, demurrer to complaint waived.

Court took a recess untill 2 o'clock.

Salt Lake Herald
February 25, 1890

DEPUTY REGISTRARS APPOINTED.

Deputy registrars, as follows, were appointed by the Utah commission yesterday: P. V. junction, J. W. Coburn. Millard county—Kanosh, Ezra Penney; Meadow, John Stredder; Holden, Nicholas Paul; Scipio, George Monroe; Leamington, C. Oveson; Oak City, George Finlinson; Deseret, William A. Ray; Oasis, Edward Webb; Smithville, W. C. Barry; Burbank, Matt M. Morrisey; Fillmore, John Kelly. Sanpete county—Fairview, J. S. Wing; Mount Pleasant, F. C. Jensen; Milburn, George Zaoriske; Thistle, W. N. Tidwell; Moroni, N. L. Eliason; Fountain Green, James A. Holman; Wales, Henry Lamb; Chester, E. J. Conrad; Spring City, Jacob Johnson; Ephraim, Peter Schwalbe; Manti, E. W. Fox; Petty, Thomas J. Patton; Gunnison, James M. Robbins; Fayette, William M. Scott; Mayfield, Henry Jensen; Winter Quarters, John B. Schimress.

Utah's Former Capital.

The action taken last Friday by the Legislature, in which they appointed a special committee to visit, Fillmore, Utah's old capital, and investigate the title to land formerly belonging to the Territory, has created a great deal of interest in the matter, and the good people of Fillmore are a little unusually exercised regarding it.

It does not appear that the Territory had secured a title to this land any other than the right by possession, or at least when the city was entered, the Territory put in no claim of ownership, consequently the city of Fillmore got the deed. The city now holds a deed for the land, and, by virtue of this, has deeded portions to individuals for building purposes, and some to a school district for a schoolhouse, which is built upon the block, and also to the county of Milliard, which has erected a fine courthouse at a cost of no less than $12.000.

The block set aside for the use of the Territorial capitol and other public buildings contains ten acres, but the city has reduced the original area by deeding out as related.

It may be a question whether the Territory now owns any land in the defunct capital but there is a stone building 45x60 feet that certainly does not belong to Filmore, it is known as the State House, and was put up by the Territory as a wing for a capitol to be enlarged upon with time. Something should be done with this structure and it is a good move made on the part of the present legislature in sending a committee to investigate matters as this property should be disposed of in some way, if still belonging to the Territory.

MR. JACKSON'S CASE.

John Jackson, of Fillmore, was put upon trial for unlawful cohabitation. He was acquitted.

Fred Allesberg made application for citizenship. He was denied that high privilege, however, for the reason that he believed the revelation on celestial marriage to be true. He said he would obey the law in the future, but his honor cut him short by remarking that no person holding such views as he did could be a good citizen.

Peter Okelberry, when called for sentence, said in answer to the question by the court, he had no promises to make and was sentenced to six months and costs of prosecution.

A motion for a new trial in the case of the United States vs. C. C. A. Christensen, recently convicted of unlawful cohabitation, was argued by Mr. Thurman for the defense and resisted by Mr. Varian. It was shown upon affidavit that one of the trial jurors had sat upon the grand jury which found the indictment. A trial de novo was allowed.

Samuel Linton was sentenced for unlawful cohabitation. He promised to obey the law, but said he would prefer not to make any promises as to teaching others to do the same. He was sentenced to three months in the penitentiary and costs of suit.

Mr. King notified the court that a motion for a new trial would be made in the case and asked that defendant be admitted to bail pending the appeal. The motion was allowed and bail was fixed at $2,000.

Mr. Varian called attention to the difficulty of the application of the territorial procedure act to these United States cases. He maintained that as Congress had legislated for these cases, the legislature could not step in and interfere. It was a complicated question he said, and one that had been decided in various ways by the different judges. His honor said until the question came directly before him he would follow the territorial practice.

Nicholas Mulestein pleaded guilty to unlawful cohabitation and will be sentenced April 4.

But four out of the forty-six jurors summoned from Ogden responded, and at 3 o'clock the impaneling of the jury in the McFarlane case was resumed. They were all challenged off by the defense and there are still three vacant chairs. The jury was sent out to further feed upon their own thoughts until three more men can be found who never read the newspapers, who have no opinion on matters in general, and whose minds are like a sheet of white paper as to this case, which may happen to-day.

A motion for a new trial was made in the case against George Jagers, lately convicted for destroying the property of the Provo Cañon road company, in removing a gate and fence that stood as an obstruction to his free passage over this road.

A FOUL SLANDER REFUTED.

On March 18th the chief anti-"Mormon" organ of this city published a communication furnished by its regular Provo correspondent, "Milo Zip," purporting to give the particulars of a case of bestial conduct upon the part of a prominent "Mormon" of Fillmore, known as Dr. North, who, however, is not, we understand, a physician. The writer represented that the county court had placed in charge of Dr. North a demented woman named Webb, that he had been in the habit of occupying her bed with the knowledge and approval of his wife, that she was about to become a mother by him, that she had been ill-fed, ill-clothed and badly cared for, that these facts had been disclosed by an official investigation on the part of the county court, and that the woman had been placed in other hands.

The statement of the foregoing particulars, as it appeared in the paper referred to, was sickening in its grossness and pruriency, and it is noticed in our columns now only because truth and justice so demand. We have been furnished with a statement by George Crane, one of the selectmen of Millard County, to the effect that the article was as false as it was filthy. The facts as given by Mr. Crane are substantially as follows: For eight or nine years Mrs. Webb had lived and been cared for in the family of Dr. North, but for several months prior to March 1st he had been sick and unable to attend to his affairs. Some of Mrs. Webb's friends complained to the probate judge that she was not being properly cared for, since he had been sick, and she was placed in charge of parties at Holden.

At the time this was done there was no rumor of any improper relation between her and Dr. North, but soon afterwards this rumor began to be whispered around. Two of the selectmen of the county, George Crane and D. R. Stevens, and the county clerk, T. C. Callister, made an investigation of the rumor and satisfied themselves that it was false. Next the matter was taken up by the ecclesiastical authorities the church of which Dr. North is a member, and thoroughly investigated by them. Any concealment or compromise of the offense, had it been proven before a Church tribunal, would have been impossible. The guilt of the accused would have been exposed and he would have been excommunicated from the Church, whose members would have felt this to be

the only method of expiating the disgrace his conduct had brought upon it. No religious society in the world more intensely detest such offenses as that which was here charged, than do the Latter-day Saints, and excommunication is the result when such guilt on the part of a member becomes known. This is the utmost extent to which any church can go in this country in the punishment of any offense on the part of a member.

But the ecclesiastical investigation, according to the statement of George Crane, exonerated Dr. North so far as the charge of improper sexual relations with Mrs. Webb was concernd. Incidental to it it was developed that she was not likely to become a mother, and a certificate to this effect from an experienced practitioner was forwarded to us with the statement from which these facts are gathered.

Salt Lake Herald
April 16, 1890

HEBER HUNTSMAN was instantly killed at Fillmore Monday by a horse falling with him.

Deseret Evening News
April 25, 1890

Railroad Notes from Nephi.

Supt. W. W. Riter and Road-master Nickerson, of the U. P., arrived in Nephi yesterday and located the grounds for their engine houses.

Yesterday morning's U. P. express brought to Nephi a gang of Utah, Nevada & California Railroad surveyors. They are now cross-sectioning this city, and deciding on the route for their line. President Tiernan is now cast floating bonds for the construction work, which commences next month.

Messrs. Probert and Holbrook, of

Messrs. Probert and Holbrook, of Provo, and J. E. Ray, of Fillmore, are working like beavers, with the U. P. men, to get them to run their line through Millard County, a vast mineral and agricultural region, taking in the towns of Scipio, Holden, Fillmore (the ancient capital), Meadow, Kanosh, Cove and the Dickert & Myers Sulphur Mills, thence in a direct line with an almost level grade to Beaver and to the coal and iron mines in Iron County. A railroad on the line indicated would pay from the start, and every mile of track laid would open a mine or tap a town.—*Ensign.*

Salt Lake Herald
May 29, 1890

MORE JUDGES OF ELECTION.

The Commissioners Appoint Those for Summit and Millard Counties.

MILLARD COUNTY.

Fillmore Precinct—Alvin L. Robinson, Edwin Bartholomew, James A Melville.

Kanosh—Ezra W. Penney, James Abraham, George Crane.

Meadow—Joseph Adams, William Bond, George H. Labaum.

Holden—Thomas Evans, Nicholas Paul, Antone Steffenson.

Scipo—Peter C. Wilson, Samuel Rowley, Orville Thompson.

Leamington—Christian Oveson, J. P. Johnson, John Talbot.

Oak Creek—George Tinlinson, George Dutson, Peter Neilson.

Deseret—W. A. Ray, D. C. Reed, Thomas W. Cropper.

Oasis—Edward Webb, Antone Christenson, S. H. Alexander.

Burbank—Matt M. Morrissey, W. Atkinson, Charles Rowland.

Smithville—W. C. Barney, Trefle Doutre, George Bishop.

THE MILLARD STAKE ACADEMY.

The Closing Exercises—Principal's Report—A Good Showing Made.

The closing exercises of the Millard Stake academy were held a few days ago. Below is the full text of the principal's report, as presented on that occasion:

To the Board of Trustees:

The attendance during the entire academic year shows a total of 191 students registered.

According to the number of students of last year, this number exceeds it by 71, thus making it the largest attendance in the history of the academy. The attendance during last term, being from January 6, shows a total of 169 registered, and they were registered in various departments as follows:

Primary Department—36 registered, 17 left.

Preparatory Department—52 registered, 12 left.

Intermediate Department—91 registered, 16 left.

The 86 remaining shows an increase of 7 students from this time last year; still this number is but a poor testimony in regard to the people's appreciation of such an institution.

The primary department has been in charge of W. E. Rydalch, wherein the following studies were taught viz: Primary theology, short studies, composition, primary arithmetic, third reader, primary geography, primary penmanship and primary hygiene.

The preparatory department, in charge of Miss Martha A. Lawisch, has been carried on according to the following statistics, viz: Preparatory theology, short studies B. and C., composition, primary geography, preparatory orthography, practital arithmetic D and E, first and second readers, preparatory penmanship and hygiene.

I have had charge of the intermediate department, but in the department there were academic and normal students, and this department has been conducted according to the following statistics: Theology, Reed & Kellogg's higher lessons in English arithmetic, A and B, elocution, standard geography, physical geography, Latin, German, bookkeeping, rapid penmanship, algebra A, B and C, normal theory, and physiology, penmanship A and B, drawing, United States history. While we were not so crowded, all departments met once a day in calisthenic drill. There have been 41 daily recitations or 205 weekly recitations, or 4,100 recitations during the term.

During the year there have been three regular teachers; aside from these, 4 normals taught daily a class of higher studies. Mr. Rydalch taught 4 and Miss Lawisch 4. During the year, 15 normals have been registered. This department promises to be the main one of this academy.

I find the purest spirits seek this department, and I will say here, you scarcely ever find an immoral person seeking a teacher's life; but those that are noble and pure in thought—those that love the rearing and directing of immortal minds.

DOMESTIC ORGANIZATION.

The students have been domestically located as follows: Fillmore, 116; Meadow Creek, 9; Kanosh, 4; Deseret, 14; Ingersoll, 1; Scipio, 2; Heden, 12; Beaver county, 6; Sanpete county, 2; Piute county, 1; Garfield county, 1; Tooele, 15; Nevada, 1, and Wyoming, 1—55 from abroad and 116; from Fillmore.

THE LADIES' DEPARTMENT,

In charge of Miss Lawisch, reports as follows: Sixty-nine ladies that have been instructed in different departments of work, viz.: sewing, knitting, crocheting, embroidering of various kinds, flowers, painting, etc.

THE MUSIC DEPARTMENT

has been under the charge of Miss Nellie Hinckley for part of the year and afterwards Miss Lawisch.

Thanks are due Mr. O. W. Andelin and members of choir for their labors, not only for singing for devotional exercises, but also at our polysophical society meetings.

THE POLYSOPHICAL SOCIETY,

under the management of W. E. Rydalch, reports eighteen sessions held, wherein lectures, songs, instrumental pieces, recitations and answers to questions were given.

The library is but small, consisting of Barnes' works, encyclopedia, text books, daily paper and two periodicals.

THEOLOGICAL ORGANIZATION.

The students during the last twenty weeks have been registered theologically as follows: Two seventies, 8 elders, 2 teachers, 31 deacons, 112 lay members, 5 not baptized, and 9 non-members—169.

The labors of the teachers and students during the past school year have been characterized by a harmony of feeling, earnestness and willingness to comply with all duties devolving upon them.

Never in the history of this academy have such feelings of unity and prayerfulness been among students; their exercising of faith in behalf of fellow students and teachers that have been sick; and a fact I have observed is, that those who have been most prayerful and have put most time on theology, have been those who have advanced faster in all other studies, and this fact has been without an exception.

The students that have remained to end of school year have received benefits that those long since discontinued never dreamed of reaping.

The students have finished their text books in nearly every instance.

CONCLUSION.

No one, I believe, will deny that God's blessings have been upon this academy, and through His kindness and the earnestness of students and teachers the labors of this year have gone forth for good, for which the teachers feel very thankful and feel to ascribe praise to God, the author and supporter of this institution. With prayerful hearts we close this school year, ever wishing the prosperity of this institution.

J. E. HICKMAN, Principal.

ARE NOW AT WORK.

The Census Enumerators Begin Their Labors.

A FULL LIST OF THEIR NAMES.

The Questions, in Brief, to Which Answers
Will be Expected—Fourteen Days
the Limit.

Below is the list of the census enumerators, as furnished by Dr. Condon, of Ogden. The enumerators commenced work yesterday, and are limited to fourteen days, unless they can give some good and sufficient reason why the time should be extended. Some of the districts will probably be completed in a week, while others will consume the entire time. The questions, in brief, to which answers will be expected:

Christian name in full and initial of middle name.

Surname.

Whether a soldier, sailor or marine during the civil war (United States or confederate) or widow of such person.

Relationship to head of family.

Whether white, black, mulatto, quadroon, octoroon, Chinese or Japanese or Indian.

Sex.

Age at nearest birthday. If under one year give age in months.

Whether single, married, widowed or divorced.

Whether married during the census year (June 1, 1889, to May 31, 1890).

Mother of how many children and number of those children living.

Place of birth.

Place of birth of father and mother.

Number of years in the United States.

Whether naturalized.

Whether naturalization papers have been taken out.

Profession, trade or occupation.

Months unemployed during the census year.

Attendance at school during the census year.

Able to read; able to write.

Able to speak English. If not, language or dialect spoken.

Whether suffering from acute or chronic diseases; with name of disease and length of time afflicted.

Whether defective in mind, sight, hearing or speech, or whether crippled, maimed or deformed, with name of defect.

Whether a prisoner, convict, homeless child or pauper.

Is the house you live in hired, or is it owned by the head or member of the family?

If owned by the head or a member of the family, is the house free from mortgaged incumbrance?

If the house is owned by head or member of family, and mortgaged, what is the postoffice address of owner?

THE ENUMERATORS AND THEIR DISTRICTS.

No	County.	Enumerator.	P.O. Address.
1	Beaver	Jas. D. Gilliard,	Beaver City
2	Beaver	Jas. H. Dupaix	Minersville
3	Beaver	W. D. Williams	Milford
4	Beaver	Henry Emerson	Beaver City
5	Box Elder	E. N. Williams	Corinne
6	Box Elder	D. D. Ryan, jr	Corinne
7	Box Elder	John Germer	Deweyville
8	Box Elder	Benj. F. Cook	Grouse Creek
9	Cache	Wm. Goodwin	Logan
10	Cache	G. W. Green	Logan
11	Cache	Benj. F. Bair	Logan
12	Cache	Robert Griffiths	Benson
13	Cache	J. E. Shortem	Smithfield
14	Cache	Sidney Allen	Smithfield
15	Cache	J. A. Christensen	Newton
16	Cache	C. C. Goodwin	Trenton
17	Cache	Aaron DeWitt	Logan
18	Cache	Geo. B. Knight	Logan
19	Cache	John G. Wright	Paradise
20	Cache	Samuel P. Hall	Wellsville
21	Davis	Eli Balderston	Bountiful
22	Davis	R. W. Haight	Farmington
23	Davis	J. B. Meredith	Kaysville
24	Emery	Don C. Robbins	Huntington
25	Emery	John F. Brown	Blake P. O
26	Garfield	Wm. O. Orton	Orton
27	Garfield	Joel Shoemaker	Moab
28	Garfield	Joel Shoemaker	Moab
30	Iron	S. R. Burton	Parowan
31	Iron	John White	Parowan
32	Juab		Nephi
33	Juab		Nephi
34	Juab	J. P. Driscoll	Eureka
35	Juab		Nephi
36	Kane	John W. Glazier	Kanab
37	Kane	B. L. Young	Kanab
38	Millard	Geo. C. Veille	Fillmore
39	Millard	John Kelly	Fillmore
40	Millard	Wm. C. Penny	Kanosh
41	Morgan	T. G. Wadsworth	Morgan City
42	Morgan	A. Rasmussen	Morgan City
43	Piute	Charles Morrill	Junction
44	Piute	Wm. L. Jones	Marysvale
45	Rich	M. A. Moffet	Meadowville
46	Rich	William Rex	Randolph
47	Salt Lake	Geo. D. Webb	Salt Lake City
48	Salt Lake	Mark Reedall	Salt Lake City
49	Salt Lake	C. W. Sells	Salt Lake City
50	Salt Lake	Leon Frank	Salt Lake City
51	Salt Lake	Joseph Foreman	Salt Lake City

52	Salt Lake	H. H. Hawthorn	Salt Lake Cty
53	Salt Lake	Henry Ames	Salt Lake City
54	Salt Lake	Ed. R. Knenig	Salt Lake Cty
55	Salt Lake	J. B. Fitzpatrick	Salt Lake Cty
56	Salt Lake	Ezra G. Stuart	Salt Lake Cty
57	Salt Lake	George Rodford	Salt Lake City
58	Salt Lake	C. H. Goddard	Salt Lake City
59	Salt Lake	J. W. Newburn	Salt Lake Cty
60	Salt Lake	Arthur O. Clark	Salt Lake Cty
61	Salt Lake	A. Jos. Johnson	Salt Lake City
62	Salt Lake	John A. Trimble	Salt Lake Cty
63	Salt Lake	C.O. Farnsworth	Salt Lake City
64	Salt Lake	Ralph L. Wilson	Salt Lake Cty
65	Salt Lake	Aug. M. Wood	Salt Lake Cty
66	Salt Lake	John W. Clark	Salt Lake Cty
67	Salt Lake		Salt Lake City
68	Salt Lake	H. H. Harrington	Salt Lake Cty
69	Salt Lake	Chas. R. Boyce	Salt Lake Cty
70	Salt Lake	Fred. A. Husted	Salt Lake Cty
71	Salt Lake	N. G. Keim	Salt Lake Cty
72	Salt Lake	Richard Hope	Salt Lake Cty
73	Salt Lake	Luke F. Wells	Sandy
74	Salt Lake	Geo. A. Burgon	Murray
75	Murray	V. Shurtliff	Butler P. O.
76	Murray	John Butter	Bingham
77	Murray	B. B. Quinn	Bingham C'n
78	Murray	Isaac E. Diehl	Salt Lake Cty
79	Murray	John F. Bledsoe	Salt Lake Cty
80	Sanpete	Abner Crane	Mt. Pleasant
81	Sanpete	Nils L. Elison	Moroni
82	Sanpete	Peter Schwalbe	Ephraim
83	Sanpete	Geo. W. Martin	Manti
84	Sanpete	E. J. Conrad	Chester
85	Sanpete	Gus M. Clarke	Dover
86	Sanpete	D. Beckstrom	Spring City
87	Sevier	John T. Leonard	Salina
88	Sevier	William H. Rex	Salina
89	Sevier	Victor E. Beane	Richfield
90	Summit	John D. Bell	Henefer
91	Summit	Miss M.A. Brown	Coalville
92	Summit	W.R. Armington	Park City
93	Summit	D. J. Williams	Park City
94	Summit	Wm. C. Wallace	Park City
95	Summit	Thomas P. Potts	Kamas
96	Tooele	E. J. Arthur	St. John
97	Tooele	F. T. Burmeister	Grantsville
98	Tooele	David B. Stover	Stockton
99	Tooele	Thomas H. Nix	Tooele City
100	Tooele	Robert Scott	Tooele City
101	Uintah	Charles C. Rich	Vernal
102	Utah	C. W. Dusehberry	Provo
103	Utah	F. D. Alexander	Provo
104	Utah	Miss P.M. Ethier	Springville
105	Utah	George I. Butts	Spanish Fork
106	Utah	Wm. McBeth	Payson
107	Utah	J. C. A. Warfield	Payson
108	Utah	Geo. H. Chappell	Provo
109	Utah	James Harwood	Lehi
110	Utah	Jas. S. McBeth	Payson
111	Utah	Mack Dougall	Springville
112	Wasatch	D. Camp Wray	Wallsburg
113	Wasatch	John Crook	Heber
114	Washington	F. L. Daggett	St. George
115	Washington	James G. Wilder	Silver Reef
116	Washington	Edw'd A. Dodge	St. George
117	Weber	W. F. Critchlow	Ogden
118	Weber	O. P. Herriman	Ogden
119	Weber	Wm. H. Dack	Ogden
120	Weber	Sanford L. Ives	Ogden
121	Weber	J. H. Humphrey	Ogden
122	Weber	George L. Corey	Ogden
123	Weber	Henry E. Steele	Ogden
124	Weber	Mrs. H. Stafford	Ogden
125	Weber	John T. Smyth	Ogden
126	Weber	Binford A. Hybee	Slaterville
127	Weber	Peter Later	Harrisville
128	Weber	Charles S. Rapp	Ogden
129	Weber	Edward P. Munn	Hooper
130	Weber	Christian P. Kar	Ogden
131	San Juan*		
132	Salt Lake	G. C. Farnsworth	Salt Lake City

* Appointed from Washington.

List of special enumerators: United States penitentiary, Salt Lake city—Dwight Colt, enumerator; Utah school for the deaf, Salt Lake city—Henry Speller, enumerator; territorial insane asylum, Provo—James Dunn, enumerator; Fort Douglas, Salt Lake city—August Lange, enumerator; Fort Du Chesne, ——————, enumerator.

AMASA S. CONDON,
Supervisor for Utah.

Utah Enquirer
June 3, 1890

SOUTHERN DOINGS.

Inducements Offered the U. N. & C. Railway—The Sevier Bridge

The people of Beaver and Millard have offered some big inducements to the Utah Nevada & California railway company to build their road through these counties. Besides monetary considerations, they now propose to demonstrate by actual survey that it will save the railroad people many dollars and miles to run a line via Fillmore and Beaver than via the Sevier Valley. From what can be learned of the natural and acquired resources of these place, it will be largely to the advantage of any railroad to run that way, and shall the U. N. & C. R. R. not take advantage of these offers now held out, we may expect soon to hear of solid negotiations being made with other lines.

The reports that the bridges of the U. P. over the Sevier were in dangerous conditions, have no foundation in fact, and now that the water has gone down several inches, and continues to lower, there is no danger from washouts this season.

The good people of Deseret have built an excellent canal, and are now supplied with plenty of water. The dam system has proven such a failure with them for so many years, that disgust and desperation have seized them and developed into a fine canal system

Salt Lake Herald
June 11, 1890

THE articles of incorporation of the Fillmore Roller Mill company were filed with Secretary Sells yesterday.

Deseret Evening News
July 28, 1890

MILLARD COUNTY.

People's Convention and County Ticket.

Correspondence of the DESERET NEWS.]

At a regularly called convention of the People's Party of Millard County, held in Fillmore, July 19th, an excellent ticket was nominated.

Owing to miscarriage of the mails or absence from home of members of the central committee, Deseret and Meadow were unrepresented in the convention, which body, after organizing, adjourned for two hours, to give time for our friends to arrive; and upon reassembling passed unanimous resolutions of regret at their absence. Certain parties having an ax to grind are taking advantage of this unfortunate incident to create dissension in the People's Party, and advise scratching the ticket.

The "Liberals" have a full ticket in the field, and would be the only ones to reap advantage from such division.

Let the People take a calm, consistent view of the situation and vote for their friends, and Millard County will be all right.

GEO. CRANE.

KANOSH, Millard County,
July 25, 1890.

Following is the ticket referred to by Mr. Crane:

Selectman, David R. Stevens; sheriff, John T. Ashman; coroner, Byron Warner; assessor and collector, Jos. A. Lyman; treasurer, Ira N. Hinckley, Jr.; county clerk and recorder, Thomas C. Callister; surveyor, Jos. S. Giles; county attorney, Jos. S. Giles.

Salt Lake Herald
July 31, 1890

THERE will be a match game of baseball played at Fillmore on election day, August 4, 1890, between the Fillmore baseball team and the Deseret Blues. Canosh, Meadow, Holden and Scipio baseball players are invited to be there. Match games will be made and played during the day.

DOINGS IN THE SOUTH

A Visit to the Former Capital of Utah.

BORING FOR WATER IN MILLARD

General Improvements about Fillmore
—Devastation by Storms—Lively
Large, Black Crickets.

[Editor Enquirer:]

To one who loves the co-mingling of intense heat and alkali will do well to take a journey into Southern Utah, for there, these articles are the chief topics. During my journey south, however, the weather took some strange freaks. Some of the awfulest thunder showers occurred that the people of the arid regions have ever experienced, and, as might be expected, the floods followed in quick succession. The way in which trees, rocks, mud and canyon debris surged down the creeks was a caution to the villagers. The old bridges in and about Fillmore and Millard county were mostly washed away to make room for better timber. The floods prevailed for the space of two days and then the parching sun began his work, and the big black crickets, that in spots carpeted the ground in various parts of Millard county, leaped with joy, and chirpped as only crickets of their genus know how. Then there were those awful swarms of flying ants. There is one instance of their covering a man and horse like bees upon a limb, and almost devouring them.

Fillmore is manifesting some enterprise in the way of putting in roller mills. The Co-op flour mills will be converted from a hopper mill to a roller mill, and the irrepressible G. Huntsman will have one of these mills.

The County court, of Millard county, made an appropriation some time ago to purchase a well-driving apparatus to be used in prospecting for flowing wells. Their first effort was a failure, but there is no discouraging such men as G. C. Veils, T. C. Callister and Chas. Crane, who have this matter in charge, and they will immediately shift quarters and bore again. Should they strike water and allow the sparkling liquid, pent up in the primeval rock, to issue forth, a cry of joy will ascend that will shake the ancient hills.

The hands of the people have been largely turned to stock raising, and a number of enterprising men are forming a syndicate for exporting stock and sheep from that region.

Mr. Jas. A. Mellville, Alma Greenwood, Geo. Veile, Geo. Nixon and others are the promoters of this move.

Politics is as usual at a rather low ebb. The liberals of Fillmore have been fighting to the tune of 60 to 300 voters so long that it is becoming monotonous and the chief works of the People's party are so pleased with their weapon, styled the noble 300, that they can recline in ease and wait for a glorious victory. There is no need for Mr. Oratorius or Grandiloquy to ring out the high sounding speeches because they have got the election bull by the horns and a down hill pull, and there is not saltpetre enough in the liberal L brigade of 60 nobles to prevent them from carrying every thing before them.

In Millard county there is one brass band, composed of both sexes, under the leadership of Mr. Don Olsen, the other members are principally his sons and daughters. They have a monopoly on music in Millard and adjoining countries and during the winter months have many engagements . In the summer this gentleman sends most of his receipts that music brings on a farm which usually produces about half that is expended upon it. For some years part the belligerent cattle and hungry rabbits have compromised the proceeds of the farm

The southern country is somewhat elated over the renewal of mining interests in Pioche and southern Utah. It affords the people a market for their products and furnishes the young men with labor.

This part of the lord's vinyard would enjoy a higher prosperity and become better known to the outside world were the railroad facilities better. The prayer for some years has been railway, but as yet their prayers has not been answered. The first company that extends its road into the country will be known as their financial redeemer.

Salt Lake Herald
August 8, 1890

FILLMORE FACTS.

A few days since, we were surprised to learn by notice in THE HERALD, that a baseball game would be played in Fillmore on election day between the Fillmore nine and the Deseret Blues. "Scipio, Kanosh and Holden were invited to attend and arrange the matches, and an offer was made to allow Fillmore to place the Kanosh chief behind the bat." This was considered by Fillmore as a Liberal suggestion on election day, and declined. The Blues really did look nice in their new attire, and feminine eyes were filled with admiration. But Fillmore rustled up a home nine, with nothing noticeable about them, but resolve upon their faces.

The election and the game waxed warm. It was scratch and scratch with both. But the People's ticket came out well on top, and the Blues went down 13 to 10.

Then they folded their azure robes and put them in their carpet sacks, and to-day we shook their hands good bye and thought there still hung around them a tinge of blue as they faded in the west.

Give us due notice, and come again boys. You are welcome to the best we can command all round—or any others of our friends with like aspirations.

OLD BAT.

A SAD CASE.

Some Dreadful Inroads Made by Diphtheria.

On Wednesday, July 30th, a funeral cortege arrived in Fillmore from Deseret with the body of Thomas Croft, a lad who had died on his tenth birth day, from disease supposed to have been induced from too frequent bathing in the river. His mother, the widow of the late George Croft, wished to bury him by the side of his father, who is interred in the Fillmore cemetery. The funeral services, conducted by Bishop Callister, were held at the house of Brother Thomas Davis, the residence of the parents of Mrs. Croft. The lad had been treated for sore throat, but no idea of contagion was thought of. The day after the funeral of the boy Mrs. Croft was taken ill, alarming symptoms developed, and Dr. Hosford from San Pete County being in town, he was summoned to the assistance of the sick woman. He instantly pronounced it a bad case of diphtheria. On the morning of August 2nd Brother Thomas Davis died,

and on the evening of the same day Sister Croft also passed away, leaving seven young children orphans in our midst. The youngest, a little boy eighteen months old, was born on the day of his father's burial. This event has cast a gloom over our community. The city authorities, under the direction of the Mayor, have taken vigorous measures to prevent the further spread of the disease, and no further development of it has appeared. Brother Thomas Davis was born in England, April 7th, 1841, has resided in Fillmore since 1852, was a faithful member in the Church. Sister Letitia Croft was born at St. Louis, Mo., November 21st, 1851, was a woman of faith, and great energy, devoted to the great responsibility of raising her fatherless children, and directing their course in the paths constantly walked in by their lamented father. There is no other case of diphtheria in our county, and we have burned it out here.   G. C.

FILLMORE, Millard County, Utah, August 7th, 1890.

AN OILY FRAUD.

He Stuffs Himself With Roast Chicken and His Dupes With Falsehoods.

About ten days ago, at about 4 o'clock a. m., a man apparently in an exhausted condition came to the house of Mr. George Day, living on a farm about a mile southwest of Kanosh. He told a doleful tale of his experience in tramping from Antelope Springs, thirty miles away, where his horse broke loose from him with the bridle on, after being relieved of the saddle, halter and other traps for the purpose of giving it a drink.

Mr. Day and his kind-hearted wife did all they could to relieve and make comfortable the unfortunate stranger, who, after being rested and refreshed, proved to be a man of great loquacity and no mean pretensions. His host and hostess were informed that he had a special mission into this neighborhood from capitalists in San Francisco, to discover and purchase a mining prospect that was said to be near by. This information was given to two of our citizens who have for years had some experience in making holes in the ground. The speech and manner of this unknown tramp satisfied our friends that there was money behind it all. They drove out to an old digging where some of your correspondent's muscle had been wasted, but it was not the place indicated on the chart. After returning to the house of our miner friend and, looking over the speci-

friend and, looking over the specimens, he seized the very kind of rock he was seeking, and which he had seen two or three sacks full of in California before leaving.

Now it must be business, as he had been from there about thirty days and had only a given number to return in. He was driven out to this barren hole, about 60 feet deep, and his eyes were filled with delight. It was the object of his search, for which he had come near losing his life, through the loss of his fractious steed. And now, boys, it must be business whitout loss of time. "Name your figures," was the commanding request of the representative of the great mining syndicate in San Francisco. After consideration the price was fixed at $50,000. "Its high boys, but I'll do the best I can for you."

He was driven back to eat some of Brother Day's chickens, etc., and express his great anxiety lest the boys should go back on the bargain. By and by he walked up to town to tell them that he would like the mine at their figures, and they must be ready next morning to take him on to the county seat (Fillmore) there they could reach the telegraph and name the bank in Salt Lake City in which the money was to be deposited. He further engaged them to haul one to the terminus of the rail road at liberal figures, started into the stores inquiring the price of goods at wholesale, arranged for shipping lumber from Nephi to build a smelter, and calculated the cost of piping a spring a long distance.

He was taken suddenly sick and could not ride to Fillmore last Saturday morning. Liquor was hunted up and administered, and he wished to dispel their anxiety by declaring that he would "be on deck in the morning boys, ready to run you a five mile race and repeat." But he would like to get that saddle and halter left at Antelope Spring and would give friend Day $10 to go and fetch them, giving a minute description of their location. The halter was in a certain corner with a little manure kicked over it. Day struck out on horseback, and during the night the representative of millions struck out on foot, taking Day's boots and shirt with him. Our mining friends got on his track, coming in this direction, and have sought him "in the highest, the lowest and loneliest spot," but the chicken, the man, the money, and the boots are all gone, and only men with broken fortunes and the hole in the ground remain with us.

The last heard of this consummate blik was from the Partridge field, above this town, where he stayed on Sunday night last, and dug and cooked potatoes. When the boys discovered him he talked glibly of being lost coming from his mining prospects in the mountains above, and offered a pocket knife in pay for the stolen potatoes, as he had no smaller change than a $10 bill. The telegraph has been freely used to discover him. He is thought to be striking through the mountains into Sevier County. He is of medium stature, about 50 years old, has a mustache sprinkled with gray, is quick with the pen, and a gentleman by manners.

Day, of course, found neither saddle nor halter at Antelope Springs, came back and found that his guest had gone. He rode on twenty-five miles north, trying to discover the man and the boots, and if he had found them there would have been a dance. We hope this scoundrel will be seized before he reaches the next county.

There is quite a flutter in real estate here, caused by the sale of twelve or fifteen thousand dollars worth from Mr. Almon Robison to the Millard County Investment Company.

Salt Lake Herald
August 31, 1890

FILLMORE FILINGS.

The farmers are busy threshing their grain.

D. D. Houtz, of Provo, was seen lately in our city.

A roller mill is in course of erection. It will fill a long felt want in the community and will be gladly welcomed.

Autumn is slowly but surely approaching. Still are the days warm, but the nights are very cool and pleasant.

The board of equalization of taxes has been busy for some time past and, in fact, court matters have been generally brisk.

The quarterly conference of the Millard stake was held here on the 25th and 26th. The meetings were very well attended and a feast of spiritual food was partaken of by all. Education and the duties of the Saints were the topics that were dwelt upon to the greatest extent.

On Monday evening, August 18, a concert and party was given in honor of Elders Frank Merrill and John Trimble who were called to foreign missions to preach the gospel to the nations of the earth. Elder Merrill goes to New Zealand and Elder Trimble will labor in Great Britain. A pleasing programme was presented and fully appreciated, and our fellow townsmen were made to feel that many warm and sympathizing friends would be left behind, who would gladly welcome the absent ones on their return.

The Millard stake academy will open Monday, September 1. The institution is a credit to the thrift and industry of the people of this county and speaks louder than words in behalf of the authorities who have labored for the education of the young folks. Last year the academy made quite a success under the direction of Principal J. E. Hickman. The same teachers have been re-engaged and a primary department will also be added for the benefit of the younger pupils who could not enjoy the privilege of attending last year because of the grade being too high, as the third reader was the lowest taught. The regular teachers with their departments are as follows: J. E. Hickman, academic studies and junior normal class; W. E. Rydalch, intermediate department; M. A. Lawisch, preparatory department.

FILLMORE, Aug. 27. DEE.

Deseret Evening News
September 3, 1890

THE LATE ANSON CALL.

It has already been announced in these columns that Elder Anson Call, Counselor in the Presidency of the Davis Stake of Zion, died at his residence on Sunday evening, Aug. 31st, at 40 minutes past 7 p.m. Having procured the necessary data, we are enabled to present the following biographical sketch, for which we are indebted to Brother George A. Lincoln:

Anson Call was born in the town of Fletcher, Franklin County, Vermont, May 13th, 1810. He was the son of Cyril and Sally Tiffany Call. The father was born in Woodstock, Windsor County, Vermont, June 29th, 1785. Joseph Call, the grandfather of Anson, was born in Oxford, Worcester County, Massachusetts, in 1742. John, the great grandfather of Anson, was also of New England birth; thus the family is known to ante-date the struggle of the American colonies for liberty for two generations.

The ancestors of Brother Call served in the Indian wars of the colonies and the brother of his great grandfather fell on the plains of Abraham, in the contest for the possession of Quebec between the French under Montcalm and the colonial army under General Wolf. His grandfather, Joseph Call, was in the battle of Bunker Hill, and afterwards served under General Washington. Thus in his veins was mingled the blood of the Teuton with that of an old New England family.

At the age of seven years the deceased, with his parents, moved to Geauga (now Lake County), Ohio. The county being new, Anson had only limited opportunites for attending school; besides, the family was much afflicted with sickness, which reduced them to low circumstances financially. Fortunately for Anson, the environment of boyhood and youth developed habits of industry and self-reliance. October 3rd, 1833, in the town of Madison, Geauga County, Ohio, he married Miss Mary Flint, daughter of Rufus and Hannah Haws Flint. She was born March 27th, 1812, in the town of Braintree, Orange County, Vermont.

He gathered with the Saints at Kirtland, Ohio, and shortly after was baptized by William Smith, brother of the Prophet. On the 21st day of May, 1835, he was confirmed, in the Kirtland Temple, by David Whitmer, one of the three witnesses of the Book of Mormon. He was administered to for an impediment in his speech, which was relieved. At the same time he was promised that his speech should be natural and proper as long as he used his tongue for the advancement of the truth, which he always has done to the day of his death. He was also ordained an Elder and preached the Gospel to his old neighbors and associates. After moving to Kirtland he was ordained into the quorum of Seventies in February, 1838. About thirty of his Methodist associates joined the Church of Jesus Christ of Latter-day Saints, and also his wife and his father's family.

On March 25th 1838, Brother Call, accompanied by his father and his brother Henry, left Kirtland for Missouri. After their arrival there they purchased land in Caldwell County. His father soon returned to Ohio for his family. After making some farther arrangements regarding land and farming, Anson started to meet his family. He found them and the company they travelled with progressing favorably. This was in July, 1838. He passed through the mobbings, persecutions and troubles preceding and connected with the exodus of the Saints from Missouri and Illinois, and was a staunch supporter of the Prophet, with his labor and means.

Brother Call was a leader of a company across the plains and, in fulfilment of predictions of Joseph the Prophet, was the founder of a number of cities and towns of this inter-mountain region. In September 1849 he was ordained Bishop and appointed to preside over North Canyon Ward in Davis County in that capacity. In 1850 he raised one thousand bushels of grain. In October of the same year he was called to assist in colonizing Little Salt Lake Valley, under the leadership of Apostle George A. Smith; left Salt Lake City on the 7th of December and camped on the present site of Parowan, Iron County, on the 12th day of January, 1851. On the 17th of the same month he was elected Justice of the Peace in the new colony; took an active part in exploring the country and in the severe labors necessary in founding a new settlement.

Brother Call returned in June and spent the summer in attending to his affairs in Davis County, and started with the colony for Pauvine Valley, in October 1851. Before starting he was appointed President of the colony by the General Conference; also at a special session of the Territorial Legislature he was appointed Probate Judge of Millard County, which he was directed to organize. He arrived on Chalk Creek, Pauvine Valley, on the 15th of November 1851 and found Brigham Young, Orson Pratt, a surveyor and about forty others on the ground. They laid out a city and called it Fillmore. By act of the Legislature it had been designated as the future capital of the Territory. Brother Call, with his usual energy and practical ability, led the infant colony along in road-making, mill-building, farming and other labors which develop the resources of a new country. At the August election of 1852 deceased was elected to represent Millard County in the Territorial Legislature. About the 2nd and 3rd of November, 1853, he, with eleven men, gathered up and buried the remains of Captain Gunnison and party, who had been massacred by the Indians on the Sevier River about ten days before.

He completed his mission to Fillmore in the spring of 1854, and on the 5th of March left that place for his home in Davis County. In the autumn of 1854 he opened a large farm in Box Elder County, Utah, at a place known as Call's Fort, for the purpose of furnishing profitable labor to the poor Saints brought from Europe by the P. E. Fund Company. At the General Conference on the 6th of April, 1855, he was sent to Fillmore to settle up some business connected with the State House, which he accomplished in twelve days and returned home. In May, the United States marshal for the Territory, Jos. L. Heywood, appointed him his deputy and afterwards took a journey to California, leaving the business of the Territory connected with that office in his hands. On the 16th of March the mother of Brother Call died at Bountiful, aged 65 years.

On the 28th of October, after his arrival home, he took charge of thirteen teams from the North Canyon Ward and went to relieve the handcart companies. After traveling 333 miles east of the city he assisted in rescuing the unfortunate handcart people. He was absent thirty-three days and returned with all those who went with him.

Towards the close of 1857, as Buchanan's army approached Utah, he and two of his sons took an active part in the defense of the people. He and his son Chester labored on the fortifications in Echo Canyon and his son Anson Vasco was employed in watching the movements of the army in the neighborhood of Green River. The former was from home four weeks and the latter

seven. With the opening of the spring of 1858 commenced that memorable move of the Saints from all their settlements north of Utah Valley, for the purpose of making a burnt offering of their houses rather than they should fall into the hands of their enemies. On the 6th of May, 1858, he evacuated his home in Davis County and gathered with the people of his ward on the Provo bottoms, near Utah Lake, where about one hundred families made the best shifts they could for temporary shelter, and awaited events, under the direction of their Bishop. Soon after, as related in general history, difficulties were arranged and he returned to his home in Davis County on the 4th of July, 1858.

On the first of the following October his Brother Josiah, from Fillmore, paid him a visit. When the latter was returning home, accompanied by Samuel Brown, both were killed by the Indians near Chicken Creek, in Juab County. Their remains were found on the 15th of October.

At the Semi-annual Conference in October, 1864, Anson was called, in connection with others, to assist in planting a colony near the Colorado River, in what was then southwestern Utah. About this time a company was formed by some of the leading merchants of

Salt Lake City and others for the purpose of building a warehouse at some suitable place on the river with a view of bringing goods into Southern Utah via that stream, and bringing the immigration of the Saints from abroad into Utah should it be demonstrated as feasable. The company constituted him their agent for the carrying out of a part of this enterprise. November 1st he was directed to take a suitable company, locate a road to the Colorado, explore the river, find a suitable place for a warehouse, build it, and form a settlement at or near the landing. This he accomplished to the entire satisfaction of those who employed him, and returned to his home in March, 1865. After remaining at home about one month, he took his wife Mary with him and was gone on another trip to the Colorado River two and a half months.

On the 4th of August, 1867, a son of Brother Call (Anson V.) died at Rock Creek, on the Laramie plains, 425 miles east of Salt Lake City, while returning from a mission to Europe, on which he had left home April 28th, 1864. His long absence and the anticipated pleasure of his return made the circumstance a very painful one. October 28th, 1870, accompanied by his wife Mary and Mrs. Hannah Holbrook, the deceased left home on a visit to numerous family relatives in Ohio, Vermont, and other parts of the country, and returned home in January, 1871.

In 1872 he accompanied the Palestine party, which was in charge of George A. Smith, to England, and employed some five months in traveling in Great Britain and Ireland, returning to Utah ahead of that company. After arriving home he presided over the home missionaries of Davis County, and was also appointed Bishop of the East Bountiful Ward.

When the Davis Stake of Zion was organized in 1877 he was appointed one of the counselors of President William R. Smith, and was succeeded in the Bishopric by his son Chester. Such men as Anson Call make history. They are peculiarly adapted to the colonization of new countries, to the laying of the foundations of empires in a wilderness. Wonderful changes have taken place since he first camped in Davis County.

He died peacefully and calmly, in possession of all his faculties. Shortly before his death he gave his son Chester instructions concerning the casket and other matters pertaining to his burial. Thus has passed away one of the leaders of men, leaving a large posterity and a host of friends to mourn his departure.

It would be difficult, after reading the foregoing sketch, to imagine how the respected deceased could have crowded into his earthly career any more work than he performed. "Labor is worship," and not only in this direction, but as a devoted religionist, Brother Call served God throughout his life.

The beauty of Brother Call's life-work lies in the fact that it was largely directed toward the benefit of others and the cause of truth. No sacrifice appeared to be too great for him to make for his religion, and the venerable patriarch goes peacefully to his rest after having made a record that will redound to his credit in eternity. We had the pleasure of being acquainted with him, and if there ever was a man of sounder integrity than he, we do not know it. May his numerous posterity follow the noble examples he has set, that in them he may still live.

Peace to his ashes.

Salt Lake Herald
September 18, 1890

FILLMORE FILINGS.

The district school teachers of this county are being examined here. Quite a number have presented themselves for certificates. The district schools of this county are being improved greatly, and in the future a marked advance can reasonably be expected.

The Millard Stake academy has opened its sixth academic year with the brightest prospects in view that have ever attended this growing institution. The Polysophical society, a society organized for the benefit of the students, held its first session last evening and creditable was the programme that was prepared carried out. For the remainder of the year weekly meetings will convene, in which lectures, songs, readings, recitations and answering of questions, will be presented.

A few weeks ago the family of Joshua Nichols went to the cañon to rusticate. While enjoying themselves an accident happened to the baby. While playing around it was poisoned in some manner. Some think a poisonous insect stung it, while others presume the child was handling poison ivy, and thus did the injury. Be that as it may, the child is dead and Brother Nichols, with his family, is again called upon to mourn. The blow falls very heavily, as last winter the dreadful disease, diphtheria, or putrid sore throat, carried off two of the children of Brother Nichols.

Deer hunting is now quite a pastime.

FILLMORE, Sept. 13.   DEE.

Salt Lake Herald
September 25, 1890

JAMES E. RAY, of Fillmore, who has been prospecting in that district, has brought some fine quartz of gold and silver, and is stopping at the White house.

Deseret Evening News
October 3, 1890

THIRD DISTRICT COURT.

Proceeding in Contempt.— Alleged Embezzler Acquitted.

Before Judge Zane this morning, a man named James Konnelly was brought in on an attachment for contempt, it being alleged that he had sought to influence a juror named Ivers, who was on the panel in the Wyman case.

Konnelly was sworn and stated that he had been a co-owner with Kelly, whom Wyman killed, of certain mining property, and that he talked with Ivers about the homicide only in an incidental and casual way. Judge Zane said he would hold the matter open until the juror Ivers could be examined further; that the latter had stated the conversation very differently from what Konnelly had just done, and that he proposed to punish severely any man who attempted to corrupt a juror.

John Yates and John Durrie were arraigned on a charge of robbing Anna Bourg alias Anna Brown, of $1 in cash and a handkerchief, and given till Monday at 10 a.m. to plead.

Joseph Deardon was tried on a charge of embezzling a span of horses belonging to John Walker. The case arose in Fillmore. Peter Huntsman testified that the team in question belonged to John Walker; that it disappeared from Fillmore, and that witness next saw it in a livery stable in this city. Witness said Walker was now in Nevada.

Barney Dority testified that he purchased the team from the defendant. There was no evidence showing how defendant came in possession of the team, and without this proof the prosecution could not, of course, make out a case. Defendant's attorney asked that the jury be instructed to return a verdict of not guilty. The court so ordered and the defendant was discharged.

Court then adjourned till 10 a.m. next Monday.

Salt Lake Herald
October 4, 1890

DEARDON RELEASED.

The case of Joseph Deardon, charged with embezzlement, was then taken up. The indictment charged the defendant with embezzling a span of horses belonging to John Walker. Peter Huntsman, of Fillmore, was the first witness. He testified that the horses in question were the property of John Walker, of Fillmore. The last time he saw them they were in Grant Brothers' stable, in this city. Mr. Walker was in Nevada, and when the officer subœpnaed witness, he told him where Walker was.

Barney Dorrity testified that he purchased the horses from the defendant some time ago.

This closed the evidence for the prosecution, and as it had not been shown that Walker did not sell the horses to the defendant, his attorney, Mr. Kroeger, moved the court to instruct the jury to return a verdict of not guilty.

J. M. Zane, who prosecuted, admitted that he had failed to make out a case, and attached the blame to the marshal's office for not subpœnaing Walker or making such a return as would enable the prosecution to get a continuance.

The jury, under instructions from the court, returned a verdict of not guilty.

Mission Notes.

ARRIVALS.—The following Elders arrived from Utah on Friday. Sept. 19th, on the S. S. *Nevada*, of Guion Line, after a very pleasant trip.

For the Scandinavian Mission: Edward H. Anderson, of Ogden; P. N. Pehrson, West Jordan; P. Crouquist, J. F. Hansen, J. Rosencrants, Logan; M. Johnson, H. Lilijenquis*, Hyrum; A. G. Johnson, Andrew Hansen, Pleasant Grove; Peter Sorensen, Jens Cofoed, Thor Nelsen, Brigham city; C. H. Poulson, Franklin, Idaho.

For Great Britain· James H. Anderson, Joshua B. Bean, Salt Lake city; Moroni England, Tooele; S. K. McMurdie, Paradise; John D. Williams, J. S. Stapley, Kanarra; John Trimble, Fillmore; John G. Webster, Cedar city; John Gibby, Morgan city.

On the same vessel were Brother Edwin Evans, of Lehi, au his way to Paris to study art, and Brother Fred Pembridge's parents in Heneford. All were well.

APPOINTMENTS.—Elder James H. Anderson is appointed to labor in the London conference.

Elder Joshua B. Bean is appointed to labor in the Leeds cenference.

Elder S. K. McMurdie is appointed to labor in the Birmingham conference.

Elder J. D. Williams is appointed to labor in Wales.

Elder J. S. Stapley is appointed to labor in the Irish mission.

Elder J. G. Webster is appointed to the Bristol conference.

Elder Moroni England is appointed to labor in the Norwich conference.

Elder John Gibby is appointed to labor in Wales.

Elder John Trimble is appointed to labor in the Newcastle conference.

Mill. Star.

DEATHS.

TAYLOR.—On Sunday morning, November 9, 1890, at the residence of her daughter, at Sandy, Salt Lake County, of general debility, Ann Maria, relict of the late John Taylor, and formerly of Fillongley and West Bromwich, England; aged 83 years.

Funeral tomorrow (Tuesday). The remains will be brought to this city, to be laid beside her husband in the cemetery.

SORENSON.—At Fillmore, October 22, 1890, of typhoid fever, Sister Bertha Caroline H. O. Sorenson, of Leamington Ward.

She was the daughter of Ror Strom; born May 9th, 1856, in Malmo, Sweden; joined the Church when sixteen years of age; emigrated to Utah in 1875, and has been a faithful teacher in the Relief Society. Her last mission to Fillmore was in behalf of her family, to educate the children who were attending the Millard Stake Academy. She was the mother of six children, two of whom are dead and four living. Sister Sorenson was a faithful Latter-day Saint, always on hand to attend to her duties. The bereft ones, husband, family and friends, mourn her loss.—[COM.

Deseret Evening News
November 15, 1890

Out of the "Pen."

This morning Brother Christian Anderson, of Fillmore, emerged from the penitentiary, after having served a sentence of a term of eighteen months imprisonment for an infraction of the Edmunds-Tucker law.

Brother W. D. Newsom, of this city, also came out at the same time, after having served a term of six months, for unlawful cohabitation.

Salt Lake Herald
November 16, 1890

CHRISTIAN ANDERSON, of Fillmore, and W. D. Newson, of this city, yesterday completed the terms of imprisonment to which they were sentenced for infraction of the Edmunds-Tucker law, and were released from the penitentiary.

Salt Lake Herald
November 27, 1890

DOWN IN MILLARD COUNTY.

A Section of Utah That is Rapidly Coming to the Front.

The present year has witnessed a little more life in Millard county than the few previous ones.

A large canal southwest of Deseret, is being excavated and a reservoir prepared for the waste water.

The roller mill erected a few months since, is increasing the prosperity in this vicinity. The flour it produces is said to equal any in the territory.

There are fair prospects of a new settlement springing up there, as the parties interested are striving for that purpose. They are sinking artesian wells and developing that region in general.

Malarial fever has kept prostrate quite a number of our friends, and although all afflicted with that disease are recovering, the grim hand of that despot—death—has carried away several from our midst.

It has been reported that a lady calling herself Inez Coalter, alias Fannie Coalter, is in Fillmore. She is supposed to be the one who reported such scandalous stories in the New York papers concerning the Mormons.

Election over, the enterprising citizens have turned their attention to a railroad. Their object is to have a branch of the Utah Central extended form Oasis to Fillmore. May they be successful, is the wish of all interested in the welfare of Millard county.

We have enjoyed quite pleasant weather, for the most part, during the autumn months, but the approach of winter is being felt now, and ere long the heavy old snow-king will put in his appearance. But the happiest of communities cannot always escape the blight of sickness.

An old gentleman named Kinney, who has been a respected resident of Fillmore many years, died about two weeks ago; also Mrs. Goddard, an elderly lady who had been bed-fast some time. Being the autumn of their life we feel to say to the friends of both: "Weep not, for they are not dead, but only gone before." The remains of Mrs. Eliza Robertson and child, of Panaca, reached here Sunday evening last, and after funeral services, were deposited in their last resting place. She was the eldest child of President Ira N. Hinckley, and we tender unto him our heartfelt sympathies in this, his hour of affliction.

The Millard Stake academy began labor this season with a larger patronage than ever before so early in the year, and though the academy has a multitude of trouble to contend with, will, we hope, keep steadily toiling on and add its mite to the educational monument of Utah and the world, and become a star among all the institutions of learning in our fair land. Physical development, mental culture and moral and religious training are the chief aims, and we wish for it all the success that it merits.

Summing it all up, the prospects of Millard county seem to brighten a little as year succeeds year, and who can say but what she will some day stand among the foremost counties of the territory for her industrial resources, as she has ever done in the line of education. May her future be as bright as the wishes of her residents would make it. J.

Salt Lake Times
December 2, 1890

The postoffice at Fillmore was robbed last week of between $500 and $600 in registered letters, by two boys of the age of 15. They succeeded in getting into the postoffice by breaking through an adjoining store.

Deseret Evening News
December 5, 1890

Millard Stake Conference.

The regular quarterly conference of the Millard Stake of Zion was held at Fillmore City, November 23rd and 24th.

We were not favored with the presence of any of the general authorities, but on the stand were the Presidency of the Stake, most of the members of the High Council, Presidents of Quorums, Bishops, etc. The meetings were well attended, and the meeting house was, as usual, too small.

The reports of the spiritual and temporal condition of the Saints in the different wards were quite favorable. The general and local authorities were presented and unanimously sustained by vote. Besides the regular conference business, the time was occupied by President I. N. Hinckley, Daniel Thompson, D. R. Stevens, Elders J. E. Hickman, C. Anderson, W. E. Ridalch, J. D. Smith and Bishop T. C. Callister, in speaking upon various topics pertaining to the duties of the Saints. A rich portion of the Spirit of God was enjoyed both by the speakers and hearers, and the manifestations were wonderful, grand and sublime. Some prophesied, others sang and spoke in tongues, followed by interpretations, others again heard singing by invisible beings. It was a time of rejoicing and strong testimony.   C. ANDERSON,
                    Stake Clerk.
November 25, 1890.

Salt Lake Herald
December 11, 1890

A GENTLEMAN at Fillmore, Millard county, says he has found a very valuable deposit of what he calls "prince mineral" or a pure quality of red fire-proof mineral paint, and has promised to forward samples of his find to the chamber of commerce in a few days. Something new is constantly being discovered in the territory and the diversity of the resources of Utah are becoming more and more wonderful every day.

Salt Lake Herald
December 18, 1890

A sample of red mineral paint has been received at the chamber of commerce from R. A. McBride, of Fillmore, Millard county. The same gentleman also sent a sample of what he terms sal soda, of which he has discoved a deposit.

Deseret Evening News
December 18, 1890

A SAMPLE of red mineral paint has been received at the Chamber of Commerce from R. A. McBride, of Fillmore, Millard County, who also sent a sample of what he terms sal soda, of which he has discovered a deposit.

Salt Lake Herald
December 31, 1890

FIRST TERM ENDED.

Closing Exercises of the Millard Stake Academy.

Friday morning, Dec. 19, the students and friends of the Millard Stake academy assembled in the court house for the closing exercises of the first term of the sixth academic year.

At 10 o'clock the congregation was called to order by head monitor, Rufus Day. The choir sang, when prayer was offered by Brother Christian Anderson. After singing by the choir an excellent programme was carried out, consisting of representations of the various departments by students, songs, instrumentals, recitations and the reading of the principal's report by the principal, Brother J. E. Hickman. The report, which shows the complete standing of the academy, is, in brief, as follows:

To the Hon. Board of Education of the Millard Stake of Zion:

As the farmer watches his growing crops and looks with anxiety to the time of gathering, that he may be the better able to judge of the fruits of his labors, whether satisfactory or otherwise, so is it with the labors of students and teachers. Although there have been threatening blasts, floods of unseen danger to the looker on, yet the results of the arduous labor are very pleasing to me. To-day closes a sixteen-week term and the results of part of the work are now before you. There is a most truly quoted saying: "The student is the reflection of the instructor," hence we have the students represent in brief the work accomplished in the academy. There have been 150 students registered during the entire term; 29 have been discontinued; 121 in attendance. This is a greater enrollment by 34 than at any previous year for the first term.

A primary grade has been added to the academy this year. The teachers have taught weekly recitations as follows:

May Cooper, twenty-five weekly recitations; May Reed, twenty-five weekly recitations; M. A. Lawisch, forty-five weekly recitations; W. E. Rydalch, fifty-five weekly recitations; J. E. Hickman, sixty weekly recitations.

With choir practices and other work the recitations would have footed to 250 weekly or 4,000 during the term.

Students as registered in departments are as follows:

Primary department	51
Preparatory department	38
Intermediate department	29
Academic department	23
Normal department	12

The students have been tabulated domestically as follows:

Fillmore	93
Holden	5
Scipio	2
Oak Creek	4
Leamington	9
Deseret	20
Ingersoll	2
Clear Creek	1
Kanosh	3
Piute county	6
Utah county	3
Sevier county	1
Nevada	1
Total	150

Students have been registered theologically as follows:

Elders	6
Priests	1
Teachers	2
Deacons	22
Lay members	94
Not baptized	15
Non-members	10

There have been three baptisms and three confirmations performed under orders of the presiding officer of the ward.

The ladies' department, under the charge of Miss M. A. Lawisch, reports the following statistics: Lady students, 72.

We acknowledge two contributions, one from Bp. Anderson, of Oak Creek, two volumes of ancient history, and a human skeleton from Charles Crockwell.

I will close, asking God's blessing upon this institution, and upon the people of this county, and that the spirit of God will speak as audibly to them as it does to me concerning the worth of these schools.

J. E. HICKMAN, Principal.
W. E. RYDALCH.
FILLMORE, Dec. 24, 1890.

Provo Daily Enquirer
January 5, 1891

Lucile, the little daughter of Mr. and Mrs. L. Holbrook, died at five o'clock last night of acute bronchial pneumonia Mr. Holbrook was called to Fillmore a few days ago, to the bedside of his sick mother, who died just five minutes before he arrived. Lucile was taken sick soon after he left and he was telegraphed for, but had not been at home more than ten minutes when his daughter died. Funeral services will be held over the remains tomorrow afternoon at 1 o'clock at the family residence.

Provo Daily Enquirer
January 27, 1891

Mr. Olson, of Fillmore, father of our musical "Ed." surprised his son last night by walking into Felt & Olson's and enquiring if he had "a boy here." The gentleman will probably remain in the city for a few days.

There are times when a feeling of

Salt Lake Herald
January 28, 1891

Up till late last evening there were 4 inches of snow at Paris, Idaho; 3 at Franklin; 4 at Logan; 4 at Ogden; 5 at Brigham; 4 at Kaysville; 6 at Nephi; 5 at Cedar City; 10 at Fillmore; 4 at Scipio; 4 at Parowan; 5 at Mount Pleasant; 5 at Glenwood; 4 at Monroe; 3 at Manti. At Gunnison, Ploche, Salina and Beaver snow was falling. It would seem as though the storm had been general throughout the territory.

Provo Daily Enquirer
February 18, 1891

Mr. J. D. Smith the leading merchant of Millard Co. spent last night in Provo and returned home to Fillmore this morning.

Provo Daily Enquirer
February 20, 1891

Mrs. McBride, who has kept the U. P. hotel for a number of years, has returned from Fillmore, where she has been for several months during her illness.

Provo Evening Dispatch
February 25, 1891

JAS. M. GEORGE, of Fillmore, was in town yesterday. As a result of his trip to town he will receive THE DISPATCH regularly hereafter.

Salt Lake Times
February 28, 1891

UTAH COMMISSION

Today Appointed the Following Deputy Registrars.

Utah county — Benjamin precinct, John Howe; Clinton, B. Wightman; Fairfield, Wm. Thomas; Lehi, Robert Gilchrist; Lake View, W. G. Williams; Lake Shore, H. S. Brooks; Pleasant Grove, John Richins; Provo Bench, D. C. Daniels; Provo, R. A. Hills; Springville, D. C. Huntington; Spanish Fork, John S. Thomas; Goshen, Geo. White; Salem, Wm. H. Taylor; Santaquin, Alex. Evans; Spring Lake, John C. Warfield; Thistle, Wm. H. Roger; P. V. Junction, P. A. Smith; Payson, John T. Stark.

Garfield county — Coyote precinct, A. V. Carpenter; Escalante, Joseph H. Liston; Hillsdale, H. P. Clove; Cannonville, Wm. E. Pierce; Paugwitch, Wm. O. Orton, jr.

Willard county — Kanosh precinct, Ezra W. Penney; Meadow, John Stredder; Holden, Nicholas Paul; Scipio, Geo. Monroe; Oak Creek, George Finlinson; Leamington, Christian Overson; Oasis, Edward Webb; Deseret, Wm. A. Ray; Smithville, W. C. Barry; Burbank, Wm. Atkinson; Fillmore, John Kelly.

Provo Daily Enquirer
March 11, 1891

Another Survey Being Made.

A corps of Utah, Nevada & California railroad surveyors under the command of Engineer Hoffman are said to be on the road making a preliminary survey for their company direct from Cedar city or Parowan, through Beaver city and Fillmore to an intersection of the line already surveyed northeast of Juab. It is understood that this action is in pursuance of an agreement spoken of in a previous issue of the *Utonian*, whereby the company in question agreed with certain prominent citizens of Beaver and Millard counties, that a survey should be made of the route as indicated, and if found satisfactory in the matter of gradients and distance, that the road would be constructed through the two counties named, instead of through Sevier and Piute counties. It is said that the chief objection to the first named route was the mountain it would be necessary to climb on the south of Scipio. This objection has, it is said, been satisfactorily met by the discovery by the engineers of an easy ascent for the grade over the hill, and that prospective big item of increased cost having been thus overcome, the parties directly interested are congratulating themselves upon the fact, as well as upon the assurance of the road being built over the newly selected route. It can't come too soon for its advent will undoubtedly inaugurate a season of prosperity throughout the entire south. One railroad is somewhat of a mixed blessing, while two roads through that country would be beneficial to all the people.—*Utonian*.

FROM FILLMORE.

THE LADIES' CO-OP STORE ENTER- ED AND ROBBED OF $200,

Total Depravity of a Champion Hoodlum —Coats and Wraps Stolen and Soaked in a Ditch.

[Editor Enquirer:]

If it was the rule to publish such incidents only as reflect credit on the society of a community, this article would prove uninteresting to Enquirer readers. It is very much to be regretted that we have any lawlessness in our quiet city; much more, that it should reach the enormity it has reached and that the world should know of our stained record. Noticing the unusual activity around the police court and observing the surprising secrecy in the actions of our marshal led your correspondent to summon his native inquisitiveness—and by boldly approaching a local Pinkerton, and bowing to the silver badge on his suspender was put on to the following items:

At the recent Academy ball the champion hoodlum so far eclipsed anything yet undertaken in his line that he ought to have a leather medal immediately. While the party was in progress, this famous scrub sneaked into the reception room, and carried off an arm full of hats, overcoats, and ladies wraps. The giant minded practical(?) joker, anxious to make a display quality, took his costly bundle and deposited it in the creek, where it was found two days later a mass of ruin. The wretch was so lost to respect that even two sealskin sacques which were among the articles taken were trampled in the mud without compunction. I speak of the low-lived specimen in the singular number as the tracks of but one person were found in the mud near the creek. A reward of $50 is offered for the apprehension of the depraved scoundrel who committed the deed; but as yet no clue has been obtained that will warrant the officers making any arrest. Prof. Hickman feels the outrage very keenly, as nothing but diabolical meanness could have prompted the act.

During the week Justice Jackson has been dealing out law to drunks, etc. to the benefit of the city treasury about $20.00.

Last night W. W. Dame, Jr. forced open the door of Greennay's saloon and helped himself to what whiskey he wanted. He was arrested and suffered the extreme penalty of one night's imprisonment at his own home. Dame talked so strong to the proprietor of the saloon that he was afraid to prosecute him. It is said that Dame scared Greennay so, that he washed his feet. This is doubted by Greennay's acquaintances, who are of the opinion that no amount of fright could induce him to make such a radical departure from his fixed habits.

The culminating act which crowns our misdeeds was the robbery of the Ladies' Co-op store. The store was entered from the rear door, which was broken open, and about $200.00 taken from the till. The police are actively working up the case, but as yet they have been unable to locate the criminal. There were a number of marked coins taken, and these have been passed into circulation again. This is the only clue the police have, but they are sanguine that they will catch their man. U. S. Detective Ray informed your correspondent that he had traced the robbery to two men; but was unable to say which one was the guilty party. He also stated that he would soon make some developments in the matter that would paralyze al opinions.

The Ladies' Co-op is a flourishing institution, under the management of Mrs. Mary Henry. It is the general opinion that the money will not be recovered.

Apostle F. M. Lyman is in town. He delivered a very interesting discourse at the meeting house to-day.

Bro. Quigly is in Millard at present, lecturing under the auspices of Y. M. M. I. association.

Edward Partridge of Provo is here.

Sam Wiele representative of Simon Bros, Salt Lake, is here taking orders for a spring and summer stock of millinery.

G. M. Hanson, Assistant county Superintendent is visiting the district schools at present. He reports great improvement in educational matters. The Teachers Institute meets regularly every month. The membership numbers twenty two teachers.

PROF.

FILLMORE, March 23, 1891.

Provo Daily Inquirer
April 8, 1891

Lost—A lady's gold watch, between Springville and Spanish Fork with the name of L. P. Winslow engraved on inside of case. The finder will be rewarded by returning the same to W. E. Maycock, Fillmore, Utah, or to EXQUIRER office.   1w

Salt Lake Times
April 16, 1891

WE AND OUR NEIGHBORS

News of the West Polished Up, Boiled
Down, so That He Who Runs
May Read.

AUT SCISSORS, AUT NULLUS.

Items of Interest and Bits of Current
Comment From the List of
Our Exchanges.

The subject of purchasing a chemical fire engine is up before the council of Logan.

The old state house at Fillmore, Utah's ex-capitol, has been leased for Millard stake academy for twenty years at a nominal figure of $2000, to be paid in improvements in the building.

A county fair is what is wanted this fall. By this means our fine horses and rich natural resources can be placed before the world in a better way than any other. Whoop the matter along.—[Provo Inquirer.

On Tuesday night, Joseph Holt, son of Samuel Holt of Millville, was thrown from the back of a wild horse he was breaking—his foot catching in the stirrup he was dragged for some distance, the thigh being fractured.

Mrs. James A. Peterson of Hyrum, while ascending a ladder leading to the loft of her residence, slipped and fell to the ground, sustaining a severe compound fracture of the left ankle joint. Amputation was found necessary.

It is a most singular thing that we are continually behind in some matters in Logan. The water was turned off one canal or more, for two days it was said, so that the headgates and platform could be fixed and the canals cleaned out. Three days went by and the streets and citizens were deprived of the light, although the needful work was done in two days, and then the fourth day went by because some one had been tardy.—[Logan Journal.

Salt Lake Herald
April 16, 1891

REPORTS received from various towns and cities in Utah, yesterday, show the state of the weather as follows: Provo, raining; Nephi, light rain and snow; Beaver, fine; Cedar city, cloudy and cold; St. George, clear and pleasant; Fillmore, cloudy; Scipio, light rain; Spring city, snowing at intervals; Mt. Pleasant, snowing and raining; Manti, cloudy; Salina, cloudy; Ephraim, looks like storm; Logan, rain and snow at intervals; Ogden, rain; Franklin, rain; Paris, Idaho, snow.

Salt Lake Herald
April 21, 1891

Harvey Warner and Sandy Reed, two boys from Fillmore, indicted for housebreaking, were arraigned and took the statutory time to plead.

TONS OF BAILED HAY

Gathered From the Best Crop Grown in
Various Parts of the Territory
of Utah

AND INTER-MOUNTAIN STATES.

Clipped With a Pair of Editorial Scissors
That Were Sharpened Up This
Morning.

Provo is complaining of irregular mails.

Millard county will this year shear 75,000 sheep.

Springville will build a fence around its public square.

Springville will have the honor of entertaining the old folks this year.

Important deposits of pumice stone have been found twenty miles west of Fillmore. Two car-loads of stone have already been shipped. The owners have contracted with Chicago parties to furnish 500 tons delivered in that city. It will net about $25 profit to the ton.

The new bridge which spans Provo river at what is known as the old ford was completed and received bo the county court on Saturday. Work on the bridge was commenced on April 2nd, making the time of the building just one month. The cost of the bridge was $1200.

CHANGED HER FAITH

A Missionary Who Came to Utah
to Convert, Converted.

CORRUPT DENVER OFFICIALS

To be Investigated—Dr. Graves Arrested and
Jailed—Harley McCoy's Trial Begins—
Outrage on an Old Lady.

EVANSTON, Wyo., May 18.—[Special telegram to THE HERALD].—News was received here at noon to-day to the effect that Miss Coulter, a mission teacher a Fillmore, Utah, under the auspices of the Home Mission board of the Presbyterian church in the United States, has given up her early faith and espoused the cause of the Latter-day Saints. This fact was sent to the Home Mission board headquarters in New York, and they at once wired the church authorities in Utah to investigate the case, and Rev. Josiah McLean, of Ogden, is now at Fillmore, in southern Utah, for that purpose. Miss Coulter is prominently connected in the east, and has been a long time in the service of mission work. She has lived in Utah for several years, and is entirely conversant with things as they are. She is the sister of President-elect Coulter, of the Indiana state university. She is known throughout the east and has figured as a zealous mission worker in the church of her choice. The news of her change of church relations has created widespread attention both in this country and New York.

Salt Lake Herald
May 23, 1891

THE Rev. McLain, of the Presbyterian church, says: "The special to THE HERALD of the 19th, from Evanston, Wyoming, in reference to Miss Coulter, has no foundation in fact. In some way a report was sent to New York from some quarter that Miss Coulter was about to join the Mormon church. I was sent to Fillmore to look into the matter. I found Miss Coulter going on quietly with her school. When the news was broken to her she was greatly astonished. She has not changed her faith."

Salt Lake Herald
June 3, 1891

THE MILLARD ACADEMY.

The Recent Commencement Exercises Held There.

The recent exercises held at the Millard stake academy at Fillmore were very interesting in their nature. A large number of the representative men of that section were present. There were the usual exercises incident upon such occasions. Miss Lama Hickman represented the theological department, Miss May Cooper the normal, Miss May Reed the literary, Mr. Callie Robinson the scientific. The principal's report was quite lengthy, and among other things showed the attendance as follows: Primary department, 53; preparatory, 34; intermediate, 49; academic, 56; normal, 16; total, 188. These departments have been in charge of Miss May Cooper, primary, Miss May Reed, preparatory; intermediate, Mr. W. E. Rydalch; academic and normal, Principal J. E. Hickman. The students came from the following places:

Fillmore, 122; Meadow, 8; Kanosh, 9; Holden, 7; Scipio, 1; Oak City 6; Leamington, 1; Deseret, 17; Ingersoll, 4; Piute county, 5; Utah county, 4; Nevada, 3; New York, 1.

The closing of the sixth academic year of the academy was one of the most pleasant affairs ever experienced in Fillmore.

Deseret Evening News
June 5, 1891

Millard Stake Conference.

The regular quarterly conference of Millard Stake was held at Deseret last Sunday and Monday, May 24th and 25th. A spacious bowery had been constructed for the occasion, and the weather was very pleasant.

On the stand were Apostle John Henry Smith and President S. B. Young, also the Stake presidency and other leading men of the Stake. The wards were all represented by Bishops or counselors, who reported health, peace, good will and good prospects in every part of the Stake.

Besides the regular conference meetings, we also had a High Priests' meeting Saturday evening and general Priesthood meeting Sunday evening. The meetings were addressed by Apostle John H. Smith, President S. B. Young, Presidents I. N. Hinckley, Daniel Thompson, D. R. Stevens, Elders J. D. Smith, C. Anderson, George Crane, J. E. Hickman, Thomas Memmott, William V. Black and Joshua Greenwood. The speakers seemed to enjoy much freedom, and a good spirit prevailed. The subjects treated on were temperance, virtue, charity, tithing, benevolence, education, faith, etc. The general and local authorities were presented and sustained by unanimous vote, and the conference was adjourned to meet at Fillmore on the 23rd and 24th of August next.

C. ANDERSON, Stake Clerk.
FILLMORE, May 27, 1891.

Provo Daily Enquirer
June 13, 1891

Programme for Commencement Exercises.

Commencement exercises of the graduation classes of the District Schools of Utah County will be held in the B. Y. Academy Hall on Friday, June 16, commencing at 10 o'clock A. M.

The following interesting programme has been prepared for the occasion, and the public should turn out to witness the exercises:

Singing "Hail Columbia",
Invocation.
Music Orchestra.
Address Frank McGraw of Provo City Graduating Class.
Song "The Kerry Dancing" Eva Frampton of Pleasant Grove.
Address by a member of Springville Graduating Class.
Duet Haydee Trane and Orinda Kerren of Lehi.
Address by a member of the Graduating Class of Spanish Fork.
Song by pupils of Provo City Schools.
Address Miss. Laura Boyle of Payson Graduating Class.
Duet by pupils of American Fork Schools.
Address John Roberts Jr. of the Lehi Graduating Class.

Quartette by the Central School Quartette Club of Springville.
Address by a member of the Graduating Class of American Fork.
Song by students of the Spanish Fork Schools.
Address Burdett Smith of the Graduating Class of Pleasant Grove.
Song Annie May Fillmore of Payson Schools.
Address to the Graduates Prof. W. M. Stewart of the University of Utah.
Music Orchestra.
Address Prof. Cluff of the B. Y. Academy.
Awarding and presentation of Diplomas by the County Sup't.
Music, Singing and Prayer.

The Graduates and their friends are invited to pic-nic with the pupils of Provo Schools after the exercises and to spend the afternoon in the grove with them.

Deseret Evening News
June 17, 1891

Unexpected Death

By private telegram to a gentleman in this city we learn that Mrs. Lois Trampton, daughter of President Ira N. Hinckley, died yesterday morning at Fillmore and will be buried on Thursday. She leaves five children.

Deseret Evening News
June 22, 1891

NOTES FROM FILLMORE.

A Large Dairy Company Organized.—Politics at Work There.

Fillmore has a dairy company organized, with a capital stock of $5000. Judge Velle is president and I. N. Hinckley, Jr., vice president. The company has purchased the old tannery rock building which is well located for dairy purposes, the Millard County Investment company are the chief movers in the concern and intend making it a success.

On Saturday, the 13th, as Mrs. M. A. Y. Greenhalgh was starting out on a tour of the county in the interest of woman suffrage, leaving the house of a friend, her horse suddenly became unmanageable and ran about a block. The light cart struck a large rock at the L. Holbrook corner. The cart was wrecked and the lady thrown to the ground. She was carried bruised and bleeding into the house of I. N. Hinckley, Jr., where she still remains. Her many friends will be glad to know that she is able to be up today, although at present she is a pitiable object to look upon. All her appointments are canceled for the present, but nothing short of death can long keep down this indefatigueable worker.

Politics are beginning to simmer in this district.

Today was burried Mrs. Lois Hinckley Frampton, a daughter of President Hinckley, whose sudden demise has cast a gloom over the entire community. Sister Lois was held in very high esteem by all, she being a lady of exceedingly pleasant address and a most exemplary wife and mother. She has left a broken-hearted husband and five little children to mourn the greatest of all losses. The bier of this loved one was tenderly borne for two blocks to the meeting house by six good and virtuous brothers of the dead. This is the second time within six months that the same six brothers have been called upon to gather home to lay in the last resting place the body of a sister, and each have left little ones behind them, to be taught and guided in life by other than a mother's hand. God bless these children and those who minister to their happiness in life.

A. BIRD.

FILLMORE, Millard county, June 18, 1891.

Salt Lake Herald
June 24, 1891

Two New Companies.

The articles of incorporation of the Fillmore Dairy company were filed with Secretary Sells yesterday. The company is organized to carry on a general dairy business at Fillmore, and is capitalized at $5,000 and the incorporators are: G. S. Giles, J. T. Ashman, the Midland Investment company, J. A. Melville, J. N. Hinckley, J. D. Smith, Joshua Greenwood, G. C. Velle and Thomas Callister.

The articles of incorporation of the Godbe Mercanticle company and the Endowment Benevolent society were also filed with the secretary yesterday.

Fillmore Dairy Company.

The articles of incorporation of this company were filed with Secretary Sells yesterday. The company is organized to carry on a general dairy business at Fillmore, and is capitalized at $5,000 and the incorporators are, G. S. Giles, J. T. Ashman, the Midland Investment company, J. A. Melville, J. N. Hinckley, J. D. Smith, Joshua Greenwood, G. C. Velle and Thomas Callister.

OUR PEDAGOGUES.

Their Names and Residences.

LECTURES BEING GIVEN

What it is to be a Scholar once Again--Questions and Answers.

At 9 o'clock a. m. on Monday morning the B. Y. A. Summer school opened at the Central school house under very flattering auspices.

After the opening exercises Prof. B. Cluff, Jr., the president of the school made a few preliminary remarks upon the object of the school, viz: To furnish practical teachers and those desirious of becoming so, an opportunity of advancing in the principles and practice of their profession.

Dr. Karl G. Maeser prefaced his lectures by an outline on "School Management and Discipline."

Professor Cluff followed with his first lecture on "History of Pedagogics," beginning with education among the Greeks and Romans under the following heads:

(1) Educational ideal. (2) Methods adopted in attaining to this ideal; (3) Result of these methods; (4) Great Educators.

Prof. Isgreen delivered a lecture on "Natural Philosophy", dwelling more particularly on the general qualities of matter.

The afternoon exercises commenced with a practical drill in the elements of vocal music after which Prof. Brimhall gave a most interesting and instructive lecture on "School Devices," under the heads: "Conduct, order and punctuality." The gentleman presented the subjective and objective phase of the subject in such an easy, simple, plain and convincing manner that each teacher present could not help but improve themselves and the schools they preside over.

The following is a list of the names and residences of the teachers who are attending the Summer institute:

G M Mumford, Big Cottonwood. Salt Lake county; George Scott, Sanpete county; Mrs Cecelia Rasmussen, Mt. Pleasant, Sanpete county; Daniel T Miller, Farmington, Davis county; Lee Bradford, Spanish Fork; Carrie Lovegren, Mt Pleasant, Sanpete county; Hattie Knowlton, Farmington, Davis county; Ruth Brimhall, Spanish Fork; Agnes Angus, Spanish Fork; Charlotte Rowbery, Grantsville, Tooele county; Phena Brimhall, Spanish Fork; Agnes Lewis, Spanish Fork; Mrs Annie M Hawkins, Benjamin; Esthma Curtis, Payson; Dora Daniels, Payson; Z S Taylor, Salem; O W Andelin, Fillmore, Millard county; Miss Jennie Smith, 603 S 2nd East Street, Salt Lake city; Kate Thomas, 443 S First west street, Salt Lake city; Zina Bennion, Salt Lake city; Emma Thatcher, Provo; Mary Nuttall, Provo; Maggie Lewis, Provo; N W Anderson, Manti, Sanpete county; Mabel Pratt, Provo; Alcesta Lewis, Payson; Eliza Wild, American Fork;

Kate DeLong, Panguitch, Garfield county; Ella Larson, Pleasant Grove; Foster Cluff, Heber city, Wasatch county; Alta; Alfred Duke, Heber city, Wasatch county; Jennie Thomas, Carrie Peterson, P C Anderson, C R Dorius, Enoch Jorgensen, Peter Graves. Jr., Ephraim, Sanpete conty; William T Taylor, Lehi; R H Thorn, Springville; J B Jensen, Draper J E Hickman, G F Hickman Benjamin; John Hanson, Riverton, Salt Lake county; John Swenson, Pleasant Grove; J L Brown, Pleasant Grove; John Foot, Provo: Thomas F Howells, 62 S. 6th West street, Salt Lake city, Samuel H Smith, Pleasant Grove.

The teachers are listening with all their ears, and their senses are on the alert, gathering many items of information, the benefits of which will be realized by their scholars during the next school year. They are relizing once again what it is to be scholars and rack their brains for correct answers and solutions to the various questions and problems that the professors fire at them.

Salt Lake Herald
July 8, 1891

Politics in Millard County.

We have had in Millard county quite a little political excitement during the past week. Hon. J. T. Caine and Prof. Paul paid us a visit in the interest of the Democratic party. Hon. J. T. Caine in a most able and effective speech explained the platform of the party and Prof. Paul expounded the tariff in his usual bright and interesting style. The meeting was well attended, and enthusiastic. Many gave in their names as adherents of the Democratic party. On Monday, July 6, a meeting will be held in Fillmore for the purpose of organizing a Democratic club and the prospect is that the organization will include the majority of the town.

On Friday, July 3d, Mr. J. A. Melville and Mr. Joshua Greenwood visited Meadow for the pupose of organizing a Democratic club in that place.

They had a good time and succeeded in enrolling the majority of the men into the club, which is the friend of liberty and of the people. Scipio, Holden and Deseret are by no means behind in responding to the call of the party, which indisputably offers the "greatest good to the greatest number."   M. A. Y. G.

The Fourth at Fillmore.

[EXQUIRER Correspondence:]

The glorious Fourth, was, as usual, celebrated at the county seat of Millard, in an enthusiastic and patriotic manner. The morning was ushered in by a salute of thirteen guns, and as the sun rose in splendor o'er the mountain top, the star spangled banner floated out on the breeze that came fresh and health-giving from the canyon. By 10 a. m. the State house was filled by an enthusiastic company anxious to hear the programme which the committee had prepared to celebrate the 115th anniversary of American independence.

The proceedings were opened by the choir, who discoursed sweet music, followed by prayer by the chaplain, Mr. A. Fortie. Then more singing by the ward choir, after which the following programme was rendered: Mr. J. Kelly read the speech of John Adams very effectively. The orator of the day, Hon. J. A. Melville in an eloquent speech gave a resume of the causes that led to the declaration of the American people, to no longer wear the British yoke, of the signing of the Declaration of Independence, and the struggle which

yoke, of the signing of the Declaration of Independence, and the struggle which ensued before they obtained it. Mr. W. A. Rydalch read the celebrated speech of Patrick Henry and gave a clever description of the noble men who on that memorable occasion, listened to his soul striving eloquence, and with him staked their lives to make their country free. A patriotic song was most agreeably rendered by Mr. Jesse Tye. "The Star Spangled Banner," was sung by T. C. Callester, Esq., in his usual effective style. Miss Ryley gave the "Red White and Blue" very sweetly, for so young a lady. At the request of the committee, Mrs. M. A. Y. Greenhaalgh read an original ode, written by herself for the occasion. Some excellent music was given by the band, and the choir added more vocal melody to close the very agreeable morning's exercises. The chaplain dismissed the meeting with prayer. Nothing occurred to mar the harmony and good feeling which prevailed throughout the day. In the afternoon the children had some amusement provided for them, in the grounds of President Hinkley, kindly thrown open to them for the purpose. In the evening a ball was given in the State House where all "went merry as a marriage bell." Ice cream was in demand and the day ended as it begun, with music, mirth and song. M. A. Y. G.

FILLMORE, July 5.

ELECTION JUDGES.

Another Batch Turned Out by the Utah Commission.

It Is Believed That the Democratic and Republican Parties Will Get Representation.

The Utah commission yesterday appointed the following judges of election:

MILLARD COUNTY.

Fillmore—Edwin Bartholemew, H. H Noyes, J. H. Melville.

Kanosh—E. W. Penney, Chas Jukes, George Crane.

Meadow—Joseph Adam, John Streder, W. H. Stott.

Holden—Nicholas Paul, Finos Dodge, George Nixon.

Scipio—P. C. Nirlson, Samuel Rowley, Orville Thompson.

Oak Cacek — Joseph Huff, Maxwell Webb, George Finlinson.

Leamington—C. Overson, August Wilson, Allen Stout.

Oasis—Edward Webb, J. B. Rawlins, John Stiler.

Politics in Deseret.

Editor Deseret News:

The people at this place held their first Republican rally last evening at which Mr. Wm. V. Black was elected temporary chairman and Joshua Bennett secretary. Mr. Thomas C. Callister of Fillmore was the first speaker. He stated that he appeared as an amateur at political speaking, but after referring to the principles of the Republican party, he fully convinced the majority of those present that he was an able advocate of the principles of Republicanism.

Mr. John Henry Smith, of Salt Lake City, then presented the benefits of Republicanism to the country and also the great evil that would come under the free trade system of Democracy. He spoke upon the great issues at stake and showed them up to the understanding of the majority of those present.

President Black then thanked the speakers and audience and invited all those that desired to connect themselves with the Republican party to step forward and sign their names. Some twenty-four availed themselves of the opportunity.

JOSHUA BENNETT,
DESERET, August 1st, 1891.

FILLMORE DEMOCRACY.

A Spirited Meeting Addressed by Hon. W. H. King.

Last evening, August 17, the people of Fillmore listened to a highly exhaustive description of the principles of Democracy and its tendency to elevate and benefit the nation, from the lips of their old townsman and fellow-citizen, Hon. W. H. King. He pointed clearly and eloquently to the advantages comparative free trade gives to the farmer and laboring classes, and showed that a high tariff benefitted only the manufacturer and the tradesman; that the latter class soon became wealthy, while those who purchased their protected goods remained poor; that the surplus product of the farm must either remains in the granary to decay or be sold at so low a rate as to be unremunerative to the farmer. That while protection helped to fill the coffers of the few, it quickly and effectually emptied the pockets of the many. He quoted history to prove that Republicanism had been a failure as a form of government from the earliest recorded dates down to the present time, and that next to a monarchy it was the most expensive to the people; that it would neutralize and render non-effective state governments and state laws; that the people were able to govern themselves, knew their own political and social needs, and referring to the constitution of the United States, pointed out its democratic character.

Of all the political orators who have visited us lately, none have been listened to with greater attention, or received a greater amount of applause than did our recently elected member to the territorial legislative council. Many of the young men from the adjacent town of Meadow, came to listen to their well known old neighbor, and expressed themselves as well repaid for their sixteen mile trip, in the information they had received. A unanimous vote of thanks was tendered to the speaker at the close of his most eloquent address. The president of the Fillmore Democratic club, occupied the chair in his usual efficient manner. The Fillmore choir gave two spirited songs, and received a well merited vote of thanks and hearty applause.

The cause of Democracy is making headway rapidly in our county, and had we a few more as able exponents of its policy as the gentleman who last night occupied the platform, the strides it would make and the hold it would take upon the hearts of the people would be still greater. While he elevated the cause of which he is an adherent and supporter, he did not attempt to depreciate any other political policy or speak disparagingly of those who differ from him in their political creeds.

M. A. Y. GREENHALGH.
FILLMORE, Aug. 18.

FILLMORE NOTES.

The Quarterly Conference.—Business, Politics and General Gossip.

The Stake conference closed yesterday, and considering the very busy season of the year was well attended, every ward being represented.

A Primary fair was held on Saturday, the 22nd, and cunning little hands made a very beautiful display of ingenuity and artistic skill.

The Millard Stake academy has opened up with very satisfactory prospects of a successful term. Professor Hickman heads a full corps of experienced teachers. The schools are located in the State house, which is cool and pleasant, with good accomodation for the various classes.

The entrance to our city from the north still has a gloomy aspect, the result of a recent flood by which many thousands of dollars worth of property was destroyed, and giving beautiful lawns and fertile gardens an appearance of desolation, wrought by the mountains avalanche of mud mixed with saw logs, brush, rocks and conglomerate debris. The door of the house of W. W. Dame Esq., was pushed open by the flowing mud, the organ was flooded into the cellar and then buried level up with sacks of sugar and many dollars worth of other provisions. Mr. Dame intends to leave all these riches where they are buried.

We have the Hon. W. H. King recuperating in our city. He has given several political lectures in the county, mostly of an educational nature, in pleasant contrast to the wild romancing of a heated campaign. The Hon. gentleman is always a most welcome visitor to our county, as a sample of our exports.

Yesterday while hurriedly preparing dinner for conference visitors the dress of Mrs. Hannah Hansen caught fire from the stove and was literally burned off her. Had it not been for the prompt action of the visiting friends a terrible disaster would have resulted.

One of Fillmore's oldest and most respected residents, Sister Anna Thomkinson Fortie has breathed her last, having suffered for many weeks since the removal of her last breast by an operation performed in Salt Lake City.   A. BIRD.

FILLMORE, Millard County, August 26, 1891.

WEATHER reports received yesterday by the Deseret Telegraph company from various parts of the territory are as follows: Paris, Idaho—Cloudy and cold; inclined to storm; one inch of snow. Franklin, Idaho—Clearing up; not so cold. Logan, Utah—Clear and calm. Spring City—Very cold; cloudy; looks like snow. Manti—Very cold; cloudy; looks like snow. Richfield—Cloudy and cold; heavy frost last night. Springville—Cold; snowing. Payson—Partly cloudy; cold; light wind. Fillmore—Very cold; snowing all morning. Parowan—Clear and calm. Cedar City—Clear and cold; snow yesterday half an inch deep. Toquerville—Clear; cold north wind. St. George—Clear and cold. Kanab—Calm and pleasant. Salina—Clear and cold.

Salt Lake Herald
October 10, 1891

E. R. Ritter undertook to pick the pockets of John Jackson, of Fillmore, during the crush at the theatre last night, and was arrested by Sergeant Donovan.

Work is being pushed rapidly on the Tintic branch of the Rio Grande Western. Goshen can now boast of a road being completed within her borders and the good people of that town can take a ride into Provo, where they do their shopping, without the burden of a team. The road will be completed to Tintic about Christmas.

James A. Melville, a prominent citizen of Millard who will represent that county in the next territorial legislature, is up from Fillmore and reports general activity in business particularly in the development of mines. Those which are becoming prominent are the gypsum and iron claims near Fillmore and also other claims are being worked near the twin peaks west of that town. Mr. Melville has over 400 acres of land under cultivation in his town which realizes a vast profit and upon which he expects to bore for water, the machinery having been received by him some time ago for that purpose. He will witness the Democratic demonstration to-night and note down some points to communicate to his constituency when he returns home.

PROVO, Oct. 9.   O.

Deseret Evening News
October 27, 1891

FILLMORE NEWS.

Lithographic Stone.—A Deer Killer and Mountain Lion Slayer.

Quite a valuable discovery has been made about three and half miles east of Fillmore, by Mr. Roof, an old-time prospector. It consists of a large deposit of lithographic rock, which Salt Lake experts class as equal to the imported Bavarian stone. A company has been formed, and shipments will be made to various points at once.

Quincy Robinson and Arthur Brunson went into the mountains two days since to hunt for deer. Quincy bagged five, Arthur none. The latter then borrowed Robinson's gun to try his luck again. In passing through some timber he noticed a fallen tree had lodged in the fork of another and there, right over his trail, sat a huge mountain lion switching its tail from side to side. He fired, piercing the lion's heart, and today he got the ten dollar bounty, proudly exhibiting the hide. He thinks the honors with "Quinb" and himself are about even.

G. C.

FILLMORE, Utah, October 23, 1891.

Salt Lake Herald
October 27, 1891

And now they have found lithographic stone near Fillmore.

Salt Lake Herald
November 3, 1891

Alma Greenwood, a prominent citizen of Fillmore, has just returned from an extended trip through Missouri, Ohio and Illinois. He went back for the purpose of disposing of some property in which he is interested and successfully accomplished the work. During his sojourn he visited the fair grounds in Chicago and other points of interest in the coming metropolis of America.

Deseret Evening News
December 1, 1891

Millard Stake Conference.

The quarterly conference of the Millard Stake of Zion convened in Fillmore city on Sunday, November 22nd, 1891, at 10 o'clock a. m. Present on the stand were the Presidency of the Stake, members of the High Council and other leading men of the Priesthood. After singing and prayer, on Sunday morning, President Daniel Thompson gave a report of the labors of the Presidency in the Stake since last conference. He spoke of the recent visits which they had made to all the wards, in company with Apostle F. D. Richards, whose kind, fatherly and much instructive talk to the people was much appreciated and had left a very favorable impression. Sister Jane Richards accompanied her husband and met with the Relief societies in all the wards.

The remainder of the forenoon was occupied with a spirited discourse on charity, by Elder Joshua Greenwood; reports by Bishops Thomas Yates of Scipio, H. B. Bennett of Meadow Creek, John Styler of Oasis, and William H. Pratt of Hinckley ward. Also a few encouraging remarks were made by President J. N. Hinckley, who expressed himself well satisfied with what had been said.

On Sunday afternoon the sacrament was administered and the wards of Holden, Kanosh, Deseret and Oak Creek were reported by Bishop Ay. Stephenson, Elder James Abraham, Counselors Isaac Whicker and George Finlinson, respectively.

Elder S. W. Western, of Deseret, who recently returned from a mission to England, reported his labors and experience in that country. He said he had been over the same ground where President Woodruff was so successful many years ago.

Elder Alma Greenwood, who has been traveling in the Eastern States during the last five months, gave an interesting account of his experience while there.

At the Monday forenoon meeting President D. R. Stevens spoke upon the danger of our becoming careless and indifferent.

President Hiram Mace reported the Forty-second quorum of Seventies, President W. V. Black the Twenty-first quorum of Seventies. Counselor James A. Melville reported Fillmore ward, Elder George Lovell Leamington ward, Elizabeth Yates as to the Relief societies, Elder Frank Hinckley reported the Y. M. M. I. A. associations.

President I. N. Hinckley expressed a hope that every department of the Stake would be alive and do its duty.

On Monday afternoon the general and local authorities of the Church were presented by C. Anderson. They were all sustained by unanimous vote.

Elder C. Anderson then addressed the conference, proving from the past history of the Lord's dealings with His people, ancient and modern, that He had never failed to fulfill His promises and His part of the covenants, while the people had failed repeatedly.

Elder J. E. Hickman spoke upon the importance of virtue and morality, and showed from history that a nation never fell until it had become immoral. He also spoke about the second coming of Christ, and said the signs of His advent had commenced. The speaker was followed by Brother Reed of Deseret.

C. ANDERSON,
Stake Clerk.
FILLMORE CITY, Nov. 25, 1891.

Salt Lake Herald
January 1, 1892

A party from Salt Lake have partly completed the arrangements for the purchase of the steam laundry plant which recently suspended business. The property will bring in the neighborhood of $1,000.

TERRITORIAL LEGISLATURE.

The XXX Session Convened at Two o'clock Today.

BOTH BRANCHES ORGANIZE.

W. H. King President of the Council and W. H. Seegmiller Speaker of the House.

COUNCIL.

Council met at 2 p.m. today in the City Hall, the same quarters the assembly has occupied at each succeeding session for many years.

Ex-chief Clerk F. J. Cannon called the Council to order and read the certified list of members prepared by the Secretary of the Territory, and the proceedings of the legislative council of the Thirtieth Utah Legislature commenced.

At roll call all the members except Evans of Ogden, Glendenning of Salt Lake, and King of Provo, responded.

On motion a committee, consisting of Lund and Baskin, were appointed to wait upon the Secretary and inform him that the members were ready to be sworn in.

Pending the arrival of the secretary, the members, by ballot, selected their seats.

The Secretary having entered the council chamber, the members stood in a circle and the oath was administered to them by that official.

King and Evans, at this juncture, entered the council chamber, and the oath was taken by them.

Melville moved that a permanent organization be effected. Carried.

Owing to the fact that a caucus had been held by the Democratic members of the Council, at which the officers had been agreed upon, the process of organization was brief.

The ballot for President of the Council resulted in the election of King, by a majority over Baskin of one, which was subsequently made unanimous.

King thanked the members for this mark of their esteem and said he would endeavor to preside with dignity and honor over the labors of the present Council.

J. W. McNutt, of Ogden, was elected chief clerk.

George Havercamp, of Provo, was installed as enrolling and engrossing clerk.

Sergeant-at-Arms— I. N. Hinkley, Jr., of Fillmore.

John Montgomery, of Salt Lake, messenger.

Watchman—Geo. R. Chase.

Chaplain—C. C. Shaw, of Cache county.

THE HOUSE.

The House was called to order at 2 p. m. by R. S. Campbell, Chief Clerk of the preceding House, who read the list of members elect.

Sargent moved the acceptance of the report as showing prima facie the membership of the body. Adopted.

The roll was called, all the members answering but Lawrence, Olsen and Pike. The first and last named came in subsequently, and on motion of Pierce, Secretary Sells was called in and the members were sworn in. They then signed the oath—the Edmunds-Tucker.

Organization being next in order, Pierce nominated for Speaker E. P. Ferry. Sargent nominated W. H. Seegmiller. The roll was called. Ferry voted for Kimball and Seegmiller did not vote, the result being—Seegmiller 14, Ferry 7, Kimball 1. Seegmiller was escorted to the chair by Sargent and Pierce. On taking the chair the Speaker returned his thanks and spoke very briefly, after which the election of a Chief Clerk was proceeded with.

Kimball nominated Clarence W. Hall, Mackey nominated J. R. Letcher. The result was Letcher was elected, 14 to 8—a strict party vote.

The Speaker announced as the next thing in order the election of a minute clerk, whereupon Kimball raised the point of order that there was no such office.

The Speaker held the point well taken, and the House proceeded to the election of a sergeant-at-arms. Moritz nominated J. J. Greenwald, Wright nominated N. W. Crookston, of Logan. The ballot resulted as before, 14 to 8 in favor of Crookston.

For enrolling clerk, John Boyden was nominated by Snow and Kenner Boreman by W. H. Irvine; 14 to 8 in favor of Boyden.

For Watchman—J. W. Judd, nominated by Tuttle; H. W. Nichols, Jr., by Lawrence. The latter said he had once held the position and could recommend his candidate as being thoroughly qualified. Judd was elected, 14 to 8.

For Messenger—Colton nominated N. G. Kimball; Pike nominated J. M. Hanson. Eight to 14 in favor of Hanson.

The strict party voting was broken into for the first time in electing a chaplain. Terry, in a short speech, in which he commended his nominee but said the latter did not dream he was the choice of the minority, named John Henry Smith. (Laughter and applause). Adams nominated D. Matthieson, of Iron County. On the vote being taken Marshall voted for Matthieson and Wright for Smith, the result being the same as before—Matthieson 14, Smith 8.

This concluded the organization except for minute clerk.

SOUTHERN UTAH

Interesting News from Sanpete

UTAH'S OLD CAPITAL

How Fillmore Appears To-day--The old Legislative Hall-Other Items.

[Enquirer Correspondence.]

Winter with plenty of snow is now reigning supreme in the green city of Sanpete. Santa Claus has made his regular tour of the season, and through the chimney of every house, descended with his rare presents for the little folks who found their stockings filled as expected. The stores, of which there are quite a respectable number, have had a rousing time just before holidays, and the saloons—yes, you may make out your own figures about them, (for I don't go there) but we have heard of no rows or arrests yet.

On Wednesday, December 23rd, while some of the boys, or young men were patronizing the bar-room, a valuable horse, with saddle, and bridle was stolen, and so far has not been recovered. Mr. Jacob Christensen, the owner, told the circumstances in this way: His oldest son was in the saloon and he (the father) sent a younger boy to get the older one home to assist him in some work. The younger boy went on horse-back, as Mr. Christensen lives on his farm some distance from town, but the older one was too interested in the saloon to leave at once. The younger brother, therefore, dismounted and tied his horse to the hitchingpost, while he went inside to get his brother out to go home. When they finally both come out,

they found only a piece of the rope, where the horse had been tied, the thief having cut it, instead of untying the animal, thus giving a plain evidence of theft, but no clue to the perpetator. Not till Friday, Dec. 25th, did anyone hear from the horse-thief, but then it was learned, that he had passed through Fairview, the next city north, at full speed early in the forenoon. Saturday morning's train took the sheriff out in pursuit, but the result is not yet learned.

On Thursday, Dec. 31st, the shareholders in the Co-op store will meet to consider whether they shall dissolve partnership or re-organize, as their charter will be void at the end of the present year. The Co-op store in Mt. Pleasant is a fine two-story building, well stocked with goods, but has not been as profitable to the shareholders as some other stores in the county; perhaps on account of its large investments of capital and also competition with the smaller and more cheaply managed stores in other localities.

A striking feature to former visitors, is the great improvements lately made on the old meeting house on the public square. A neat belfry or tower with a fine bell weighing some 600 or 700 pounds, gives the old familiar structure quite an aristocratic appearance, and speaks well for the church, the sound of the bell being both pleasant and strong. The square, a full block, is surrounded with a neat and substantial picket fence, and shade trees are plentiful both outside the block and inside the fence, which in time will give that city a fine park, and another gem in her crown earned by her energetic citizens.

FELIUS.

MT. PLEASANT, Dec. 27, 1891.

Old Capital of Utah.

[Enquirer Correspondence:]

From Holden is ten miles to Fillmore the county seat of Millard county and former capital of Utah. Here we find the old Legislative hall, still the peer of its younger surroundings, looming up as a giant veteran and witness of former-days' glory, when the law-makers, coming by teams from all parts of our then still more extensive territory gathered under its roof to give us the benefit of their experiment and learning. Oh! if they could speak to day and, like the monophon, repeat the speeches made then, but now lost for ever! It is now an institution of modern learning, being used for the Stake Academy under the able management of Fred. Hickman and a corps of qualified teachers. It seemed well nigh a bee-hive, comparatively speaking, as everybody seemed actively engaged and interested, and kept the most perfect order throughout.

There is no Co-op store in that city, the old organization having dissolved and sold out to another private party but the store business is seemingly in able hands and is well patronized. Some of the effects of the destructive flood of last spring are still to be seen. Large trunks of trees, some broken off squarely by the force of the maddened waters that carried everything before them, are still seen along the bank of the creek; some of them nearly two feet thick. The bridge on Main street is being rebuilt as the old one was entirely destroyed. Here resides the President of Millard Stake, we found him and his councilors and stake clerk making their quarterly visit through the various wards, holding meetings with the people and also investigating the conduct of the church officers, which seems to have a very good effect generally. The word of wisdom is more generally observed in Millard Stake, than in other stakes that we have any knowledge of, and the people seem to get along just as well as others anyhow.

Some eight miles farther south is a small village called Meadow Creek, presided over by Bishop Bennet, whose wife is a full cousin of Joseph Smith, the Prophet. She is a daughter of Aziel Smith, uncle to the Prophet. She was remarkably bright and active for her age, being nearly eighty years old; yet she could sew and direct her grand-children in dressmaking without the least difficulty. Her features are regular and remarkably fine, very much resembling the familiar profile of the martyr.

There is not much of interest to be seen in the little quiet burg, though there is a good public building used both for church and school purposes. It is owned by the ward.

Kanosh, or Corn Creek, still farther south, some seven miles; is the last village or settlement in Millard county. In by-gone years, an Indian agency was kept here, and the present settlement derives its name from the tribal chief of that time. An old, very unsightly adobe building is all the people have for religious and social gatherings, but there is talk about building a new one some time.

C. C. A. CHRISTENSEN,

EPHRAIM, Dec. 29, 1891.

Fairview Items.

[Enquirer Correspondence.]

The past year has been an eventful one for Fairview in many ways and will long be remembered by many as one of sickness, snow and death. Yet, however, we have many things to be grateful for. Good crops have been raised, especially of hay,' and now our farming community can sit by the fire and laugh at the storm, while they think of the good prospects for another year. The snow is now about a foot deep and prospects are good for more in the near future. Our reservoir did good service this year, and as a consequence hundreds of tons of lucern hay have been hauled from the former sage brush flat north and east of town.

Our sickness began with the year and during the year we have added over fifty mounds to the little village over the way; most of the deaths have been caused by diptherhia and typhoid fever. During the summer the diptherhia had such a start that our City Council employed Dr. Johnson of Fountain Green. We would advise other settlements troubled with this disease to do as we have done. There is little or no sickness in our midst at the present time.

Quite an interesting law suit has just been brought to a termination in Justice Guy C. Wilson's court, wherein Wm. F. Young and Swen O. Nielson figured as plaintiff and defendant respectively. Wm. Zabriskie represented the former and Jacob Johnson the latter. At 3 o'clock in the morning the jury returned a verdict for the defendant of $44.23.

The prospects are that our District Schools will be more of a success this winter than any previous year, on account of the corps of teachers employed by our trustees.

The schools are at present under the principalship of Guy C. Wilson, who has the able assistance of Eliza Day, Joseph Hanson and Miss Maggie Lewir, the latter of Provo.

All of our people have had a "Merry Christmas" and expect a "Happy New Year. "DAVE."

FAIRVIEW, Dec. 31, 1891.

Salt Lake Herald
January 19, 1892

Fillmore has a newly organized brass band with fifteen members. They are equipped with a fine set of new instruments and uniforms and are under the tutorship and direction of Prof. Dan Olson, of this place. Those who have heard this combination in quickstep selections have many compliments to offer.

THE WARM CREEK TRAGEDY.

Doutre Terrorized the Neighborhood and Has Now Killed An Objector.

In order to give the readers of THE HERALD a better understanding of the Warm Creek tragedy, a brief notice of which was telegraphed to you yesterday, it will be necessary to go back several years. Warm Creek is situated in the northwest corner of Millard county, and furnishes about as much water as Parley's cañon creek, and s presumably used on a half dozen or so ranches, and as is the custom in eastern Nevada and the west of this county, it has been the policy to claim all the water possible, thus keeping settlers at a distance, and any one expecting to appropriate any water must do so under protest, often of a rather forcible nature.

At the place of which we are writing, Mr. Rhodes' ranch of 160 acres lies highest up on the stream. Below and adjacent is an Indian farm of eighty acres, under fence, and which has been tilled by the reds for many years, and who claim a priority of appropriation of the water which they take out of the main creek near and on the lower side of the Rhodes' ranch. About one and one-half miles down the creek from the Indian farm is located the ranch of the Doutre Bros., who are represented as being .

A TERROR TO THAT REGION.

Three years ago last July a dispute over some land between some of the settlers and the Doutre Bros. culminated in the killing of Tom Noakes. Alex. and Treflle Doutre and Jerry Patnode were arrested for the murder. The grand jury ignored the case against Treflle and held Alex. and Patnode under the charge of murder. They were tried at Provo and found guilty of murder in the second degree. A new trial was obtained. The killing was admitted by Alex. Doutre, but the theory of self defense was set up and the prisoners discharged.

Several years ago the Doutre Brothers put a dam and head gates in the creek about a half a mile above Mr. Rhodes' place and ran the water around and north of the Rhodes farm and emptied the water into the main channel below the point where the Indians take out water for their farm, and allowing only that portion claimed by Mr. Rhodes to run down the creek from the Doutre dam. By a system of bulldozing the reds were terrified into letting their crops burn up several years in succession. This was a matter which two years ago Governor A. L. Thomas reported to the Washington authorities and asked for remedial measures. During this time Mr. Rhodes' farm was leased and he was in Utah county. On his return he collected some of the Indians and

TORE OUT THE DOUTRE DAM.

Some six weeks ago Mr. Stevens and family left Spring Valley, White Pine county, Nev., and settled at Warm Creek, purchasing a half interest in the Rhodes farm.

Last Saturday at about 4 p. m. Messrs. Rhodes and Stevens noticed a man at the Doutre dam and went up to see what was going on. It proved to be Treflle Doutre, who was putting the dam in shape to turn the water. Mr. Rhodes is a man over sixty years old, and it was presumed that Mr. Stevens was the chief objector and forbid Doutre from turning the water, but little is known of the occurence more than Doutre shot Stevens a few inches below the heart while standing so near the double-acting "bull-dog" as to have his jumper burned by the powder. After the shooting Doutre went home, while Mr. Stevens walked back to the Rhodes place, a distance of over half a mile. He lived until 9 a. m. the next morning.

Sheriff John T. Ashman, of Fillmore, has gone out to Warm creek and if the bird hasn't flown, will likely bring Doutre in here for examination. IGNOT.

A PIONEER GONE.

William King Died at the Deseret Hospital Yesterday Morning.

At 11 o'clock yesterday morning, William King, father of the Hon. W. H. King, president of the legislative Council, died at the Deseret hospital in this city, and the event was entirely unexpected. The deceased had been in temporary charge of the colony of Sandwich Islanders, located in Skull valley, Tooele county. Years ago, while acting as sheriff of Millard county, he was wounded in his leg by a desperado whom he was endeavoring to place under arrest. On Monday last he came to this city for surgical treatment in connection with this trouble, and was operated upon by Drs. Richards and Wilcox. Late Tuesday evening everything pointed to a complete recovery; therefore his death yesterday morning caused a severe shock to his relatives and friends in this city. The deceased was an old and esteemed resident of Utah, having come to this territory nearly two score years ago, and lived at Fillmore during most of the time. He was in his fifty-seventh year. The remains will be sent to Fillmore on Friday. As a mark of respect, both houses of the legislature adjourned yesterday until today at 2 o'clock.

The news of the death of William King, formerly of Kingston, Utah, but later of Skull Valley, was received by his children and friends in Provo as a great shock. It was not known that he was seriously ill, although he has been for some time suffering from a bullet wound in the leg. The wound was inflicted about twenty years ago from the hands of Willis Bartholomew, whom he was attempting to arrest in Fillmore, and it has been a source of trouble to him ever since.

Mr. King has always been distinguished for his enterprise, and has done much toward building up southern Utah. About ten years of his life was spent in the Sandwich Islands, where he was laboring with the natives.

He is the father of the Hon. William H. King, president of the legislative council. The news of his death came from Salt Lake yesterday, where he was being treated at the hospital.

Ira N. Hinckley, of Fillmore, was arraigned charged with unlawful cohabitation. He made a statement that he had not lived with the plural wife for over three years and that he would obey the law in the future. The judge inflicted a fine of $50 and costs.

Salt Lake Herald
February 21, 1892

The body of William King was taken to Fillmore yesterday, where the funeral will be held and interment take place. The relatives of Mr. King, who are very numerous in Southern Utah, will be present to pay their last respects to the departed. Hon. W. H. and Samuel A. King, together with other younger members of the family, accompanied the body to Fillmore.

Salt Lake Herald
February 26, 1892

Joseph E. Ray was in Provo yesterday. He is a part owner of the lithographic stone quarries in Millard county, over which there is at present considerable excitement. He is confident that the discoveries west of Fillmore and at Deseret will send a wave of prosperity over that region.

G. HUNTSMAN, a merchant of Fillmore, who has been in the city a few days, left for home yesterday.

Deseret Evening News
March 19, 1892

NO LONGER A "LIBERAL."

THE following letter was handed to us this morning by a friend, who thought it worthy of publication because the writer has been such a well known, pronounced "Liberal," and it shows the drift of feeling in reference to division which prevails in most parts of the Territory. As to the writer's views in reference to Republicanism and Democracy, they should be taken, if at all, with a grain of salt. He is a sheepowner whose opinions are largely governed by his pecuniary interests, and also a person of rash assertion and wild conclusion. We give his letter for what it is worth:

"SALT LAKE CITY, UTAH,
February 6th, 1892.

"George Velte, Esq., Chairman Millard County Liberal Committee, Fillmore, Utah:

Dear Sir—Your letter of February 1st, asking me to represent Millard County in the Territorial Liberal Convention, to hand. In reply will say, that first I am unable to comply with your request for reasons herein set forth.

I have, as you well know, always been a Liberal, and have been identified with that party since its inception. I have always, and am today, opposed to the union of Church and State, and have ever opposed ecclesiastical interference in any manner with politics, believing that priestcraft and statecraft are as opposite as the polls. I was a Liberal when to be so meant social ostracism, a state of society that ninety per cent. of the Liberal party knew nothing about, but I know this state of things could not always remain so. As the people became intelligent, and the free school system planted in every hamlet in our Territory, the ideas, thoughts, principles and opinions of the masses would be broadened and uplifted from the rut they had for so many years been grovelling in, and when the electric light of American ideas and principles became impregnated and diffused in their midst, they would follow the new light, and if not already so, become loyal, true and faithful to the great and grand principles of American institutions. That hope that I then had has been in a measure realized, and today I find the people dividing on party lines in national politics. I also note that the Democratic party, to whom the people of Utah were led to believe they owed allegiance to, and the success of whose policy they were told was the Mecca of all their hopes, has taken an aggressive stand, and made such an active cam-

paign, that today the Territorial Legislature is overwhelmingly Democratic,
and they can pass any measure they
choose, to foster the interests of their
party upon the people. Utah should
naturally and geographically be Republican, and when a proper presentation of
the facts are laid before the people, when
the people understand that the Republican party is the party of loyalty, of
progress, and of protection to all American interests, and when we can show
them that the Democratic party is a party
of promises ever holding the cup to their
lips, but breaking it to their hearts; that
they are being led by men who for years
trailed our country's flag in the mire, and
who caused tens of thousands of lives
to be sacrificed, made tens of thousands
of widows, filled the land with
orphans, and almost bankrupted the nation. When these facts are made known
to them, and their intelligence and justice
appealed to, we need have no fear of the
result; their loyalty to the flag and country will never again be questioned. By
longer adhering to the Liberal party we
are giving the Democrats an open field;
and when the former party is disrupted,
which it surely must be, we will be found
with the bag to hold, the game having
long since been captured. If the Liberals
of Salt Lake county wish to retain their
Liberal organization, I have nothing to
say. They are strong enough to hold
their own, and can elect their own repre-

sentatives to the Legislature; but we who
number only fifty in Millard county can
only stand and look on at the turmoil of
political strife, without daring to take
action with them. We can, I feel confident, carry Millard county for that glorious old Republican party. We can
place a man in the Legislature that
will be an honor to us, that
will represent a principle, who will be
honest and aggressive for our best interests, who will not be subservient to the
wishes of the majority, but who though
he stands alone will stand fearlessly for
the right for loyalty, and for the best interests of his constituents. For these
and other reasons equally pertinent, I
could not longer affiliate with, or enter
the late convention of the Liberal party,
and I feel confident that you and the
Liberals of Millard county will, when
you weigh the great issue at stake at the
coming election, agree with me, and
henceforth throw our influence, and lend
our voice and pen, and give our votes for
the success of that loyal party that never
yet had a traitor in its ranks, that have
ever stood for American interests and
American industries, for American men
and women and their prosperity, and for
the honor of that splendid emblem of
our country in every clime—Our Flag.
Yours truly,
CHARLES CRANE.

Salt Lake Herald
May 8, 1892

John Jackson and wife of Fillmore are
spending a few days in Provo.

Salt Lake Herald
May 25, 1892

Accident at Deseret.

Francis M. Lyman came up from Deseret
with the distressing news that Mrs. Martha
Robison of Fillmore had received some
frightful injuries caused by a team running
away while she and Mrs. Lizzie Henry
were out for a ride. They alighted at the
residence of William Black and Mrs.
Robison went to the head of the team and
took hold of the horses. They became
frightened and made a dash forward,
knocking her to the ground and tramping
upon her body. The woman was unconscious when picked up and sustained an
ugly wound in the head and side. After
being attended for some time she was
restored to consciousness but suffered
great pain. Up to last accounts the unfortunate woman was resting more easy.

AN ASSAULT CASE.

It Occupies the Attention of Judge Blackburn at Provo.

UTAH COUNTY COURT MATTERS.

Satisfactory Opening of the Lake Resort. — Other Items of Interest.

Justice Alexander's court was engaged the greater portion of yesterday in the case of Provo City vs. J. W. Siebolt and Joseph Hobbs. The defendants were charged with assaulting A. J. Stewart, Jr., on Tuesday, May 24th, '8. A. King prosecuted and E. B. Jones defended. A. J. Stewart, Jr., was the first witness. He stated that on Friday last he called at Mr. Siebolt's meat market on Center street, and presented an order for $8.75 for payment, Mr. Siebolt said he could not pay the bill then, but to call on Monday and he would pay it. Tuesday morning he called, presented the order, Mr. Siebolt took the order, and placed upon the counter $7.25 in cash and a bill against Mr. Stewart for $1.50. The latter said he did not owe the bill and demanded the full amount of money or the order returned. Mr. Siebolt then took from his desk the order, and commenced reading the same. Mr. Stewart reached over the desk and took the order out of Mr. Siebolt's hands and turned to leave the shop. Mr. Siebolt now made a lunge for Stewart and grappled with him, at the same time his hired man, Mr. Hobbs, caught hold of Mr. Stewart and held him and while holding him Mr. Siebolt struck him several blows on the face and head. Mr. Stewart finally got hold of a weight and tried to strike Siebolt, but the weight was taken from him. Andy Stewart corroborated the testimony of his father and stated he endeavored to stop the fight.

The defense claimed that Mr. Siebolt had a right to the order after it was presented, that it was his property, and that Mr. Stewart, instead of taking the order out of his hands, struck the order to the floor; at this Mr. Siebolt endeavored to get the order from the floor, but was not successful, and while Mr. Stewart was stooping to pick up the order he also grabbed a weight and tried to strike the defendant who then grabbed Mr. Stewart and held him solid. In other words Mr. Stewart assailed Mr. Siebolt and the latter then had the right to protect himself. In the melee Mr. Siebolt received a wound on the head which he alleges was cut by Mr. Stewart striking him with a weight. After arguments by council, the court held Mr. Siebolt guilty as charged and dismissed the charge against Mr. Hobbs. Mr. Siebolt was fined $10, he gave notice of an appeal. A complaint had been sworn out against Mr. Stewart by Mr. Siebolt, but when the verdict was rendered, finding Mr. Siebolt guilty, the case against Stewart on motion of the prosecution was dismissed.

There was a special meeting of the county court yesterday. The main business was the discussion of the recent laws passed by the legislature in reference to the leasing of school lands. The county attorney was requested to report on its provisions at the next regular meeting.

A Springville couple, William Johnson and Jane Kendall, were brought before Commissioner Hill yesterday on the charge of adultery. Soren Christensen appeared as their counsel. They waived examination and were bound over to await the action of the grand jury. Their bonds were placed at $1000 and $600 respectively.

Dr. F. B. Bickford, one of our leading physicians, leaves for Europe tonight. The gentleman has not been in our midst very long, but while here he has made many warm friends, and worked up an excellent practice. He is a graduate of the Michigan University and he now visits the continent to pursue his studies. The Doctor will go direct to Berlin where he will spend most of the summer, after which he will visit many of the principal cities and go perhaps as far as Palestine. We wish the gentleman a pleasant and successful sojourn and a safe return.

A meeting of the stockholders of the Provo West Co-op. was held yesterday, to hear a report of the condition of the institution and an explanation of what led to the assignment. The assignment was attributed to a partial loss by fire; many improvements had been made and times were hard, $10,000 becoming due, they could not meet the demand promptly. Times being hard, merchants cut prices, and collections could not be made. When the assignment was made their assets were $35,000 and their liabilities were placed at $27,000. They had outstanding book accounts to the amount of $9115.

The opening at the Lake resort yesterday, was satisfactory. The Republican drum corps rallied quite a crowd. Various outdoor sports were indulged in. Some young men received an unexpected bath by being capsized while out for a row, but they managed to right the boat and reached the shore in safety. A party was enjoyed at night. Jefferson's quadrille band was in attendance.

The beautiful residence of President A. O. Smoot, was the scene of festivity and happiness last evening, the occasion being the wedding reception of his daughter Ella to Mr. George Robinson, of Fillmore.

The bride was attired in a lovely white silk princess with shell trimming and natural flowers.

The presents were many and varied, some of them being of a most beautiful and costly nature. About fifty members of the family and intimate friends sat down to the first table at supper, which was a perfect picture of delicacies, surrounding a large and beautifully ornamented wedding cake, the whole table being set off with delicately perfumed flowers.

PROVO, May 28.

Ben Stewart of Fillmore, who has been suffering for a long time from internal troubles, died on Monday evening at Mrs. Waters' residence in this city. A wife and two small children are left to grieve. The remains will be buried at Fillmore.

AN ICE SPRING.

Millard County Has the Greatest Natural Curiosity in Utah.

Probate Judge Velle Writes of Volcanic Craters and Other Marvelous Productions.

In response to a request for information, Probate Judge George C. Velle writes Secretary McDaniels, of the World's Fair commission, as follows:

The principal industry of Millard county is farming and stock raising. We have about half a million acres of the best kind of farming land, but owing to lack of water we have not so far been able to bring it under cultivation. We are now experimenting with artesian wells, having one of the largest rock drillers in the territory at work, and if water can be had at reasonable figures ours will be one of the very best counties in Utah.

Of undeveloped resources we have mines of coal, iron, aluminum, also mines containing silver and gold, some of which are now being developed. Of quarries we have some of the best lithograph rock found in America, the supply being almost inexhaustible and only needing capital to develop it. We have gypsum enough to do the world for one hundred years to come. Of building rock we have the best kind of red sandstone in inexhaustible quantities, also sulphur. We have a great supply of timber, not hard wood, but suitable for lumber, and lime enough to run the whole world for a thousand years.

Our mountain streams could furnish water power enough to run 100 factories, but we have not one yet.

We need a railroad first of all to help us bring some of our resources to the front. We are setting a large cheese factory here at Fillmore and expect to add a cannery for putting up fruits and vegetables. Of stock, we are coming to the front with some good grades of horses and cattle, but do not raise thoroughbreds.

In the line of sheep our enterprising friend, Mr. Charles Crane of Kanosh, has stood pre-eminent, both as importer and breeder of the merinos for years. A letter directed to that gentleman would be answered promptly giving full details. We have the finest sheep range in Utah and the most of it. There are over 3,000,000 acres of land that can be used for anything but grazing purposes.

In connection with the farming industry I forgot to mention that mammoth enterprise at Swan lake, thirty-five miles west of here on the Sevier river, where the surplus water of that stream has been turned into a huge reservoir, containing some 11,000 acres of land. Dikes to hold the same and canals for conveying it to the lands to be cultivated are now being prosecuted and are to be completed this summer at a cost of over $2,000.

It is calculated to water some 50,000 acres of land from this source alone.

The boundaries of our county is also well adapted to raising fruit and will be so utilized as soon as a railroad shall admit us as competitors in the markets of the world.

Of curiosities we have an extinct crater and within a few miles of it a spring that produces ice even in the hottest weather; a few miles from there a warm spring said by Mr. Crane to be good for medical purposes; a short distance from there, a solid rock some eight or nine feet, nearly square, with human foot-prints well defined up one side of it, the best of which was cut out about a year ago, but some still remain. On top of it is what look like imprints of two large serpents coiled, also more foot-prints, of which the heel is the best defined. This curiosity I examined about six years ago. These foot-prints were made while the rock was yet in a

plastic state, and to me speaks of antiquity of the human race so remote that the Genesis of the Bible compared to it is like examining a last year's almanac to find the announcement of Columbus discovering America.

REPUBLICANS RATIFY.

They Hold a Meeting at Provo, Last Night.

THE ST. LOUIS BUNCO MAN ARRESTED.

Arthur Halliday Sustains a Broken Leg. — General Provo News.

Our City Recorder Mr. Geo. Havercamp accompanied by his wife left for Denver today. They will be gone about a week.

Court matters have been very quiet during the past few days.

The farmers are very busy putting up their hay.

Few idle men are seen on our streets during these hot days.

Mr. James Melville, of Fillmore, one of the gentlemen who was "buncoed" at St. Louis a few days ago out of a band of horses, passed through Provo last evening on his way home from the East. He reported that the person who beat him and Mr. Greenwood out of their horses had been arrested, and is now held at St. Louis on a charge of fraud. Mr. Greenwood remained there to appear against him. The hearing will take place today. The horses had been disposed of before the offender was arrested, and at present it is not known whether the horses or their value can be recovered.

Mr. Melville says he is now a little wiser than when he left home, and thinks he will be able to avoid affairs of this kind in the future. The horse market, Mr. Melville states, is quite dull at the present time.

For the past few days rumors have been afloat that the strictest propriety was not being observed at our Lake Resort by the bathers. Some of our leading citizens who are interested in the resort are somewhat concerned about this matter and an investigation is being made by them into the conditions of affairs. This resort has of late become quite popular, and the owners of the property are desirous that its former good reputation may be maintained.

Quite a number of our old people joined the Old Folks' Excursion yesterday and went to Payson.

Last evening the Republicans of Provo ratified the nomination of Harrison and Reid. During the afternoon and evening the Republican Drum Corps paraded the streets with banners and succeeded in bringing out a fair-sized audience, composed of both Republicans and Democrats. It had been announced that Hon. Frank J. Cannon of Ogden and Hon. Arthur Brown of Salt Lake would be present, and the people seemed quite anxious to hear what these gentlemen had to say about the convention at Minneapolis.

Mr. J. E. Booth called the meeting to order and stated its object. He predicted the success of Harrison and Reid, and concluded by eulogizing Ex-Speaker Reed and his action as Speaker of the House of Representatives.

Hon. A. G. Sutherland was introduced as a representative of the old "Liberal" Republican party. The gentleman spoke for about ten minutes, dwelling on the birth of the party and the policy it had always pursued in protecting the liberties of the people. He referred to protection and reciprocity as the foundation of the Republican party, and on that basis they should win the coming election. Referring to the past the gentleman said that the "clouds had cleared away, and brightness is before us—Harrison will have no slaves in America. We can't vote for him, but on the same day we can vote for a Delegate to Congress and thereby place ourselves in harmony with the great national party."

Judge J. D. Jones talked of the past administration, characterising it as successful, and predicted victory in November.

Hon. Frank J. Cannon was intro-

Hon. Frank J. Cannon was introduced as a product of "home industry." The gentleman stated he was pleased to ratify the nomination of the candidates of the Republican party. He called attention to Harrison's popularity in Indiana and Cleveland's unpopularity in New York, and from this reasoned that Harrison's election was sure.

Speaking of local affairs he said he was satisfied with the result of the Minneapolis convention, and that he believed that it would tend to harmonize the two Republican parties here in Utah. "And when the Republicans will not have a ripple to trouble them—Powers will not have forgotten his treatment at Chicago." At the conclusion of his speech the gentleman was handed a beautiful bouquet of roses.

Hon. Arthur Brown said it was the truth that the Republicans had been called on to ratify the action of their conventions. He spoke of protection and liberty as fundamental principles of the Republican party. "This was its platform in 1856—this is its platform in 1892."

He spoke at some length on the platforms of the two parties and compared them and their principles.

The public lands and silver questions occupied considerable of his time at the Minneapolis convention, he said. "We ratify the actions of the convention all through. We did not get quite all we wanted, and for a time felt bad; but I can now see the wisdom of only giving us half a vote. The convention held out the olive branch and asked us here in Utah to take hold of it together, and I am willing to do it."

Governor A. L. Thomas who had been to Payson on the Old Folks' excursion, stopped off for the rally, and was now introduced. He said he "welcomed the audience in the broad sense of American citizens." He predicted the success of the Republican party.

Last night about 8 o'clock, Arthur Holliday, the son of Abram Holliday, one of our city councilmen, caught hold of the hind end of a buggy that was being driven rapidly down Centre street, and some how his foot caught in the wheel, and his leg was broken above the knee. Drs. Pike and Shores were called in and set the injured limb, and at last account the boy was resting well.

Provo, June 30.

Salt Lake Herald
July 6, 1892

Joshua Greenwood dropped off on his return from Salt Lake to Fillmore. He has been in attendance at the district school teachers' convention in Salt Lake city.

Provo Daily Enquirer
July 7, 1892

S A, King goes to Fillmore to-day. He will ship a train load of horses east from Millard county, but does not propose to exchange them for real estate.

Salt Lake Herald
July 8, 1892

Samuel A. King has gone to Fillmore, his former home. He is making arrangements for the shipment of a train load of horses east.

Salt Lake Times
July 26, 1892

THE UTAH COMMISSON.

Down to Business Today — Registration Officers for Four Counties Appointed

The Utah commission today made the following appointments for deputy registration officers:

MILLARD COUNTY—Kanosh precinct, E. W. Penney; Meadow precinct, John Stredder; Holden precinct, Nicholas Paul; Scipio precinct, Andrew Peterson; Leamington precinct, Joseph Overton; Oasis precinct, John Styler; Deseret precinct, James H. Mace; Oak City precinct, Joseph A. Lyman; Hinckley precinct, George A. Black; Smithville precinct, W. C. Barry; Burbank precinct, Charles Rowland; Fillmore precinct, John Kelly.

CACHE COUNTY—Logan precinct, G. H. Keyson and L. D. Martin; Providence precinct, Mark Fletcher; Millville precinct, Joseph Harvey; College precinct, C. C. Brindrup, jr.; Hyrum precinct, C. H. Bwans; Paradise precinct, Dan Bickmore; Wellsville precinct, S. P. Hall; Mendon precinct, Fred Larsen; Peterboro precinct, Peter Petersen; Benson precinct, Robert Hawthorn; Newton precinct, John A. Christensen; Clarkston precinct, Frank Griffiths; Trenton precinct, C. C. Goodwin; Coveville precinct, Herchell Bullen; Richmond precinct, John Anderson; Smithfield precinct, Newton Woodruff; Lewiston precinct, J. W. Knowles; Hyde Park precinct, Steven Thurston; La Plata precinct, Joseph Watson.

BEAVER COUNTY—Beaver precinct, W. P. Smith; Greenville precinct, William Hurst; Adamsville precinct, John J. Jones; Minersville precinct, John Lightner; Star precinct, W. J. Kennedy; Grampion precinct, David James.

RICH COUNTY—Woodruff precinct, A. W. Nebeher; Laketown precinct, John Nebeher; Meadowville precinct, George T. Judd; Garden City, Edward Calder.

The commission is still at work on appointments as THE TIMES goes to press.

Provo Daily Enquirer

July 28, 1892

JOHN TRIMBLE, of Fillmore, lately re
turned from a mission to England, is
spending a few days in the Garden city
visiting friends. He is thinking per-
manently of locating in our city.

Deseret Evening News

August 1, 1892

FIRE AT FILLMORE.

Bishop Thomas Callister Sustains a $3,000 Loss.—He Carried No Insurance.

[Special to the DESERET NEWS.]

A serious fire occurred here yesterday afternoon at the farm of Bishop
Thomas Callister, situated about five
miles northwest of town. One hundred and fifty tons of hay, three sets of
harness, some farm machinery and one
imported bull together with all of Mr.
Callister's corrals, stacks and feed
sheds were consumed. The loss is estimated at about $3,000. There is no
insurance. The origin of the fire is
unknown. It required hard work to
save Mr. Callister's houses and
grainary.

FILLMORE, U. T., Aug. 1.

Salt Lake Herald

August 2, 1892

A FIRE at Fillmore on Sunday caused a loss
to Mr. Thomas C. Callister of about $3,000—no
insurance. One imported bull, 150 tons of hay,
three sets of harness and a large amount of
farm machinery were consumed.

George Hanson of Fillmore is a Provo
visitor. He is in attendance at the summer school.

Salt Lake Herald

August 4, 1892

Miscellaneous.
Joshua Greenwood and wife are up from
Fillmore.

Salt Lake Times
August 6, 1892

MUNICIPAL ELECTIONS.

List of Towns Whose Municipal Election Falls on the General Election Day.

The Utah commission has made the following list of the towns whose municipal election comes on the same day as the general election, in accordance with the provisions of an act of the last legislature, providing that elections shall be held in November next in each city, town, village and school district in the territory not having held an election since January 1, and prior to January 31, 1892:

Alpine, American Fork, Beaver, Bear River, Cedar, Coalville, Corinne, Ephraim, Elsinore, Fairview, Fillmore, Grantsville, Hyrum, Heber, Richfield, Springville, Washington, Willard, Huntington, Kanab, Lehi, Maroni, Morgan, Mendon, Manti, Monroe, Midway, Nephi, Ogden, Payson, Pleasant Grove, Park City, Salina, Santaquin, Spring and Salem.

Deseret Evening News
August 22, 1892

ALLEGED FORGERY CASE.

A Couple of Youthful Candy Thieves are Candidates

TO THE REFORM SCHOOL.

Extensive Sheep Transaction Made and
More in Contemplation.—Other
Items of Interest.

The case of Brooks, the alleged
forger of Springville, was resumed on
Saturday before Commissioner Hills.
The defense submitted their evidence
which was to the effect that Brooks
was manager for Klingler, and that he
contracted some lumber, and when he
came to fill the orders Klingler did not
have the kind of material necessary to
complete it, so he was compelled to
make purchases elsewhere, and when
the money to pay these accounts was
collected Brooks withheld sufficient to
pay for what he had purchased from
other firms, and so did not report to
Klingler the full amount collected.
The court thought defendant's conduct
suspicious and so bound him over to
await the actin of the grand jury.

Hank Johnson and Joe Baberg, two
small boys, were brought before Justice Gash yesterday evening, charged
with stealing five pounds of candy
from John Holdaway's candy stand.
The evidence against them was convincing to the court and they were
held to appear before Judge Blackburn
to see if they were not fit subjects for
the reform school. They are rather
tough boys.

Mr. John C. Witbeck came up yesterday from Manti, bringing with him
three of his children, who will attend
the Academy this year. Mr. Witbeck
reports things as being in a flourishing
condition at the Temple city. Mr. Witbeck and his sons have been engaged
rather extensively in the sheep business of late years and they seem to have
made it pay. He states that they
have just made a big sale to Phil-
brick & Grant of Idaho. About 12,000
head of sheep changed hands in
this one transaction. The sheep
were delivered about the first of
this month on the San Pete mountains. Two of this gentleman's sons
are now in Arizona negotiating for
about 30,000 head, which they expect
to drive into Utah. If the number
they desire cannot be obtained in
Arizona the gentlemen will go as far
as Texas. Mr. Witbeck thinks that
sheep can be purchased pretty cheap in
the south, and that by careful management they can be worked slowly into
this Territory, being brought in for
just about what it would cost to tend
them during the same length of time if
right here. Mr. Witbeck thinks the
outlook for the sheep men is very
bright.

Mr. and Mrs. James F. Babcock, of
New Hampton, Iowa, attended the
conclave at Denver and then came on
to Utah to visit some of their relatives
who have been in this Territory since
the early days. They came to Provo
yesterday and were the guests of Mr.
and Mrs. W. H. King. They will continue as far south as Fillmore, where
they have a great many relatives. Mr.
Babcock was raised at Kirtland, and
his parents were Mormons in the early
days of the Church, his father being a
Seventy. This is the gentleman's
first visit to Utah and he is very much
pleased with our surroundings and
states that if he could sell out reasonably well in Iowa, he would be
tempted to make his future home in
Zion.

Apostle Lyman paid Provo a visit
last night, he is en route to Southern
Utah, where he will attend a number
of Stake Conferences.

The ball game between the newspaper men and the lawyers of Provo
will be played this afternoon.

PROVO, Aug. 20, 1892.

LADY MANAGERS.

Presidents of County Organizations Elected Last Evening.

The Utah Building Is Highly Praised by All
the World's Fair Officials—Good
Work Being Done.

The board of lady managers for Utah held a meeting yesterday at the commission rooms, all the members being present except Mrs. Lyman, who was unavoidably detained. Mrs. Salisbury, Mrs. Whalen and Miss Keogh of the national board were also present.

The following presidents or organizers were appointed: Lucy A. Clark, Farmington, Davis county; Mary Pitchforth, Nephi, Juab county; Sarah Pieston, Ephraim, Sanpete county; Sarah H. Crosby, Panguitch, Garfield county; Amy E. Cook, Laketown, Rich county; Ann C. Woodbury, St. George, Washington county; Mary Howard, Huntington, Emery county; Harriett D. Bunting, Kanab, Kane county; Mrs. Ruth Hatch, Heber City, Wasatch county; Rhoda A. Lyman, Tooele, Tooele county; Mrs. E. Crane Watson, Parawan, Iron county; Dailah K. Olsen, Fillmore, Millard county; Martha T. Hammond, Bluff, San Juan county; Mamie J. Snow, Brigham, Box Elder county; Ann Cluff, Coalville, Summit county; Esler E. C. Francis, Morgan, Morgan county; Celia E. Bean, Richfield, Sevier county; Sarah M. Dell, Beaver, Beaver county; Sarah Stewart, Moab, Grand county; Mrs. C. C. Bartlett, Vernal, Uintah county; Sarah S. Studweeks, Junction, Piute county; Mrs. Emeline B. Wells, Salt Lake city, Salt Lake county; Mrs. Thomas Whalen, Ogden, Weber county; Mrs. Marrilla Daniels, Provo, Utah county; Mrs. Moses Thatcher, Logan, Cache county.

A meeting was called for the Templeton parlors for Saturday afternoon at 1 o'clock to organize Salt Lake county.

It was decided to collect funds and make a silk portier for the woman's building at Chicago, the portier to be made of native silk.

Mrs. Thatcher was appointed a committee of one to make a report on candidates for the floral emblem to be selected for the territory.

A large amount of routine business was transacted, and the board adjourned subject to call.

Salt Lake Times
September 9, 1892

WORLD'S FAIR COMMISSION.

Special Meeting Held to Hear the Report of the Secretary.

A special meeting of the Utah World's Fair commission was held last night to hear the report of Secretary McDaniel on his trip to Chicago in the interest of the Utah exhibit.

Secretary McDaniel stated that he had called for bids in accordance with the plans and specifications adopted for the erection of the Utah building. A number of bids had been submitted, all of which were wired to Executive Commissioner Empey. The bid had been awarded to Harvey & Son for $10,500 for the building complete. The contract calls for the completion of the building by October 20. The action of the secretary was formally approved by the commission.

THE LADY MANAGERS.

The board of lady managers of World's fair for Utah met yesterday afternoon at Secretary McDaniel's office and began the work of forming county associations of ladies to look after the work. The following ladies were appointed organizers in the several counties:

Salt Lake, Mrs. Emily B. Wells, Salt Lake; Davis, Lucy A. Clark, Farmington; Juab, Mary Pitchforth, Nephi; San Pete, Sarah Preston, Ephraim; Garfield, Sarah H. Crosby, Pauguich; Rich, Amy E. Cook, Laketown; Washington, Mrs. M. C. Woodbury, St. George; Emery, Mary Howard, Huntington; Kane, Harriet T. Bunting, Kanab; Wasatch, Mrs. Ruth Hatch, Heber; Tooele, Rhoda A. Lyman, Tooele City; Iron, Mrs. E. C. Watson, Parowan; Millard, Delia K. Olsen, Fillmore; San Juan, Martha T. Hammond, Bluff; Box Elder, Minnie J. Snow, Brigham; Summit, Ann Cluff, Coalville; Morgan, Esther E. C. Francis, Morgan; Sevier, Cecelia E. Bean, Richfield; Beaver, Sarah M. Bell, Beaver City; Grand, Sarah Stewart, Moab; Uintah, C. C. Bartlett, Vernal; Piute, Sarah P. Studweeks, Yunkton; Utah, Merilla Daniels, Provo; Weber, Mrs. Thomas Whalen, Ogden; Cache, Mrs. Moses Thatcher, Logan.

It was decided at the meeting to prepare a silk portiere of native silk for exhibition in the women's department. Mrs. Bullock was appointed a committee of one to look into the silk culture industry of the territory, for the purpose of gathering material for this piece of work.

Provo Daily Enquirer
September 10, 1892

THE JURORS SUBPOENED

For the September Term of the First District Court.

Deputy Marshal Bachman returned last night from the southern counties of the district. He has subpoenaed the following jurors for the September term of court:

GRAND JURORS.

Geo. W. Mickel, Provo.
E. J. Ward, "
Thomas Beesely, "
Heber Allred, Lehi.
Andrew Adamson, American Fork.
L. J. Deal, Springville.
J. Frank Bringhurst, Springville.
J. J. Banks, Spanish Fork.
Wm. Jex " "
George Carter, Fountain Green.
Parley R. Allred, Sr., " "
Henry Green, Ephraim.
E. T. Barry, Manti.
J. W. Lowe, Mount Pleasant.
James Rigby, Jr., Fairview.
Nephi Reese, Wales.
Wm. Lisenbee, Annabella.
Samuel Sprague, Richfield.
Mads Christensen, "
Frank Carroll; Orangeville.
Arthur Van Buren, "
Thomas C. Miles, Huntington.
Wm. Memmoth, Jr., Scipio.
George Crane, Kanosh.

PETIT JURORS.

R. A. Hill, Jr., Provo Bench.
Chas. E. Crandall, Provo Bench.
Robert Dugdale, Provo.
Albert Glazier, Provo.
J. S. Fiddler, Provo.
Wm. P. Bennett, Provo.
Chas. J. Taylor, Provo.
John F. Westfall, Pleasant Grove.
J. B. Seleck, Provo.
George Dorton, Lehi.
Newell Brown, Lehi.
Leo. T. Shelly, American Fork.
James H. Clark, American Fork.
Albert G. Thomas, Fairfield.
George McKinzey. Springville.
Morgan Warner, Spanish Fork.
John O. Thomas, Spanish Fork.
Henry Fairbanks, Payson.
O. H. Pulver, Payson.
James Leetham, Lake Shore.
John F. Williams, Lake Shore.
Levi Openshaw. Santaquin.
J. M. Halladay, Santaquin.
Luke Hickman, Silver City.
H. H. Sorvles, Silver City.
Joseph Hoff, Lemington,
Frank Holbrook, Fillmore.
G. W. Cropper. Deseret.
La Fiber Ouddeback, Vermillion,
Asa R. Harvley, Central.
Wm. H. McKenna; Redmond.
James P. Christensen, Ephraim.
August Anderson, Ephraim.
Edward Reed, Manti.
John A. Larsen, Mt. Pleasant.
John Ford. Wallsburgh.

Salt Lake Times
September 13, 1892

BACK FROM THE SOUTH.

Millard County Will Go Largely Republican This Fall.

Hon. J. S. Painter returned yesterday from Millard county, where he, in connection with Will Hall Poore of THE SALT LAKE TIMES, have been campaigning for a week.

The eloquent speakers addressed large and enthusiastic audiences at Deseret, Oak Creek, Holden, Fillmore, Meadow, Kanosh and Scipio and made a number of converts to Republicanism.

Millard county is Republican by at least 100 majority. There is a large neutral vote, and it is rapidly giving its adherence to the party of protection. The leading industry of the county is sheep-growing, and the voters are fully advised as to the benefits of a tariff on wool and mutton.—*Ogden Standard.*

Salt Lake Herald
September 18, 1892

Miss Lillian Hinckley of Fillmore stopped off at Provo on her way to the wedding reception of her brother, Samuel A. King, at Salt Lake.

Salt Lake Herald
September 24, 1892

There were two heated terms, about the 1st to the 5th, and the 14th to the 17th days. During these hot spells the temperature reached 113 at St. George on the 4th (maximum for the month), 107 at Cisco on the 4th, 103 at Fillmore on the 18th, 100 at Salt Lake city on the 15th. There was a cool spell from the 24th to the 30th in various localities.

Salt Lake Herald
September 27, 1892

POLITICS IN MILLARD COUNTY.

To the Editor of THE HERALD:

The Democrats of Millard county have, at last, "got a move" on themselves, and good, hard work has been done for Democracy during the past eight days by H. J. Webber, Esq., of Ogden.

Mr. Webber began the labor of "pulling the wool" away from the optics that have been covered by the numerous Republican stumpers that seemed to have made a special prey of Millard county, by delivering his opening speech at Scipio, and proceeding south, delivered speeches at Holden, Fillmore, Meadow and Kanosh.

Fillmore had a fine parade and a lively rally. Several members of the g. o. p. getting full and satisfactory replies to their questions.

Night before last Mr. Webber held forth in a rally at the Hinckly ward, where Chairman W. H. Pratt had made ample arrangements for the comfort of the people who went over from Oasis and Deseret. Hinckly has about sixty voters, eight of whom are Republicans.

Last evening a rally was held in Deseret, which drew largely from our neighboring wards, all standing room being occupied and many appearing at the windows as interested listeners.

Mr. Webber is a fluent, logical and forceful speaker at any time, but surpassed himself last evening, holding the attention of his large audience for nearly two hours, and the hearty applause as point after point was made proved how much in sympathy were the people with the sentiments enunciated by the speaker. Tonight Mr. Webber speaks at Oak Creek, and tomorrow evening will close his tour through Millard by speaking to the people of Leamington. Aside from our local stumpers, Mr. Webber is the only Democratic speaker that has visited this section, while the Republicans have had Messrs. John Henry Smith, Calvin Reasoner, Colonel Miller, Judge Painter and others who have labored through the entire lists of Republican arguments, and yet, it is safe to predict that this and our sister towns will give a satisfactory majority for the party of Jefferson.   Respectfully,

Iσxoτ.

Deseret, Sept. 23, 1892.

Salt Lake Herald
October 9, 1892

PUBLIC SPEAKING.

List of Appointments of J. L. Rawlins to Address the People of Utah.

J. L. Rawlins, Democratic nominee for delegate to Congress, will address the people of Utah on the issues of the day at the following times and places. Other gentlemen are expected to be present and speak. County Democratic committees will please make the necessary arrangements.

Monday, Oct. 10, Park City.
Tuesday, Oct. 11, Heber.
Wednesday, Oct. 12, Wanship and Coalville.
Thursday, Oct. 13, Morgan and Echo.
Friday, Oct. 14, Logan.
Saturday, Oct. 15, Ogden.
Monday, Oct. 17, Brigham and Willard.
Tuesday, Oct. 18, Terrace and Box Elder county.
Wednesday, Oct. 19, Scipio.
Thursday, Oct. 20, Fillmore.
Friday, Oct. 21 Beaver.
Saturday, Oct. 22, Minersville.
Monday, Oct. 24, Sevier.
Tuesday Oct. 25, Sevier.
Wednesday, Oct. 26, Sevier.
Thursday, Oct. 27, Sanpete.
Friday, Oct. 28, —
Saturday, Oct. 29, Fountain Green and Nephi.
Monday, Oct. 31, Price.
Tuesday, Nov. 1, Springville and Provo.
Wednesday, Nov. 2, Payson and Lehi.
Thursday, Nov. 3, Bingham.
Friday, Nov. 4, Bountiful and Murray.
Saturday, Nov. 5, Grantsville.

Deseret Evening News
October 11, 1892

Departing Missionaries.

Elders H. M. Rawlins, Jr., of Lewiston, Cache county, who recently returned from the territory bringing home with him Elder F. F. Merrill, of Fillmore, who was ill at the time, and Elders John A. Lowe, of Franklin, Idaho, Joseph H. Lowe, of the same place and Joseph Hyrum Holmes, of Montpelier, Idaho, all leave this city over the Rio Grande Western at 9:25 tonight on missions to the Indian Territory.

Deseret Evening News
October 17, 1892

FROM MILLARD COUNTY.

A Complaint Against Sheep.—Politics Stir the Peaceful, Rural Air.

[Special correspondence of the NEWS.]

MEADOW, Millard Co., Oct. 13,—Our county, like all others, is in a state of commotion and ferment over politics. We have had political "stumpers" of both parties to visit us, and try to convert us to their own views, while local politicians are airing their lungs and booming wool to an extent that would almost lead us to believe it was the only article left in the wide world worth thinking or talking about.

We have had a surfeit of sheep during the past few weeks for they have been herded on our one solitary creek, and made its water so foul that it has produced among the inhabitants of Meadow an amount of epidemic disease that has alarmed us. First we had diphtheria from which four deaths resulted; then malarial fever and diarrhœa, from which complaint many are now suffering.

No doubt the sheep industry is a most useful and profitable one to the community, but where the owners are so neglectful or so devoid of all feelings of humanity, so intensely selfish as to endanger the lives of their neighbors by persistently fouling our water, they become an unmitigated nuisance, and it is about time something was done to protect us from their cruelty. It is bad enough to have pigs, calves and other animals wallowing in our ditches, corrals, hog pens and chicken coops in close proximity to our homes, without our drinking water being fouled from its very source.

Fillmore is making great preparation for receiving the Democratic candidate for Congress, Mr. Rawlins, and those who may accompany him. They are expected next week, and as we have just had speakers on the Republican side, we are kept pretty busy getting up receptions. Cleveland and Harrison hats give a somewhat picturesque air to our streets, and it is a novelty to see our sturdy citizens of all ages with tall, grey stovepipes on their heads. The political tile is not only in great demand, but many wearers have also a portrait of the Presidential candidate stuck on the side of their ordinary head gear. All the other towns in the county are equally enthusiastic and earnest in striving to give a welcome to the speakers who come among us. The young especially are beginning to take an interest in politics, to read more, and make themselves acquainted with what is occurring outside their own immediate neighborhood. The present campaign has sent among us many able men, and will be a great educator, both politically and socially.

The fruit and potato crops are partial failures, but the grain harvest has been a bountiful one, and the people generally are cheerful and contented. There is considerable excitement over our local election, especially among those who are aspirants for office.

M. A. Y. G.

A DRY SEPTEMBER.

Less Precipitation In Our Locality Than Ever Before, so Far as Known.

The United States department of agriculture and weather bureau says in its monthly review of Utah weather for September, 1892:

Temperature, etc. — The month could be properly characterized as a very dry one, and one above the average September in warmth. The atmospheric movement was sluggish, resulting in absence of storms and a prevailing dryness.

The amount of sunshine was unusual, even for September. The photographic record at Salt Lake City, shows a total sunshine of 325 hours, or about 90 per cent of the possible amount.

There were two hot spells, one from the 14th to 19th, and the other from 28th to the 30th. During the former of these periods the maximum temperature of 102 was reached at St. George, on the 16th; a temperature of 104 reported from Fillmore on the 28th, appears erroneous. During the cold spell on the 21st of the month the mercury at Scofield sank to twenty degrees; the extreme range at Scofield was thirty-seven degrees, the greatest reported from any station. Grouse Creek had a monthly range of thirty-six, the least range recorded by self-registering instruments.

The average temperature of the Territory was 64.6 degrees; a mean of from twenty stations. The monthly mean at St. George was 79; at Fillmore 71.7; Ogden 69.9; Moab 66.8; Scofield 53.

Precipitation. — Reports agree that the month was one of the dryest Septembers ever known. Many localities had absolutely no precipitation, and even where rain fell it was only a few light showers, the greatest amounts being 0.54 inch at Ogden, and 0.49 at Snowville. The average of all stations was 0.09 inches.

Light frosts occurred at Loa on the 10th and 11th; at Levan on the 21st, and at Snowville on the 29th and 30th.

Light thunderstorms occurred at various stations on the 2nd, 20th, 28th, 29th and 30th.

The observer at Levan writes—The month has been unusually dry, with hot days and cold nights. Ranges dry and bare; no show for stock living out this winter without feeding.

Observer at Loseoo writes—The month has been very dry. No high winds; clear sky nearly all the month, with light breezes from the southwest.

Observer at Mt. Carrol—This has been the driest month of the year; only a sprinkle on the 30th.

Observer at Richfield—This has been the driest season known in this county. Crops have stood it well, as the yield is about the average. Cattle ranges on the mountains have been poor for lack of rain.

Observer at St. George — Weather sultry, atmosphere rather smoky. The driest time for over four years.

RAWLINS' TOUR.

Big Crowds Greet Him Everywhere and the Greatest Enthusiasm Manifested.

FILLMORE, U. T., Oct. 20.—[Special telegram to THE HERALD.]—The campaign now being waged by the Democrats of Utah is bringing out great crowds of people, and this portion of the territory is like the rest, anxious to hear the truths of Democracy expounded.

Yesterday afternoon Hons. J. L. Rawlins and John T. Caine addressed a large audience at Oasis, and at Deseret in the evening, while Alfales Young spoke at Scipio the same evening. Today all three were at Holden and tonight Fillmore is filled with people who have listened to these Democratic orators.

Mr. Rawlins' tour has been a remarkable one. Everywhere the greatest enthusiasm is manifested. The meetings have been immense ones and great inroads have been made in the Republican strongholds.

Salt Lake Times
November 3, 1892

New Election Judges.

The commission today made the following changes in the judges of election:

Thomas J. Marley was appointed at Moroni to fill the vacancy occasioned by some man, whose name was not given, resigning on account of being a candidate.

J. M. Clark of Birch Creek, Box Elder county, was appointed to fill the place of R. M. Burch, resigned.

Will R. Thompson was appointed to fill the vacancy caused by the resignation of Orville Thompson, candidate for office at Scipio, Millard county.

George P. Brown was appointed to take the place of William I. Hatch, another candidate at Scipio.

George M. Hansen, Edward Bartholomew and Alma Greenwood were appointed at Fillmore to fill the places of the three judges formerly appointed, all of whom were candidates. They were James King, John B. Williams and James A. Mellville.

Deseret Evening News
November 25, 1892

AGRICULTURAL LAND PATENTS.

The Last List Received from Washington by the Local Land Office.

Subjoined is the last list of agricultural land patents received from Washington by the local land office:

C. E. No. 3934, to Francis H. Grice of Salt Lake county, 160 acres.

C. E. No. 4000, to Alexander McKenan of Salt Lake county, 160 acres.

C. E. No. 4002, to Ludwig Felt of Weber county, 160 acres.

C. E. No. 4005, to Warren D. Smith of Wasatch county, 160 acres.

C. E. No. 4012, to Thomas George of Salt Lake county, 160 acres.

C. E. No. 4020, to Susan Weyland of Tooele county, 160 acres.

C. E. No. 4027, to Neils Monson of Utah county, 80 acres.

H. E. No. 4753, to Edwin W. Beckwith, 166 acres.

H. E. No. 4754, to George Yates, 100 acres.

H. E. No. 4755, to John W. Gibson, 80 acres.

H. E. No. 4756, to James Forbes, 40 acres.

H. E. No. 4757, to Elizabeth M. Quimby, 160 acres.

H. E. No. 4758, to Lee Byber, 160 acres.

H. E. No. 4759, to Samuel D. Nicholas, 80 acres.

H. E. No. 4760, to Jorger C. Peterson, 160 acres.

H. E. No. 4761, to Julia A. Davis, 160 acres.

H. E. No. 4762, to David Provost, 160 acres.

H. E. No. 4763, to Ephriam Hansen, 160 acres.

H. E. No. 4764, to Andrew Christensen, 160 acres.

H. E. No. 4765, to William F. House, 50 acres.

H. E. No. 4766, to John Ray, 40 acres.

H. E. No. 4767, to Myron A. Abbott, 160 acres.

H. E. No. 4768, to Edgar Fillmore, 160 acres.

H. E. No. 4769, to Thomas J. Parkinson, 160 acres.

H. E. No. 4770, to David T. Rees, 160 acres.

H. E. No. 4771, to Edward S. Underwood, 160 acres.

H. E. No. 4772, to Hyrum Thomas, 160 acres.

H. E. No. 4773, to Joseph H. Craghead, 160 acres.

H. E. No. 4774, to Charles Hayborne, 161 acres.

H. E. No. 4775, to Johanna Peterson, 157 acres.

H. E. No. 4776, to Alvin D. Terry, 160 acres.

H. E. No. 4777, to Orson Kelsey, Jr., 160 acres.

H. E. No. 4778, to Simon Webb, 160 acres.

H. E. No. 4779, to Mary Pohlson, 160 acres.

H. E. No. 4780, to Andrew Russell, 160 acres.

H. E. No. 4781, to Clemence H. Martin, 160 acres.

H. E. No. 4782, to Charles J. Conley, 40 acres.

H. E. No. 4783, to Elizabeth Tipton, 161 acres.

H. E. No. 4784, to William Thomas, 160 acres.

H. E. No. 4786, to Hans C. Jenson, 160 acres.

H. E. No. 4787, to James Chantrill, 160 acres.

H. E. No. 4788, to Jas. W. Thomas, 160 acres.

H. E. No. 4789, to Wm. H. Jolley, 160 acres.

H. E. No. 4790, to Rees Griffith, 160 acres.

H. E. No. 4791, to John G. Shields, 172 acres.

H. E. No. 4792, to Joseph Colby, 160 acres.

H. E. No. 4793, to Carl Y. Svenson, 160 acres.

H. E. No. 4794, to Erick Erickson, 160 acres.

H. E. No. 4795, to James A. Holman, 160 acres.

H. E. No. 4796, to Martin A. Taylor, 160 acres.

H. E. No. 4797, to Wm. L. Smith, 160 acres.

H. E. No. 4799, to Daniel B. Woodland, 160 acres.

H. E. No. 4800, to Robert Spray, 160 acres.

H. E. No. 4802, Elizabeth Miller, 80 acres.

H. E. No. 4803, to Zenos Whittaker, 80 acres.

H. E. No. 4804, to Frands C. Grundvig, 155 acres.

H. E. No. 4805, to the heirs of Hyrum Thayer, deceased, 160 acres.

The following two patents have been received issued to Indians under act of Congress of July 4, 1884:

H. E. No. 4801, to Richard Nebeker, for 160 acres of land near Bear Lake.

H. E. No. 6406, to Peaunum, an Indian, 160 acres in township 15 south, range 19 west.

A Sharp Query From Millard.

Oasis, Millard Co., Dec. 20, 1892.

Editor Deseret News:

On the morning of December 17th two men left Swan Lake, 18 miles below here, for Salt Lake on foot. They passed through here about 5 p. m., following the railroad track, and reached Riverside, a small station further north, about 8 o'clock p. m. By this time both were badly frozen, and one of them, it is since learned, will be likely to lose both his feet. The section men at Riverside took them in, dressed their frosted members and kindly cared for them during the night. The conductor of the train having refused to carry them, a man on horseback was sent back to Oasis next morning with a letter to the constable, who immediately sent a wagon for them, brought them to this place and had them taken to a hotel. He then telegraphed, upon advice of the selectman, to the county prosecuting attorney at Fillmore, stating that the poor fellows could not travel, and were in need of medical aid, and asking what should be done with them. The answer was to the effect that "we cannot do anything with such men, get rid of them the best way you can!"

Now, Mr. Editor, does the law compel the counties to take care of such unfortunates? If so, it ought to be enforced. If not, ought not such a law to be enacted at once in the interest of civilization and common humanity? As to the advice to "get rid of them the best way you can," we are in a quandary as to which of the two ways would be the better: to turn them out in the snow and let them die like dogs, or to cast them into a pit and secure their death and burial at once. The latter plan would certainly be most effective as a means of getting rid of them.

I need scarcely say the advice has not been acted upon.   Oasis.

When Seward Was Governor.

One of the best stories William H. Seward used to tell was of a reception he had while governor of the state. He gave it in honor of Millard Fillmore. A great many people knew neither Seward nor Fillmore by sight. Fillmore was a splendid specimen of sturdy manhood, nearly six feet in height. He stood at Seward's left, and the difference between the men was striking. Of the throng that passed by those who were not acquainted with either Seward or Fillmore saluted Fillmore as governor, and he turned to Seward and said, "Why do so many people mistake and call me governor?"

"Ah," said Seward, "it is because in the popular mind there is an instinctive feeling that a great office should be filled by a man who is physically great, as you are, Fillmore. When people see me they think some mistake has been made, and that in some way or other a boy has been chosen governor."—New York Sun.

Fillmore Paragraphs.

Editor Deseret News:

We have had a great influx of visitors to our city today, on account of a horse race between Fred Bird's Corn Creek sorrel, and Doyley Huntsman's Baldy. The enthusiasm gradually waned as the crowd watched the struggles of Baldy to keep in sight of the sorrel. But the main attraction was a foot race. A great unknown sent a challenge from Deseret to run any one in the county seventy-five yards for money—quite a stake. A lad from Scipio was backed against this mystery. When the biped speeders appeared upon the track the disparity in size was marked. The mystery is a large, angular and rangey fellow. Scip is a compact, well muscled high stepper, of Caledonian pedigree with a mountain cross. As they pranced up and down the track money went begging for investment on the unknown. Demure faces looked anxiously on.

But how they come, like a cyclone; the mystery is solved. The money goes to Scipio and the honors remain in Millard, which generally "gets there," when she makes an effort.

The two saloons and a large dance hall are but too well patronized considering how dull times are and the class of goods they carry.

The old State House has found a grand and legitimate use as a district school building, presided over by County Superintendent Professor Joshua Greenwood. The new, rustling assessor has been chasing sheep in the western wilderness and counting noses of about half a million of that lately timid animal. He looks well and is cheerful about the future.

Millard has many signs of coming prosperity, although at present but little snow is stored in the mountains.

A. BIRD.

FILLMORE, Millard county, Jan. 28, 1893.

BEFORE BLACKBURN.

Grand and Petit Jurors Empaneled—A Youthful Burglar.

PROVO, Feb. 1.—The February term of the First district court opened today, and after sending John Martin, a youthful house breaker, to the reform school, Judge Blackburn began the work of empaneling the grand and petit juries with the following result:

GRAND JURY.

Ezra Shoemaker, Manti.
C. A. Larsen, Ephraim.
Samuel Thomson.
J. H. McLenehan, Salina.
Ed Bennett, Holden.
John C. Kelly, Fillmore.
J. A. Allred, Deseret.
James Evans, Lehi.
A. B. Okey, Nephi.
James Ivy, Salina.
A. Mortensen, jr., Monroe.
D. McArthur, Mt. Pleasant.
Jonas H. Erickson, Mt. Pleasant.
Mathias Jorgensen, Mt. Pleasant.
W. J. Van Horn, Castle Gate.
E. T. Cook, Eureka.
Albert Marsh, Alpine.
Theodore Jepperson, Midway.
Isaac Wall, Wallsburg.
William Ward, Castle Gate.
Thomas Coswell, Silver City.
J. Murdock, Heber.
P. C. Scomp.

PETIT JURY.

J. I. Chatwin, Santaquin.
S. P. Christensen, Salem.
J. S. Page, jr., Payson.
Joseph Bells, Payson.
J. M. Creer, Spanish Fork.
S. Wanless, Spanish Fork.
J. B. Mitchell, Mammoth.
Peter Thompson, Richfield.
William Guther, Eureka.
J. E. Jensen, American Fork.
E. A. Harvey, Eureka.
George Robbins, Scipio.
Orvil Thompson, Scipio.
J. E. Daniels, Provo.
R. Turner, Nephi.
E. H. Davis, jr., Lehi.
S. J. Taylor, Lehi.
E. H. Boley, American Fork.
P. C. Christensen, Moroni.
Richard Velton, Vernal.
Fred Mann, Nephi.
N. S. Holliday, Santaquin.
John O. Dixon, Provo.
John Sidwell, Nephi.
William Homer, Eureka.
R. J. Llewellyn, Fort Green.
Thomas Fitch, Helper.
Willard Pierson, Ephraim.
J. P. Mustard, Spanish Fork.
George Hayes, Eureka.
M. N. Andrews, American Fork.
R. S. Wilson, Eureka.
Enoch Bowles, Nephi.
George Kerwell, Mona.
Stephen D. Johnson, Springville.
William T. Brown, Alpine.

Provo Daily Enquirer
February 4, 1893

It is understood that Ira N. Hinckley of Fillmore has been chosen as the fifth member of the Jordan Dam Commission.

Deseret Evening News
February 10, 1893

PROVO LETTER.

A Painful Arrest Through the Defendant Not Understanding Our Language.—Other Notes of Interest.

Special Correspondence of the News.

PROVO, Feb. 9.—Albert Revel, the Frenchman who swore out a complaint of assault against Postmaster McCauslin last week, was arrested yesterday on a counter complaint of disturbing the peace, sworn to by the postmaster. The arrest was made by Deputy Marshals Clark and Monehan. He did not understand, and resisted the officers. It became necessary to use force; the handcuffs were placed on his wrists, and he was dragged through the streets to Commissioner Dudley's office, his wife following closely behind, talking and scolding with all a woman's tongue; but it was all lost on the deputies, who do not know a word of French. Arrived at the commissioner's office, an interpreter was sent for. Awaiting his arrival, Mrs. Revel occupied the time scoring the officers, the government, etc. The fact that handcuffs had been used seemed to be considered especially severe; it was explained that they were never used on gentlemen in France. Mr. Revel had less to say, but the disgrace evidently preyed on his mind, for suddenly his head dropped to one side and he fell to the floor, writhing and foaming in a fit. Water was brought, and he was gradually restored to consciousness. The sympathy of the court and attorneys had been aroused; on motion of the prosecuting attorney, the case was dismissed, and the respective officers "knock off" the costs. Revel appears to be an educated man, but he is not used to the manners and customs of the United States. He is a professor of languages.

The case of James Inglefield vs. ex-Officer White, a suit brought to recover $250 damages, alleged to have been sustained by plaintiff from blows received from the officer, when he (plaintiff) was arrested, December 23, 1892, was tried last night before Commissioner Dudley. Plaintiff and a number of other witnesses testified to the striking. The striking was denied by White and a fellow officer. A decision was rendered in favor of defendant.

John Lunceford has been found guilty in the court of Justice Craig of Lake View, of cruelty to animals, in beating his horse. Another trial has been asked for.

A county bridge is to be constructed across Provo river near the mouth of Provo canyon. This will be of great convenience to Lake View and Provo Bench residents, who have heretofore been compelled to make a circuit of several miles by way of Provo to reach the canyon.

Ira Hinkley, of Fillmore, has been appointed the fifth member of the Jordan dam commission. The appointment gives general satisfaction among those interested in this county.

"Red Riding Hood," presented by local artists, is the attraction at the Opera House on Saturday evening.

The Provo Mandolin and Guitar club go to Heber to give a musical performance on the 18th inst.

Provo Daily Enquirer
February 14, 1893

Territorial Items.

A colonization scheme for this vicinity [Fillmore] is now under consideration. A company of some 300 hundred Hebrews from Germany proposes to establish a colony on the flat, in a northerly direction and about four or five miles distant from Lemington. The colony therefore would be situated within the confines of Juab county. As the new settlers would not own any of the water right, that contingency is provided for in the proposition in which they contemplate the building of a huge reservoir on the Sevier river, in the neighborhood of Doyer and Fayette. This syndicate intends to purchase the farm of Daver and Warm creek, which would be inundated by the water of the reservoir. They propose to build the dam of masonry, principally of rock and brick, laid in mortar. Surveys are now under way and some of the land already purchased. This enterprise promises to be a vast project, and if successful it will be a grand achievment as an engineering triumph.—Salina Press.

Mr. Birchall of Nephi was accidentally shot in the side last Friday by his son Ben. The wound is not dangerous Ben was shooting at a chicken, and it is supposed the ball glanced.

Mr. Hoyden, formerly station agent on the U. P. at Juab, has been removed to American Fork. Mr. Hoyden is succeeded at Juab by R, F. Moher of Omaha.

Casady, the adulterer found guilty in Judge Zane's court, was yesterday sentenced to six months' imprisonment in the penitentiary.

The Press club masquerade ball at Salt Lake last evening was a great success. It netted the boys of over a thousand dollars. The receipts were about eighteen hundred.

Patrick C. Kearns committed suicide early yesterday morning at Park City by shooting himself through the mouth with a revolver.

Salt Lake Herald
February 21, 1893

A JORDAN DAM MEETING.

A meeting of the Jordan dam commissioners was held this morning at the county court house. Those present were Ira N. Hinckley, Fillmore; W. H. Wilson and D. W. Thomas of Utah county, and Joseph L. Rawlins and Eliza A. Smith of Salt Lake.

After organization, James Aiken of Lake Shore presented a damage claim, caused by flooding, which was laid over until next meeting, which will convene March 27 to consider important business.

Colonel James F. Woodman of Salt Lake is a visitor in Provo.

Five tramps were let loose from the city jail this morning and ordered to leave town.

A full account of the grand masquerade tonight at the opera house will appear in the country society cotumn. The next great social event is the telegraphers' ball at Springville Wednesday night.

ANOTHER GOLD STAMPEDE.

Detroit District Ore That Assays Fifty Thousand Dollars.

DESERET WAS DESERTED.

The Eureka Miners Reject a Bullion-Beck Proposition.

The Directors Offered to Restore Wages
When Silver Remained at 95 Cents
for a Month—Rich Indian Creek
Ore—Mining Notes.

HOLDEN, Feb. 20.—Why has not the new strike in Drum district been noised abroad? Two weeks ago some prospectors of Deseret struck a vien on the south side of Quartz hill, the ore of which, within one foot of the surface, assays (by Mr. Paxton of Kanosh) $50,043 in gold. Before an assay was made Mr. Almond Robison of Fillmore gave $5,000 for a one-fourth interest.

The vein was found under an eight-inch capping of white spar and between two solid lime ledges. It is fourteen inches thick, with a two-inch central germ, as it were, of gold.

I have a small specimen of the ore, from which I have broken a mite and enclose to you.

DESERET STAMPEDED.

Now we, of Deseret, have always differed more or less from the judgment of Fillmore on account of its age, hard streets and shade trees, and when teams began arriving from the county seat, it created a suspicion in the minds of conservative people that there was "something in it"—the gold boom. Reports stated that a Fillmore capitalist had invested $5,000 for a fifth interest in one bonanza, and excitement reached nearly the top round, and when a conservative and well-known stock man arrived at 11 p. m., with his lines held high in his left hand, and his right wielding a black whip on the jaded team, excitement went a round higher. But when he was seen to hold a whispered conversation with a leading saloon man here, and then told his acquaintances that he was "on the road for Snake valley, on important business connected with the projected reservoir," excitement went clean over the ladder, for all knew he had "fibbed."

Our staid justice of the peace, who runs a hay press, left his press with a bale half completed and at midnight was on the road to the gold belt, leaving instructions to forward lunch next day. Staid merchants, farmers and artisans went out, pell mell, and are now doubtless millionaires, and in town we have a second edition of "Deseret Deserted."

Sheriff H. W. Hawley has just arrived form the "diggins," and reports the "boom is busted," and will go on to Fillmore to condole with the capitalist who invested and prevent the payment of further cash by the gentleman.

A Land and Water Company.

The Snake Valley Land and Water company filed articles of incorporation in the county clerk's office yesterday.

The object of this company is to conduct the business of owning and reclaiming desert land and improving it, also for the purpose of building and purchasing reservoirs and canals, irrigating land and to do anything that may be deemed necessary or profitable for the advancement of the purposes named in the articles.

Their capital stock is placed at $500,000, which is divided into 50,000 shares of the par value of $10 each.

The officers are James A. Melville, president; R. T. Pettingill, vice-president; James W. Searles, secretary and treasurer. These gentlemen and D. F. Walker, jr., are the incorporators. All are residents of this city except James A. Melville, who is of Fillmore. Their general office will be in Salt Lake.

Salt Lake Herald
May 13, 1893

MILLARD COUNTY ITEMS.

A Reservoir for Snake Valley—$3,000 for a Salted Mine.

FILMORE, May 12.—[Special.]—The cry of quiet times is heard in Millard county, although there are some enterprises being carried on which will add very materially to the growth of the country. At Swan Lake, near Oasis, there are 100 teams and about the same number of men employed in preparing the soil for raising crops. Every satisfaction is expressed by those interested in the company over the success of their project, and it is expected that a live town will spring up within a very short period.

Mrs. Joseph Ray, who was among the first to suggest the building of a reservoir at Swan lake, has, now, in company with James A. Melville, begun a similar piece of work at Snake Valley. About $50,000 was cleared up on the former scheme, and this one promises equal success.

A SALTED MINE.

If all reports are true, Mr. Almon Robinson, the financial king of Millard county, has either been swindled out of $5,000 or else made the poorest speculation he ever made in his life. Some time ago he purchased a mine west of the town of Deseret, the ore from which was reported to be very rich. After seeing the certificate of a responsible assayer to that effect, Robinson made the purchase, paying in cash and notes. It was not long before a thorough investigation proved that the claim was not worth the powder used in blowing out a blast. The question uppermost in his mind is, was the mine salted or was that a float the assayer got hold of.

DEATH OF A PIONEER.

Funeral services were held on Wednesday over the remains of Daniel Olson a highly esteemed citizen of Fillmore. The people came out en masse and every possible favor and attention was shown the mourners by them.

Mr. Olson is an old Salt Laker, arriving there in 1852. He was engaged in musical pursuits and will be well remembered by all classes who lived there in the early days. He died at the age of 59 years.

Provo Daily Enquirer
May 13, 1893

Mr. Ed. Olson has returned from Fillmore, where he went to attend the funeral services over the remains of his father, Daniel Olson.

High Water at Fillmore.

FILLMORE, Millard Co., May 17.—
High water is doing some damage
here, through the choking up of a
ditch. The water flowed in at the
cellar window of the rock house occupied by John T. Ashman, Sen. He
and his wife were in bed in the east
room, and at about four o'clock yesterday morning, the west end of the house
with part of the partition wall fell
with a tremendous crash carrying the
floor and contents of the room into the
flooded cellar. Once before her marriage Mrs. A. lost her clothing in a
similar way. John is seeking higher
ground as the water is not up to the
highest yet.   A. B.

FILLMORE HAPPENINGS.

Two Sad Deaths. — Serious Fire. — A Meeting House of Onyx.

Correspondence Deseret News.

FILLMORE, June 19.—Quite a gloom
has brooded over us for a number of
days past owing to several cases of
sickness of women, and two deaths.
Mrs. Mercy Croft Callister, the twenty-
year-old wife of John W. Callister,
died on the evening of the 13th under
circumstances that created great
sympathy for the young husband, who
was 200 miles from home in Nevada.
Messengers were sent by team to
inform him of his wife's sickness. Dr.
Tilson came down from Payson on
the 12th and gave encouragement for
her recovery but hope was blighted in
death. Bishop T. C. Callister started
off in the night to bear the still sadder
news to his young brother, whom he
hoped to meet at Deseret, thirty-five
miles away. Not finding him he got
a fresh team loaned by Brother
Dan Black and drove it ninety miles
that day, and the same team seventy
miles more the next day. The Bishop
tells how he prayed to the Lord to sustain that team that they might endure
the heat and thirst of that long and
tedious journey. Our God does not
sleep and doubtless heard his prayer.
When Johnny saw his brother he cried
out: "Tell me the worst, I know my
Mert is dead, or you would be at her
side!" The young man was entirely
prostrated with grief and fatigue when
he arrived here.

The funeral was a large one, as the
young lady was a great favorite in
public esteem and a school teacher of
remarkable ability. For a number of
terms she has taught in Kanosh, and
possessed that special charm of commanding obedience with attractive
admiration. She was the daughter
of the well known and respected Jacob
Croft, who sat like a familiar monarch
in the face of death, this being the
twelfth child that had fallen before
the reaper's sickle, with the last one
sobbing at his side; four wives had
been gathered in, and the lonely whit-
ened octogenarian sat and mutely
wept, the embodiment of faith in God
and the Gospel restored to earth in
this dispensation, sustained by the
peace of a virtuous life and the comforting influence of the Holy Ghost.

Sunday at 9 o'clock a. m., Millisa,
wife of Brother Alma Greenwood,
died after years of suffering. About
ten days since she was stricken with
paralysis and has shown little signs of
consciousness since. She was thirty-
six years old and leaves three children.
Brother Alma has the sympathy of all.

About 3 o'clock p.m. on the 17th,
the corrals of Jesse Millgate were discovered on fire, on the west side of
town. The wind was blowing directly towards the house and it seems
almost a miracle that the building
was saved. Another house near by in
direct line with the wind contained a
very sick aged sister and another an
invalid and blind. The poor creatures
became somewhat excited at the smell
and sound of the burning. Brother
Millgate lost besides his corrals a plow,
two sets of harness and a young horse
which was literally cremated—quite a
loss for a poor man.

The Fillmore creamery has just
started up. Some difficulty is experienced in obtaining sufficient milk for
successful operation. This institution
certainly ought to be fostered by the
people, and give the proprietors,
who have put their money into
it for public good, a chance to
redeem their promises of producing
an article that could be eaten with a
relish, in distinction from the fearful
mossagate article of unmeasured
strength made in most of the one-cow
dairies and misnamed butter. Some
of this stuff would make oleomargarine
melt with shame at being classed with
the same article.

Your esteemed historical correspondent recently gave us a deserved re-
minder of the antiquity of our meeting
house, but this very close observer
seems to have overlooked the fact that
we have the partially prepared foundations of two meeting houses in repose.
It is now suggested that we build one
entirely of onyx, as a very large body
of that beautiful stone has been discovered near by and many of our citizens
are carrying a polished specimen in
their pockets. Such an edifice would
certainly be a resplendent attraction to
the weary traveler as he approached
the capital from the west.   A. BIRD.

COUNTY REGISTRARS.

A Rather Strange Proceeding in the Case of Beaver County.

The Choice of the Democrats Ignored and a Republican Appointed for a Democratic County—The Appointees.

The Utah commissioners yesterday took up the matter of the appointment of county registration officers, with the understanding that only such counties from which the recommendations of the Democratic and Republican committees had been received would be taken up. The recommendations of the Salt Lake county committee, including the names of J. B. Timmony, E. L. Sloan and C. E. Angell, have been sent in, but Salt Lake county was not reached yesterday.

The following registrars were appointed:

Millard County—James A. Melville, Fillmore.

Juab—F. W. Chappell, Nephi.

Rich—A. C. Call, Woodruff.

Tasele—David B. Stover, Stockton.

Washington—Edward N. Snow, St. George.

Weber—John Seaman, Ogden.

Beaver—George H. Fennemore, Beaver City.

Box Elder—William Lowe, Willard.

Garfield—Samuel O. Crosby, Panguitch.

Emery—John W. Williams, Ferran.

Iron—N. W. Pryor, Cedar City.

Sanpete—J. P. Christiansen, Ephraim.

Utah—W. C. Schen, Springville.

A PECULIAR APPOINTMENT.

The session on the whole was a harmonious one, although there was some disagreement on a few of the candidates. The appointment of George H. Fennemore of Beaver county, was a very peculiar and inexplicable proceeding, in the light of all the circumstances. Beaver is a Democratic county and clearly entitled to a Democratic registration officer. The Democratic county committee had recommended Professor Maeser, William M. Lowe and Walter M. Christian, with preference in the order named. Fennemore, who was selected as registrar, was a candidate for county superintendent of schools last year on the Republican ticket, and was defeated by Professor Maeser, the first choice of the Democrats for registration officer.

A HERALD reporter asked Commissioner Lett, after the commission had adjourned, why a commission, composed of three Democrats and two Republicans, should ignore the recommendation of the county committee and appoint a Republican registrar for a Democratic county.

"I do not understand that the three Democrats did it," was the reply. "My impression is that two of the Democrats voted against it, but they were in the minority."

It is learned that Chairman Williams insisted that Fennemore was a Democrat, notwithstanding the fact that he was a candidate on the Republican ticket last year, and his appointment was brought about by Williams voting with the Republican commissioners.

THE EMERY COUNTY CASE.

The commissioners seem to have been imposed upon in the Emery county case. Three names were read, purporting to be the recommendations of the Democratic committee, at least some of the commissioners so understood it. One of the persons recommended was John W. Williams, the registration officer of last year, and he was vouched for as a straight Democrat by Chairman Williams and appointed. It now turns out that the appointee is a nephew of Chairman Williams, that he was not recommended by the Democratic committee, but by some person without authority to express the wishes of the Emery county Democrats. The Democracy of Emery county is divided into two factions, the independents and the regulars. One faction had sent in its recommendations to the territorial committee, but the other had not, and the territorial committee was holding back the names for a few days for that county until each side had been heard from. The commissioners were imposed upon, and the appointments made before the Democratic committee had been heard from.

David P. Stoner, the Tooele county appointee, it a Republican, that being one of the few Republican counties.

WILLIAMS ON THE CLERKSHIP.

Chairman Williams takes exceptions to a statement which appeared in Sunday's HERALD, to the effect that he had said he would do as he pleased in the matter of the appointment of a chief clerk, and that any efforts to secure his removal would be unsuccessful, "What I did say," said he yesterday, "was that I was going to do what I thought was right, and when I had done that I did not care. Whenever Mr. Cleveland desires my resignation, he can have it."

Judge Williams admitted that the other portion of the statement, to the effect that he would not consent to the appointment of a Democratic chief clerk, was correct.

Salt Lake Herald
July 21, 1893

TWO MORE COUNTIES.

Deputy Registrars Appointed Yesterday For Kane and Summit.

The Utah commission met yesterday and appointed the following deputy registrars:

KANE COUNTY.

Kanab—Fuller Broadbent.
Mount Carmel—R. M. Englested.
Orderville—C. W. Carroll.
Glendale—John S. Carpenter.
Ranch—G. D. McDonald (R).
Johnson—Nephi Johnson, Jr. (R).
Georgetown—A. S. Workman.
Pahreah—George W. Adair.

SUMMIT COUNTY.

Henefer—R. A. Jones.
Echo—James Hopkins.
Grass Creek—Jacob James.
Coalville—J. L. Boyden.
Hoytsville—Chas. W. West.
Wanship—George W. Young.
Rockport—Wm. Brown.
Peoa—Arthur Maxwell.
Oakley—Marvin Frazier.
Kamas—Jesse Burbidge.
Woodland—Daniel Mitchell.
Castle Rock (or Wasatch)—Jos. J. Ball.
Upton—George Randall.
Snyderville—J. W. Scott.
Park City—John W. Girger.

MILLARD COUNTY.

Fillmore—Alexander Kelly substituted for H. C. Jackson.

C. P. Sorenson was appointed registrar of San Juan county, in place C. E. Walton, who is absent from the territory.

George D. Alder was appointed deputy registrar for the First precinct of this city, vice J. B. Timmony, declined.

IN MILLARD COUNTY.

Some Important Enterprises — Mining, Farming and Irrigation.

Undoubtedly Millard county is in a much better condition today, than many of her northern neighbors. Here the ravages of the "boom" with all its attendant evils were not experienced, and as a result the people are not laboring under the burden of having mortgages, long since due. True, money is a scarce article, but many of our good citizens have not forgotten the days when cabbages, turnips, pumpkins, etc., served as a circulating medium in this territory, and as something must be had, they have again adopted their old style currency to satisfy their local requirements, until the "hardier materials" will be obtainable. The now common talk of "hard times," "no work" and free silver," is indulged in to a limited extent, but the majority of the people seem disposed to work their farms, care for their flocks and herds and produce the necessaries of life, rather than complain about existing circumstances and do nothing to relieve the situation. Those who have no farms or herds and want work, if they cannot labor for money, are disposed to accept hay, grain or produce, and thus you see in Millard today few idlers and less suffering for want of necessaries.

The crops throughout the county are generally good. In Scipio a scarcity of water was beginning to be felt, but a heavy rain on 23rd inst., was sufficient to mature their grain, and will undoubtedly increase the water supply enough to save the fall crops.

Throughout the whole county the hay and grain crop will not be quite as heavy as usual, but when compared with that of ten or fifteen years ago it will be considerably in advance, for every year a few more acres are being cultivated. It was thought ten years ago that there was then more land in use than there was water to supply, but time has shown that by careful handling and a correct distribution of the water there is still plenty to satisfy the requirements of the farmers. It is now observable that within a very few years, Millard, by reason of her typography, is destined to become one of the greatest agricultural localities in our territory. Hundreds and thousands of acres of land today remain uncultivated that in time will yield abundant harvests. The water supply is not great, but there are special advantages for the construction of reservoirs, in which water may be stored sufficient to irrigate large tracts of land. One of these reservoirs is now already completed, at Swan Lake, a few miles southwest of Deseret. It was one of Fillmore's worthy citizens, Mr. J. E. Ray, who commenced this labor. Capitalists came to his aid, purchased his interests and carried to a successful termination a scheme that will bring thousands of acres into use. When Mr. Ray severed his connection with this enterprise it was not because he did not believe in his undertaking, but because he knew of a still better field—one in which more abundant harvests could be gleaned. This time he was joined by Hon. James A. Melville of Fillmore, in his endeavor, and their energies were exerted in Snake valley at the extreme west of Millard county near the Nevada line and at the base of the Jeff Davis range of mountains. Their reservoir will tap Lake creek, Lexington and Big Wash canyons, together with a few minor streams. It will cover four square miles at a depth of forty-five feet. This, Mr. Melville says, will furnish water for 50,000 acres, and there is at least 100,000 acres of good land in this valley.

At the present time there are several ranches in this vicinity, at which places the soil has been fully tested and it is found that all kinds of grains, and vegtables can be raised, while it is especially adapted for fruits of all kinds. Mr. Alma Rhodes and Mr. Baker have now fine orchards and speak in the highest terms of that section of the country. A company has now been formed with a capital of $50,000, and with A. Melville as president, R. J. Pettingill of Salt Lake city, vice president, J. W. Searles of Salt Lake city, secretary and treasurer, and J. E. Ray, manager. These gentlemen are now working at their enterprise and hope to have it completed by the autumn of 1894.

While the mining interests of Millard are quiet at present, a good many of her cititizens are still hopeful, and look forward to better times in the near future. Onyx and black marble are the latest discoveries around Fillmore, and indications are that there is an abundance of these stones. Pumice stone is also found in Willard on the line of the Union Pacific railway near Blackrock. The Mr. Ray above referred to has a mine at the place indicated. He has expended $3,600 in work, and has shipped three carloads to San Francisco and two to Chicago, which netted him $30 per ton. The gentleman claims he has a vast amount of the material in sight and that it is a valuable piece of property.

Kanosh is now boasting of a fine new school house, furnished completely and with all the modern improvements. It is the best in the county. Now that the good people of this ward have a school house, they think it time to have a new church and a move is on foot to this end, but I can't say whether "Apostle Charley Crane," as he has been pleased to call himself, is directing it or not. Hinkley district is erecting a new school house and Fillmore has succeeded in securing the old state house for a like purpose. The trustees will expend $600 in improvements on it.

Provo Daily Enquirer
August 7, 1893

AT THE TABERNACLE.

Services Held There on the Sabbath Day.

Among those present on the stand at the Tabernacle Sunday services was Dr. Baldwin of the University of Texas.

Elder Joshua Greenwood of Fillmore addressed the congregation. He referred to words uttered by Dr. Baldwin in the First ward Sunday school. If the children could only continue to be as clean and sweet and pure as they now are, what a delightful condition of things would exist. It is for the purpose of making ourselves as nearly like children as possible in these things that we meet together often. Christ took a little child and said, "except ye become as a little child, ye cannot enter into Kingdom of Heaven." But it is also our duty to make advancement in life. We are here to gain experience in passing through this vale of tears. When we come to leave this sphere of action, it should be with the cleanness, sweetness and purity of little children, with the experience of a well spent life added.

God has told us to seek first the Kingdom of God and all other things shall be added. But we are inclined to rush to the front, sometimes even throwing our neighbors back, in our efforts to grasp the first handful of the opportunities thrown among us. The promises of God do not appear to be quite tangible enough for us. We are not willing to trust in Him. But we will have to work up to a higher plane—laying up treasures in heaven, not silver dollars, but virtues which shall be an everlasting inheritance to us.

Elder M. L. Pratt was the next speaker. He made reference to the prevalent cry of "hard times". He compared the present "hard times" with those of the early days of Utah. Now abundance smiles around us, but we are heavily indebted. Then we had but very little around us; true, we were not indebted to the banks and great firms of the east as we now are. The present crisis will pass away as have others before. There is one thing for us to remember to keep the commandments of the Lord.

Elder B. Cluff Jr. shoke of the great enthusiasm which had existed at Beaver at the branch of the B. Y. A. Summer school held there. True education, the speaker thought, was the only sure foundation to a firm faith in the gospel.

THE JUNCTION CITY.

Probate of the Alleged Will of John Broom Refused.

OGDEN, Aug. 8.—[Special.] — This morning Judge A. C. Bishop in the probate court denied admission to probate of the alleged will of John Broom deceased, said will not having been legally executed. The executors named in the document gave notice of appeal. The ground for the contest was that should the provisions of the will be carried out (to sell the Broom hotel property within one year) that the estate would suffer great loss. Mrs. Broom, widow of the deceased, has filed a petition asking for the appointment as special administratrix of the estate. The petition was granted and letters will be issued to her upon filing a bond of $12,000. Mrs. Broom also applied for appointment as regular administratrix and hearing on petition was set for Aug. 21.

Sheriff Hawley of Millard county, Utah, was in Ogden, today, on his return from Nevada, where he captured an alleged horse thief. The man was captured about fifty miles this side of Lovelock, that place being his former home. Sheriff Hawley left for Fillmore this evening.

MAIL SERVICE IN THE SOUTH.

Complaints still come from the region south of Milford in regard to the unsatisfactory mail service and we are not surprised that the people there are out of patience and want the parties who are responsible for their troubles "roasted." A correspondent from the extreme south explains that though a tri-weekly mail service is now supposed to run, in reality it is only twice a week in practice. "For three weeks running," he says, the mail which leaves Milford "at a fixed hour" has "started after the train arrived."

This is a source of great vexation. It ought to be remedied. If the fault is with the railroad, that ought to be known. If it is with the mail carrier, that should be made clear. It is bad enough to be deprived of the daily train and daily mail. But when only a tri-weekly service is had and that is spoiled in the manner described, it is almost enough to make even the Dixie rocks cry out.

The suggestion is renewed that an effort be made for a daily mail via Juab and Fillmore by the Union Pacific, or via Salina and Richfield by the Rio Grande Western. We understand that petitions are in progress for a change of that character. THE HERALD endorses the proposition. We have no doubt that our Delegate in Congress, Hon. J. L. RAWLINS, will render all the aid in his power to forward the movement, if the people of the South will forward to him the particulars of their grievance and a copy of their petition.

Southern Utah badly needs a railroad. If St. George were within rail connection of this city, the South would not only bloom with beauty, but boom with prosperity. Its fruits and wines, its copper and other minerals would come to market, and Our Dixie would be a comparatively rich land. Push on the movement for a daily mail, friends, and still hope and work for a railroad. You will get the former soon and the latter after awhile, and don't you begin to doubt it.

Millard County Onyx.

Mr. R. A. McBride of Fillmore has presented this office with a beautiful paper weight of native onyx, which was shaped and polished by the donor. The most pleasing feature in connection with this subject is that the onyx is a Millard county product, the quarry being situated in the southern termination of the Detroit range, about thirty miles northwest of Deseret. The ledge is about five feet thick and of various hues, from light to a lowly dark, the veins and shades, while being strongly marked, merge into each other in a marvelously beautiful manner. Mr. McBride assures us that he has sent numerous polished specimens to eastern experts who pronounce it equal in every respect and superior in some to Mexican onyx, which is considered the finest in the world, and negotiations are now pending which, it is confidently believed, will result in the opening of the quarries and exportation of the product to the east and west, the advantages of which in the employment of our people and the attraction of capital to our almost unlimited resources and natural wealth cannot be estimated. The same gentleman has also located near the onyx quarries a ledge of fine grained black marble, 25 to 30 feet thick, which, on account of its rarity in the United States, is destined to become valuable. The *Blade* heartily congratulates Mr. McBride on his find, and his perseverance manifested in his mastering the art of polishing, and wish him and Millard county success in this important enterprise.—*Millard County Blade.*

Salt Lake Herald
September 14, 1893

MILLARD COUNTY ONYX.

It Is Said to Be Equal to the Mexican Article.

Mr. D. McMaster of Denver and Mr. A. A. McMaster of Salt Lake city arrived in Deseret yesterday from Osceola, where they have been for a number of days, inspecting the gold ledges of that camp with a view to starting up the gold mill. The gentlemen have obtained a lease and bond on the mill, also on several gold-bearing quartz veins, and believe the outlook to be very favorable for the success of their enterprise. The gentlemen will go on to Salt Lake tonight. Mr. D. McMaster will take to Denver several fine specimens of polished onyx from the quarries of Messrs. R. A. McBride and C. Anderson, of Fillmore. These quarries are situated in the southern portion of the Detroit range, and about twenty-two miles northwest from Deseret. Mr. McMaster is enthusiastic in his praise of the onyx, which varies from a rosewood to a mahogany color. The gentleman says the onyx used in Brown's hotel, Denver, was imported from Old Mexico, and resembles very strongly the Millard county product, and which, if of the requisite hardness, can undoubtedly be put on the market in a short time. On Mr. McMaster's return to Denver, the specimens will be given a thorough test, which will be awaited with considerable interest by the entire community.

Sheriff Hawley returned from Fillmore Wednesday, bringing with him the man, Miles, arrested some time ago by the sheriff, and who is now awaiting his trial in the upper court on the charge of horsestealing. The prisoner will remain in the custody of the sheriff until Tuesday next, when he will be taken to Provo.— *Millard County Blade.*

Salt Lake Herald
September 17, 1893

CITY DISINCORPORATION.

We learn that in some remote places there is an attempt being made to destroy the town incorporations that have been organized in the interest of public order. This is rather surprising and is evidence of a spirit of lawlessness or a lack of good judgment.

In a small village or a scattered farming district such incorporations are perhaps not necessary. But in every place where people have congregated in sufficient numbers to form a town, it seems to us that the most orderly and progressive among them would consider some kind of municipal government essential. It was with this view that the laws authorizing the organization of towns and their incorporation were enacted. It is possible, of course, that some of them may have been conducted in a manner that displeases the inhabitants and that good people may think disincorporation desirable. But we should think they would hesitate before endorsing so destructive a measure. It is a retrograde movement. It is in opposition to progress and the spirit of the times.

The people in any town or city have it in their power to institute reforms in the government of the place. The voters are the ruling power. If the officers elected or appointed do not suit them, they can make a change and institute such policies as they deem necessary. To do this would be far better and more sensible than to endeavor to break up the corporation.

We understand that those who are moving for disincorporation represent that the people in many of the towns and cities of Utah are taking steps in the same direction, and that among those cities and towns are Salt Lake, Provo, Ogden, Lehi, St. George, Nephi, Spring City, Manti, Fillmore, etc. If that is the story, somebody is playing upon the credulity of the citizens. We have heard of no such movement in any of the cities specified. And the very fact that such a tale is being told is evidence that unreliable and untrustworthy persons are at the back of the scheme.

Our friends who feel concern over this matter should understand that no city or town can be disincorporated without: First, a petition in writing to the city council signed by not less than one-half of the electors of the city, as shown by last year's registration list. Second, the publication once a week for four weeks in a newspaper or by posting notices, of an election to determine the question. Third, the votes of three-fourths of the electors in favor of disincorporation.

Thus it will be seen that no faction can accomplish the work of destruction, but that a large majority of the voting citizens must be converted to the movement before it can have the ghost of a chance of success. It is not likely that so large a proportion of the people would support a movement for dissolution unless it was really the proper thing to do under the circumstances. The friends of law and order may rely on this, but all the same they should not allow the enemy to steal a march on them.

THE CONVENTIONS.

Meeting of the Democratic Territorial Committee Yesterday.

Counties Represented — Dates Fixed for the Representative and Council Conventions—Other Business.

At the meeting of the Democratic territorial committee, held at the Union club yesterday afternoon, Beaver, Emery, Garfield, Grand, Iron, Juab, Kane, Millard, Sevier, Tooele, Uintah and Wayne counties were unrepresented. Box Elder was represented by R. H. Baty and William Lowe, Cache by C. H. Hart, Davis by Thomas J. Brandon, Morgan by Samuel Francis, Piute by L. W. Shurtliff, proxy for L. G. Long, Salt Lake by W. C. A. Smoot, jr., A. G. Norrell, Elias A. Smith, F. S. Richards, C. W. West, F. S. Fernstrom, I. M. Waddell and E. B. Quinn, Sanpete by Peter Greaves and John Reid, Utah by A. J. Evans, W. N. Dusenberry and J. B. Milner, Washington by R. C. Lund and James Andrus, Weber by C. C. Richards, John G. Tyler, O. J. Swenson and A. J. Weber, proxy by Thomas D. Dee, and Wasatch by William Buyes.

LEGISLATIVE CONVENTIONS.

It was decided to hold the representative conventions in all the districts on the 16th of October, and the council conventions on the 21st inst. Representations to said conventions shall be on a basis of one member to every ten votes cast at the last election in representative districts and one to fifty in the council districts.

The conventions will be held at the following places:

First district, Logan; second, Brigham city; third and fourth, Ogden; fifth, Salt Lake; sixth, Farmington; seventh, American Fork; eighth, Mill creek; ninth, Nephi; tenth, Coalville; eleventh, Provo; twelfth, Spanish Fork; thirteenth, Ephraim; fourteenth, Price; fifteenth, Fillmore; sixteenth, Beaver; seventeenth, Toquerville.

The council conventions will be held in the following places:

First, Logan; second, Ogden; third, Hot Spring, Box Elder county; fourth and fifth, Salt Lake; sixth, Pleasant Grove; seventh, Park City; eighth, Fairview; Ninth, Spanish Fork, and tenth, Parowan.

The subject of calling primaries for the election of delegates to conventions was left to the county committees.

ATTENTION, DEMOCRATS

Call of the Territorial Central Committee.

For Council and Representative Conventions to Nominate Members of the Legislative Assembly.

HEADQUARTERS DEMOCRATIC TERRITORIAL CENTRAL COMMITTEE.
SALT LAKE CITY, SEPT. 27, 1893.

Council and representative district conventions of the Democratic party of Utah are hereby called to convene at the times and places hereinafter named, for the purpose of placing in nomination candidates for members of Council and House of Representatives of the thirty-first session of the Legislative Assembly to be voted for at the general election to be held on the Tuesday next after the first Monday in November 1893.

The council and representative district conventions will be composed of the numbers of delegates hereinafter named, to be selected from the several precincts of the district to be allotted by the County Central committee of the respective counties.

The representative district conventions will meet at the places indicated on Monday, the 16th of October, A. D. 1893, at 12 o'clock noon. The council district conventions will meet at the places indicated on Saturday the 21st day of October, A. D. 1893, at 12 o'clock noon, and nominate candidates to represent their several districts in the council of the legislative assembly. Said council district convention will in addition to nominating a candidate to represent the district in the legislative council select not less than five persons to act as a campaign committee to conduct the campaign for the election of members of the legislature within their respective districts. In the election of these committees it is recommended that each county within the district be represented thereon.

REPRESENTATIVE CONVENTIONS, OCTOBER 16, 1893.

Plans of Meeting and Apportionment:

First district, consisting of Cache and Rich counties, and entitled to two representatives. Convention to be held in Logan City, at the county court house. Delegates allotted as follows:

Rich county	15
Cache county	142

Second district, consisting of Box Elder county. Convention to be held in Brigham City at the county court house. Delegates as follows:

Box Elder county	56

Third district, consisting of Ogden City in Weber county, and entitled to two representatives. (Convention to be held at such time and place and be composed of as many members as the county central committee of Weber county shall designate.)

Fourth district, consisting of all of Weber county excepting Ogden city. Convention to be held at Ogden at such time and place and to consist of as many members as the county central committee may designate.

Fifth district, consisting of Salt Lake city and entitled to six representatives. Convention to be held in Salt Lake city at such time and place and to be composed of as many members as the county central committee of Salt Lake county may designate.

Sixth district, consisting of Davis and Morgan counties and Pleasant Green, Hunter and North Point precincts in Salt Lake county. Convention to be held in Farmington, Davis county, at the county court house, and to consist of 72 members, allotted as follows:

Davis county	56
Morgan county	16
Precincts in Salt Lake county	7

Seventh district, consisting of West Jordan, South Jordan, North Jordan, Herriman, Riverton, Bluff Dale and Draper. Precincts of Salt Lake county and Cedar Fort, Alpine, Lehi, American Fork and Pleasant Grove, precincts of Utah county convention to be held at American Fork, Utah county, and to consist of eighty-two members, allotted as follows:

Precincts in Salt Lake county	25
Precincts in Utah county	57

Eighth district, consisting of Brighton, Granger, Farmers, Mill Creek, Sugar House, Mountain Dell, East Mill Creek, Union, South Cottonwood, Butler, Sandy, Granite, Little Cottonwood and Silver precincts of Salt Lake county. Convention to be held in Mill Creek ward house and to consist of fifty-four members.

Ninth district, consisting of Juab county, excepting Mona precinct, Tooele county and Bingham precinct, Salt Lake county. Convention to be held in Nephi city at the county court house and to consist of seventy-five members, allotted as follows:

Tooele county..................................25
Juab county......................................46
Bingham precinct, Salt Lake county.......... 4

Tenth district, consisting of Summit and Uintah counties; convention to be held at Coalville, Summit county, in the county court house, and to consist of 92 members allotted as follows:

Summit county..................................... 70
Uintah county.................................... 22

Eleventh district, consisting of Provo Bench, Provo, Lake Shore, Lakeview and Springville, precincts of Utah county; convention to be held at Provo city in the county court house, and to consist of 80 members.

Twelfth district, consisting of Spanish Fork, Thistle, Pleasant Valley, Benjamin, Salem, Goshen, Santaquin, Payson, Fairfield and Spring Lake, precincts of Utah county; Mona precinct of Juab county and Thistle, Milburn, Fountain Green, and Fairview precincts of Sanpete county; convention to be held at Spanish Fork, Utah county, and to consist of eighty-two members, allotted as follows:

Precincts in Utah county.................... 71
Mona precinct in Juab county............... 4
Precincts in San Pete county................ 7

Thirteenth district, consisting of Sanpete county (excepting the precincts of Thistle, Milburn, Fountain Green and Fairview) convention to be held in Ephraim and to consist of 90 members.

Fourteenth district, consisting of Wasatch, Emery and Grand counties, convention to be held at Price, Emery county, and to consist of 76 members, allotted as follows:

Wasatch county............. 26
Emery county 45
Grand county 5

Fifteenth district, consisting of Sevier and Millard counties, convention to be held at Fillmore, Millard county, and to consist of 75 members, allotted as follows:
Sevier county 42
Millard county 33

Sixteenth district, consisting of Beaver, Piute, Iron and Wayne counties, convention to be held at Beaver city, Beaver county, in the county court house, and to consist of seventy members, allotted as follows:

Beaver county..................... 26
Piute county...................................... 11
Iron county...................................... 20
Wayne county.................................... 13

Seventeenth district, consisting of Garfield, Washington, Kane and San Juan counties, convention to be held at Toquerville, Washington county, and to consist of sixty-six members, allotted as follows:

Garfield county............. 17
Washington county............................. 41
Kane county 6
San Juan county........... 2

COUNCIL DISTRICT CONVENTIONS.

First district, consisting of first representative district, councilman to be nominated at same time and place and by same convention as representatives.

Second district, consisting of third representative district, councilman to be nominated at same time and place and by same convention as representatives.

Third district, consisting of second and fourth representative districts, convention to be held at Hot Springs, Weber county, and to consist of twenty-four members, allotted as follows:

Box Elder county.................. 11
Weber county....................................... 13

Fourth district, consisting of fifth representative district, and entitled to three councilmen, to be nominated at same time and place and by same convention as representatives.

Fifth district, consisting of Sixth and Ninth representative districts. Convention to be held in Salt Lake city and to consist of thirty members allotted as follows:

Davis county...................................... 11
Morgan county..................................... 3
Tooele county..................................... 5
Juab county........ 9
Precincts in Salt Lake county............... 2

Sixth district, consisting of Seventh and Eleventh representative districts. Convention to be held at Pleasant Grove, Utah county, and to consist of thirty-two members allotted as follows:

Precincts in Salt Lake county.................. 5
Precincts in Utah county... 27

Seventh district, consisting of Eighth

Seventh district, consisting of Eighth and Tenth representative districts. Convention to be held at Park City, Summit county, and to consist of twenty-nine members allotted as follows:

Precincts in Salt Lake county.............. 11
Summit county................................ 14
Uintah county................................ 4

Eighth district, consisting of Twelfth and Thirteenth representative districts. Convention to be held in Fairview, Sanpete county and to consist of thirty-four members allotted as follows:

Sanpete county............................... 19
Precincts in Utah county..................... 14
Mono precinct, Juab county................... 1

Ninth district, consisting of Fourteenth and Fifteenth representative districts. Convention to be held at Spanish Fork, Utah county, and to consist of thirty members allotted as follows:

Wasatch county............................... 6
Emery county................................. 9
Grand county................................. 1
Sevier county................................ 8
Millard county............................... 6

Tenth district, consisting of sixteenth and seventeenth representative districts, convention to be held at Parowan, Iron county, and to consist of twenty-seven members allotted as follows:

Beaver county................................ 5
Piute county................................. 2
Iron county.................................. 4
Wayne county................................. 3
Garfield county.............................. 2
Washington county........................... 5
Kane county.................................. 5
San Juan county.............................. 1

THE COUNTY COMMITTEES.

The county committees of the several counties are requested to make an apportionment of the delegates allotted to their respective counties according to the vote cast for the Democratic nominee for delegate to Congress in November, 1892, and where no building has been named to hold the convention in, the county central committee of the county in which the same is to be held will please make the necessary arrangements for holding the convention.

By order of the territorial central committee.　　　C. C. RICHARDS,
ELIAS A. SMITH,　　　　　　　Chairman.
　　Secretary.

Salt Lake Herald
October 19, 1893

UTAH COMMISSION.

Attorney Baldwin Appointed to Hear Objections to Voters.

General McClernand Arrives — Election Judges Appointed for Emery, Sevier, Millard and Garfield Counties.

The Utah commission met yesterday, with all the members present, General McClernand having arrived from Springfield, Ill.

The commission decided to appoint Attorney Charles Baldwin to hear objections to right of voters in Salt Lake city to remain on the registration lists.

Mr. Baldwin will commence work at his rooms, Nos. 81 and 82 Commercial block, next Monday morning, and will be prepared to hear objections from day to day until five days before the election.

The following additional judges of election were appointed:

EMERY COUTNY.

Price—L. M. Olson, D., Hy Frack, D., J. D Milburn, R.
Cleveland—Lewis Larsing, D., H. H. Oviatt, Jr., D., John Eden, R.
Lawrence—A. D. Dimmic, D., Ole N. Tufts, D., Llewellyn Lewis, R.
Castle Dale — Samuel Jackson, D., Andrew Rasmussen, D., Casper Anderson, R.
Blake—R. P. Johnson, D., A. D. Thompson, D., Thomas Farrer, R.
Spring Glen—Heber J. Stowell, D., George N. Perkins, D., F. M. Ewell, R.
Wellington—Edgar Thayer, D., E. E. Branch, D., J. R. Roberts, R.
Woodside—Eli Randall, D., James N. Coleman, D., J. A. Curtis, R.
Molen—L. S. Beach, D., H. P. Rasmussen, D., E. H. Barton, R.
Orangeville—E M. Moore, D., J. B. Crawford, D., Henry M. Reid, R.
Muddy—Nephi Williams, D., N. C. Anderson, D., P. V. Bunderson, R.
Ferron—John C. Duncan, D., Chester Bryan, D., Thomas Fugate, R.
Castle Gate—B. F. Coffey, D., Reese Lewis, D., Alex. McClain, R.
Minnie Maud—W. J. Russell, D., E. L. Hannon, D., E. C. Lee, R.
Winter Quarters—T. J. Parmley, D., John Potter, D., Samuel Padfield, R.
Scofield—W. S. McClain, D., T. H. Thomas, D., W. D. McLain, R.
Huntington—D. M. Tyler, D., D. C. Woodward, D., H. Loveless, R.

SEVIER COUNTY.

Richfield—John Hellstrom, D., Holger Ramlose, D., W. H. Clark, R.
Joseph—James H. Wells, D., Jas. Billingsley, D., A. E. Shipp, R.
Monro— Alphonzo Winget, D., Christian Swenson, D., J. H. McCarty, R.
Annabella—Ralph Fairbanks, D. William S. Parks, D., Samuel Thompson, R.
Vermillion—Peter Gottfredson, D., Christian Meyer, D., Samuel Nebeker, R.
Aurora—J. D. Whipple, D., W. M. Palmer, D. [...]n Larson, R.
Glenwo[...] R. Hipler, D., C. W. Powell, [...] A. W. Buchanan, R.
Elsin[...] Soren Sorenson, D., Peter Christe[...]on, D., Charles Anderson, R.
Centr[...] Asa R. Hawley, D., E. T. Rapp[...], D., W. [...] Stewart, R.
Salina—W. [...] Robinson, D., Joseph Lapish, D., J. W. Phillips, R.
Redmond—A. P. Anderson, D., N. L. Christensen, D., Hy. McKenna, R.
Burrville—Joseph Whitehead, D., J. B. Waters, D., Edgar Felmore, R.
Gooseberry—F. M. Jackson, R. T. W. Simpers, K. W. Bird, R.

MILLARD COUNTY.

Scipio—Jorgen Brown, D., W. J. Hatch, D., Ole Madsen, R.

Oak Creek—John Levell, D., Hy. Roper, D., F. R. Lyman, R.

Leamington—C. Overson, D. B. P. Lextorious, D., John Stronge, R.

Deseret—H. W. Davis, D., L. R. Cropper, D., John R. Bennett, R.

Hinckley—R. W. Reeves, D., Leroy Young, D. Alonzo Hinckley, R.

Smithville—George Bishop, D., W. E. Meecham, D., S. G. Earl, R.

Meadow—John Beckstrand, D., N. M. Stewart, D., Edwin Stott, R.

Kanosh — Chris Christianson, D., Dennis Dorritz, D., Wiliam F. Hunter, R.

Fillmore—H. C. Jackson, D., A. Greenwood, D., J. M. Hanson, R.

Holden—Charles Wood, Jr., D., J. J. Stephenson, D., George Nixon, R.

GARFIELD COUNTY.

Panguitch—John Houston, D., Leonard C. Sargent, D., Brigham Knight, R.

Cannonville—K. A. Fletcher, D., John Hatch, D., Elias Smith, R.

Coyote—Volney King, D., James Farmer, D., A. L. Hunter, R.

Escalante—Edward Wilcox, D., William Alvy, D., William Lay, R.

Henrieville— W. W. Roundy, D., Ebenezer Savage, D., Samuel J. Littlefield, R.

Hillsdale—James Johnson, D., Peter Clove, D., David Hatch, R.

Orton—James Veater , D., Andrew Lamreaux, D., John Lefevre, R.

Tropic—John Spendlove, D., Levison Hancock, D., Wilford Holiday, R.

Salt Lake Herald
October 21, 1893

The monthly weather review issued by Observer Salisbury, yesterday shows that last month the atmospheric pressure here was the lowest of any September on record, being 25.57 inches, or 29.90 inches reduced to sea level. The average sunshine was 10.3 hours per day, being about the average. The monthly mean temperature from twenty-five stations was 58 degrees, the highest monthly mean being 69.4 at St. George and the lowest monthly mean 46.5 at Scofield. The maximum for the month was 99 at Fillmore on the 24th and the minimum 12 at Scofield on Sept. 24. The average rainfall from twenty-five stations was .84 inches.

Salt Lake Herald
October 25, 1893

Hon. William H. King, of Provo, and Mr. Joshua Greenwood, from Fillmore, held forth in American Fork last evening. The Democrats were out in full force and a splendid meeting was held. Reports from that locality indicate large Democratic gains.

Salt Lake Herald
November 2, 1893

THE HOUSE.

First District—Joseph Monsen, Cache county, Aquilla Nebeker, Rich county.

Second District—A. D. Hubbard, Willard.

Third District—J. N. Perkins, M. S. Browning, Ogden.

Fourth District—George F. Hunter, West Weber.

Fifth District—E. W. Wilson, S. A. Kenner, W. H. Dale, H. A. Smith, O. H. Hardy, J. C. McNally, Salt Lake.

Sixth District—David Stoker, Bountiful.

Seventh District—D. O. Rideout, jr., Draper.

Eighth District—R. E. Miller, Mill Creek.

Ninth District—George L. Stockey, Tooele county.

Tenth District—John McDonald, Park City.

Eleventh District— Alexander Robertson, Springville.

Twelfth District—John Moore,

Thirteenth District—W. K. Reid, Manti.

Fourteenth District—J. R. Murdock, Heber.

Fifteenth District—I. J. Stewart, Richfield.

Sixteenth District—F. J. Tolton, Beaver.

Seventeenth District—A. W. Evens, St. George.

LEGISLATIVE TICKET.

Complete List of Democratic Candidates for Council and House.

COUNCIL.

First District—Charles H. Hart, Logan.

Second District— Ransford Smith, Ogden.

Third District—John Seaman, Ogden.

Fourth District—P. L. Williams, J. H. Moyle, I. M. Waddell, Salt Lake.

Fifth District—H. F. McCune, Nephi.

Sixth District—E. A. Wilson, Provo.

Seventh District—W. W. Cluff, Coalville.

Eighth District—C. H. Lund, Mt. Pleasant.

Ninth District—Joshua Greenwood, Fillmore.

Tenth District—Charles Adams, Parowan.

Salt Lake Herald
November 5, 1893

At Fillmore.

Fillmore, Nov. 4.—If reports and appearances count for anything, Millard county 's safely Democratic and on Nov. 7, a good round majority will be held up for the Democratic Nominees.

LEGISLATIVE TICKET.

Complete List of Democratic Candidates
for Council and House.

COUNCIL.

First District—Charles H. Hart, Logan.

Sec_nd District— Ransford Smith, Ogden.

Third District—John Seaman, Ogden.

Fourth District—P. L. Williams, J. H. Moyle, I. M. Waddell, Salt Lake.

Fifth District—H. F. McCune, Nephi.

Sixth District—E. A. Wilson, Provo.

Seventh District—W. W. Cluff, Coalville.

Eighth District—C. N. Lund, Mt. Pleasant.

Ninth District—Joshua Greenwood, Fillmore.

Tenth District—Charles Adams, Parowan.

THE HOUSE.

First District—Joseph Monsen, Cache county, Aquilla Nebeker, Rich county.

Second District—A. D. Hubbard, Willard.

Third District—J. N. Perkins, M. S. Browning, Ogden.

Fourth District—George F. Hunter, West Weber.

Fifth District—E. W. Wilson, S. A. Kenner, W. H. Dale, H. A. Smith, O. H. Hardy, J. C. McNally, Salt Lake.

Sixth District—David Stoker, Bountiful.

Seventh District—D. O. Rideout, jr., Draper.

Eighth District—R. E. Miller, Mill Creek.

Ninth District—George L. Stockey, Tooele county.

Tenth District—John McDonald, Park City.

Eleventh District— Alexander Robertson, Springville.

Twelfth District—John Moore.

Thirteenth District—W. K. Reid, Manti.

Fourteenth District—J. R. Murdock, Heber.

Fifteenth District—L. J. Stewart, Richfield.

Sixteenth District—F. J. Tolton, Beaver.

Seventeenth District—A. W. Evens, St. George.

Salt Lake Herald
November 13, 1893

Temple Marriages.

The following marriages took place at the Manti temple on Wednesday:

Edward Alfred Wood and Ada Jane Ashby, both of Holden.

John Julius Thuesen and Julia Maria Larsen, both of Monroe.

Francis Arden Elmer and Inez Estelle Fillmore, both of Payson.

James Henry Mellor, of Fayette, and Sarah Erickson, of Dover.

Salt Lake Herald
November 26, 1893

William Probert, of Holden, and Gabrel Huntsman, of Fillmore, two staunch Democrats, are in town, attending court.

A NEW RAILROAD

To Be Built From Neel's Station, on the U. P., to Fillmore.

BIG BUSINESS ENTERPRISE.

Besides This the Capital of Millard Is to Have a Chamber of Commerce and Newspaper.

J. P. Jacobson, recent editor and publisher of the Millard County *Blade*, was in Salt Lake today. To a News representative he stated that there was a grand revival in business in that part of southern Utah from which he hailed.

The citizens of Fillmore, he said, would next week organize a chamber of commerce, its purpose being to develop the resources of Millard county. The chamber would be incorporated as a large business concern with a capital stock sufficient to carry out the projects of those who were promoting it. The first stroke will be to build a branch railroad from Fillmore to Neel's station, on the Union Pacific, a distance of between thirty and thirty-five miles. The estimated cost, apart from the work of construction, is about $30,000. All labor is to be performed by citizens and turned in as stock, making it a great co-operative enterprise.

The principal movers in the scheme are James A. Melville, Joseph E. Ray, Joshua and Alma Greenwood, Almon Robinson and Charles Crane. He says these gentlemen are backed by the people with the utmost unanimity. It seems to be the determination of everyone to add his or her mite to the enterprise.

To further assist in this great work of contemplated development, a new weekly paper is to be started at Fillmore immediately. It will be called the Southern Utah *Times*, and will be non-partisan in politics.

Mr. Jacobson's business in the capital is to purchase a complete printing plant which he will take back with him at once. He will be the editor of the new newspaper venture and he says, as the whole county is back of it, success is sure to follow.

Salt Lake Herald
December 14, 1893

A Newspaper for Fillmore.

J. C. Jacobson, a Millard county newspaper man, is in the city for the purpose of purchasing a printing plant which will be used in publishing a new weekly paper at Fillmore to be known as the Southern Utah Times. The gentleman will be editor of the new paper and proposes to let the people of the world know of the many resources of Millard county.

The people of Fillmore and southern Utah in general are pushing to the front and intend to let the country know what they have got in sight. At Fillmore, Mr. Jacobson stated, a chamber of commerce will be organized next week for the purpose of aiding in the development of the resources of the country. The first work will be to build a branch railroad from Fillmore to Neel's station, on the Union Pacific a distance of between thirty and thirty-five miles. The estimated cost, apart from the work of construction, is about $30,000. All labor is to be performed by citizens and turned in as stock, making it a great co-operative enterprise. The principal movers in the enterprise are James A. Melville, Joseph E. Ray, Joshua and Alma Greenwood, Almon Robinson and Chas. Crane. He says these gentlemen are backed by the people with the utmost unanimity.

Salt Lake Herald
December 21, 1893

Land Office Items.

Heber L. Bishop, of Hinckley Millard county, made final proof in the land office yesterday to his homestead entry to 160 acres in section 25, township 17 south, range 8 west, in Millard county.

John Duncan, of Meadow, Millard county, made final proof of homestead entry to 160 acres in section 7, township 22 south, range 5 west, in Millard county.

Jacob Croft, of Fillmore, Millard county, made desert entry to 40 acres in section 13, township 21 south, range 5 west, in Millard county. Irrigating water is to be taken from Chalk creek by a ditch two miles long.

The monthly mean temperature of 34.4 was about the normal. Highest mean 64.3 at St. George; lowest mean, 25.4 at Soldier's Summit. Highest maximum, 86 at Fillmore on the 7th; lowest minimum, 16 below zero at Scofield on the 22nd. Greatest monthly range, 77 at Randolph; least monthly range, 47 at Lake Park.

Salt Lake Herald
January 6, 1894

J. M. Hanson, of Fillmore, well known as one of the prominent citizens of that place, is at the White.

Salt Lake Herald
January 12, 1894

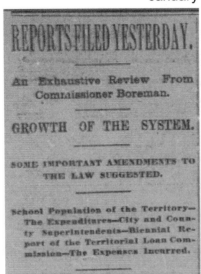

REPORTS FILED YESTERDAY.

An Exhaustive Review From Commissioner Boreman.

GROWTH OF THE SYSTEM.

SOME IMPORTANT AMENDMENTS TO THE LAW SUGGESTED.

School Population of the Territory—The Expenditures—City and County Superintendents—Biennial Report of the Territorial Loan Commission—The Expenses Incurred.

The biennial report of Commissioner of Schools Boreman was sent in to the Legislature yesterday.

GROWTH OF THE SCHOOLS.

The communication says: It is with profound pleasure that I can state that the law making the district schools free to all of school age, is daily growing in popularity and the system is becoming each year, more and more firmly fixed in the affections of the people of the territory. The growth of the system is extremely gratifying to the friends of education, and its growth is rapidly developing a deep and abiding interest in the cause of education all over the territory. The advance in many quarters has been as wonderful as it has been satisfactory. New and more commodious buildings have been and are being erected throughout the territory, and a great many of them are large and admirably adapted to the purpose for which they have been erected, and are justly the pride of the whole people. There is no disposition manifested anywhere to give up the free school system, but the anxiety is to see the law which gave us the system, improved and made as nearly perfect as it is possible to make it.

DEFECTS IN THE LAW.

He then goes on to review his work during the past two years, and suggests some radical changes in the school law, one of which is in regard to the selection and discharge of teachers. On this subject he says: Any system that should be adopted might be abused, but the one least likely to be abused, would certainly be the preferable one. Where the whole matter is left to the school board, local and social influences sometimes have too much to do with the selection and also the discharge of teachers. And some school boards allow one of their number—or he is allowed to assume the authority—to select and discharge teachers at his pleasure. As a consequence it is possible that social or other local influence will lead to the selection of teachers who would not do the best work, and to the discharge of good teachers from some mere whim, thus causing injustice to be done to competent and worthy teachers. A central authority should exist in every county, whose consent should be necessary to the selection and discharge of every teacher. This central authority might consist of the county superintendent and chairman of the school board.

UNION INSTITUTES.

The commissioner is inclined to think that authority for holding union institutes is carried beyond what was intended by the section giving the authority. He believes that if teachers are required to attend these institutes, their expenses, at least, should be paid, and no charge should be allowed to be made against anyone for any lecture or other matters at any such institute, and no one should be denied admission to any lecture or other matters in the line of instruction at the institute.

CERTIFICATES TO TEACH

As to certificates to teach, the commissioner says that all should specify the grade or class of teaching to which they apply. There should also be some authority, although not obligatory, for the examining boards to consider the certificates coming from other states and territories. As the law now stands, no one coming from outside the territory, no matter what his experience and standing or qualifications, can teach without an examination in the territory, and that examination without regard to the well known and acknowledged qualifications of the party.

ISSUANCE OF BONDS.

Conflicting requirements in the law referring to the issuance of school bonds are called attention to, and amendments suggested.

DENOMINATIONAL SCHOOLS.

concerning schedules attached to the report, Mr. Boreman says: I regret that I have again to call attention to the meagreness of the reports from the denominational and private schools. I have exhausted every means at my command to get full reports, but without success. It evidently will have to be made the duty of some local officer, perhaps the superintendent in every county and city, to gather the statistics regarding all denominational and private schools. There seems to be no other way in which the necessary information can be obtained.

SCHOOL LIBRARIES.

As to school libraries, the report says: The time has arrived in the history of our territory, when attention should be given to the creation and maintenance of district school libraries. The thirst for knowledge in the young minds must be met with good books and the best current literature. Thus their tastes and their morals will be trained in the right direction. I hope that authority may be given the school boards to establish such libraries and that a reasonable per centage of the school funds be made available for this purpose.

SCHOOL POPULATION.

The following report is given of the number of school children of the territory between the ages of 6 and 18 years, the enumeration being made between August 1 and 10, 1893:

Beaver, 1,227; Box Elder, 2,665; Cache, outside of Logan, 4,265; Logan, 1,616; Davis, 2,505; Emery, 2,046; Garfield, 1,118; Grand, 165; Iron, 957; Juab, 1,565; Kane, 687; Millard, 1,531; Morgan, 652; Piute, 554; Rich, 634; Salt Lake, outside of city, 5,906; Salt Lake city, 11,294; San Juan, 144; Sanpete, 4,842; Sevier, 2,484; Summit, 2,622; Tooele, 1,505; Uintah, 1,190; Utah, outside of Provo, 7,364; Provo, 1,822; Wasatch, 1,441; Washington, 1,451; Wayne, 681; Weber, outside of Ogden, 3,067; Ogden, 5,265. Total, 71,798.

DISBURSEMENTS.

Beaver, $9,127.49; Box Elder, $35,903.16; Cache, $75,601.90; Davis, $33,463.54; Emery, $26,166.87; Garfield, $10,052.65; Grand, $2,531.65; Iron, $11,296.95; Juab, $16,931.41; Kane, $8,321.02; Millard, $15,478.41; Morgan, $6,718.77; Piute, $4,275.74; Rich, $5,366.06; Salt Lake (outside of city), $130,931.52; Salt Lake city, $610,025.28; San Juan, $2,129.01; Sanpete, $46,796.11; Sevier, $45,954.65; Summit, $38,318.54; Tooele, $19,761.39; Uintah, $13,992.09; Utah (outside of Provo), $22,555.15; Provo city, $23,543.94; Wasatch, $27,891.61; Washington, $9,486.03; Wayne, $5,277.31; Weber (outside of Ogden), $45,144.31; Ogden city, $170,675.83; total, $1,560,812.45.

CITY AND COUNTY SUPERINTENDENTS.

Beaver, R. Maeser, Beaver city; Box Elder, Angus Vance, Box Elder; Cache, Samuel Oldham, Logan; Davis, David O. Willey, Jr., Bountiful; Emery, James Scott, Huntington; Garfield, M. M. Steel, Panguitch; Grand, F. A. Manville, Moab; Iron, M. H. Dalley, Cedar city; Juab, John Foote, Nephi; Kane, Edwin R. Cutler, Kanab; Millard, T. C. Callister, Fillmore, Morgan, Thomas

R. Condie, Croydon; Piute, Samuel L. Page, Greenwich; Rich, James W. Fackrell, Randolph; Salt Lake, D. R. Allen, Salt Lake city; San Juan, A. P. Sorensen, Monticello; Sanpete, Peter Greaves, Jr., Ephraim; Sevier, Henry N. Hayes, Salina; Summit, D. S. L. McCorkle, Park City; Tooele, P. P. Christensen, Grantsville; Uintah, E. G. DeFriez, Vernal; Utah, D. H. Christensen, Provo; Wasatch, Attewall Wootton, Midway; Washington, Levi N. Harmon, Toquerville; Wayne (new county), Willis E. Robison, Loa; Weber, Mosiah Hall, Ogden city.

Salt Lake city, J. F. Millspaugh, Salt Lake city; Ogden city, R. S. Page, Ogden city; Provo city, W. E. Rawlings, Provo city; Logan city, Ida J. Cook, Logan city.

In conformity with an act entitled "An Act Providing for the Issuing and Disposal of Territorial Bonds, Approved March 16, 1892," the territorial loan commission, consisting of George A. Lowe, James Glendenning and R. C. Chambers, appointed by the governor, yesterday submitted their report to the Legislature.

It sets out that said board of loan commissioners met at Salt Lake city on April 5, 1892, and organized by electing George A. Lowe, chairman, and James Glendenning, secretary.

It was decided to issue bonds to the amount of $250,000 and the territorial treasurer was instructed to advertise for their sale as directed in the act authorizing the issue of said bonds for a period of one month in two daily newspapers published in Salt Lake city, Utah territory, and said advertisements were duly inserted in the Salt Lake Daily Tribune and the Salt Lake Daily Herald.

Provo Daily Enquirer
January 16, 1894

BIDS RECEIVED.

The report then goes on to state that the commission met on June 16, 1892, and opened eleven bids as follows:

Utah National bank, Ogden....$$251,000
Utah Title Insurance & Trust Co., Salt Lake................... 251,026
W. I. Quintard, New York...... 258,000
N. W. Harris & Co., Chicago... 260,700
E. H. Rollins & Son, Denver.... 263,850
Lamprecht Bros. & Co., Cleveland 256,783
W. I. Harper & Son, Cleveland.. 259,625
Spetses & Co., Toledo............ 257,650
Farson. Leach & Co., New York 250,625
Blair & Co., New York......... 261,375
Equitable Mortgage Co., New York 263,000

The offer of Rollins & Sons was accepted and on June 30, 1892, a resolution was adopted ratifying the action. The bonds were executed in strict compliance with the act authorizing their issuance and sale.

THE EXPENSES.

The expense incurred in issuing and negotiating the sale of territorial bonds is shown in the following exhibit:

Expenses incurred in issuing and negotiating sale of territorial bonds.

Paid for telegraphing, $12.65.

Paid for expressage on bids, $13.95.

Paid Elijah Sells, secretary, papers relating to appointment and duties of commission, $7.00.

Paid for printing notices of sale and copies of "Act" relating to bonds, $102.50.

Paid for clerk and messenger hire, $23.00.

Paid American Bank Note company for printing bonds, $675.00.

Paid for rent of safety deposit box, $4.50.

Paid for sundries for secretay, blank book, $7.00.

Paid for stamps, $1.00.

Paid Robert Harkness, counsel for Loan commission, $60. Total, $887.

Mrs. Norton, formerly a Miss Palmer of this city, now living at Fillmore, fell into a fireplace on the 10th inst. while in a fit. She is badly burned and it is not expected she will live.

Fillmore.

The county seat of Millard, is situated forty-five miles south of Juab, a station on the the Union Pacific line. The city comprises an area of sixteen square miles and has an assessed valuation of $97,174.00.

Situated, as Fillmore is, at the foot-hills of the imposing Wasatch range, sheltered on all sides, it is exceedingly well adapted to fruit raising, and large quantities of apples, pears, apricots, peaches, plums, cherries and small fruits are annually produced.

Owing to the want of water, or rather to a lack of economy of the water available, a large tract of the very best fruit-producing land in the world is as yet unreclaimed.

These acres of land could, and undoubtedly will, at no distant date, be turned into smiling orchards when the necessity for storing the waters which now run to waste, and economizing its use, becomes apparent.

Our water for irrigating purposes we obtain from mountain streams, and much water is lost by seepage through the coarse gravel with which the beds are filled as well as through the transmissions from the creeks by ditches to the lands.

A reservoir constructed with a view to save the volume of water that flows to waste during the months of May and June, would irrigate countless acres of soil now lying barren for want of the precious fluid.

A number of excellent prosperous farms are situated within a few miles of the city limits, aggregating some 10,000 acres, among which are prominent the Thomas O., Wheeler, Russell, Melville and Greenwood's farm and the Hinckley ranch.

THE MINERAL SPRINGS.

Southwest of the city, afford splendid bathing; it is 75x40 feet, and has a depth of from 4 to 28 feet. These springs will eventually become an attractive health and bathing resort. A pleasant one and a half hours' drive will convey visitors to these springs.

THE STATE HOUSE.

In the centre of the city, on what is known as the State House block, stands the first Capitol of Utah Territory.

It is a large three-story brown sandstone structure, and was erected 1852-1853 at a cost of $100,000. $60,000 of which was furnished by the National Government, the balance by the people of the Territory.

The building at the present time is the property of the city of Fillmore, and is occupied by the City Council on the first floor, while the upper floor or hall has been divided into three spacious school rooms, which are now occupied by the District school.

Two rooms on the first floor, also, have been granted for the use of THE MILLARD PROGRESS, and this paper is now being printed in the same rooms that were once used by the Deseret News company for the printing of that journal.

THE COUNTY COURT HOUSE.

Which occupies the southeast corner of the State House block, is a fine brick structure with a large spacious court room and offices for the various county officials. It was erected 1871-1872 at a cost of $9,000.

FILLMORE'S ENTERPRISE

Fillmore has a number of progressive and enterprising business men and women, and goods of all descriptions can be purchased here cheaper than anywhere in the county.

Among the leading business houses, we may here mention the People's Store, J. D. Smith, Supt.; Geo. Greenway's store, Wm. Beeston, Supt.; the Ladies' Co-op., Mrs. Mamie Henry, Manager; John Kelly's general merchandise establishment; Julia Merril's millinery department, etc.; G. Huntsman's store, C. Anderson's drugstore and meat market, A. O. Robison, watches and jewelry, etc., etc.

Lack of space prevents us giving detailed write-ups of these at the present time.

There are here three saw mills, two run by steam, one by water power; a planing mill which, however, is not running at the present time, but will be started up again in the spring; a first-class roller flouring mill, whose products have gained fame all over this section and Eastern Nevada; a burr mill, which will be fitted with rollers by next season. A dairy, where cheese of a flavor that cannot be surpassed in quality any where, is produced.

Two hotels, the Robison House and the Huntsman Hotel, will be found as pleasant and accommodating houses as can be found anywhere. One barber shop, a large Pavilion, 36x65 feet, owned by Rasmussen Bros.

Besides these there are a number of blacksmith and machine shops, boot and shoe makers, harness and saddlers, lumber dealers, brickyards, carpenters, and lastly two saloons.

These last institutions we do not mention because of the large amount of good they accomplish in a community, but simply because they are here, and as it seems that saloons have become a necessity to most communities.

We shall from time to time call attention to each and every industry singly.

We now pass on to our beautiful neighbor on the North.

Provo Evening Dispatch
February 1, 1894

THE Millard Progress, a new eight column weekly from Fillmore, graces our exchange table this morning. It starts out with a good line of advertising and if it gets a rate and maintains it, it will thrive and do well. THE DISPATCH welcomes the new comer warmly. J. P. Jacobson is editor and manager.

Salt Lake Herald
February 3, 1894

TERRITORIAL NEWS.

The Value of Our Onyx—A Curiosity —General Items.

Heber and John Williams came in from Fillmore on Saturday and the next morning went out to the Detroit district. The gentlemen will do some work on a black onyx claim owned by themselves and James S. Giles, of Fillmore. The gentlemen will also get samples from their quarry for shipment to eastern investigators of the onyx.

The Belgian black onyx, which is not a whit superior to the Millard county product, costs $3 per cubic foot laid down in the United States. This fact illustrates the value of the onyx find in the Detroit mountains and shows the possibilities that will come with the starting up of the home industry of quarrying, stoping and shipping the native onyx.—Millard County Blade.

Salt Lake Herald
February 10, 1894

Deputy Marshal W. P. Payne is up from Fillmore on court matters.

Provo Daily Enquirer
February 13, 1894

This morning's Tribune contains accounts of extremely cold blizzards in Beaver, Millard and Iron Counties.

Mrs. L. A. Kimball has been appointed Postmaster at Kanosh, Millard county.

Provo Evening Dispatch
February 13, 1894

THE STORM KING.

He is Raging Viciously All Over the Southern Part of Our Fair Territory.

A fearful blizzard has been sweeping over Illinois and other states in that vicinity the past two days. The storm in fact seems to have reached across the entire continent, and Utah has had its share of it. Yesterday the great storm north of Salt Lake and in Sanpete was reported in these columns. Today a special to the Salt Lake Tribune among other things says:

"At noon on Saturday, the stage with the Salt Lake mail, left Beaver for Milford, reaching Minersville with great difficulty between 3 and 4 o'clock, where the storm was raging worse than here. Leaving there before 4 p. m., and about five miles northwest the snow was falling so thick, the blizzard whirling snow in every direction that the horses refused to face it, the driver lost the road and about dusk dropped into a gulch eight or ten feet deep, full of drifted snow. After a while he got one of his horses loose and got back to Minersville at 10 o'clock the next morning. When starting back to his abandoned horse, buggy and mail he learned of two Salt Lake drummers that had also got lost and spent the night in the bed of the river, sheltered by the banks, one of them having both feet badly frozen. The driver found his horse alive, and mail all right, and reached Milford at noon. Here he learned that the driver that should have left Deseret Springs on Saturday morning for Milford had not yet arrived or been heard of, and it is certain that if he had started he got lost and perhaps perished in the storm, which, if possible, was worse at Milford and Pioche than east."

News of the same voilent storm is received from Toquerville, Cedar City, Parowan, Kanosh, Fillmore, Scipio and other settlements in various parts of southern Utah.

Deseret Evening News
February 15, 1894

Fillmore Chamber of Commerce.

"A Bird" writes from Fillmore, Millard county, Feb. 10th, 1894, that the organization of a chamber of commerce was effected in that city that day with the following named officers:

Alma Greenwood, president; Jas. E. Ray, vice-president; Jas. A. Melville, O. C. Holbrook, Joshua Greenwood, John T. Ashman and J. P. Jacobson, directors; J. P. Jacobson, secretary; George C. Viele, treasurer; and Joseph S. Giles, corresponding secretary.

The same day Fillmore was having the worst snowstorm of the winter.

Deseret Evening News
February 16, 1894

Fillmore Chamber of Commerce.

"A Bird" writes from Fillmore, Millard county, Feb. 10th, 1894, that the organization of a chamber of commerce was effected in that city that day with the following named officers:

Alma Greenwood, president; Jos. E. Ray, vice-president; Jas. A. Melville, O. C. Holbrook, Joshua Greenwood, John T. Ashman and J. P. Jacobson, directors; J. P. Jacobson, secretary; George C. Viele, treasurer; and Joseph S. Giles, corresponding secretary.

The same day Fillmore was having the worst snowstorm of the winter.

Salt Lake Herald
February 21, 1894

Fillmore Board of Trade.

Fillmore has just organized a board of trade, with the following officers:

President—Alma Greenwood. Vice-presidents—Joseph E. Ray, of Fillmore; George Crane, Kanosh; Neil M. Stewart, Meadow; O. L. Thompson, Scipio, and D. R. Stevens, Holden. Recording secretary—J. P. Jacobson. Corresponding secretary—J. S. Giles. Treasurer—George C. Veile. Executive committee—James A .Melville, Joshua Greenwood, J. P. Jacobson, J. T. Ashman and O. C. Holbrook.

TERRITORIAL NEWS.

A BIG MOUNTAIN LION KILLED NEAR FILLMORE CITY.

A Stage Driver Has His Hands Frozen—The Fillmore Board of Trade Organized—General Items.

Wednesday morning, Aruthur Day of this city triumphantly exhibited to the gaze of a Progress reporter, the carcas of a huge puma, which he had killed near Maple Hollow, three miles southeast of the city the evening previous, when Arthur, in company of his father John Day, were hunting in that vicinity.

The animals tracks had been followed for about three miles, when he was overtaken in a thick patch of mahogany brush. Arthur dismounted and, while the animal watched his every movement, approached to within fifteen yards, took deliberate aim and sent a bullet through the cranium of the brute. He made a jump straight in the air, about four feet, run fifty yards, when he fell. Burying his head in the snow. Arthur followed him, and when he fell, sent another bullet through his body, from right back of the left shoulder. The dimensions of the animal were as follows: Length, from nose to tip of tail, 7 feet 4½ inches, weight, 168 pounds; measurement around body, 3 feet 1 inch; around forearm, 12 inches; around head, 23 inches, across paw, 7 inches, claws, lenght, 1¾ inch.

Arthur received $10 bounty from the county, and with his feet on the rug made from the monster's pelt, will in time to come be able to tell his grandchildren of the thrilling adventure in Maple Hollow.—Millard Progress.

SOUTHERN IRRIGATION ENTER-
PRISES.

Two Prominent Millard County Citi-
zens Here on the Business.

Hon. James A. Melville, of Fillmore, member of the former session of the Legislature, and Joseph E. Ray, also of Fillmore, are in the city on business connected with two great irrigation enterprises in which they are interested in connection with a number of Salt Lake capitalists. During the coming week another company will be incorporated in this city for the purpose of constructing and maintaining an immense reservoir and long stretch of canal in Piute county. This is part of the business which brings the gentlemen to Salt Lake at this particular time.

"We have just commenced active operations upon our reservoir in Snake valley, Millard county," said Mr. Ray, who is general manager of the Snake Valley Land and Reservoir company, whose articles of incorporation were recently filed with the secretary of the territory and whose capital stock is placed at $500,000, yesterday to a Herald reporter. "This reservoir is situated in the upper end of the valley and its water will reclaim over 50,000 acres of what is now arid land. The company does not own all of this land, but will furnish the settlers a perpetual water right. Our dam is to be forty-five feet wide at the top and so constructed that all of the floods in the world combined could not break it. It will cost over $10,000. From the canal a ten mile canal will lead the water over the vast extent of land which it is to water. At one point on the canal it will be necessary to tunnel 200 feet through solid rock, at an expense of $2,000. The company has guaranteed to expend not less than $40,000 on the work. The name of the company which is to be organized by us during the week has not quite been agreed upon. The reservoir of the corporation will be constructed in Piute county and its water will also reclaim 50,000 acres of now arid lands."

Erickson, the sawmill man, this week came in from Clear Lake with the tails of 247 muskrats, receiving in bounty for the same, $17.35. He also shipped to Salt Lake 293 ducks, which he had brought down in twenty-seven shots. These bring him 12½ cents apiece in Salt Lake. He says he killed 50 ducks in two shots on Monday morning. Some of our young men might emulate this example these hard times.—Fillmore Progress.

Millard County Progress
March 3, 1894

No. 1992.

NOTICE FOR PUBLICATION.

United States Land Office,
Salt Lake City, Utah, Feb. 9, 1894.

Notice is hereby given that Ann E. Giles, of Fillmore, Millard county, Utah, has filed notice of intention to make proof on her desert-land claim No. ____ for the north half south-east quarter of section 18, township 21 so., range 4 west, before the Clerk of the County Court at Fillmore, Millard county, Utah, on the 24th day of March, 1894.

She names the following witnesses to prove the complete irrigation and reclamation of said land: Joseph Carling, Arthur M. Bronson, John T. Ashman, Abraham E. Carling, all of Fillmore, Millard county, Utah.

ALSO

Notice is hereby given that William L. Brown, has filed notice of intention to make proof on his desert-land claim No. 2717, for the lots 1 and 2, section 19, township 28 south of range 5 west, and east half of north-east quarter section 24, township 28 south, of range 6 west, before the Clerk of the County Court at Fillmore, Millard county, Utah, on the 24th day of March, 1894.

He names the following witnesses to prove the complete irrigation and reclamation of said land: Charles Crane, Owen Crane, John Kendall and Charles J. Reinhold, all of Kanosh, Millard Co., Utah.

ALSO

At the same time and before the same officer, viz. George Stewart, H. E. No. 368, for the so. half, south-east quarter of section 13, north-east quarter, north-east quarter of section 24, north-west quarter, north-west quarter section 23, township 22 south, range 5 west.

He names the following witnesses to prove his continuous residence upon and cultivation of said land, viz: James Duncan, John Duncan, Peter Greenhalgh, Joseph N. Davis, all of Meadow, Millard county, Utah.

BYRON GROO, Register.
G. W. Parks, Attorney for claimants.

Brands and Marks.

The list of brands appearing below, are used by stockmen of Millard county, having cattle and horses on the range. Poundkeepers, Constables, and officers of the Peace, will please notice the brands and if estrays, bearing the same, are brought to them for damage, notify the owners of said brands, whose postoffice address appears with the brand, by mail.

The circulation of THE PROGRESS in Millard and surrounding counties, makes this journal a valuable advertising medium, and owners of stock should have their brand in our columns. For particulars, address, THE PROGRESS, Fillmore City, Utah.

JOHN T. ASHMAN,

Brand appears on either side.
Square crop off each ear.
Postoffice address, Fillmore, Utah.

J. D. SMITH,

Postoffice
Address:

Fillmore City,
Millard Co,
Utah.

Brand appears on left hip or ribs and thigh.

Ear mark—Crop off and two slits in right ear; swallow fork in left.

GEO. C. VEILE,

Brand appears on left hip and thigh on horses and cattle.

Postoffice address—Fillmore, Millard county, Utah.

C. HUNTSMAN,

Postoffice
Address:

Fillmore City,
Millard Co.,
Utah.

Brand appears on right thigh.

Ear mark—Crop off left and under bit in right ear.

HANS PETERSON & SONS,

Postoffice
Address:

Fillmore City,
Millard Co.,
Utah.

Cattle brand appears on left hip. Horses branded on left thigh.

Ear marks—Square crop off left and under half off right; slit in each ear.

The Millard Progress.

Issued every Saturday morning at FILLMORE, MILLARD COUNTY, UTAH.

J. P. JACOBSON,

Editor and Mngr.

SUBSCRIPTION TERMS:

One Year........................$1.50
Six Months.....................85 Cts.
Three Months.................50 "
   Invariably in Advance.

ADVERTISING RATES:

LOCALS—Ten cents a line for each insertion.

MARRIAGE NOTICES.—Rates according to the social position and financial condition of the groom.

BIRTH NOTICES—Will be charged for according to the enthusiasm of the father and child.

DEATH NOTICES.—Notices of the death of any resident of this county published free.

DISPLAY "ADS."—Rates furnished upon application.

Salt Lake Herald
March 9, 1894

Hon. Joshua Greenwood came up from Fillmore yesterday evening, and today he is frequenting the legal haunts. Mr. Greenwood reports everything favorable in the southern country. The whole of Millard county has been visited recently with very heavy storms, and while it may be a little hard on the range stock, prospects are good for next season's crops.

Attorney I. I. Stewart is up today

Provo Evening Dispatch
March 13, 1894

Millard Mites.

MEADOW, March 10.—Once in a while some one crops up with a pean of praise for the country of their birth or adoption. I have a patriotic streak just now, and feel like saying a few words in behalf of Millard, and her onward march. Money is as scarce here as elsewhere, yet we have suffered as little from the panic as most places in the territory, which goes to prove that the farmer is much better off than the tradesman or mechanic during hard times.

Even when produce is sold at the low price it is at present, he does not want for food for he grows nearly all he requires. If he purchased no article of food from the store he may always have a substantial meal on the table from the products of his own farm, garden and orchard.

The people down here are generally thrifty, industrious and persevering in their endeavor to improve their land and homes, and thereby their financial condition, while a panic like the present one is calculated to teach them a stricter economy.

In Meadow two of our young farmers have made a reservoir large enough to hold all the waste water which runs past their land, thus by their industry and economy they can bring more land under cultivation. One of these men has irrigated twenty-seven acres with one claim of water, in years when water was abundant, and he had good crops. These are examples it would be well if many others would follow they would find it would pay, and in many instances save them having to adopt that most ruinous practice of mortgaging.

Meadow is to have a new school house and amusement hall and the meeting house must be enlarged to meet the needs of the increasing population. Nor is this to be wondered at, seeing there were six weddings within twelve month, out of a population consisting of fifty two families, and units are often added to the family record.

Some of the boys have recently purchased instruments for a band, and are making rapid progress in their musical education under an able instructor. The instruments are silver plated and are very handsome.

We have a civil government class, the members of which hold semi-weekly debates which are interesting and instructive.

Our district school is large enough to employ two teachers during the winter months.

Every year more land is being taken up and better homes built.

We have a saw mill, and one for finishing lumber and cracking feed. There is cooperative sheep herd and several individual herds. Not much stock is kept for the sheep, which pass through in great numbers, have destroyed the range and the poor man's cow can hardly find a tuft of grass

There are many good orchards and the fruit grown is of excellent quality. The people are sober and industrious, and we have neither saloons nor gambling dens in Meadow. A board of trade has been established for Millard county. Fillmore has a creamery, and we ought to have a canning factory, which would provide a market for our fruit and vegetables instead of labor and time expended in taking them to Provo, Salt Lake city, or westward to the mining camps. It would also find employment for some of the rising generation.

M. A, Y. G.

Salt Lake Herald
March 17, 1894

Messrs. Melville and Ray of Fillmore are working like beavers on their two resorvoir schemes at Marysvale and Snake creek. The latter gentleman is now in Denver. Prospects good.—Millard County Blade.

Provo Daily Enquirer
March 17, 1894

Rejected Supreme Bench Nominees.

The record shows that there have been thirteen nominees for the United States supreme bench rejected by the senate besides Mr. Hornblower. Those were John J. Crittenden of Kentucky, nominated by John Quincy Adams; Roger B. Taney of Maryland, by Jackson; John C. Spencer and Reuben H. Walworth of New York, Edward King of Pennsylvania, and John M. Read of Pennsylvania, by Tyler; George N. Woodward of Pennsylvania, by Polk; E A. Bradford of Pennsylvania, by Fillmore; Jeremiah S. Black of Pennsylvania, by Buchanan; Stanberry of Ohio, by Johnson; Caleb Cushing of Massachusetts, E. Rockwood Hoar of Massachusetts, and George H. Williams of Oregon, by Grant.

ATTENTION, DEMOCRATS!

There will be a meeting of the Fillmore Democratic Club on Monday evening, March 19, at 8 o'clock sharp, in the lower room of the Court House, for the purpose of organizing a Democratic Brass Band, and for such other business, as may come before the Club.

Alma Greenwood Pres.

Dan Stevens, Sec.

OUR CITY SOLONS.

The City Council of Fillmore City convened in the Council room, Mayor Callister presiding. Of the Councilors there were present, O. C. Holbrook, J. C. Kelly and N. S. Bishop; also marshal Alexander and Recorder Kelly.

Mrs. Powell, M. D., presented her bill for attendance on Mrs. McNorton who, while in a fit, fell into the fire and was severely burned. The matter was laid over until the County Court should again be in session, so as to have it properly adjusted. R. A. McBride, J. P., presented the following bill of costs in the case of Fillmore City vs. G. R. Huntsman. Justice's fees $24.45, Jury fees $24.00, Witness fees $16.80, bailiff fees $6.00, Marshals fees $24.00, Board of Jury $3.00 total $103.65, which was allowed.

W. J. Goulter was allowed $1.00 for hauling away a dead horse.

The Council appointed G. Huntsman and J. V. Robison a committee to be associated with a committee of one to be appointed by the Roller Mill Company to make specification for the construction of a dam to be built at the head of the New City ditch.

Mr. McMahon stated that he intended to pull up some of his apple trees, and asked permission to deposit them on the side-walk adjoining his orchard until he could move them away. Granted

On motion the Mayor was authorized to receive the specifications of the dam committee, and accept or reject them.

Ora Peterson was allowed $3.00 for extra labor on the South ditch.

Rasmussen Bros. were allowed a rebate of three dollars on their dance licenses.

The committee of the Franklin Society dance was allowed a rebate of one dollar on their license.

The recorder was allowed ten dollar on salary.

On motion the conducting of the waste water into the waste ditch was referred to the Irrigating Company.

N. S. Bishop and J. T. Ashman were appointed a committee to let by contract the work of cleaning out the water ditches. They were also required to see to the construction of flumes under the Melville and Beaton ditches, to carry the waste water into the Sink ditch.

G. R. Huntsman was given a rebate of $25.00 on his license for two Pool tables for the quarter ending March 17, 1894.

George Greenway was given a rebate of ten dollars on his last licence for one billiard table.

G. R. Huntsman made application for a liquor license on the expiration of his present one.

On motion, the Council decided to hold an executive session on Thursday evening next.

The minutes of the previous meeting were read and approved.

On motion the compensation for labor for City purpose was fixed as follows: Hand without team $1.00 per day, with team $1.50. Adjourned until next Thursday at 7 P. M.

Salt Lake Herald
March 22, 1894

Harvey W. King, of Fillmore, Millard county, filed homestead entry No. 10,871, for 160 acres in section 11, township 21 south, range 5 west.

Church Chimes.

The services last Sunday were opened by the choir singing:

"Oh, ye mountains high,
Where the clear blue sky."

Prayer was offered by Elder Joshua Greenwood, after which the choir sang a beautiful sentence entitled:

"Go, when the morning shineth."

The sacrement was then administered by Elders Joseph Swallow and Abram Carling, during which the choir sang:

"He died, the Great Redeemer died."

Elder Jas. A. Melville was the first speaker. He was pleased to see so large a congregation present. Said we all had objects in life, and the good objects should be encouraged. We should all be united in matters that were of benefit to the ward. Many of our young people were spending too much time to no purpose. Spoke of the condition of the people in Salt Lake and compared them with those of Fillmore. The speaker advised the people to employ their spare time beautifying their homes. Too many criminal cases had been coming before the people lately. This should not be. Difficulties between Latter-day Saints should be settled before the authorities if they could not be amicably settled among themselves. As a community we should seek to be more united; in union is strength. Here is a considerable amount of disunion even in our little ward. Let us unite one and all in an effort to encourage the upbuilding of our town and county and establish home industries. Here is a market for the products of farms, and if nothing more lucrative could be gotten to do, we should take advantage of the fact that land is plentiful, and crops large. The mineral resources of our Territory have so far as yet been barely commenced. A million of people would come here at no distant future, our mountain streams would be dotted with machine shops and factories. The speaker had but one desire—to be of benefit to the masses of the people, to establish unity. We should build up each other, strengthen and patronize each other. That we might all reach this point was his desire.

President Hinckley said he had listened with much interest to the remarks of Brother Melville. We should seriously consider the advise given by him this Sabbath. Spoke ... unity of effort to ... little too ... like the present, would make us ... oping home industries. The backbone of all mankind was farming. Why did we not properly develop the land we have; we were land poor. We would find that if we did not take advantage of opportunities offered us at home, we would find strangers coming here, who would make us their servants and handmaidens. We should have a creamery in each town in the county. We should have woolen mills here. Not one sheep of ten wintering in Millard County was owned here; we are letting too many opportunities pass unnoticed; let us look to our streams and water power. Complimented THE PROGRESS for its labor. Spoke on the aid promised by the people to help complete the Deseret meeting house. Let each one do according to his ability.

Bishop Callister then spoke a few moments. He said he had secured work for every man in Fillmore, who would assist bringing the waters from Dry Creek into the city. Said if the people would work to that end, we could have a woolen factory here by next fall.

The choir sang:

"Guide us, oh, thou Great Jehovah."

Benediction by Elder C. Anderson.

Salt Lake Herald
April 7, 1894

The wires of the Deseret Telegraph line south of Fillmore were not working yesterday on account of a break somewhere between that place and Kanosh. The repairs will be made at once.

Provo, April 12.—Henry W. Hawley, sheriff of Millard county, today filed suit against J. S. Giles, county clerk of Millard county, for $10,100 damages. The complaint sets forth that plaintiff as sheriff of said county, was authorized by the county court to collect amounts due for license throughout said Millard county; that he collected the sum of $30 from W. A. Ray and Alonzo Hinckley on the 15th day of July, 1893, and afterwards turned this amount over to defendant in the presence of Daniel Stevens, county treasurer of Millard county, and defendant thereupon issued to said Ray and Hinckley their license. "Defendant, well knowing these facts and mali-

well knowing these facts and maliciously intending and desiring to injure the said plaintiff in his reputation, did falsely state on February 4, 1894, at Fillmore city, in the presence of a large number of persons, the following slanderous words: 'That said plaintiff had procured licenses for said Ray and Hinckley by fraudulently pretending that he would turn over the money for said licenses, and then having thus fraudulently obtained the licenses, kept the money which the said plaintiff had collected therefor.'"

Plaintiff claims that these words were uttered to injure his reputation and therefore demands relief. Zane & Zane represent the plaintiff.

A Fillmore Sensation.

Last week Fillmore had an overgrown sensation in which a semi-civilized red, several semi-civilized whites, several Pahvant squaws and forty gallons, or so, of cider became inextricably mixed up in a most disgusting carouse. United States Commissioner George C. Veile sat on the unsavory case two days, and on account of the conflicting testimony, dismissed the case in disgust.

The man who sold the cider was fined $25.

The people of Fillmore are so indignant and mortified over the nauseous affair that the Blade would not, out of respect to their feelings, mention it, did not its duty as a news gatherer insist upon it.—Millard County Blade.

Elizabeth Robinson, of Fillmore, Millard county, filed final proof on her desert entry of the northeast quarter of the northwest quarter of section 7, township 21 south, range 5 west.

Several specimens of gold bearing rock have lately been found in the vicinity of Fillmore and Meadow; and specimens have been sent off for assay, the results of which are anxiously awaited. A number of prospectors have arrived from the north. Watch out for developments.

The following letters, remaining at the Fillmore postoffice, will, if not claimed within thirty days, be forwarded the Dead Letter office at Washington: Ezra Madison, George Francotth, Martin F. Hynes, Francis Jenson, C. E. Johnson, Frank Keller, N. T. Nyberg, Henry Otterström, A. Richardson, Andrew Thorp.

Salt Lake Herald
April 17, 1894

Mining Notes.

Silver, 63½; lead, $3.20.

T. R. Jones & Co. received yesterday: Bullion, $2,500.

McCornick & Co. received: Hanauer bullion, $3,200.

Wells, Fargo & Co. received: Pennsylvania bullion, $3,444; Ontario bullion, $15,011.

Just as we were going to press a fine specimen of gold-bearing quartz, which was found immediately east of the city, was exhibited to a Progress reporter. The rock is fairly bristling with free gold, and will go above $1,500 to the ton. A party of six prospectors have already started in search of the ledge, each one being confident of locating it. There is no doubt of the hills east of the city being thoroughly prospected, as men are arriving daily, each one being more sanguine than the other about our mineral outlook.—Millard County Progress.

Samples from C. Anderson's mine, which was worked some last year, have just been assayed in Salt Lake, and show $11.85 in gold to the ton. It is understood that Mr. Goss and other mining men will arrive from Salt Lake today.—Millard County Progress.

Mining locations are being made by the score, east of Fillmore, and the county recorder is being kept busy recording the same.—Millard County Progress.

Millard County Progress
April 21, 1894

It is understood that Fillmore is to have a military company. Judge Greenwood has taken the preliminary steps for its organization.

Writes Mr. C. Overson from Leamington: "I like to read THE PROGRESS, and when I have read it, I send it to old friends in Kansas, who have lived in Fillmore. Have just returned from Detroit, where I accompanied three mining men to look at o'er group. Think soon to be able to make a sale. The Drum mines will soon come to the front; but it is as elsewhere, it will take capital."

AN UNFAIR STATEMENT MADE.

That "Fillmore Sensation" Invented by the Blade.

ITS CLAIM AS A NEWSGATHERER.

It Publishes Nothing in the Line of News "Gathered" While Visiting Our Settlements, but Slander.

Last week Fillmore had an overgrown sensation in which a semi-civilized red, several semi-civilized whites, several Pahvant squaws and forty gallons, or so, of cider become inextricably mixed up in a most disgusting carouse. United States Commissioner George C. Veile sat on the unsavory case two days, and on account of the conflicting testimony, dismissed the case in disgust.

The man who sold the cider was fined $25.

The people of Fillmore are so indignant and mortified over the nauseous affair that The Blade would not, out of respect to their feelings, mention it, did not its duty as a news-gatherer insist upon it.—Deseret Blade.

We notice the above for two reasons, first, because of its utter and absolute falsity and lack of truth, second, because of the evident desire on the part of the writer, who penned that article, to publish statements detrimental to our fair city, and at the same time suppress any and all items of benefit to this eastern part of our county. The writer says, that a "semi-civilized red, several semi-civilized whites, several Pahvant squaws, 40 gallons or so, of cider became inextractible mixed up in a most disgusting carouse."

These are utterances and assertions, which are absolutely without foundation in truth, and which were not proven in the examination before the United States commissioner. It was, however, proven, that some Indians—bucks and squaws—had been indulging in intoxicants at their camps—from whom obtained was not brought out, and certain it is that none of the defendants were charged with furnishing them said liquor—that they were determined upon having some fun, and came to town. The officers of the peace hearing of the matter, set to work to investigate, and, of course, to shield themselves, the Indians implicated some white men. These were arrested, tried and, and proved their innocense

The Blade says further, that United States Commissioner Veile sat on the case two days and "dismissed it in disgust." That is a direct slur to our people. The case was not dismissed in disgust, but after all the evidence was in, the attorney for the prosecution moved defendants be discharged, as there was no cause for action.

Further it says, the "man who sold the cider was fined $25.00." This is another characteristic of that writer. No one was found guilty, and the man who "was fined $25.00 for selling cider," exists only in the imagination of the Blade.

Then follows the assertion, that the "people of Fillmore are so indignant," etc., and "did not its (The Blade) duty as a newsgatherer" insist upon it, it would not publish the story.

The claim of the Blade of being a "news-gatherer" is rather amusing; but like the tattle-tale and slanderer, well-known in most communities, it gathers up various bits of information, and covering them with its venom it sends them abroad to poison the communities which lend it succor.

"There was no testimony that the Indians has been drinking forty gallons of cider, nor half that amount, nor one-twentieth part of that quanity. No white man did furnish them any, so far as the testimony went, and the "disgusting carouse "exists merely in the mind of the writer, who gloatingly penned that infamous paragraph.

While the paper referred to time and again has shown its desire and wish to run down the editor of this paper, without cause or provocation, and while we have continually overlooked said attacks, considering the source, we can not consistely allow any writer, however insignificant, to unchallenged misrepresent any part of our fair county, and we offer this as our only excuse for noticing that most contemptible article and thus give it publicity, rather than keeping it quiet by permitting it to appear in the Blade only.

Did not the Blade's "duty as a newsgatherer" insist that it publish items from the trip on which its reporter was taken by our water-master? why did not they appear? Did not its "duty" insist that it publish something about our mines and minerals, shown its reporter by one of our citizens? Why did not they appear? Why does the Blade say something on the County-Fair proposition. Does not its "duty as a news-gatherer insist upon that being mentioned?

But then, to ask the Blade for its reticence on many public topics, and to enumerate them, would require too much of our space.

The Progress does not mean to afford the Blade too much free advertising, but when its virulence is vented at the people of Millard, this paper will see to it that justice is done.

THE CITY CHARTER.

Sec. 1. All that portion of Millard county embraced in the following boundaries, to-wit: Begining at a point two miles due east of the southeast corner of the public square in said city, thence south two miles, thence west four miles, thence north four miles, thence east four miles, thence south two miles, to the place of beginning, shall be known and designated under the name and style of Fillmore city, and the inhabitants thereof are hereby constituted a body corporate and politic by the same aforesaid and may have and use a common seal which they may change and alter at pleasure.

Sec. 2. The inhabitants of said city, by the name and style aforesaid, shall shall have power to sue and be sued, to plead and be impleaded, defend and be defended in all courts of law and equity, and in all actions whatsoever; to purchase, receive and hold property real and personal; to purchase, receive and hold real property beyond the city for burying grounds or other public purposes for the use of the inhabitants of said city; to sell, lease, convey or dispose of property real and personal for the benefit of said city; to improve and protect such property, and to do all other things in relation thereto as natural persons.

Sec. 3. There shall be a city council, to consist of a mayor and five councilors, who shall have the qualifications of electors of said city, and shall be chosen by the qualified voters thereof, and shall hold their offices for two years and until their successors shall be elected and qualified.

The City Council shall judge of the qualifications, elections and returns of their own members, and a majority of them shall form a quorum to do business; but a smaller number may adjourn from day to day, and compel the attendance of absent members under such penalties as may be prescribed by ordinance; there shall also be elected in like manner two justices of the peace, who shall have the qualifications of voters, be commissioned by the Governor and have jurisdiction in all cases arising under the ordinances of the city.

Sec. 4. The mayor and councilors, before entering upon the duties of their offices, shall take and subscribe an oath or affirmation that they will support the Constitution of the United States and the laws of this Territory, and that they will well and truly perform all the duties of their offices to the best of their skill and abilities.

Sec. 5. One mayor and five councilors shall be elected biennially, and the first election under this act shall be at such time and place as the probate judge of Millard county shall direct: Provided, said election shall be on or before the first Monday in August next. Said election shall be held and conducted as now is provided by law for the holding of elections for county and Territorial officers; and, at the said first election, all electors within said city limits shall be entitled to vote.

Sec. 6. The clerks of election shall leave with each person elected, or at usual place of residence, within five days after the election, a written notice of his election; and each person so notified shall, within ten days after the election, take the oath or affirmation hereinbefore mentioned, a certificate of which oath shall be deposited with the recorder, and by him preserved; and all subsequent elections shall be held, conducted and returns thereof be made as may be provided for by ordinance of the city council.

Sec. 7. The city council shall have authority to levy and collect taxes for city purposes upon all taxable property, real and personal, within the limits of the city, not exceeding one-half of one per cent. per annum upon the assessed value thereof, and may assess, and collect, and expend the necessary taxes to furnish the city with water for irrigation and other purposes, and to regulate and control the same for the use and benefit of the inhabitants thereof, and may inforce the payment of taxes in any manner to be provided for by ordinance not repugnant to the Constitution of the United States, or the laws of this Territory.

Sec. 8. The city council shall have power to appoint a supervisor of streets. They shall also have power to appoint such other officers, by ordinance, as may be necessary, define the duties of all city officers and remove them from office at pleasure.

Salt Lake Herald
April 25, 1894

Sheep shearing has commenced in Millard county.

Fillmore is to have a military company. General Judge Greenwood is at the head of the movement.

Charles Crane tells the Salina Press editor that he is going to leave politics alone and attend strictly to his own private business. He is now devoting his attention to mining and expects to give employment to 300 men during the summer in developing his properties.

Between fifty and seventy-five persons are at present busily at work at Swan Lake, "the coming capital of Millard county and possibly of Utah territory," as Superintendent Aldrach enthusiastically puts it. Upward of 1,000 acres of wheat, barley and oats have been planted, besides a large tract of land seeded to lucern. The grain is looking well, and there is no danger of floods or bursting of reservoirs. Some building is also going on.—Fillmore Progress.

James McNorton was this week arrested on a charge of having stolen $1,000 from John Kelly's store. He was brought before Justice McBride and demanded a jury trial. Almon Robinson, Thomas C. Callister, F. C. Melville, John Jackson, jr., J. B. Williams and J. D. Smith were chosen as jurors. James A. Melville appeared for the prosecution and James King for the defendant. The accused made a very flimsy defense, and a verdict was brought in, finding the defendant guilty as charged. He was fined $50 with an alternative of fifty days in jail. He paid the fine.—Fillmore Progress.

Salt Lake Herald
May 10, 1894

Kanosh industrial army, consisting of your correspondent and six other men, one of whom is past 71 years of age, and another 65 years old and an invalid, were engaged during the past week in putting up and repairing some forty rods of joint field fencing, the property of a stalwart person 35 years old, who married a widow and got the fence thrown in. If your paper would help the industrials to wake up the loafers in the community to a sense of duty, it would be a good evidence of progress in our midst.—Kanosh correspondence Fillmore Progress.

Salt Lake Herald
May 13, 1894

I west.
By Orson C. Holbrook, of Fillmore, Millard county, on west one-half of the northeast one-quarter and south one-half of the northwest one-quarter of section 15, township 21 south, range 5 west.

Salt Lake Herald
May 14, 1894

Mayor Holbrook, of Provo, yesterday received a telegram from Joshua Greenwood, of Fillmore, asking him to forward two caskets on the first train. It appears that on Saturday the little daughter of Orson C. Holbrook and the son of Joseph E. Ray were drowned at Fillmore.

Salt Lake Herald
May 21, 1894

BACK FROM MILLARD.

Hon. John T. Caine Spends a Week With Southern Democrats.

Hon. John T. Caine has just returned from Millard county, where he has been for the past week in the interests of Democracy. Democratic clubs have now been organized in every precinct in the county and this is only the starter for the territory.

The gentleman left the city on Monday last and at Nephi was joined by Hon. W. K. Reid, of Sanpete county, who accompanied him during the tour of the county. The first meeting was held at Scipio on Monday night and then followed enthusiastic meetings at Fillmore, Kanosh, Holden, Meadow, Oak Creek, and Leamington. At each of the places named clubs were organized with heavy memberships. The Democrats of Millard are confident of victory at the coming election and already have opened the campaign. It is now the intention of the Democracy to organize societies in every precinct of the territory in conformity with the national organization.

Millard County Progress
May 19, 1894

Tuesday held a Democratic rally in the upper room of the Court House to organize a Democratic Society. Alma Greenwood acted as chairman and I. N. Hinkley, Jr, as secretary; Hon. Jno. T. Caine outlined a course of procedure, after which the Democratic club was disorganized and an organization known as Democratic Society of Fillmore was formed with the following officers Pres. Alma Greenwood, First Vice-president, I. N. Hinckley, Jr., second vice-president, Jas. A. Melville; Secretary, J. S. Jiles; Treasurer, Miss Edith Huntsman. A committee on membership, consisting of J. T. Ashman, J. E. Ray and Daniel Stevens was then elected, after which Judge Reid delivered an address on the principles of Democracy. The Society will meet next Tuesday evening at the same place.

Provo Enquirer: Mayor Holbrook got a telegram from Fillmore last Saturday evening, telling him that his brother's little girl and Mr. Joseph Ray's child had both been drowned, and asking him to forward two caskets. Mrs. Holbrook went down with the coffins yesterday.

Salt Lake Herald
May 22, 1894

Hon. J. T. Caine and Judge Reed, Tuesday, held a Democratic rally in the upper room of the court house, to organize a Democratic society. Alma Greenwood acted as chairman and I. N. Hinkley, jr., as secretary, Hon. John T. Caine outlined a course of procedure, after which the Democratic club was disorganized and an organization known as the Democratic Society of Fillmore was formed with the following officers: President, Alma Greenwood; first vice-president, I. N. Hinckley, jr.; second vice-president, Jas. A. Melville; secretary, J. S. Jiles; treasurer, Miss Edith Huntsman. A committee on membership consisting of J. T. Ashman, J. E. Ray and Daniel Stevens was then elected, after which Judge Reid delivered an address on the principles of Democracy. The society will meet next Tuesday evening at the same place.—Fillmore Progress.

Edward Trimble, while plowing last week, unearthed on his farm in the old field, an Indian grave. Various pieces of utensils were uncovered, and articles composed of some kind of clay or metal were left with the Progress, where they can be seen. Mr. Trimble made an agreement with our reporter, that if anything in the line was found, he would present us with a complete skeleton, in place of the one demolished by the Deseret dentist, whereas if any gold was found, he would keep that himself.—Fillmore Progress.

ROBINSON'S SALTED MINE.

How a Fillmore Man Was Swindled Out of $2,000.

The story of Alma Robinson and the salted mine is being revived through proceedings in the grand jury which is now holding session in Nephi.

Some two years ago, Mr. Robinson, a wealthy citizen of Fillmore, and the wealthiest man in Millard county, was approached by one of the Greenhalgh family of Meadow, and asked for an extension on a note, says the Millard Blade. In justification of his request, the Meadow man said he had struck it rich out in the Detroit district, and for proof exhibited a sample of ore which fairly glittered with the precious metal. The ore had been assayed by an assayer living in Meadow at the time, and although it bore the returns of fabulous wealth, there is no proof that it was other than a correct analysis of the ore submitted for examination.

Naturally such a story excited the cupidity of the wealthy Fillmore man, increased by his well-known desire to own a rich mine. With every confidence in Greenhalgh, Mr. Robinson made him an offer for his share in the bonanza, but the offer was refused. Mr. Greenhalgh could not part with his fortune; he had too good a thing. The refusal only intensified the other's resolve to purchase, and the Meadow man knew it full well. The trap was set and the victim was an easy prey. Greenhalgh told Robinson that he would not part with his share, but the other owners might be induced to do so. In fact, the other owners were prepared to receive an offer.

So long as Mr. Robinson could not buy out Greenhalgh, he sought the other partners in company with the Meadow man. These proved to be the Jennings brothers, of Juab county. Placing implicit confidence in Greenhalgh, Mr. Robinson, without going to the fake mine to examine it, concluded a bargain with the Jennings brothers, and deposited notes to the amount of $3,000 in W. A. Ray's safe, instructing our Deseret merchant to let the Jenningses have what supplies they desired against the amount deposited.

For a time there was great excitement over the fabulous discovery, and the camp was full of men looking for rock like unto Robinson's mine. At last it began to dawn upon the prospectors that they had been sold as well as Robinson; but the Fillmore man was the first to find it out, his suspicions having been aroused through a letter from Mr. Ray.

Notwithstanding Mr. Robinson knew he had been defrauded, his conscientious regard for the name of Alma Robinson across the back of a note or check constrained him from repudiating the fraudulent bargain. He came up to Deseret and in W. A. Ray's store paid over in checks and money to the Jennings brothers the price agreed upon for what he himself knew was a salted mine.

It is alleged now that Mr. Robinson has in his possession evidence which shows that the rock assayed and upon which he based his faith, was obtained from the Monkey Wrench district; that it was a deliberate plan to swindle him, and he therefore preferred complaint against the Jennings brothers and Greenhalgh for obtaining money under false pretenses. This complaint is now before the grand jury at Nephi, and Mr. Ray gave in his testimony on Monday. Ed Stewart, out at the Ibex, has also been subpenaed.

Salt Lake Herald
May 27, 1894

Notes from Provo.

Provo, May 25.—The B. Y. academy closed another successful year yesterday and today the students are leaving the town for their homes. A farewell party was given last evening and a large number were present. The closing exercises occupied all of last week and a very pleasant time was had.

J. F. Noyes returned a day or two ago from Louisville, Ky., bringing with him his sheepskin, which will in future give him the appellation of Doctor. Mr. Noyes is a Utah boy; he was born and raised at Fillmore, but during the last few years he has resided at Provo.

Judge Dusenberry received word yes-

Provo Evening Dispatch
May 29, 1894

MRS. SAM. A. KING of this city leaves this afternoon for a few weeks visit with her mother in Salt Lake county.

SAM. A KING left this morning for Fillmore on legal business and will be absent from the city perhaps a week.

Salt Lake Herald
May 31, 1894

W. H. King, while attending court here is spending his spare moments organizing Democratic clubs. Last evening he in company with Hon. Joshua Greenwood, of Fillmore, held a rousing meeting at Levan. The people were enthusiastic and after attending to business matters cheered lustily for the principles of Democracy. The night before, Judge Judd and Mr. King held forth at Nephi.

Millard County Progress
June 2, 1894

Miss A. L. Dillon Thursday, left for the East, where she will spend the summer months in the interest of education. She will resume her duties in the Fillmore Primary department next fall.

J. T. Ashman this week shipped 11500 pounds of cheese from the Fillmore dairy to Salt Lake City. The demand for Fillmore cheese is rapidly growing and promises to be greater than the supply.

The Fillmore Democracy on Saturday elected the following delegates to attend the county convention to be held to-day, which will elect three delegates to the Territorial Democratic convention to be held in Logan, June 16th: J. S. Giles, Joshua Greenwood, Alma Greenwood, Jas. A. Melville, Jos. E. Hay, J. T. Ashman, Ova Peterson and John Jackson. Alternates: John Jackson, Jr., Walter Rowley and G. C. Wade.

Live stock men in the vicinity of Fillmore should remember that they can always secure as low rates from Salina and Gunnison to eastern markets vio the D. & R. G. railroad, as by any other route. Before shipping it will be to your interest to write B. F. Nevius, General Agent, D. & R. G. railroad, Salt Lake City.   tf

Provo Evening Dispatch
June 4, 1894

SIGNS OF THRIFT

And Substantial Progress Down in Millard County.

LANDS BEING FENCED

And Reservoirs Being Built and Constructed—The Dairy Business Prosperous—There are No Idle Men and all are Comparatively Oblivious of the Hard Times.

FILLMORE, Utah, June 1.—[Correspondence DISPATCH.]—The ex capital of Utah, in one respect, is better off to-day than the present capital, it is not troubled with the so-called "industrials" and professional tramps. The people of this city may not possess all of the luxuries of life and indulge in all of the pleasurable excesses of the age, but they are quiet and industrious, working day by day at such matters as are common to farming communities, making but little money, yet obtaining plenty of the common necessaries of life and dwelling comparatively oblivious of the much talked of hard times.

The Fillmore creamery, managed by A. W. Ensign of Davis county, is now in active operation, and is producing a vast amount of cheese, which finds a ready market in all parts of the territory. Nearly 1000 pounds of milk is being used daily, and many of the citizens are now engaging in the dairy business.

President Ira N Hinckley of the Millard stake, together with his sons, are at present engaged in fencing a large and valuable tract of farming land, situated about five miles west of of Fillmore. Mr. Hinkley for years has possessed the finest farm in this section of the country, but recently, he and his sons have purchased both from the government and individuals, about 3000 acres, which will now increase their possessions to about 5000 acres, and before a month passes by the whole amount will be inclosed. The farm is now well stocked with hogs and cattle and this year they expect to put up about six hundred and nifty tons of hay.

Messrs. Melville & Ray have just completed a small reservoir on the sink of Meadow creek, and have fenced in that immediate vicinity about fifteen hundred acres of fine agricultural land and have commenced some extensive improvements.

Some others of the Fillmore citizens are now at work on a reservoir, the site being at the Bald Mountain, situated about seven miles northwest of the town. This is considered as one of the most feasible schemes in this section of the country. The water for the reservoir will come from Chalk creek during the winter and spring months, and will be sufficient to irrigate several thousand acres of land, and there is any quantity of valuable land within from one to four miles of the reservoir site

It has long been known that Millard county would yet become a great farming center, and that it has within its confines more good land "lying out doors" than any other two counties in the territory. All that is needed is a little energy and some capital directed towards the development of its vast resources and it will become a desirable place in which to live.

GNI KAS.

Salt Lake Herald
June 15, 1894

At the Democratic county convention, held in the court house Saturday, W. A. Ray, of Deseret; Joshua Greenwood, of Fillmore, and Edward Stevens, of Holden, were elected delegates to attend the territorial convention to be held in Salt Lake June 16. Phil Corcoran, B. J. Stringham and George Crane were elected alternates. The county Democratic society was organized with Joshua Greenwood as president; George Crane, first vice-president; J. C. Hawley, second vice-president; C. Anderson, secretary, and John Cherrington, treasurer.—Fillmore Progress.

Millard County Progress
June 16, 1894

Opposite the County Court House is the residence of J. V. Robison. At this time of the year, particularly, this place presents a most attractive appearance. With the stately shade trees surrounding the house on all sides, the well-kept lawns and flower beds, the odor of many flowers, and the well kept kitchen garden in the rear, it presents a picture of taste and untiring labor. All our inhabitants might have residences and surroundings like this, but it takes labor, and much of it. With the sun Mr. Robison is around his premises, beautifying here and there, cutting down or trimming a tree and replacing it with a more choice one. This residence is one of the attractions of Fillmore and its beauty and neatness attracts the admiration of all strangers who visit our city.

Salt Lake Herald
June 22, 1894

Omaha, June 21.—There are a thousand delegates in the Democratic conference opened today for the purpose of organizing the state free coinage league.

The wildest cheering followed the reading of the call, declaring for free and unlimited coinage of the white metal.

While the committee on resolutions was out, officers were elected as follows: President, J. E. Ong, Fillmore county; secretary, T. J. Morgan, Cass county; treasurer, G. A. Luikhart, Madison county, and an executive committee of ten. The resolution committee's report was adopted as follows:

"We send greetings to our fellow Democrats of Nebraska, and invite their earnest co-operation and aid in electing delegates from every county in the state to the Democratic state convention of 1894, pledged to vote for the insertion in the Democratic state platform of the following plank:

"We send greetings to our fellow Democrats of Nebraska, and invite their earnest co-operation and aid in electing delegates from every county in the state to the Democratic state convention of 1894, pledged to vote for the insertion in the Democratic state platform of the following plank:

" 'We favor the immediate restoration of the free and unlimited coinage of gold and silver at the present ratio of 16 to 1, without waiting for the aid or consent of any other nation on earth.'

"In the effort to obtain a fair expression of Democratic sentiment, we urge upon every Democrat who believes in the principle herein enunciated to participate actively and vigorously in the selection of delegates to the state convention.

"We recommend that in every county of the state, the Democrats who oppose this proposed plank be invited to a thorough discussion of its merits, to the end that the Democratic party may act intelligently and harmoniously upon this great question.

"We propose that this contest shall be fought out upon clean lines and with intelligent methods; but, confident in the correctness of our position, we also propose that the fight shall be vigorous, and that no effort shall be spared to place in the platform of the Democratic party the same emphasis, the same unmistakable utterance concerning the great question of finance as has been lastingly imprinted upon our party platforms concerning the great question of tariff reform."

Then the convention adjourned.

Salt Lake Herald
June 23, 1894

Rufus Day, of Fillmore, Millard county, homestead entry of lots 2, 3, 6 and 7, southwest quarter of the northeast quarter, and the southeast quarter of the northwest quarter of section 32, township 21 south, range 4 west.

Salt Lake Herald
July 26, 1894

Arrived With His Prisoners.

Officer Hawley, of Millard county, arrived in the city yesterday morning, having in his custody Tom Morgan, an Indian, and Mat Dunn, the fellow who committed a terrible assault upon a sheepherder in the western part of Millard county some time ago. They were arrested near Reno by Hawley and held there while the officer returned to Utah for requisition papers. This morning the sheriff will leave for Fillmore with his prisoners.

Salt Lake Herald
July 27, 1894

THE LAND OFFICE.

Yesterday's Filings—Decisions Handed Down in Two Cases.

Yesterday the following filings were received at the local land office:

James E. Mellville, of Fillmore, desert land entry of the east half of the northwest quarter of the north half of the southeast quarter of the southeast quarter of the southwest quarter and lot 7 of section 1, and the northeast quarter of section 12, township 22 south, range 20 west.

Mary E. Roy, of Fillmore, desert land entry of the east half of the northeast quarter and the north half of the southeast quarter of the northeast quarter of the southwest quarter and lot 1, 2 and 3, section 12, township 22 south, range 20 west.

Decisions were handed down......

Gone South With Prisoners.

Sheriff Hawley, of Millard county, left yesterday morning with his two prisoners, captured in Nevada. The men are to be arraigned at Fillmore.

Millard County Progress
July 14, 1894

Orders for Fillmore cheese continue to come rushing from outside places. The Nebo Salt Company, Nephi, Holden Co-op, W. M. Ray, Deseret, Mansfield, Murdock and Co., Beaver, and several others, sent in their orders this week.

The day that the President signs the Statehood bill for Utah, a new railroad line will be commenced for the Coast, and it will come through Fillmore! Hurrah.

On Monday last, the sad tidings reached the city that Esther McCullough, aged 14 years, and Nettie Nichols, a girl aged 15, had been drowned in Grass Valley on the 6th inst. Esther is a grand daughter of Mrs. Callister of this city and a niece of Bishop Thomas C. Callister. Mr. McCullough is an old Fillmore resident, and lived in this city for a number of years, and a host of friends and relatives in this vicinity join with the bereaved parents in their mourning. The girls, it is understood, went in bathing in the Sevier river, and must have gone beyond their depth. Full particulars of the sad affair have not yet been received.

Music hath charms! What! Say, have you listened during the past week to the the silvery strains of that new Fillmore acquisition? Have you heard the new bass drum—boom, boom, and the snare—r-r-r-r! Have your nerves been soothed, or have you felt like attacking the performers with a double-barrelled gattling-gun? Have you listened to the sweet strains of Annie Rooney, Sweet Marie, Three Little Girls in Blue and Tra-ra-ra-boom-de-aye! and still survived? Go and watch the boys as they wend their way homeward with protruding eyes and swolen lips and forgive them. They are practicing that they furnish political enthusiasm at the next campaign.

Salt Lake Herald
August 25, 1894

Mrs. Minnie Greenway, formerly Mrs. Bottomfield, writes from Fillmore to Desk Sergeant Macintosh at the police office stating that the boy Johnny Green, who was picked up as a waif at the depot by Officer Milner some few days ago, belongs to Fillmore, that his mother lives there and will be glad if the police will send him home to her and she will pay all expenses. The little fellow when taken in said he was a newsboy and the police turned him loose, but last night he again put in an appearance at police headquarters and was taken care of and will be sent to his mother today.

Salt Lake Herald
August 26, 1894

Land Office.

The following filings were received at the local land office yesterday:

Susannah T. Robinson, of Fillmore county, homestead entry of the east half of the northwest quarter and the east half of the southwest quarter of section 28, township 21 south, range 3 west.

Harriett P. Drewbey, of Tooele county, desert land entry of lots 4 and the south half of the northwest quarter of section 1 and the southeast quarter and lots 1 and 2, of the south half of the southwest quarter of section 2, township 3 south, range 4 west.

James M. Gallocher, of Tooele county, desert land entry of the south half, the southwest quarter of the southwest quarter and the south half of the northwest quarter of section 14, township 2 south, range 5 west.

Salt Lake Herald
August 30, 1894

FILLMORE MODIFIES.

Just a Little Sorry He Was a Trifle too Brash.

San Francisco, Cal., Aug. 29.—Superintendent J. A. Fillmore, of the Southern Pacific company, has modified his attitude towards those engaged in the recent strike. Just after the strike he was quoted as declaring that none of the leading strikers should ever obtain work in California if he could help it. These threats caused much indignation, and President C. P. Huntington wrote a sharp reproof from New York. This letter caused Mr. Fillmore to make a supplementary statement in which he denies that he said he would hunt down the ex-strikers and deprive them of their positions.

"I am not interfering with anybody," explained Mr. Fillmore. "The men who destroyed our property, stole our trains and killed our employees are on the black list. This list goes to other roads. It is a caution that has been in vogue twenty years."

"If an ex-striker can get work you do not propose to interfere then?" Mr. Fillmore was asked.

"Certainly not," he replied, "except in so far as the black list may come against him. There are ex-strikers now scattered all over the state picking fruit or hops."

Millard County Progress
August 31, 1894

R. & L. Collier and family have taken up their residence in Fillmore City. The Progress says welcome.

The Republicans of Fillmore have chosen T. C. Callister and G. M. Hanson as Delegates to the Territorial Convention at Provo, September 15.

The People's Party of Fillmore Wednesday evening organized their club with Albert Day as Chairman, Finley Randolph, vice-chairmen, A. F. ___ ford, Secretary and Geo. C. Wade treasurer.

Salt Lake Herald
September 2, 1894

Mrs. D. K. Olson, of Fillmore, is in town for a few days attending her son Frank, who has been quite ill, but is rapidly recovering.

WILL GIVE RELIEF

The Befouling of Fillmore's Culinary Waters Must Cease.

A Mass Meeting Held and a Committee Appointed to Visit the Sheep Herds.

On Sunday last a large number of our citizens met in the meeting house to discuss the terrible condition of our drinking water and to take steps to call a halt in the matter of the sheep herd's intolerable nuisance and menace to the health of our people.

A Committee of twelve, consisting of our leading people, were appointed to visit the herds and request them to at once abate the nuisance.

The said committee started on their mission Monday morning and returned Tuesday evening.

Another mass meeting was called Wednesday evening at which the committee presented the following report:

To the People of Fillmore City:

Your committee appointed to examine into the matter of the befouling of the waters flowing through Fillmore City, respectfully report: That we have visited one sheep herd, belonging to Mathias Knudsen, of Fountain Green, Sanpete County, in Bear canyon, and notified the parties in charge, Messrs. Angell and Johnson, to remove their sheep from the water sheds of Chalk Creek, and they have agreed to so remove, and are removing, their sheep to our satisfaction.

We also visited two herds in charge of Charley Frome, of Scipio, Millard County, and notified them to leave inside of three days, and they at once began making preparations to remove their sheep.

We also notified the parties in charge of Hans Eskeland's herd, which is situated in White Pine, to leave the water sheds, and they have began removing their sheep.

We further report that the sheep herd belonging to the Holden Co-op., under the management of John E. Hunter, has been camped in "Cherry," at what is known as the "Bull Corral," for the past four weeks, and all the debris, incident to a sheep camp, was, during the recent floods, washed into the waters of Chalk Creek and swept down the same into this city.

We further report that the water of the right hand fork is clear, while that coming from the left hand fork is muddy and in a befouled condition. And that along the left hand fork there are a number of sheep herds which time and circumstances would not allow us to visit, and your committee is informed and believes, and therefore states, that these sheep are befouling the waters used by this city for culinary purposes.

We further report that there are numerous piles of float-wood, and decaying matter, lying in the bottom of the right hand fork and through which the waters of the creek are flowing. And we recommend that a committee be appointed to notify the sheep camps to at once remove their herds from the water sheds along the creek, and that a like committee be appointed to remove the debris, which undoubtedly contains cattle or sheep, along the right hand fork, either by burning or otherwise removing the same, and also to see whether or not the parties notified have removed their sheep.

We are all of the opinion that the floods are caused by the sheep, tramping the ground so hard that the rains will not penetrate it, and eating out the grass and underbrush so that there is nothing to catch the rains; for we have noticed that in canyons where sheep have never been herded, no floods have ever occurred.

We further report, that in our opinion all of the said sheep are within the seven-mile limit.

Very respectfully.

J. E. RAY,
Chairman.

FILLMORE, Utah, Sept. 5, 1894.

Speeches were made by many leading citizens which were to the effect that the herds must be moved.

The old committee with additional members consented to go again and they will report on Monday evening at 8 o'clock.

It looks as though several herders would be arrested for befouling waters.

Millard County Progress
September 21, 1894

Two of Fillmore's bright boys, whose names will be heard in the future in connection with Millard County's affairs, left Wednesday to attend the Academy at Provo. Harvey Melville and Samuel Greenwood. The best wishes of The Progress goes with the lads.

Live stock men in the vicinity of Fillmore should remember that they can always secure as low rates from Salina and Gunnison to eastern markets vio the D. & R. G. railroad, as by any other route. Before shipping, it will be to your interest to write B. F. Nevins, General Agent, D. & R. G. railroad, Salt Lake City.　tf

Wm. Bangs of Arimo, Idaho, is spending a few days in Fillmore, the guest of Mr. and Mrs. Thomas C. Callister.

Millard County Progress
September 28, 1894

FINANCIAL STATEMENT

—OF—

Fillmore City for the Year Ending December 31, 1893.

RECEIPTS.

On Liquor Licenses	$ 900 00
On Pool Table Licenses	140 00
On Merchants' Licenses	70 25
On Ice Cream Parlor License	6 00
On Pedlers Licenses	1 50
From Cemetery	12 24
From Loan Society, per E. Bartholomew	48 25
From Assessor and Collector, J. A. Lyman	247 67
From Collector Wm. Jackson on Revenue Tax	371 24
From Collector Wm. Jackson on Water Tax	436 75
From Thomas Turner, on New Ditch	14 65
From Roller Mill Company	220 00
Total	$2,463 55

DISBURSEMENTS.

To Sexton	$ 5 24
To Attorneys	35 00
To Recorder	60 06
To Marshal and Police	44 93
To Mayor and City Council	107 25
To Watermaster	175 00
To Road Supervisor	45 75
To E. Bartholomew, on New Ditch	110 51
To Carling & Tomkinson, New Ditch	182 86
To J. S. Giles, on note	71 82
To A. Robison, on note	60 18
Treasurer's Salary	20 00
To Rebates on Liquor Licenses	500 00
To Rebates on Pool Tables	35 00
To Expenses for Headgates and Ditches	360 25
To Expenses Waste Ditch, per J. V. Robison	36 00
Incidental Expenses	118 05
Total	$1,963 43

RESOURCES.

Amount Due on Revenue Tax, by J. A. Lyman	100 00
Amount Due on Revenue Tax, for 1893	25 57
Amount Due on Cash Water Tax	82 80
Amount Due on New Ditch, by J. T. Ashman	9 00
Amount Due by the Several Water Districts:	
First District	125 82
Second District	110 23
Third District	2 31
Fourth District	60 23
Fifth District	2 10
Sixth District	2 21
Value of Water Right for Two City Lots	64 55
Cash in Recorder's Hands	23 70
Checks in Treasury	114 59
Note against Alma Greenwood	6 63
Approximate Value of Cemetery Lots	250 00
Total	$1,027 21

LIABILITIES.

Amount Due Almon Robison, on note	$206 16
Approximate Value of Unredeemed Warrants	200 00
Balance in Favor of the City	621 05
Total	$1,027 21

Salt Lake Herald
September 29, 1894

John Hansen was next called. He said the defendant had shown him a piece of rock which looked very good; was shown some rock from the mine and asked if that was it. He said it was not; was shown another piece and said that it was the piece shown him before or very much like it.

Sid Black also testified as to the value of the mine. He had gone to the district to locate claims on the strength of the sale made. The rock in the mine was what is called crystalized lime. The piece of rock shown the witness was quartz, and never came out of the mine. There is a difference in the looks of the rock and also in the cutting and scraping.

Charles Howard was next sworn and said: I am superintendent of Mercur mine. I was down at Detroit and done some prospecting. I have considerable experience in metal-bearing rock; I am familiar with the rock in the immediate vicinity of the mine in question. The rock shown me did not come from that vicinity. (The rock shown witness was the rock shown to Mr. Robinson at the time of purchase). The witness stated that no quartz was to be found in that vicinity. That no rock like that from which the assay was taken was to be found in the vicinity of the mine in question.

The case is still in progress.

The case of the people vs. Peter Greenhalch et. al., who are accused of selling a "salted" mine to Mr. Robinson, of Fillmore, was then called up.

It is alleged that the defendants, Peter Greenhalch, Nephi Jennings, Alex Jennings and Thomas Goff, obtained $2,000 from Robinson under false pretenses. Aimon Robinson paid the defendants $500 at one time and $2,500 at another. The defendants had shown Mr. Robinson a piece of rock and represented to him that it came from the mine in question, when in reality it came from Colorado. The defendants also showed an assay said to be rock from the mine assaying $50,000 to the ton.

James Paxman was sworn and testified that he assayed the rock and it assayed over $50,000 to the ton.

H. W. Hawley was next sworn and testified as to the mine. He had been to the mine and took up several prospects on the strength of the report circulated by the defendants. He said the mine was no good.

Salt Lake Herald
October 1, 1894

Some fine iron-gold fluxing ore, which assays $8.20 in gold to the ton and a trace of silver, and goes 75 per cent iron, was this week located near Leamington by Fillmore parties.—Millard Progress.

Salt Lake Herald
October 9, 1894

The news was received here yesterday of the death of Mrs. Alma Greenwood, at Fillmore, on Sunday. The deceased was the wife of the assessor and collector of Millard county and a daughter of Dan Olsen, an old time musician well known in this city.

Deseret Evening News
October 10, 1894

Word has been received from Fillmore that Mrs. Eva Olson Greenwood, wife of Alma Greenwood, died on Sunday last from childbirth. The deceased had many friends and relatives in this city who sympathize with the bereaved husband in his great loss.

Salt Lake Herald
October 11, 1894

DEMOCRATIC WORKINGMEN.

A Rousing Meeting Held By Them Last Night.

At the meeting of the Workingmen's Central Democratic club last night, P. W. McCaffrey answered a weekly newspaper and made a brilliant speech to the workingmen, showing why they should be Democrats.

At the conclusion of his address, through the chair, he issued a challenge to the president of the Workingmen's Republican club to debate the issues of Democracy and Republicanism.

Angus M. Cannon, jr., made a brief speech on Jeffersonian principles.

The Chamberlain children's quartette rendered a beautiful vocal selection and J. B. Rawlings followed with a rousing Democratic speech.

He was followed by Mr. H. Huntsman, of Fillmore, who made a telling speech, and the meeting closed with a duet by Messrs. Gleason and McCaffrey and a selection by the Chamberlain quartette.

The attendance was large and the meeting was one of the most enthusiastic yet held by the workingmen.

MILLARD COUNTY.

Hon. A. G. Webber will speak in Millard county as follows:

Holden, Thursday afternoon, Oct.11.
Scipio, Thursday evening, Oct. 11.
Kanosh, Friday evening, Oct. 12.
Meadow, Saturday afternoon, Oct 13.
Fillmore, Saturday evening, Oct.13.

In the European Mission.

[Millenial Star, October 8.]

Arrivals—The following missionaries arrived in Liverpool from Utah, via Glasgow, per Anchor steamship Ethiopia, Wednesday, September 26, 1894: For Scandinavia—Peter Jensen, of Mantua, Box Elder county; H. S. Rasmussen, of Salt Lake city; Christopher Iversen, of Ephraim, Sanpete county; C. E. Cederstrom, of Salt Lake city. For Great Britain—Daniel Stevens, of Fillmore, Millard county; Reuben Gardner, of Pine Valley, Washington county; Samuel H. Parker, of Taylorsville, Salt Lake county; Edwin J. Winder, of Mill Creek, Salt Lake county.

Releases and Appointments—Elder William T. Jones has been honorably released from his labors as traveling elder in the Welsh conference, owing to ill-health, and is permitted to return home October 11, 1894.

Elder Andrew Wallwork has been honorably released from his labors as traveling elder in the Manchester conference, to return home October 11, 1894.

Elder Daniel Stevens and Reuben Gardner have been appointed to labor as traveling elders in the Scottish conference.

Elder Samuel H. Parker has been appointed to labor as traveling elder in the Manchester conference.

Elder Edwin J. Winder has been appointed to labor as traveling elder in the London conference.

Millard County Democrats.

The Democrats of Millard county held their convention in Fillmore recently, and in most instances emphasized their recognition of the past services of their Democratic county officers by a renomination.

Following is the ticket:

Selectmen—J. C. Hawley, William J. Hatch, J. M. Robinson.

Clerk and Recorder—J. S. Giles.

Assessor and Collector—Alma Greenwood.

Treasurer—Christian Anderson.

Attorney—James A. Melville.

Sheriff—G. W. Cropper.

Surveyor—Willard Rogers.

Coroner—Sidney Teeples.

G. W. Cropper, the nominee for sheriff, has been endorsed by the Populists, or "Independents." His nomination is a tower of strength in the western division of the county.

The Colonel Heard From.

In the Saddle,

Headquarters, Beaver City, Utah,
October 22, 1894.

To the Editor of The Herald:

Will charge the enemy—Republican forces—here tonight. They have entrenched themselves behind cross-toed boots, McKinley breeches and "Nuggets of Truth," but before 11 o'clock will plant 'Our Joe's' banner on the breast works! This is the prettiest town I have struck since I left Provo. The people all along the line are kind, generous and hospitable. It is truly a land where a man can travel without "script or purse"; that is, if he is a Democrat. Wouldn't advise any Republican brother to try the same thing; he'd find it too far between eating-houses unless the good Democrats took compassion on him! Rawlins and Democracy solid in southern Utah. The funniest and richest thing I have heard in the entire campaign happened here in Beaver a week ago, when Cannon and Booth were here. Cannon during his speech was reading from the card the Democratic county committee have out, asking "Who got the university lands?" "Who got statehood?" etc., etc., and ending with "Rawlins." Cannon was reading all the questions out, and when he came to the last and said, "Rawlins," the large audience, two-thirds of whom were Democrats, commenced to go wild and cheered to the echo at the mention of Rawlins' name. This nearly set F. J. and the Republicans crazy. It came so sudden it paralyzed them.

Am working my way homeward and hope to enter the Webe. campaign next Monday. Judge Boreman will speak at Fillmore next Thursday, the same date that I am booked for there. My heart goes out in tender, tearful, prayerful sympathy for the judge! We'll treat him well there, though. Hastily,

W. L. P. PEYTON.

CRANE'S BOOMERANG.

Villainous Conduct Towards His Brother Will Cause His Defeat.

Fillmore, Nov. 3.—[Special.]—Charles Crane's infamous attack on his brother, George, insures Charlie's defeat in Millard county.

Republicans who have received the circular for distribution have consigned them to the flames, not daring to distribute them where George is known.

Fillmore.

Fillmore, Nov. 7.—Charles Crane runs behind his running mate, Thompson, in nearly every precinct of the county.

Millard County News
November 9, 1894

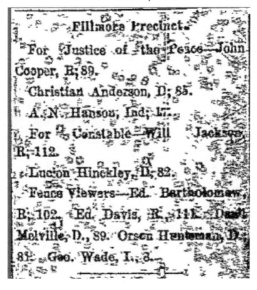

Fillmore Precinct.

For Justice of the Peace—John Cooper, R, 89.

Christian Anderson, D, 85.

A. N. Hanson, Ind, 17.

For Constable—Will Jackson, R, 112.

Lucton Hinckley, D, 82.

Fence Viewers—Ed. Bartholomew, R, 102. Ed. Davis, R, 115. Dan Melville, D., 89. Orsen Huntsman, D, 81. Geo. Wade, I., 3.

Salt Lake Herald
November 14, 1894

Mr. Virgil Kelly, of Millard county, contractor on the projected Snake Valley irrigation scheme, was in the city yesterday. When he left Deseret the returns from the Snake Valley precincts had not been received. The impression prevailed these returns would count in Wise Cropper, the Democratic nominee for sheriff, but elect Charles Crane for constitutional delegate. The Democrats elected their nominees for assessor, Alma Greenwood, of Fillmore.

Millard County Progress
November 16, 1894

The Directors of the Fillmore Roller mills held a meeting Wednesday evening, only routine business was transacted.

The Clerk this week issued licences to marry to Richard T. Asbby and Minnie Colegrove, aged both 22 years and both of Fillmore city; also to G. R. Hickerson of Snake Valley, aged 23 and Miss Zettie Ramsey of Meadow, aged 19.

Brigham Young and Wm. J. Barney, of Snake Valley, were Fillmore visitors this week. They came on land office business.

The Fillmore boys, who went to Snake valley to run a race against "Baldy Sackel" with Hans Peterson "Mandy," came out winners, though thought their expense took away almost all of the profits.

Bicycles are beginning to be of considerable interest in Fillmore. Both ladies and gentlemen are seen on our streets daily riding the silent steed.

The Fillmore Franklin Society convened at the Robison Hotel Saturday evg, Nov. 10th, for the purpose of re-organizing. Mr. John Kelly was elected Chairman and Miss Margie King Secretary. The society will meet hereafter on Thursday at 7:30 p. m. A cordial invitation is extended to all wishing to join.

U. S. Deputy Marshal Payne, on the morning of the 6th left Fillmore to summon witnesses in the case of the U. S. vs. Alma Hague. He drove from here to Clear Lake, Beaver River to Black Rock, thence to the Hockman ranch, Snake Valley, 140 miles distant, from there due south Burnt Canyon, 30 miles this side of Pioche, thence northeast to the Wilds, to Snake valley, thence to Snak Creek and from there east to Kanosh, in all a distance of nearly 500 miles, and returned on the afternoon of the fifth day. Pretty good driving that. It was learned yesterday that the indictment against Alma Hague had been quashed, and the case resubmitted to the grand jury.

News has just reached this office that the owners of the Lucky Strike mine, situated in Millard County, 25 miles north of Fillmore, have struck a large body of the finest iron ore that has ever been struck in this Territory, and gives a fine report of the prospects of both gold and silver. This property is owned by six of Fillmore's people, and they are ready to furnish all the fluxing ores for the Leamington smelter in any quantity they desire, and cheaper than they can buy it for elsewhere. They say they can compete with any iron mine in Utah.

Live stock men in the vicinity of Fillmore should remember that they can always secure as low rates from Salina and Gunnison to eastern markets via the D. & R. G. railroad, as by any other route. Before shipping, it will be to your interest to write B. F. Nevins, General Agent, D. & R. G. railroad, Salt Lake City.   tf

Iron Mine Strike.

Millard Progress—News has just reached this office that the owners of the Lucky Strike mine, situated in Millard county, twenty-five miles north of Fillmore, have struck a large body of the finest iron ore that has ever been struck in this territory, and gives a fine report of the prospects of both gold and silver. This property is owned by six of Fillmore's people, and they are ready to furnish all the fluxing ores for the Leamington smelter in any quantity they desire, and cheaper than they can buy it for elsewhere. They say they can compete with any iron mine in Utah.

B.Y.A. GRADUATES.

What Pursuits They are Pursuing.

SOME SUCCESSFUL BOYS

Their Acts speak in Loud Praise of their Excellent Alma Mater.

Let those who will praise or disparage an institution of learning, there are unimpeachable evidences of it just claims of superiority that are patent to even the most casual observer, or if it be unworthy, there is no need of any criticism beyond the enquiry: "What kind of citizens, business and professianal men and women do its graduates become?" The profiieney and number of its professors, the elegance of its buildings, the cost and extent of its apparatus, are good prefaces to a recommendation of the school to those who have children to educate, but the most vital question asked by parents will be: "What are they, who have graduated from that institution."

It is not alone the intellectual training that makes the man or woman that is most admired; for who has not seen scholarly fools, as well as scolarly scoundrel. Not even practical training, lead so that hand and eye, co operate with; all the intellectual polish and proficiency, the mind is capable of receiving is the ideal, although it approaches. But when we see the disciple of an institution of learning, walking bravely and nobily along the path of life in which he is called to walk, doing his whole duty, honored for his usefulness respected for his honest sincerity, and loved for his unfeigned and unselfish love for his fellow men, then not only the merits of the intellect trainers received at the alma mater, may be determined, but also those potent undercurrents of truth, honor, humanity and unselfishness, that can not be catalogued and offered to the public as inducements to trust the all important training of their children to its care.

By way of applying this theory practically, here is a list of the graduates from the Normal department of the Brigham Young Academy for last year and a partial list of those graduates from the Commercial department. There were seven graduates from the Normal department, viz:

Henry Peterson, of Ogden; now principal of the Central school at Montpelier Idaho; Mary Woodruff, of Smithfield, teaching the sixth grade in the preparatory department of the Brigham Young Academy; Collie Robinson of Fillmore, teacher of the eighth grade, in central school, Beaver, W. M. McKendrick, of Tooele, assistant teacher of mathematics in Brigham Young Academy; W. E. Rydalch, of Grantsville, chemistry teacher at the Brigham Young Academy, and H. S. Tanner, of Payson, who succeeded Dr. Karl G. Maeser as president of the California mission

A very great many who enters this department do not graduate principally for want of means. Having studied until they are able to take out a teach- er's certificate, say for one, two or three years, they enter the field of workers and wage earners, in the hope f being able in a few years to come .ack a d complete their course. Many ave by their own efforts, after leaving school, progressed commendably along model lines.

The list of graduates from the com- mercial department is much larger, and the entire list is not necessary, but the following are fair samples of that de- partment: Harry McGraw and Hamner

Magelby of Monroe, Heber Christen- sen of Richfield, and Leo Bird of Spring ville are on missions; Robert Holt of West Jordan, railroad contractor; Ray Scoville of Ogden, manufacturing and merchandising; George Harrison of Springville, hotel business; Joseph Sharp of Salt Lake, commission and forwarding merchant; Herman Martin of Provo, partner and cashier with Swasey & Martin, bankers; Jacob Mag- elly of Monroe, commission merchant and lumber dealer; Daniel Welch of Arizona, book keeper and salesman.

It can be truthfully said that each of these young men are making a grand success in their chosen vocation, a credit to their parents, their native state and the institution that graduated them.

Salt Lake Herald
December 13, 1894

BRIGHAM YOUNG ACADEMY.

Graduates from the Normal Depart- ment and the Success They Have Met.

Your correspondent has been look- ing up the record of those who grad- uated from the Normal department of the Brigham Young academy last year, in the belief that the very best evi- dence of what an institution is, may be obtained by finding out what its children are.

The proficiency and number of the professors employed, the elegance of its buildings, the cost and extent of its apparatus, etc., are good prefaces to a recommendation of the school to those who have children to educate, but the most vital question that will be asked by parents who intelligently consider the future of their children will be: "Who are they who have graduated from that institution?"

Parents, communities and nations have learned to their cost that it is not the most brilliantly gifted and elaborately taught that make the best citizens, for where is there an epoch of time or an inhabited place that has not produced its scholarly fool, as well as the intellectual rascal. Not even the conditions of manual training so that hand and eye co-ordinate per- fectly with the best efforts of the brain, gives us the ideal man or wo- man, though it approaches nearer; in- deed the greater the proficiency, the greater the power of wrong-doing if the heart and impulses be wrong. Only when we see disciples of an institution of learning walking bravely and nobly along the path of life in which they are called to walk, doing their whole duty, honored for their usefulness, re- spected for their honest sincerity, and loved for their unselfish love for their fellow men, can we form a proper esti- mate of those deep undercurrents of honor, truth, unselfishness and hu- manity, that are largely taught by per- sonal example, and spiritual purity,

which cannot be catalogued and offer- ed to the public as inducements to trust the all important training of their children to its course.

There were but seven graduates from the normal department of the Brigham Young academy last year. They are: Henry Peterson, of Ogden, who is now principal of the Central school at Montpelier, Idaho; Mary Woodruff, of Smithfield, teaching the sixth grade of the preparatory department in the Brigham Young academy; Collie Rob- inson, of Fillmore, teacher of the eighth grade of the Central school, Beaver City; W. M. McKendrick, of Tooele, assistant teacher of mathe- matics in the Brigham Young acad- emy; W. E. Rydalch, of Grantsville, chemistry teacher at the Brigham Young academy; and H. S. Tanner, of Payson, who succeeded Dr. Carl G. Maeser as president of the California mission. A great many who have taken one, two and three years as normal students have been unable to gradu- ate for want of means. Quite a num- ber have taken out teachers' certifi- cates and are endeavoring to overcome the financial difficulty, and return and complete their course. Commendable progress along the proper lines has been made by many of those who did not graduate, their love of learning leading to personal effort when ad- verse circumstances closed their school days prematurely. In almost every case, at least 95 per cent. of these un- der graduates have made splendid rec- ords as teachers, reflecting credit on the institution that graduated them, as well as those who have taken the full course.

ELLEN JAKEMAN.

The special stage of John F. Ashman leaves Juab, Saturday afternoon Dec. 22, at one o'clock, and comes straight through to Fillmore, for the accommodation of students away from home.

Jas. W. Huntsman and Antone Carlson of Fillmore became engaged in a fistic encounter while playing a game of pool Tuesday night. Both parties were badly bruised, Huntsman having a portion of his left ear bitten off during the scrimmage. They paid $7.50 each in Justice R. A. McBride's court Wednesday morning for their evenings' fun.

A gentleman entered our sanctum this morning and showed us a wallet handsomely lined with "Long green" and containing an almost inexhaustible supply of "yellow boys." All this, he solemnly affirmed, was procured by pouring milk into the Fillmore Dairy. Let every resident of Fillmore look into this matter and give it a fair trial.

I have for sale, excellent lime, in quantities to suit purchaser, which I will sell at 25 cts. per bushel. Virgil Baldwin, Fillmore.

Mr. Saunders, the popular cattle man of Salt Lake City, passed through Fillmore Wednesday, on his way south where he intends to buy cattle.

THE WEATHER.

Observer Smith's Summary of the November Climatic Conditions.

The weather during November, 1894, was unusually fine and pleasant throughout the entire month. The days were warm and clear with moderately light winds, and less than the average amount of precipitation.

The mean temperature for the territory, 40 degrees, is about the normal, and six degrees higher than the mean for November, 1893. The highest temperature, 82 degrees, was recorded at St. George on the 8th, and the lowest, 9 degrees below zero, was recorded at Soldier Summit on the 13th, making a range of temperature for the territory, 91 degrees. The highest monthly mean was 48.5, at St. George, and the lowest, 30.8, at Soldier Summit; greatest local monthly range of temperature 70 degrees, at Fillmore; least local monthly range of temperature, 29 degrees, at Levan. The mean maximum temperature was 66.4, and the mean minimum temperature, 16.9.

The editor of the Progress received a pleasant call this week from Mr. E. W. Kelly, who has charge of the intermediate department of our city schools. Mr. Kelly reports the pupils to be progressing nicely in their studies. He has kindly agreed to furnish the People of Fillmore through the Progress, a weekly report of the advance made by the students. To further increase the interest of the pupils in their work the Progress will occasionally publish a composition or essay by some Fillmore boy or girl. The heads of the departments will decide upon the merits of these writings.

A gentleman has been in Fillmore this week buying saddle horses. Horses that were well broke, and weighed from 800 pounds up brought $20.00 and upwards. Boys, get up your good horses, and break them. They are worthless to you running wild on the range, and you can make good wages breaking them. There will be more chances to sell by spring.

The special stage of John T. Ashman leaves Juab, Saturday afternoon Dec. 22, at one o'clock, and comes straight through to Fillmore, for the accommodation of students away from home.

The Fillmore brass band practices a great deal nowadays, and there is a marked improvement in the way that they exude their melodious compound. That's right, boys, keep at it, you're doing well.

The Progress this week received communications from parties residing in Colorado, requesting the names of Fillmore people having real estate for sale. They want the land for the cultivating of fruit. Fillmore is bound to boom yet.

A gentleman has been in Fillmore this week buying saddle horses. Horses that were well broke, and weighed from 800 pounds up brought $20 and upward. Boys, get up your good horses, and break them. They are worthless to you running wild on the range, and you can make good wages breaking them. There will be more chances to sell by spring.—Millard Progress.

Mr. Frank Holbrook, one of our Fillmore boys, now stopping in Deseret, has been visiting friends and relatives in Fillmore this week. Frankie started the New Year right by subscribing for THE PROGRESS. Mr. Orson Holbrook, Jr., of Rock Springs, is spending the holidays with us.

A petition for a road running west from Fillmore to the Sevier via "the sinks," Clear Lake and Swan Lake, was signed by the citizens of Fillmore, as well as by parties outside of Fillmore, for presentation to the county court this week.

The people of our vicinity, though very public spirited, have not thoroughly learned the value of favoring home products. Ye scribe is informed that Salt Lake nurserymen sold about $1400 worth of fruit trees in Fillmore last fall, and now hear the people howl! If all agreements was inserted a clause stating that the nursery men should substitute something else in case the article ordered was not carried in stock. We are informed that the "something else" came all too frequently. Mr. Albert Shall, of our city, has has hundreds of good fruit and shade trees, trees that are acclimated, which he sells at figures far below Salt Lake prices. We trust that our good citizens will bear this in mind when they need anything more in this line.

...en, of Spring City, for 160 acres.
Patent No. 5132, to Susannah T. Robison, of Fillmore City, for 160 acres.

Land Office.

The following filings were made in the local land office under date of Feb. 2:

Peter Hansen, of Draper, Salt Lake county, homestead entry of the southwest quarter of the southeast quarter, and the southeast quarter of the southwest quarter of section 5, and the northwest quarter of the northeast quarter and the northeast quarter of the northwest quarter of section 8, township 3 south, range 6 east.

Ira Sutton Jr., of Blake, Emery county, final proof of homestead entry of lots 3 and 4 of section 29, and lots 1, 2 and 4 of section 32, township 20 south, range 16 east.

John Meade, of Salt Lake City, desert entry of the south half of the northwest quarter, the west half of the southeast quarter, and the southwest quarter of section 33, township 23 south, range 9 west.

Charles E. Warr, of Tooele City, Tooele county, homestead entry of the southwest quarter of section 29, township 2 south, range 4 west.

Lotle Taylor, of Salt Lake City, coal entry of the southeast quarter of the northeast quarter of section 33, the southwest quarter of the northwest quarter, and the west half of the southwest quarter of section 34, township 36 south, range 10 west, in Iron county.

Homestead patents have been received from Washington as follows:

No. 5149, Emma E. Porter, of Farmington, Davis county, 160 acres.

No. 5090, Peter F. Rollo, of Huntsville, Weber county, 160 acres.

No. 5125, Samuel Adams Jr., of Randolph, Rich county, 120 acres.

No. 5115, Swanty Beng'ton, of Randolph, Rich county, 160.40 acres.

No. 5138, Thomas H. Best, of Panguitch, Garfield county, 160 acres.

No. 5034, Frederick Cazier, of Eden, Weber county, 149.89 acres.

No. 5090, Christen N. Christensen, of Huntington, Emery county, 159.64 acres.

No. 5081, Wm. A. Chamberlain, of Hot Springs, Weber county, 160 acres.

No. 5064, Matthew Evans, of Lawrence, Emery county, 160 acres.

No. 5180, Dexter Litchfield, of Randolph, Rich county, 160 acres.

No. 5122, John Losee, of Spanish Fork, Utah county, 160 acres.

No. 5087, Lyman O. Porter, of Morgan, Morgan county, 160.08 acres.

No. 4977, Thomas Robb, of Paragoonah, Iron county, 120 acres.

No. 5138, Samuel L. Cornaby, of Tucker, Utah county, 160 acres.

No. 4077, James A. S. Smith, of Tooele county, 160 acres.

No. 5089, Joseph Southwick, of Liberty, 160.16 acres.

No. 5076, Peter Smith, of American Fork, Utah county, 160 acres.

No. 5019, Charles S. Wood, of Huntsville, Weber county, 80 acres.

No. 5052, Jeremiah W. Whitehouse, of Tooele, Tooele county, 160 acres.

No. 5110, Joseph Kippen, of Peterson, Morgan county, 160 acres.

No. 5473, James Burns of Wallsburg, Wasatch county, 40 acres.

No. 5075, Richard Smith, of Heber City, Wasatch county, 80 acres.

No. 5108, James Watson, of Heber City, Wasatch county, 160 acres.

No. 5148, Isaac S. Goodwin, of Teasdale, 160 acres.

No. 5149, Parley M. Grigg, of Loa, Wayne county, 160 acres.

No. 5049, Edwin C. Freston, of Mt. Pleasant, Sanpete county, 82.48 acres.

No. 5131, James Barton, of Mt. Pleasant, Sanpete county, 160 acres.

No. 5094, Freeman E. Allred, of Spring City, Sanpete county, 160 acres.

No. 5132, Susannah T. Robison, of Fillmore, Millard county, 160 acres.

Millard county *Blade:* During Sunday afternoon the work of heating up the Leamington smelter began. Wood was used and the heat gradually increased until Monday forenoon. The fluxings had been carefully arranged in piles and rows, and every precaution taken to insure a successful start. Quite a number of spectators had assembled to witness the inauguration of an industry that will yet make Millard one of the most important counties in Utah.....A couple of weeks since Wallace C. Tilton and Miss Effie Shaw came down from Salt Lake and put up at the Huff hotel, Oasis. They represented to the proprietor of the hotel that they were man and wife and occupied the same room. After a few boys Tilton went out to Detroit and secured work in the Ibex mine and Miss Effie sought employment as a domestic. On Friday last U. S. Marshal Paine came over from Fillmore and went on to Detroit and arrested Tilton who is a married man, on the charge of adultery and has brought his prisoner to Deseret and on Monday took him over to Fillmore where Miss Effie is now also in durance vile, or rather boarding with the marshal. Marshal Paine returned on Sunday bringing with him Mr. Tilton and went on to Fillmore the next morning. Tilton claims that he is an unmarried man

claims that he is an unmarried man and first became acquainted with Effie Shaw through correspondence while he was in California. At the urgent request of Effie who stated that her mother was dead and her father was in the "pen" Tilton came from California and met her for the first time at American Fork. He also learned that "Miss" Shaw was a married woman and that her husband, Wm. Shaw, is working at the Sandy smelters. Mr. Tilton says that he also learned that her mother was alive and hearty and her father was at his own fireside and not boarding at the expense of Uncle Sam. Notwithstanding these allegations, Tilton came down to the Leamington smelter and represented that Effie and himself were married. After a few days' sojourn, Tilton went back to American Fork and secured the marriage certificate of Effie and Mr. Shaw and returned. Thereafter, instead of being Mr. Tilton, he became Mr. Shaw—Wm. Shaw—and came on to Oasis as related above.

Wasatch Wave
February 5, 1895

AN OASIS SCANDAL.

American Fork Woman and a Californian Under Arrest.

A couple of weeks since, Wallace C. Tilton and Miss Effie Shaw came down from Salt Lake and put up at the Huff Hotel, Oasis. They represented to the proprietor of the hotel that they were man and wife and occupied the same room. After a few days Tilton went out to Detroit and secured work in the Ibex mine and Miss Effie sought employment as a domestic. On Friday last United States Marshal Paine came over from Fillmore, and went on to Detroit and arrested Tilton, who is a married man, on the charge of adultery, and has brought his prisoner to Deseret, and on Monday took him over to Fillmore, where Miss Effie is now also in durance vile, or rather boarding with the Marshal.

Provo Evening Dispatch
February 13, 1895

NOTICE TO CREDITORS—ESTATE OF
Daniel Fillmore, deceased. Notice is
hereby given by the undersigned executor of
the estate of Daniel Fillmore, deceased,
to the creditors of, and all persons having
claims against the said deceased, to exhibit
them with the necessary vouchers within four
months after the first publication of this notice to the said executor at his residence in
Payson, Utah.
                    THOMAS H. WILSON,
    Executor of the estate of Daniel Fillmore,
deceased.
    Dated February 11, 1895.

Salt Lake Herald
February 18, 1895

    The Fillmore Progress is pulling for
the establishment of a small electric
light plant in that village. It could be
put in at a comparatively small expense, it is argued, and would be a
great advantage in more ways than
one.

    There is trouble among the editorial
brethren of the South. The Deseret
Blade accuses the Fillmore Progress of
stealing editorials and palming them
off on its readers as original; then the
Progress goes after the Blade man and
calls his attention to the fact that a
series of articles running in the latter
paper on "Genesis and Geology" bear a
striking, very striking, in fact, resem-
blance to essays written by Hugh
Miller, 40 years or more ago, on the
same subject, and which were compiled and printed in a book that is now
a rara avis. Accompanying the re-
minder is a hint that the Blade man
might have got hold of the book, while
in a trance.

Salt Lake Herald
February 22, 1895

    Lucian Hinckley, a prominent stock
man from Fillmore, is here as a witness before the grand jury.

Salt Lake Herald
March 5, 1895

EDWARD PARTRIDGE,
Of Provo City, was born in Independence Jackson county, Mo., June 25, 1833,
and is the son of Edward and Lydia
Clisbee Partridge. Being early deprived

of a father's fostering and protecting
care, he had to encounter the hard and
rugged edge of adversity from his youth
up, with but little chance for education.
Mr. Partridge arrived in Utah in 1848.
    He has served as a member of the city
council of Fillmore; held the office of
city recorder, mayor, county clerk, and
county recorder, and for a number of
years was county and probate judge. In
1874, was a member of the territorial legislature, and again in 1881 was elected a
representative, and served as such in the
winter of 1881-2. He has been engaged in
merchandising for several years, and connected with several co-operative enterprises—sometimes manager, member of

EDWARD PARTRIDGE.

the board, or president. Has worked at
mason work, freighting and other pursuits. Mr. Partridge is a Democrat.

EXCITEMENT IN DESERET.

A HERALD CORRESPONDENT VISITS THE IBEX SMELTER.

One Hundred Men Are Now Employed There—Talk of Building a Narrow Gauge Road to the Mines—Free Gold Found in the Detroit District—The Sevier on a Rampage.

Deseret, Utah, March 6.—[Special Correspondence to The Herald.]—Looking through a car window on the southern extension of the Union Pacific, one begins to think that all there is to Utah in the rose blossom, he leaves behind at Nephi in Juab county. From there on the eye becomes tired of the endless miles of sagebrush on either side, patches of saleratus mineral spread out like duck ponds, with here and there a farm house of the rudest architecture, built on the green spot—all bearing evidence of unrequited toil and the courageous but hopeless efforts of the farmer to overcome nature.

Beside the railroad rushes the Sevier in its mad spring rampage, throwing up large cakes of ice on one side or the other wherever the crooks and eddies of the river afford the best designs for a blockade. "There will be plenty of excitement in Deseret in less than a week," said Hon. Joshua Greenwood, of Fillmore, to your correspondent, pointing his finger in the direction indicated, and sure enough his prediction proved true.

The brakeman tells us the next station is Leamington, and we crane our necks to catch a first view of the Ibex smelter.

Six months ago there was nothing to Leamington but a few scattered houses, barring that a man lived there named Chris. Overson, and whenever a Millard county man heard Leamington pronounced, he invariably answered "Oh, you mean Chris. Overson, don't you?" Now Leamington has the Ibex smelter, and there it stands out in the sage brush like a pillar of cloud by day and a pillar of fire by night—a monument to the glory of Millard county's mines.

Going south the train stops at the Leamington station sometimes an hour, sometimes two hours. Accompanied by Hon. Joshua Greenwood and Sam Godbe of Salt Lake, your correspondent walked the quarter-mile distance over the railroad sidings to the smelter, and looked into the roaring furnace which was kept alive night and day melting the ores from the Ibex mines, from the Horn Silver and from Tintic and Bingham. Including the flux, the smelter turns out a product of from 70 to 90 tons every twenty-four hours. In and about the smelter, in one capacity or another, 100 men are employed, and $4,000 are distributed every month in earnings. Fifty-five of the employees are boarders in Chris. Overson's boarding house, and the remainder belong to the little town and its surroundings. It is safe to estimate that these 100 breadwinners means a population of at least 300 in Leamington that owe their living to the establishment of the Ibex smelter.

Nor is this all. The plan is seriously entertained of building a narrow-guage road from the smelter over the desert direct to the mines—a distance of 35 or 40 miles, which will cut off the wagon haul from the mines to Oasis and thence by U. P. rail to Leamington. While this will have the effect of blighting the Deseret country in the freighting industry, it will enhance the value of Leamington property. Already town lots have been platted in Leamington, and the shrewd Overson takes pleasure in submitting a map of the city of Leamington to visitors. Howbeit, whether Leamington becomes a city or not in the broad sense of the word, it is soon destined to be the largest town in Millard county.

In company with Virgil Kelly, of Deseret, one of the "hustlers" of Millard county, and at present engaged in the construction of irrigation enterprises in the Snake valley and Beaver, your correspondent set out on Thursday last for the mines in the Detroit district. The roads were heavy from the deep snows which had just melted away, but Kelly's team were untamed bronchos, and the distance of thirty-five miles was covered in less than seven hours, including a stop for a camp lunch at the "old smelter," which was burned some three years ago and never rebuilt.

This ruined structure, with its demoralized machinery rusting through exposure to the elements, has been a "hoodoo" to the district, and has invariably turned away capital when its story was told—the story of lavish expenditure in rainbow mines and tunnels; the story of claims that were located by night and abandoned by day, of mining recorders who never qualified and of records that were kept wherever you could find the recorder, so that today, it is said, half a dozen men claim to own the district whose title does not rest on stakes or monuments, but on records, which, it is alleged, were manipulated by themselves. Up to the election of S. F. Mount as recorder, ex-County Clerk Giles, of Fillmore, states that no recorder of Detroit district ever qualified. Thus it is that many of the claims of Detroit district are recorded in Fillmore instead of in the district records, by men who placed no faith in the records of Detroit district. No end of litigation is promised so soon as the ball commences rolling.

About the center of the district and a mile south of the great Ibex, we come to the Charmed, better known as the Busby, by reason of its owner, George Busby, of Salt Lake. This mine is next to the Ibex in importance, and is operated by the Ibex syndicate. Around the mine are comfortable quarters for the miners, newly erected boarding houses and a restaurant where one may obtain a square meal for 35 cents. The work of development began but a few months ago, but already ore is being hoisted to the top by means of a whim from a solid vein 35 feet square. The shipping ore from the Busby, according to the Ibex assayer, runs from 1 to 10 ounces in gold, but less in copper than the Ibex.

Your correspondent found the little camp electrified over the discovery of free gold which happened the day before, and right on top of the ground directly behind the main shaft of the Charmed. Free gold had been found in the shaft a day or two previous, but nobody ever dreamed that one could really walk over it and almost stick his knife into it from the "grass roots," to speak in miners' parlance. There it was, however, plainly visible to the naked eye, and dug out of a hole scarcely two feet in depth. Mr. Busby was overjoyed to find a newspaper man around, and gleefully exclaimed that The Herald would be the first to announce the discovery.

But the Busby mine is not the sole possessor of the precious metal in its free state. Over in the Copperhead, a claim that is being developed by Messrs. Davis, Hawkins, Stewart and Ludlow, of Payson, free gold had been found a week ago, so Mr. Davis told your correspondent, and his statement was verified by others around the Ibex camp. The Copperhead is a promising property, even if it never bore an ounce of free gold. Ore is being shipped from the mine that assays from 2 to 6 ounces in gold and from 2 to 24 per cent copper.

Friday your correspondent camped at the Ibex, and was amazed at the work accomplished since his visit last summer. Then it was that No. 1 tunnel was commenced and cut through until it terminated at a distance of 290 feet from the opening, after reaching immense bodies of ore. This winter work was begun on a lower tunnel, and already 200 feet has opened daylight into the solid rock, and 200 feet more will be cut away, when it is expected that the ore body they are after will be reached. Already the Ibex is a wonder. In less than three months it will be the marvel of the Rocky mountains.

A force of carpenters are now employed in the erection of a three-rail tramway, built at an agle of 45 degrees, and which will convey the ore from the mine on cars, where the contents will be dumped into wagons to be freighted over the country. This idea was put into execution since Superintendent Marx took charge of the mine, and will solve the problem of expeditious delivery when the Ibex gets ready to pour out its treasures. The tramway will be 480 feet long. Already 140 feet had been run up the hill on Friday, and the whole will be completed in a short time. Until its completion about half of the Ibex miners are given a vacation. Mr. Alf Mikesell is now foreman of the Ibex and Mr. Fred Redmond assayer.

Mr. Redmond informed your correspondent that there is a claim located four miles from the Drum Springs, owned by a Mr. Giles, which assays 189 ounces in silver and $2 in gold. There are a large number of other claims in the district which carry on the surface ore which varies from $2 to $20 per ton.

Fifteen men are working on the Rattler, owned by Alf Mikesell and others, and bonded by St. Paul parties. They were down Saturday to make another payment on their bond.

Jack Barrett and his partner brought into camp some of the finest specimens of oxide of copper we ever saw. It was tested on a knife blade by the application of a strong solution of acid vinegar, leaving no doubt as to its genuineness. Barrett found it in the Dugway district, and says it is as easily worked as the gravity sewer in Salt Lake.

Returning to Deseret your correspondent had an opportunity to examine the improvements that had taken place within the past year. He found it in the renewed hope of the people inspired by the mining industry in Detroit district. He found it in the ambition of the young men to assist in the reclamation of lands around Leamington and the bench. He found it in the desire for higher education of the young. He found a strong sentiment existing against the saloon element and for a vigorous prosecution in behalf of law and order. In one word, the people talked better, dressed smarter, and were rapidly acquiring the style of their northern neighbors.

Deseret has the finest meeting house in the county, but the glory of the town is in its school house. It is a structure that would reflect honor upon such towns as Payson or Springville. A large share of the credit for this belongs to G. W. Cropper, Joseph Damron and W. A. Ray, the trustees. The school is under the charge of Professor H. P. Brown, a gentleman whose experience was gained in the Ogden public schools. Milton Moody, bishop of the ward, is in the intermediate department, and Miss Dona Cropper, graduate of the Provo academy, in the primary.

Deseret has a bright little newspaper and a cheese factory, and the product turned out by the latter tastes better to a New Yorker than what he ate at home in his youth. Then there are two hotels—the Webb and the Deseret house. And, last, it has a bridge with a gap through the center just now, as Joshua Greenwood said would happen when he saw the ice gorge at Leamington.   P. C.

Salt Lake Herald
March 10, 1895

GOULTER'S CLOSE CALL.

TWO YOUNG FELLOWS ATTEMPT TO POISON HIM.

Strychnine Put in His Milk—A Forged Will Found Afterwards Gives the Key to the Mystery.

A sensational case of attempted poisoning and forgery is the latest for Fillmorites to pause and think of, says the Progress.

It all occurred in our peaceful little burg last Tuesday night and was kept very quiet for some reason. We do not think there are a dozen people who will know of it until they read the ever wide-awake Progress.

It seems that a young man of Fillmore, who but a short time ago was married, has been on very intimate terms with Mr. William Goulter, who is pretty well to do.

Tuesday night he was at Mr. Goulter's house, and by one way or another found out what he was going to have for supper.

Goulter was obliged to step out for a moment, and when he returned he sat down to eat his peaceful meal. As he did so, he noticed a knife that was lying by his plate wet with milk. He thought it was kind of strange, as he knew he hadn't used it. A few moments later he started to drink some milk that was on the table.

What was his horror after drinking a little to find that it tasted very bitter.

His horror increased when he had examined the contents that were left and found them deadly poison.

He rushed around and procured a remedy for what little he had taken. After feeling somewhat better, he began an investigation. About the first thing he found was a will purporting to be his own and the last one he had written.

The will was gotten up in a very crude form, and in substance, was as follows:

I, William Goulter, give to ——— at my death, this place that I am now living in and the four adjoining lots and all the stock that I own; also all notes that are out at the time of my death.

(Signed.) WILLIAM GOULTER.

PROVO PARAGRAPHS.

MYSTERIOUS MESSAGE AND PACKAGE FROM FILLMORE.

Jerry Richardson is Convicted of Rape, and Will Be Sentenced March 14—The Co-op Burglarized.

Provo, March 9, 1895.—Deputy Marshal Fowler received a package yesterday by express from Deputy Payne and T. C. Callister, of Fillmore. It contained a bottle of milk and some white substance found in the bottom of a bowl. A request made of Marshal Fowler to have the contents carefully analyzed and report results, as the evidence was to be used against a man. No other particulars could be learned. Prof. Hydalch and Dr. J. F. Noyes made the analysis, and reported that strychnine was contained in the milk and also in the sediments from the bowl.

Salt Lake Herald
March 17, 1895

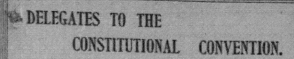

DELEGATES TO THE CONSTITUTIONAL CONVENTION.

WILLIS E. ROBISON,

Of Wayne county, was born in Will county, Ill., March 1, 1854. At an early age he emigrated with his parents, to Utah, and settled at Fillmore, Millard county; he was raised to manhood, receiving the limited education that was given in the district schools of that time. His early life was spent in farming, freighting, caring for stock and such avocations as were common to boys on the frontier. At the age of 21 he married and, with his wife, moved to Scipio, where he resided for twelve years. In 1888, he moved to Piute county, where land was plentiful. That portion in which he settled was organized into a new county under the name of Wayne, and to Mr. Robison was accorded the honor of naming it. He has filled many positions of trust. Is now and for some time has been superintendent of schools. Served as a member of the territorial legislature in 1896. Is a member of the Mormon church. Spent two years in the southern states advocating its doctrines. Filled the position of bishop for a number of years and now presides over the interests of the county

WILLIS E. ROBISON.

in which he resides. In political matters Mr. Robison is a Democrat.

JOHN R. MURDOCK,

Of Beaver, Republican, is one of the pioneers of Utah, having arrived here in 1847. He was born September 13, 1826, in Orange township, Cuyahoga county, O. Parents from New England. Was married in 1850 to A. H. Lott, in Salt Lake city. Business, stock raiser and farmer. Left Ohio and went to Missouri, 1832; from there

JOHN R. MURDOCK.

to Illinois; left there in 1846 to emigrate to the Ricky mountains. Enlisted in the Mormon Battalion at Council Bluffs, and went to California; was discharged in 1847 and returned to Utah. Took part in the Indian war during the winter of 1849-50. Carried the United States mail from Salt Lake city to Independence, Mo.; sixty miles a day was about the average speed. In the summer of 1857, traveled from Salt Lake city to Independence, Mo., in fifteen days, at the rate of eighty miles per day, the distance between those points being 1,200 miles. The trip was accomplished with but three changes of animals, grass fed; four twenty miles drives being made each day. Has brought overland five trains of immigrants from the Missouri river, and it is safe to say that he has brought more immigrants by team to Utah than any other man. He has been successful in business. Was a member of the legislature for several terms.

RICHARD G. LAMBERT,

Of Salt Lake city, and elected, as a Republican, in the Second precinct, was born in Salt Lake city, June 2, 1850. He is the son of Charles and Mary Alice Cannon Lambert, and is one of seven brothers. His early days were spent amid the trying scenes of pioneer life. H toiled on the farm; worked in the canyons, and, in the winter of 1868, he entered the Deseret News printing office, where he served until October 1873. He was then sent to the Sandwich islands, on a mission, and returned in November, 1877. He

RICHARD G. LAMBERT.

again entered the business department of the Deseret News, and remained there until October 1892. He was quite active in People's party, and when the division came he joined the Republican ranks. Was elected chaplain of the council of the last legislature.

Provo Daily Enquirer
March 18, 1895

THERE is talk of holding the next session of court at Fillmore instead of Nephi. There will be very little to do, judging from the way Judge King is clearing up the cases.

Going Out to Snake Valley.

President Melville, of the Snake Valley Land and Water company, whose reservoir and canal systems are in the extreme western part of the county of Millard, left for the south yesterday afternoon and after a short stay at Fillmore will go out to the scene of his company's operations. Word was received yesterday afternoon from General Manager Holloway, who has been in Texas for some weeks interesting some of his old friends in the Utah enterprise, to the effect that he would leave for Utah with a good sized colony within the next day or two. He should reach here some time during the present week or the first of the coming.

DANIEL THOMPSON,

Of Scipio, was born in Canada, Markim Township, December 25, 1834. Was married in Fillmore City, Utah, May 4, 1854, to Lorinda E. Brunson; served as a counselor to Bishop Brunson, of Fillmore ward; was a member of the legislature in Utah for two sessions; served under Captain Henry Stondage during the Indian war of 1853-54; was one of the party that accompanied President Anson Call to obtain the remains of Captain Gunnison, who was killed by the Indians in this county; Mr. Thompson was also a member of the county court for a number of years; also a bishop of the Scipio ward about fifteen years, and first counselor to President Hinckley, of Millard stake, for the last twelve years.

DANIEL THOMPSON.

Governor West yesterday issued a proclamation fixing the times and places of holding the First judicial district court. A term will be held in Provo City on the first Monday in February; one at Nephi, in Juab county, on the second Monday in May; one at Fillmore in Millard county on the second Monday in July; and one at Provo on the second Monday in September. The time for opening the sessions is fixed at 11 a. m. on the days designated.

Salt Lake Herald

April 6, 1895

Homestead entry of John A. Taylor, of
Fillmore, Milard county, to the south
half of the southeast quarter and the
south half of the southwest quarter of
section 27, in township 20 south of range
5 west, containing 160 acres

Salt Lake Herald

April 13, 1895

Homestead entry of John L. Brunson, of Fillmore city, to the northeast
quarter of section 33, township 20
south, range 5 west, containing 160
acres.

Salt Lake Herald

April 18, 1895

Southern Hogs Received.

The first receipts at the Union stock-
yards for the week, was a carload of
hogs for the Utah Slaughtering company. There were eighty hogs in the
consignment, and they came from the
ranch of Messrs. Melville and Greenwood
near Fillmore. They were in splendid
shape and brought top notch prices—in
the neighborhood of $3.75 per hundred
pounds.

T. W. Jennings yesterday shipped two
carloads of his fat cattle onto the Omaha
market. He will have two or three more
cars to move soon.

Salt Lake Herald

April 24, 1895

LAND OFFICE.

The local land office yesterday received
entries as follows:

Homestead entry of Edward Davis of
Fillmore to the south half of the northwest quarter and the north half of the
southwest quarter of section 28 in township 20 south of range 5 west, containing 160 acres.

HAS DONE UNTOLD GOOD.

STORM WAS GENERAL THROUGHOUT THE TERRITORY.

Country Much in Need of Just Such Soaking Rains—Southern Part of the Territory Visited by Welcome Showers—Abundant Crops and Good Ranges Are Assured—Idaho and Nevada Also in the Storm Belt

The rains of the past two days, warm and soaking in their nature, have been of untold value to the territory, for the storm has been general. From the southern boundary of Utah to the southern Idaho counties come reports of splendid showers, and they were much needed, for the warm weather and drying winds of the month just closed had rendered the country extremely dry. Especially was this the case in the extreme north and extreme south. The rains will give the grass and other vegetation a fresh start and abundant crops and good ranges are assured. May flowers are now in order.

Inquiries sent out from the Salt Lake office of the Deseret Telegraph company yesterday afternoon to its branch offices, as to the condition of the weather, elicited the following interesting information:

Paris, Idaho—Raining nearly all day.

Franklin, Idaho—Been raining all day; still rains.

Logan, Utah—Raining hard and has been all day.

Mendon, Utah—Raining all day.

Brigham, Utah—Has been raining ever since last night and still raining.

Ogden, Utah—Cloudy; calm; raining all day.

Sandy, Utah—Cloudy; been raining all day.

Lehi, Utah—Been raining all day; calm.

Provo, Utah—Rained all day.

Springville, Utah—Cloudy and calm; has been raining all morning.

Payson, Utah—Cloudy and gloomy; rained all morning; looks like more rain.

Nephi, Utah—Rain been falling all day; mild.

Scipio, Utah—Cold and stormy; just stopped raining; looks like more storm.

Fillmore, Utah—Been raining all day.

Kanosh, Utah—Rained all night last night and all day; still raining.

Sulphurdale, Utah—Raining hard.

Beaver, Utah—Rained at intervals all last night and till now, 2 p. m.; cloudy; cold.

Parowan, Utah—Rained some yesterday afternoon, all night and is still raining.

Cedar City, Utah—Cloudy, rainy and cold wind.

Toquerville, Utah—Some clouds; been showery for two days; warm.

Rockville, Utah—Some clouds; been showery for two days; cool.

Kanab, Utah—Some clouds; been showery for two days; cool.

St. George, Utah—Cloudy and stormy; rained Monday.

Pine Valley, Utah—Cloudy and warm; rained yesterday; none today.

Bullionville, Nevada—Clear and pleasant; have had some rain.

FILLMORE TO THE FRONT.

We will commence spraying our fruit trees on Monday next, May 20th. Every fruit tree owner must spray. Let's have no half-way business, but all come forward like men, and "Yankee-doodle-do-it." I shall be around to see that it is properly done. Let's show the other settlements that Fillmore is strictly in it.

Yours Truly,

GEO. A. SHAIL,

Fruit Tree Inspector.

BUSINESS DIRECTORY.

Those whose names are not found in this directory can arrange for their insertion, if so desired.

The Robison House; Fillmore.

Fillmore Roller Mill; Fillmore.

L. M. Warner, Lumber; Fillmore.

Wm. H. Statt; Dentist, Meadow.

Azariah Mikesell; Surveyor, Kanosh.

H. W. Hawlaw; Money to Lend, Oasis.

Fillmore Dairy Co., J. S. Giles, Sec'y.

Ashman & Co., Meat Market; Fillmore.

Jas. M. Hanson, Att'y at Law; Fillmore.

B. B. L. Collier, Civil Engineer; Fillmore.

Sorenson Sisters, Dressmakers; Fillmore.

J. S. Giles, Abstractor and Att'y; Fillmore.

Nadauld & Paxton; General Mdse., Kanosh.

C. Anderson, Druggist and Merchant; Fillmore.

A. Q. Robison, Watches and Jewelry; Fillmore.

B. N. Whitman, Contractor and Builder; Fillmore.

Mrs. Merrill, Milliner and Supply Store; Fillmore.

The People's Store, General Merchandise; Jas. D. Smith, Supt., Fillmore.

One Price Store, General Merchandise; G. R. Huntsman, Fillmore.

Holden Co-op; Gen'l Mdse., A. Y. Stephenson, Supt., Holden.

Miss Huntsman, Dressmaking and Millinery; Fillmore.

Greenway's Store, General Merchandise; Fillmore.

Hinckley Co-op; Gen'l. Mdse., A. A. Hinckley, Supt., Hinckley.

Thos. C. Callister, all Kinds of Conveyances attended to; Fillmore.

The Fillmore Dairy Store, General Merchandise, J. S. Giles, Mgr.; Fillmore.

OUR WATER.

The people of Fillmore are at last beginning to realize that they must do something to improve our water. A petition has been circulated the last few days, asking the City Council to enforce the law and compel sheepmen to keep their herds a certain distance from our streams.

It is reported that several herds are working their way to the hills east of us, hence the petition.

Our water is bad enough as it is, and if the sheep are allowed to feed near the streams, the water will be unfit for hogs to drink, let alone human beings.

We are glad to see the people take this step—it is one forward—and we hope they will take another in the same direction and have the water piped down from the springs.

Then we can say "Fillmore is in it," and she will be.

BUILD FILLMORE UP.

There are a great many people in this neighborhood who are busily engaged in the manufacture of brick. Quite the proper thing that they should be. Fillmore is very short of houses and people coming in from other parts of the country find it very hard at times to obtain shelter for themselves and their belongings.

Again, while times are as dull as they are at present, what better use can a man find for his time than in spending all his spare moments in improving his home? If the people were to take a little more pride in the appearance of their houses, fences, etc.; than they do, and set out more shade trees, Fillmore would look like another place.

Brick are easily obtained now, and sand, gravel and rock can be had for the hauling. Tear down some of these old "shanties" and erect neat, modern buildings in their place. Now is a good time to do it.

The May term of the First district court, which has been held at Nephi, adjourned today. The jurors were discharged on Wednesday evening. Judge Smith heard a habeas corpus case today against a person from Eureka who is confined in the county jail at Nephi. The July term will be opened at Fillmore, Millard county, the first Monday in July.

Joseph Giles, the baker at the asylum is happy today over the arrival at his house this morning of a new baby girl. All doing well.

Provo Evening Dispatch
June 7, 1895

THE conjoint meeting, Y. L. and Y. M. M. I. A. of the Fourth ward to be held on Monday evening next in the Fourth Ward meeting-house is to be an exceptionally interesting one and will be profitable to all who attend. Professor J. B. Walton will deliver an illustrated scientific lecture. Professor Gillman in a clarionet solo, the Fourth Ward Glee club in popular selections, and several other interesting numbers will also be on the program.

J. V. Robison of Fillmore, is in Provo for a few days on a visit. When he returns, his daughter Eva, wife of Professor Rydalch, lately departed on a mission to the southern states, will return with him where she will remain during the term of her husband's mission.

Provo Evening Dispatch
June 8, 1895

No. 1 of volume 3 of the Blade, a sprightly weekly paper heretofore published at Fillmore will be published at Nephi next week. Hereafter the Blade will issue regularly from Nephi.

Provo Evening Dispatch
June 10, 1895

DISTRICT COURT.

An Early Session Was Held This Morning.

TWENTY JURORS DRAWN

For Services at the Fillmore Term—One Divorce Granted—A Number of U. S. Commissioners' Accounts Approved—New Cases Filed.

A brief session of the First District court was held this morning before 8 o'clock. At 8:35 Judge King left over the R. G. W. Ry. for Salt Lake city.

Twenty jurors for service at the term of court to be held at Fillmore to convene on July 8th, were drawn from the box as follows:

Samuel Davis, Springville.
John R. Wilson, Spanish Fork.
C. W. Brewerton, Payson.
John Jackson, Fillmore.
Cornelius M. Fairbanks, Glenwood.
C. H. Sperry, Nephi.
C. W. Watts, Kanosh.
Niels Thompson, Ephraim.
H. P. Cushing, Santaquin.
John Ray, Mona.
Elmer Taylor, Juab.
N. P. Nielsen, Mount Pleasant.
Samuel Curtis, Salem.
Frederick Lewis, Spanish Fork.
Amasa Bird, Springville.
Wm. Andrews, Provo Bench.
Levi Snow, Provo.
C. B. Harper, Pleasant Grove.
Llewellyn Jones, Spanish Fork.
A. P. Harmon, Holden.

A decree of divorce, with $50 00 attorney's fee and $20 00 per month alimony, was granted in the suit of Mary Pierce vs. Nephi Pierce. Parties of Pleasant Grove.

Execution was ordered stayed ten days in the case of Dennis Sullivan vs. Edwards.

The accounts of the following named U. S. Commissioners were approved: J. W. Morehouse, William Zabriskie, Peter Jensen, R. C. Camp, Peter Jensen, Jacob Johnson, Ed. Pike.

Court adjourned to June 19th.

NEW CASES.

The following new cases have been filed:

Almon Robison vs. Peter Greenhalgh and Jenet Greenhalgh, his wife. Suit for the recovery of the possession of lot 2 in block 17, plat "A," town of Meadow survey; for $100.00 damages for witholding possession; for $275.15 balance rents due and for $9.00 per month rent from date. Sam A. King and E. A. Wilson, attorneys for plaintiff.

H. J. Christensen vs Sine P. Christensen. Suit for divorce. Parties of Sanpete. Grounds, desertion. Jacob Johnson, attorney for plaintiff.

N J. Nielsen vs. John Dallin and Hannah Dallin his wife. Defendants of Springville, plaintiff of Provo. Suit for recovery on a promissory note for $600.00 signed at Provo on June 20, 1890, and for foreclosure of mortgage given to secure payment. L. W. Kenward, attorney for plaintiff.

Jesse Knight vs. H. K. Roundy and John Roundy. Suit for judgment on $500.00 promissory note signed at Provo on June 10, 18.0. No mortgage. J E. Booth, attorney for plaintiff.

Alma Robison vs. Peter Greenhalgh and Jenet Greenhalgh, his wife. Suit for recovery of possession of certain farming land in Millard county; for $100.00 damages for witholding possession; for $466.58 rents due; for $11.40 per month from date, as rents. Sam A. King and E. A. Wison, attorneys for plaintiff.

R. G. Wilson vs. Silas W. Bennett. Parties of Eureka. Suit for $369.71 balance due on account of goods, wares, merchandise sold and board and lodings. J. W N. Whitecotton, attorney for plaintiff.

Provo Evening Dispatch
June 22, 1895

NEW CASES.

The following new cases have been filed:

James Day et al vs. Joseph Turner et al. Suit for $500.00 damages and for order restraining defendants from diverting waters of Dame creek near Fillmore, in Millard county.

Zion's Co-op. Mer. Inst. vs. Mons Peterson of Moab. Suit for judgment for $132.87, balance account, and $2675.-85 on promissory note and for foreclosure of mortgage.

Provo Evening Dispatch
June 29, 1895

GEO. E. ROBISON and wife went south on the Union Pacific this morning, bound for Fillmore, to visit relatives and friends.

MRS. ADA HINCKLEY who has been visiting relatives in Provo for some time, departed for home in Fillmore this morning.

Provo Daily Enquirer
July 12, 1895

Mission Notes.

Arrivals.—The Cunard steamer "Lucania" arrived in Liverpool on June 21, having on board Mrs. Chloe Eldredge, Ernest Eldredge, Harold Eldredge, Guy Eldredge, and Miss Mamie Eldredge, all of Salt Lake city, who came on a pleasure trip to England and the Continent.

Also there arrived in Liverpool per American Line Steamer "Kensington" on June 25, 1895. the following named Elders from Utah: For the British mission—John H. Burrows and W. S. Romney of Salt Lake city; O. D. Smith of Fillmore; D. C. Stephenson of Nephi; Edwin Price of Greenville.

For the Scandinavian Mission—Ole Anderson of Pleasant Grove; Andrew Bjorkman of Salt Lake city.

Accompanying these were Mrs. John H. Burrows of Salt Lake City; Mrs. John L. Fackrell of Bountiful; Mrs. Mary J. Dean and son Joseph H. Dean of Almy, Wyoming; Miss Nora Bennion of Taylorsville; Mrs. A. K. Bartlett of Vernal. The last named accompanied the Scandinavian Elders to Copenhagen. leaving Liverpool in the afternoon of June 26. and the other ladies will spend some time in England, and on the Continent.

Appointments.—Elder John H. Burrows has been appointed to labor in the business department of the Millennial Star office.

Elder W. S. Romney has been appointed to labor as Traveling Elder in the Sheffield Conference.

Elders O. D. Smith and D. C. Stephenson have been appointed to labor as traveling elders in the Newcastle conference.

Elder Edwin Price has been appointed to labor as traveling elder in the Welsh conference.—Millenial Star.

Salt Lake Herald
June 12, 1895

The sheriff reports that several new clues have been found, and he believes the guilty parties will eventually be convicted.

The following jurors have been called to serve the July term at Fillmore: Samuel Davis, Springville; John R. Wilson, Spanish Fork; C. W. Brewerton, Payson; John Jackson, Fillmore; C. M. Fairbanks, Glenwood; C. H. Sperry, Nephi; C. W. Watts, Kanosh; Niels Thompson, Ephraim; H. P. Cushing, Santaquin; John Hay, Mona; Elmer Taylor, Juab; N. P. Nielsen, Mt. Pleasant; Samuel Curtis, Salem; F. Lewis, Spanish Fork; Amassa Bird, Springville; Wm. Andrews, Provo Bench; Levi Snow, Provo; C. B. Harper, Pleasant Grove; Llewelly Jones, Spanish Fork; A. P. Harmon, Holden.

A decree of divorce was granted to Mary Pierce of Pleasant Grove against Nephi Pierce.

Salt Lake Herald
June 16, 1895

S. M. Duggins, of Provo, has filed suit in the First district court against Joseph E. Ray, of Fillmore, and L. Holbrook, of Provo, for $400, alleged to be due on a promissory note.

The Salt Lake Herald
June 29, 1895

PROVO PARAGRAPHS.

Mrs. Ada Hinckley, who has been visiting relatives here for some time, leaves for her home in Fillmore tomorrow.

Salt Lake Herald
July 7, 1895

Judge W. H. King, Marshal Fowler, Attorneys D. D. Houtz and S. A. King will go south to Fillmore tomorrow morning to be in attendance on the First district court, which convenes there on Monday next.

Salt Lake Herald
July 12, 1895

ARRIVED IN ENGLAND.

Eldredge Party Is Now Sight-Seeing in Europe.

Arrivals—The Cunard steamer Lucani arrived in Liverpool on June 21, having on board Mrs. Chloe Eldredge, Ernest Eldredge, Harold Eldredge, Guy Eldredge and Miss Mamie Eldredge, all of Salt Lake city, who came on a pleasure trip to England and the continent.

Also there arrived in Liverpool per American line steamer Kensington on June 26, 1895, the following named elders from Utah: For the British mission—John H. Burrows and W. S. Romney, of Salt Lake city; C. D. Smith, of Fillmore; D. C. Stephenson, of Nephi; Edwin Price, of Greenville. For the Scandinavian mission—Ole Anderson, of Pleasant Grove; Andrew Bjorkman, of Salt Lake city. Accompanying these were Mrs. John H. Burrows, of Salt Lake city; Mrs. John L. Fackrell, of Bountiful; Mrs. Mary J. Dean and son, Joseph H. Dean, of Almy, Wyo.; Miss Nora Bennion, of Taylorsville; Mrs. A. K. Bartlett, of Vernal. The last named accompanied the Scandinavian elders to Copenhagen, leaving Liverpool in the afternoon of June 26, and the other ladies will spend some time in England and on the continent.

Appointments—Elder John H. Burrows has been appointed to labor in the business department of the Millennial Star office.

Elder W. S. Romney has been appointed to labor as traveling elder in the Sheffield conference.

Elders C. D. Smith and D. C. Stephenson have been appointed to labor as traveling elders in the Newcastle conference.

Elder Edwin Price has been appointed to labor as traveling elder in the Welsh conference.—Millennial Star, June 27.

Provo Evening Dispatch
July 13, 1895

VERILY is it quiet Saturday in Provo today with the majority of the legal fraternity at Fillmore, many families camping up the canyon, the base ball team and many of their friends gone to Park City and scores of democrats gone up to Salt Lake city to attend the convention.

Provo Daily Enquirer
July 15, 1895

Court at Fillmore.

FILLMORE, Utah, July 13.—Special to Tribune.—Court convened this morning at 10 o'clock, and the arguments in the case of Dodge vs. Johnson et al. were resumed by D. D. Houtz for defense, and Judge Baum for plaintiff. The Court charged the jury, and they retired in charge of the bailiff. After being out for twenty minutes the jury came into court and rendered a verdict in favor of the defendant, the verdict being "no cause of action." A stay of execution for forty days was granted.

The case of A. Robison vs. Peter Greenhalgh and Jennett Greenhalgh was called, and a jury impaneled. This suit is brought to eject defendants from certain property in Meadow. It appears that Greenhalgh gave Robison a deed to the property to secure the payment of $150 for which Greenhalgh had, previous to the execution of the deed, given his promissory note, and subsequently gave the deed, and the note was returned to him. Greenhalgh having come into possession of the note, claimed that he paid of the obligation, and demanded that Robison reconvey the property to him, which he refused to do, setting forth that the obligation had not been paid. A great amount of testimony was given, both direct and rebuttal, and a large number of witnesses were sworn for plaintiff, who all testified that the reputation of Greenhalgh in the community in which he lived for honesty, integrity and veracity was bad. At this time the court took a recess. This evening the case had not been given to the jury. The arguments will be made this evening at 8:30, and the case given to the jury.

The case of the People vs. Peterson was dismissed on the ground that no conviction could be had. Court is not expected to finish its business until the middle of next week.

The people of Fillmore are making it as pleasant as possible for the court officials and attorneys while they remain. Dancing and other amusements are given in their honor every night.

Fillmore's Court.

FILLMORE, Utah, July 15—Special to Tribune—Saturday evening the jury in the Robison-Greenhalgh case returned a verdict giving Robinson the possession of the premises prayed for. Today at 10 o'clock the case of Robinson vs. Jeannette Greenhalgh, a suit for defendant's house, was called, and a jury of nine men, by consent of parties, was sworn to try the case. The case has

been hotly contested on both sides all day. At 6:30 p. m. court took an adjournment until tomorrow morning at 9:30 at which time the court will charge the jury. Jurors Bird, Davies, Curtis Taylor, Watts and Thompson were excused for the term.

It is said that Edward Stevens and E. E. Dodge, litigants in the Holden water case, while returning from Fillmore to Holden, both leading citizens of that place, partook generously of the contents of a flask, and wound up with a fist-fight, resulting in soiled clothes, blackened eyes and broken noses. No arrests were made.

Court Cullings.

The court officials are all back from Fillmore, but Judge King had to go to Nephi this morning to hear arguments in a case tried last May. All the officials praise Fillmore for its sociability. Deputy Clerk Havercamp is back in the office again. The following cases have been filed:

Laurekkee Thompson wants a divorce from Niels Peter Thompson, on the ground that the defendant was convicted of the crime of polygamy at Provo Feb. 27, 1894, and is serving a term at the penitentiary. The couple were married in Denmark, Nov. 22, 1882.

David McPherson has filed his answer, through his attorneys, Brown & Henderson, in the damage suit brought against him by Phillip Speckart.

Defendant says he has not information or belief sufficient to enable him to answer and therefore denies that plaintiff enjoyed a good reputation for honesty, fair dealing, decency or respectability at the time of the commencement of the suit.

He denies in like manner that plaintiff has ever been suspected of selling or offering for sale unwholesome meat—flesh of horses, or big-jawed cows.

While thus denying all allegations in the form and manner alleged, the defendant further denies of his own personal knowledge, that the plaintiff has enjoyed a good reputation for fair dealings, etc., and alleges that his correspondence with defendant illustrates the truth of plaintiff not having a reputation for fair dealing.

Defendant denies that the flesh of horses is regarded as unfit, unwholesome or improper for human food in Provo. He denies that the flesh of cattle suffering from a disease known as big jaw is unfit for human food, unless such big jaw has developed into a disease so as to affect the blood. He denies that plaintiff's business was a large and lucrative one. He denies that his publication of ads. were false and malicious concerning plaintiff, and admits he published them. He says it was not with the intention of injuring plaintiff and denies it has injured him. Therefore he asks the case be dismissed.

Hans S. Nielsen has begun suit against John T. Henninger et al on a $600 promissory note secured by a mortgdge.

Salt Lake Herald
July 20, 1895

The Progress appeals to the express company, in behalf of the people of Fillmore, to locate an office here or remove the would-be agent at Juab and put a man in there who will attend to business. It is outrageous the way our people are treated by the express company or their agent at that point, and they will certainly not stand it much longer. We give our 4th of July supplement this week (just fourteen days late) on account of carelessness on the agent's part, who let our express lay at Juab since June 30—telling the stage drivers that there was no express for Fillmore. We could mention several other cases similar to ours, but is is unnecessary. If our patrons can get any satisfaction out of our supplement at this late date they are welcome to it.—Millard Progress.

Provo Even Dispatch
July 20, 1895

First District Court.

George Havercamp, deputy clerk of the First District court, returned on Thursday from Fillmore and the work of the office here is again caught up. Among the pile of filings of interest to the public are the following:

Fairview Co-op. vs. Nels Youngdell. Abstract of judgment confessed for $63.65 in Justice Sells' court in Fairview.

Fred Aurbach & Brothers. Abstract of judgment for $189.25 and $15.15 costs, filed from Justice Veltman's court at Vernal.

THEY LIKE FILLMORE

And Fillmore's People—Our Legal People Full of Praise for Them—Judge King Honored in His Old Home—Millard County Democrats Confident of Success.

On Tuesday afternoon Judge King, D. D. Houtz, E. A. Wilson and S. A. King, Clerk Havercamp and Marshal Fowler returned from Fillmore where the First District court has been in session for the past two weeks. Others of the attorneys had returned before.

They are unanimous and earnest in their praise of the hospitality and generosity with which they were received and entertained by the people of Fillmore. Fillmore they say is on an equal socially and intellectually with any part of the territory. Social gatherings and entertainments of various kinds were held while they were there and the boys had a most enjoyable time. Judge King was royally received, and most flattering marks of esteem, respect and honor were shown him.

On Monday evening a public reception was tendered the judge. The good people of Fillmore turned out en masse to do him honor. He was not only covered with encomiums and bid God-speed by his old time friends, but was showered with flowers by the hands of Fillmore's fair daughters. The evening was spent in music both instrumental and vocal, speeches and recitations. The judge responded in a feeling and eloquent way and the event was a complete success in every way.

The democrats of Fillmore held a rally on last Thursday evening at which Hon. S. R. Thurman, Messrs. D. D. Houtz and E. A. Wilson of Provo addressed the meeting. The meeting was well attended and was enthusiastic from beginning to end.

The democrats of Milliard county, though beaten last fall, are sanguine of capturing that county at the coming election.

Salt Lake Herald
July 22, 1895

A SCIENTIFIC EXPEDITION.

It Will Leave Today for Southern Utah.

Today a scientific expedition, under the auspices of the department of geology of the University of Utah and the Deseret museum, leave for the high plateau region of southern Utah. The party consists of Dr. J. E. Talmage as director, Professor G. R. Mathews, vice-director; Instructor W. D. Neal, secretary, and Messrs. Chamberlin, Poulson, Woodbury, Doxey, Riter and Ridges. Other members will be enrolled in the course of the journey and it is expected that a second detachment will leave the city in charge of Profesor Kingsbury immediately after the close of the university summer school, joining the main division in Garfield county. The purpose of the undertaking is primarily geological and generally scientific. The party will go to Salina by rail, there fitting out with riding horses, mules and pack donkeys, and traveling in a manner independent of wagon roads or beaten routes of travel. The equipment is well adapted for field work in science, comprising geological instruments, collecting apparatus for botanical, zoological and microscopical subjects, a complete photographic outfit, etc. The route of travel as at present arranged will carry the party to Fish lake, thence into Rabbit valley and via the Thousand Lake mountain to the site of the selenite deposit, for the development of which the Deseret museum has become famous; thence to the Henry mountains, Kaipawirtz plateau and the Grand canyon of the Colorado. The return may be made by way of Kanab, Panguitch lake, Beaver and Fillmore.

A COURT CHANGE.

Clerk J. W. Beasley is Deposed.

BONDSMEN RELEASED.

No Record Made of the Court's Order--Mr. Beasley Interviewed.

There has been rumors in the air for many days of dissatisfaction on the part of John W. Beasley's bondsmen, in his office of clerk of the First District court Ever since Hon. John T. Caine paid a visit to Provo in the latter part of June, the bondsmen have been uneasy. He gave them notice that Clerk Beasley was behind about $300 in his Territorial remittances, and he would hold them responsible for this dereliction in duty.

The bondsmen got together and concluded to seek their release, and on July 3 they went into open court and made a request of Judge King to release them. Judge King made an order for their release, and the bondsmen were of the belief that they had been released. Soon they learned that no record of their release had been made, and they again notified Judge King of the fact. He said the order had been made and should have been entered. When the bondsmen again came before him last Saturday and showed up the fact that the order had not been entered, Judge King was wrathy and immediately deposed Clerk Beasley and put in his deputy Geo. Havercamp.

An Enquirer reporter saw the bondsmen about the matter, and some said they demanded their release because Clerk Beasley was leading a fast life and was behind in his remittance to the Territory, while it was impossible to find out how he stood with the government, because he had made no report while in office, yet the law provides for a semi-annual report. They said that it was learned a $200 fine had been paid him as a fine from Will March and no record was made of it in the office. Clerk Beasley left at once for Salt Lake when he received this money, and had not returned to Provo when this precipitate action was taken.

The bondsmen feared he was up there on a spree, and that they would have to pay for the music, so they concluded that if their release was not granted forthwith they would telegraph to the attorney-general to release them and appoint a receiver for the office. They also feared a shortage anywhere within a thousand dollars, for they said he had never been able to recover from some $900 which he lost on the last Delegate election.

Clerk Havercamp, when seen in reference to the shortage, said he did not believe the bondsmen would have to foot any bills. The government owes Mr. Beasley a lot of fees and many attorneys are indebted to him for filings. When all is collected, he believes Mr. Beasley will be square with the world.

The Salt Lake Tribune has the following interview this morning with Clerk Beasley in Salt Lake:

"It is stated, Mr. Beasley," said the interviewer, "that you lost $900 on the election, and it is then your first shortage began. Is that true?"

"I lost about $700. There was no shortage," was the answer.

"Did Mr. Caine go to Provo and demand of you $300, or any other sum, as being due?"

"No; there was no money due at that time, and no demand made for money at the time. Mr. Caine said he had come at the instance of some parties, and he had heard several times that I was leading a somewhat sporting life. Matters were satisfactorily arranged at the time. I paid him $50 on what would be my remittance for the quarter ending June 30th. I also sent him an order on the Territorial Treasurer for the amount of my salary, $75, a receipt for which I hold."

"Why did you give him the $50 and an order for your salary?"

"I sent it all as part of my account, sending in the warrant as a credit and retaining so much cash."

"What amount was due the Territory after you had paid Mr. Caine the $125?"

"I cannot say exactly, without reference to my books, but something in the neighborhood of $400.

"Why did you not promptly remit the amount due at the end of the quarter?"

"I did not at that time have the cash on hand."

"How was it that you did not have the cash on hand, when it must have been paid you?"

"My office expenses were high, credit had been given attorneys and marked as paid, and I had loaned considerable money to friends. Nor had I received any money from the Government that was due as fees."

"Why should what you owed the Territory depend upon the amount the Government owed you?"

"Because for every law case that is filed there must be a jury fee of $3 paid to the Territory."

"Do you not collect this fee from those filing a suit?"

"In a great many cases no; perhaps not in half."

"What made your bondsmen become uneasy?"

"Unsuccessful competitors did all they could to make them uneasy, and if I was at all indiscreet they magnified it as much as they could."

"It is charged, Mr. Beasley, that on Tuesday last you received from City Attorney Whitecotton of Provo $200 that one Will March had paid as a fine, and that the records of the court fail to show that you so received it."

"I gave Mr. Whiteotton...

"show that you so received it."

"I gave Mr. Whitecotton a receipt for the amount, stating it was for fine and costs. It was my receipt as Clerk of the Court, and bore the seal of the Court."

"Why do not the record show this also?"

'If it is not on the records it is thought inadvertance, and nothing else. Mr Havercamp, who was my deputy, made all the entries on the records, but he was in Fillmore at the time attending court. This is why it was not entered. The stub of my receipt book will show that it was paid, and these stubs I consider as part of the record of the court."

"Why did Judge King dismiss you as Clerk?"

"I do not care to answer that question at present."

"Have you anything you wish to say, generally?"

"I have been raised in Provo, and never had an enemy in my life until I entered the clerk's office. Since being there I have been in hot water, caused by political jealousy and some indiscretions on my own part."

"Are you ready and able to at any time settle any balances due the Territory from you as clerk?"

"Yes, sir."

The auditor, John T. Caine, was also interviewed and said only $50 had been remitted by Clerk Beasley while in office, and he believed there was a shortage on his books of about $400.

Salt Lake Herald
July 29, 1895

Judge King's Dance.

Speaking of the Ogden Standard's comment on the dance given by the choir and band boys of Fillmore, that "the judge's recognition of 'song and dance' methods is not without political significance," the Millard Progress says: "A man now days, according to the Standard, cannot even give a sociable in the town he was born without political significance.' Shame on such talk."

Salt Lake Herald
July 31, 1895

KILLED IN THE CANYON.

Frink Scottern Meets Sudden Death Near Fillmore.

[Special to The Herald.]

BEAVER CITY, July 30.—An accident near Fillmore caused the death of Frink Scottern, his neck and back being broken by the falling on him of a portion of a tree he had felled. His parents live in Provo. Deceased was about 25 years of age, and had been married only a short time.

Deseret Evening News
July 31, 1895

Fatal Accident Near Fillmore.

Tim Scottern, of this city, received a telegram yesterday to the effect that his son, Frink A. Scottern, met his death yesterday morning while he was cutting timber in the mountains, east of Fillmore. A tree which he was cutting lodged in the top of another tree, and a part of the standing tree was broken off and struck Mr. Scottern on the head inflicting fatal injuries. Mr. Scottern was a young man, 24 years of age, and married last winter. He was getting out timber to build a house at the time of the accident. His father went to Fillmore with a coffin on this morning's train.

Salt Lake Herald
September 5, 1895

A decree of divorce was also granted to Laura Dean Mace against Hiram Mace, of Fillmore. The grounds alleged being cruel and inhuman treatment.

Salt Lake Herald
September 19, 1895

Young Carling was arraigned on an indictment charging attempted murder. This is the Fillmore poisoning case.

Salt Lake Herald
September 20, 1895

The People vs. Frank Carling; defendant pleaded not guilty. He is accused of administering 15 grains of strychnine to W. C. Goulter, of Fillmore, with intent to kill.

DISTRICT COURT.

A Number of Cases Reset For Trial.

SPECKART VS. M'PHERSON

Libel Suit Between Provo Butchers to be Heard on Monday—Fillmore Poisoning Case Set For October 1st—Thompson Damage Case—Verdict not Yet Returned.

Cases were reset for trial last evening by Judge King as follows:

Friday September 20th—James H. Mynders vs. R. G. W. Ry. Co. Anna Marks vs. Bullion-Beck & Champion Mining company.

Saturday, September 21st—Oliver A. beth E. Berry vs. R. G. W. Ry. Co.

Monday, September 23d.—The People vs Joseph McCune. W. L. Elwood vs. Edward Malmquist. Philip Speckart vs. David McPherson.

Tuesday, September 24th.—Peter L. Greenhalgh, an infant, vs. Meadow Irrigation company. Joseph Greenhalgh vs. Meadow Irrigation company. Heber McNeill vs. Harry Hayes et al.

Wednesday, September 25th.—T. L. Vincent vs. R. G. W. Ry. Co. Joseph A. Smith vs. R. G. W. Ry. Co. Martinus Nelson vs. C. H. Blomsterberg et al.

Thursday, September 26th—Eureka City vs. R. G. Wilson. B. K. Block & Co. vs. H. E. Rawlings et al. M. N. Patten vs. Richard Dowdle. Bank of Montreal vs. Ed. Kearns.

Friday, September 27th.—The People vs. H. E. Sturgeon. The People vs. Lewis McCarty and Henry Malmgreen (four cases.)

Saturday, September 28th.—U. S. vs. Norman Bean.

Tuesday, October 1st.—The People vs. Frank Carlin.

The damage case of R. H. Thompson vs. R. G. W. Ry. Co. has been on trial again all day. At 4 o'clock the attorneys were arguing the case before the jury.

Deputy United States Marshal Payne came to Provo today from Fillmore. He brought with him Frank Wilson, who is charged with grand larceny in stealing a horse from W. L. Lott. The prisoner was at once arraigned and entered a plea of not guilty, and Joshua Greenwood was appointed by the court to defend him.

G. W. Cropper and Butler Allred are up from Deseret in Millard county. They speak hopefully of the project which was begun last spring towards reclaiming those vast tracts of arid lands beginning at a point near Leamington and extending along the bench towards Fillmore. In the opinion of the gentlemen, with the completion of the irrigation enterprises now under way, Millard county will have a population of not less than 30,000 five years hence.

Alleged Poisoning.

The witnesses in the case of the people vs. Frank Carling are all here and it is expected the case will be called tomorrow. The case is of great importance and is attracting much attention. Carling is a boy about 18 years old and is indicted for attempting to murder William Goulter, of Fillmore, by putting strychnine in some milk, which Goulter had prepared for his supper.

The evidence will show that a will had been made out by someone and forged, willing all of Goulter's property to young Carling.

POISONING CASE.

Frank Carling of Fillmore On Trial Today.

MR. GOULTER'S STORY

Of How the Attempt was Made and How It Failed—Found a Forged Will Among His Papers—McNeill Wins His Case—Other Business.

Judge King delivered his instructions to the jury in the McCarty-Malmgreen case this forenoon beginning at 9:30 o'clock. The jury retired and the jury in the McNeil vs. Hansen case were called to the box and heard the arguments of the attorneys and afterwards the instructions of the court and they too retired.

The last named jury soon returned with a verdict of $32.65 for the plaintiff.

The next case called was the noted poisoning case from Fillmore. Readers will remember that in March last the papers were all filled with elaborate accounts in which Frank Carling, a boy aged 19, with another named Shail were accused with having administered strychnine in some milk to one William G. Goulter. At the preliminary trial Shail was discharged. It appearing from the evidence that the only connection he had in the matter was that he had signed as a witness a certain paper purporting to be a will made out in favor of Carling by Goulter which read as follows:

FILLMORE, July 12, 1890

This is to certify that I, on July 12, 1894 give to Frank Carling at my death, whenever that might be, my home which I am now living in, and its surroundings; also the four lots which are adjoining and all the animals which I own.

This is my wish if not changed.

WILLIAM G. GOULTER.

FRANK CARLING.

On the back of this paper appears the following: Fillmore Dec. 7, 1894 The undersigned witness to this will James Shail.

Mr. Shail it is said proved at the preliminary hearing that he signed this paper at the request of Carling, upon the representation by Carling that it was the old man Goulter's request that he should do so. The paper is said to be in Carling's hand-writing. Goulter denies ever having written it. Carling it is alleged was in the habit of working in and upon Mr. Goulter's lots and was frequently in Mr. Goulter's house. Mr. Goulter was batching it and on sitting down to his frugal supper of bread and milk on the evening of March 5th last after having been about the house in different rooms, getting wood straining milk etc., Carling, who had been in the room, went out. Goulter looked at a knife lying on the table and found the knife wet with milk. He looked to see if the milk had been spilled on the table but found no evidence of any having been spilled. He then drank some of the milk and found it bitter. He ran and got some salt and water and drank this mixture which made him vomit. He was very sick during the balance of the night. He went for his brother and they two fished up a small portion of white substance from the bottom of the bowl of milk. When he went to retire he reached for his account book to make some entries and while searching for the book found the will above referred to among his papers.

All of the forenoon was occupied in getting a jury. Mr. Goulter was the first witness put upon the stand. He is still there. He testified to all of the above at considerable detail and to more, detailing what transpired on the evening of March 4th, when he found his tea very bitter after Frank Carling had been in the house and lit the fire for Goulter and placed the water with which the tea was made on the stove to boil.

What the theory of the defense is has not yet been divulged, but from the nature of the cross-examination it would appear that they will contend Goulter suffers from a mania which leads him to believe people want to poison him; that he left his wife because he was afraid she was going to poison him, and that no attempt whatever was made by Carling or anyone else to poison him.

S. R. Thurman is prosecuting, and S. A. King, D. D. Houtz and James Melville are defending.

THE CARLING CASE

Did The Boy Poison Coulter?

A COPY OF THE WILL.

Millard County's Sensational Case Begun—Jury in McCarty-Malmgreen Case Out.

The case of the People vs McCarty and Malmgreen, charged with stealing cattle, was given to the jury this morning. It is still out.

Arguments were then made in the case of McNeil vs Hansen, and the jury retired at 10:30 a.m.

At 11 a.m. the jury in the case of Mc Neil vs Hansen brought in a verdict of $32,65 for plaintiff.

The next case to come up was that of the people vs Frank Carling. Mr. Carling is a young man, 19 years of age, and is accused of administering poison with intent to kill. The complaint charges that Carling on the 5th of March, 1865, in the city of Fillmore, Millard county, Utah, unlawfully, wilfully and feloniously, did administer, and caused and procured to be administered to one William J. Goulter, a large quantity of deadly poison, to wit; fifteen grains of strychnine, with intent to kill and murder said William J. Goulter.

Mr. Goulter is an aged gentleman, past 60, also of Fillmore, having resided at that place for the last thirty-two years. The poison administered to him did not cause his death, but he suffered intense pain throughout the night, and by aid of physicians his life was saved.

There is a will purported to have been made out by Mr. Goulter, which will figure prominently in the case. The will reads thus:

Fillmore, July 12. 1894.

This is to certify that I on July 12th, 1894, give to Frank Carling at my death, whenever that might be, my house which I am now living in, and its surroundings, also the four lots which are adjoining, and all the animals which I own. This is my wishes if not changed.

WILLIAM J. GOULTER.
FRANK CARLING.

On the back of the purported will appears the writing

Fillmore. Dec. 7. 1894.

The undersigned witness to this will.

JAMES SHAIL.

James Shail, whose name appears as witness to the will, was also arrested, but the grand jury ignored the charge against him.

J. A. Melville of Millard county, D. D. Houtz, and S. A. King, appear for defendant, and Prosecuting Attorney Thurman and John M. Hanson represent the people.

Salt Lake Herald
October 10, 1895

LEGAL GRIND AT PROVO.

FRANK CARLING CHARGED WITH POISONING W. J. GOULTER.

Alleged That He Put Strychnine in Milk, After a Will Had Been in Favor of Carling—Mrs. Haight Adjudged Insane.

PROVO, Oct. 9, 1895.—At 11 o'clock this morning the case of the people vs. Frank Carling was called. S. R. Thurman prosecuting and Sam A. King, James A. Melville and D. D. Houtz appeared for the defendant. The defendant sat beside his counsel and appeared very dejected and down hearted, and fully realizes the position he is in. The boy's father, brothers and friends are in attendance in his behalf and will see that no evidence in the boy's favor will be left out. The crime charged is a very grave one and the boy and his friends fully sense the enormity of the offense. The indictment charges Frank Carling with administering fifteen grains of strychnine to William J. Goulter, of Fillmore, with intent to kill Goulter. Goulter is a man about 54 years of age and is possessed of considerable property. A motive for the crime will be introduced in the shape of a will in the defendant's favor. This will, Mr. Goulter says is a forgery. Following is a copy of the will:

"FILLMORE CITY, July 12, 1894.
"This is to certify that I, on July the 12th, 1894, give to Frank Carling, at my death, whenever that might be, my house which I am now living in, and its surroundings and 'alleo' the 'fowr' lots which is joining and all the animals which I 'one.'
"This is my wishes if not changed.
"WILLIAM J. GOULTER.
"FRANK CARLING."

On the back of this paper appears the following:
"FILLMORE, Dec. 7, 1894.
"The undersigned witness to this will,   "JAMES SHAIL."

The boy does not look nor act in any way like one who would commit so grave a crime. He looks to be a quiet, inoffensive young man.

The defense will attempt to prove that Carling was in the opposite end of town on the evening of the 5th of March, when the poison is alleged to have been placed in the milk. They will also put evidence on to prove that Mr. Goulter actually did make the will in favor of the defendant and afterwards regretted the transaction and trumped up this charge against the young man.

William Goulter, the prosecuting witness, was the first sworn. He testified that he was 54 years old, has known the defendant a number of years. His business is freighting. Saw Frank Carling on the 2d of March. On that day he came to me, said the witness, and asked to borrow my horse to go to Deseret; saw him again on Monday following. I was away all day and in the evening came home and found Mr. Carling at the house. He had brought the horse back; myself and Carling went to the house together; I said that I wanted a cup of tea; he said for me to go to the yard and feed my stock and he would make a fire to heat some water for the tea; when I came back the water was boiling and Carling at once said he must go home; he then went; I poured some tea and put sugar and milk in it and after stirring it with a spoon, drank some and found it to be bitter and spat it out and threw the balance away; the water in the pail tasted all right; the next evening when I was preparing my supper Carling came to my place; I invited him in; he sat by the table; before he came I milked the cow and strained it in a bowl which would not hold it all; the milk was sweet; I tasted it; when he (Carling) came, I said come in; he sat down by the table; I made a fire; I put the milk on the table near the defendant; he asked if I was going to have milk for supper; I said yes and went into another room for some cake; I then went after some wood for the evening; when I got in with the wood, the milk was sitting in front of him; he then said he must go; I went out to the gate with him; there he offered me something to drink; he said it was brandy; I tasted it; I then went to the house and proceeded to eat my supper; found the milk spilled upon the cake; I looked to see how it could come there; I took a mouthful and found it to be as bitter as gall.

The witness seemed to be very anxious to tell his story in his own way and was stopped by the judge and told to answer the questions put to him. The witness proceeding said: My brother came to my house and we examined the milk; I was too sick before this to see for myself; when my brother came I put a spoon into the milk and drew out a small white substance about the size of a pea; I left the milk with my brother and went home; before going to bed I took down a small account book and found a paper or document (the purported will.) Witness identified the paper as being the one found.

Cross-examination elicited nothing new in the evidence. Witness stated that he did not sign the paper produced as the will; said that his name was spelled wrong.

The case is being contested step by step and will likely not be terminated before Thursday evening.

Provo Evening Dispatch
October 10, 1895

CARLING IS GUILTY

He Says So Himself and Gets Five Years.

SUDDEN TERMINATION

Of the Important Attempted Poisoning Case From Fillmore—The Jury in the McCarty-Malmgreen Case Failed to Agree—Nelson vs. Johansen Trespass Case—Other Business.

The jury in the McCarty-Malmgreen cattle stealing case retired at 10 o'clock yesterday (Wednesday) morning to consider their verdict. They remained out all day and until this afternoon when they returned into court and reported that they were unable to agree and were discharged.

Upon the opening of court this morning a surprise was perpetrated upon the court, the prosecution, the jury and all interested in the Carling poisoning case by the defense which arose and asked the privilege of withdrawing its plea of not guilty to the indictment. This was granted and a plea of guilty was thereupon entered. The young man was called up before the judge who asked him if he had anything to say why the sentence of the court should not now be passed upon him. His attorneys made a plea for leniency, setting forth his youth, the fact that he has a young wife depending upon him, the fact that he is repentant, has all along, but for this circumstance borne an exceptionally good character and reputation, and the deed was done as the rash conclusion of a boyish and immature mind, which did not realize the enormity of the attempted crime nor its awful consequences. The judge sentenced the boy to a term of five years in the pententiary and he was taken up to that bastile today.

The next case taken up was the one entitled Marinus Nelson vs. Lars A. Johansen. C. H. Blomsterberg, David Vincent, Joseph Smith and A. E. Veatch. The particulars are that plaintiff sold to one Johansen a piece of ground in the southwestern part of the city on the installment plan. Mr. Johansen had erected thereon a rough lumber house and later failed in his contract. The property reverted back to Nelson including all improvements. The house was removed by these defendants by and under the advice of A. E. Veatch, attorney-at-law, whose advice was asked and paid for. Mr. Nelson now sues for $250.00 damages for the house, and for trees, fences, corrals, etc., destroyed. The jury found for plaintiff awarding damages at $100 00.

Provo Daily Enquirer
October 15, 1895

ELIZABETH Robison of Fillmore has filed an action against Fillmore city for the recovery of $500 damages, alleged to have been sustained by defendant municipal corporation depriving her of using water for irrigation purposes, by having graded a street by her property and making it impossible for her to get water on her land.

Salt Lake Herald
October 17, 1895

WEATHER AND CROPS.

The Report of Observer Smith For Last Month.

Following is the weather and crop report for the month of September:

Temperature—The mean temperature for the territory was 60.8 degrees; highest monthly mean, 70.2 degrees, at St. George; lowest, 52.1 degrees, at Grouse Creek. The highest temperature, 103 degrees, was recorded at St. George, on the 8th, and the lowest, 9 degrees, at Fillmore, on the 22nd, making the range of temperature for the territory 94 degrees. The greatest local monthly range of temperature, was 90 degrees, at Fillmore, and the least, 60 degrees, at Logan. The average maximum temperature was 91 degrees, and the minimum 22 degrees.

Elizabeth Robison has begun suit against Fillmore City to recover damages in the sum of $500, alleged to have been sustained by reason of defendant grading a street and preventing the water to flow upon land owned by plaintiff.

Precipitation—The average precipitation for the territory was .69 of an inch; greatest monthly amount recorded was 2.28 inches at Millville, and the least amount recorded, was a trace at Orton. The principal part of the precipitation was in the shape of snow which fell on the 20th and 21st. The average number of days on which one-hundredth of an inch or more of rain, or melted snow fell, was three.

Wind—Prevailing direction southwest. Total movement at Salt Lake City, 5,140 miles; maximum velocity, 38 miles per hour from the south on the 10th; average hourly velocity, 7 miles per hour.

Weather—The weather was generally clear to fair from the 1st to the 6th, cloudy and stormy from the 17th to the 21st, and generally clear the remainder of the month. The heavy snow storm on the 20th and 21st, and the severe cold wave on the 22nd, were the most notable features of the weather during the month. The storm was general over the northern portion of the territory, and caused great damage to late fruits and vegetables.

The average number of clear days was 20; partly cloudy, 7, and cloudy, 3. There was 72 per cent of sunshine at Salt Lake city, and 81 per cent (estimated) at Grover, Wayne county, during the month.

Salt Lake Herald
October 22, 1895

Dr. Moyes returned from Fillmore Saturday, where he went to attend his sick father, but was too late to do any good as the old gentleman died before he arrived there.

Salt Lake Herald
October 25, 1895

Gabriel Huntsman, a prominent Democrat from Fillmore, was a Provo visitor today.

Salt Lake Herald
October 29, 1895

KING IN MILLARD.

The Eloquent Judge Making Democrats in His Old Home.

FILLMORE. Oct. 26.—Judge King of Provo began his campaign in Millard county on October 24 at Sciplo and Holden. On Friday night he spoke at Fillmore to a crowded house, and in two hours delivered one of the ablest addresses of his life. He spoke first on church and state, showing that they must be separated, and that union will only heap trouble on the people in the future. He spoke on silver and the tariff, showing that the Democratic party was most in favor of silver and the harm done the working men by a high tariff.

He showed plainly that Republican legislation brought on the hard times. The Republicans passed tariff bills and demonetized silver. He defied Republicans to show that such legislation had not brought hard times. He spoke of the qualifications of the men on both tickets, and showed the Democrats were by far the best for the offices.

Judge King goes to Meadow and Kanosh today. He is doing lots of good for the Democratic cause. The Democrats meet tonight to name a city ticket. Republicans will have a rally Monday night.

Provo Daily Enquirer
October 31, 1895

Big Three at Fillmore.

[Enquirer Correspondence.]

Fillmore, Millard County, Utah, Oct. 28, 95.—The "Big Three" and party left Kanosh this morning for Fillmore, they were met four miles out of town by a large delegation of Republicans from Fillmore in carriages, also by about 30 young ladies on horseback in uniform, and the brass and string band, all under the direction of John Hanson, marshal of the day.

The party was driven to Mrs. E. M. Collister's for dinner. When the party halted, Cannon was called for, responding with a short speech. The quartette was called for, responding with "onward marching"

The Democrats here are downcast, some blaming the church for interfering in political matters; others are cursing Boss Powers for the mess he has drawn the Democratic party into. The Democrats here concede the election of Orvil Thomson the Republican candidate to the Legislature. They also concede that the entire Republican state ticket will be elected, blaming Powers and the church for their defeat. Judge King, it is said, conceded that the Democracy were beaten. Mr. Thurman, has been here and tacitly admitted the same thing. The Republicans are jubilant and say they will carry the county by at least 250 majority.

At 7:30 p. m. a hugh torch light procession, was formed, headed by the brass band. They marched down the street to where the party was staying escorting the party to the Liberty Hall, which was packed to suffocation. Never in the history of Fillmore has such a monstrous political been held. The Republicans are to be congratulated upon the success of the whole day's proceedings. Hon. H. M. Wells and Hon. C. E. Allen were the speakers, Hon. F. J. Cannon leaving the party for Holden where he speaks tonight.

The young ladies' glee club, of Fillmore, the string band and the quartette furnished the music. The quartette received an ov.t on having to respond three times in succession.

SCARLL.

Salt Lake Herald
November 1, 1895

AS TO CHURCH INFLUENCE

How It Has Been Used by Apostle Francis M. Lyman.

In the address issued by the reconvened Democratic state convention, reference was made to the action of Apostle F. M. Lyman, a Republican, as an instance where church influence had been used in political affairs. Since then Mr. Lyman has published a card, denying in a general way, these charges. This put the Democratic party on its proof, and as a starter, two affidavits are published this morning.

The first is from J. F. Tolton, a man who has held many positions of trust, and whose veracity cannot be questioned. The gentleman is a member of the presidency of the Beaver stake conference.

J. F. TOLTON'S AFFIDAVIT.

The Proof Has Been Called for--- Here It Is.

In a Private Priesthood Meeting, This Apostle Advised People to Ally Themselves With the Republican Party—A Plain Statement From Alma Greenwood.

J. F. Tolton's Affidavit.

Mr. Tolton's affidavit is as follows:
Territory of Utah, County of Beaver—ss.
J. F. Tolton, of Beaver City, Beaver county, Utah, being first duly sworn, on oath says:
That on or about the twenty-second day of June A. D. 1891, he was present at a private and special priesthood meeting held in Beaver City, Utah, at which there were present Apostles F. M. Lyman and A. H. Cannon; also representatives of the stake presidencies of the following stakes, to-wit: Beaver, Panguitch, Kanab, Parowan and Millard.

That said meeting was called and presided over by said Lyman, ostensibly for the purpose of dictating in matters political. Said Lyman then and there stated that he had convened said meeting for the purpose of talking politics. He then inquired, addressing himself more particularly to M. L. Shepherd, "How is it that so many of you leading brethren in Beaver are Democrats?" He then resumed by saying: "This is not as it should be. The authorities desire that the people should divide themselves about equally between the two great national parties," and said it would be proper for some to remain independent or neutral "That the object in such a division is that we will then have more power in the nation, and get a more honest administration from the party in power. Each party will then cater to us more or less in order to secure control of the territory."

He further stated that it was desired that brethren who had not taken an active part in discussing politics or who had not openly declared themselves Democrats, should ally themselves with the Republican party.

Deponent further avers that while said Lyman was thus speaking, Apostle Cannon endeavored to check and restrain the speaker by saying: "Brother Lyman, don't go too far," and then placed his hands upon said Lyman by way of restraint.

J. F. TOLTON,

Subscribed and sworn to before me, this 29th day of October, A. D., 1895.
(Seal)   R. MAESER,
                                    Notary Public.
My commission expires July 21, 1896

From Alma Greenwood.

The second statement is from Alma Greenwood and tells its own story. It is as follows:

Oct. 28, 1895.

On the day that William King, father of Judge King, was buried at Fillmore, Utah, Apostle Francis M. Lyman called at my residence, Fillmore, Millard county, Utah. After some conversation he invited me to walk with him, which I did. We walked along Main street northward for some considerable distance. During the same Apostle Lyman conversed freely upon the political outlook and the prospects of obtaining statehood for Utah. Among other things he remarked: "Your brother, Joshua Greenwood, is a staunch Democrat, and it is only right that you should be a Republican, as it would hardly be fair for both of you to be on one side of the fence," continuing: "We will never get statehood unless we have more Republicans in Utah, and in fact Zion needs it.

(Signed)   "ALMA GREENWOOD."

Salt Lake Herald
November 5, 1895

A GENERAL STORM.

Weather Report, via the Deseret Telegraph Company,

American Fork—Cloudy; cold; raining.

Salina—Cloudy, wet; snowed some last night and this morning.

Manti—Snowed last night; cloudy; snowed some this morning.

Nephi—Been snowing this morning; rained all night; very wet.

Payson—Cold and windy; snowing this evening.

Provo—Raining nearly all day; snowing tonight.

Fillmore—Snowing hard.

Kanosh—Been snowing all afternoon.

Cedar City—Snow this morning; cold and cloudy.

Kanab—Heavy rain.

Beaver—Sleeting and snowing.

Ogden—Snowing and raining at intervals all day.

Franklin—Snowing; quite cold.

Paris—Snowing; inch and a half on ground.

Logan—Snowing at intervals all day.

Parowan—Snowing at intervals all the morning; very cold north wind; raining this evening.

Toquerville—Weather stormy, rainy and sun shining at intervals during the day.

Salt Lake Herald
November 19, 1895

Accidental Poisoning.

FILLMORE, Nov. 17.—At Hinckley ward, Millard county, on Saturday last, a 3-year-old daughter of A. A. Hinckley accidentally took strychnine and died in a very few hours afterwards, despite the utmost care. The father was in Fillmore at the time, and did not reach home until 5 p. m.

Salt Lake Herald
November 22, 1895

Utah Boy Honored.

Utah has been honored at the college of physicians and surgeons, Baltimore, Md., by the election of George E. Robison, of Provo, as president of the class graduating in 1899. Mr. Robison was born in Fillmore, Utah, where his parents now reside. He left Provo September 17 last to take a four years' course in medicine at the college above mentioned. His many friends are highly elated over the honor conferred upon him and Utah.

Salt Lake Herald
November 27, 1895

Frank Olson, of Fillmore, and Miss May Cluff of Coalville are to be married tomorrow. The bride is the daughter of W. W. Cluff of Coalville.

Provo Evening Dispatch
December 6, 1895

E. B. Bushnell, of Fillmore was arraigned last evening on an indictment charging perjury. He pleaded not guilty. He is accused of testifying in a trial at Fillmore of a suit entitled Almon Robison vs. Peter Greenhalgh et al that a payment of $500.00 was made on a note in 1889 when, in fact the payment was made in 1892.

Provo Daily Enquirer
December 9, 1895

A. E. Kilpatrick; of Fillmore, Cal., had the misfortune to have his leg caught between a cart and a stone and badly bruised. Ordinarly he would have been laid up for two or three weeks, but says: "After using one bottle of Chamberlain's Pain Balm I began to feel better, and in three days was entirely well. The peculiar soothing qualities which Chamberlain's Pain Balm possesses I have never noticed in any other liniment. I take pleasure in recommending it." This liniment is also of great value for rheumatism and lame back. For sale by Smoot Drug Co.

Deseret Evening News
December 10, 1895

CERTIFICATES OF ELECTION.

Issued by Secretary Richards to the Successful Candidates for Municipal Offices.

Great credit is due Secretary C. C. Richards and assistants for the expeditious manner in which they have handled the work of issuing certificates of election, to the municipal officers whose election the count which was finished last week shows. All have been issued and sent out to the victors, in good time for them to take upon themselves the incumbencies of their respective offices. There are seventeen parties effected by ties, and the secretary requests them to appear at his office on Saturday next at 11 a. m. and cast lots to determine the winner. In Wellsville, Cache county, five councilmen were to be elected, but the returns showed an election of only three, with a tie vote between three others. It now remains for these three to cast lots, and decide which two of them will get the places. Following is a list of the tie votes:

Sandy City—Charles Tripton and W. D. Kuhre, councilmen, 82 each.

Logan—Evan Jones and Peter Eliason, councilmen, Third ward, 81 each.

Hyrum — Earn J. William[?] and Hans H. Petersen, treasurer, 132 each.

Smithfield—James Meikle and William Thornley, councilmen, 119 each.

Wellsville—George Bankhead, David A. Kerr and Daniel T. Stuart, councilmen, 90 each.

Pleasant Grove—Alex Bullock and James O. Bullock, mayor, 113 each.

Fillmore—J. S. Giles and George C. Veile, justice of the peace, 110 each.

Morgan—George A. Taggart and William Robinson Jr., marshal, 63 each.

Salt Lake Herald
December 18, 1895

WEATHER REPORT.

Observer Smith's Review For the Month of November.

Temperature.—The average temperature for the state was 32.7 degrees; highest monthly mean, 42.2 degrees at St. George; lowest, 23.4 degrees at Soldier Summit. The highest temperature recorded was 75 degrees at Fillmore, on the 2nd, and the lowest, 24 degrees below zero at Koosharem on the 3rd, making the monthly range for the state, 99 degrees. The warmest days were the 1st, 2nd and 3rd, and the coldest, 22nd, 23rd, 24th, 25th and 26th.

Precipitation.—The average for the state was 1.47 inches, which is about normal. The greatest monthly amount, 2.44 inches, was recorded at Salt Lake City, and the least amount recorded, was 0.49 of an inch at Loa. The average snowfall for the month was 11 inches.

Weather.—Average number of clear days 12; partly cloudy, 7; cloudy, 10, and days on which one-hundredth of an inch or more rain fell, 5. There was 50 per cent of sunshine at Salt Lake City, and 66 per cent (estimated) at Grover, Wayne county, during the month.

Wind.—Prevailing direction southwest. The total movement at Salt Lake City was 2,512 miles, and the maximum velocity, 30 miles per hour from the south on the 3rd.

Miscellaneous phenomena.—Sun dogs, Levan, 24th; hail, Levan 4th, 12th; Moab, 4th; thunderstorms, Moab, 4th.

Salt Lake Herald
December 20, 1895

Marriage licenses were issued yesterday for Dewis Critchley, aged 21, of this city, and Ada Christopherson, aged 19, of Fillmore; William E. Gabbott, aged 25, and Ellen Snedaker, aged 24, both of this city; August Larson, aged 28, and Tillie Johnson, aged 18, both of Murray.

Salt Lake Herald
December 23, 1895

Albert Isra'sky, of San Francisco, aged 26, died at Fillmore, where he had gone for his health, on Saturday, of consumption. The body will be shipped to San Francisco by Undertaker Evans today.

Salt Lake Herald
January 5, 1896

At Fillmore.

(Special to The Herald.)

FILLMORE, Jan. 4.—The advent of Utah's admission into statehood was observed by a fitting demonstration by the patriotic people of Fillmore today. At 11 a. m. guns and cannon were fired, bells were rung, while a multitude of people surrounded the court house where short speeches were made by a number of leading citizens. National airs were rendered by the Fillmore brass band, and cheer after cheer given for the new state.

Salt Lake Herald
January 8, 1896

(Special to The Herald.)
FILLMORE, Jan. 7.—Between 2 and 3 o'clock this morning, Liberty hall, one of the largest public buildings in this city, used principally for dancing and other amusements, and owned by Rasmussen Bros., was burned to the ground. Not more than fifteen minutes had passed since the inaugural ball which was given in this hall had come to an end and the dancers had dispersed to their homes when the entire building was a mass of flames. People living near were aroused and soon the place was in a state of great excitement, as the fire was so intense and as there was no possible way of getting it under control. Fears were had that it would spread to Greenway's general merchandise store and to a saloon which was almost adjoining it and had it done this it was believed that nearly half of the town would have been endangered. As it happened there was no breeze from any direction and the buildings near by were saved, but only by the work of a bucket brigade of about fifty men. The building was erected about three years ago and cost near three thousand dollars. There was probably $1,200 insurance upon it. It is almost certain the fire was started by the explosion of a lamp, although many believe it to have been of incendiary origin.

Deseret Evening News
February 1, 1896

OBITUARY.

JOHN THOMAS ASHMAN,

Died at Fillmore, January 24th, 1896, John Thomas Ashman, son of Patriarch John Ashman and Ann his wife. Deceased was born at Woodhouse, near Leeds, Yorkshire, England, March 29, 1852, and came to Fillmore with his parents in 1864. He married at the age of seventeen years Elizabeth Steel, who has borne him eleven children, eight of whom—six boys and two girls, now mourn the loss of an indulgent father.

Brother Ashman was an energetic and valued citizen, and has been elected to many offices of trust, both municipal and county, all of which he filled with honor.

He had a lingering sickness (muscular rheumatism) and suffered with heroic fortitude for many months. All was done for him that science and loving friendship could suggest, until at last he knew that he must cross the span which separates this from a higher life. Then he called his family and friends around him, like unto one about to leave for a foreign mission; he counseled his sons as to their future course in life, and gave instructions to his friends about his temporal affairs, as one who had borrowed strength from beyond the veil; he even named those who should wash his body after death, then resignedly passed away.

There was a very large gathering at the funeral on Sunday the 26th. The long cortege was led by the Fillmore brass band playing appropriate music. The speakers chosen by the deceased were Elders Joshua Greenwood, James A. Melville and Bishop T. C. Callister, all of whom spoke of their long and honorable acquaintance with the dead, and gave lessons of counsel to the living. The Holden choir came over to do the singing, as the deceased, his mother, and sister and other relatives were members of our choir. The aged father is resigned, with the knowledge that his son is clothed with the Holy Priesthood in preceding him to the new field of labor.

A. Bird.

Salt Lake Herald
February 4, 1896

Daniel Funk, L. J. Clark and Dr. G. W. Shores have just completed a deal for an interest in a new mineral discovery in the mountains near Fillmore, in Millard county. The ore from the new discovery goes $13 in gold, 12 ounces silver and quite a large per cent. in copper, and the new purchasers think they have a bonanza in an embyrotic state.

Salt Lake Herald
February 9, 1896

Homestead entry 12066 by William Lambert, of Fillmore, for north one-half of northeast one-quarter and north one-half of northwest one-quarter of section 34 in township 20 south of range 5 west.

Homestead entry 12065 by George W.

Salt Lake Herald
February 29, 1896

LAND OFFICE.

The following entries were made in the land office yesterday:

Homestead entry No. 12105, by A. R. Nichols, of Fillmore, north half of northeast quarter, southeast quarter of northeast quarter and northeast quarter of southeast quarter of section 25, township 21 south, range 4 west.

Salt Lake Herald
March 5, 1896

Court at Fillmore.

(Special to The Herald.)

FILLMORE, Utah, March 4.—The business in Judge Higgins' court today was not characterized by anything of great moment.

The case of the State vs. F. Appleman was reset for trial for the 7th.

The People vs. E. B. Bushnell, for perjury, was dismissed on motion of the prosecution, on the ground that the evidence would not warrant a conviction.

Carlos Young and George Young were each arraigned on separate indictments and their cases were set for trial tomorrow.

The State vs. James Croasmer; set for the 5th.

In the case of the People vs. Virgil Barron, bonds in the sum of $750 were forfeited.

Samuel A. King was employed by the county today to assist in the prosecution of criminal cases, and it is expected that matters criminally will be pushed with vigor.

Judge Higgins, in the cases against the Youngs, held that defendants must set out in their affidavit the names of the witnesses desired and a brief statement of what they would swear to if present, so that the expense of unnecessary witnesses could be avoided.

COURT AT FILLMORE.

A Sheep Stealing Case Occupies Judge Higgins' Time.

(Special to The Herald).

FILLMORE. March 6.—In the Crossman rape case mentioned yesterday, the jury were out about fifteen minutes and returned a verdict of not guilty.

The state vs. Carlos and George Young, charged with stealing 19 sheep from James Hatton, of Petersburg. Samuel King and the county attorney for the prosecution, and O. H. Foster, with Greenwood & Melville, for the defense, has occupied the court all day. Foster tried to hinder progress upon plea of abatement, which was overruled. Then he demurred to the indictment. After about an hour's war of words and another adverse ruling by Judge Higgins, the defendants were ordered to stand up, but under instructions from their counsel refused to plead. The judge ordered a plea of not guilty to be entered and the case proceeded.

E. A. Mortensen, of Kanosh testified that the Youngs drove the sheep up to his place on the night of the 12th of April and asked if any one but his wife was in the house. Upon being told that no one else was there, he said he had got Hatton's sheep outside and his son was holding them there. He wanted Mortensen to get up and help to shear them. Mortensen refused to do this, but as Young was hungry he told him to go to the cupboard and help himself to food. Mrs. Mortensen corroborated her husband's statements in every particular. The sheep were driven into the hills east of Kanosh that night Alvin Penny and his wife testified to seeing the Youngs driving the sheep towards Mortensen's between 12 and 1 o'clock on the night of the 12th of April. James Paxton, of Kanosh, testified to buying 12 sheep of Carlos Young in July. William George, superintendent of the Kanosh co-op store, testified to buying wool from Young and Mortensen. There are a number of witnesses on both sides and the evidence is very conflicting. The defense is seeking to show that the case is one of conspiracy on the part of some of the prosecuting witnesses who have been engaged in a criminal combine, suddenly dissolved by a disagreement and a fight.

Died at Fillmore.

Mrs. Lewis P. Lund received a telegraph message on Friday, the 6 h, that her brother, Henry McArthur of Scipio, was dead, having expired March 5, 1896. Mrs. Lund took the first train to be present at his funeral which was held Saturday, and was largely attended, every mark of respect being shown the deceased. From a letter just received by Mr. Lund from his wife, the following particulars are learned of his death: Mr. McArthur was a member of the jury of the court being held at Fillmore; he complained of a heart ache and went to his hotel, took a dose of soda, hoping to get relief. He repaired to the barn, feeling sick at his s omarl, presumably to throw up. This was near dinner time. When called to his meal, not responding, search was made, and his lifeless body was found lying in a barn, apparently having died without a struggle.

Mr. McArthur was a brother of Pres. D. D. McArthur of St. George stake. Deceased became identified with the Mormon church at Kirtland. Ohio, and shared in common with his adopted people. He was a member of the famous Mormon Battalion and endured the arduous hardships of that expedition; he was overcome on the journey with fatigue and thirst, and left by the way side until some of his comrades procured water and returned to him with food and liquid.

Brother McArthur, after being disbanded in California, remained in that State until the summer of 1856, when he came to Utah and found his parents brothers and sisters at Pleasant Grove, after a separation of ten years. Mr. McArthur leaves a large family of children, his wife having died two years since.   X.

Pleasant Grove, March 9, 1896.

(Special to The Herald.)

FILLMORE, March 9.—In the Fifth judicial district court the case of the State vs. Carlos and George Young, charged with sheep stealing, occupied the court all day Saturday. At 9:30 on Sunday the court reconvened and Foreman Ed Stevens handed in a sealed verdict finding Carlos Young guilty as charged and his son George not guilty. At 8:30 today the prisoner was brought in for sentence. Defense sought an arrest of judgment, which was denied, as was also an application for a new trial. Judge Higgins gave him some good counsel, ostensibly with a view to redemption; then "Five years in the state prison!" fell upon his ear like a thunder clap and honest citizens breathed with new hopes.

Attorney Greenwood applied for letters of administration in the estate of John T. Ashman to Joseph G. Giles.

A similar application was made by Attorney Melville in the estate of George Croft.

Both cases were set for hearing on June 2, 1896.

Charles A. Thompson of Oasis was admitted to citizenship.

Court adjourned until June 2. Judge Higgins, Clerk Cook and Attorney Foster have gone to Beaver.

LET IT GO TO—DIXEY.

In a talk with Mr. A. H. Cannon, prominently connected with the company about to commence railroad building from this city in the direction of Deep Creek mining country and Los Angeles, California, published in yesterday's Herald, it was stated that the possible route of the line to Los Angeles would be to start from Lemington, on the Union Pacific, thence through nearly all the towns of Iron county and thence on to St. George. But this route is contingent upon the earnestness and effort of the people in the far south of Utah. In the event that they do not make the concessions and render what assistance to the enterprise they can, then the most likely route of the road will be over the Union Pacific south to Ploche, thence on to southern California, but with a branch road to Cedar City, in order to make use of the great deposits of coal and iron in the vicinity of that place.

This latter plan ought not to be thought of. It is of the utmost importance that this road be made to benefit southern Utah, and especially Utah's Dixey, the St. George country. If it starts south from Leamington it can easily be made to touch nearly all the settlements of Millard county—Oak City, Holden, Fillmore, Meadow and Kanosh; Minersville in Beaver county, thence on to Parowan, Cedar City, in Iron county; and so via Kanarra to St. George; thence to Los Angeles. We hope the people in that part of Utah will be alive to their own interests, to the development of the resources of that part of the state. We don't want to see our Dixey left off on one side, but have this trunk line go right through the line of settlements named, and to this end we urge the people down there to do everything that is reasonable to do in order to secure the advantages that this road will bring to them; and with reasonable concessions and proper effort we believe they can secure the road. Let the branch line run to Ploche, the main one through St. George.

Provo Daily Enquirer
March 16, 1896

CARLOS Young, convicted of sheep stealing on the 7th inst. at Fillmore, managed to get away from Sheriff Holbrook on Saturday night, and is still at large, and there is no trace of his whereabouts. The sheriff and a posse are still on the hunt.

Salt Lake Herald
March 27, 1896

LAND OFFICE.

The following entries were filed at the land office yesterday:

Homestead entry 12,156, by Charles H. Harding, of Taylorsville, for northwest quarter of section 12 in township 3 south of range 2 west, containing 160 acres.

Desert land entry 4,422 by Mary Ann Leigh, of Cedar City, for northwest quarter and south half of northeast quarter of section 24 in township 36 south of range 12 west, containing 240 acres.

Desert land entry 4,423 by Martha A. Snow Keate, of St. George, for southwest quarter of southeast quarter of section 19 in township 42, south of range 15 west, containing 40 acres.

Final homestead entry 8,921 by Henry Roof, of Fillmore, for lot 6 and northeast quarter of southeast quarter and north half of southeast quarter of section 11 in township 22 south of range 6 west.

Homestead entry 12,158 by Carl Albrechton, of Emery, for east half of southeast quarter and east half of northeast quarter of section 31 in township 22 south of range 6 east, containing 160 acres.

Salt Lake Herald
April 14, 1896

LAND OFFICE.

The following papers were filed in the land office yesterday:

Homestead 12,210 by John Starley of Fillmore, for north half of northwest quarter; southeast quarter of northwest quarter of section 26, and northeast quarter of northeast quarter of section 29, township 20 south, range 5 west, containing 160 acres.

Homestead 12,209 by Peter Beaugard, of Fillmore, for northwest quarter of northwest quarter of section 26, and southeast quarter of northwest quarter of section 27, township 20 south, range 5 west, containing 160 acres.

Provo Daily Enquirer
April 14, 1896

BOOK-KEEPER J. S. Peterson was laid to rest yesterday afternoon. The funeral took place at his residence in the First ward. He was one of the best book-keepers in his day, in the State, having worked for the First National Bank, Jennings & Co., Z. C. M. I, and other large institutions of Salt Lake. He was born in Copenhagen, 53 years ago, and came to Provo 25 years ago. About 10 years ago he came to Provo, and has worked here for S. S. Jones Co., J. W. Hoover and others. He was a well educated man, and leaves a wife and eight children. The speakers at the funeral were O. H. Berg, S. S. Jones, and I. W. Hinckley of Fillmore.

Salt Lake Herald
April 15, 1896

J. T. Ashman and Roy James, of Fillmore, were in the city yesterday on mining business. Mr. Ashman states that there is considerable activity just now at Antelope, a few miles east of Fillmore, and that nearly all of the desirable ground in that locality has been taken.

The Union
April 16, 1896

UTAH PUMICE STONE

The News correspondent at Fillmore, Millard county—"A Bird"— sends the following under date of the 6th inst.:

It may interest some of your readers to know that President Quigley of the Chicago Pumice company, a large concern owning a $300,000 plant in that city, has made arrangements with Mr. Joseph E. Ray (the discoverer of vast beds of pumice stone near Coyote Springs, this county) whereby that gentleman expects to ship to Chicago 3.000 tons of pumice this year. A number of hands are now engaged getting it ready for shipment and Mr. Ray has assurance that a like amount or more will be shipped yearly for an indefinite period.

Mr. Ray gave this information just as he was starting out to inspect the Marysvale reservoir, previous to a meeting of the company to be held in Salt Lake City on the 12th. The reservoir is a success, and the different irrigation companies in Sevier Vally are already competing for the use of its water. Irrigation water is becoming a serious question right here also, as very little snow is in the mountains and the days are warm. Frost has killed the apricots, but other fruit is safe as yet.— Deseret Evening News.

The Union
April 17, 1896

FIRE AT FILLMORE.

FILLMORE, Utah, April 7th, 7:15 p. m.—Between 12 and 1 o'clock last night a fire broke out in and consumed Day's dance hall and confectionery store. Nothing was saved. Mr. Day was at Kanosh. Loss is $1,500, insurance $800 in the Hartford Connecticut.

The fire caught and licked up a new lumber building to Mrs. Levi Warner, which the lady had occupied only two days; loss $200, no insurance.

The butcher's shop belonging to the People's store was damaged $100, covered by insurance.—*Desert News.*

Salt Lake Herald
May 26, 1896

FEDERAL COURTS.

List of Old Cases Dismissed—Other Business.

Judge Marshall, having formulated the rules of the United States circuit and district courts governing the practice therein, handed them to Clerk Letcher, with the direction that they be spread upon the records. They will take effect from yesterday. The rules were entitled in the circuit court, but, so far as applicable, apply to the district court as well.

Joseph S. Giles of Fillmore, Millard county, was appointed a commissioner of the circuit court of the United States.

Samuel H. Lewis of Salt Lake City was appointed master in chancery and examiner of the circuit court.

On motion of Mr. J. W. Judd, Mr. E. D. R. Thompson was admitted as an attorney in both courts, and took the required oath.

METROPOLITAN FILLMORE.

A Prize Ring Set to, Bicycle Track and Other Evidences of Progress.

FILLMORE, Millard Co., May 23, 1896.—There are many persons scattered abroad who remember and frequently inquire after the welfare and progress of this the ancient capital of Utah; and some of these will be surprised to learn of our efforts to keep in touch with the popular march of modern civilization. We cannot point to anything to induce a boom in real estate, or invite the penniless home-seeker to drop down in a land flowing with milk and honey. Yet there are evidences that we still possess the metropolitan instinct, and put on airs to attract notice, and keep step in the march of progress. The old State house is now surrounded by a bicycle track. I enclose clipping from a local paper describing the same:

The wheel craze has struck Fillmore with cyclone force. A track is being made on the public square where the cyclists in the future expect to break all possible records. The track is to be made of dirt with a top layer of thick dust, excepting in stormy weather, when mud will be the sticking feature. The cyclists organized a club and agreed to assess each person owning or riding a wheel one ounce of castor oil to rub on skinned noses and sore joints.

Then we have people who think that the fastest mare ever raised in the state is owned here, and they are ready to back her against anything that "wears hair" to the extent of their limited "pile." You see we are strictly in the modern run of things.

But the latest and most unlooked for innovation is the introduction of the prize ring, regularly advertised. Your correspondent witnessed this grand exhibition today, and as such like affairs are considered of sufficient importance for the Associated Press to dish up for the nation's breakfast every morning, and as few of the NEWS readers have ever seen a show of the kind, I will try to give them an idea of its nature. This was a licensed show; the city charged two whole silver dollars for the privilege, and it took place one block south of the court house on a lot east of the old Giles place on

...east of the old circus place on Main street. Here a frail stockade was formed of small poles and dilapidated wagon covers, which a stiff breeze frequently brought down, rendering the application of twine and baling necessary to hold the flappy walls in place. The whole affair looked like the abandoned remnants of a tornado-stricken circus tent. High up on derricks were boys perched, getting a free sight at what was going on inside the walled arena; and high up in an apple tree the crowd discovered a rich man perched, and cheered him. William smiled like a fledgling crow at his vantage over the fifty cent crowd below.

Inside the ducking walls are seats of planks and boxes to accommodate the patrons, among whom are a few ladies. In the center is a twenty-foot ring, composed of four stakes and two strands of rope. Time-keepers, referee and two seconds are announced for each participant in the big event. The band plays and two local aspirants to fistic fame step into the ring and are instructed in the etiquette of nose pounding. Then they attempt its actual accomplishment with varying success for fifteen minutes and retire. Then the announcement is made that two of the great men's seconds will give a display of the manly art, which was about as artistic as would be the gambols of a giraffe and hippopotamus. The crowd shouted "get out," and they did so.

Next the great event was announced; and shortly the "Boston Kid," as he calls himself, tripped over the ropes and did honor to the city of "Colchaw" by a graceful bow to the ladies. He was a dandy, in black hose and black silk trunks, a drab undershirt trimmed with pink ribbon and rosettes, and a wide pink belt which was well padded. He looked more like a trapeze performer than a gladiator, and weighed 140 pounds. McKinney was helping fix up the wagon covers, but shortly stepped into the arena in blue trunks, black stockings, a red belt and undershirt. He recently came here from Kansas, and the contrast between the two men was marked—McKinney weighs 190 pounds. It looked like a bantam rooster and a turkey gobbler in a war for dunghill control.

The men took their seats on a chair in their respective corners, after tossing for choice; then it was amusing to see their respective seconds gravely anoint them with what looked like alcohol and vinegar, place a towel over their shoulders, and we all grinned our admiration until time was called. Both then stepped to the middle of the ring, touched their 8-ounce mittens together,

... stepped back and began to saw the air with their arms, Boston on the outside of the ring and Kansas following around, pretending to want to hit each other but not meaning to. McKinney accidentally hit the æsthetic youth on the mouth which nearly "sent him to grass," then they slapped each other with the gloves until time was called, three minutes. They retired to the corner for one minute, to be salved again on the nose, chin and arms. The seconds did this with all the gravity and bustle of a city shoeblack, until time was called, when they met and circled all as before, sparring and dancing the time away. That McKinney did not intend to hurt the athenian youth was apparent, as he did not close his hand, but dabbed at him with the open mitten.

This continued for a round or two, and the smart easterner, seeing a chance, landed a straight one on McKinney's forehead and strewed the "prairie flower" upon the grass. "First knock down" and a spot of blood on McKinney's lip gave the bantam two points and cheers. The big fellow arose with a cloud upon the seat of his blue trunks, which boded a storm in Boston; and in the eighth round the cyclone came and the silk and pink went through the ropes. The time-keeper counted ten (seconds), the Bean-eater opened one eye with a melancholy twinkle and was glad to see himself out. Nobody hurt, nor was it ever intended there should be. The result could be foreseen as well as that of a collision between a pleasure yacht and battering ram. McKinney is 22 years old, a Hercules in physical form, and could have done the "knock out" at any moment he desired. But the people wanted to be humbugged, and they were. The whole business was a fake exhibition of licensed brutality, got up for the gate money, which fell far short of anticipation. Its tendency is coarse and immoral, appealing to the animal in masculine youth, flattering to brutes with brawn, and a blight upon the beautiful and refined in human life. Give it no welcome or license in country towns.

A. Bird.

Salt Lake Herald
June 10, 1896

Advices from Fillmore state that the store of George Greenway was entered on the night of June 7 and $150 abstracted from the safe. Three young men, Will Aldrich, Todd Ashmore and Frank O'Neill are in jail charged with the crime. It is said Frank Merrill, a clerk in the store, gave the keys of the store to Aldrich who, after he had gotten the money refused to divide up and the others peached.

Provo Daily Enquirer
June 11, 1896

S. A. KING is back from Fillmore where he attended Judge Higgins' court. He says members of the bar speak in very complimentary terms of his Honor. He is a man of good moral character and high integrity. The people of Fillmore gave him a public reception Tuesday evening at the residence of J. V. Robinson. Judge Higgins opens court at Nephi next Monday.

Salt Lake Herald
June 22, 1896

Bitten By a Rattler.

"Joe" S. Smith, while logging at the sawmill Friday was bitten by a rattlesnake. He was in the act of picking up a spike between two logs when the snake struck him; not getting its fangs in deep enough, it struck at him a second time, but Joe was too quick for his snakeship, and got out of its way. His hand immediately swelled to an enormous size and turned black, but with the assistance of mud and other remedies the poison was drawn out and nothing serious resulted from the bite.—Fillmore Progress.

Deseret Evening News
June 22, 1896

FILLMORE ITEMS.

A Thrilling Canyon Runaway—Mining
Property Bonded.

FILLMORE CITY, Utah,
June 20, 1896.

To the Editor:

Quite an exciting runaway occurred here yesterday, the 19th. Mr. Joseph Payne needed some new bows in his hay rack, and accompanied by his wife (who was ailing, and thought the trip to the canyon would do her good) and also Judge Greenwood, his wife and two children, they went to where the timber grew to enjoy a quiet outing. About a mile and a half from town the horses were tied to a sapling, and the passengers scattered. Mrs. Greenwood, her mother and the two children returned to the wagon first, and got on the hay rack in the shade. Shortly after something started the horses, and they broke loose and started just as Mr. Greenwood was approaching them. His efforts to catch them failed and his wife and babe jumped, receiving bruises and torn clothes; Mrs. Payne clung to the wagon and a little three year old girl, as the horses sped down the canyon. Nearing town Mrs. P., knowing of a deep ditch to cross, dropped the little girl to the ground, and she escaped without serious injury. The lady still clung to the wagon until it came uncoupled, when she was thrown to the ground, bruised and shaken almost to death.

Dr. Kean being called pronounced one rib fractured. Judge Greenwood lost his hat in the chase and had a frantic wife and babe upon his hands, she expecting to find her child and mother dashed to death. She now calls it a miracle, in answer to her prayer, and she broke down in relating the occurrence to your correspondent.

Mr. Kirby of the Bullion Beck mine made our county a visit this week to inspect some mining property, about fifteen or twenty miles southwest from Kanosh, the property of Charley Jukes, his brother John, and Gus Howlet. The inspection appears to have been satisfactory, and Mr. Kirby has a $10,000 option on the property, upon which the boys have done a large amount of work and exposed large bodies of low grade ore, which, with favorable railroad rates, can be developed by its new owners.

A. B.

Salt Lake Herald
June 30, 1896

LIST OF COUNTY QUEENS.

Sarah Dowding, Sandy, Salt Lake county; Georgia Warburton, Tooele, Tooele county; Clara Kirkman, Richfield, Sevier county; Sarah Bowen, Logan, Cache county; Winnie Smith, Beaver, Beaver county; Annie Sorrenson, Nephi, Juab county; Fannie Bone, Kaysville, Davis county; Annie Stewart, Moab, Grand county; Amelia Hammond, Monticello, San Juan county; Florence Kimball, Scofield, Carbon county; Ada Wood, Cedar City, Iron county; Emma Hatch, Heber, Wasatch county; Octavia Cheney, Randolph, Rich county; Mrs. W. H. Olsten, Manti, Sanpete county; Fannie West, Brigham City, Box Elder county; Angie Callister, Fillmore, Millard county.

Provo Daily News
July 9, 1896

Warrant for J. B. Rawlings.

FILLMORE, Utah, July 8.—Tribune Special—It has just leaked out that a warrant has been placed in the hands of Sheriff Holbrook for the arrest of J. B. Rawlings, ex-mine inspector of Utah, for obtaining money under false pretenses.

Last August the ex-mine inspector was down here and is said to have passed a worthless check to Almon Robison for $10.

Mr. Robison sent the check to the bank ot Salt Lake, but it was returned with the words "no funds." Since then Mr. Robison has made other efforts to collect the amount but failed, so he placed the matter in the hands of the officers, who are now trying to locate Rawlings.

Salt Lake Herald
July 14, 1896

(Special to The Herald.)

FILLMORE, Utah, July 13—The biggest flood in the history of Millard county visited Fillmore today at about 5:15 p. m.

Boys came down from the mouth of the canyon, crying as they ran through town that a flood was coming, and besides the warning given in that way the people could smell the destructive flood as it ground immense rocks together, uprooting trees and carrying everything in its path.

All along the bottom lands for about one mile in width the flood destroyed every vestige of grain, lucern and garden truck.

Stables and outhouses were washed away and in some of them were horses and cows, which were also destroyed. At 6.15 the flood began to recede. Hundreds of cords of driftwood is scattered along the path of the flood in the streets, in doorways and other places. The damage done cannot yet be estimated, but will run well up into the thousands. At this writing it is not known whether any lives were lost or not.

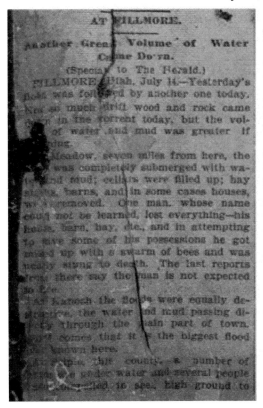

AT FILLMORE.

Another Great Volume of Water Came Down.

(Special to The Herald.)

FILLMORE, Utah, July 14.—Yesterday's flood was followed by another one today. Not so much drift wood and rock came down in the torrent today, but the volume of water and mud was greater if anything.

At Meadow, seven miles from here, the town was completely submerged with water and mud; cellars were filled up; hay stacks, barns, and in some cases houses, were removed. One man, whose name could not be learned, lost everything—his house, barn, hay, etc., and in attempting to save some of his possessions he got mixed up with a swarm of bees and was nearly stung to death. The last reports from there say the man is not expected to live.

At Kanosh the floods were equally destructive, the water and mud passing directly through the main part of town. Report comes that it is the biggest flood ever known here.

At Scipio, this county, a number of homes are under water and several people were compelled to seek high ground to save their lives. Here in Fillmore all who live in the lower part of town are moving out and in order to do so they are compelled to go through water and mud from three to four feet deep. The loss throughout the county is estimated at not less than $75,000 to $100,000. A vast scope of country, with growing crops, is under water and the water is still coming in great torrents. The people here are expecting another rush this evening, as it is still raining. Three saw mills have been washed away—one belonging to Joseph Hanson, one to John Jackson, another to Levi Warner, besides all the necessary implements for running the same. The mills were all situated in the canyons east of Fillmore. The poor farmers and stock raisers are, as usual, the greatest sufferers, and the loss in some cases includes their all. These floods are becoming a yearly menace, and the people are loud in their condemnation of the sheep, which they say is the principal cause. They have eaten up the grass, destroyed vegetation in the mountains, leaving nothing to retain the moisture as it falls, and the rain runs off as fast as it would from a duck's back.

Fillmore Again Flooded.

FILLMORE, Utah, July 14.—[Tribune Special.]—The disastrous effects of yesterday's flood have been augmented today by another of equal dimensions. A much larger body of water came down from the mountains today between 3 and 5 o,clock than that which caused such consternation here yesterday, but owing to the torrent being comparatively free from timber and debris and the channels being cut wider and brides, dams and other obstructions being all removed, the waters swept more rapidly down, without much additional destruction of property.

Many homes have been vacated, houses and lots being filled several feet with mud and water.

Two sawmills are known to be entirely destroyed—Warner's a water-power mill, and the Hanson Bros.', a fine steam sawmill, are swept away, and the third, a steam sawmill, owned by John Jackson, is very much damaged.

There is considerable feeling here regarding the petted sheep industry, and it is charged that it is responsible for much of the damage caused by recent floods. The whole country being almost entirely denuded of vegetation and every hillside mapped with beaten trails, afford, it is claimed, a ready passage for water to the lower channels, when previous to the advent of sheep it was retarded by vegetation and absorbed and retained in the soil. The smell attending the first rush of the water easily suggested that sheep were in it.

If all reports are true that we hear from Meadow, Kanosh and Scipio, the aggregate of damage will be enormous and some suffering may be experienced.

Very little rain fell in the valley here yesterday, but a heavy downpour has occurred today, which will in some measure compensate for the loss occasioned by the floods.

SEARCH THE MOUNTAINS.

Peter Huntsman of Fillmore Not Heard from Since Monday's Storm.

Another Account of the Great Flood Which struck Fillmore on Monday Last.

FILLMORE CITY, Utah,
July 15th, 1896.

To the Editor:

A party of men is going out now to try to find Peter Huntsman, who was in the mountains and has not been heard from since Monday.

FILLMORE, July 14th, 1896.—Yesterday about 5 o'clock p. m. excited men on horseback were seen galloping in many directions warning the people of this city that a flood was coming down the canyon and a terrible stench and a roar told told of its near approach. Few people thought it could be but a small affair until the unusual noise dispelled the thought, when hundreds of people repaired to the Chalk creek banks to watch its approach.

This was a sight not easily to be forgotten. The mighty torrent had little the appearance of water for in its precipitous career down the steep canyon it had torn the black and red soil from the creek banks and, mixing them to a consistency of thick mud and bearing on its bosom uprooted trees and saw logs with debris everywhere, it looked as though the mountains above had spewed forth a world of undigested matter to stifle and destroy everything below. Large trees were tossed high to dash against every dam and bridge that offered an impediment.

In looking over the ground this morning the potent evidences that a calamity has befallen our city are before us. Many homes that yesterday were surrounded with everything to make the heart glad with prospective harvest are now standing in a sea of mud from one to two feet deep. From the Rock bridge on Main street to the last house on the north, about a half a mile away, teams have to wade knee deep in a slimy mass of thick mud. The homes of Lucean Noyes, Dr. Kees, George Greenway, Ed. Hibbiman, Albert Smiler, John Kelly, Mrs. Jesse Huntsman, William Beaston, Tod Ashman, Charley Christopherson, Riley Huntsman, the old Bartholomew place, and many others are damaged from one to many hundreds of dollars. Grain and gardens are destroyed from the top city waters to the fields miles below. The creamery is surrounded with mud and debris, and inside the two lower shelves filled with cheese are buried in the same filth. Hogs, chickens and some cattle were seen to

go down the stream. Three wagons
and several sets of harness are known
to be lost, also a road cart belonging to
John Kelly. The wagons and harness
belonged to saw mill hands working in
the mountains.

Frank Russell, just down from the
Hansen Brothers saw mill, tell me
that not a vestige of it is left in place
and only the smoke stack was seen by
the owners, the belt was found today
in the field twelve miles from the mill
site; 30,000 feet of lumber was swept
from this mill.

The Warner (water power) saw mill
is also cleaned out. The road is gone
and the hands, men and women, have
made new trails to get down home as
best they could.

John Jackson, another steam saw
mill owner with a force at work, has
not been heard from but we hope for
the best.

This is the worst flood ever known
here and estimates of damage run from
$20,000 to $30,000.

Meadow is suffering from a similar
disaster, and Kanosh is damaged to
some extent.

Several frightened and bedraggled
women and children have just got to
town on foot having had a night of experience never to be forgotten. They
report the remains of the Hansen
steam engine to be a mile above town.

Hon. F. M. Lyman was an eye witness of yesterday's disaster.

Dick Russell reports hail stones falling near the saw mill as big as his fist.

Another large torrent of water is
rushing down the creek this afternoon,
equal to that of yesterday but it is
more free from timber and debris, consequently will not do as much damage.

We can stand on Main street and
see the water rushing down the mountain sides four miles south. It will go
down the old Pine creek channel to
President I. N. Hinckley's farm.

A. BIRD.

A METHOD TO AVERT DROUTH.

Our method of averting drouth, says
a writer in the American Agriculturist,
is to first plow eight inches deep with
an ordinary 14-inch plow, following this
with a subsoil plow running in the same
furrow and loosening the soil to a
depth of eight inches or more, but
throwing none of it on the surface. This
gives us a reservoir sixteen inches deep
to catch and retain all the moisture
which falls, and we are convinced during the twenty-three years we have resided in Fillmore county that there has
never been a season when the rainfall
was not sufficient to fill this reservoir
before the growing season commenced.
We harrow each evening all the land
plowed during the day. This breaks
up the clogs before they become hard-
ened and prevents drying by evapora-
tion. Before planting we again harrow and pulverize the surface with
a "float." Plant three or four inches
deep, following the planter with a harrow. Practice shallow cultivation, running the cultivator just deep enough
to destroy weeds and break the surface
soil. We cultivate the ground just as
soon after a rain as the condition of the
soil will permit. If the rain is a heavy
one, the soil is firmly packed. It is of
the utmost importance that the crust be
broken as soon as possible, in order to

... as soon as possible, in order to retain the moisture in the soil, the loose upper layer acting as a mulch. We find that it is not necessary to subsoil each season. Once every three years will answer all practical puruposes. If the field is subsoiled and planted to corn the first or the second year, then followed by oats or wheat, the results will be satisfactory, though a slight falling off will be noticed in the third crop after subsoiling.

As to results, land subsoiled in the fall of 1892 and planted to corn the next spring, yielded 75 bushels per acre. Other land not subsoiled, but otherwise treated in identically the same manner, yielded about 35 bushels. In 1893 potatoes on the subsoiled soil produced 125 bushels to the acre. The crop on unsubsoiled land was practically a failure. Last year rye yielded thirty and one-half bushels on subsoiled and on not subsoiled two and one-half. Oats on corn ground one year from subsoiling, forty-four and one-third bushels, two years from subsoiling thirty-nine and one-quarter bushels, not subsoiled seventeen bushels. We are convinced that if there is a fair amount of moisture in the soil hot winds are not necessarily fatal to the corn crop.

Salt Lake Herald
July 28, 1896

FILLMORE

suffered greater loss than any of the towns before named. A flood down the canyon took three saw mills and left the fourth so washed around that no one could get to it. It is a wonder that nobody was hurt, for several families were living near the mills, but all escaped.

Salt Lake Herald
July 30, 1896

PAYSON EXCITED.

Two Couple of Alleged Sinners Are Now on Trial.

PAYSON, Utah, July 29.—Our quiet city has been in a fomentation of excitement for the past few days over a case of lasciviousness.

William Potter and Maurice Potter, brothers, with Miss Lillie Webb from Goshen and Miss Cyntha Fillmore of this place, are the defendants. They were apprehended in the night time, or early morning hours, and taken in custody by Marshal F. M. Ballard. The investigation is still going on.

A great deal of damage was done here to the farms by the last heavy rain storms, and the loss will prove more serious than was at first supposed.

The city hall is being provided with a neat structure on top for a belfry. The new bell lately purchased by the city is placed in position and was rung on July 24 the first time. The tower will improve the city building.

Bishop Page is rustling to complete the Second ward meeting house so as to make it possible for it to be used next winter. Every effort is being made.

The "Hell Hole."

Millard county has a number of curiosities in the way of petrifications, old craters, hot and cold springs and caves.

Last spring I had the opportunity of exploring one of the latter, and have been asked to describe it.

It is known as the "Hell Hole," or the Old Spanish mine, and is located east of the Saw Tooth mountains, in the western part of the county, about three miles south of the Margin Pass road, and perhaps a mile from the foot-hills. It is a large hole in a gently sloping plain, with no brush, stones or any other natural marks by which to distinguish the place, and it is not easily found. The hole cannot be seen more than 100 yards. We drove quite close to it before we knew we had found the place we were looking for. As we came near and looked in, one of the party pronounced it the "Hell Hole," and I thought it very well named. It has a very treacherous appearance.

We had brought a cable and tackle and we rigged it to let a man down the middle of the shaft to avoid falling rocks. None of us cared to go down, so it fell to me, being the lightest, to make the descent. I took notes and measurements that show it to be 62 feet in diameter at the top. For 20 feet below the surface the formation is coarse gravel, cemented together by lime. The sides slope in, so that at this depth the diameter is 50 feet. Here the formation changes. A little more sand and clay, and less lime with the gravel, making the earth looser, so the sides slope out for the next 40 feet, making the diameter at 60 feet below the surface 60 feet. Here is black sand and gravel for about 10 feet. Immediately under this, very fine black and yellow sand, with some clay. Here the debris falling from the sides and the sand caving from the west side have formed a mound, filling the original shaft, and leaving another space to the west. One can climb or roll (as he wishes) from here to the end of the cave.

When at the bottom one can see the sky over about fifteen feet of the surface edge of the hole. Here one is 24 feet west of a line let fall from the west side, and 35 feet below the base of the east wall, making the perpendicular depth 112 feet.

There is quite a romantic story told by those who think it is the Old Spanish mine. Years ago, when Fillmore was young, the Mexicans used to come in from the west at regular intervals with gold dust to buy provisions.

There is an old Indian now living near Fillmore who has told of a pool of water on the south of Saw Tooth, where the Mexicans brought the gold to wash. They packed it in every day from the north on burros. These Mexicans finally stole a squaw off the Indians, for which they either killed or drove off all the Mexicans, and none ever came back.

The Indians do not know where the mine is, but believe it was less than a day's drive north of the pool. There are no water drains into the hole, and its origin is still a mystery.

Our party, consisting of Peter Huntsman, August Meyers and myself, were looking for the "shining metal" and had "prospectors' luck." The best samples, when tested, showed "a trace of gold."—Millard Progress.

BOARD OF EDUCATION

Annual Meeting of the Members Held Last Evening.

OFFICERS MAKE REPORT

RECEIPTS AND DISBURSEMENTS AS SHOWN BY THE CLERK.

Finance Committee Makes an Estimate for the Coming Year—Buildings and Grounds Committee—Teachers Committee Makes a Good Report—Routine Business of Last Night—Contractors' Agreements Ratified—Other Business of the Board—Adjourned for Two Weeks.

The annual meeting of the board of education was held last evening at which the president, clerk and chairmen of the various committees made their reports for the school year ending June 30, 1896.

These reports cover all the subjects relating to government of the schools of this city in a very exhaustive and comprehensive manner, and so complete are they that were they printed in their entirety they would fill a page of this issue. As it is, with the exception of the report of President Dooly, which is given in full in another column, they are summarized.

CLERK'S REPORT.

Clerk Moreton submitted the following report:

"In accordance with the requirements of school law and your honorable body, I have the honor to submit the following, my sixth annual report of the receipts and disbursements of the board of education of Salt Lake city for the year ending June 30, 1896:

RECEIPTS.

City school tax 1895 maintenance	$148,152 95
City school tax 1895, interest	41,250 00
City school tax 1895, sinking fund	16,500 00
City school tax 1893-4, redemptions	2...
County school tax 1895	50,261 99
Territorial apportionment	41,151 20
Seventeenth ward Ecc. Assc'n	2,730 00
Miscellaneous	78 60
Furniture sold	282 25
Tuition received	29 00
Rents	89 50
Books and school supplies	69 60
On hand July 1, 1895	7,518 60

Total $310,241 51
By warrant issued for the purchase of bonds as an investment of the sinking fund returned cancelled 10,000 00

Total $320,241 51

DISBURSEMENTS.

Teachers' salaries	$146,000 76
Janitors' salaries	13,231 50
Janitors' supplies	1,532 90
Fuel and lights	6,096 23
Maintenance and repairs	12,097 43
Rents	5,078 50
Books and supplies	8,029 14
General expense	14,370 03
Interest on overdraft	612 21
Furniture	1,440 85
Buildings	144 50
Suspense account	139 20

Total $208,462 25
Interest on bonds 41,285 62
Sinking fund investment—
Bonds Salt Lake school district redeemed 51 to 70 inclusive series 2 denomination $1,000........$20,000 00
Premium paid 581 00
Bonds of Salt Lake city purchased for investment No's 101 and 122 to 140 both inclusive $20,000 00
Premium paid 400 00
Accrued interest 141 67 $41,122 67
Treasurer for warrant unpaid .. 10,000 00

Total $300,870 54
Balance July 1, 1896................ 1... ...

Total $320,241 51

FINANCE REPORT.

The report of the finance committee as to receipts and disbursements is identical with that of the clerk. The committee adds:

"For the school year 1896-7 the following estimate is submitted:

ESTIMATED REVENUE.

State apportionment 1896..........$ 40,000 00
County school tax 1896.............. 50,000 00
City school tax 1896 for mainten-
ance 160,000 00

Total for maintenance...........$250,000 00
City school tax 1896 interest on
bonds 40,250 00
City school tax 1896 sinking fund. 16,100 00

Total revenue $306,350 00

ESTIMATED EXPENDITURES.

Teachers' salaries $165,000 00
Janitors salaries 14,000 00
Janitors' supplies 2,000 00
Fuel and lights 7,500 00
Maintenance and repairs.......... 25,000 00
Rents 6,000 00
Books and supplies 13,000 00
General expense 15,600 00
Furniture 2,000 00

Estimate for maintenance......$250,000 00
Interest on bonds 40,250 00
Sinking fund 16,100 00

Total expense $306,350 00

ASSETS.

Cash (treasurer) ....$ 19,822 82
Furniture 47,485 25
Real estate and buildings.......... 907,931 09
Sewer tax 3,799 30
Water scrip 1,429 40
Building fund 13,484 01
Bonds of Salt Lake city............ 20,000 00
Premium on bonds bought........ 981 00
Accrued interest 141 67

Total $1,015,084 54

LIABILITIES.

School fund ....$ 13,484 01
Suspense account 6,631 22
Sinking fund 21,877 32
Sinking fund investments........ 41,122 67
Warrants 461 85
Bonds 805,000 00
Income account 126,507 45

Total $1,015,084 54

BUILDINGS AND GROUNDS.

The report of this committee cites that no new buildings have been erected this year although the need of two or three is urgent. The Tenth and Eighteenth wards need new buildings, but the law will not admit of a levy for the purpose, but contains provisions restricting the use of funds to taxes and repairs.

The new school law made a provision for a levy of this kind but not containing an emergency clause, this same did not go into effect until it was too late to make a levy.

In the Tenth ward a building is needed very badly and ere another year it is to be hoped this board will be able to construct one. The president in his report covers all the essential points in this one.

TEACHERS AND SCHOOL WORK.

This committee announces that the work in the schools continues to improve and their efficiency increases, and it is with great satisfaction that the committee recognizes they take rank among the best in the nation.

The committee notes the increase of 64 children over the number last year, making a total of 12,604.

The cost of text books and supplies per capita of children enrolled was 74½ cents.

The cost of maintenance of schools during the year was $19.19.

The committee calls attention to the need of a high school and cites that during the year 221 students were admitted, making a total of 458. From indications it would appear that by September there will be a total attendance of about 690.

The corps of teachers is 227, of which 184 have been re-employed, 23 new teachers engaged and 20 vacancies remain to be filled, the average salary being $515 per annum, which the committee believe is as low as it can be placed.

The average age of beginners is 6 years and 10 months; of eighth grade graduates 15 years and 5 months; of high school graduates 18 years and 6 months.

The committee suggests the curtailing of years of study so as to advance by one year the time of entrance into the high school and suggests a commission of eleven members, of which the superintendent, the principal of the high school, one principal of grade schools, be appointed to make a report on this matter.

The committee closed its report by

commending the work of the superintendent.

COMMUNICATIONS.

The city council sent in notice of the action of Tuesday evening relating to the sewers of the Sumner and Franklin schools, and on motion of Mr. Westerfield the expense was authorized.

The board of regents' action on the matter of training school was communicated by Prof. Talmage, and the buildings and grounds committee appointed to furnish the rooms in the building occupied by the school for the deaf; also so to furnish the Sumner and Franklin schools.

Grace Robertson, Chehalea Walsh, W. J. Dean and Cora Truitt of this city; R. H. Hough of Shwab, Tenn.; Sarah M. Gillett, Winifred Whitehead and Claire Whitehead of this city; Viola Kelly of Fillmore, Utah; A. F. Senter of Salma, Kan.; Nettie Treadwell, Ann Arbor, Mich.; Blanche Atherton, Carson, Nev.; Louise Rose, Yonkers, N. Y., and Grace Stevenson, of Butte, applied for positions as teachers.

ROUTINE WORK.

The committee on supplies was authorized to ask for bids for supplies for schools.

Contracts for furnishing certain changes and improvements in the Franklin and Sumner schools were read and awarded as follows:

C. J. Brain, annex to Franklin......$ 3,527
C. J. Brain, annex to Sumner........ 3,893
Midgley Bros., plumbing Franklin.. 2,488
Midgley Bros., plumbing Sumner... 2,276
P. J. Moran, heating Franklin...... 4,547
P. J. Moran, heating Sumner........ 4,547
_____
Total $21,278

The buildings and grounds committee was authorized to sell the old furnace and furniture at the Franklin school.

John Reynolds was appointed temporary janitor at the Thirteenth school at $8 per month; James Lee, high school, $10 per month; C. J. Larsen at the Richards building at $10 per month; Mr. Hollister at the Emerson, vice F. Groves, at $12.50 per month, during vacation.

Miss Harriet M. Goodrich, Miss Bertha J. Curtis, Mrs. Mattie B. Prosser and Miss Bessie M. Eurgins were granted leave of absence during the school year 1896-7 as per request.

____ per request.

Chas. Erickson was promoted from janitor of the Bryant school to that of storekeeper, at a salary of $70 per month.

The committee on teachers and school supplies reported that Parsons, Derge & Co. could not furnish Faber pencils at the bid submitted; that the Lambert Paper company could not furnish paper at price quoted, $102, but would furnish the same at $172.50; that Geo. Q. Cannon & Sons Co. made an error in their bid for manilla paper of the difference between $67.50 and $116.80, and the Acme School Supply Co. a mistake on 1,000 gross of crayon amounting to the difference between $196 and $130. Parsons & Derge's offer and that of Geo. Q. Cannon & Sons Co. were accepted, and the contract for crayons given to B. A. McMillan, and the 120,000 sheets of examination paper to W. A. Olmstead for $145.

At the conclusion of the regular business the board adjourned for two weeks.

FILLMORE FlOOD.

Jennie Robison Loses Her Life.

A SUICIDE AT HOLDEN.

Joseph Turner Found Hanging in His Barn—Mrs. McBride is Dead.

FILLMORE, Aug. 17.—Special.—Fillmore was visited by another flood last evening, caused by heavy rains in the mountains. At 5:30 p. m., while attempting to ford the swollen creek, Joseph Segwine, his son Robert, daughter Alta and Miss Jennie Robison were all tossed into the stream, and the latter drowned. Miss Robison's body was recovered at 8 30 p. m. about three miles below town. Miss Segwine lies in a critical condition.

Mrs. Mary A. McBride, whose daughter and several grand children reside at Provo, died last evening. She was aged 79, and was with the church through all the trials at Nauvoo and Illinoie.

FILLMORE PARAGRAPHS.

Miss Jennie Robison Meets Death in the Creek—Suicide at Holden.

Special to the News via Deseret Telegraph.

FILLMORE, Utah, Aug. 17.—In attempting to ford the creek in town yesterday, Joseph Segwine, his son Robert, a daughter, Alta, and Miss Jennie Robison were all tossed into the water. Miss Robison's body was recovered three miles below town.

At Holden this morning, Joseph Turner, about forty years old, committed suicide by hanging.

Grandma McBride died last night at the home of Bishop Callister.

We just learn by telegram from Provo that one of our citizens, Henry Davis, aged 72, was found dead in his wagon. He is known as Sawyer Davis.

IT WAS HEART FAILURE.

Henry Day's Found Dead at Provo This Morning.

The Old Gentleman's Home Was Fillmore, and He Was En Route to Salt Lake on Business.

This morning, about 8 o'clock, Mr. John Grier found the dead body of Henry Davis back of the post office block. He was lying across the front end gate of his wagon, with his arms around some bedding, and death had apparently come to him as was getting out of the wagon. His team was unhitched and tied behind the wagon, and a box of provisions and some cooking utensils had been removed from the wagon and placed under an adjoining sled. When Mayor Holbrook became acquainted with the death and came on the ground, he recognized the deceased as being from Fillmore, and said he had for several years past been engaged in bringing produce from the People's store of Fillmore to Salt Lake and Provo and taking merchandise back, and he was evidently on a trip of that kind now as he had some wool and eggs in his wagon. The supposition is that he was preparing camp for the night last evening, and was seized with an attack of heart failure which caused his death. Mayor Holbrook further informed the News correspondent that the deceased was over seventy years of age and leaves two daughters and three sons. He was an Englishman by birth and an honorable, hard-working old gentleman. The mayor telegraphed J. D. Smith of the People's store, acquainting him with the circumstances. Coroner Berg was also notified and an inquest is being held, wringing out nothing different from the facts suggested above. Several parties saw him yesterday evening when he was unhitching his horses and moving his effects from the wagon. His remains will be held till his relatives can be heard from.

FILMORE CITY, August 17, 1896.

Yesterday, Sunday, Robert and Alta Seguine and Miss Jennie Robison, daughter of Willie Robison (son of the venerable "Uncle Peter") left Petersburg (Corn Creek) on a visit to Filmore. Joseph Seguine, father of Robert and Alta, went from town with them to the farm of Mayor Smith, to see some old friends just arrived from Kansas, Mr. and Mrs. Cummings, whose sons are working the farm, one of whom is a son-in-law of Joseph Seguine. During the day thunder clouds had deposited considerable water in the mountains which concentrated in the creek making a very large volume, swift and muddy, which reached town about 6 o'clock p. m. when the above named were returning to the city in their wagon.

At the junction of the Sunday waste ditch and the old creek, a block north of the creamery on First West street, is a crossing. Brigham Melville and Walter Rowley saw the travelers coming towards it, and pulled off their hats and waved them back, knowing the danger of the swift current. The girls sensed the danger, but Robert whipped up the horses for the venture, and they plunged into the water, which lifted the wagon bed from its place and turned it completely over, depositing the four passengers in the muddy torrent beneath it. They were carried down the stream and the Seguines were all rescued, but Miss Robison could not be reached. Walter Rowley heard her scream, "O save me!" He ran to the rescue but when about ten yards from her he lost sight of the body. Scores of people were attracted to the scene ready to assist, and searched the creek for two miles, until they came to a large body of driftwood, left by a previous flood, where they knew the body could not pass. This was pulled apart piece by piece until the body was liberated and was seen to start down the current again and could be seen at intervals for half a mile further, when a young man, Frank, son of Delle Webb, caught sight of it and made a heroic plunge and caught the drowned girl's foot, to which he hung with a grip of despair, unable to pull it to the bank until Heber Mitchell reached out and caught his hand when they drew it to the land, limp, bruised and dead.

Mayor Smith went down to Petersburg to apprise the parents of the loss of their daughter, who had left home a few hours previously full of happy anticipation.

Jennie was an exemplary young lady, one of the chief workers in the Sunday school, the affianced of Bob Seguine and the first born in the family, for whom all the people feel the deepest sympathy.

Joseph Turner of Holden, about 46 years old, the father of a large family, six or seven of whom are living, some few years since showed signs of mental trouble, and became listless in care for progress or work; but for the last few years he has assumed his normal condition and been active and energetic. He has had some sickness in his family lately; one boy about 6 years old has required careful attention for several weeks, but appeared to be improving lately. Friends were at the house last night and offered to remain all night but Joseph said he did not wish them to do so as he could not sleep if he went to bed. He and his wife could do all that was necessary.

Quite early in the morning he left the house, and his wife thinking his stay long, took a lantern to try to see where he had gone, and soon discovered his body hanging under a shed near the barn, dead. He had evidently made an unsuccessful effort to cut his throat, as signs clearly showed. The good people of Holden are much distressed over this very sad affair. Mr. Turner served as a juror at the last term of the district court held in Filmore, and was generally considered a kind, indulgent parent, and a good and honorable citizen.

A. BIRD.

GREAT FLOODS IN THE SOUTH

Much Property Damage and at Least One Life Lost.

CITIZENS ARE INDIGNANT

Cause of the Floods Laid to the Sheepmen.

They Will Be Given Notice to Remove Their Muttons, and If They Fail to Heed It, Trouble May Ensue—Holden Visited by a Flood, and Many Persons Have a Narrow Escape—Boulders, Stumps, Logs and Animals Carried Along.

(Special to The Herald.)

FILLMORE, Utah, Aug. 17.—During the flood here last evening and while the big creek that runs through the town was full of mud and water, a wagon containing J. S. Segwine, his grown son and daughter and Miss Jennie Robison, 15 years old, all of Petersburg, tried to cross.

Just as the wagon got in the water, the wagon box tipped over and all were thrown out. The three Segwines, AFTER A TERRIBLE STRUGGLE, saved themselves, but Miss Robison was drowned and her body was carried down the stream four miles before it was caught. The body was taken to Kanosh this morning, where it will be buried. This is the third person drowned here in the last two years during floods. The people throughout the county are worked up considerably over these floods occurring so often, and they lay the blame to the sheep in the hills. It is said the sheep men will be given due notice, in the next few days, to leave and not to return. If they refuse to go,

of his wagon here this morning. He had been engaged in the business of freighting from Salt Lake to Fillmore, and last evening about 6:30 he was seen to drive into the open yard just behind the Central building and unhitch and feed his horses. That was the last seen of him till this morning at about 8 o'clock, when his dead body was found partly in the wagon, as if he was in the act of climbing in or out for his bedding. The verdict of the coroner's jury was "death from heart failure."

The body was shipped to Fillmore tonight.

A telegram was received here today stating that Joseph Turner of Holden, a man about 45 years of age, had committed suicide by hanging himself to the beam of his barn.

Joseph K. Crater, aged 55, and Charles Odd, aged 71, both inmates of the asylum, died last evening and were buried today.

Dave Clark of Grand Junction, Col., formerly a resident of Provo, is in town for a few days.

Provo Points

PROVO, Aug. 17.—Henry Davis, a man 72 years of age, whose home was in Fillmore, was found dead in the front

WEATHER AND CROPS.

The Conditions Favorable For Growth, Harvesting and Threshing.

The first five days of the week ending August 17 were hot and dry; the last two showery and much cooler. The conditions were favorable for growth, harvesting, thrashing and general farm work. Harvesting continues in all districts, and in the southern portion of the state thrashing has been vigorously pushed during the week. The yield is reported uniformly light in Washington and portions of Millard counties, owing to drought early in the season. Haying is well under way and a good crop of timothy and wild hay has been cured and saved in fine condition. The second cutting of lucerne is in full blast, with indications of a fair crop. Corn and potatoes doing well; vegetables of all kinds plentiful; fruit prospects not very good.

The summary of the report for the month of July is as follows:

The most notable feature of the weather during the month of July, 1896, was the heavy rains in the southern part of the state about the middle of the month, which caused destructive floods in Sanpete, Sevier and Millard counties, where great damage was done to crops, canals, ditches, farm and railroad property. In the vicinity of Fillmore, Fairview, Kanosh, Richfield and Holden, the most damage was done, though in other localities considerable hay and grain was destroyed by the excessive rains and high winds.

The mean temperature for the state was 72 degrees, which is about one degree below the normal; highest monthly mean, 81 degrees at Corinne; lowest monthly mean 62 degrees at Soldier's Summit. The highest temperature recorded during the month was 111 degrees at St. George on the 11th, and the lowest 37 degrees at Park City on the 2nd. Range of temperature for the state, 78 degrees. The warm days were the 1st, 5th, 6th, 7th, 8th, 9th, 10th, 11th, 12th, 18th, 19th and 21st.

The average precipitation was 1.81 inches; greatest monthly amount recorded, 3.83 inches at Koosharen; least amount recorded, .12 of an inch at Cisco. The principal part of the rainfall fell on the 13th and 14th. The average number of days on which one-hundredth of an inch or more of rain fell was 7.

Tere was an average of 13 clear, 11 fair and 7 cloudy days during the month. At Salt Lake City there was 71 per cent. of sunshine, and at Grover, Wayne county, 43 per cent., during the month.

The prevailing wind for the state was from the southwest, and the total movement at Salt Lake City, 4,108 miles; average hourly velocity, 6 miles an hour.

NEWS FROM NEARBY CITIES AND TOWNS

Deseret Finds a Bonanza in Lucerne Seed.

IT BRINGS IN THOUSANDS

CACHE COUNTY CONVENTION WAS VERY HARMONIOUS.

A Good Story Now Going the Rounds in Provo — Rio Grande Railway's Big Suit—Democrats at Panguitch —Many Pleasure Seekers Flock Into Morgan—A Mecca for Sportsmen.

DESERET, Sept., 12.—Not since the days when the Deseret country was a vast range with the grass growing up to a horse's belly, have the people been promised such hope for getting out of debt, and laying by a stake for the future; and it's all owing to the lucerne crop. Never before had such a crop grown in this end of Millard county, and the seed alone which will be stacked up in the granaries, providing Jack Frost remains out of the country just ten days, will bring the farmers about $30,000, even at last year's prices. Estimating the number of inhabitants at 2,000, in the three wards of Oasis, Hinckley and Deseret, this means a per capita of $15 for every man, woman and child in the Deseret country. Lucerne seed has a staple market value, and generally commands a cash price; hence if the producer holds his seed until the buyer approaches, he can make farming pay well in Millard county.

When a farmer told me today that the lucerne crop of the Deseret country would exceed in value the agricultural product of Iron and Beaver counties along with the other end of Millard county, I scarcely believed him, but he had facts and figures at his fingers' ends. The recent floods have played havoc with everything that grew above ground along the bench lands of Millard in the east, saving not enough to feed the people of Fillmore and the beautiful and thrifty little towns at the foot of the mountains. Therefore the Deseret country is called upon to supply its neighbors and the supremacy of the western end as a reliable producer is again established. No wonder the people of Fillmore are up in arms against the sheep.

Can the farmer hold his crop of lucerne seed until he gets the top market price? This is the question that is now agitating the Deseret granger. About a week ago a meeting was held in the tabernacle here and an agreement reached to organize a trust on the lines of the grange plan of the farmers of the middle, west and south. One speaker cited an instance which occurred a year ago. He sold his lucerne to a storekeeper for $3.90 and drove it down to the station two miles away and unloaded it. There somebody else received it who paid the storekeeper $5.50 for the consignment. Two or three others at the meeting told similar stories, and the result is that another meeting is called for next Tuesday evening, when a code of laws will be presented for the government of the organization and the support of the ecclesiastical heads of the three wards is promised.   P. C.

Deseret Evening News
September 16, 1896

BURIAL OF SUICIDES.

A correspondent writing from Fillmore makes inquiry concerning the clothing and burial ceremony of one who is a member of the Church who has committed suicide. In reply to the questions we note the fact that it is beyond comprehension how a member of the Church, understanding the genius of the Gospel even to the most limited extent that any member of ordinary perceptive faculties can, should commit suicide while in a sound state of mind. The doctrine of the Church is so utterly at enmity with the terrible crime of self murder that no one capable of membership should fail to recognize the abhorrence in which the suicide is held.

So far as concerns the inquiries made, it is difficult to give a pointed reply, because each case has peculiar features that affect its determination. If there were a deliberate suicide, where it was evident that no unsoundness of mind had interposed to lead to the crime, the quieter the funeral ceremony the better. In case there were such a lamentable act as the taking of one's own life, one thing should be remembered, and that is that the dead person can have no hearing in a mortal court; therefore each doubt should be resolved in his favor. This would be a general rule concerning the robing and preparation for the grave. As to public funeral services, the Stake authorities have their instructions on the subject from the general authorities, and we presume the Bishops in each Stake have them in turn, so that there ought to be no question as to what to do. Certainly there should be nothing that would cause the crime of self murder to be looked upon with the least degree of allowance or palliation.

Salt Lake Herald
October 7, 1896

Court at Fillmore.
(Special to The Herald.)

FILLMORE, Utah, Oct. 6.—Judge Higgins opened the regular October term here today and did the following business:

A petit jury of twenty names was drawn and summoned to be in attendance at court tomorrow at 2 o'clock.

Frank Holbrook and Frank Hanson were appointed bailiffs.

Fillmore city et. al. vs. Albert Nichols; set for trial October 7.

Elizabeth Robinson vs. Fillmore city; set for trial October 7.

George M. Velle vs. A. Q. Robinson; set for trial October 7.

Mrs. D. K. Olson vs. Culbert King et. al.; John W. Thornley was appointed guardian ad litem for minor defendants—Norma Thornley, Mattie Thornley and William J. Thornley.

H. G. Labrum et. al. vs. Peter Greenhalgh; set for trial October 7.

State vs. Peter Patnode; arraigned on charge of assult to commit murder; set for trial October 8.

Samuel G. Nye was granted a divorce from Carry M. Dye on the ground of desertion and the defendant, by agreement, was given the custody of the minor child.

State vs. Thomas Morgan; arraigned on charge of assault to commit murder; case set for October 9.

State vs. E. W. Workman; set for trial October 9.

There are in attendance upon court here beside the local attorneys, Judge Gilchrist, W. F. Knox, Colonel Tatlock and Dan Houtz.

From the looks of the calendar, the court will be in session about ten days.

Fillmore Court.
(Special to The Herald.)

FILLMORE, Utah, Oct. 7.—Judge Higgins did a good deal of miscellaneous business of a non-important public nature today.

The case of George M. Velle against A. Q. Robinson, was set for trial for the 12th instant.

H. G. Labrum vs. Peter Greenhalgh; suit to quiet title to land and water; judgment for plaintiff by default.

In the case of Elizabeth Robinson against Fillmore City; E. A. Wedgwood and Dan Houtz took up the afternoon in arguing a demurrer, and the decision thereon was reserved by the court.

Colonel Tatlock has been employed by County Attorney Hansen to assist in the prosecution of the criminal cases.

Higgins Talks to Justices.
(Special to The Herald.)

FILLMORE, Utah, Oct. 8, 1896.— Judge Higgins had another day of hearing law and motion matters.

Christian Thompson, a native of Sweden, was naturalized.

Elizabeth Robinson vs. Fillmore city; demurrer sustained.

Fillmore city vs. Albert Nichols et al.; demurrer overruled; five days to answer.

State vs. Jerry Patnode; demurrer overruled and motion to quash information denied.

State vs. Tom Morgan; motion to quash information because of the irregularity of the papers and proceedings from committing magistrate sustained and defendant discharged. The facts in relation to the setting aside of this information prompted Judge Higgins to caution justices of the peace in making their returns on cases held to the district court. He said that justices of the peace in their preliminary examinations, should follow the statute literally, and see that their proceedings were directed by law; that the authority of the county attorney to file an information depended solely upon the fact of a legal preliminary examination having been held, and that the court had no jurisdiction to go into a hearing of a case unless it affirmatively appeared from the transcript of the justice that the law relating to such examinations had been complied with, and in order to save the expense to the state and trouble to parties, justices should proceed with more care than they apparently were in the habit of doing.

E. M. Workman pleaded guilty to burglary with intent to commit rape, and his time for sentence was fixed for Saturday next.

Salt Lake Herald
October 10, 1896

Court at Fillmore.

(Special to the Herald.)

FILLMORE, Utah, Oct. 9.—Court convened at 9:30. In the case of Labrum vs. Peter Greenhalgh, his honor ruled that the default and judgment should be set aside. The defendant was given until tomorrow morning to answer.

In the case of the State vs. Jerry Patnode, defendant was granted continuance until next term.

In the case of Fillmore City vs. Nichols et al., the entire afternoon has been consumed in taking depositions of witnesses for the plaintiff.

Salt Lake Herald
October 11, 1896

FOR ONE YEAR.

Workman, Who Pleaded Guilty of Burglary, With Attempt to Commit Rape, is Sentenced.

(Special to The Herald.)

FILLMORE, Utah, Oct. 10.—Niels Anderson, a native of Denmark, and Walter Maycock, a native of England, were naturalized today by Judge Higgins.

E. W. Workman, who pleaded guilty last week to burglary with intent to commit rape, was sentenced to one year's imprisonment in the penitentiary. Workman's friends made a strong plea for leniency, by showing that he had previously borne a good character, and that the circumstances showed the offense not to be an aggravated one.

The largest part of the day was consumed in taking testimony in the water case of Fillmore city et al. vs. Albert Nichols et al.

Colonel E. W. Tatlock presented the public school here with a beautiful flag, and the Central school today gave an interesting programme upon the occasion.

Bishop Callister responded eloquently to the sentiment "Patriotism in the Public Schools," and that, with other appropriate exercises, made a very pleasant occasion.

Deseret Evening News
October 12, 1896

AN AFFECTING SCENE.

Sentence of a Young Man at Fillmore—Other Court News.

Special Correspondence of the News.

FILLMORE CITY, Utah, Oct. 11th, 1896.—In the Fifth Judicial district court, justice drags its slow course along, owing to lack of preparation on the part of council. No jury trial has been had and Judge Higgins discharged the jury for the term.

Tom Morgan, charged with assault with intent to kill, was set at liberty and his bondsmen discharged.

The case of assault with intent to kill against Jerry Painode went over until next term.

In the case of E. M. Norkman, charged with burglary with intent to commit a rape defendant came into court and pleaded guilty. Judge Higgins asked defendant if he knew the nature of the charge and the penalty attached thereto, defendant answering that he did. Saturday, the 10th, being set for the judgment, at 2 o'clock the young man, 24 years old, came into court. Asked if he had anything to say why sentence should not be passed, Attorney Joshua Greenwood arose as a citizen and addressed the court on behalf of the young man, reviewing his past life which had been without spot or blemish. Without any attempt to cover up the facts in the case, Greenwood spoke of many circumstances of a mitigating nature in connection therewith. The young man stood before the court an object of pity; he gave to the law the whole facts of his wrong-doing, acknowledging that he himself alone was guilty of all the wrong-doing in connection with this lamentable affair, and he tried to choke down his emotion and take the consequence of the sin, as though he welcomed justice as a guide to a better life in future. But when Greenwood referred to his honorable parents living in the south, he broke down, and by tears of remorse showed the effect of good parental training.

Judge Higgins reviewed the case and spoke of his unpleasant duty. He would take into consideration the exceptional good character of the defendant, and after giving high moral counsel to the young man, he sentenced him to one year in the state prison. The young fellow sobbed out, "Thank you, sir," and although the sentence in the case may appear to some to be a light one, all who are acquainted with it feel that justice is served and a warning given to night-prowling around the homes of other people.

The case of Fillmore City against Albert Nichols and others, wherein defendants are charged with appropriating water unlawfully, is under way. Greenwood and Melville have associated with them Attorney Wedgewood from Provo for the city, and D. D. Houtz, E. W. Tatlock and John Hanson are handling the case for Nichols et al. The case will probably continue another day or two, as quite a number of witnesses have been summoned on both sides.

A. BIRD.

Salt Lake Herald
October 13, 1896

WORKMAN REPENTS.

Apparently Sorry That He Pleaded Guilty to the Charge.

(Special to The Herald.)

FILLMORE, Utah, Oct. 12.—E. M. Workman, who pleaded guilty the other day to burglary with intent to commit rape, this morning filed a petition for a writ of habeas corpus, stating as a ground for the same that the information to which he pleaded guilty did not charge an offense known to the law, and that he was illegally restrained of his liberty under the commitment issued. The writ was granted by the court, and the matter argued by Messrs. D. D. Houtz and E. A. Wedgwood for the relator and County Attorney Hanson and Colonel Tatlock for the respondent. The particular point relied upon by the relator is that the information did not charge that the burglary was committed with the intent to ravish, etc., a female, being a person other than the wife of the accused.

The court reserved his decision in the matter till tomorrow.

George M. Velle vs. A. Q. Robinson; judgment for defendant.

The balance of the day was consumed in the hearing of testimony in the water case of Fillmore City et al. against Albert Nichols et al.

Salt Lake Herald
October 14, 1896

COURT AT FILLMORE.

(Special to The Herald.)

FILLMORE, Utah, Oct. 13.—Judge Higgins' court at this point is drawing to a close. The testimony and arguments in the case of Fillmore City and Irrigation Co. vs. Albert Nichols was concluded after four days' continuous work, and the court took the case under advisement, reserving his decision. In the habeas corpus proceeding of E. M. Workman, the county attorney this morning conceded the claims, and asked that the court discharge the prisoner, which was done.

The case of George W. Velle against A. G. Robinson will be tried the first thing tomorrow, when court will adjourn, and Judge Higgins will leave for Nephi to open court there next Monday.

E. A. Wedgewood, who has been here during the entire term trying cases, leaves tonight for Provo, and Dan Houtz will leave for the same place tomorrow night.

Salt Lake Herald
December 8, 1896

Present indications are that Utah will be well represented at the fifth annual session of the National Irrigation congress, which meets at Phoenix, Ariz., on December 15, 16 and 17. Among those who have already signified their intentions of going are Senator L. W. Shurtliff and Judge Thomas D. Dee of Ogden; Colonel C. L. Stevenson, Hon. George Q. Cannon and wife, E. G. Rognon, J. W. Culley, W. R. Cutler, Charles T. Loback and Van H. Brooks of Salt Lake; Hon. James A. Melville of Fillmore and John R. Barnes and wife of Kaysville. The local committee is working hard to get others to go and a rate of $59.70 for the round trip has been made by the Southern Pacific Railway company.

Salt Lake Herald
December 15, 1896

Fillmore, Utah, Dec. 14.—The regular December term of court opened here this morning, with Judge Higgins on the bench.

Nelson Beauregard and James Kelly were appointed bailiffs.

The information charging Jerry Patnode with assault with intent to kill was dismissed on motion of the county attorney, who stated that the evidence was not sufficient to warrant a verdict of guilty.

A petit jury had been previously drawn and summoned and were examined upon their statutory qualifications.

Thomas Barrett, for assaulting John Charlesworth of Kanosh and inflicting some ugly wounds upon his body and neck with a knife, was arraigned and pleaded not guilty. His case will be tried tomorrow.

Estate of Lewis Brunson; order to sell certain real property.

James Alexander Melville was admitted to the bar upon an open court examination today. He showed considerable native ability in his answers and intends taking an extended course at Ann Arbor.

George M. Velie vs. A. Q. Robinson; motion for new trial overruled.

The court entered an order fixing county commissioners' bonds at $5,000.

Charles H. Howard vs. Lydia Busby; dismissed at plaintiff's cost.

Mary Charlsworth has brought suit for divorce against James Charlsworth, alleging such cruel treatment as flogging her at times, and for which she asks for a divorce, their two children, a share of the property, alimony and costs.

The calendar was called. But few of the attorneys being present, they were passed on first call.

Tomorrow on the second call they will be disposed of one way or another.

Deseret Evening News
December 16, 1896

FILLMORE COURT NOTES

A Dance Hall Row Trouble Investigated Before Judge Higgins.

Special Correspondence to the NEWS:

FILLMORE CITY, Utah, Dec. 12.— The Fifth Judicial District court opened here yesterday, Judge Higgins presiding; a jury was empaneled to try a case from Kanosh, the State vs Thomas Barrett, charged with assault with intent to kill. This case arose out of a row at a dance, and the evidence went to show that the defendant received very disgusting provocation. The dance hall is approached by a long flight of stairs leading up to the second floor of the building. From the platform at the entrance door the first assault appears to have come, which angered the defendant, who under the influence of drink hastened up the stairs to find his assailant, who proved to be John Charlesworth, and then the fight commenced. Both men claim that their opponent used a knife, although no very serious wounds were received by either. Attorney Greenwood was appointed by the court to defend Barrett. Melville and J. M. Hanson prosecuted the case, which was well argued by both sides and given to the jury just as the mail is about to leave.

Several minor cases have been dis-

Several minor cases have been disposed of.

Mr. James Alexander Melville passed a very successful examination and was admitted to the bar. The young man intends shortly to go to Michigan for further study, and his many friends here expect to welcome his return therefrom in honor to himself and profession.

Mrs. Armanda C. Carling through Attorney Hansen made application for divorce; her husband Frank Carling is now serving a term of five years in the State prison for felony.

Joseph Hyram Labram was admitted to citizenship.

Salt Lake Herald
January 8, 1897

Fillmore Court.

(Special to The Herald.)

FILLMORE, Utah, Oct. 7.—Judge Higgins did a good deal of miscellaneous business of a non-important public nature today.

The case of George M. Yelle against A. Q. Robinson, was set for trial for the 12th instant.

H. G. Labrum vs. Peter Greenhalgh; suit to quiet title to land and water; judgment for plaintiff by default.

In the case of Elizabeth Robinson against Fillmore City; E. A. Wedgwood and Dan Houtz took up the afternoon in arguing a demurrer, and the decision thereon was reserved by the court.

Colonel Tatlock has been employed by County Attorney Hansen to assist in the prosecution of the criminal cases.

THE MILLER GOLD STRIKE.

Satisfactory Developments in Gold Mountain District.

Some very important developments have been made in Gold Mountain district, in Piute county, during the past few months and from a letter just received from a resident of that camp it is learned that there is considerable excitement there at the present time over the recent rich discovery in the Miller group, adjoining the Sevier mine on the west.

The discovery was made by John T. Miller, the owner of the property, who has since bonded the same to Joe Ray, of Fillmore.

The new find is a most important one, and comprises a 5-foot ledge in which free gold is visible through and through the quartz. The rock is very similar in appearance to the ore found in the Sevier mine, and there is every reason to believe that the deposit is a permanent one, and that the property will develop into one of the most prolific producers in the district.

The news of the rich find has resulted in attracting considerable attention to the camp and has given an impetus to mining affairs throughout the district.

On the Breckinridge group, which is being developed under the management of John Long, a commodious building has been erected which will be used as a boarding house for the operatives of the mine, which, it is said, is looking in a most promising condition.

Besides other work that is going on in the camp at present, developments are being pushed in the extension of the Annie Laurie and Blue Bird tunnels, while on the Sevier and the Golden Eagle there seems to be no let up in the improvements now in hand.

The writer of the letter states that there is more work going on in the district this winter than ever before, and he is confident that with the coming spring there will be wonderful activity in the camp.

The extension of the Rio Grande Western railroad to Richfield and to the narrows will assist materially in the upbuilding of the district and there is no reason why it should not make regular shipments the coming year.

SENT TO MILLARD COUNTY.

Callister-Tatlock Criminal Libel Case So Disposed Of.

The criminal libel case against T. C. Callister and Attorney E. W. Tatlock on the complaint of George A. Henry, was called up yesterday for a preliminary hearing before Judge Sommer, but on motion of Assistant County Attorney Eichnor it was transferred to Millard county, where the offense is alleged to have been committed. The preliminary hearing will be had before some justice of the peace at Fillmore.

Marriage licenses were issued yesterday to David Dupins, 41, Chicago, and Mrs. Mary Knapp, 38, Eureka; William D. Edmond, 23, Salt Lake, and C. Rosella Stout, 18, Farmers; Charles A. Brunson, 22, Fillmore, and Christina Fackrell, 20, Bountiful; John A. Caley, 22, Boston, and Amelia Lamoreaux, 20, Lincoln, Neb.

Salt Lake Herald
February 7, 1897

Provo, Feb. 7.—Senator Robison, of Fillmore, was quite badly hurt at Clear Lake Friday night. He fell from the platform, broke his collar bone and otherwise injured himself. He passed through here this morning on his way to Salt Lake for treatment. He can be found at Bellvue avenue, on Sixth South, between Fifth and Sixth East.

Fillmore.—Rained considerable during the night; none on ground.

Salt Lake Herald
February 14, 1897

THE JAKE MILLER MINE.

Valuable Gold Property Sold to Montana Parties.

Mention has been made in these columns from time to time regarding the Jake Miller gold mine, in Gold Mountain district, and this property, from all accounts, is one of the most promising bonanzas in the district.

The Miller group comprises eight claims, and it is stated that the property adjoins the noted Sevier mine, which is principally owned by Charlie Lammersdorf and his associates. About $2,000 has been expended in the development of the Miller ground, and The Herald is informed that this work has disclosed eight feet of solid ore that averages $100 in gold to the ton, while there are chutes through the vein that goes as high as $500 to $10,000 in the yellow metal.

This property has been held under bond for the past month or so, but it is learned that since his visit to this city Mr. Joseph E. Ray of Fillmore, has made a sale of the mine to Montana capitalists, the purchase price ranging up near the $75,000 mark, a payment being made at the time of the deal, while the balance of the money is to be paid in installments, the whole to be paid in by the first of July.

It is possible that the new purchasers will put in a mill during the season, and if they do, there is no doubt but that the district will make a fine record this year, as it is understood that there are other projects in contemplation for the camp which, if consummated, will give it a wonderful impetus.

A prominent mining expert, who has recently visited the camp, states that in his opinion the district will develop into another Cripple Creek.

At Fillmore, where Judge McCarty opens court Tuesday next, a case of burglary where three men broke into a store at Deseret and are charged with stealing money and clothing, will be tried. A water suit between Fillmore City and Mr. Nicholas, and three or four divorce suits, are also on the docket.

D. D. Houtz and S. A. King, two of Provo's foremost attorneys, started for Fillmore today on legal business which will be brought before Judge McCarty.

The dog tax bill passed the council

Deseret Evening News
March 3, 1896

FILLMORE NEWS.

Water Case Settled — Burglars Had Guilty — Adorning the Public Square.

FILLMORE, Millard Co., March 2, 1897.—The district court opened here today, Judge McCarty, owing to several important water suits coming up in his own district in which he was interested, presiding, and our own Judge Higgins presiding over the district court now being held in Richfield.

After attending to the arrangement of the calendar to suit the convenience of attorneys, and calling up the water case of Fillmore city vs Albert Nichols et al, the report of Special Commissioner George Crane was handed in, and the case was settled by giving defendants fifty inches of water once in every ten days during the irrigation season.

The three safe blowers who operated in Deseret several weeks ago were arraigned and knowing that the web of evidence had them safe, they concluded to plead guilty and will come up tomorrow for sentence.

The city council has got a move on to embellish the public square, and men and teams are plowing and scraping preparatory to planting grass and trees. A. BIRD.

Salt Lake Herald
March 4, 1897

MILLARD COUNTY.

Court Matters Before Judge McCarty at Fillmore.

Fillmore, March 2.—The regular March term of court opened here this morning, with Judge W. M. McCarty of the Sixth district presiding as judge pro tem. The following miscellaneous business was transacted:

In the case of the state against Thomas Manti, Fred Black and Charles Sheppard, the defendants each pleaded guilty to a charge of burglary. On Dec. 25, 1896, these three men broke into the Salt Lake Equitable Co-op. at Deseret and blowed the safe all to pieces, and got away with $90 and some clothing. The time of sentence was fixed for tomorrow morning at 10 o'clock.

State vs. John Bottomfield; set for hearing March 4, at 9:30.

In the matter of the estate of John T. Ashman; hearing report of administrator set for March 3.

Manda Carling vs. Frank Carling; set for trial tomorrow at 2 p. m.

Caroline Block vs. Salt Lake Equitable Co-op.; set for trial March 5.

C. Andrews vs. J. P. Johnson; set for trial March 4, at 2 p. m.

Delilah K. Olson vs. Culbert King et al.; set for trial March 3, at 10 a. m.

Almon Robinson vs. Charles C. Beauregard; set for trial March 3.

Fillmore City et al. vs. Albert Nichols et al.; order entered approving the report of the commissioner appointed to take testimony in relation to the amount of water used respectively by plaintiff and defendant from Dry creek; and it was further ordered that judgment be entered accordingly.

In the matter of the estate of Charity Prows; ordered that due and legal notice to creditors had been given.

Salt Lake Herald
March 6, 1897

MILLARD COUNTY.

Three Burglars Sentenced at Fillmore—Brave Little Fellow.

Fillmore, Utah, March 4.—Yesterday the three burglars who pleaded guilty to cracking the safe at Deseret, were sentenced—Thomas Manti and Fred Black to two years in the penitentiary, and Charles Sheppard to 18 months in the pen, the latter getting the benefit of the six months from his age, being only 19.

Delilah K. Olsen vs. Culbert King et al.; judgment for plaintiff.

Estate of John T. Ashman, deceased; ordered that due and legal notice had been given to creditors, and that the administrator's report be referred to J. M. Hanson for examination and report; and it was further ordered that the administrator sell all the personal property of the estate not exempt from execution.

John E. Walker, a native of Scotland, was admitted to citizenship.

Hans Esklund vs. Scipio Irrigation district et al.; demurrer overruled and April 3 allowed within which to answer.

Deseret Evening News
March 6, 1897

A Letter From England.

FILLMORE Millard County,
February 28th, 1897.

To the Editor:

I enclose a letter which came under my notice today, the writer is eighty-two years old, and "Emily" (Frampton) is a widow sixty two years old, a twenty-four year resident of this city.

MENDHAM, February 10th, 1897.

Dear Emily:—This comes with my kind love to you, and I want to know if you got the books and my letter. I sent the books off on the 16th of December, and the letter on the 19th of December. I had a newspaper on the 29th of January from you, and I have been looking for a letter every day since, to know if you got them. I hope they are not lost. Write and let me know.

Well, dear Emily, my dear brother and I do enjoy your papers, for I can tell you he is a real Mormon and he believes that to be the work of the living God, and no other. He and

Court at Fillmore.

FILLMORE CITY, Utah, March 4, 1897.—The Fifth judicial district court, in the matter of the estate of John T. Ashman, deceased, ordered that due notice be given to creditors, and that J. M. Hanson examine and report. It was further ordered that the administrators sell all the personal property of the estate not exempt from execution.

John E. Walker, a native of Scotland, was admitted to citizenship.

Hans Esklund vs Scipio Irrigation district et al; demurrer overruled and to April 3rd allowed to answer.

Almon Robison vs Chas. and Nels J. Beauregard; dismissed on motion of plaintiff's counsel as to N. J. Beauregard, and judgment given against Chas. C. Beauregard for $363 principal and $523 interest.

In the case reported yesterday wherein little Jack Bottomfield was mentioned as sent to the Reform school, Judge McCarty appointed Attorney Greenwood to defend the boy and it was clearly shown that the little fellow was more sinned against than sinning. The court gave the boy's stepfather and his mother some very good advice as to the future care of little Jack, who is evidently a bright lad and with proper direction will yet make a good man. Several of our citizens were impressed with the ready wit and honest explanations of the boy, and would give him a home and a chance in the world if they could get him.   A. BIRD.

MILLARD COUNTY.

Decree Against the Salt Lake Equitable Co-op.

Fillmore, Utah, March 5.—The case of Caroline Black against the Salt Lake Equitable Co-operative Institution was taken up for trial today before Judge McCarty, and resulted in a decree for plaintiff as prayed. This is an action brought to declare a deed executed in 1891, by Caroline Black, in favor of the Equitable Co-op, to be, in fact, a mortgage, also to secure a decree declaring the payment of the debt it was given to secure, and to have the mortgage cancelled. Mr. J. T. Richards represented the defendant, and occupied the whole forenoon in trying to get a continuance, and being denied his continuance, withdrew from the case, and the defendant not desiring to fight the case by employing additional counsel, made the matter very easy sailing for Dan Houtz, attorney for the plaintiff.

This is the last case here for trial at this term, and so Judge Higgins will return home tomorrow, and immediately proceed to Kanab, where he has several important cases to try.

Senator J. V. Robison.

Joseph V. Robison is a Knickerbocker by birth, and was born in Onondaga county, New York, December 20, 1832. His parents moved to Il-

linois when he was 12 years of age, where they lived for ten years or until 1854, when they came west and settled at Fillmore. Mr. Robison took in the possibilities of the country and established a fruit tree nursery, which has supplied thousands with fruit trees. He also engaged in stock raising, and at one time was one of the heaviest owners in this state. He has been mayor of Fillmore and probate judge and county judge for several terms. In 1882 and 1883 he represented Millard, Piute and Beaver counties in the legislature. He declined the nomination as member of the constitutional convention from Millard county and at his own expense made a campaign opposing the financial policy of the administration. He is a man of ripe judgment and his opinions are much sought after by his colleagues.

Salt Lake Herald
April 1, 1897

A MAN WITH A HISTORY.

Chairman Clawson recently received a letter from G. Huntsman of Fillmore, Millard county, in which he asked for information concerning the proposed appointment of commissioners to represent the counties of the state in the Jubilee celebration. Mr. Huntsman volunteers his services for any duty imposed. He has an interesting history. He came to Utah in 1851, and in 1852 he removed from Fort Hall to this city wagons and supplies the church had purchased from the government. He was the first merchant to open a store in Millard county, and was appointed quartermaster-general of the Nauvoo Legion, and held that position, under Colonel Thomas Callister, until the disbanding of that famous organization. He also was one of the 72 elders who was called to go on a mission by President Brigham Young in 1857, and among the duties imposed upon him was the pulling of a handcart from this city to a settlement in Nebraska, a distance of 1,013 miles. The trip was made in 41 days.

F. J. Rodgers, representing Macondray & Co. of San Francisco, called at headquarters yesterday and ordered five Jubilee cups for friends in the Golden state, who gave him the commission. This is an evidence of the interest manifested abroad in the celebration.

Deseret Evening News
April 8, 1896

FIRE AT FILLMORE.

It Destroyes a Store and Residence and Does Other Damage.

Special to the News:

FILLMORE, Utah, April 7th, 7:15 p. m.—Between 12 and 1 o'clock last night a fire broke out in and consumed Day's dance hall and confectionery store. Nothing was saved. Mr. Day was at Kanosh. Loss is $1,500, insurance $800 in the Hartford of Connecticut.

The fire caught and licked up a new lumber building belonging to Mrs. Levi Warner, which the lady had occupied only two days; loss $200, no insurance.

The butcher's shop belonging to the People's store was damaged $100, covered by insurance.

Provo Daily Enquirer
April 9, 1897

Fire at Fillmore.

FILLMORE, Utah, April 7, 7:15 p. m, —Between 12 and 1 oclock last night a fire broke out in and consumed Day's dance hall and confectionery store. Nothing was saved. Mr. Day was at Kanosh. Loss is $1,500, insurance $800 in the Hartford of Connecticut.

The fire caught and licked up a new lumber building belonging to Mrs. Levi Warner, which the lady had occupied only two days; loss $200, no insurance.

The butcher's shop belonging to the People's store was damaged $100; covered by insurance.

Deseret Evening News
April 12, 1897

Pioneer Names.

A correspondent writes: "I am requested to hand in the name of Helen Mar Callister of Fillmore and her daughter, Helen Mar McCullough of Marion ward, Garfield county, as Pioneers of 1847. They are the wife and eldest daughter of the late President Thomas Callister of Millard Stake. They arrived upon the site of Salt Lake City, September 25th, 1847. They crossed the plains from Winter Quarters in the company of Father John Smith, the Patriarch."

Deseret Evening News
April 15, 1897

Fourth District Court.

Judge Dusenberry rendered his decision in the divorce suit of Ella Erickson vs Nils G. Erickson submitted some time ago. Plaintiff is granted a decree of divorce and the custody of the minor children together with the use of the house and lot in Santaquin, upon which she reside, until further order of the court.

A decision was handed down in the case of Ann E. M. Monroe vs Jane Memmott, involving title to some land in the southern part of the county. The decision was in favor of plaintiff as to the possession of the land and as to damages in favor of defendant.

The cases of James B. Edmunds vs James Thompson, and Tacitus Gough vs Julius Van Ausdale were set for April 26th.

The divorce suit of Thankful Fillmore vs Reuben Fillmore was set for April 26th; plaintiff's default therefore entered being withdrawn on motion of defendant's attorney, with plaintiff's consent.

Provo Daily Enquirer
May 22, 1897

District Court.

The following orders have been made in the Third district court:

Fillmore vs. Fillmore; motion for a new trial ordered filed.

Gough vs. VanAusDale; motion for a new trial ordered filed.

Geo. T. Tunnecliff vs. Geo. T. Peay; time to answer extended five days.

Estate of Sarah Mayhew, deceased; order of sale of personal property.

Estate of Geo. Weaver, deceased; Josie Kempton appointed administratrix.

Estate and Guardianship of Annis Crandall et al; hearing a petition to sell real estate set for June 19, 1897.

Fillmore vs. Fillmore; motion for stay of proceedings denied.

COUNTIES' SHARE.

Commissioners to Distribute Jubilee Fund.

Gov. Wells yesterday appointed the commissioners in each county under whom the amounts appropriated for the semi-centennial celebration are to be expended. The joint resolution passed by the last Legislature appropriated $15,000 for the semi-centennial. Ten thousand of this goes to the commission, and the other five thousand is divided up among the counties, and the Governor has now appointed the commissioners to supervise the expenditure of these amounts. The sum to which each county is entitled and the name of the respective commissioners are as follows:

Beaver county, $150, John R. Murdock of Beaver.

Box Elder, $250, Rudger Clawson of Brigham City.

Cache, $250, Lyman R. Martineau of Logan.

Carbon. $150, W. G. Sharp of Castle Gate.

Davis, $250, John W. Hess of Farmington.

Emery, $150, O. G. Larson, Castle Dale.

Grand. $150, M. W. Warner of Moab.

Garfield, $150, Thomas Sevy of Panguitch.

Iron, $150, Francis Webster of Cedar,

Juab, $250, C. H. Blanchard of Silver City.

Kane. $150, Thomas Chamberlain of Orderville.

Millard, $200, Ira N. Hinckley of Fillmore.

Morgan, $150. Richard Fry of Morgan.

Piute, $150, Charles Morrill of Junction.

Rich, $150. Archibald McKinnon, Sr., of Randolph.

Sanpete, $250, William D. Livingston of Manti.

San Juan, $150, F. A. Hammond of Bluff.

Sevier, $200, Theodore Brandley of Richfield.

Summit, $250, A. D. Moffatt of Park City.

Tooele, $200, Hugh S. Gowans of Tooele City.

Uintah, $150, R. S. Collett of Vernal.

Utah, $300, Lafayette Holbrook of Provo.

Washington, $150, David H. Cannon of St. George.

Wasatch, $150, Abram Hatch of Heber.

Wayne, $150, W. E. Robison of Loa,

Weber. $350, G. H. Islaub of Ogden.

On account of the refusal of several commissioners to serve, Governor Wells yesterday appointed the following to supervise the expenditure of money appropriated to the different counties for a display at the coming Jubilee: B. Christensen of Eureka, vice C. H. Blanchard, resigned; James M. Beatie of Carbon county, vice William G. Sharp, resigned; Thomas C. Callister of Fillmore, vice Ira N. Hinckley, resigned.

Mr. A. V. Robison is preparing to go to Fillmore next week to witness the race between Mandy and Nelly Gray, which takes place at that burg. It is stated that the Millard county people have unbounded faith in Mandy and are willing to loose large sums of money if any animal can be brought in to beat her. She has defeated every horse of note in the state and has a record equal with the best.

THE FILLMORE RACE.

Stranger Carries Off the Prize as a Little Dreamer Predicted.

FILLMORE CITY, Utah, May 25.—5:30 p.m.—The largest gathering of people ever seen in Millard county were gathered together today to witness a horse race between Millard county's pet mare Maudy and a grey mare which came in here about a month since, owned by a Mr. Hammond and called Nelly Grey, alias Humming Bird. The local sports made up a purse of $300 and the main bet was for that amount, but some $1,000 changed hands on the event. The stranger got away with all the money in sight and the idol of our local sports is down in the dust.

Kanosh sports were here in force and are feeling gleeful at the result of the race. They are returning home with many large dollars in their pockets as a result of acting upon the suggestion of a little dreamer, a child about 7 years old, named Penney. Her father told in public that his little girl had dreamed now seventeen times as seeing the outcome of horse races, and they had all come out as dreamed by her.

The father told me before the race the grey would beat Maudy, and I went to a buggy and saw the little dreamy miss. She modestly told me, "Yes, the grey mare will beat Maudy but not much. I am sure she will." Of course I did not bet upon this suggestion and will leave it to wiser heads than mine to figure out where such dreams come from.

Many people are feeling real good here today judging by the hilarious away they carry through the dust.

Maudy is the property of Mr. Almon Robison and has been thought to be a record breaker hitherto.

A. BIRD.

Salt Lake Herald
May 29, 1897

Fillmore Progress: Last fall Mr. R. A. McBride and Joseph Payne discovered in the mountains east of this place some good looking rock, and a few days ago those gentlemen took Mr. J. M. Hanson and John McBride as interested parties in the claim, and a small amount of development work was done; an average sample of the ledge, which was uncovered about three feet below the surface, was sent to Mr. Seckles, an assayer at Salt Lake, and returns show the value of the rock to be $5.80. All the parties are quite elated over their good fortune and considerable development work will be done at once.

Deseret Evening News
June 5, 1897

Fillmore News.

FILLMORE CITY, Utah, June 4, 1897.—An adjourned session of the Fifth judicial district court (Judge E. V. Higgins presiding) commenced here yesterday, June 3rd. The docket is a light one. There are several probate cases of little public interest. Besides our local lawyers there are present Attorneys Foster and Knox from Beaver, and D. D. Houtz and S. A. King from Provo.

Nellie A. Tomlin, upon the grounds of desertion and failure to provide, obtained a divorce from John E. Tomlin.

Reuben M. Keen obtained a divorce from his wife Ida A. Keen, upon the ground of desertion. This is a case of a mother deserting her husband and two small children.

All parties to the above named divorce suits are somewhat recent arrivals to Millard county.

Amanda Carling was today granted a divorce from Frank Carling, upon the grounds of conviction of felony. The young fellow is now serving five years' sentence in the penitentiary for attempting to poison one William Goulter.

No jury trials will be had this term of court and the county commissioners appreciate Judge Higgins' assistance in helping keep down expenses.

Mrs. Holbrook, the wife of the mayor of Provo city, is on a visit to her parents. Her father, I. N. Hinckley, president of this Stake, is moving among the people, still plainly wearing the effects of the recent accident which befel him in Utah county.

A very unpleasant hitch frequently occurs in mail matters lately. The DESERET EVENING NEWS arrives at the office sometimes in batches of two and three dates by the same mail, some papers do not come at all, and some will arrive tardily, marked "missent" and as the NEWS gives us news twenty-four hours ahead of the other dailies, its non-arrival causes disappointment especially when there is much public anxiety about the condition of our sick friends as recently has been the case.

After the noon recess the district court was adjourned until the October term, and our city again lapsed into the grave-like quiet which has prevailed since the late exciting horse race, when Millard's favorite got beaten, and the sly stranger walked off with the honor and dollars. A certain lawyer here is cruelly quiet, when he sees a Faber pusher approaching; he looks admiringly down at his own feet encased in a pair of Victoria calf shoes, won from the latter on the horse race, then he suddenly becomes anxious about the time of day, and pulls out a bright and shining Elgin watch obtained from the same source. The one man smiles, the other leaves in search of an item to refresh or dull the memory of a former venture.

The crop prospect here is very good, both for fruit and grain, and a cheerful spirit pervades the husbandman.

A. BIRD.

Salt Lake Herald
June 19, 1897

Up to date about one-third the population of Fillmore has expressed their intention of visiting Salt Lake during the jubilee week. A large number will go the old fashioned way—by wagon.

Washington County News
June 26, 1897

PRIZE FIGHTER M'KINNEY.

HE IS WANTED DOWN IN MILLARD COUNTY.

His Accuser is a Fillmore Girl and His Arrival is Expected.

H. H. McKinney, the prize fighter, who is now in this city, bragging about who he can lick, is wanted at Fillmore on a charge of fornication, and will doubtless be arrested as soon as the papers arrive here from Millard county.

His accuser is a girl in Fillmore, who is about to become a mother, and who claims he is the father of her child.

The offense is said to have been committed in this city. The officers of Millard county are anxious to get him back and make him right the wrong so far as is possible, by marrying the girl whom he has ruined, and the warrant will doubtless reach here this morning.

Salt Lake Herald
June 29, 1897

SOME LIVING PIONEERS.

President George Q. Cannon, of the first presidency of the Mormon church
is another member of the pioneer band of '47. He was born in Liverpool,
Jan. 11, 1827. When he was 12 years of age his parents joined the church and
emigrated to Nauvoo, where President Cannon for a number of years
worked in the newspaper offices of the Nauvoo Neighbor and Times. For
two years after coming to Utah he engaged in the roughest kind of work,
afterwards going to California with Apostle C. C. Rich, where he worked in
the gold mines. In 1850 he was called on a mission to the Sandwich Islands,
where he labored for the next four years, and on returning to his home in
Utah was almost immediately sent to California on a mission, and while there

PRESIDENT GEORGE Q. CANNON.

he published the Western Standard. The "Utah war" called him back to Salt Lake and in 1859 he took the Deseret News plant to Fillmore City.

In 1855 he was made an apostle, afterwards filling many missions.

In 1862 President Cannon was elected United States senator from the inchoate state of Deseret, but the honor was empty owing to the failure to get Utah admitted into the Union. He was subsequently private secretary to Brigham Young, with whom his relations were very intimate. President Cannon took charge of the Deseret News as editor in 1867, which position he held until 1872, when he was elected delegate to congress, and on the death of Brigham Young was called to the first presidency.

From the records compiled by Chairman Clawson of the Pioneer Jubilee commission, it is learned that there are now 24 surviving members of Brigham Young's company of pioneers. Their names, nativity, date of birth and residence are:

Name.	Born.	Nativity.	Residence.
Brown, George W	1827	New York	Charleston, Utah
Cloward, Thomas P	1823	Pennsylvania	Payson, Utah
Curtis, Lyman	1812	Massachusetts	Salem, Utah
Dewey, Franklin B.	1829	Massachusetts	White Hills, Ariz.
Eastman, Ozra F.	1828	Vermont	Idaho Falls, Ida.
Egbert, Joseph	1818	Indiana	Kaysville, Utah
Farr, Aaron F., sr.	1818	Vermont	Ogden, Utah
Flake, Green (colored)	1828	North Carolina	George Lake, Ida.
Gleason, John S.	1819	New York	Pleasant Grove, Utah
Godard, Stephen B.	1810	New York	Fruitvale, Cal.
Harper, Charles A.	1817	Pennsylvania	Halliday, Utah
Krisey, Stephen	1817	Ohio	Paris, Ida.
Kendall, Levi N.	1822	New York	Mapleton, Utah
Klineman, Conrad	1815	Bavern	Maricopa, Ariz.
Norton, John W.	1820	Indiana	Panguitch, Utah
Shumway, Charles	1806	Massachusetts	Shumway, Ariz.
Shumway, A. P.		Massachusetts	Franklin, Idaho
Smoot, W. C. A.	1825	Tennessee	Sugar House, Utah
Taylor, Norman	1828	Ohio	Moab, Utah
Thornton, Horace	1822	New York	Manti, Utah
Vance, W. P.	1822	Tennessee	Pine Valley, Utah
Walker, Henson, sr.	1820	New York	Pleasant Grove, Utah
Woodruff, Wilford	1807	Connecticut	Salt Lake City, Utah
Woodard, George	1819	New Jersey	St. George, Utah

Salt Lake Herald
July 11, 1897

COPPER IN DEEP CREEK.

A Promising Property in Those Regions Changes Hands.

An important mining deal was closed yesterday upon the Coleman group, located in the Deep Creek country. The group embraces three claims. Walter C. Coleman was the owner of an undivided one-half interest in the property and he sold all of his right and title to State Senator Joseph V. Robinson of Fillmore. The consideration was $2,500, which was paid by Mr. Robinson in cash.

The property is a copper and gold proposition and shipments have been made from it which run up to values of $35 per ton.

Colonel George A. Henry is part owner of the property.

Edward Partridge, President Utah Stake.

In a revelation to Joseph Smith, Feb. 4, 1831, occurs the following passage:

"And again, I have called my servant, Edward Partridge, and give a commandment that he should be appointed by the voice of the Church, and ordained a Bishop unto the Church, to leave his merchandise and to spend all his time in the labors of the Church * * * and this because his heart is pure before me, for he is like unto Nathaniel of old, in whom there is no guile." Such, by the testimony of the Lord himself, was the character of Edward Partridge, whose son is now President of the Utah Stake of Zion.

President Partridge was born June 25, 1833, at Independence, Jackson County, Mo. When eight years old his father died, and as a boy he passed through all the persecutions and privations incident to the expulsion of the Saints from Missouri and Illinois. He reached Salt Lake valley in 1848. Six years later he went on his first mission to the Sandwich Islands, returning in 1857. He now married Sarah L. Clayton, and removed to Fillmore, where he resided till 1885, when he removed to Utah county.

During three years, 1882-85, he was President of the Sandwich Island mission and superintendent of the sugar plantation, and had the honor of entertaining the king and his suite, who attended the dedicatory services of a costly meeting house built by the Saints. His life has been a most active one, both in civil and ecclesiastical affairs. In Fillmore he acted successively as member of city council, mayor, county clerk and recorder, and probate judge, and was twice elected to the Territorial Legislature. He was also elected a member of the Constitutional convention from Utah county.

In an ecclesiastical capacity, he was a member of the High Council of Salt Lake Stake in 1855; Bishop of Fillmore, and afterward first counselor to President of the Stake. On moving to Provo he was made second counselor to President A. O. Smoot, and after President Smoot's death, was chosen, April 21, 1894, to be President of the Utah Stake.

In uprightness and singleness of character President Partridge resembles his father. A man of kindly disposition and clear practical judgment, one goes to him instinctively for counsel. Though conservative in many things, he is a staunch supporter of education and has made many sacrifices to give his own sons a university training. One of them is now professor of mathematics in the Brigham Young Academy.

Samuel A. King, Attorney-at-Law.

The legal profession is partly compensated for the withdrawal of Congressman W. H. King, by the able services of his brother Mr. Samuel A. King, of Provo, who has already risen to an enviable rank in his profession. If one word more than another characterizes the work of the Kings it is brilliancy. In manners and bearing they win by suavity and courtesy, and inspire confidence, by temperate habits, and a careful, painstaking attention to the interests of clients.

Samuel A. King was born at Fillmore, Jan. 9, 1868, received a high school education at the B. Y. Academy, spent two years on a mission to England, then entered the Michigan law school, graduating in 1891, since which time he has constantly been before the public in one capacity or another. He was last year elected county prosecuting attorney

and appointed attorney for Provo city—positions which it is needless to say he fills with marked ability.

Salt Lake Herald
August 8, 1897

Senator Robison's Damage Suit.

Millard Progress: On Monday, Aug. 2, Senator J. V. Robison, by his attorneys, Brown & Henderson, filed papers for a damage suit in the sum of $995 against S. H. Clark et al., receivers of the Oregon Short Line & Utah Northern Railway company.

This suit is the result of an accident Mr. Robison met with at Clear Lake Feb. 5, 1897, while on his way from Salt Lake to Fillmore. Upon arriving at Clear Lake station about 3 o'clock in the morning on that date, he alighted from the train. It was quite dark, and as he took a few steps forward he fell off the platform, breaking his collar bone and three ribs. This laid him up for a number of days, and in the meantime he was unable to attend the legislature, which was then in session.

It is alleged that carelessness and negligence on the part of the railroad company in not having lights and a railing around the platform was the cause of the accident. The case is expected to be heard at the next session of the district court held here.

Big Deals In Sheep.

Millard Progress: During the past month Bishop T. C. Callister has purchased 14,000 head of stock sheep in this county, paying from $1.55 to $1.60 per head, and is now looking for 6,000 more. Mr. Callister is buying these sheep for D. F. Saunders, of Salt Lake. If successful in buying 6,000 more, some $31,500 will be left in the county. As it now stands about $23,450 has changed hands.

Salt Lake Herald
September 15, 1897

MILLARD COUNTY BUDGET.

McKinleyites Are Non-Partisans—Important Irrigation Enterprises.

Fillmore, Utah, Sept. 13.—Notwithstanding we have experienced one of the most prolonged and severe drouths known to Millard county since its early settlement, the crops of all kinds, grain, hay, vegetables and fruit, have been unusually abundant, with fine prospects of bringing good prices. What, in common with other sections of our state, is demanding already a high cash price.

Many of the sheep owners have disposed of their entire flocks at good prices. Various opinions are entertained respecting the results of the wholesale disposition of sheep. Some claim that a benefit will arise therefrom in the fact that the destruction of ranges, water supply, water sheds, etc., will be stopped, while others claim that a cash revenue to our people will cease.

All classes of cattle are in great demand and bringing prices not paid here for some time in the past.

Bricklaying on the schoolhouse was commenced today by the Critchley brothers. It is expected that this magnificent building will be up and roofed in this fall.

All the schools will open one week from today with Professor Christensen, late of Utah county, principal, with the assistance of Miss Poulsen of Richfield, Miss Maud Crane of Kanosh, Mr. G. D. Olsen and Miss Lillian Powell of Fillmore.

Mrs. Ella Reese and Miss Annie Colegrove are at present very dangerously ill.

In the political realm there are two characteristic features observable—the partisan and the non-partisan. The Democrats adhere to the former view and the Republicans, especially McKinleyites, to the latter.

It is expected that work will soon commence on the White Mountain reservoir plant and also on the Lake Bonneville works. Both of these enterprises, it appears, will be a go, and if so Millard county will be one of the most inviting of state for settlers, investment of capital, location of business and enterprising people.

Salt Lake Herald
September 24, 1897

MILLARD CATTLE THIEVES.

Walter Webb Arrested and His Accomplices Wanted.

Fillmore, Utah, Sept. 23.—On complaint being filed in Justice Giles' court, Walter Webb of Oasis was arrested on a charge of grand larceny. He was admitted to bail in the sum of $500. The alleged crime is stealing cattle belonging to persons residing at the towns of Oak City and Leamington. Other parties, supposed accomplices in the crime, will be arrested in the near future.

Lewis Tarbuck, an aged veteran and pioneer, was stricken with paralysis last evening. While he is somewhat improved, he is still in a precarious condition.

Deseret Evening News
September 24, 1897

Fillmore Notes.

Millard Progress: Last Tuesday in the neighborhood of some 200 head of cattle were shipped out of Fillmore. A Mr. Lunt, of Nephi, was the purchaser. This will leave considerable money in town, tho' it has drained Fillmore of all salable cattle for the present, but we understand that from 200 to 600 head of cattle will likely be brought here from the south and from Nevada in a few days. Mr. Almon Robison is at the head of this deal.

D. P. Callister, who has made Salt Lake his home the past eight years, arrived in the city Saturday. It is his intention to make Fillmore his future home and will move his family down in about a month.

Salt Lake Herald
September 29, 1897

Fillmore, Utah, Sept. 28.—Ex-United States Deputy Marshal W. P. Payne arrested today at Robison's ranch, about 8 miles west of Fillmore, E. E. Livingston, who escaped from the Salt Lake county jail on the 21st of August, while intrusted with painting the public building.

Livingston came direct to Millard county and has worked on the Robison farm and in the vicinity for three weeks. He states that on his arrival here the first person he met was the sheriff of Millard county, with whom he talked for some time. Livingston will be taken back to Salt Lake tomorrow.

Sheriff Lewis went to Fillmore yesterday to escort Ed Livingston, who escaped from the county jail a few weeks ago, back to Salt Lake. Livingston was awaiting trial on a charge of grand larceny and his arrest was accomplished through descriptions furnished the Millard county officers.

Salt Lake Herald
October 2, 1897

Sheriff Lewis returned yesterday morning from Fillmore with Ed Livingston, the escaped jail bird. The sheriff believes that Livingston tells the truth when he denies that he ever made the statement that a deputy consented to and encouraged his levanting while painting the exterior of the county bastile, over a month ago.

Deseret Evening News
October 2, 1897

NEWS FROM FILLMORE.

The Cattle Stealing Case—Sheriff Lewis Returning With the Fugitive Livingston.

Fillmore, Sept. 30, 1897.

To the Editor:

More recent developments in cattle stealing case at Oasis have resulted in finding several hides of animals, shipped to C. Andrews at Nephi, and bearing the brands of Samuel and William McIntyre, George Nixon, Ben Kinney, Bishop Stephenson and others. A warrant for the arrest of E. M. Webb is issued, and proof is at hand that Walter Webb, the man whose wife's innocent communication to the local paper put the officers and cattle men on the scent, have been freely disposing of other people's property, and will have to give explanation to the matter in the district court.

Walter Webb is at large on $500 bail, and will appear before Justice J. S. Giles on Saturday, to answer to the charge of stealing cattle.

Livingston, the jail bird who escaped from Salt Lake county prison, has been stopping around here in and near town for the past two or three weeks. He is in the county jail and will leave this evening for Salt Lake City in custody of Sheriff Lewis. The prisoner talks freely of his recent experiences. He tell that about the first man he visited here was the county sheriff to make inquiry for the whereabouts of one Baker, who has been working upon the White Mountain reservoir. He laughingly tells that at the time he spoke with the sheriff he had a Salt Lake paper with his likeness and an account of his escape in his pocket. He also kindly assisted our genial county prosecuting attorney to brand a cow (it was the attorney's cow). Livingston appears to have just come this way for a horse back ride and to wait around until he was wanted, as he disposed of his sorrel steed to young Edgar Turner at Holden.

The county commissioners have been busy for the last four days with important county affairs.

Your observing canvasser, Mr. Jones, has caused a ripple in the stagnant waters here by telling very nicely what he saw when here; but he certainly missed to notice the foundation of our fine new school house which was then in and upon which is now laid most of the first story of what will be the finest school building in the county, and which will compare favorably with the best in Salt Lake City. Thanks to the efforts of a few energetic men here and the perservering school trustees, Judge Greenwood, Christian Andersen, and Mrs. Birdie Robison. Fillmore always has been noted for its educational facilities, is determined to keep up its good name, and the people are making sacrifices to have suitable building accomodations.

A. BIRD.

Provo Daily Enquirer
October 2, 1897

Terrific Storm at Fillmore.

FILLMORE, Utah, Oct. 1—Tribune Special—A continuous gale blew here last night, and this morning about 10 o'clock Critchlow's new one-story brick house, situated in the northern part of the city, was struck by what appeared to be a small cyclone; the roof was torn off and landed in a lot on the opposite side of the street, and the gabled ends of the house blown in on the family—Lew Critchlow, wife and baby, and his mother who is here on a visit.

The older members escaped with a few bruises, but the little baby was buried under two feet of brick and mortar, and when gotten out was still alive, but it is doubtful if it will live.

Just before the house was struck, what appeared to be a dark cloud was seen coming from the west at a terrific speed, thirty yards wide and 100 feet high.

Salt Lake Herald
October 3, 1897

MILLARD IMPROVEMENTS.

Much Can Be Said to the Credit of the People.

Fillmore, Utah, Sept. 30.—A correspondent of a Salt Lake paper, in a recent article, created the impression that what are known as the mountain towns of Millard county are in a state of lethargy and are not progressive. While Millard county, in common with many other Utah counties, is in need of a great many things, there is much that can be said to the credit of the people in their desire for improvements. There are neat and convenient meeting houses and modern and commodious school houses in each of the towns of Scipio, Holden, Meadow and Kanosh, and also all the towns in the western part of the county, while here in Fillmore we have the time-honored state house, court and other public buildings, with an excellent school house and a meeting house in course of erection.

There are two cheese factories, a roller mill, planing mill, two saw mills, eight stores and an excellent system of graded schools. In the last four or five years there have been erected in Fillmore some 40 or 50 neat dwelling houses of brick, adobe and lumber.

Lewis Tarbuck, who was stricken with paralysis and subsequently succumbed, was buried on the 26th past. The funeral ceremonies were held in the meeting house, a large number attending.

The 13-year-old daughter of Josiah Trimble of Fillmore died very suddenly this morning. She had been subject to fits all her life, which reduced her to a physical and mental wreck, and caused her death.

Fillmore Cattle Sales.

Millard Progress: It is reported to us that William George has sold some $12,000 worth of cattle and sheep the past ten days, Antone Paxton about the same amount and Charles Whitaker some $7,000 worth. Last week we reported that on account of over 200 head of cattle being sold in Fillmore it had drained this city of all saleable cattle at present. We are told that this is not correct, and that there are yet a considerable number of cattle for sale in Fillmore.

Deseret Evening News
October 4, 1897

News From Fillmore.

Fillmore City, Oct. 2, 1897.—The cattle stealing case against Walter Webb came up before Justice J. S. Giles. Attorney Greenwood for the defense asked for a continuance for forty days. And after some objection by the prosecution an agreement to continue till Nov. 5, 1897, was arrived at. The bonds were increased from $500 to $1,000; securities, G. R. Huntsman, Amos Maxfield and Samuel Rutherford, and the defendant was liberated.

Sheriff Holbrook now has here, in addition to the six head of live cattle, seven hides brought down from Nephi. Several of the owners of the cattle from which these hides were taken were examining them on the street today. The defense claims that Walter Webb was simply the innocent agent of his brother, E. M. Webb, who is at present buying cattle near White river in Nevada.

Attorney S. A. King came on today with his brother-in-law, L. N. Hinckley, bringing for burial here the body of the latter gentleman's 19-months-old baby girl, who died suddenly from a cold contracted by its playful action in the water upon a lawn in Provo. The babe was buried in the family plot in Fillmore cemetery.

The Critchley baby, hurt badly by the falling house yesterday, is doing nicely and will recover.

A. BIRD.

Salt Lake Herald
October 6, 1897

COURT AT FILLMORE.

Efforts to Reinstate a Personal Damage Case.

Fillmore, Oct. 5.—The regular term of the 5th judicial district court opened here today with Judge Higgins on the bench. The calendar was called, some cases were continued for the term and others were passed temporarily on account of the absence of counsel.

The case of James Whitaker vs. Joshua Greenwood was set for trial for the 9th inst.

C. Andrews vs. J. P. Johnson, set for the 6th inst. J. M. Hanson, attorney for defendant, withdrew as counsel in the case and defendant was requested to employ other counsel.

Peter Greenhalch vs. Almond Robison, set for 7th inst.

Peter Huntsman vs. R. G. Huntsman, set for 8th inst. This is a case of personal damages for $10,000. The defendant through some mistake allowed the case to go by default. A vigorous effort will be made to set the default aside and have the case tried on its merits.

Marragh Palmer vs. Pauline Mila Jorgenson; plaintiff was given a decree of divorce on the ground of desertion.

Lancaster Savings bank vs. Thomas C. Callister et al; set for trial for the 7th inst.

Lindesey Prous et al vs. Watum Hardy, dismissed at cost of plaintiff, defendants having filed disclaimers.

James Whitaker vs. Joshua Greenwood et al, demurrer overruled.

A jury of 18 names was drawn and the venire made returnable Thursday next.

From the books of the calendar this term it would seem that court would be in session here for about ten days.

Salt Lake Herald
October 7, 1897

COURT AT FILLMORE.

Suit For Rebate on a Wool Shipment.

Fillmore, Utah, Oct. 6.—Judge Higgins transacted the following business today:

Maretta Palmer of Kanosh vs. William Palmer; plaintiff was granted a divorce on the ground of desertion and failure to support.

C. Andrews & Co. vs. J. P. Johnson; judgment was given the plaintiff for $545, costs and interest from March, 1894. This suit was brought to recover a rebate on a wool transaction, it being claimed that the wool was shipped on commission and the defendant claiming that it was sold to plaintiff outright.

The case of C. Andrews & Co. vs. Hans and K. Lund, a similar suit to the former, was settled by the parties and dismissed.

FILLMORE DAMAGE SUIT.

Six Thousand Dollars Wanted For False Imprisonment.

(Special to The Herald.

Fillmore, Utah, Oct. 7.—After the jury was examined this morning on their statutory qualifications, the case of Peter Greenhalgh against Almond Robison was taken up for trial. This case is developing into quite an interesting suit. The plaintiff is suing Robison for six thousand odd dollars for malicious prosecution and false imprisonment. The defendant had the plaintiff arrested some months ago for removing and hauling away a fence. The case was tried and resulted in a nonconviction.

In his testimony today the plaintiff showed that an old feud has existed between himself and defendant for years, and that after the fence had been partly removed, defendant was arrested, and that Mrs. Ernst went to defendant and tried to get the case dismissed, saying to defendant that she had ordered Greenhalgh to remove the fence, and if anyone was to blame for it, she was. The case, however, was gone ahead with, with the result as stated above.

Colonel Tatlock and McBride have the case for the plaintiff and S. A. King and Greenwood & Melville are conducting the defense and the case is being closely tried and is causing considerable public interest.

Joseph H. Diorden, a native of England, was today admitted to citizenship.

News From Fillmore.

Fillmore, Oct. 7, 1897.—The case of Peter Greenhalgh against Almond Robison is being stubbornly fought with Attorneys Tatlock and McBride for plaintiff and Attorneys Greenwood and S. A. King for defendant. It appears that Mr. Robison owned land in Meadow and believed that the fence upon it was his also, and when Peter Greenhalgh removed it he, Robison, had him arrested. He was in custody of the sheriff at his house one night. Next day, finding the fence was not his, Robison's, but the property of Mrs. Ernst of Meadow, who had employed Greenhalgh to remove it, Mr. Robison withdrew his prosecution. For this imprisonment Mr. Greenhalgh now asks $6,000. It looks as though the case will consume the time of the court tomorrow.

The lawyers here are somewhat amused to note in one of your morning cotemporaries the information that "Marigetto Palmer vs Pauline Mila Jorgenson; plaintiff was given a decree of divorce on the ground of desertion." These are supposed to be both ladies. Mrs. Mary Ettie Palmer did obtain a divorce from William Palmer, and Soren Jorgenson also obtained a divorce from Pauline Nielsen Jorgenson, upon the grounds of desertion.

There is something wrong with the mails, for your paper frequently comes in batches. Some papers never appear at the postoffice at all. I am inclined to think that the trouble is in transit, and not at your office. It would appear that there is an incompetent or lazy clerk somewhere.

A. BIRD.

Fillmore Damage Case.

(Special to The Herald.)

Fillmore, Utah, Oct. 8.—The damage suit for false imprisonment and malicious prosecution of Peter Greenhalgh vs. Almon Robison has been in progress all day in Judge Higgins' court.

The plaintiff closed this afternoon, and while the defense is well under headway the case will take at least all day tomorrow to finish.

DESERET RESERVOIR.

Will Reclaim Lands For Hundreds of Settlers.

Deseret correspondence Fillmore Progress: The Deseret and Salt Lake Irrigation company met Saturday, Oct. 2, at Deseret. Hon. John T. Caine, Bishop Solomans, John Nicholson, Charles Wilknes, Attorney Ferguson representing the Salt Lake company and Attorney Thurman, of Provo, with our citizens, representing Deseret. An agreement was reached between the two companies that the Salt Lake company should build a reservoir to hold sufficient water to irrigate all lands belonging to the people of both companies. It is supposed the cost will be $15,000. The Deseret company owning four-sevenths, the Salt Lake company three-sevenths. If such an agreement is perfected work will be commenced in 60 days, and will be completed in one year. The president of the Deseret Irrigation company has gone to Salt Lake and the agreement will be consummated before his return, at least we hope so. This will develop our country and enable us to take in hundreds of people more than live here at the present time.

DISAPPROVED AT FILLMORE.

President Woodruff's Remarks the Subject of Discussion.

(Special to The Herald.)

Fillmore, Utah, Oct. 8.—The Herald, which arrived here this morning, containing the report of President Woodruff's remarkable political address before the conference at Salt Lake caused considerable consternation and a widespread feeling of disapproval throughout the community.

The question has been very generally discussed all day by little groups of men in front of the hotels and on the corners of streets. Many think there is some mistake about the affair, others predict a restoration of the old condition of affairs, while still others attribute this remarkable speech to the president's old age. The fact that such an address would be made, however, during the close of conference, had been whispered to several, and when The Herald arrived this morning their expressions were: "Didn't I tell you so?"

If this speech of President Woodruff's means that the leaders are going to hereafter dictate in political affairs, contrary to their pledges to the contrary, they will find a strong opposition in this part of the country, for the sentiment expressed here has been general, and in many cases from men in high standing in the church, that church control in politics will be resisted to the bitter end.

Deseret Evening News
October 19, 1897

Burglary at Abe Hunter's.

It was reported at the police station this morning that a burglary had been committed during the night at the Hunter's place, 623 west, North Temple street. The police department investigated the matter and found that an apartment occupied by Mrs. Fillmore had been entered by unknown parties and several bottles of fruit and other household necessitis taken. Mrs. Fillmore recently secured a decree of divorce from her husband and was preparing to move out when the theft occurred. The officers believe that the guilty parties are none others than some of the lady's friends.

Salt Lake Herald
October 26, 1897

MAN LOST NEAR FILLMORE.

Aged Resident Out All Night in a Storm.

Fillmore, Utah, Oct. 25.—John Mitchell started from Fillmore to a sheep camp about five miles away Sunday morning at 10:30 for the purpose of taking medicine to his son, who was herding sheep for Nichols Brothers. Being quite aged, near-sighted and deaf, he lost his way and wandered around in the foothills. The report of his being lost was made at 7 p. m. by the ringing of the bell on the county court house. Men and boys rushed into the hills on horseback, endeavoring to rescue the lost man, as great fears were entertained that he would perish if not found before morning, as one of the most severe storms of wind, snow and rain was raging all night long. Bright lights shone from the top of the dome of the county court house to enable the unfortunate man to return to town.

The effort of the anxious hunters proved fruitless, as no trace of him could be found until 10 a. m. today, when he was found by P. D. Callister in a chilled, half frozen condition, scarcely able to move. Brandy was administered immediately, when he revived and was brought into town.

Salt Lake Herald
November 1, 1897

A FRIGHTFUL WOUND.

Ram Rod of a Gun Shot Into Partridge's Body.

(Special to The Herald.)

Fillmore, Utah, Oct. 31. — William Partridge of Oak City, while hunting in the mountains near Fool Creek peak, was accidentally shot while riding through the timber. The cleaning rod of the gun being in the barrel at the time of the discharge, passed into his body near the floating rib, ranging upwards into the cavity of the lungs, taking a curve therein. As the rod passed upwards it struck one of the ribs, causing splinters to fly therefrom, and lodging in the muscles covering the shoulder blade.

The unfortunate sufferer traveled 12 miles from the scene of the accident to Oak City. Dr. Keen of Fillmore was immediately sent for. On his arrival he found the accident one of the worst kind. A piece of the rod 17 inches in length was extracted from the body, bringing with it indications that it had entered the colon. Twelve incisions were made in the back and pieces of wood taken therefrom. The patient at last accounts was doing as well as could be expected, but grave doubts as to his recovery are entertained.

Salt Lake Herald
November 4, 1897

FOR STEALING CATTLE.

Walter and Edward Webb of Oasis Under Bonds.

Fillmore, Nov. 3.—Walter and Edward M. Webb of Oasis, are held to the district court in the sum of $1,000 each, to answer for the charge of stealing cattle. This case was reported some time ago. These persons were charged with stealing cattle near Leamington, and driving them to Milford, where a portion of them were butchered and others recovered by the officers.

Deseret Evening News
November 5, 1897

Millard Progress: About 6:30 Thursday evening, the Fillmore meeting house was the scene of a small blaze, creating some excitement. The fire was quickly brought under subjection, and no damage to speak of was done. The fire started near the roof, on account of a shortage of stove pipe. The organ and part of the benches were quickly taken out after the alarm was given.

Salt Lake Herald
November 16, 1897

POSTMASTER FOR FILLMORE.

Marshal Glen Miller Has Selected Frank E. Hansen.

(Special to The Herald.)

Washington, Nov. 15.—Frank E. Hansen was today appointed postmaster at Fillmore, Millard county, Utah, vice Ira N. Hinkley, removed.

Comptroller Eckels today decided a final dividend of 7.05 per cent in favor of the creditors of the First National bank of Sundance, Wyo., making in all 52.05 per cent on claims proved, amounting to $48,502.

An original pension is granted Joseph McCrosky of Sundance, Wyo.

[From The Herald's Correspondents.]

Fillmore, Nov. 15.—The 7-year-old son of Silas M. Smith, at Meadow, Utah, while playing, fell from the doorstep, a distance of about 18 inches, on to a small express wagon. One of the wheels being broken, one of the spokes entered the brain near the temple. The child, after making one scream, expired instantly. This sudden death, which occurred Sunday at 5 p. m., was a most terrific blow to the griefstricken parents, who have the sympathy of the entire community.

TOO MUCH COUGH MEDICINE.

Child at Meadow Has a Narrow Escape From Death.

Fillmore, Nov. 16.—Peter Greenalch of Meadow has been making a cough medicine, containing morphine in large quantities. Mrs. Veatch, of the same town, gave some to her two-months' old boy, with the result that she called Dr. Keen, who administered an antidote which acted admirably. The child may recover.

Salt Lake Herald
November 26, 1897

PANIC AT FILLMORE

Meeting House Ablaze During a Thanksgiving Entertainment.

TERRIBLE SCENE ENSUED

WOMEN TRAMPLED ON AND BABIES THROWN OUT.

Scenery and Draperies Caught Fire and the Whole Stage Was a Mass of Flame—Women and Children Knocked Down and Furniture Smashed—Many Cut and Bruised.

(Special to The Herald.)

Fillmore, Utah, Nov. 25.—Last evening a concert was given in the meeting house under the management of the teachers of Fillmore district schools. The entertainment was largely attended, especially by the children of the town. Reasonable estimates place the number in attendance at 500. The children, who were mostly all small, were near the stage and on it.

The programme, which consisted of songs, recitations, tableaux, etc., was completed, with the exception of the last tableaux, when the combustibles used for illumination caught fire, which spread to the scenery and bunting running across the ceiling, causing the stage to present the appearance of one mass of flame.

The people became panic stricken, rushing for the door, windows were smashed, through which women threw their babies, others jumping out with children in their arms. Women and little children were knocked down and jumped upon, benches and other furniture were broken to pieces by this struggling mass of human beings piled up in confusion.

While this horrifying scene was going on in the main part of the building, the men and women on the stage were fighting the flames, which they finally brought under control.

After the excitement had abated and the hall nearly emptied, it was learned that no one was seriously injured, but many suffered cuts and bruises, caused by the breaking of windows and falling over benches. While it was a dangerous position for people to be in, all rejoice that it is no worse than it is. The breaking of the windows enabled quite a number to escape, and allowed the suffocating fumes to pass out, thereby saving some from suffocation.

Salt Lake Herald
December 3, 1897

ACCIDENT AT DESERET.

Alpha Cahoon's Leg and Ankle Crushed—Heavy Storm.

Deseret, Dec. 1.—While on the road coming from Fillmore here with a load of flour, Alpha Cahoon was thrown from his wagon and his leg broken in two places just below the knee and the ankle was crushed. He is doing as well as could be expected with the aid he could get.

A heavy snow has been falling all day and is still falling. The work on the Gunnison Bend reservoir had to be discontinued today on account of the storm. The company has decided not to fill the reservoir until spring. Consequently the work will not last as long as expected at first.

The supply of lucern and hay so far exceeds the demand that there will be a large quantity on hand and no sale for it.

There are, according to rumor, several weddings to be celebrated during the holidays.

Deseret Evening News
December 3, 1897

One Held, the Other Discharged.

George Harmon and A. M. Fillmore were before Justice McMaster today to answer the charge of grand larceny. The complaint was sworn to by Victor Erfurt, who alleged that the defendants stole a horse and saddle belonging to him. Fillmore waived examination and was held to the district court in $500 bonds. Harmon stood the siege of a preliminary hearing and secured a dismissal.

Deseret Evening News
December 10, 1897

What of This Wheat?

Cedar City, Iron Co., Utah,
Dec. 8, 1897.

To the Editor:

Some time ago, I got a sample of curious looking wheat from a friend who said it had been found in a cave near Fillmore, but he could give me no further information about it. I have been making inquiries, but can learn nothing more.

I sent a few grains to the American Miller, who submitted it to Prof. Latto, an expert in these matters, but he did not appear to be sure whether it was really wheat or not.

Perhaps your genial correspondent, A. Bird, or others of your readers in that locality will kindly throw some light on this matter.

ALEX MATHESON, Miller.

FILLMORE PARAGRAPHS.

Proceedings in the Fifth Judicial District Court

Filmore, Dec. 14, 1897.

The Fifth judicial district court convened here today, Judge E. V. Higgins presiding. Among the attorneys present was D. D. Houtz and Wedgewood of Provo, Knox of Beaver and John M. Zane of Salt Lake City. The case of the Deseret Irrigation company vs Samuel McIntire et al was argued, Zane for defendants and Wedgewood for plaintiff, and the complaint dismissed as to the Fayette Irrigation company, Robins & Kearns, Edward Robins and Henry A. Kearns for want of jurisdiction, the defendants residing out of the county. At 2 p. m. S. H. King, attorney, Provo, came in.

Jury drawn to try the Webb Cattle stealing case, which is set for Thursday, Dec. 16th.

The case of W. A. Ray vs Boregard et al; continued for the term.

Decree denied for the distribution of the estate of Appleton S. Harmon.

Lancaster Bank vs T. C. Callister; demurrer overruled.

In the case of Lawler vs Fox; defendants have and to include the 4th of January A. D. 1898.   A. BIRD.

COURT OPENS AT FILLMORE.

A Lively Term Predicted—Webb Brothers Arraigned.

Fillmore, Utah, Dec. 14.—Judge Higgins opened court at this point today and the number of leading attorneys present indicates a lively term. The attorneys behind the bar at the calling of the calendar were J. M. Zane, E. A. Wedgwood, D. D. Houtz, Sam King and W. F. Knox, as well as local attorneys, Joshua Greenwood, J. M. Hanson and County Attorney Melville. Only a partial setting of the calendar was made.

In the matter of the estate of George Croft, Dec. 17 was set for final settlement and distribution, and the 18th inst. for some orders in the estate of George Monroe.

Peter Huntsman vs. G. R. Huntsman; set for 18th inst.

Joseph V. Robison vs. S. A. Clark et al., receivers of the Oregon Short Line Railway company; set for the 18th.

James A. George vs. Almon Robison et al.; demurrer argued and submitted.

State vs. Walter Webb; arraigned and defendant took statutory time to plead.

State vs. Edward M. Webb; same order.

These two defendants were also arraigned on six different informations, charging them jointly with grand larcenies in stealing cattle.

Lancaster Savings bank vs. Thomas Callister et al.; demurrer overruled.

Lawler vs. Jesse W. Fox, jr., et al.; demurrer overruled.

A petit jury of 24 names was drawn and the venire made returnable Thursday next at 10 o'clock.

FINE POINT DECIDED

Suit Involving Most of the Waters of the Sevier.

JURISDICTION QUESTION

SUIT MUST BE BROUGHT WHERE WATERS ARE DIVERTED.

Judge Higgins Decides an Important Question Raised Under a Peculiar Provision of the Constitution— Sevier County's Finances—A Whitecap's Warning at Richfield —Davis County Offender.

[From The Herald Correspondents.]
Fillmore, Utah, Dec. 14.—A very important question was argued by Wedgewood for the plaintiffs and J. M. Zane for the defendants and decided by Judge Higgins today in a big suit pending here, entitled the Deseret Irrigation company and the Lemington Irrigation company vs. Samuel McIntyre, William H. McIntyre, the Wellington Irrigation company, the Dover Irrigation company, the Fayette Irrigation company, Edward Robbins, Henry A. Kearnes and the Deseret & Salt Lake Agricultural & Manufacturing company.

This is a case involving pretty much all the waters of the Sevier river from Sanpete county down to its sinks in Millard county. The action was brought to determine the rights of the several water owners. The attorneys for defendants, the Fayette Irrigation company, the Robbins Dam & Canal company and Albert Robbins, moved the court to dismiss action against their clients for the reason that the complaint shows that any interference by their clients with the water of the river took place in Sanpete county, and that the court sitting in Millard county has no jurisdiction in the matter, owing to that provision in the constitution which provides that all criminal and civil business arising in any county shall be tried in the county where such business arises.

It was contended by Mr. Zane that the wrong by interference with the waters of a running stream must be taken as having been done at the point and in the county where the injured party receives his water from the natural channel, and notwithstanding the water may have been diverted from the natural channel in another county, the county in which the party injured received his water being the place where the cause of action arose. The court, after hearing the arguments, decided that interference with the right to the use of water in a running stream was a trespass, and the cause of action arose in the county where the trespass took place. Secondly, the wrong complained of having taken place in Sanpete county, and the action having been brought in Millard county, this court is without jurisdiction, and hence dismissed the case as to the parties moving a dismissal.

By consent of all parties nothing further is to be done in the case until the question is determined in the supreme court on an appeal from the order dismissing the action. Steps for an immediate appeal will be taken on this question, which, under the new and somewhat peculiar phrasion of the constitution seems to be very uncertain.

THE X-RAY AT PROVO.

Used By Doctors to Examine a Fractured Bone.

Provo, Dec. 14.—The X-ray aparatus belonging to the B. Y. academy is of great convenience to doctors. Recently a son of Mr. Miller, who had received a fracture of the leg, was examined by Dr. Allen with the aid of this apparatus. The doctor was enabled to see plainly the break in the bone and became satisfied that the bone was not splintered, as had been feared.

Samuel A. King started last evening for Fillmore, where he has some legal matters to look after.

Business houses are beginning to take on holiday atire.

A local minstrel company, under the management of Thomas Osborne, is rehearsing for an entertainment during the holidays.

Provo rooters will be out in full force to witness the game of football to be played by the academy and 'varsity teams.

Salt Lake Herald
December 16, 1897

NEWS OF THE STATE

Webb Brothers Arraigned For Cattle Stealing at Fillmore.

CATTLE THEFTS IN EMERY

THIRTY HEAD RECOVERED BY THE IRELAND COMPANY.

Two Hundred Thousand Sheep On the Eastern Utah Range—Gun Play at Payson Lands Ab. Gough In Jail—Outrage at Scofield—Logan Postmaster Demands the Office.

[From The Herald Correspondents.]

Fillmore, Utah, Dec. 15.—The only business of any importance before Judge Higgins today was the arraignment of the Webb brothers of Oasis on eight different informations, charging them with stealing cattle. They pleaded not guilty to each charge and their cases were set for trial Thursday, Friday and Saturday next.

Some of the cattle alleged to have been stolen belong to the McIntyre brothers, who evidently intend to prosecute these cases for all there is in them, they having hired C. O. Whittemore of Salt Lake as special counsel to assist in prosecuting at the preliminary hearing before the justice and also to assist in the trial in the district court.

Salt Lake Herald
December 17, 1897

TRIAL OF EDWARD WEBB.

Explains How He Came Into Possession of Other People's Cattle.

Fillmore, Dec. 16.—The venire for petit jurors was returned today in Judge Higgins' court, and the first case, that of the state vs. Walter Webb, was called for trial. The prosecuting attorney stated that he was not ready in the case of the state against Edward M. Webb. The defendants' counsel, Mr. Houtz, objected to taking up the cases out of their order, and so the state asked to have the first named case dismissed, which was done, and the case of Edward M. Webb, being the next on the docket, was proceeded with.

It appeared from the evidence that defendant and another man were partners, keeping a butcher shop at Milford last August, and that Webb brought in about a dozen cattle with a bill of sale from one Nielson. These cattle proved to be stolen from divers persons in Millard county, and this fact becoming known to the officers, and Webb having the cattle in his possession, he was arrested for stealing them. The prosecution showed several suspicious circumstances tending to connect the defendant with the theft, but when they rested at noon had not the strongest case in the world. The defense asked for an instruction to bring in a verdict of not guilty, which was overruled.

The defendant then took the stand in his own behalf, and made an elaborate and minute explanation of how he bought the cattle from others, and verified his statement by bills of sale for the cattle. If the defendant does not fall down tomorrow on cross-examination he will without doubt be acquitted. The McIntyre brothers, who are the alleged owners of some of the cattle, have C. O. Whittemore here to help prosecute the case, and much interest is being taken, both by the parties directly interested, and by the public generally.

Salt Lake Herald
December 18, 1897

WEBB LARCENY CASE.

Bill of Sale and Check Said to Be Forgeries.

Fillmore, Dec. 17.—The larceny case against Edward M. Webb was submitted to the jury at the close of tonight's session. The cross examination of the defendant was resumed this morning by Mr. Whittemore at considerable length, but without any material inroads on his first story. Two or three witnesses were then sworn to corroborate different circumstances of the defendant's story as to how he came by the cattle. The prosecution followed up with several witnesses to show that the bills of sale of the alleged cattle and a check that Webb claims was given in part payment for the cattle were forgeries.

Judge Higgins wrote to the clerk at Nephi to adjourn court at that point till Monday the 27th instant. Next Monday is the time that the regular December term should begin at Nephi, but it became apparent to the judge that he would not be through here in time to conform to regular time of convening court at Nephi on Monday next, hence court will reconvene just one week later.

Deseret Evening News
December 21, 1897

A THOUSAND DOLLAR KICK.

What it Cost Peter Huntsman for Injuring His Uncle.

Special to the "News:"

Fillmore, Dec. 21.—In the suit of Peter Huntsman vs G. R. Huntsman, Attorney Houtz for plaintiff and Attorneys Knox and Hansen for defendant, the jury today gave Peter Huntsman one thousand dollars for the damage for being kicked in the head by his nephew.

Court Matters at Fillmore.

Fillmore, Dec. 29, 1897.

To the Editor:

The rather notorious case State of Utah vs E. M. Webb, wherein the defendant was charged with stealing cattle, has resulted in a verdict of guilty, and Judge Higgins has passed a sentence of two years in the State prison upon the man.

The case has created much interest in this county, owing to the large quantity of cattle and hides traced to the possession of Mr. Webb, who, in company with another man, was running a butcher shop at Milford, this county. The defense was that Webb had corresponded with one N. C. Neilson, who professed to have cattle to sell, and would hold them on the Sevier river, some six miles above Leamington. There are a number of Neilsons living at Leamington, among them the Bishop and several of his sons. Webb told it around that he was going to Leamington to purchase cattle from Mr. Neilson, a name well known there, but this Neilson and Johnson appear to be myths. Mr. Webb's wife was a correspondent of the Millard Progress, and among the items sent was one to the effect that E. M. Webb had gone to Milford with a nice bunch of cattle purchased at Leamington. This caused inquiry as to who had sold cattle, and no person could be found who had made a sale. The inquiry resulted in stolen cattle being found at Milford and hides at Nephi, shipped to Merchant Anderson. These cattle and hides bore upon them the brands of well-known stock men such as Mr. Wm. McIntire, George Nixon, Bishop Stephenson and others. The defense was that Neilson had traded young stock for McIntire's beef cattle and thus got possession of his brand not vented. Two bills of sale were produced, one signed by N. C. Neilson and another signed by his purported partner, one Johnson. These bills of sale were shown to be signed by the same hand that also signed a check said to have been paid in part payment to Neilson for the cattle. D. D. Houtz worked like a trojan for his client, the defendant, and C. O. Whittemore showed up well on the part of the State.

E. M. Webb is a bright and pleasant spoken young man, who stood well in the county, and was thought to be going straight and no one can look upon him in his present position without regret.

The case of Peter Huntsman vs G. R. Huntsman, wherein the plaintiff seeks to recover $10,000 damages for trespass upon his person, has occupied the court yesterday and today and arguments have yet to be made. D. D. Houtz, for plaintiff, is addressing the jury, among whom is Hon. I. N. Hinckley, as the mail closes.

A. BIRD.

Salt Lake Herald
December 22, 1897

VERDICT FOR THE UNCLE.

Huntsman Gets $1,000 Injuries In An Assault.

Fillmore, Dec. 21.—The jury in the personal damage case of Peter Huntsman against G. R. Huntsman, his nephew, after being out one hour and a half, returned into court last night with a verdict of $1,000 for the plaintiff. The case grew out of an assault.

The defendant moved for a new trial and 50 days' time in which to make a statement. The public in general consider the verdict a just one, as the assault was a most brutal one.

Lars Jensen, a native of Denmark, was admitted to citizenship.

This morning Samuel Rowley was granted a divorce from his wife, Emily Rowley, on the grounds of desertion. Court then adjourned for the term, Judge Higgins and the visiting attorneys leaving for their respective homes this evening.

Salt Lake Herald
January 8, 1898

Millard Progress: For some time past a most deplorable state of affairs has existed in Fillmore and the evil is now growing to alarming proportions. We refer to the drink habit, which is getting a strong hold on many of our young men.

Salt Lake Herald
January 22, 1898

CHILD BURNED AT FILLMORE.

Clothes Caught Fire While She Stood By the Stove.

Fillmore, Jan. 21.—The 3-year-old daughter of Mr. and Mrs. James Swallow of Fillmore, while standing by the stove warming an apple, was severely burned by her clothes catching fire from the blaze coming out through the stove door. The right arm and hand were burned to the elbow and the right side of the face. At the time the accident occurred there were only two little girls in the house. The father was notified and put out the flames. The little sufferer will recover.

Deseret Evening News
February 5, 1898

Voted a Two Per Cent School Tax.

Millard County Progress: The citizens of Fillmore met at the state house on Saturday and heard the report of the school trustees as the building committtee of the fine new building now being erected.

The amount of taxes for the year 1898 was $5,019.43; remittances $153.04. Contracts already made amount to $7,000, this includes the steel covering to be put on the roof.

Deseret Evening News
February 10, 1898

WANT A TOWN ORGANIZATION.

Effort of Kanosh Citizens—Deep Snow, Heavy Rains, Dying Sheep and Horses.

Correspondence of the "News:"

Fillmore City, Utah, Feb. 8.—Many of the citizens of the little town of Kanosh think it advisable to have an incorporated town organization, and at a mass meeting, at which was present by invitation, Judge Greenwood, a committee consisting of E. W. Penny, James M. Gardner and George Crane, was appointed to make inquiry as to successful working in other places in this State, and report in the near future.

The unprecedented winter is still with us with all its blessings and disadvantages, as I write, 7:20 a. m., everything in sight is wrapt in the mantle of white, wet, soggy snow, ten inches deep and still falling. On the 6th and 7th a rapid thaw set in and the deep snow had disappeared from some spots in the beaten roads which spoiled the sleighing; last night a heavy rain set in, followed by this heavy snow; the result, when it clears up, will be bad for travelers, and I fear the sheep men will continue to lose heavily. Mr. George A. George, of Kanosh, told me Saturday, that there would be but few sheep left in this part of the country, if this weather continued long; he said, "I expect to lose 30 head again tonight—have been losing from that to 50 head some nights." Many of the sheep are being hauled into town in wagons and fed on hay at $5 per ton, and still they die after being fed. Mr. Charles Jukes, who is in the business with Mr. Bland of Brooklyn, Sevier county, is also losing heavily.

Horses are also rapidly dying off on the range, with few regrets to settlers, as they had become a nuisance, without value to anybody, and consequently hundreds of unbranded, wild, and dwarfed ponies were to be found all over this county.

Many people have lost large quantities of apples and potatoes, for Jack Frost has got down to unprecedented low acts here, unexpectedly entering cellars, and in many instances solidifying all the bottled fruit in sight. And 23 below zero is not a healthful sign for our next season's crop, as the tender wood has no doubt suffered some; 35 below zero has been reached at Oasis, this county, and yet a few of our citizens have an itching for the Klondike. The farmers who got their wheat in the ground last fall do not want to go there.

A. BIRD.

Salt Lake Herald
February 22, 1898

COURT AT FILLMORE.

New Rule Governing Jury Trials— Huntsman Case.

Fillmore, Utah, Feb. 21.—The February term of court opened today, with Judge Higgins presiding. The clerk read the new rules just promulgated by the judge governing the practice in this court. There were some important changes from the old rules of practice.

The following business was transacted today, which would indicate that the term here would be of short duration:

J. C. Stadham vs. G. W. Lacy; demurrer to complaint sustained, and the 23rd inst. given to amend.

W. A. Ray vs. M. J. Beauregard; set for trial tomorrow. This case was set for trial at the calling of the calendar in the forenoon, and in the afternoon J. M. Hanson, attorney for the defendant, asked for a jury in the case, but the court denied it, on the ground that a jury was not demanded within the time prescribed by law or the rules of the court, which require that parties wanting a jury trial must make a demand either before the setting of the case or within a reasonable time thereafter, or orally in open court at the time of such setting. The attorney was present at the setting of the case and did not demand a jury, or at any time previous.

The case of George M. Hanson vs. H. M. Johnson was set for trial today, but not reached.

The whole of the afternoon was taken up in arguing the motion for a new trial in the damage suit of Peter Huntsman vs. R. G. Huntsman, and arguments will be resumed again tomorrow. The principal ground supporting the motion is newly discovered evidence and misconduct of the jury while engaged in the trial of the cause.

The larger part of the business has been continued for the term.

The roads in this part of the country are almost impassable, which accounts for most of the continuances, the parties being unable to get here. The attorneys in attendance are J. A. Melville, Joshua Greenwood, J. M. Hanson, R. A. McBride, Sam Thurman, E. O. Lee, W. P. Knox and D. D. Houtz.

Salt Lake Herald
February 24, 1898

TWO DIVORCES GRANTED.

Principal Business Disposed of by Judge Higgins at Fillmore.

Fillmore, Feb. 23.—But little business was transacted in the district court today.

Hannah Quarnberg was granted a divorce from her husband on the ground of failure to provide.

Mrs. Lizzie Huntsman was granted a divorce from Lafayette Huntsman, on the grounds of desertion and failure to provide. The custody of the only child was granted to Mrs. Huntsman.

The case of Ray vs. Beauregard went over till next term of court, on account of the defendant filing an amended answer.

Some probate matters were attended to and court adjourned until June 20. Judge Higgins and the visiting attorneys left for the north this evening.

Salt Lake Herald
February 25, 1898

SLAUGHTER OF HORSES.

Animals Killed For Their Hides In Southern Utah.

Milford, Utah, Feb. 22.—At Cedar City they are driving range horses up by the hundreds and skinning them. A peddler here today from Holden, Utah, says that all the way from Holden to Fillmore and the surrounding range they are slaughtering the horses on all sides. They do not shoot the animals outright, but, finding them weak from lack of food, throw a rope over their heads and then drag them to death. From the report of the peddler, they are doing this on a large scale. This manner of killing the horses saves about 3 cents per hide.

Sheriff Barton of Beaver goes to Provo tonight, with a Mr. Olcott of Beaver, who has recently become demented.

Mrs. Wolfenton of Beaver left on the night train for Salt Lake, where she joins her husband, and the two will make a journey throughout England, Mr. Wolfenton having answered a call to the missionary field. He gives up one of the best mercantile businesses in southern Utah.

The first Milford man to go to Klondike is James Ward, who leaves here tomorrow night direct for Seattle. A big dance is given tonight in honor of the occasion.

Several teams of heavy De Lamar freight are stranded a few miles out from Milford, and will not be moved for a few days.

Deseret Evening News
February 25, 1898

A JUROR TO ANSWER.

Cited to Appear in Court for Contempt—Young Couple Divorced.

Correspondence of the "News:"

Fillmore, Feb. 24.—Very little business has been done here at the term of the district court which closed yesterday. The case of W.A. Ray vs N. J. Boregard went over for the term; court ordered that an amended answer may be filed on the payment of $10 costs to plaintiff by the defendant.

Peter Huntsman vs S. R. Huntsman, application for a new trial still under advisement.

The court ordered the clerk to issue citation to Samuel W. Western, a petit juror at the December term, to appear at this court on the first day of the June term, A. D. 1898, to show cause why he should not be punished for contempt of court. The trouble has arisen from the fact that Mr. Western was one of jurors on the panel which tried the Huntsman case, and as such sought a clearer insight upon the subject, by going into the saloon where the fracas took place, and making a personal examination as to how certain falls occurred. To hear some of the lawyers talk, it appears that in this case "innocence is not bliss" and may be the peg upon which a new trial will be hung.

Elizabeth McMahon Huntsman asked for and obtained a divorce from Lafayette E. Huntsman. These young people had been married about two years, but the little lady did not approve of Lafayette's bed and board, and shortly after the marriage she sought the shelter of the parental roof, where she and her babe have been provided for ever since. It appears to be a clear case of mesalliance and against parental counsel, from which the young wife deserved liberation. Lafayette sat smiling in court and like "Barkis, was willin'" to make another capture.

The M. I. A. missionaries under the guidance of Elder Clyde have been doing a splendid work all through the county. They have carried the war into Africa by making house to house visits, shaking up the dry bones, and making lazy manhood look upon itself, and in many instances acknowledge the corn with a smile of glad you came. The results are already apparent in many directions, in happier homes, brighter eyes, higher aims, better citizenship, and a sure success in life. God speed the boys who do battle for the truth.   A. BIRD.

WANTED TO GO CAMPING.

Wires Warmed Over the Case of a Young Adventurer.

The authorities of Fillmore are anxious about the case of Bert Penrose, a lad of 12 or 13, who was apprehended down there and held until some word could be received from this city. The boy is a son of a well known gentleman, and some days ago asked his mother if he could make a trip to Stateline with two young men who were going down there to do some work on a claim. The young men are amply able to take care of him, and all that sort of thing, but the mother did not want the lad to go.

However, he packed his bundle and went without further parley. The father received a telegram from Nephi, asking if it was all right, and replied that as the boy had gotten that far, and the trip was not going to consume over three weeks longer, or thereabouts, he might as well go on. When the boy got to Fillmore the authorities there stopped him, and asked what should be done with him.

The father wired last evening and told them to let him go on. The young men are perfectly safe companions, and the father thinks that a couple of weeks out in the hills, with common miners' diet, will make the youth sigh for home and mother ere the time has elapsed, and do much toward keeping him home in the future.

Millard County Happenings.

Fillmore, March 28, 1898.

To the Editor:

Something of the old-time spirit of self-help has been shown during the last three months by the people of Hinckley precinct, located in the northwest section of Millard county, which deserves notice as a commendable example of united effort. The energetic citizens of that precinct wanted a bridge across the Sevier river, to save them about five miles of travel via Deseret to the depot at Oasis, and also to the firewood districts in the foothills; and of course they had an eye to business travel also. In mass meeting they appointed a bridge committee, consisting of Mahonri Bishop, J. C. Webb and Arthur Talbot. These men did not stand upon the dignity of appointment, but went to work like beavers, and, knowing the weak financial condition of the county, they modestly asked and obtained assistance from that source to the amount of $100 worth of lumber. They now have in use a good, substantial bridge similar to that at Deseret, which cost the county something like $1,400.

Hinckley has a population of 500 people, all farmers, and their quality may be judged by the above description of their works. When they want something they go to work with brain, muscle, and means and get it.

We continue to have our weekly snowstorms here, which keep the roads in bad condition and prevent anxious farmers from putting in their grain crops.

Last Monday Elders F. M. Lyman and J. G. Kimball arrived at Kanosh from Beaver county in a rough snowstorm; and on Tuesday, the 22nd, in the forenoon, they held meeting in that ward. The people turned out en masse to welcome them and attend the ordination of Elder C. F. Christensen (who for some months had been acting by appointment) as Bishop of the Kanosh ward, under the hands of Elder Lyman and the presidency of the Stake, with Jas. M. Gardner and Joseph M. Robison as his counselors. Then a six-mile drive through the mud and snow was had to Meadow, and a meeting was held at 2 p.m.; then another wallow through the mud was made, eight miles, to Fillmore, and on Wednesday evening meeting was held and both Elders addressed the congregation. Thursday morning Elder Kimball met with the Forty-second quorum of Seventies, and gave them much clear and pointed instruction as to their duties—afterwards coming on to Holden to continue the work. Elder Lyman remained, going around amongst old friends, and warming them up with a pleasant grip and words of counsel. Saturday morning the usual Priesthood meeting was held with Elder Lyman also present, and at 2 p.m. he met with the High Council in a lengthy session. Yesterday (Sunday) he attended Sunday school in the forenoon and at 2 p.m. he faced a well-filled meeting house, and for an hour and thirty minutes talked in that characteristic and logical manner upon the principles of the Gospel which sticks to people after they get out of meeting. Directly after the meeting he departed for Holden, ten muddy miles away, and held meeting in the evening at that place, and Monday will continue his journey towards Salt Lake.

It may interest some of your readers

It may interest some of your readers to know that the lady who a few years ago did considerable literary work in Utah of the initials of M. A. Y. G., has sold her property in this county and has left the State with her husband, Mr. Erst, and in future will reside in California.   A. B.

STILL MORE NAMES.

The "News" is in receipt of the following:

To the Editor:

In re-christening the joint city and county building the name proposed should be short, euphonious and expressive. Let someone improve on—"Union Court House."

FRIEND SHIPP.

Here are some criticisms and suggestions "combined."

To the Editor:

I have watched with loyal solicitude the result of your suggestion for a suitable name for your city and county building, and have become sufficiently agitated to obtrude my crude ideas with rural impudence before the public. That magnificent structure should have a name euphonious, surely not suggestive of uncertainty, or mischief. "Combine," O, horrors! many of us bitten, country people would fear to enter it. "Capitola" is very good, but a probable metropolitan abridgement would make it "The Cap," often applied to hangers-on around public offices.

"Onyx building" is cumbersome and misleading and whilst the profuse display of that beautiful stone is much admired, its lack of arrangement is offensive to the trained, not to say cultivated eye. Its confused jumble of various sized slabs, with the conspicuous joints without pleasing contrast or harmonious blending, produces a symmetrical void suggestive of a gorgeous display in a mason's yard.

One tenth of the present amount of that beautiful onyx, set in wood or metalic paneling, would have made a rich and attractive display. Now it is rich without taste, (shoddy extravagance) and not calculated to suggest its use in the chaste and beautiful homes of the wealthy, and in contrast with the rough, hungry walls, makes an unpleasant "combine."

Permit me to suggest the (not original) name "Valhalla." This would not call up unpleasant memories connected with the building, but would have a semi-sacred, soothing influence, and admonish to eschew evil thoughts.

The present incumbents, and all others when they retire, having done justly, would feel a reflected honor from its occupancy.

If an original name is desired, call it the "Vallah" suggestive of the glorious valley of the great Salt Lake.

A. B.

Fillmore, March 28, 1898.

Salt Lake Herald
April 4, 1898

FILLMORE NOTES.

A Golden Wedding Celebrated—New School House.

Fillmore, April 2.—Yesterday Mr. and Mrs. C. P. Beauregard celebrated the fiftieth anniversary of their marriage day by giving a golden wedding. A large number of friends and relatives were present, and an enjoyable time was had by all.

The farmers are now busily engaged in planting their crops. The mountains are heavily laden with snow, and the prospects for the Millard farmers are bright.

Fillmore's new school house is nearing completion, the masons having completed their work. The building is an undoubted credit and ornament to the town, and will be a long stride in the educational progress and advancement of this section of the country. It will by fall be in a condition to hold school in. The old state house, now occupied by the schools, will be remodeled and the upper floor, now petitioned into three rooms, will be made into one large, commodious hall.

A Joyous Golden Wedding.

Fillmore, April 2nd, 1898.

To the Editor:

A very pleasant family re-union has just taken place at the residence of C. P. Beauregard, one of the old and respected citizens of this place. The gathering was to celebrate the golden wedding of Brother Beauregard and his wife Anna K. This venerable couple were married in Jutland, and received the Gospel in that land some 15 years after. Mr. B. related to your correspondent some incidents of the time of his wedding: The Danish priest desired to put off the marriage for a time, owing to his own nervous excitement caused by the fact that a declaration of war had that day been made between Prussia and Denmark. Mr. B. tells of the demand made upon his labor of that time—he being a blacksmith, was called upon to cut up old iron into ugly shapes to be fixed from cannon, the latter to mutilate the enemy with; he tells how they cut up old scythes to make spears and all kinds of rude implements of warfare for those who had no guns. What a contrast to the weapons of the present day!

Brother Beauregard has been a prominent citizen of Fillmore for 36 years and filled many offices of trust and honor, and for about 20 years he has been a High Councilor of the Millard Stake. Today he continues to work at his trade as a blacksmith, whilst his wife is lively as a girl of sixteen in many of her movements. Her greatest trouble yesterday was caused because she was not permitted to help in the work of cooking, etc., going on; and she smiled and showed her good natural teeth as she told me of her son Nelson leading her in from the labor of feeding her little chickens. Then she showed me the very nice presents she and her 50-year companion in life had received at the hands of their offspring, for every grandchild gave her some little token of love upon this memorable occasion—these consisting of rocking chairs, a beautiful lo[unge] and a nice oil painting, the wo[rk of]

an eleven-year-old grandson. All who were present hoped that they would have the pleasure of assembling to celebrate the diamond wedding of this good old Christian couple.

A. BIRD.

Scandinavian Star, please copy.

Fillmore City, April 6.—The farmers of Deseret, Oasis and Hinckley have suffered considerable loss for many years on account of the failure of the water supply during the months of July, August and September, but with the completion of the Deseret and Salt Lake Agricultural and Manufacturing and Canal company's reservoir and canals, the prospects are changed, and farmers are now practically sure of a constant supply of water during the entire season.

This enterprise was not projected for the purpose of creating a boom, but to enable settlers to reclaim the desert and to make for themselves comfortable homes, and a visit to the works will convince anyone that it is a substantial affair and built to stay.

The improvement consists of a reservoir covering 940 acres, and holding water sufficient to cover 10,000 acres to a depth of one foot, with dam, headgates, canals and a conduit for letting the river flow through when the reservoir is full.

The old river bed coming from the north turns to the east and back again, forming a horseshoe bend. This bend, with the dam at the lower end, forms the reservoir. At the end of the bend, corresponding to the heels of a horseshoe, the river is separated from itself only by a bank of earth about 400 feet wide, so that the two ends of the reservoir are really only about that distance apart. And the overflow is cut through this bank, so that when the reservoir is full, or when no more water is wanted in the same, the river cuts across the ends of the horseshoe bend and does not enter the reservoir at all.

The dam is the most imposing part of the works. It is 1,200 feet long, 120 feet wide at the base, 30 feet wide at the top, and 20 feet high. The overflow was the most particular part to construct, and required the most skilful engineering. It consists, first, of a channel 400 feet long, 100 feet wide and seven feet deep, cut through the bank of earth separating the river bed at the two points; and, second, of the "drop." This "drop" is at the lower end of the cut-off channel, where the water finds its way into the old bed of the river. The "drop" is the large gateway to let the water out through the cut-off chan-

nel. The floor is 60 feet long and is made of two layers of 2-inch plank, laid on 12x12 timbers, bolted securely to two rows of piling.

Two "drop aprons," extending six feet into the ground and filled in with gravel and rock, will keep the water from washing backward under the floor and cutting under the proper place of outlet. From this floor the water will drop 15 feet, and this is where the danger lies. Water in falling this far is apt to cut and wash a big hole and take the headgate away. In order to prevent this, a deep excavation 100 feet long and 33 feet wide was made, where the water is to fall, and four rows of 12x12 timbers were laid down. On top of these were laid a layer of heavy cedar posts, covered with slag, and then alternate layers of timber and cedar posts till four layers of each was in, all bolted together, and to two rows of piling extending across the channel. Then, on these three thousand posts and four layers of timbers was piled three thousand tons of slag and gravel, to receive the water when it falls from the floor of the "drop," 15 feet above. But even this was not considered safe enough, and so the receiving basin was made sufficiently low to be under two feet of standing water from the river bed, and

this will serve to protect the basin from the water falling from above. The two headgates through which the water is drawn from the reservoir to the canals which lead to the farms are 27 feet wide and 16 feet high, and are expected to hold a wall of water ten feet high. They, too, were made solid with tons of gravel and slag.

On the whole, this entire construction bears the appearance of solidity and stability; and it is confidently expected that it will add materially to the farming wealth of Millard county, and furnish a desirable place for those who desire to make comfortable homes. Mr. Charles Wilkins is president of the company which has this enterprise in hand.

Fillmore is now without a licensed saloon, the license having expired last Monday. Both saloons closed their doors.

On account of lack of funds, the public schools of Fillmore will close next Friday for the summer vacation.

Salt Lake Herald
April 20, 1898

NEW ROLLER MILL.

Deseret Irrigation Company Decides to Build It.

Deseret, April 18.—The Deseret Irrigation company held a meeting last night for the purpose of considering a proposition to build a roller mill. Some of the stockholders wanted to build it by taxing the stock, while the others favored selling the water rights to some individual to run a mill. It was put to a vote and was decided to build by assessment on the stock. A roller mill here will catch all the trade from the western country and surrounding places where now they are compelled to take grain to Fillmore to mill. It has not been decided when the work will begin, but it will be soon.

Salt Lake Herald
April 22, 1898

FILLMORE'S PROGRESS.

New Meeting House and Many Dwellings to Be Built.

Fillmore City, Utah, April 20.—The Fillmore meeting house committee met last night and formulated a plan upon which to work in the erection of a new meeting house. A brickyard was started this morning that will be actively worked until the required amount of brick are made. It is expected that the corner-stone will be laid some time the latter part of this week.

Editor L. W. Gaisford of the Millard Progress left last Saturday for the north, where he will sojourn for about two weeks.

The number of residences in Fillmore will be increased by at least ten this spring. All are neat brick houses.

Salt Lake Herald
April 28, 1898

Russel K. Callister of Fillmore, and Melvie Smith of Centerville, have been granted a marriage license.

Salt Lake Herald
May 1, 1898

Southern Utah Heard From.

Governor Wells yesterday received a telegram from a Mr. Callister at Fillmore, stating that there 20 men there who desired to enlist in the cavalry. E. D. Woolley of Kanab also sent word to the effect that two patriots there desired to be enrolled and more could be secured.

Salt Lake Herald
May 4, 1898

MILLARD'S SONS ENLIST.

Bishop Callister Secures Fourteen Volunteers at Fillmore.

(Special to The Herald.)

Fillmore, Utah, May 3.—Fillmore has been full of enthusiasm for the past few days. By authority from Governor Wells, Bishop T. C. Callister has been acting as recruiting officer, and yesterday and today 14 sons of Millard have offered their services to their country. They are: W. E. Jukes, A. W. Dickinson, Edward Day, Raymond Ray, D. P. Callister, J. W. Callister, Walter Maycock, L. E. Huntsman, George M. Velle, J. W. Huntsman, Will Huntsman, James H. Maycock, John T. Ashman, C. A. Walch.

The event has been celebrated by the raising of flags, a big parade and firing of guns. There are many more of Millard's sons who are willing to enlist.

Some six inches of snow fell in the valley this morning.

In the European Mission.

Millennial Star, April 28, 1898.

Arrivals.—The following named missionaries from Zion arrived in Liverpool on April 27, 1898, per American line mission—James Briggs, Salt Lake; Job Hemsley, John S. Smith, Sugar House; Henry Crane, Herriman; James Laird, Mountain Dell; Thomas Nichols, Riverton; Franklin G. Burton, Almy, Wyo.; William H. Thomas, W. E. Jones, Malad, Idaho; Joshua R. Hodson, Provo; John S. Painter, Nephi; Lewis Williams, Samaria, Idaho. For the Scandinavian Mission—Charles E. Forsberg, Bengt T. Bengtson, Salt Lake City; Andrew Gustav Erickson, Peter Hanson, Heber; Erick A. Modeen, Gunnison; Severin Swensen, Mt. Pleasant; Noar S. Pond, Pocatello, Idaho. For the German Mission—Walter Hasler, Mt. Pleasant, Isaac Edinborough, of Nephi; John Jackson of Fillmore, and H. Le Bailey of Montpelier, Idaho, who are on a visit to this country, came with this company.

Releases and Appointments—John Hirst has been honorable released from laboring as a traveling Elder in the Leeds conference to return home May 21, 1898.

Mark Austin has been released from the Manchester conference and appointed to labor as a traveling Elder in the London conference.

James Blake has been released from the Liverpool conference and appointed to labor as a traveling Elder in the Manchester conference, from hence he was called some time since to assist in the Millennial Star office.

George E. Carpenter has been released from laboring as a traveling Elder in the London conference and appointed to the Liverpool conference to assist in the Millennial Star office.

James Briggs has been appointed to labor as a traveling Elder in the Manchester conference.

Job Hemsley has been appointed to labor as a traveling Elder in the London conference.

Henry Crane has been appointed to labor as a traveling Elder in the Norwich conference.

James Laird has been appointed to labor as a traveling Elder in the Leeds conference.

Thomas Nichols has been appointed to labor as a traveling Elder in the Cheltenham conference.

Franklin G. Burton has been appointed to labor as a traveling Elder in the Nottingham conference.

William H. Thomas, W. E. Jones and Lewis Williams have been appointed to labor as traveling Elders in the Welsh conference.

Joshua R. Hodson has been appointed to labor as a traveling Elder in the Liverpool conference.

John S. Painter has been appointed to labor as a traveling Elder in the Birmingham conference.

John S. Smith has been appointed to labor as a traveling Elder in the Scottish conference.

A Narrow Escape.

Fillmore, May 18.—Postmaster Hanson had a narrow escape last evening. His team ran away and began to circle around, when he sprang out of the buggy to grab the bridle bits. His foot caught in the wheel and threw him to the ground. The fall rendered him unconscious, but it is not thought his injuries are serious.

Their Only Doctor Going.

Fillmore, May 18.—The only physician in Millard county, Dr. E. R. Keen, has decided to remove to Eureka, Nev. There is an opening here for a good doctor, who will attend strictly to business.

Water Is Not Free.

Fillmore, May 18.—A suit was filed today in the district court here in which the Scipio Irrigation company is plaintiff and Hans Ecklund defendant. Complaint is made that Hans has used water without making arrangements or settling for it.

Salt Lake Herald
May 28, 1898

DRUNKEN INDIANS.

Somebody In the Neighborhood of Fillmore Sells Them Liquor.

Millard Progress: The band of Indians which were camped in the city west of town departed northward Wednesday, but only got out about three miles when they got so drunk that further travel was out of the question. One Hunter of Holden reports that he was stopped several times by a number of them and he had quite a time to get by. Just before reaching Holden, Hunter met the United States mail coming in and told the driver, Tom Nielson, that he would likely have trouble, as they were in a crazed condition. Tom drove to within hearing distance of the band. The squaws were crying and the bucks hollering. He unhitched and slipped around them on his horse, being compelled to leave his cart there for the night. Thursday morning the Indians were still quite drunk, but preparing to move northward.

Salt Lake Herald
May 29, 1898

SOLD LIQUOR TO INDIANS.

Jackson Clothier, Seventy Years of Age, Confessed His Guilt.

Fillmore, May 28.—A few days ago a band of Indians secured several bottles of alcohol while in Fillmore and proceeded northward. They had not driven over four miles when the majority of them became beastly drunk, camped and held an all-night powwow. The night was made hideous with their war whoops. The mail carrier was compelled to leave his cart and make a detour to get in with the mail. Sheriff Holbrook started after the band yesterday and today brought in two of them. Upon being pressed to tell who sold them the liquor, they named Jackson Clothier, who is 70 years of age, and an old-time resident of Fillmore. "Jack" denied the charge, but when brought before the Indians admitted the crime, and this evening plead guilty. Sentence was withheld until the county attorney returns from the north.

COURT IN MILLARD.

Several Orders Made By Judge Higgins On Opening Day.

Fillmore, June 20.—The June term of court was begun here this morning by Judge Higgins. It appears from the calendar that court will be in session at this point about one week.

A number of probate and other orders were made, besides the following:

Alexander and Trelle Dotre vs. Almond Rhoads et al.; demurrer to complaint overruled and 15 days given to answer.

William B. Lowler vs. Jesse W. Fox, jr., et al.; cause transferred to the Third district court for trial.

Scipio Irrigation company vs. Hans Esklud; set for trial June 21.

Joseph V. Robison vs. S. H. Clark et al.; receivers; set for trial for 23rd inst.

William A. Ray vs. N. J. Beauregard; set for trial for 23rd.

Jacob Huntsman vs. Jesse Huntsman and Fanny Allen; dismissed as to Fanny Allen.

Other settings will be made tomorrow.

D. D. Houtz is as yet the only attorney from abroad who has put in an appearance, although most of the cases are represented by outside counsel.

THAT RAILROAD PASS.

Senator Robison Used It—The U. P. Uses It Now.

Fillmore, June 23.—In the damage case of Joseph V. Robison against the receivers of the Union Pacific Railway company, a jury was empaneled and evidence introduced on both sides which showed very little conflict and was substantially to the effect that Robison, a legislator, was returning from Salt Lake to his home in Fillmore and used for his transportation a pass given to him by the defendant company, on the back of which was the regular contract signed by plaintiff to the effect that he would release the defendant from all damages against said company. The plaintiff had reached Clear Lake station and went into the office, which was an old car sidetracked for that purpose. He waited there until the stage called for him, when he left the room, went out on to the platform and proceeded to where he thought the steps were going down from the platform, but the night being very dark he missed the steps and fell from the platform about six feet, breaking his collar bone and otherwise injuring him.

The main question in the case and which is being argued at great length to the court on the instructions to the jury is as to the force of the contract accompanying the pass upon which plaintiff was riding. A night session is on, but the case will not go to the jury until tomorrow.

In order to prevent the case from going to the United States courts the plaintiff has made the amount of his damages claimed but $1,995. Judge Henderson is conducting the case for the plaintiff and J. W. N. Whitecotton is representing the defendant company.

SENATOR ROBISON LOSES.

His Suit Against the Railway Decided Against Him.

Fillmore, June 24.—Judge Henderson, on behalf of the plaintiff, and J. W. N. Whitecotton for the Oregon Short Line railroad, this morning resumed their arguments on the law of the case of the railroad and cited numerous authorities, after which the court charged the jury that the contract upon the back of the pass that plaintiff used was a valid contract, so far as it went, and it went to the extent of releasing the defendants from ordinary negligence. He also instructed them that such a contract was not against public policy, as was contended by counsel for plaintiff, but that if the plaintiff recovered it must be from the gross negligence of the defendants, and upon the question as to whether or not the injury to plaintiff was the result of gross negligence on the part of the defendants. After arguments by counsel the case was given to the jury, and after being out about two hours and a half returned with a verdict for defendants of no cause of action.

After some other miscellaneous work the court adjourned until the October term.

Salt Lake Herald
July 5, 1898

Beaver Blade: A party consisting of Messrs. J. A. Melvin and Al Greenwood of Fillmore, D. D. Houtz of Provo, and W. L. Cook of this place, left last Saturday morning with a well filled wagon and behind a spanking pair of grays, for Stateline. The glittering gold-plated rumors of hidden wealth which have emanated from that district recently was the incentive which urged them on. They expect to reach Beaver tomorrow on their return, unless they experience unexpected delay in making use of the supply of location notices procured of the Blade before their departure.

Commencing today, Stateline has a daily mail service running from Milford to Pioche and De Lamar, via Stateline.

D. Houtz of Provo paid the camp a visit this week; also Messrs. Melville and Greenwood of Fillmore.

Salt Lake Herald
July 7, 1898

Innocents United.

Coalville, July 6.—A marriage license has been issued by County Clerk Boyden to Mr. C. A. Fillmore, aged 24, of Kamas, and Miss Ellanore Davis, aged 18, also of Kamas. They were married in the clerk's office by Elder E. H. Rhead, and the happy couple went on their way rejoicing. The young man volunteered the information that though he was born and raised in Kamas, Summit county, he had never as yet been to Salt Lake City, nor hardly that distance from his home in any direction.

Salt Lake Herald
July 9, 1898

MILLARD COUNTY MATTERS.

Salaries Cut and Slashed By the Commissioners.

Fillmore, July 6.—For the past two days the county commissioners have been in session and transacted the routine business. Today they levied a tax of 5 mills on the dollar on all taxable property in Millard county for the year 1898, and a tax of 2½ mills on the dollar for county and school purposes.

For the past year the citizens of Millard have been "kicking" at what they consider the high salaries drawn by our Millard county officers for the work they have performed. Today the commissioners took the matter up, and after an executive session lasting some four hours, made a great slashing, cutting some of the officers down one-half in fixing their salaries for the coming year.

Following is a table showing the salaries now drawn by our officers, the new salary for 1899, and the saving to Millard county in this reduction:

	Old Salary.	New Salary.	Saving.
County attorney	$700	$300	$400
County assessor	750	400	350
County fish and game commissioner	25	30*	
County surveyor	60	100**	
County recorder	400	350	50
County clerk	720	500	220
County treasurer and collector	800	500	300
County sheriff	700	400	300

*Raise of $5.00.
**Raise of $40.00.

The commissioners' salaries were left at the same figures as during the past two years, $120 per year each.

Salt Lake Herald
July 11, 1898

A PROMISING PROPERTY.

Valuable Claims On Whisky Creek Near Fillmore.

Richfield, July 9.—Colonel S. F. Mount has just returned to this city from Whisky creek, where he and Thomas Ainesworth, also of this city, have what they think to be one of the coming mines of southern Utah. The mine has been worked for the past four months by the two owners, and last week a one-car shipment was made, which paid all expense of mining and the freight to the railroad, with a few dollars over to act as an encouragement for them to keep working.

Mr. Mount, on being interviewed by The Herald correspondent, claims that his partner and himself have no doubt they have struck a rich deposit of lead and silver-bearing quartz. Their ledge is about 20 feet from wall to wall, but the rich streak is surely two and one-half feet wide. Mr. Mount has one more carload on the dump ready for shipment so soon as he can return, and he feels that he has one of the best milling propositions in this section of the country; and as the property is so easily gotten at in the winter, a force of men will soon be put at steady work to develop the property more fully.

Whisky creek, the location of the new mine, is in Willard county, some few miles east of Fillmore. It is in no mining district, and has never been prospected in the least, and more new strikes are expected at any time.

FLOOD AT FILLMORE.

Creek Overflowing and Water On the Rise.

Fillmore, July 11.—At 2:45 today the first flood of the season came down from the mountains above Fillmore. Little damage is done crops thus far although the big creek filled to almost overflowing. Great big boulders were swept along like so many chips and more came down than known at any previous flood, while it is estimated that 100 cords of timber came with them. The big creek is still half full and rain is pouring down, while dark and threatening clouds still hang over the mountains, which indicate that a larger volume of water will reach us tonight. It is just two years ago today when we experienced the largest and most disastrous flood in this county.

At 8 o'clock another small flood reached the town but no damage will be done.

Salt Lake Herald
July 22, 1898

Alexander Melville of Fillmore has just graduated from the law school of Ann Arbor, Mich., with honors, and will enter upon the practice of his profession in the Fifth judicial district of this state.

Salt Lake Herald
August 12, 1898

HORRIBLE ACCIDENTS

Two Men Carved Up In Millard Saw Mills.

FELL AGAINST BUZZ SAWS

THE THIRD VICTIM WAS A BOY ON A HORSE.

Thrown Against a Tree and Rendered Unconscious For Ten Hours—The Men Mutilated In a Sickening Manner, But All Were Alive at Last Accounts.

(Special to The Herald.)

Fillmore, Aug. 11.—Yesterday was a day of accidents for Fillmore, three occuring, and they were all _____ The first was at the lower saw mill and the victim Charlie Gull of Meadow.

While picking up lumber near the saw mill he became overbalanced and in throwing up his hand it came in contact with the saw; his thumb was ripped up, the first and second fingers seriously cut, while the third was almost taken off.

THE SECOND VICTIM.

Frank Rogers of Fillmore, was the victim of the second accident. While employed as off-bearer at what is known as the Waterbury mill, and carrying a slab from the saw he slipped, his left leg striking the saw, which was in rapid motion, and he was thrown in the air over the saw to the trestle work on the other side, miraculously escaping a horrible death. As it is he is cut and slashed almost beyond human endurance. The left arm was cut and all the muscles and sinews laid bare from the palm of the hand to the elbow, his left leg, from the knee down about eight inches, was cut to the bone and all the muscles exposed to view.

He has probably the worst cut in his left foot, that member being sawed through from the toe to the instep, severing one toe completely and splitting the foot in a horrible condition. He was brought to his home late last night in good spirits, submitting to his injuries with heroism. There being no surgeon in the county his wounds have been dressed temporarily. Friends left with him tonight for Salt Lake.

THE THIRD CASUALTY.

Last evening the third accident happened to Marion Greenwood, son of Judge J. Greenwood, caused by a vicious horse. In the act of riding him to the barn the animal became frightened, running at full speed around the corner and dashing up the street, the lad using every effort to stop him without success. Two blocks farther on the beast suddenly darted towards the sidewalk, jumping the ditch and throwing the boy violently against a shade tree, rendering him unconscious, in which condition he remained ten hours. The only injuries visible are a badly bruised head, although he may be hurt internally.

Salt Lake Herald
September 5, 1898

Dying at Fillmore.

Fillmore, Sept. 4.—Mrs. Lizzie Partridge of this city, wife of Edward Partridge, stake president of Utah county, is at the point of death. Heart trouble is the cause. Her husband, sons and daughters were sent for and arrived last night.

Salt Lake Herald
September 9, 1898

Fillmore, Sept. 8.—The biennial ghost dance of the Indians living east of Kanosh is being held and has continued since Sunday night. A great many Indians and squaws from the surrounding country, bringing with them their dogs, horses and vermin, are congregated at that place and are holding their hideous incantations during the night time and in the interval exchanging courtesies with the resident Indians—and squaws.

Their number is about 350 and their picturesque appearance during the dancing hours would do credit to a Spanish bullfighter. Large crowds of young people from the surrounding towns go nightly to witness the weird spectacle, which is as good as a circus or a Republican convention trying to harmonize the silver and McKinley forces.

Your correspondent visited the camp last evening and witnessed the maneuvers from the beginning to the close, and while there was nothing happened which could be repeated at a Sunday school, yet the whole can be called a picturesque and howling success.

The most picturesque of all the bucks is "Marcus-Hanna-Long-Tailed-Horse" from Nevada, who has a strong desire for distilled vapor, and who struck his squaw Tuesday night with a two-gallon cuspidor on the face, for which he was immediately tied down and remained so during the balance of the evening.

The squaw had been "flirting" with a Uintah Indian, in a manner not quite orthodox, and this morning the hubby reminded her of the fact by cutting an under-half-crop and two slits in her left ear.

The dance will last all this week and part of next unless the home Indians become so jealous they run the others off before that time.

Salt Lake Herald
September 17, 1898

Alonzo Froman, who left Colorado over a year ago to make his home here, has returned to Provo after an extended pleasure trip through the northern part of the state and Yellowstone park.

Salt Lake Herald
September 20, 1898

FREE NORMAL SCHOLARSHIPS,

TWENTY-EIGHT STUDENTS AP- POINTED AT UNIVERSITY.

Still Twenty-two Vacancies to Be Filled—Names of Those Who Have Been Appointed.

State Superintendent Park of the department of public instruction yesterday notified President Kingsbury of the Utah university of the appointment of 28 students for the free normal scholarships at the university for the ensuing two years, in pursuance of nominations made by the boards of examiners in the several counties and the metropolitan cities.

Out of the 50 free normal scholarships apportioned to the counties and the four large cities, there are still 22 vacancies, caused by the failure of boards of examiners to report, and these will be filled by the president of the university from any locality. The 28 appointments made yesterday are as follows:

Cache county—Vilate E. Lewis of Richmond.

Emery county—Katie Loveless of Huntington.

Millard county—Reuben Clark McBride of Fillmore.

Salt Lake county— ther Pearson of West Jordan, Electa Jensen of Sandy, Ethel A. Smithen of Farmer's Ward and J. F. Anderson of Sandy.

Sanpete county—Ida Watt and Anna Erickson of Manti.

Sevier county—Eliza Heppler of Glenwood.

Tooele county—Lillian Durfee of Grantsville.

Utah county—Emma Fenton, Alvin F. Sundberg, May West and Hattie Beck of Pleasant Grove, and Mary Adamson of American Fork.

Weber county—David H. Fowler of Hooper and Thomas E. McKay of Huntsville.

Salt Lake City—Lotta Dinwoodey, Serene Sylvestersen, Lean Martin, Rebekah Edward, Thomas J. Howells, Bertha Schwin and Lydia Smithen.

Ogden—Mae Carter, Rachel E. Woodcock and Isabella Slater.

Salt Lake Herald
September 23, 1898

MILLARD CONVENTIONS.

Both Parties Will Nominate Tickets Next Week.

Fillmore, Sept. 22.—Both the Republican and Democratic parties will hold county conventions here next week for the purpose of nominating state representatives and county officers. The political situation promises to become lively before the campaign is over.

The Democratic nominees for congressman and supreme judge are giving general satisfaction throughout the county.

MILLARD REPUBLICANS.

Nominated a Weak Ticket That Causes General Dissatisfaction.

(Special to The Herald.)

Fillmore, Sept. 26.—The Republican county convention was held here today, for the purpose of nominating a state representative and county officers. But eight precincts were represented out of 14.

T. C. Callister of Fillmore received the nomination for representative. The county officers are:

Commissioners—J. R. Bennett, Deseret; James Gardner, Kanosh; D. R. Stevens, Holden.

Clerk—J. M. Hanson.

Treasurer—George C. Velle.

Recorder—Mrs J. E. Robison.

Attorney—John Cooper; all of Fillmore.

Assessor—Joseph L. Stott, Meadow.

Sheriff—Virgil Kelley, Deseret.

Surveyor—O. N. Parson, Clear Lake.

After some difficulty a resolution was passed endorsing the platform of the recent state convention. At one time it looked as though some of the delegates would leave the convention hall. Trading was done in every possible way, and dissatisfaction is the result. As it is the ticket is not considered a very strong one, and the Democrats feel confident of defeating it next November.

MILLARD COUNTY JUDGES.

List of Those Appointed By the Commissioners.

(Special to The Herald.)

Fillmore, Oct. 17.—The county commissioners appointed the following election judges for Millard county today. The first two in each precinct are Democrats and the third Republicans:

Fillmore—John Jackson, O. H. Huntsmand and J. F. Holbrook.

Meadow—H. G. Labrum, sr., William H. Gull and Edwin Stott.

Kanosh—Henry Whatcott, Mrs. Ann Hopkinson and Anthony Paxton, jr.

Holden—J. F. Giles, Lillie Crosland and Harry Hughes.

Scipio—Charles Memmott, Orson Wasden and William Memmott, sr.

Deseret—Parley Allred, Joseph W. Damron and William V. Black.

Hinckley—George Walker, N. M. Peterson and Frank T. Slaughter.

Oasis—J. C. Hawley, Daniel Rutherford and David Day.

Leamington—Jens Jensen, B. P. Textorious and Joseph Overson.

Oak Creek—Simeon Walker, Eddie Dutson and Peter Anderson.

Clear Lake—C. J. Aldrach, John Bowen and C. W. Aldrach.

Burbank—Erick P. Hockman, Rufus Pack and E. W. Clay.

Smithville—Alfred J. Bishop, Isaac Gandy and Almond Rhoads.

Black Rock—Walter James de Witt, C. Reed and William Armstrong.

Salt Lake Herald
October 24, 1898

Fillmore Progress: "In view of the meeting of the state legislature in the near future, and the fact that a senator from this great state will be elected by that body to the congress of the United States, we have carefully considered the adaptability of the honorable gentlemen whose names have been mentioned by the papers as candidates for that office, and we are of the opinion that in the person of the Hon. A. W. McCune the people would find the senator who could and would give them the best service."

Salt Lake Herald
October 27, 1898

UNANSWERABLE.

The Republican organ, commenting on its "frost" stories from Fillmore and elsewhere, wonders: "What is the matter? Mr. Roberts is a natural orator; what is the spell upon him?"

What can the matter be? What is it that causes people to leave a hall in Fillmore when Mr. Roberts is speaking in Bountiful? Why is there such a frost in Millard meetings when Mr. Roberts is in Davis?

Echo answers, "What, indeed!"

It is one of those inscrutable mysteries known only to the oracle of Republicanism. Providence, isn't it?

Salt Lake Herald
October 30, 1898

ANOTHER EXPLANATION DUE.

When our neighbor described the reception, in Fillmore, of a speaker who was actually in Bountiful, 150 miles distant, there was a discrepancy similar to those it found in Mr. Fisher's figures.

It made an explanation, of course, for the same fertile mind that gets up a story can generally be depended upon to supply a plausible sequel.

The plea was that the tale was 24 hours old, and the blame was placed upon the telegraph company.

Then it told about a railroad meeting in New York, and said that "E. H. Harriman had been elected president of the Oregon Short Line, to succeed Samuel Carr."

It was another "Tribune special," just as the "frost" story from Fillmore purported to be.

As a matter of fact, W. D. Cornish was elected president of the Short Line.

Probably the telegraph company is again to blame. We await our neighbor's explanation of this fake, confident that it will be as plausible and ingenious as its excuses are for the others.

Salt Lake Herald
October 31, 1898

Political Notes.

One week from tomorrow is election day. This week will complete the work of the campaign.

The Great Campaign will issue again today and it is going to be a warm number, from all accounts.

The reception given by the Broad Ax will take place tomorrow evening at 23 West First South street.

Al Eklund has returned from his mine in Star valley and will from this time forward devote his time and attention toward electing the entire Democratic ticket.

Tomorrow is the last day for registration and the county committee especially urges all who have not attended to this important duty to see their names are on the lists.

J. C. Nordstram has written two excellent campaign songs, which will be sung during the coming week at the several meetings in the county. These songs are especially for Scandinavian singers, but translated in English will have a splendid effect.

Alma Eldredge and his aggregation are going to open the campaign on their behalf in Milford today. On Tuesday they will recite at Fillmore and on Wednesday at Holden and Deseret. The troupe will play at Nephi on the 3rd. Dates afterward will be announced later on, as soon as the secretary can get matters untangled.

Salt Lake Herald
November 2, 1898

ELDREDGE AT FILLMORE.

Having Heard Both Candidates, People Will Vote For Roberts.

(Special to The Herald.)

Fillmore, Nov. 1.—Alma Eldredge and his aggregation arrived at the ex-capital this afternoon, and tonight he appeared before a large audience at the old meeting-house, but fully half of them were Democrats, who were out to hear Professor J. P. Meakin. Mr. Eldredge was the first speaker. His voice is greatly impaired and for five minutes the audience could hardly hear him half way across the room, but he improved as he went along, and gave the same old talk as has been his custom nightly since taking the stump. His speech was received with some applause, but John Henry was always the one to start it.

Mr. Eldredge occupied about 20 minutes. Then Professor Meakin entertained the audience. John Henry Smith filled in the balance of the time with a long-winded speech on the tariff, and the show adjourned.

The people here have now had a chance to compare both congressional aspirants, and, if talk goes for anything, B. H. Roberts will receive a large majority in this county on Nov. 8. Judging from conservative reports from all over the county, Millard will again go Democratic this year.

WHY FILLMORE WENT WILD.

Our morning contemporary printed another "special" from Fillmore yesterday. It was quite as enthusiastic as its former "special" was disparaging. However, the Democratic speakers whose Fillmore reception it covered with frost, were not within a hundred miles of where it located them. If the Republican speakers were present when the people of Fillmore "applauded vociferously," they were indeed fortunate.

"Fillmore went wild," says the Republican organ, and in glaring headlines it thus proclaims the cause: "Eldredge and Smith speak."

Certainly that was enough to make Fillmore seem wild, whether it really was or not. And it may be that the attempt of the Hon. Alma to prove that the St. Louis platform was a silver declaration, actually drove the people wild, for the time being. Or, when he entered the ex-capital of the state, people may have taken up with one accord that popular refrain, "The wild man from Borneo has just come to town." It may have spread like a contagion, until the specialist wired, "Fillmore went wild."

Still, one is inclined to suspect that, after all, if there was enthusiasm, it was due to Professor Meakin—Alma's tutor and John Henry's chaperone.

GREAT OVATION TO KING.

Biggest Demonstration of the Campaign at Fillmore.

(Special to The Herald.)

Fillmore, Nov. 4.—The greatest rally Fillmore has witnessed in this campaign was held tonight, and the ovation that Congressman King received on his arrival here this afternoon and at the meeting house tonight would have gave the impression to a stranger that the president of the United States, or some other great personage was visiting the ex-capital.

At 5:20 a big procession formed and drove out of town some two miles, when Mr. King was met. On the way back to town he was cheered on every hand. At 7:30 by far the largest audience ever assembled in the old meeting house greeted him. And it cheered him time and again. He spoke for over three hours on the silver question, while the audience listened with rapt attention. During his speech he quoted from the Salt Lake Tribune, and showed what a back somersault that paper had taken on the silver question. He also said that paper was trying hard to bring the old fight on again in Utah between Mormons and Gentiles. His talk tonight was the best that has ever been heard in Fillmore, and has done the Democratic party more good than all former rallies together.

The Democratic speakers are receiving ovations wherever they appear in Millard. The Hon. R. N. Baskin and C. W. Penrose held meetings at Kanosh last night and Meadow today, and they were enthusiastic ones. Packed houses welcomed the speakers at both places. Tonight Mr. Baskin held forth at Holden, while Mr. Penrose and Joshua Greenwood, the Democratic nominee for state representative, held a rousing and thoroughly satisfactory meeting at Scipio. That Mr. Baskin is popular and making a good impression on the people of Millard, is evidenced by the hearty applause he receives everywhere.

Millard County Claims.

(Fillmore Progress.)

Judging from conservative reports from all over the county, this election will be a very close one. Up to date, leaders of both parties fail to claim everything in sight, as is usually the case.

In an interview with the chairman of the Republican party, E. W. Kelly, yesterday, he said: "Without doubt the Republicans will elect two-thirds of the county ticket."

While we have been unable to interview the Democratic county chairman, leading Democrats claim an easy victory for the majority of their ticket.

From the outlook now there will be considerable scratching on both tickets, and with one or two exceptions, one can take his choice from either ticket and have an even chance of picking the winners.

Salt Lake Herald
November 6, 1898

Fillmore Progress: The Progress has no politics, but, like other people, we have preferences, and feel at liberty to express them, and support any man, regardless of party affiliations, and it is with pleasure we view the candidacy of A. W. McCune for the United States senatorship, and would be more than pleased to see him selected. Should the legislature so honor Mr. McCune, the people of this state will have a senator of whom they will be justly proud and on whom they can implicitly rely.

Salt Lake Herald
November 7, 1898

CLOSE FIGHT IN MILLARD.

Democratic Chairman Claims a Small Majority.

(Special to The Herald.)

Fillmore, Nov. 6.—Conservative reports from all parts of Millard indicate that next Tuesday will witness one of the closest elections ever held in this county. In an interview today with the Democratic county chairman, J. S. Giles, he said:

"We claim majorities in Hinckley, Deseret, Oasis, Leamington, Oak Creek, Clear Lake, Holden and Kanosh. While Fillmore, Meadow and Scipio are uncertain, they will be very close. As yet we have not heard from Black Rock, Burbank, nor Smithville, but these precincts are small and I expect Black Rock will go Republican, while Smithville and Burbank will go Democratic, as usual. Millard county will go Democratic by a small majority."

REPUBLICAN ESTIMATE.

E. W. Kelly, Republican county chairman, made this statement: "The vote for Roberts and Eldredge will be very close in Millard this election. Zane will carry the county by a large majority. T. C. Callister, for state representative, will be elected by a small majority. We will also elect a majority of the county ticket."

Salt Lake Herald
November 9, 1898

WELLS' ATTACK ON ROBERTS.

Cost Eldredge One Hundred Votes In Millard.

(Special to The Herald.)

Fillmore, Nov. 8.—The papers have just arrived and the uncalled for and dirty attack of Governor Wells on B. H. Roberts has caused considerable excitement, and will lose Eldredge over 100 votes in Millard.

Salt Lake Herald
November 11, 1898

MILLARD IS CLOSE.

Result on State Representative Not Yet Decided.

(Special to The Herald.)

Fillmore, Nov. 11.—Complete returns from 12 districts out of 14 in Millard give Roberts a majority of 127; Baskin a majority of 21; Callister (R.), for legislature, 3. Commissioners: Ed Stevens (D.), 204; John A. Beckstrand (D.), 288; E. F. Pack (D.), 41. County attorney: James Alex Melville (D.), 206, Clerk: J. S. Giles (D.), 259. Recorder: Mrs. D. K. Olson (D.), 143. Sheriff: Virgil Kelly (R.), 9. Treasurer: Rufus Day (D.), 223. Assessor: J. L. Stott (R.), 37. Surveyor: Willard Rogers (D.), 149.

Burbank and Smithville precincts yet to hear from. These two precincts can only change the result on legislature and sheriff. They went two-thirds Democratic in 1896. Returns not expected from these precincts till tomorhow. Both Democratic and Republican chairmen claim majorities there. Very few voted on the constitutional amendments in county.

Holmgren (R.) for representative, has 148 majority, with five precincts to hear from, which, combined gave King 25 majority last election.

THE MAJORITIES INCREASING

Roberts Leads Eldredge By 5,228, and Baskin Is 3,022 Ahead of Zane.

At 2 o'clock Wednesday morning, eight hours after the polls had closed, The Herald estimated the total vote of the state at 65,000 and Roberts' plurality at 6,300. The returns now show 64,217 votes, with a few sparsely settled districts to hear from, and The Herald's estimate will come within 100 of the official figures. Roberts' plurality has reached 5,228, and will probably fall 800 below the first estimate. Baskin's plurality is over 3,000. The returns show that Zane ran 1,595 votes ahead of Eldredge, while Roberts leads Baskin by 611. Foster received 2,397 votes and Bowman, Populist, for judge, 1,198. There were 215 more votes cast for congressman than for judge.

The following revised table shows the vote by counties:

VOTE BY COUNTIES.

	CONGRESS.						JUDGE.		
	1896.			1898.					
	King, D.	Holbrook, R.	Foster, Pop.	D. Foster,	Roberts, R.	Eldredge, Pop.	Baskin, D.	Zane, R.	Bowman, Pop.
Beaver	646	594	2	643	529	9	627	587	....
Box Elder	1411	1188	19	1141	1048	9	1068	1094	6
Cache	3468	1439	163	2588	2289	....	2488	2354	....
Carbon	359	353	20	114	127	....	104	136	.. ..
Davis	1416	677	79	1284	766	17	1223	937	5
Emery	788	389	27	647	366	....	592	392	..
Garfield	411	499	2	366	571	....	318	487	.. ..
Grand	111	154	16	132	101	....	111	116	.. ..
Iron	611	393	12	576	361	....	529	314	..
Juab	1823	909	46	1247	1045	51	1181	1175	23
Kane	195	317	2	178	303	....	156	314	..
Millard	954	581	17	820	683	3	761	748	1
Morgan	412	285	21	308	309	....	339	316	..
Piute	422	158	9	252	212	82	249	237	15
*Rich	323	229	2	66	....	....	45	....	....
Salt Lake	12888	7471	686	8569	6865	1349	8730	7547	581
Sanpete	2718	2440	34	2124	2447	17	2122	2484	8
Sevier	1336	944	52	1056	1101	....	1002	1116	..
Summit	2344	1114	130	1....	1272	110	1398	1159	25
Tooele	1165	232	46	729	769	54	713	830	3
Uintah	529	201	254	420	281	76	393	239	74
Utah	5744	3534	151	4943	3349	65	3956	3528	33
Wasatch	982	326	13	725	497	6	715	499	5
Washington	1075	283	5	722	287	....	713	242	.. ....
Wayne	326	158	2	94	126	....	83	121	..
Weber	4766	2382	447	3463	2649	589	3296	2889	413
Total	47362	27813	2	33524	28296	2397	32913	29891	1198
Plurality	19549	....	....	5228	....	....	3022	....	....

*Majorities

WEBER COUNTY.

	King, D.	Holbrook, R.	Foster, Pop.	D.	Roberts, R.	Eldredge, Pop.	Baskin, D.	Zane, R.	Bowman, Pop.
Ogden									
First Ward	676	286	39	444	293	73	413	300	....
Second ward	534	248	39	373	275	53	350	305	....
Third ward	480	194	71	332	261	52	328	275	....
Fourth ward	792	499	53	562	474	95	555	522	....
Fifth ward	668	265	40	518	323	119	516	370	....
Warren	26	14	9	25	30	2	25	20	....
Burch Creek	61	8	2	47	22	4	46	10	....
Eden	116	17	6	66	18	12	63	29	....
Farr West	57	34	11	37	43	3	33	45	..
Harrisville	72	21	4	74	22	2	68	26	....
Hooper	161	45	14	115	73	12	114	62	....
Huntsville	185	195	46	161	142	28	156	177	....
Kanesville	41	14	1	23	42	1	19	54	....
Liberty	49	8	3	21	39	0	21	28	....
Marriotts	50	32	0	38	48	1	33	54	....
North Ogden	169	124	12	142	102	9	128	110	....
Plain City	177	82	21	129	102	32	128	196	....
Pleasant View	93	21	7	88	20	0	77	26	....
Riverdale	51	27	7	22	51	10	20	53	....
Roy	25	6	1	22	30	0	20	30	....
Slaterville	81	42	20	43	68	17	33	76	....
Uintah	54	37	4	21	27	16	21	28	....
West Weber	119	109	10	88	141	..	84	145	....
Wilson	118	29	9	81	36	3	67	51	....
Total	4792	2382	423	3468	2643	593	3399	2889	413
Plurality	2410	....	....	719	....	....	410	....	....

EMERY COUNTY.

	King, D.	Holbrook, R.	Foster, Pop.	D.	Roberts, R.	Eldredge, Pop.	Baskin, D.	Zane, R.	Bowman, Pop.
Emery	63	65	2	62	53	....	57	58	....
Ferron	72	78	4	87	58	....	82	62	....
Cleveland	89	14	5	64	32	....	62	30	....
Woodside	15	7	2	10	5	....	11	1	....
Green River	17	30	....	6	26	7	4	32	2
Total	788	369	27	647	366	7	592	392	....
Plurality	397	.. ..	....	281	....	....	200	....	....

Total includes complete returns.

Total includes complete returns.

GARFIELD COUNTY.

Hillsdale	43	20	....	55	28	....	....	....	....
Panguitch	249	151	2	135	213	....	136	211	....
Orton	11	31	....	19	53	....	....	....	....
Three precincts	....	....	....	186	277	....	182	276	....
Total	411	449	2	269	571	....	318	487	....
Plurality	....	38	....	....	211	....	....	169	....

MILLARD COUNTY.

Fillmore	234	161	2	199	228	....	196	228	....
Meadow	51	33	4	43	52	1	45	55	1
Kanosh	126	99	6	125	85	....	108	101	....
Black Rock	4	9	..	4	8	....	4	8	....
Hinckley	71	51	....	73	41	....	70	44	....
Deseret	76	69	1	57	65	....	52	71	....
Oasis	33	24	2	33	25	....	31	26	....
Oak Creek	53	5	....	25	24	....	26	33	....
Leamington	61	9	....	34	26	....	31	28	....
Scipio	139	71	....	121	81	....	117	86	....
Holden	75	32	....	86	35	....	77	43	....
*Clear Lake	..	..	....	4	13	2	4	15	....
Total	954	581	17	829	683	3	761	748	1
Plurality	373	....	....	137	....	....	13	....	....

*New precinct.

PIUTE COUNTY.

Koosharem	112	8	....	61	24	....	52	32	....
Bullion	126	29	5	34	34	23	45	33	10
Kingston	25	20	....	16	21	....	14	22	....
Circleville	103	43	..	98	39	....	96	57	....
Junction	44	40	....	30	57	1	29	40	....
Wilmot	12	18	....	4	11	2	4	12	2
Dewey	....	..	..	9	5	6	9	7	3
Total	422	158	9	252	212	32	249	227	15
Plurality	264	....	....	40	....	....	22	....	....

WAYNE COUNTY.

Fremont	51	19	....	41	34	....	39	35	....
Loa	70	64	2	53	86	....	54	86	....
Total	326	158	2	94	120	....	83	121	....
Plurality	168	....	....	....	....	....	....	....	....

Millard County Returns.

(Special to The Herald.)

Fillmore, Utah, Nov. 11.—Burbank precinct gives Roberts 9, Eldredge 16, Baskin 8, Zane 18, J. Greenwood (Dem.) 9, T. C. Callister (Rep.) 18.

Salt Lake Herald
November 18, 1898

UTAH'S THIRD LEGISLATURE.

MRS. ALICE SMITH MERRILL HORNE.

Mrs. Alice Smith Merrill Horne, representative-elect, is the daughter of Clarence and Bathsheba Merrill, and a granddaughter of the late President George A. Smith.

Mrs. Horne was born in Fillmore, Millard county, in 1868, and afterwards spent several years on a ranch in Piute county. At the age of 15 she removed to this city and entered the University of Utah (then the Deseret university), graduating with honors. She was the second woman chosen to represent a graduating class as valedictorian. She has since been a prominent member of the Alumni association, and was the first of her sex to be elected vice president.

Naturally taking up educational work, she became a leader in that field and is known as one of the best instructors in this region. In art, music and literary circles she is also prominent, adding to her store of knowledge by traveling in the east. She is a regular exhibitor at displays of the Society of Utah Artists, and is said to have originated the local Shakespeare society. Mrs. Horne is a charter member of the Daughters of the Revolution, is a good parliamentarian, and will prove a useful member of the lower house. She is a typical daughter of the pioneers and a lifelong Democrat.

Washington County News
November 19, 1898

DEMOCRATS ARE VICTORIOUS

Elect Roberts and Baskin by a Small Majority.

The Legislature Will Consist of Forty-two Democrats, Sixteen Republicans and Five Cannon Fusionists—An Unusually Light Vote Cast.

Salt Lake City, Utah, Nov. 12.—Returns from nearly all the counties in the state show the election of Roberts to congress and Baskin to the supreme bench, by a majority of from 5,000 to 6,000.

There were many surprises in various parts of the state, and the Democratic majority is much less than was counted upon by the Democratic leaders.

The legislature is Democratic by a majority of two to one. The Populists have one member, S. S. Smith of Weber, the Republicans sixteen and the Democrats forty-two. Seven of the latter are hold-overs), and O. F. Whitney, D. H. Peery, jr., and R. K. Thomas, Salt Lake; Seventh district, A. O. Smoot, Provo, and A. J. Evans, Lehi; Eighth district, J. V. Robinson, Fillmore (hold-over); Tenth district, Isaac K. Wright, Richfield (hold-over); Eleventh district, R. R. Tanner, Beaver; Twelfth district, Hardin Bennion, Vernal. Total, 15.

Republicans—Second district, Joseph Howells, Wellsville; Ninth district, Ferdinand Alder, Manti. Total, 2.

Cannon Fusion—Third district, Fred J. Kiesel, Ogden. 1.

Total, 18.

LOWER HOUSE.

DEMOCRATS.

Cache County—A. F. Farr, Logan.
Davis County—John Fisher, Bountiful.
Emery County—Joseph Robertson.
Iron County—John Parry, Cedar.
Juab County—C. V. Wheeler, Silver City.
Piute County—J. H. Fullmer.
Rich County.—D. S. Cook.
Salt Lake County—Heber Bennion, Taylorsville; A. W. Forman, Bingham; Joseph G. Bywater, Sugar; Horace Cummings, Mill Creek; Mrs. Alice M. Horne, H. B. Shephard, C. M. Jackson, R. T. Lloyd, John E. Hanson, S. W. Stewart, Salt Lake.
Sevier County—B. H. Greenwood, Central.
Utah County—Joseph Lapish, American Fork; John E. Betts, Payson; M. Larsen, Spanish Fork; W. M. Roylance, Springville.

B. H. ROBERTS.

holdover senators, the Democrats electing the other thirty-five at this election.

The Cannon legislative ticket was elected in Weber county, the Republicans electing the county ticket.

Salt Lake county is Democratic, majorities ranging from 1,500 to 2,000. There was a heavy scratched vote.

A large percentage of the Gentile vote remained away from the polls.

There was much scratching on all tickets, it appearing at present that both judiciary candidates outran their congressional nominees.

The vote throughout the state was very light. In this city not more than two-thirds of the regular vote was polled.

Uintah County — William O'Neill, Vernal.

Wasatch County—J. W. Clyde, Heber.

Wayne County—Matthew Mansfield.

Washington County—John G. McQuarrie, St. George.

Total, 26.

CLOSE CALL FOR CALLISTER.

Elected In Millard County By Only Eight Votes.

(Special to The Herald.)

Fillmore, Nov. 22.—The official canvass of Millard county was finished at 5 o'clock this evening and shows that the whole Democratic ticket was elected with the exception of assessor, sheriff and legislative candidate. T. C. Callister, Republican candidate for the legislature, has a majority of eight over Joshua Greenwood, Democrat. The canvass showed many irregularities made by the various judges in sending returns in and this caused considerable trouble, but the board counted all with the exception of Black Rock precinct and this was thrown out as no tally sheet could be found so as to determine the vote cast there. Smithville, another precinct, failed to receive their ballots and no election was held there. All kinds of reports are being circulated about contests for the legislative seat but Mr. Greenwood informs The Herald correspondent that he will not make any, although believing if he should the result would be changed in his favor. He bases this assertion on what can be learned from the judges of election that in the different precincts there were thrown out between twenty-five and thirty ballots, two-thirds of which were Democratic tickets. The report appearing in the Tribune this morning that several precincts had been thrown out by the canvassing board yesterday was untrue. There was no ground whatever for such a statement.

Salt Lake Herald
December 8, 1898

UTAH'S THIRD LEGISLATURE.

HON. THOMAS C. CALLISTER.

Thomas C. Callister, representative-elect from Millard county, was born in Salt Lake City, Aug. 2, 1852. His parents came to Utah with the foremost pioneers, moving to Fillmore in May, 1861. Mr. Callister is a self-made man, and his record stands above reproach. In politics he is a Republican. He is also a staunch silver man.

Mr. Callister can be relied upon to work for a man to sit in the United States senate chamber who will best represent the interests of the people of Utah, a man who will lend his vote for the cause of silver upon each and every occasion.

Mr. Callister has served the people in many ways during the past, having acted in the capacity of probate judge, county clerk, recorder and superintendent of schools. He has also been mayor of Fillmore City. In any election where he has been a candidate, he has been counted a "hot number," always hard to beat, and often running away ahead of his ticket.

He has for many years acted as bishop of Fillmore ward. He is also well and favorably known as a farmer and stockraiser, having a large ranch within a couple of miles of the former state capital.

UTAH'S THIRD LEGISLATURE.

HON. JOSEPH V. ROBISON.

Joseph V. Robison is a Knickerbocker by birth, and was born in Onondaga county, New York, Dec. 30, 1832. His parents moved to Illinois when he was 12 years of age, where they lived for ten years, or until 1854, when they came west and settled at Fillmore. Mr. Robison took in the possibilities of the country and established a fruit tree nursery, which has supplied thousands with fruit trees. He also engaged in stock-raising, and at one time was one of the heaviest owners in this state. He has been mayor of Fillmore and probate judge and county judge for several terms. In 1882 and 1883 he represented Millard, Piute and Beaver counties in the legislature. He declined the nomination as member of the constitutional convention from Millard county, and, at his own expense, made a campaign opposing the financial policy of the administration. He is a man of ripe judgment, and his opinions are much sought after by his colleagues. He was elected to the senate of the second state legislature, and is a hold-over. He is a Democrat.

Salt Lake Herald
December 16, 1898

Jurors For Millard County.

(Special Correspondence.)

Fillmore, Dec. 13.—Jury Commissioners Andrew Peterson and L. R. Cropper have made the selection of jurors for this county for 1899.

Deseret Evening News
January 3, 1899

FILLMORE.

Special to the "News."

Fillmore, Jan. 3.—The new year has dawned upon us here filled with brightness and hope for a prosperous ending. The festive Christmas season has passed with the usual pleasantness; amongst the social gatherings of our people, we have had Sunday school exhibitions, and the teachers of the district schools have vied with each other in entertaining the parents of the students with intelligent exercises, displays of acquired knowledge amongst the little ones, which has made the parental hearts beat with pride for their offspring. A better dressed and better fed horde of little ones cannot be found than those of our city and vicinity. We are at peace with all mankind and wish our friend the "Deseret News" a prosperous and happy New Year.

Deseret Evening News
January 7, 1899

FILLMORE.

An examination for county teachers' certificates was held in the State house Monday and Tuesday. Nine teachers took the examination.

At last four rooms of the new school building are ready for occupancy, and the four higher departments will begin the new year there next Monday.

Fillmore is likely to have another creamery in the near future, in fact Mr. Abe Carling informs us that he will erect and run one on his own accord very soon.

The administration of Millard county the past two years has been clean and business-like. Economy has been the watchword with the county commissioners and as a result they have left quite a little money in the treasury for their successors, with all bills paid. What has been said about the outgoing commissioners may also be said of each official during the past two years. They have all worked for the interests of the county, and leave the burdens of office with a knowledge that they have betrayed no trust and have studiously tried to serve the people well. We say, hats off, to the old officers; may their successors do as well.

The new officials are particularly capable men whose reputation is such that the people are assured of an honest, capable and economical administration of county affairs.—Millard Progress.

FILLMORE.

There will be held next Monday evening a meeting for the purpose of organizing a farmers' institute. All interested should attend. At meeting house.

FILLMORE'S NEW SCHOOL BUILDING.

Fillmore Central School building is so near completed that the four lower rooms are now occupied by the fourth, fifth, sixth, seventh and eighth grades.

It is the finest school building south of Provo City, and although it has been a hard struggle for some of the taxpayers to meet the heavy tax, few have complained and all now point with pride to this magnificent house.

It has just been a little over two years since our citizens decided to erect this building and at a regularly called meeting of the taxpayers of Fillmore school district, held Dec. 20th, 1896, it was decided to build a suitable school house, the necessity of which was plainly explained by the trustees, and a tax of two per cent for that purpose was voted by a great majority of those present.

It has cost up to date $8,650, and the estimated cost for the completed building is $10,000.

The people of Fillmore deserve much credit for their liberality in taxing themselves two per cent per annum for two consecutive years, and the principal taxpayers, and in fact, nearly all, are in favor of pushing the work to completion.

AMUSEMENTS.

A very swell party was given at the home of Mrs. Helen M. Callister Wednesday evening. The guests were received in a very cordial way by the hostess and the rooms presented a most cheerful aspect. The guests were: Messrs. and Mesdames John T. Ashman, Abe Carling, A. Q. Robison, Thomas Phelps, Henry Jackson, Mesdames Hinckley, Rydalch, Lyman, Misses Ethel Olson, Edith Robison, Zina Robison, Edith Huntsman, Pearl Huntsman, Maud Crane, Frantie Thompson, Hattie Carling, Nellie Ashman; Messrs. Geo. Melville, Bert King, Will Ashman, David Melville, Charles Warren, Herbert Sömner, Lafayette Huntsman, Alex Melville and John Callister. At ten o'clock a delightful supper was served. The rest of the evening was spent in singing, games, etc.

Mrs. Mamie Henry entertained the members of the F. L. T. club at her home last evening.

Mrs. Hannah Hanson will give a card party Saturday evening.

UNITY AND DIVISION.

What a splendid and profitable thing it would be for the people of Fillmore and Millard county if they would only be united! Not united in religion or politics, but in the practical and business affairs of life. United in the promotion of those things which tend to the material welfare and progress of the community. In these matters diversity of sentiment is healthful and beneficial, but in private and public enterprises, in the physical and practical labor of improvement and advancement there should be unity; the

people should stand shoulder to shoulder, and so to speak, all heave together.—Millard Progress.

YOUNG LADY'S SUDDEN DEATH.

Sad Ending of Miss Laura Holbrook of Fillmore.

(Special to The Herald.)

Fillmore, Jan. 14.—One of the most sudden deaths that has ever been known in this community occurred this morning. Miss Laura Holbrook, daughter of ex-Sheriff and Mrs. Virgin Holbrook took sick last night about 12 o'clock and at 5:15 this morning breathed her last. Miss Holbrook had been ailing some for several months, but her ailment was not considered serious and she was out as usual yesterday and last night called at the postoffice.

After being there a short time she took seriously ill and a few minutes later went into convulsions. Aid was called and the young lady carried home and everything possible done to relieve her, but to no avail. She would have an attack every fifteen or twenty minutes. Her last words were, "Oh, am I going to die, I want to live so much." Miss Holbrook was 22 years old Dec. 2. She was born and raised in Fillmore and had many friends. She was engaged to Postmaster Frank Hanson of this city. Her funeral will be held Tuesday.

Salt Lake Herald
January 25, 1899

GILES IS REMOVED

Action Taken On Millard's Missing Clerk.

HIS SUCCESSOR NAMED

CHRISTIAN ANDERSON OF FILL-MORE GIVEN THE PLACE.

No Trace Yet of the Disappeared Of-ficial—Some Fear Foul Play—Search Parties Return to City—Land Entries Being Investigated—Mrs. Giles' Bondsmen Uneasy.

(Special to The Herald.)

Fillmore, Jan. 24—The county com-missioners met in special session yester-day and the chairman stated that the bondsmen of J. S. Giles asked to be re-leased. The board then passed this resolution:

"Whereas, J. S. Giles, county clerk in and for Millard county, Utah, on the 11th day of January, A. D. 1899, aban-doned his office as said county clerk, and has since that time absented him-self from said office, without providing any deputy or assistant to perform the duties of said office, and his where-about being unknown to the board of county commissioners, or any of his relatives, and

"Whereas, The business in said office is such as to require the officer to be present on each and every business day, to perform the duties of said of-fice; therefore, be it

"Resolved, By the board of county commissioners in and for Millard coun-ty, Utah, that the office of county clerk of Millard county, Utah, be and the same is hereby declared to be aban-doned and vacant."

Christian Anderson of Fillmore was then appointed county clerk for the un-expired term of two years. Mr. Ander-son stated this evening that he has made a hurried investigation of the books and papers of the missing county clerk, and everything seems to be all right, with the exception that Mr. Giles' bond cannot be found.

Giles is still missing. No word of any kind has been received from him, nor has any one seen or heard of him since one week ago tonight. The searching parties which have been out scouring the country with the expectation of finding his body have returned, and it is now generally believed he is alive and out of the county, although others still hold to the idea that his mind was turned and he wandered off, or that he killed himself in some out-of-the-way place. Again the broad assertion has been made that Giles has met with foul play, but there is no ground on which to base such an assertion. For the past several days people have been coming in from all parts of the county to investigate their land entries, etc., but so far nothing wrong has been found concerning them.

Today the bondsmen of Mrs. J. S. Giles, who has a lease on the Fillmore dairy and whose husband was the man-ager, made a demand on the stockhold-ers of that company that they be re-leased and the stockholders take charge of the plant and business at once.

Salt Lake Herald
January 29, 1899

FILLMORE STORE CLOSED.

Giles' Departure Made Creditors Un-easy, Hence the Trouble.

(Special to The Herald.)

Fillmore, Jan. 28.—On account of J. S. Giles' sudden departure from this city several days ago, the Fillmore Mercan-tile company's store, of which he was manager, was compelled to close its doors this morning.

James Currie, representative of the Co-op Wagon & Machine company, has been here in the interest of his house, trying to get a settlement, and only this morning began preparing attach-ment papers, but before they could be gotten out the smaller creditors of the store swooped down and purchased al-most the entire stock, leaving Mr. Cur-rie out. Those interested claim this was not allowed to defraud Mr. Cur-rie's house, but to give the smaller creditors a chance. Nothing yet has been heard from the missing county clerk.

Big Copper Proposition.

Joseph E. Ray of Fillmore, who is in the city, informs The Herald that he is interested in a copper proposition near the north end of the Buckskin mountains and not far from Kanab, which promises to develop into a world-beater.

There are five claims in the group, which endline on each other along the vein, and Mr. Ray states that there are three parallel ledges within fifty feet of each other, each about four feet in width, all of which will carry average values of from 11 to 15 per cent copper to the ton.

The property is easily accessible, and the ground is heavily timbered, while there is a good water supply in the near vicinity.

Federal Court Orders.

Judge Marshall yesterday ordered the removal of J. S. Giles as United States commissioner at Fillmore. Giles was clerk of Millard county and recently disappeared under circumstances suspicious of official crookedness.

J. F. Tolton, United States commissioner at Beaver, filed his resignation in the federal court yesterday, stating that he had held the position for a long time and had transacted no business. The court accepted his resignation.

Judge Marshall ordered that the appointment of J. S. Snow as United States commissioner at St. George be vacated. Mr. Snow left on a mission in August last.

In the case of Wells, Fargo & Co. and Fred J. Kiesel, plaintiffs, vs. the Simmons Hardware company, defendants, an attachment suit for $3,020, filed in 1896, a stipulation was filed for the dismissal of the case.

United States vs. O. J. Salisbury and Monroe Salisbury; plaintiff allowed ten days in which to elect whether it will amend the complaint as to first count against Monroe Salisbury, and defendants given seven days in which to prepare and file answer as they shall be advised.

Rosenbaum-Buchanon company vs. W. S. McCornick; depositions of defendant and plaintiff on file ordered opened and published, and P. L. Williams was given leave to withdraw depositions from files for forty-eight hours on leaving receipt.

Irving M. Herkimer vs. Silver King Mining company; damage suit for taking water, $24,030; on motion of plaintiff the case was ordered dismissed at his cost as to second cause of action pending.

Leon Goldberg vs. Nathan Tanner, jr., report of master in chancery, S. H. Lewis, of the sale of mortgaged premises confirmed.

W. K. Sullivan, receiver American Loan & Investment company vs. Anna E. Loomis and Judd H. Loomis; evidence introduced and decree entered for plaintiff, fixing amount at $1,239.55 and sales fee at 10 per cent.

W. K. Sullivan, receiver American Building Loan & Investment company vs. Enoch Farr, jr., et al.; called for trial on proof on default. Evidence introduced. Decree ordered entered for plaintiff for $812.21 and 10 per cent attorneys' fees.

The supplemental account of United States Marshal Glen Miller for fees and writs, $20.75, for quarter ending Dec. 31, 1898, was presented and approved.

FILLMORE.

Friday County Clerk C. Anderson issued a marriage license to Geo. Crane and Mrs. Ann Hopkinson, both of Kanosh. They left this week for the north end will be married in the Salt Lake Temple.

The hall in the old State House is almost completed. The new floor is laid, the stage up and the stairs leading up from both the north rooms finished. With some finishing touches it will be ready for use. The masons are now engaged in laying the stone wall in the lower hallway. The council could not have put the people's money to any better advantage.

The speakers at the ward meeting Sunday afternoon were: Mr. Knight, of Salt Lake, and messrs. Holbrook, Kirkham and Richardson, Y. M. M. I. A. missionaries. The house was packed and the sermons were interesting and instructive, more especially for the young. In the evening conjoint meeting was well attended, with the same speakers. The services were interspersed with music, songs and recitations.

FARMERS' INSTITUTE MEETING.

Quite a number turned out to the regular meeting of the Farmers' Institute last Thursday evening. Two new names were added to the list and the association is making headway.

A very instructive lecture was given by N. S. Fishop on profits of dairying and feeding. Another lecture by Mayor Geo. C. Yeile on raising pigs feeding artichokes, etc., was instructive and interesting.

A number of questions were asked and answered and the meeting adjourned for one week.

NO WORD FROM GILES.

The whereabouts of J. S. Giles is still unknown. No word of any kind been received from him by his family. From what can be learned it is almost certain that after leaving Fillmore he went almost direct to Salina, then took the railroad.

The Fillmore Mercantile Co. store, or better known as the old Dairy store, closed its doors last Saturday and went out of business. Mr. Giles was manager and part owner of this store, and when the news reached certain creditors that he had turned up missing, they sent representatives here to look after their interests.

The store is now closed for good, but Jesse Giles informs us that they will try and settle all just claims against the store without any law suits.

Judge Marshall Monday ordered the removal as United States commissioner of J. S. Giles, late county clerk of Millard county, and who disappeared on the night of January 17th.

It is expected that T. C. Callister will be appointed to fill the vacancy.—Millard Progress.

Extreme Cold at Fillmore.
(Special to The Herald.)

Fillmore, Feb. 6.—One of the coldest snaps that we have experienced here for many years reached us last night, 17 below zero.

GILES IS STILL ALIVE.

Millard County's Missing Clerk Is Heard From.
(Special to The Herald.)

Fillmore, Utah, Feb. 6.—At last J. S. Giles, the missing county clerk of Millard, who so mysteriously disappeared three weeks ago, has been heard of, but in an indirect way. The message was to his wife, and was to the effect that he is well and all right. This is a great relief to his family and many friends throughout the state.

Salt Lake Herald
February 8, 1899

COURT AT FILLMORE.

Several Matters Passed On By Judge Higgins.

(Special to The Herald.)

Fillmore, Feb. 7.—A regular term of the Fifth district court opened here this morning with Judge Higgins presiding. There is little business here on the calendar and only a small part of that to be tried at this term.

The case of James A. George against Almon Robison was set for trial for the 8th inst.

W. A. Ray vs. N. J. Beauregard; continued for term on the plaintiff paying to defendant $7 and half of the costs.

Alex Dontre et al. vs. A. Rhodes et al.; restraining order granted prohibiting defendant from interfering with the waters in controversy.

Richard Hatton vs. M. A. Hatton; set for trial for tomorrow at 2 o'clock.

Peter Grienhalgh vs. Meadow Irrigation company; demurrer of defendant sustained. Court will likely adjourn tomorrow.

IDAHO MOURNS THE LOSS OF HER BRAVE SONS

Draped Flags at the State Capitol---Casualty List Includes a Utah Man.

MAJOR E. McCONVILLE

(Special to The Herald.)

Boise, Ida., Feb. 7.—Crepe-draped flags placed at various points about the legislative halls today symbolized the sorrow of the legislators over the death in Manila of the Idaho boys. In the lower hall the flag of company B, which sustained the heaviest loss, was prominently displayed, encircled with a badge of mourning. The flag on top of the state house was placed at half-mast, and everywhere were seen evidences of the sadness pervading the legislative assembly over the loss of sons of the state. Arrangements were made for suitable memorials to be presented tomorrow at the forenoon session in each house, after which, as a further mark of respect, the legislature will adjourn for the day.

Governor Steunenberg today wired Senator Shoup, asking him to make a special effort to have Private McConville of the Idaho volunteers discharged. He is a son of Major McConville, one of those killed.

Boise, Feb. 7.—The following data concerning Idaho boys wounded at Manila was taken from the adjutant general's record:

Corporal Lewis B. Bloch, company F, age, 25; born in Montgomery county, Mo.; enlisted from Wardner. Nearest relative, J. B. Bloch, Cranmer, Cal.

Musician Fred W. Beck, company C, age, 22; born at Huntsville, Ala.; enlisted from Grangeville; nearest relative, Sophia L. Taylor, Grangeville.

Fred H. Streeter, company C, aged 24; born at Catoba, Mo.; enlisted from Boise. Nearest relative, M. J. Streeter, Hamilton, Mo.

Howard C. Holler, company C, aged 19; born in Kirkville, Mo.; enlisted from Albion; nearest relative, T. C. Holler, Albion.

Quartermaster Sergeant Ernest Scott, company B, aged 21; born at Bracebridge, Canada; enlisted from Lewis-ton. Nearest relative, Henry Scott, Ashland, Wis.

Harry Rutherford, company C, aged 18; born at Leadville, Colo.; enlisted from Pocatello. Nearest relative, Mrs. J. H. Meadows, Pocatello.

Fred J. Schell, company G, aged 22; born in Monroe county, O.; enlisted from Pocatello. Nearest relative, Jacob Schell, Ransom, Kan.

William C. Payne, company G, aged 22; born at Fillmore, Utah; enlisted from Pocatello. Nearest relative, William Payne, Rockland, Ida.

Enoch S. Koth, company F, 22 years old; born in St. Louis; enlisted from Coeur d'Alene. Nearest relative, Mrs. Belle Koth, Kansas City, Mo.

Sidney C. Bailey, company C, aged 21; born at London, Canada; enlisted from Pocatello. Nearest relative, William Bailey, Ogden, Utah.

James C. Henson, company H, aged 25; born at Overton, Tenn.; enlisted from Boise. Nearest relative, Simpson Henson, Intho, Mo.

Corporal Frank A. McCall, company B, aged 27; born at Pleasant Hill, Mo.; enlisted from Rathdrum. Nearest relative, D. McCall, Ord, Neb. He resigned the position of principal of the Rathdrum school to enlist.

Thomas P. Burke, company C, aged 25; born at Montpelier, Vt.; enlisted from Boise Valley. Nearest relative, Miss Sarah Parkens, Boise.

Sergeant William M. Kellar, company B, aged 24; born at Fountain City, Wis.; enlisted from Lewiston. Nearest relative, C. Kellar, Portland, Ore.

The other names in the list are not found on the adjutant general's books. There are several Jones', but none in company D.

Wesley Walton is in the regiment, coming from Albion, but no Riley Walter. There is no John Switzons, but a John F. Swank, company A, from Shoshone. There is no F. H. Lewis, and no James Payne.

Salt Lake Herald
February 9, 1899

COURT AT FILLMORE.

Night Session, and Adjournment Taken Until April.

(Special to The Herald.)

Fillmore, Feb. 8.—There was little business transacted in the district court here today. There will be a night session tonight and court will then adjourn till the special session in April.

The first business today was Almon Robison et al. vs. Ann Dorrity; dismissed at cost of plaintiff.

The case of Hatton vs. Hatton, divorce; dismissed at plaintiff's cost.

Case of J. W. Jackson vs. J. B. Davis, suit on two promissory notes; judgment rendered as asked for.

The case of Deseret Irrigation company vs. Samuel McIntyre; set for April 4th in special session.

All the other cases were postponed for the term.

CASUALTIES TO UTAH MEN

FOURTEEN KILLED, WOUNDED, OR DIED IN HOSPITALS.

Private C. S. Hill of Carbon County, Shot Yesterday—Lieutenant Grow Probably In San Francisco.

The list of Utah's heroes, killed, died and wounded at Manila was augmented yesterday, when news came that Private Charles S. Hill of battery B had been shot. How serious is his wound is not known, but so many have been shot that it is not likely all of the injured ones can recover.

So far as reported the list now is:

Killed—Assistant Surgeon Harry A. Young, Corporal John Granger Young, Private William Goodman. These men all died in the recent fight. Private George H. Hudson was shot and killed at Cavite, making the number killed four.

Besides, two Utah men died of disease, Morley Hassard, the well-known Salt Lake bicycle rider, and Albert Luff, the total dead being six.

The list of wounded includes Corporal George B. Wardlaw of Ogden, Private Peter Anderson of Richfield, Private Isaac Russell of Salt Lake, Private Charles S. Hill of Wellington, Carbon county; Private Benjamin A. Harbour, ex-state senator, now serving with the Fourteenth regulars; William C. Pyne of Fillmore, serving with the Idaho volunteers; Private J. G. Winkler, wounded at Malate, and Corporal William Anderson of Logan, wounded at Cavite.

The casualties so far sustained by Utah men are, therefore: Killed and died, 6; wounded, 8. Total casualties, 14.

It is reported that Lieutenant Orrin A. Grow, a gallant officer of battery B, arrived in San Francisco on the last vessel, reaching there on Friday. So far, his parents have not heard from him, but letters stated that he had been in the hospital with typhoid fever and was sent home on sick leave. If he arrived, the fact that his father has not yet heard from him is no cause for the least alarm, as the ship would, of course, be in quarantine for a short time.

Private Charles S. Hill, wounded yesterday, enlisted in Ogden. He was 24 years of age, single and was born at Wellington, Carbon county. His nearest relative is W. J. Hill of Wellington.

FILLMORE.

Natural Wealth of Millard Capital, and Need of Railroad.

[Clear-Lake Review.]

Fillmore is situated three miles west from the base of the mountain. The great natural wealth at, and near this place, should induce capital to investigate our resources, among the many that might be mentioned, and to which I will call special attention, are our large stone quarries, their enormity, quality and the easy access to them. The red sand stone belt, of which I shall now treat, commences at the base of the mountain and extends in width two miles towards the east, paralleling the base of the mountain north and south a distance of twelve miles in length. Its color is a bright red and the texture is of fine grain. It is solid and durable, and can be quarried out either in slate form or in blocks of any desired size or dimensions.

It cannot be surpassed either for building or flagging purposes. Its quantity is without limit, and in quality and beauty, it is equal if not superior to that of the far famed stone taken from Red Butte or Cyune, which has found its way by rail, to the great metropolis of our sister states, thereby giving greater impetus to railroad traffic, besides paying the promoters of the enterprise liberally. Access to the quarries here, can be had without hindrance. A railroad grade could be built that would require no more than an ascension of twenty-five feet to the mile, and there would be no heavy cuts or fills in its construction.

The people of this municipality are frugal, industrious and intelligent; and are always willing to contribute liberally to a public enterprise. They want a railroad from here to Clear Lake, and they seem pleased to learn that Engineer O. N. Parsons has taken the initial step in this direction by making an estimate of the probable cost of its construction.

Salt Lake Herald
February 21, 1899

TOOK SALTPETRE.

Mayor Veile and His Son Nearly Killed By a Mistake.

(Special to The Herald.)

Fillmore, Feb. 20.—About 2 o'clock this afternoon Mayor George C. Veile of this city had a close call from death by taking saltpetre, and his oldest son, George M., was badly affected from the same cause. Both have been ill for several days, and under the impression that they were taking salts they took a large dose of saltpetre. The mayor mixed the stuff up and drank two-thirds of a glass, and his son swallowed the balance. A few moments later both became seriously ill, and for some twenty minutes it was a question whether the older gentleman would survive. Dr. Merrill, who was immediately summoned, had his hands full for half an hour, but at the end of that time pronounced him out of danger. The dose the younger man took made him very ill, but not dangerously so.

Deseret Evening News
March 11, 1899

FILLMORE.

Will Build a New Tabernacle—Plowing Begun.

Special Correspondence.

Fillmore, Millard Co., March 8.—The county commissioners were in session on the 6th and 7th inst. Besides the regular routine of business, they had under consideration the advisability of building a vault in which to keep the county records. The people generally favor the proposition, and it is hoped the county commissioners will soon build the vault.

The people here have united, regardless of religious belief in an effort to construct a new and modern tabernacle in which to worship God. It is expected that vigorous work will be done on the same this coming summer.

The farmers have commenced work preparing the ground for spring sowing. The outlook for water this irrigation season is good.

Deseret Evening News
March 17, 1899

FILLMORE.

Tabernacle Services—Death of Mrs. Elizabeth Peterson.

Special Correspondence.

Fillmore, Millard Co., March 15.— At the tabernacle last Sunday the people were addressed by Elder Joshua Greenwood upon the subject of repentance. Elders David Melville and John W. Callister, who have been called to perform missions in the Southern States, expressed themselves as being well pleased with their appointments.

Stake President Ira N. Hinckley and his counsellors are visiting the different wards of Millard Stake of Zion.

Mrs. Elizabeth Peterson died suddenly the night of the 13th inst. There appears to have been no particular cause for her death except old age, she being eighty-three years old. Mrs. Peterson was one of the early pioneers of Fillmore; her many acts of kindness have endeared her to the hearts of all who knew her.

Deseret Evening News
March 21, 1899

FILLMORE.

Miscellaneous Budget of News.

Special Correspondence.

Fillmore, Millard Co., Utah, March 20.—The speakers at the tabernacle Sunday were James A. Melville, Alma Greenwood and Bishop T. C. Callister. They have been in Salt Lake City during the senatorial contest.

State Senator Joseph V. Robison is expected home in a few days.

Two teachers of our district school have been dismissed on account of shortage of the school fund.

Quite a number of people are locating dry farms in Millard county this season. It is believed by many that grain and alfalfa seed can be raised without artificial irrigation.

The old State House at Fillmore, in which the first Legislature of Utah met, has been remodeled. The upper story is used as a dancing hall and the lower story for offices.

Merchants report business in a flourishing condition.

FILLMORE.

Heaviest Storm of Years—Streets Impassable and Traffic Suspended.

Special Correspondence.

Fillmore, Millard Co., March 27.—Priesthood meeting was held here on the 25th instant. Many persons from outside settlements were in attendance. Some of them remained over Sunday to visit their friends. The Young Men's Mutual Improvement association will close for the season after their next meeting, which will be held conjointly with the young ladies on April 2nd.

The infant child of Mrs. [Dan] Wixom died last Sunday.

HEAVIEST STORM OF YEARS.

The snow which fell Saturday night and Sunday caused considerable loss to stockmen who had their cattle in the open fields. Quite a number are reported to have died. The creek raised nearly to high water mark and came rushing down the mountain slopes in torrents; the streets were a perfect lake of water and communication with the outside towns was suspended. It was impossible for the children to get to Sunday school and the Clear Lake mail was seven hours late. There has not been such a storm in this vicinity for years.

IS GARDNER DEAD OR ALIVE

HE LEFT FOR THE MOUNTAINS WHILE INSANE.

May Have Perished In Snow or Been Murdered By Half-witted Companion—Searchers Out.

(Special to The Herald.)

Fillmore, March 29.—The following is taken from a private letter which has just reached Kanosh from parties in Snake valley: "One morning last week at 5 o'clock Alma J. W. Gardner of Kanosh, employed as a sheepherder by Mr. Gregory, went insane, took his gun and started for the mountains, stating that a mob was coming from Snake valley to kill him." Nothing further has been heard of him, and it is feared he has perished, as it is stormy in the mountains.

Gardner has been heard of since the letter quoted was received, and it was stated that he was near Osceola with his herd, and his companion was James Egan, a half-witted person who, it is said, shot a former partner in the same business several years ago. It is therefore thought by some that Gardner made for the camp and fell a victim to foul play.

Parties from Kanosh, immediately upon receiving this word, took Gardner's trail, but nothing has been heard from them, and as there is no telegraph line in that part of the country their return will have to be awaited for full particulars.

Gardner has always been a good citizen and much respected by the people of Kanosh, and his poor mother and sister are almost wild with grief under the uncertainty and dreadful suspense.

Deseret Evening News
April 4, 1899

FILLMORE.

Teachers' Institute—Was Alma Gardner Murdered?—Grave Suspicions.

Special Correspondence.

Fillmore, Millard Co., April 3.—The teachers of Millard county met here on Saturday and held an institute; they wer addressed by Profs. Cluff and Brimhall of the B. Y. academy. The enthusiasm manifested by the teachers is indicative of the good work they are doing in our public schools.

The postoffice is to be removed from its present site to a point lower down on Main street. The building it now occupies has been purchased by Alma Greenwood and will be used for a residence.

Conjoint Mutual was held last Sunday evening at the tabernacle and an excellent program was rendered. This will be the last conjoint meeting this season.

ALMA GARDNER STILL MISSING.

The friends of Alma Gardner know nothing further of his whereabouts. It was reported that he had gone insane and left a sheep camp near Seroola, going into the mountains. His companion, Mr. Egan, who was charged with having shot a former companion in the same business, has a brother living at Fillmore, who is very indignant to think that his brother, James Egan, had been accused of murder.

Deseret Evening News
April 8, 1899

FILLMORE.

Will Build a Road to Gunnison—Stockmen in Clover.

Special Correspondence.

Fillmore, Millard County, April 4.—

The county commissioners were in session on the 3rd and 4th inst. Very little business was transacted, but they expect to commence the construction of a wagon road from Scipio to Gunnison before long, the last Legislature having made an appropriation to build the same.

The Kelly Brothers have taken the contract to run the mail from Fillmore to Clear Lake, the present contractor, Marsellous Webb, having sub-let the same.

Stock men are turning their cattle on the ranges since the recent storm.

Mrs. Gabriel Huntsman has been sick for the past week with a severe attack of la grip. All members of the family were telegraphed for, but at present she is improving.

FILLMORE.

Teachers' Institute—Was Alma Gardner
Murdered?—Grave Suspicions.

Special Correspondence.

Fillmore, Millard Co., April 5.—The
teachers of Millard county met here on
Saturday and held an institute; they
were addressed by Profs. Cluff and
Brimhall of the B. Y. academy. The
enthusiasm manifested by the teachers is indicative of the good work they
are doing in our public schools.

The postoffice is to be removed from
its present site to a point lower down
on Main street. The building it now
occupies has been purchased by Alma
Greenwood and will be used for a residence.

Conjoint Mutual was held last Sunday evening at the tabernacle and an
excellent program was rendered. This
will be the last conjoint meeting this
season.

ALMA GARDNER STILL MISSING.
The friends of Alma Gardner know

nothing further of his whereabouts. It
was reported that he had gone insane
and left a sheep camp near Osceola, going into the mountains. His companion, Mr. Egan, who was charged with
having shot a former companion in the
same business, has a brother living at
Fillmore, who is very indignant to
think that his brother, James Egan,
had been accused of murder.

FILLMORE.

Prospectors Happy—Illicit Whiskey Selling
—Alma Gardner Heard From.

Special Correspondence.

Fillmore City, Millard Co., April 9.—
Several parties have been out prospecting the last few days and brought in
some fine specimens of ore.

Report comes from Kanosh that Alma
Gardner, the gentleman who recently
left a sheep camp in Snake valley, and
who was supposed to have been lost or
to have met foul play, has been found.
He went west instead of east, as was
supposed at first, and wandered off into
Nevada.

The speakers at the Tabernacle Sunday were Rufus Day and Alman Robison.

ILLICIT WHISKEY SELLING.

One of our young men took a little
too much "booze" Saturday and was
lodged in the county jail. It is reported that he will swear to a complaint
charging one of our citizens with selling liquor without a license.

Hans C. Hansen of Fillmore, Millard
county, 160 acres in section 7, in township 22 south, of range 4 west.
Roy H. McBride of Paragoonah, Iron

Deseret Evening News
April 15, 1899

FILLMORE.

An Unsavory Scandal—Unlicensed Liquor Selling.

Fillmore, Millard County, April 14. —The county attorney, J. A. Melville, received word from Kanosh the morning of the 13th inst. that three young men went out to the Indian camps a few nights before and remained nearly all night. They had a supply of whisky with them and got an Indian and two squaws drunk, and an unsavory scandal is the result of the spree. The boys may be arrested for furnishing liquor to Indians.

L. E. Huntsman of Fillmore has been arrested for selling liquor without a license. His trial will come up some time next week.

At a special session of the city council last Wednesday, the resignation of John M. Hanson as city attorney was accepted, and Joshua Greenwood was appointed to supercede him.

Salt Lake Herald
April 21, 1899

CLERK GILES WILL COME BACK

MISSING OFFICER OF MILLARD COUNTY IS LOCATED.

Tells Friends That He Intends to Return and Face Charges—Didn't Mean to Do Wrong.

(Special to The Herald.)

Fillmore, April 20.—It is just learned that J. S. Giles, late county clerk of Millard, who, on the night of Jan. 16 so mysteriously disappeared on account of irregularities coming to light in his land business, has been visited by friends, to whom he freely talked.

He said he was considering the advisability of returning to Fillmore and face the charges. He protests against any criminal intent, but said the condition and circumstances surrounding certain acts connected with his land business were such that he could not at the time fully explain them. He further says that the act most seriously complained of—forgery—was committed for the temporary benefit of the individual concerned, more than to injure, or violate the law.

These parties refuse to give Giles' whereabouts at the present time.

FILLMORE.

Closing Exercises of the District Schools— J. S. Giles Reported in Town.

Special Correspondence.

Fillmore, Millard County, April 22.— The funds of the district school have been exhausted and all departments closed on the 21st inst. An excellent program was had in the morning and the afternoon was spent by indulging in physical sports. Miss Maud Crane, who had charge of the third and fourth grades, left for her home at Kanab last Saturday.

The weather has been extremely cold the last week, and fruit growers predict a total failure of the fruit crop.

The report that J. S. Giles was in town has had quite a general circulation. If the rumor be true, only his immediate friends and relatives know where to find him.

Sheriff Kelly made a visit to Elsinore recently for the purpose of obtaining evidence against parties who are suspected to have been engaged in the business of killing horses for their hides. As yet no arrests have been made.

The case of the city of Fillmore vs L. E. Huntsman, charged with selling liquor without license, came on for hearing Saturday at 10 a. m. The defendant demurred to the complaint, and the demurrer was sustained.

ILLEGAL LIQUOR SELLING.

Hot Two Days' Trial Down In Fillmore.

(Special to The Herald.)

Fillmore, April 24.—The case of Fillmore City vs. L. E. Huntsman, charged with unlawfully selling liquors on the 8th inst., came up before Justice Cooper Saturday morning. Attorneys Greenwood and Hanson appeared for the prosecution while Attorney Warner of Provo represented the defendant, and true to public expectation there has been a battle royal in progress up to tonight, when the case was given to the jury, who are still out. Two long days and a night's session have been taken up with this case, and the evidence almost conclusively shows the defendant guilty.

The case has attracted considerable attention, for unlicensed liquor selling is alleged to have been going on for years in this city, but it has been impossible for the authorities to get evidence to convict.

Voted Special School Tax.

(Special to The Herald.)

Fillmore, April 24.—Today the taxpayers of this city met and voted a special school tax of three-quarters of a mill to complete the new school building, which is recognized as the finest south of Provo.

Deseret Evening News
April 26, 1899

FILLMORE.

Jury Acquits L. E. Huntsman of the Charge of Illegal Whisky Selling.

Special Correspondence.

Fillmore, Millard Co., April 25.—The case of Fillmore City vs L. E. Huntsman, came on regularly for hearing at 10 o'clock last Saturday morning, after disposing of the demurrer a new complaint was filed and defendant entered a plea of not guilty to the complaint, which charges him with selling liquor without a license. The evidence for the prosecution tended to show that defendant had sold liquor at various times, on the 8th of April to Frederick Maycock, the complaining witness.

The defendant attempted to make it appear that the liquor had been stolen from the premises. Last night at 11 o'clock the jury returned a verdict of not guilty.

The wind has been blowing almost continuously the last ten days. Everything is very dry and unless some rain falls soon there is apt to be a shortage in the harvest.

Salt Lake Herald
April 27, 1899

a county charge.

Mrs. Thankful Fillmore died Sunday morning at the home of her daughter, Mrs. Annie Cushing, she was 85 years of age, and was the wife of Daniel Fillmore deceased. She lived in Payson since 1869. The funeral was held this afternoon at the First ward meeting house. The speakers were Charles Brewerton, H. E. Gardner and Bishop J. S. Page, jr.

Deseret Evening News
May 5, 1899

FILLMORE.

Grand County Ball Given in the State House—Stormy Weather.

Special Correspondence.

Fillmore, Millard County, May 2.—Last night the ladies' physical culture club of Fillmore, under the auspices of the Y. L. M. I. A. gave a grand ball in the old State House building. The walls were appropriately decorated with bunting and evergreens. Invitations were sent to the members of the dancing community in almost every town of the county, and a very large crowd was in attendance. The first number of the program was a grand march by the members of the physical culture club under the instructor; both the members and the instructor received many compliments. Following this were several fancy dances, including the cake walk. Refreshments were served in the small rooms on the first floor. All expressed themselves as having had an excellent time.

During the last few days there has been a remarkable change in the weather. A great deal of snow has fallen and cattle on the range are suffering.

Deseret Evening News
May 11, 1899

FILLMORE.

Millard County as a Promising Dairy District.

Special Correspondence.

Fillmore, Millard Co., May 9.—The treasurer of Millard county is sending out the statements to the taxpayers.

Millard county is, at present, exporting large quantities of dairy products. People who supply milk to the dairies find the returns entirely satisfactory, and before long that industry will be a great source of revenue to the inhabitants of this part of the State.

The city council of Fillmore will not permit the physical culture class to use the Old State House building any longer for their exercises, as they tend to impair the floor for dancing.

Deseret Evening News
May 17, 1899

FILLMORE.

Bernard Robinson Still Remains in a Critical Condition

Special Correspondence.

Fillmore, Millard Co., May 16.—Bernard Robison, the son of F. A. Robison, who was kicked by a horse on Saturday evening last, is still in a critical condition. Dr. Robison of Provo is in attendance and thinks the case a serious one. The boy's skull is fractured just above the eyes, leaving a wound about three inches long. An operation was performed yesterday morning by removing that portion of the skull bearing on the brain. The boy is still conscious, although a large part of the skull on the forehead has been removed.

SUNDAY SERVICES.

Alex Forte occupied the time at the Sunday services of the 14th, speaking on the subject of the God-head.

Clinton D. Rey, who has been employed as a teacher in the academy at Preston, Idaho, returned home last week. He is looking well and expressed himself as having enjoyed his labors in the Church school very much.

The Y. L. M. I. A. is still in a flourishing condition although warm weather has set in. Considerable enthusiasm is manifested by the young ladies in studying the principles of the Gospel and storing their minds with a knowledge of the divine teachings of the Savior.

Salt Lake Herald
May 18, 1899

Killed By a Horse.

(Special to The Herald.)

Fillmore, May 17.—The little child of F. A. Robison, who was kicked on the forehead by a horse last Saturday, died this morning. Dr. George E. Robison of Provo, who has been here attending him all the week, said it was one of the most frightful injuries he had ever seen a child have.

Salt Lake Herald
May 19, 1899

COPPER NEAR KANAB.

Joseph E. Ray Speaks of His Property In Buckskin Mountains.

Joseph E. Ray, the well-known mining operator of Fillmore, is in the city. He has just come up from the southern part of the state, where he has recently acquired a large group of claims in the Buckskin mountains near Kanab. Mr. Ray owns over twenty claims in one group, and, judging from what he has to say about them, he has the foundation for a big copper mine.

He has a force of men at work taking out ore, some of which is high grade and rich enough to stand transportation charges to Salt Lake and net a handsome profit. He expects to start shipments at once, and if they pan out as he believes they will, he will keep them up regularly.

It is the ultimate intention of Mr. Ray to put up a smelting plant. This he will probably do this summer. He says he has an immense showing of copper on his property, and with a smelter on the ground he could furnish employment for several hundred men to take out pay ore.

The location of his claims is convenient to water and fuel, making the cost of smelting a matter of comparatively little importance.

Deseret Evening News
May 24, 1899

WILL ARRIVE AT FILLMORE TONIGHT

President Snow's Party Gradually Pushing Back to the North.

WARM WELCOME AT KANOSH

People are Everywhere Glad to See the Honored Pilgrims on Their Mission of Doing Good.

Special per Deseret Telegraph.

Kanosh, Utah, May 24.—Yesterday morning, Tuesday, at 8:30, President Snow's party left Beaver, after a most interesting visit with the hospitable people. The weather was most favorable and the roads fine. The country shows very perceptibly the effects of the severe drouth. The fruit has suffered greatly from the late frosts. The historical spot known as the old Cove Creek fort was reached at 11 o'clock, when a halt of an hour and a half was made for lunch. This is 25 miles from Beaver. The old fort is an interesting structure, built during the troubles with the Indians. The rock walls are about twenty feet high. The fort, in connection with the land, cost about $25,000. It belongs to the Church; 1:30 p. m., and we were again on the way. The party was due in Kanosh at 4 o'clock, but through skillful driving we reached there at 4 p. m. A grand procession of seventy-five ladies and gentlemen on horses met the President several miles from the city and escorted the party in.

It was a beautiful sight; about 300 children greeted the President on his arrival, and he shook hands with all after addressing them. In the evening a three hour meeting was held. The house was crowded; the speakers were, President Snow, President Richards, Dr. Young, Bishop Preston, Elders L. C. Snow, Apostle Woodruff and President Smith. The law of tithing, return to Zion and the Word of Wisdom were the subjects spoken upon. A few members of the party show signs of fatigue, but the President not only feels better, but looks much better than when he left Salt Lake. He has been much improved by the trip so far; he has attended every meeting, even the ladies' meetings. He eats hearty and rests well, and delights in visiting the people. The entire country has become enthused with his visit, and the good that has already been accomplished cannot be estimated. The people of Nephi very much desire President Snow to hold meeting in their city, so he has decided to do so Friday evening; note this change in program. Meadow is 6 miles from here; meeting will be held there at 10 this morning. Then we shall continue to Fillmore, 4 miles, for afternoon and evening meetings.

Deseret Evening News
May 25, 1899

ENROUTE TO FILLMORE.

Party Given the Same Warm Welcome as It Has Received Everywhere.

Special per Deseret Telegraph.

Fillmore, Utah, May 24.—The ride from Kanosh to Meadow was delightful. All the members of President Snow's party are well and much refreshed today. While President Snow was approaching the meeting house at 10 o'clock this morning he was met by all the people of the town who carried banners and flags. The Sunday school children made a pretty showing. The President addressed them a few moments and then shook hands with all of them. Meeting commenced at 10:30. President Snow said he had been inspired by the Lord to present the law of tithing to the Saints and he intends to visit all the Stakes in Zion and awaken the people to their duty in this regard. The 119th section of the Doctrine and Covenant was read to the meeting. "If the people," said he, "whom we have visited will observe this law my life will be preserved and I shall see you all again but if you do not I shall not see you again."

Bishop Preston, during his remarks, said the people here, and in other places, do not show the Lord proper respect by not improving the surroundings of their meeting houses and tithing houses. President Smith advised a change here in the Bishopric as Bishop Bennett is getting old and the responsibilities are too great for him.

Fillmore, May 24.—President Snow's party has just arrived. Received royally from all the people and Sunday school children who presented the President with a beautiful souvenir. He is now shaking hands with the children. The freedom of the city has been tendered him.

Salt Lake Herald
May 25, 1899

EMPHATIC ON POLYGAMY.

Apostle Lyman's Discussion of the Subject.

(Special to The Herald.)

Kanosh, May 23.—The denial of President Lorenzo Snow on the subject of plural marriage was repeated and emphasized by Apostle Francis M. Lyman at Beaver where overflow meetings were necessary to accommodate the throng of special conference visitors last night.

The meetings lasted until after 10 o'clock. After urging obedience to the tithing law and appealing to the Saints for their earnest support in the plan of liquidating church indebtedness, Apostle Lyman said: "I want to declare unto this people that plural marriage is not a live ordinance in the Church of Jesus Christ of Latter-day Saints today. The law has been taken from us, and the practice is suspended by the manifesto of President Wilford Woodruff. Even before that was issued we find that only 3 per cent of the people accepted of the doctrine, although our leaders were hounded and persecuted year after year.

"Again I say it has been suspended, and," continued the apostle, in great earnestness, "I challenge any man to say it has been encouraged by the leaders or officers of this church since the manifesto came forth. I, as an apostle in this church, have been consulted hundreds of times by faithful believers as to the law of plural marriage, and my answer to them has invariably been that it could not be done; that plural marriages had ceased in the church of God at his own command. My associates will testify to the same experience, but the time is coming when God will have it otherwise."

A drive of fifty-five miles brought President Snow and party to Kanosh from Beaver today. They were met on the outskirts of the town by fifty young men and ladies, mounted on horses, and led by Major B. H. Watts and a number of prominent residents on horses, who headed the procession, carrying a large flag and a handsome banner, upon which was inscribed: "Zion's youth are made glad and the gray beards bid you welcome."

On Main street President Snow met the children, who followed to the meeting-house, all the time cheering their beloved leader. The president spoke for a few moments, afterwards shaking hands with 256 people.

A meeting at Meadow in the afternoon and the evening at Fillmore is the programme for tomorrow. The party lunched today at the old Cove Creek fortress, erected in 1867, which is still in a good state of preservation.

END OF TOUR IS IN SIGHT

PRESIDENT SNOW'S PARTY WILL REACH HOME SATURDAY.

Handsome Present Made Church President By Fillmore Sunday School.

(Special to The Herald.)

Fillmore, May 24.—President Snow and party met with a warm reception both here and at Meadow today. Crowds of people, both young and old, gathered to bid him welcome. Upon coming into the city this afternoon, the president was escorted by a band of horsemen and about thirty carriages of prominent citizens. The Sunday school representatives presented him with a beautiful copy of the articles of faith, printed in gold on fine satin. The emblem bore these words: "To our honored and beloved president, Lorenzo Snow. We, the members of the Fillmore Sunday school ward, herewith express our love and respect to you on this occasion of your visit to our city, May 24, 1899, and we pray that God will preserve you long upon earth as a prophet and seer to his people."

Flags are flying all over town in honor of the visitors. Hundreds are unable to gain admission to the meetings, and many will go on to Holden with the party tomorrow, in order to hear the president speak.

The end of the tour is in sight. Saturday noon will bring the party into Salt Lake. The last meeting is to be held at Nephi.

Salt Lake Herald
May 26, 1899

J. E. Ray of Fillmore is at the Cullen. He has a group of copper mines down near the Arizona line, and has made shipments to this city for assay. Some of the ore runs from 15 to 20 per cent in copper and carries from ten to twenty ounces of silver.

Salt Lake Herald
May 27, 1899

Fine Farming Country.

From Parowan to Fillmore, a distance of over 125 miles, it is gratifying to note the land is more under cultivation than in the country surrounding Dixie. Irrigation facilities are much more adequate. Parowan, since last year has become a field of flowing wells, over 100 being in use at present, although the residents have never be-

"buttonholing" visitors to "move here." T. Marioneaux, the newly appointed district attorney, is a most aggressive enthusiast in this regard. His dissertations and briefs upon Beaver's beauties and imposing prospects would fill a volume to make Blackstone shudder.

At present the Branch Normal students are unable to contain their exuberance over the defeat of the Cedar City high-kicking team. The residents, too, are jubilant.

Beaver's nearest neighbor is Greenville, sometimes called Pancake, because of the peculiar shape of its buildings. It is situated near the west fence of Packard's dry farm. A sudden seizure of ennui caused the death of a tramp here once, one of two casualties with which the town is credited.

Pancake's population has been variously estimated at from 31 to 97 souls. Only one census was ever taken, and that during a performance of "Uncle Tom's Cabin," when, it is claimed, little Eva and all the bloodhounds were included in the count. Adamsville, a town to the right, has twice threatened suit against Pancake for taking the names of her prominent residents, who were in the audience simply as spectators. The record, it appears, was subsequently destroyed by a charivari party attending the city recorder's wedding. He died. His predecessor, however, claims the above figures were legitimate and correct, and he is corroborated.

The Rob Roy mine is located near Beaver. Development work is going on under P. T. Farnsworth, who owns the controlling interest. A few miles from the Rob Roy is the Big mine, in Granite district, owned by J. F. Tolton and others of Beaver, who have assays showing 12 7-10 per cent copper 22 per cent lead, seven ounces silver and some gold. Great interest is being taken in the Beaver county mines at present, and a bright future is predicted for the locality.

On the road to Kanosh, the party had the pleasure of visiting Cove Creek Ranch fort, which was erected as a protection from Indians in 1867. It could at this day be turned to use as a barricade in which twelve men could stand off an army of infantry. It is built of solid rock and the living rooms, constructed together on either side of the field inside, are still in good condition. Port holes extend along the sides and ends and, being funnel-shaped, gave the defenders ample room to operate a rifle with practically no exposure to themselves. They stood on the roof of a house, and yet were protected by the wall, which stands five feet higher than the roof. The fort has been the scene of many an attack, successfully withstood. It is owned by the church, with 125 acres adjoining.

The sulphur mines between Beaver and the fort were an object of great interest, and very entertaining was the village of prairie dogs and owls in Dog valley.

Kanosh is perhaps the quietest settlement along the road, but it has a history. It was named for the famous chief of the Parowan tribe, who always was friendly to the Mormon people. The present site of the town was once roamed by Kanosh and his band of braves, but they willingly parted with the land at President Brigham Young's request. The Parowan tribe is almost extinct. Hunkhop (pronounced Hunkup) is one soul remaining. He was Kanosh's own cousin. Hunkhop is thoroughly Americanized, speaks good English, and lives with his squaw and family on a farm near the city. He has another relative in the town, called Pete, who also has taken to the ways of the white man.

Twenty-three miles from Kanosh the Miller group of claims is located. The ore shows about $111 gold to the ton, and a shaft 125 feet deep has been sunk. William George owns the property.

PRESIDENT SNOW'S TRIP.

Description of Country Included In the Tour.

(Special Correspondence.)

Fillmore, May 24.—But few days remain of the most pleasurable tour of the president's party, and as the end manifests itself, the members realize more thoroughly what an uncommon experience it has been. The demonstrations on every hand, the great outpourings of people to meet the beloved leader, and the cordial welcomes and hospitality extended, are justly appreciated, being as they are a powerful factor in making the trip what it has been.

With journeys of forty or forty-five miles each day, over the roughest mountain roads and in the hot sun and desert sands, the oldest members of the party have showed remarkable endurance. Not one case of illness or even serious fatigue has been known during the trip, and President Snow, who remarked today that he has not met a man older than himself in the south— insists that he is holding up better than anybody, and his appearance bears out the assertion. If solicited as to his welfare, he will cheerfully reply: "Never mind me; I am old and tough, and can stand it. But," he will add, "do look after these young people. We do not want them sick on our hands."

The tour has gone merrily on.

Deseret Evening News
May 27, 1899

FILLMORE.

Good Effect of President Snow's Visit— News Briefs.

Special Correspondence.

Fillmore, Millard Co., May 22.—The visit from the President of the Church was very much appreciated here; his remarks were timely and appropriate, as were also the remarks of the brethren who were associated with him. Many expressions of gratitude were heard today as a result of the visit of the presidential party, and many resolutions have been made to live nearer to God in the future than in the past.

Preparations are being made for the celebration of Memorial day; it is expected that a large number of our citizens will visit the cemetery and decorate the graves of the loved ones who have passed away.

Levi W. Arner, who has been working for the Holbrook Land and Irrigation company, at Snake valley, returned home last Monday. He says that work is being pushed vigorously on that enterprise.

Salt Lake Mining Review
May 30, 1899

Hinckley Correspondence Fillmore Progress: Your correspondent has just returned from Sawtooth mountains, where he found some very good specimens of platinum, copper and gold. Sawtooth has a very curious formation; it is cut right into at Granite Pass and shows any kind of formation you wish, and you can get mineral of any description in small quantities, enough to show that somewhere concealed are rich bodies of ore. I am informed that the mountain has never been very thoroughly prospected, and the near future may make some material developments, as quite a number have their attention turned in that direction.

Deseret Evening News
May 31, 1899

FILLMORE.

Memorial Day Duly Remembered—Sunday Services.

Special Correspondence.

Fillmore, Millard Co., May 30.—The people are celebrating Memorial Day in a very appropriate manner here this afternoon. A large number of our citizens have gone to the cemetery with baskets full of flowers prepared to decorate the graves of the loved ones there interred; preparations are being made to give a grand ball in the Old State House.

Deseret Evening News
June 2, 1899

FILLMORE

Court at Scipio—Walch Case Dismissed—Social Ball.

Special Correspondence:

Fillmore, Millard County, Utah, June 1.—The case of the State of Utah vs Franklin Walch, called at Scipio yesterday, was dismissed by County Attorney Melville. The defendant was charged with an assault with a deadly weapon with intent to do bodily harm on the person of one Levmaster. The evidence was insufficient to warrant the prosecution in proceeding with the case. It appeared from an examination of the witnesses that the complainant took an aggressive stand during the unpleasantness which occured, and a portion of the time forced the fighting.

There will be a ball given this evening at the State House under the auspices of the Primary association.

Salt Lake Herald
June 7, 1899

COURT AT FILLMORE.

Important Water Case Set For Trial —Another Compromised.

(Special to The Herald.)

Fillmore, June 6.—Judge Higgins arrived here today and opened the regular June term of court, with a good-sized calendar to work upon. He was busy the greater part of the day in disposing of the following matters:

On the petition of the trustees of Kanosh school district, certain lands in the town of Kanosh entered by the probate judge under the townsite law, the title of which is vested in the district judge as trustee, were set aside for school purposes and a deed ordered issued therefor.

The same order was made with reference to a piece of land in Holden, the object of the trustees being, as they say, to erect new schoolhouses.

Upon application of District Attorney Thomas Marioneaux, the court ordered a commitment issued for the commitment of Edward M. Webb. Webb was convicted several months ago of stealing about seventeen head of cattle and was sentenced to two years in the state prison. He appealed to the supreme court, but the case was affirmed.

Salt Lake Herald
June 8, 1899

YOUNG GETS VERDICT.

Judgment at Fillmore For Salt Lake Man.

(Special to The Herald.)

Fillmore, June 7.—Court reconvened this morning at 10 o'clock. After some probate business, the case of O. R. Young vs. John A. Ruxton was called. Judgment by default was entered in favor of the plaintiff for the sum of $3,054.90, attorney's fees $150, and costs.

The Deseret Irrigation company vs. Sam McIntyre et al. was continued for the term by agreement of all the attorneys interested, upon the suggestion of defendants that Cazier Bros. of Juab county, R. C. Roberts, Benjamin and Reuben Christensen, L. H. Erickson and the Dover Irrigation company of Sanpete county, and the Westview Irrigation company of Sevier county, and other persons whose names are unknown, are interested in the subject matter of the action, and that their presence as parties to the suit is necessary to its complete determination. The court ordered as suggested.

Court adjourned until October term.

Deseret Evening News
June 8, 1899

FILLMORE

District Court Cases Passed for the Term—Adjusting Taxes.

Special Correspondence.

Fillmore, Utah, June 7.—All cases on the calendar have been passed for the time and the court adjourned today at 4 o'clock p. m.

It was expected that the case of the Deseret Irrigation company et al vs Samuel McIntyre et al would have been tried. A large number of witnesses were present, and many attorneys were in attendance, but on stipulation of the attorneys for the respective parties, the case was postponed.

The board of equalization is still in session and transacting a large amount of business.

Deseret Evening News
June 13, 1899

FILLMORE.

County Court—Wedding of Harvey King and Mrs. Katie McBride.

Special Correspondence.

Fillmore, Millard Co., June 12.—The county court is still in session and transacting some business in relation to the taxes.

The contract for building the county vault was awarded to Hanson and Rasmussen of Fillmore.

The county clerk issued a marriage license last week to Harvey King and Katie McBride, both of Fillmore; the wedding will take place tomorrow evening at the residence of Mr. and Mrs. Dan Melville.

Dr. George E. Robison of Provo spent a few days this week with his relatives here.

Deseret Evening News
June 16, 1899

BARN BURNED AT FILLMORE.

Special per Deseret Telegraph.

Fillmore, June 16.—The large and beautiful barn owned by Walter Jukes, situated on lower Main street was burned to the ground last night. The cause of the fire, which started about 11 o'clock, is unknown. Mr. Jukes is absent at Nephi; loss about $500.

Salt Lake Herald
June 17, 1899

Joshua Greenwood and wife of Fillmore were circulating among friends in the city yesterday.

Deseret Evening News
June 21, 1899

FILLMORE.

Sunday Services—Fourth of July Celebration.

Special Correspondence.

Fillmore City, Utah, June 20.—Hyrum Beckstrand, of Meadow, passed through here today on his way home from Ann Arbor, Mich., where he has been studying electrical engineering.

SUNDAY SERVICES.

President Cluff of the B. Y. A. spoke to the congregation at the Church service last Sunday. He emphasized the necessity of education of a spiritual nature, and advised the Saints to instill in the minds of the children the principles of the Gospel.

FOURTH OF JULY CELEBRATION.

The program for the Fourth of July has been arranged, and the committees have done excellent work in the preparation of the same. Every effort has been, and will be, made to make the occasion a memorable one. An invitation has been extended to the other towns in the county to participate in the pleasures of the day.

Deseret Evening News
June 30, 1899

FILLMORE.

Hay Crop Light—Sunday School Conference.

Special Correspondence.

Fillmore City, Utah, June 29, 1899.—The contractors have commenced the construction of the county vault on the west side of the county court house. They expect to have it completed about the 15th of October.

Farmers are engaged hauling their hay; the yield this season is much lighter than usual but there will probably be enough for home consumption.

Two public school buildings, to-wit: the school house and state-house, are receiving a coat of paint this week.

Jas. A. Melville and Alma Greenwood left for Deep Creek last Monday on mining business.

Those who attended the Sunday school conference at Oak City last Sunday were very loud in their praises for the hospitality of the citizens of that place. All visitors were very cordially welcomed and entertained.

Salt Lake Herald
July 4, 1899

DR. J. F. NOYES of American Fork was born in Fillmore, Utah. He went through the public and high schools. In 1883 his mother moved to Provo that they might have better advantages for an education. Here he attended the Brigham Young academy until the spring of 1889, when he was called on a mission to Great Britain.

After his mission closed he spent some time in seeing the sights of various countries. During the school year of 1890-1 he was principal of Juab stake academy at Nephi. The following fall he went to the College of Physicians and Surgeons at Baltimore to study medicine and afterwards to the university at Louisville, Ky., from which he graduated in the spring of 1894.

He practiced medicine in the city of Louisville for about three months before his return home to Provo, where he practiced for some months. On Jan. 20, 1897, he located in American Fork, and has had a good practice ever since. Last fall he married an accomplished young lady, Miss Sydie Chipman.

Deseret Evening News
July 8, 1899

FILLMORE.

Fourth Celebration—Fire—Sunday School Jubilee—Wedding Announced.

Special Correspondence:

Fillmore City, Utah, July 6.—The Fourth of July celebration passed off very pleasantly. The parade in the morning was a grand success; every person did all within their power to make it surpass all previous efforts in that direction.

Yesterday Mrs. John Hansen was burning some rubbish in the back yard of her premises, and the fire accidentally spread to the shed and corral, a short distance away, and consumed the same. The alarm was given, and the many friends who came to her assistance, prevented the house from being destroyed in the conflagration.

Patriarch John Ashman and John Cooper, both of Fillmore, visited the Kanosh Sunday school on the 2nd inst., in the interests of the Sunday school jubilee, recently held at Oak City.

The county commissioners were in session last Monday. Very little business was transacted.

Cards are out announcing the wedding of Mr. George Melville to Miss Nellie Ashman, which will occur at the groom's residence on July 11th.

Deseret Evening News
July 12, 1899

FILLMORE.

School Election—Death of Isaac Mitchell —Beneficent Rains

Special Correspondence.

Fillmore City, Utah, July 11, 1899.—The citizens of Fillmore placed in nomination, and yesterday elected, Alma Greenwood school trustee to succeed Joslin Greenwood, whose term of office has expired.

DEATH OF ISAAC MITCHELL.

At 6 p. m. yesterday Isaac Mitchell departed this life. He was born in England and came to Utah with the early pioneers and has always been a faithful and devoted member of the Church of Jesus Christ of Latter-day Saints. His death was due to old age, being past eighty.

BENEFICENT RAINS.

The recent storms in the mountains have cooled the atmosphere considerably and given relief to the suffering animals ranging in the hot deserts.

At the Sunday services President Hinckley addressed the congregation on the subject of tithing and gave some practical illustration of the operation of that law. He referred to the instructions given at the priesthood meeting recently held at Salt Lake City.

Deseret Evening News
July 15, 1899

OLD "STATE HOUSE," FILLMORE.

The building shown in this picture is one of the historic edifices of Utah. It was erected by the government as a Territorial capital at Fillmore in the early fifties. A short time before that a board of commissioners, appointed by Governor Young under the authority of the Legislature, left Salt Lake City for Pauvan Valley—Millard county—to select a site for the proposed capital of the Territory. The Legislature, by resolution, had previously located the seat of government within that county, but the exact spot had not yet been determined. The commissioners were Orson Pratt, Albert Carrington, Jesse W. Fox, William C. Staines and Joseph L. Robinson. Governor Young, Hon. Heber C. Kimball, Hon. George A. Smith and others went also, to assist in the selection. They directed their course to Chalk Creek, in Pauvan valley, to which place Anson Call, of Davis county, and later one of the founders of Parowan, had been directed by President Young to lead a colony. Chalk Creek was about one hundred and fifty miles south of Salt Lake City. There on the 28th of October, a site was selected for the capital and the city laid out. That city, as previously ordered by the Legislature, was named Fillmore.

Millard county was chosen as the place for the capital owing to its central geographical location, but was afterwards abandoned for that purpose as the bulk of the population was contained in the northern counties.

On the 10th of December, 1855, the Utah Legislature in its fifth annual session convened at Fillmore, the new capital of the Territory, and organized by electing Heber C. Kimball president of the Council, and Jedediah M. Grant speaker of the House. This was the first and last session of the Legislature held at Fillmore. Though it afterwards convened there more than once, it immediately adjourned to Salt Lake City to hold its sessions.

Among the acts passed by the Assembly that winter was one authorizing an election of delegates to a Territorial convention, the purpose of which was to prepare a State Constitution and memorialize Congress for the admission of Utah into the Union. This convention assembled at Salt Lake City on March 17, 1856. Ten days later the Constitution and memorial were adopted, and Hon. George A. Smith and Hon. John Taylor—the latter then editing a paper in New York called The Mormon—were elected delegates to present the same to Congress.

During the same session of the Legislature, acts were passed creating the counties of Cache and Boxelder. Cache Valley was then unsettled, and mainly used for haying and pasturing cattle. Among those who had visited the valley for that purpose were Samuel Roskelley, Andrew Moffatt, Brigham Young Jr., Bryant Stringham, Stephen Taylor, Seymour B. Young, and Simon and Joseph Baker. Peter Maughan, the pioneer of Cache county—then living at Tooele—was just about to lead a colony northward and found Maughan's Fort, on the site of the present town of Wellsville. Boxelder county, which had belonged to Weber, was, as seen, partly settled, and had recently been strengthened by fifty additional families lead by Lorenzo Snow. Other counties, now defunct, or beyond the present boundaries of Utah, created by the Legislature during the winter of 1855-56, were those of Greasewood, Humboldt, St. Mary's, Shambip, Cedar and Malad.

It is only recently that the title of the capital building passed into the absolute possession of the municipal authorities of Fillmore. The structure was never completed and while it is very substantial and commodious, is but one wing of the building as designed, the main body and other wing being left for future construction. Since its abandonment for capital purposes it has been put to almost every use known to the people of Millard county. At times it has contained county and municipal offices, been used as a jail and a place of detention for insane persons. Schools, religious, political and business meetings, ward entertainments, dances, and various other kinds of amusements have taken place in its sturdy old walls. Today a newspaper is published in it. To what other uses it will be put only the future can tell.

Deseret Evening News
July 29, 1899

FILLMORE.

Honor for Returning Volunteers — Plead Guilty to and Fined for a Serious Offense.

Special Correspondence.

Fillmore City, Millard Co., July 28.— A committee has been appointed consisting of citizens from various parts of the county to arrange for the reception of Will F. Aldrich on his return from the Philippines. Mr. Aldrich was the only volunteer from Millard county; he has been in several engagements, including the capture of the city of Manila, and has distinguished himself for bravery and heroism.

James Thompson, of Oasis, plead guilty to the charge of fornication before Justice Bennett, of Deseret, last week. A fine of $60 was imposed.

Deseret Evening News
August 5, 1899

FILLMORE.

Rains Washing Fertility from Mountains— Notes and Personals.

Special Correspondence.

Fillmore, Millard Co., Aug. 4.—The recent storms in the mountains have caused considerable mud and debris to be deposited along the banks of our streams and farming land that has been recently irrigated. However, people are not complaining much, but feel grateful that they did not get such a flood as Manti had.

State Senator Joseph V. Robison, who is operating some mining claims at Deep Creek, came home on a visit, and to obtain supplies, a few days ago. He left again yesterday for his mineral deposits.

E. M. Crandall from the Tintic mining district, is spending a few days at the ex-capital of Utah.

County Attorney of Sevier County J. H. Erickson spent Monday here for the purpose of effecting a settlement with Millard county on the division of the taxes on transit sheep for the year 1898.

TORNADO NEAR FILLMORE.

People Scared By a Frightful Storm —Damage Done.

(Special to The Herald.)

Fillmore, Aug. 5.—One of the worst hailstorms that ever visited this country occurred this afternoon, and has done considerable damage to crops, as well as scaring the people half out of their wits.

A few minutes before 2 o'clock the sky west of here was dark and threatening, and a deep rumbling sound was heard, resembling the noise of a cyclone. It lasted fully eight minutes, and could be heard for miles. People here rushed for their children, then to cellars, and the cry of "cyclone" was heard on all sides.

But the storm did not strike us; it passed two miles to the northwest, taking a northeasterly direction towards Holden and Scipio. At what is known as the old field, three miles northwest of here, corn was stripped bare, and the wheat and lucern-crops badly damaged. A little further on fully six inches of hail, half as large as hens' eggs, fell.

Word comes from Holden that the storm passed through that town, doing great damage to crops. Word has been received from Scipio that the storm did not strike the place at all, but the roaring was heard miles away.

Later—News from the "old field" estimates that at least one-fourth the crops are destroyed. Birds by the hundreds were killed.

FILLMORE.

Disastrous Hail Storm — Returned Missionaries—County Court.

Special Correspondence.

Fillmore City, Millard Co., Aug. 9.— A hail storm passed through the fields just west of here a few days ago and destroyed much hay and corn. It came up with a thundering noise and sounds of heavy winds. The people were much frightened and many of them thought a cyclone had come and sought refuge in their cellars. The estimated loss to crops is about $2,000.

James A. Kelly and J. Harvey Melville returned home this morning from their missionary fields of labor in the Southern States. Elder Kelly has been laboring in Tennessee and Elder Melville in Alabama. They left home in May, 1897, to work for the advancement of truth. Many friends and relatives are glad to welcome them home again.

COUNTY COURT.

The county court was in session on the 7th and 8th inst., and transacted considerable business. An order was made directing the county treasurer to advertise for redemption all contingent warrants issued during the months of April, May and June.

FILLMORE.

The Love of Watermelons Leads to Jail—Quarterly Conference.

Special Correspondence.

Fillmore, Millard Co., Aug. 16.—Seven large boys of our town were brought before Justice Jukes on a charge of petit larceny today. The boys had a love for watermelons, and one of our townsmen had devoted considerable time and a little surplus energy in the production of a superior quality of the same; the temptation was stronger than the will power of the boys to resist. They pleaded guilty and were fined $2 each. Two of the culprits failed to produce the necessary amount of circulating medium and are now dining at the expense of the tax payers.

QUARTERLY CONFERENCE.

The quarterly conference of Millard Stake convenes here next Sunday and Monday. Much credit is due the acting Teachers of this ward for the efforts they are making to comfortably entertain the brethren and sisters of our neighboring towns, who may feel inspired to visit us and drink from the fountain of eternal knowledge, and be instructed by officers of this Church, who hold their position by divine authority.

A BABE ACCIDENTALLY SHOT

MEADOW BOY DIDN'T KNOW GUN WAS LOADED.

Pointed It Playfully at the Child and Pulled Trigger—Infant Is In Critical Condition.

(Special to The Herald.)

Fillmore City, Aug. 17.—At Meadow last evening the 3-year-old baby of Mrs. Shaw received a load of shot in his thigh and stomach and now lies at death's door.

The gun was fired by a 9-year-old brother who not knowing it was loaded, said he would snap a cap and pointing the gun toward the bed pulled the trigger. The little babe lying there received the full charge and his clothes were set afire. There is little hope for his recovery. The family is in destitute circumstances, the father was but recently released from the Utah penitentiary where he served a two years' sentence for adultery, but up to date he has failed to return to his family.

Millard Awaits Volunteers.

(Special to The Herald.)

Fillmore, Aug. 17.—Millard will do honor to her volunteers next Thursday. A county reception awaits them.

Salt Lake Herald
August 24, 1899

GILES RETURNS.

Millard's Missing Clerk Comes Back to Fillmore.

(Special to The Herald.)

Fillmore, Aug. 22.—J. S. Giles, ex-county clerk of Millard, who left here very suddenly last January, returned to Fillmore today. Since he left here Mr. Giles has been living in Bunkerville, Nev.

Salt Lake Herald
August 26, 1899

ALDRICH'S GREAT TIME.

Millard County Turns Out to Do Him Honor.

(Special to The Herald.)

Fillmore, Aug. 25.—A county reception was given at the ex-capital of the territory today to Millard's volunteer, W. F. Aldrich. In enthusiasm, good feeling and patriotism all former occasions were surpassed, and our volunteer will have cause to remember his welcome home as long as life lasts. People from every town in the county were here to show him honor. A parade fully one and a half miles long in the morning, an excellent programme this afternoon and the grand military ball tonight, where an elegant gold medal was presented to the volunteer, finish up the day's demonstrations.

Deseret Evening News
August 26, 1899

FILLMORE.

Embezzlement Charge Dismissed Against J. S. Giles—Will F. Aldrich Feted.

Special per Deseret Telegraph.

Fillmore, Utah, Aug. 26.—The grandest reception ever tendered any person in Millard county was given Will F. Aldrich, our returned volunteer from the Philippines, at Fillmore, yesterday. All business houses, hotels, and many residences were appropriately decorated. A parade was organized in the morning, which met Aldrich four miles west of the city and escorted him to town. An appropriate program of exercises was rendered in the afternoon, followed by a military ball in the evening. Every part of the exercises was a grand success.

Aldrich is still in our city and will remain here a few days visiting his many friends, who bid him thrice welcome to our midst again.

The charge of embezzlement against J. S. Giles, ex-county clerk of Millard county, was dismissed today on motion of the county attorney, because the complaint which had been filed against him was defective in substance. Another complaint may be sworn to and proceedings commence anew.

FILLMORE.

Further Details of the Life and Character of the late Mrs. Robison.

Special Correspondence.

Fillmore, Sept. 1.—Mrs. Bird Robison writes the "News" asking that a correction be made in the item previously published regarding the death of Mrs. Lucretia Robison. She says the deceased lady had not lost the use of her mental faculties, but was like many, if not all very aged people are, forgetful of the present, to some extent, her mind going back to childhood and youth, and dwelling on events of long ago. She adds:

Lucretia Hancock Robison was the daughter of Lucretia Proctor and Benjamin Hancock. She was born Aug. 24th, 1807, in Shrewsbury, Vermont. Moved from Vermont to New York in 1818. Was married to Joseph Robison Feb. 5th, 1829. Both joined the Church in 1844. Started to Nauvoo, but hearing of the death of Joseph Smith, they stopped at a small town, called Crete, in Illinois. They started to Utah in April, 1864, arriving here in July of the same year. Came direct to Fillmore; lived seven years in the old fort, forted up to defend themselves from attacks by the Indians. Her husband died June 3rd, 1868, leaving her a widow for thirty-one years.

"Grandma" Robison, as she was familiarly called, was a strong character, and inherited independence, firmness, determination and patience to as great an extent as John Hancock, (the signer of the Declaration of Independence), to whom she was closely related. She kept the Word of Wisdom from the time that she first heard of it; and would have helped throw the tea overboard as readily as did her ancestor. She was the mother of thirteen children, nine sons and four daughters. Seven have preceded her to the spirit world. She was also grandmother to seventy-one, great-grandmother to ninety, and great-great-grandmother to two. She was a gentle, loving mother, a true and generous friend, and charitable to a fault. She loved little children, and did not wish to live where she could not see them playing around. She was also devotional; and while modest and unassuming admired the talents and eloquence of others. In one of her last nights on earth she expressed the wish to attend meeting once more, saying it had been so long since she was able to go.

FILLMORE.

Wedding of Orson Holbrook and Miss Eva Kelly—Other Items.

Fillmore City, Millard Co., Sept. 7.—Mr. Orson Holbrook and Miss Eva Kelly, both of this city, were united in the holy bond of matrimony last evening by Bishop T. C. Callister. The bride's home was appropriately decorated for the occasion and hundreds of guests were in attendance. After the ceremony had been performed and congratulations offered, all indulged in a festive repast which must have been enjoyed immensely—judging from the quantity of viands consumed.

COUNTY COURT BUSINESS.

The county court was in session this week but had very little business to dispose of.

Work on our new tabernacle has again been resumed; much credit is due our Bishop for the energy he manifests in furthering the completion of the same.

Deseret Evening News
September 13, 1899

FILLMORE.

Robert Barrows Wandered off on Sunday Last and Not Seen Since.

Special per Deseret Telegraph.

Fillmore, Millard Co., Sept. 13.—Robert Barrows, an old gentleman of 65 or 70 years, left this city last Monday morning about 9 a. m. and has not been heard of since. The gentleman was living with his sister, Hannah Rowley, and appeared to be very comfortably situated and surrounded with all the necessaries of life. He took a few matches and said he was going to the cedars and did not care if he never returned. His course was then eastward into the foot-hills, where all traces of him have disappeared. He was, perhaps, laboring under some mental delusion. A searching party is being organized to search for him.

Deseret Evening News
September 20, 1899

FILLMORE.

Returned Missionary—Missing Man Found —Work on Tabernacle.

Fillmore, Millard Co., Sept. 19.—John Peterson, who recently returned from the Southern States, occupied the time at meeting last Sunday. He referred with pleasure to his experience in the South.

MISSING MAN FOUND

Mr. Barrows, who recently left Fillmore so unexpectedly for the hills, was found near Kanosh with some of his relatives.

The committee that has been supervising the construction of our new tabernacle are beginning to see the fruits of their labor materialize; it is expected that the foundation will be completed in about two weeks.

Quite a number of our young people were in attendance at the M. I. A. conference held at Kanosh on the 16th and 17th inst.

Deseret Evening News
September 26, 1899

FILLMORE.

Reception to Missionaries and Others— Light Crops but Prices Good.

Special Correspondence.

Fillmore City, Utah, Sept. 23.—Last Friday a public reception was tendered James Kelly, John Peterson, Harvey Millville, returned missionaries, and Frank Rogers, who has been confined in a hospital at Salt Lake for more than a year. The meeting house was appropriately decorated for the occasion and a varied program, consisting of speeches, recitations, vocal and instrumental solos, was rendered. The boys were much pleased and honored by such a grand demonstration and manifested their gratitude in many ways. At the conclusion of the exercises, luncheon was served by the young ladies.

FILLMORE SCHOOLS.

The lower grades in our public schools are again in operation: Miss Vern Robinson of Kanosh and Miss Herma Robinson of this city, are the instructors. The people feel to congratulate themselves in securing the services of such efficient teachers.

Elmer Hinkley and Christian Anderson occupied the time at meeting Sunday.

LIGHT CROPS BUT PRICES GOOD.

Our crops have been nearly all harvested this season and are considerably lighter than last year; however, we are expecting better prices for our product.

Salt Lake Herald
October 5, 1899

CHARGED WITH ASSAULT.

Richard Duncan of Meadow On Trial at Fillmore.

(Special to The Herald.)

Fillmore, Oct. 4.—Today Richard Duncan of Meadow was arrested for assault and battery on the person of Almon Robison, one of Fillmore's leading citizens. His trial has occupied the whole day and has just been given to the jury, which is still out. The evidence went to show that defendant went to Robison's house in a drunken condition and when ordered out brutally assaulted him.

WILL BE ARRESTED.

Fillmore Man Believed to Have Sold Indians Liquor.

(Special to The Herald.)

Fillmore, Oct. 4.—Lee Boder, a rock mason by trade and a recent resident of Salt Lake, will be arrested in the morning on the charge of selling Indians liquor. The officers claim a sure case against him, saying he was caught in the act. The officers are also gathering evidence against another party, who purchased liquor for Indians last Monday. Lately Indians have been seen drunk in this city quite often and everything to stop such traffic is being made by officers.

Salt Lake Herald
October 6, 1899

FINED TWO DOLLARS.

Priest For Assaulting a Man—Fillmore Indian Liquor Case.

(Special to The Herald.)

Fillmore, Utah, Oct. 5.—Richard Duncan, who was tried yesterday for assault and battery on the person of Almon Robison, was found guilty and fined $2 today.

Lee Baker was arrested today on the charge of giving Indians liquor. He waived his preliminary hearing and was held to the district court, his bonds being $100.

Deseret Evening News
October 6, 1899

FILLMORE.

A Tempest in a Teapot Settled by a Jury in Eight Hours.

Special per Deseret Telegraph.

Fillmore, Millard Co., Oct. 5th.—The case of the State of Utah vs Richard Duncan came on for trial yesterday at 1 o'clock p. m. The charge preferred was battery alleged to have been committed on the person of Almon Robison at his residence by Mr. Duncan, who refused to leave the house when requested. Mr. Robison then proceeded to eject him and Mr. Duncan offered resistance. The jury returned a verdict of guilty about 2 a. m. this morning after having been out about eight hours. Judgment was rendered imposed a fine of $2.

A complaint has been filed against Lee Baker charging him with disposing of liquor to Indians and a warrant has been issued for his arrest. The preliminary examination will probably be held today unless the same is waived.

Deseret Evening News
October 11, 1899

COURT AT FILLMORE.

List of Cases Disposed of by Judge Higgins.

Special per Deseret Telegraph.

Fillmore, Oct. 11.—Court adjourned here last evening. Judge E. V. Higgins presided. After setting the time for hearing the cases on the calendar, some preliminary matters were disposed of.

In the case of The Holden Irrigation company et al vs Nicols Paul et al, a motion to confirm the report of the commissioner previously appointed to make measurement of certain waters was granted.

In the matter of the estate of Anna Galloway, deceased, a decree was rendered approving the final accounting and granting final distribution.

In the matter of the application of school board for conveyance of a certain parcel of land for school grounds and on which to erect a school building, an order was made granting a conveyance of the same.

In the case of James A. George vs Almon Robison and Josephine Robison, demurrer to the complaint was overruled.

In the case of Wood vs Wood a decree was rendered annulling the marriage relation.

No jury was summoned as the other cases on the calendar were postponed for the term. Court adjourned at 4:30 p. m. until December.

Salt Lake Herald
October 19, 1899

FILLMORE'S FIGHT.

Citizens and Republicans Having a Hot Campaign.

(Special to The Herald.)

Fillmore City, Oct. 18.—The past four days have been of importance in political circles in this city, and the municipal campaign is now in full sway. The battle is between two tickets—the Citizens', which is composed of Democrats, Republicans and independents, and the other of straight Republicans. This coming election will be the hardest fought one ever witnessed here. Following are the tickets:

Citizens' ticket—
Mayor—E. W. Kelly.
Councilmen—Daniel Stevens, George Rose, J. G. Starley, James McMahon, John Curling.
City Marshal—John C. Kelly.
Recorder—Richard Russell.
Treasurer—Frank Rogers.
City Justice—Alma Greenwood.
Republican ticket—
Mayor—T. C. Callister.
Councilmen—Peter Beauregard, Clarence Merril, Edwin Bartholomew, Hans Peterson, J. M. Warner.
Recorder—John Kelly.
Treasurer—Frank Rogers.
Marshal—John W. Callister.
Justice of Peace—George C. Veiler.

Deseret Evening News
October 20, 1899

FILLMORE.

Joseph Neilson Held for Grand Larceny—
Declines the Nomination.

Special per Deseret Telegraph.

Fillmore, Millard County, Oct. 19.—
Joseph Nielson, of Leamington, who
was arrested recently on a charge of
grand larceny, was bound over to appear for trial in the district court. His
bonds were fixed at $200, which were
promptly furnished by his brothers.

DECLINES THE NOMINATION.

E. W. Kelly, who was nominated by
acclamation as a candidate for mayor
of Fillmore on the Citizen's ticket, has
declined the nomination.

Salt Lake Herald
November 3, 1899

ELOPEMENT AT FILLMORE.

Girl's Parents Obdurate and She Flies With Lover to Manti.

Fillmore, Nov. 2—It has just come to
light that there was an elopement from
this city last evening. The parties are
Miss Esther Anderson, daughter of County Clerk Anderson, and William Huntsman, nephew of Gabriel Huntsman, both
of this city. The young couple have been
keeping company for the past year,
against the wishes of the girl's parents.
Several months ago the young man went
to Manti to work, but he visited Fillmore
quite often, and when he came again on
Tuesday nothing was thought of his visit,
but it appears they had everything arranged, for he hadn't been in town but a short
time when he asked the consent of the
parents to marry the girl. They refused.
Yesterday he visited the father at the
court house, and again asked for the girl
and also for a marriage license and got a
refusal for both. Last night they skipped
out for Manti, giving it out to a few intimate friends that they would be married
there today.

Deseret Evening News
November 4, 1899

FILLMORE.

Very Quiet Campaign — Marriage of Miss Ester Anderson—Good Roads.

Special Correspondence.

Fillmore, Millard Co., Nov. 3.—All indications point to a peaceable and quiet city election; no political meetings of a public nature have been held yet, and it is not thought likely that either party will place any political speakers in the field. A majority of the voters express themselves as though they would vote for the candidate whom they believe will discharge the duties of the office incumbent upon them, in the most satisfactory and economical manner consistent with progressive city government.

Will Huntsman and Ester Anderson left for Manti last Tuesday, where they will be united in matrimony.

Heber J. Mitchell, our district road supervisor, deserves considerable credit for the great improvement that is being made on our public highways; never before were they in as good a condition as at the present time. No doubt this is due to the fact that the men who work poll taxes are compelled to perform eight hours of honest labor.

Washington County News
November 5, 1899

STATE EDUCATION BOARD.

Diplomas and Certificates Granted at Yesterday's Meeting.

A meeting of the state board of education was held yesterday in the office of State Superintendent Park, there being present President J. T. Kingsbury, President Tanner, Superintendent A. C. Nelson and Dr. Park, Principal Bennion being absent.

Bills were presented and allowed covering expenses incident to the state examination of teachers in August, after which business of a routine character was transacted.

Diplomas and certificates were granted as follows:

A high school diploma to Mrs. Mattie J. Prosser of Salt Lake; a grammar grade diploma to C. E. Marks, Mill Creek, and to E. M. Mumford, Palouse, Washington.

State certificates were issued to Albert N. Hanson, Fillmore; G. N. Child, Lehi; Mathilda Monteith, Tooele; Hannah Allen, Salt Lake, and Mrs. Rena E. Stone, Ogden.

Deseret Evening News
November 8, 1899

FILLMORE.

Eugene W. Kelly, the Citizen Nominee for Mayor, Wins It.

Special per Deseret Telegraph.

Fillmore, Millard Co., Nov. 8.—The Citizens' ticket triumphed. At the city election held yesterday the Republican party went to defeat, only electing one councilman. All was peaceable and quiet during the day, the weather was fine and a large number of votes were cast. Eugene W. Kelly, the candidate for mayor on the Citizens' ticket, defeated Thomas C. Callister, the Republican candidate, by a small majority.

Mostly Republican.

Special per Deseret Telegraph.

Smithfield, Nov. 8.—The Republicans will occupy the heaviest side of the next city administration, they having elected the mayor, recorder, treasurer and three councilmen. The Democrats getting the marshal, justice and two councilmen.

Hyrum Democratic.

Special per Deseret Telegraph.

Hyrum, Nov. 8.—The Democratic ticket went in with a clean sweep. The majorities ranging from 21 to 65.

Salt Lake Herald
November 9, 1899

FILLMORE'S OFFICERS.

Citizens' Ticket Wins Against the Republicans.

(Special to The Herald.)

Fillmore, Nov. 8.—Our city election was the most exciting one held here for years. There were two tickets in the field—Citizens' and straight Republican. Each side worked hard for victory, but the Citizens' ticket won out with the exception of one councilman. The names of those elected were:

Mayor—Eugene W. Kelly.
Recorder—Richard Russel.
Treasurer—Frank Rogers.
Marshal—John C. Kelly.
Justice of the Peace—Alma Greenwood.
Councilmen—Daniel Stevens, John Carling, George Reese, John J. Starley and Clarence Merrill (Rep.).

The Citizens declared that politics should be eliminated from our city election and won on that stand.

Deseret Evening News
November 18, 1899

FILLMORE.

Conference at Scipio — Ames - Littlewood Nuptials - Enterprise at Snake Valley.

Special Correspondence.

Fillmore City, Millard Co., Nov. 17.—A marriage license was issued on the 10th inst. to Samuel Ames, 27, and Dorah Littlewood, 28, both of Meadow, Utah.

CONFERENCE AT SCIPIO.

Quite a number of our citizens are making preparations to attend conference at Scipio on the 19th and 20th of this month. A special effort is being made to secure a large attendance of the members of the Seventies' quorums.

Patriarch John Ashman was slightly injured in the spine recently, while working around his wood pile, but is now convalescent.

SNAKE VALLEY ENTERPRISE.

J. F. Holbrook, who has had charge of the work on the Holbrook land and irrigation enterprise, at Snake valley, has been visiting with his relatives and friends the last week. He reports business in that section of the country in a very pleasing condition.

Washington County News
November 25, 1899

The home of Mrs. Joseph H. Hanson of Fillmore, together with everything in it, were destroyed by fire, which in some manner was started by her four-year-old girl while Mrs. Hanson was absent. A fund was immediately raised to build the woman a new home.

Deseret Evening News
November 27, 1899

forenoon. The court adjourned in the afternoon in honor of the funeral of Vice President Hobart.

Jacob F. Gates, of Provo and Joseph E. Wilkins, of Spanish Fork were appointed jury commissioners for 1900.

Estate of R. S. Hines, deceased; sale of drug store stock confirmed.

Estate of Sarah C. Lambson, deceased; final account approved and distribution ordered.

Estate of John V. Smith, deceased; Mrs. Julia E. Smith appointed administratrix with bonds at $2,500.

Estate of Esther E. Davis, deceased; petition for probate of will and letters testamentary came on to be heard. Will admitted and Marinus Larson and Peter Nielson appointed executors with bonds at $1,000 each.

Estate of James Hunter, deceased; final account approved and distribution ordered.

PROVO.

Probate Matters — Utah County Business —
Damage Suit Compromised.

Special Correspondence.

Provo City, Nov. 25.—Judge Booth transacted the following business in the Fourth district court Saturday

COUNTY BUSINESS.

The board of county commissioners held a special session Saturday.

The Enquirer Company was awarded the contract for publishing the delinquent tax list.

James E. Hall, mayor of Springville, appeared before the board and claimed that Springville city had been assessed and had paid taxes for the years 1896-7-8 amounting to $162.18, the same being illegal and erroneous, and asked that the same be refunded. Referred to the county attorney.

E. C. Lackner, attorney for the Telluride Power Company, called attention of the board to the bad condition of the county road in Provo canyon near the Ferguson place. Taken under advisement for investigation.

Berg & Alexander were allowed $2,000 and Homer & Watkins $500 on county infirmary contracts.

The Rio Grande Western Railway Company asked to be allowed to build an overhead wooden bridge at the mouth of Spanish Fork canyon over the large cut just completed. The petition was granted on condition that the company maintain and keep the bridge in repair, and that it be not less than 14 feet wide with railing on the sides high enough to prevent cattle or sheep from jumping off.

FILLMORE.

Experimental Dry Farming — Success will Mean Much for Millard County.

Special Correspondence.

Fillmore City, Millard Co., Nov. 24.— Considerable dry wheat is being planted this autumn by many of our citizens who expect, by proper cultivation, to reap a harvest that will remunerate them for their labor and expense. The soil, generally, is rich and fertile and should dry farming prove a success, this county is destined to become rich and populous, because the natural resources exist here and only need development to exhibit their immensity.

The treasurer of Millard county, Rufus Day, has been busy the last week preparing the delinquent list of tax payers, while there are quite a number of delinquencies, the list will probably not exceed those of other years.

An entertainment to raise funds for the Sunday school is in a progressive condition, the exercises will probably be rendered in the early part of December.

LAND ENTRIES.

FINAL HOMESTEAD.

Nov. 25.—James Gurr, Vernal; 80 acres, section 2, township 50, range 21 east.

Daniel M. Rees, Brigham City; 160 acres, section 14, township 8 north, range 1 west.

Niels C. Sorenson, Koosarem; 80 acres, section 11, township 27 south, range 1 west.

Nov. 27.—Walter James, Black Rock; 160 acres, section 15, township 24 south, range 10 west.

John J. Steed, Point Lookout; 160 acres, section 8, township 11 north, range 3 west.

Nov. 28.—Kimball Sorenson, Fillmore; 161.60 acres, section 5, township 21 south, range 5 west.

William O. Smith, Smithfield; 160 acres, section 25, township 13 north, range 4 east.

MINERAL ENTRY.

Nov. 22.—John T. Hobson, Salt Lake City; Cape Cod mine, West Mountain mining district, section 27, township 3 south, range 3 west.

FILLMORE.

County Surplus — Grand Larceny — New School Building to be Dedicated.

Special Correspondence.

Fillmore City, Millard Co., Dec. 7.— The county court was in session three days this week and disposed of the business on the table with their usual alacrity and scrutiny; there will likely be a surplus of money on hand after the county obligations have been met, which the commissioners contemplate expending in making public improvements on and around the court house.

ACCUSED OF GRAND LARCENY.

District Attorney S. Marioneaux today filed with the clerk of the district court, an information charging Joseph Nelson with grand larceny.

FINE NEW SCHOOL BUILDING.

Preparations are being made for the dedication of our new school house, which will occur the 22nd of this month. There will be an appropriate program of exercises under the auspices of the school, and impromptu remarks from some of our leading citizens. The building is one that would adorn the school grounds of any city in our State; it is constructed according to modern plans of school building, and is furnished with the latest improved school apparatus.

FILLMORE.

Wintry Weather—Happy Marriages—Sunday School Jubilee.

Special Correspondence.

Fillmore, Millard Co., Dec. 15.—Considerable snow has fallen the last few days and the ground is frozen hard.

HAPPY MARRIAGES.

Walter Maycock, 29, and Lizzie Day, 26, were united in the holy bonds of matrimony on the 13th inst. at the home of Mr. and Mrs. John Day, the bride's parents. They were both born and raised in Fillmore and expect to make this city their future home.

Willie Trimble and Katie Beeslar, two popular young people of this city, will be married in the Manti Temple today.

The local Sunday school jubilee, held here last Sunday, was a grand success.

Conjoint mutual will be held at the meeting house next Sunday. An excellent program, both entertaining and instructive has been arranged.

FILLMORE.

Sunday School Concert—Interest in Mutual Organizations Increasing.

Fillmore City, Millard County, Dec. 25.—The Sunday school concert last Monday night was the greatest social event of the season. The program was furnished exclusively by the organization. The little boys and girls did honor to the school, and distinguished themselves as entertainers by the excellent rendition of the exercises assigned them.

MUTUAL ATTRACTIONS.

Our Mutual Improvement associations are in a thriving condition, as was manifest by the large attendance at the conjoint session last Sunday evening. The officers are much gratified by the increased attendance and interest.

Students who have been absent attending school, are returning home for vacation.

FILLMORE.

Holiday Festivities—Weddings—Great Increase in Business.

Special Correspondence.

Fillmore, Millard County, Jan. 1.—The holidays have been spent very pleasantly by a majority of our citizens; the time has been utilized in such a manner as to be both instructive and pleasurable.

WEDDINGS.

George Rowley and Emma Chesley, and Mr. Dunn and Mary Sorenson were joined in wedlock today. Receptions were held at the residences of the brides' parents respectively.

Business the past month has been rushing with our local merchants; they report a much larger trade this year than for many years preceding.

FILLMORE.

Delightful Weather — Students Returning to their Alma Maters.

Special Correspondence.

Fillmore, Millard Co., Jan. 5.—Prof. Roylance of the State University, arrived in our city the 3rd inst. He came as a representative of State Superintendent of Public Instructions John R. Park.

The weather is just delightful, like that usually prevailing in April. The snow has all disappeared, and the ground is drying rapidly.

Students who have been home spending the holiday vacation, will return to their respective schools tomorrow, and resume their mental labor during the coming winter. Fillmore has made a reputation for the number and quality of students who have attended various institutions of learning, of the higher type, both in our own and other States, and this year is no exception. Many of the students are destined by pluck and courage to become leaders in society, wherever they may go.

LAND ENTRIES.

FINAL HOMESTEAD.

Jan. 5—George Kinsey, Park City, 40 acres, section 25, township 20 south, range 1 east.

Josias Jensen Jr., Axtel, 40 acres, section 17, township 20 south, range 1 east.

Andrew A. Kruse, Moroni, 155.72 acres, sections 12 and 7, township 15 south, range 2 east.

ORIGINAL HOMESTEAD.

Jan. 10—Niels Christensen, Mayfield, 80 acres, section 28, township 19 south, range 2 east.

James W. Brunson, Fillmore, 160 acres, section 8, township 21 south, range 4 west.

Ella Walker, Kamas, 160 acres, sections 33 and 34, township 2 south, range 5 east.

Charles R. Cooper, Torrey, 157.76 acres, section 8, township 3 south, range 4 east.

Jan. 11.—George Day, Fillmore, 160 acres, sections 10 and 11, township 21 south, range 4 west.

Jan. 12.—Carl Christensen, Molen, 120 acres, section 17, township 20 south, range 4 east.

Deseret Evening News
January 16, 1900

JUDGE TIMMONY'S COURT.

A. M. Fillmore, alias "Bob" Fortune, was in the act of making some excuse for being drunk yesterday, but he was cut short by the court saying, "$5."

* * *

Ed. Price forfeited $10 for fighting, while Joe Kimberley, the other principal, was discharged because there were no witnesses to appear against him.

* * *

Spectators in the court room were totally absent today, the smallpox scare proved too much for them.

WANTS NEW SCHEDULE.

Western Trying for Better Train Service for Itself and Connections.

On Thursday in this city there will be held a meeting of passenger officials representing some of the transcontinental railways. The systems which will have representation at the meeting will be the Southern Pacific, Burlington, Rio Grande Western, Rock Island, Colorado Midland and Denver & Rio Grande. Third Vice President J. C. Stubbs, Fourth Vice President J. Kruttschnitt, Manager J. A. Fillmore, General Passenger Agent T. H. Goodman of the Southern Pacific, left San Francisco yesterday evening, and they will be met here by Passenger Traffic Manager E. O. McCormick, from the East. Officials of the other lines mentioned will also be here to meet with General Superintendent Welby, Traffic Manager Babcock and General Passenger Agent Heintz of the Western. General Passenger Agent Bailey of the Colorado Midland has already arrived.

The meeting will consider the feasibility of a modification of the schedule now controlling train service affected by the overland limited. When the Southern Pacific made its change to accommodate the overland the Rio Grande Western and its eastern connections were considerably discommoded and were compelled to adopt very uncomfortable schedules. An effort to arrange a better through car service for the Western and connections via Salt Lake and Grand Junction will be made at this meeting.

Deseret Evening News
January 17, 1900

FILLMORE.

Mrs. G. R. Huntsman Seriously Ill—Streets Almost Impassable.

Special Correspondence.

Fillmore, Millard Co., Jan. 16.—Mrs. G. R. Huntsman has contracted a case of pneumonia, due, no doubt, to the damp, rainy weather that has prevailed here during the last week. Her many friends are keeping anxious watch by her bedside and rendering all assistance possible to alleviate her suffering.

The speakers at the Sunday service were Orange Warner, John Peterson, James A. Kelly and Harvey Melville. Elder Warner is a resident of Benjamin, Utah county, and is spending a few weeks here visiting his relatives and many friends.

The mud on our streets and sidewalks makes traveling very laborious, both for pedestrians and teams; it is expected that our new city council will adopt some vigorous and aggressive measure to improve the same. A small tax, payable in labor, and judiciously expended, would enhance the beauty of our city, the value of our property, render traveling easier and burden no one

Deseret Evening News
January 19, 1900

FILLMORE.

J. S. Giles Arrested on a Charge of Forgery on Grand Jury Indictment.

Special per Deseret Telegraph.

Fillmore, Millard Co., Utah, Jan. 19.— Mr. J. S. Giles returned from Bunkerville this week, and late yesterday afternoon was arrested by Deputy U. S. Marshal Smith on the charge of forgery, the Federal grand jury having found an indictment against him the 6th of this month. The arrest is the outcome of charges made against Mr. Giles, one year ago this month, by Geo. Bishop of Smithville. Mr. Giles gave a bond in the sum of one thousand dollars for his appearance before the Federal court, whenever his case is called up. The bond was furnished by several leading citizens of Fillmore.

Salt Lake Herald
January 21, 1900

GILES IS ARRESTED

Former County Clerk is Charged With Forgery.

LAND OFFICE RECEIPT

AMOUNT INVOLVED AMOUNTS TO BUT $40.

Deputy United States Marshal Smyth Returned Yesterday From Fillmore, Where He Had Gone to Secure the Warrant — Defendant Promptly Furnished $1,000 Bail.

When the United States grand jury completed its work on the 6th of this month five indictments were returned. The nature of but four of them was disclosed at that time, as the fifth person was still at large. Yesterday, however, Deputy Marshal Smyth returned from Fillmore with a warrant of arrest, which he had served upon Joseph S. Giles, who was at one time United States commissioner and clerk of Millard county, and who was the man wanted.

The crime which Giles is alleged to have committed is the forgery of a land office receipt for $40 a year ago this month. He was United States commissioner at that time and was accustomed to receive money for land entries and to forward them to the land office in this city. The complaint against him was sworn to by George Bishop of Snake valley, who claims that he gave Giles $40 to send to the land office. In due course of time Giles gave Bishop a receipt for his money with the name of the land office receiver appended. It turned out that the signature was a forgery, and a correspondence with the land office developed the fact that the money had not been received there.

Disappearance of Giles.

Bishop immediately confronted Giles with the evidence which he had collected against the commissioner. They discussed the matter and decided to wait a day or two and see if they couldn't affect a compromise. That night Giles mysteriously disappeared from Fillmore. His most intimate acquaintances had no knowledge of his whereabouts. His standing in the community was so high and his reputation for integrity was such that his fellow citizens couldn't believe that he had committed any wrong.

For some time Fillmore was in suspense as to the whereabouts of Giles. There were many who claimed that he had been murdered, and the idea gained currency. In no other way could the people account for his disappearance. Finally one of his friends heard that he had gone south, but where no one knew.

Last September Giles returned to Fillmore, and the news of his return reached the complainant, Bishop. A warrant for his arrest was made out before Judge Twomey and Deputy Marshal Smyth made a journey to Fillmore to serve it. But Giles had gone south again, and the report was that he was in Bunkerville, a little town in the southern portion of Nevada. The officers decided that his arrest and requisition would have entailed more expense than the crime would justify, so no further action was taken at that time.

Comes Back Again.

When Deputy Marshal Hardy went to Kanosh in December to serve subpoenas, he overheard a remark of a stage driver to the effect that Giles was coming back to Fillmore. The grand jury then met and Bishop appeared before it with his evidence, and the indictment against Giles was issued. Day before yesterday Smyth went to Fillmore and served the warrant, just two days after Giles had returned. The neighbors of the accused still have unbroken faith in him, and a number of them came forward to sign a bond of $1,000 for his appearance. Giles is 57 years old and is one of most popular men in Millard county. His neighbors say that his life has been exemplary, and he himself admits that the forging of the receipt was a misstep that he cannot account for. He says that he does not know why he did it, and that the remorse and shame he has suffered has been almost too much for him.

The case will not come up for the consideration of the court before the May term.

Deseret Evening News
January 22, 1900

J. S. GILES ARRESTED.

Prominent Fillmore Man Brought Here and Gives Bonds.

Mr. J. S. Giles returned from Bunkerville, Nev., this week, and late yesterday afternoon was arrested by Deputy United States Marshal Smith on the charge of forgery, the federal grand jury having found an indictment against him the 6th of this month.

The arrest is the outcome of the charges made against Mr. Giles, one year ago this month, by Geo. Bishop, of Smithville.

Mr. Giles gave a bond in the sum of $1,000 for his appearance before the Federal court, whenever his case is called up.

The bond was furnished by several leading citizens of Fillmore.—Fillmore Progress.

It will be remembered that some time ago Bishop sent some money by Giles to be paid into the land office here. Giles gave Bishop a receipt for the money, which as a matter of fact, seems never to have been paid, and Receiver Smith says the receipt is fraudulent.

Deputy Marshal L. A. Smith brought Giles from Fillmore to Salt Lake Saturday and the man was released on giving bonds in the sum of $1,000.

Salt Lake Herald
January 30, 1900

(Special to The Herald.)

Fillmore, Jan. 29.—No news of E. W. Penney and son has been received, but all kinds of speculation is indulged in by the people of Kanosh. The majority believe they have met with foul play. They base this supposition on the fact that the younger Penney had trouble with a Mexican at Wah Wah Springs some time ago, giving the Mexican a terrible beating. Sheriff Kelly, upon the advice of the county attorney, started for the Wah Wah range last night and will make a thorough investigation.

Deseret Evening News
January 30, 1900

FILLMORE.

Searching for Missing Men—An Attractive Mutual.

Special Correspondence.

Fillmore, Millard Co., Jan. 29.—Sheriff Kelley has gone to Wah Wah Springs, just west of Frisco, in Beaver county, Utah, to ascertain, if possible, some information concerning E. W. Penney and son of Kanosh, whose mysterious disappearance has caused considerable anxiety.

LOCAL IMPROVEMENTS.

Some much-needed improvements are being made on our sidewalks surrounding the public square. Now the citizens have a practical example of the benefits of improvements, it is to be expected that no more time will be spent on the sunny side of our public buildings by the progressive people of this city.

AN ATTRACTIVE ASSOCIATION.

The M. I. associations of this ward are in a flourishing condition. Every effort possible is being exercised by those presiding in authority to make them a success, and at present the inducements to attend the same are stronger than any outside temptation to remain away.

Deseret Evening News
February 2, 1900

HOTEL AND PERSONAL.

Speaking of cheese, Mr. G. R. Huntsman of Fillmore is here and reports great success in that Millard county industry.

Salt Lake Herald
February 8, 1900

COURT AT FILLMORE.

Several Criminal and Civil Cases Receive Attention.

(Special Correspondence.)

Fillmore, Feb. 7.—Judge Higgins opened court here yesterday and disposed of a large batch of probate and other matters. In the case of the state against Leo Baker, charged with selling liquor to an Indian, the defendant being called for arraignment but not appearing, upon motion of District Attorney Marioneaux, his bond was declared forfeited and a bench warrant ordered issued for defendant. The defendant voluntarily appeared later in the day and the court set aside the forfeiture of the bond upon the defendant paying the cost of the attachment. Whereupon the defendant was arraigned and entered a plea of not guilty and upon application of defendant the case was continued until the next term of court.

William A. Ray vs. N. J. Beauregard; set for trial on the 8th instant.

James A. George vs. Almon Robison et al.; default set aside and defendant allowed to answer.

Almon Robison vs. Peter Greenhalgh et al.; demurrer overruled and defendant given until Feb. 20 to answer.

Jane E. Ketcham et al. vs. W. H. Jones et al.; demurrer argued and submitted.

Rufus Pack vs. Samuel Pargman et al.; judgment by default quieting the title to certain real estate.

In the case of the state vs. Joseph Nielsen, District Attorney Marioneaux stated to the court that upon investigation of the case made by himself and County Attorney Melville, he was convinced that the facts would not warrant a conviction and asked the court to dismiss the case, which was done.

M. W. McDonald vs. Myrtle M. McDonald; set for trial for the 9th instant.

Catherine Haycock vs. Samuel Haycock; the plaintiff was granted a decree of divorce and given the custody of the child upon the ground of desertion and failure to support. Later on it appearing to the court that the time for defendant to answer had not expired the default and decree were set aside and the case continued for the term.

Laura E. Lowery vs. LeRoy Lowery; decree of divorce granted upon the default of defendant on the grounds of desertion, which decree was afterwards set aside and the case continued until Feb. 9 for the reason that the default was improperly entered.

The Scipio Relief society upon petition, was granted a piece of the public square for charitable purposes. Among the attorneys attending court are D. D. Houtz, Thomas Marioneaux, N. F. Knox, C. W. Collins, S. A. King and Josiah Greenwood.

Deseret Evening News
February 14, 1900

SHERIFF KELLEY'S FIND.

Discovered the Spot Where It is Believed E. W. Penney and Son Were Murdered.

No Trace Has Yet Been Found of the Bodies—Suspicion Points to Evidence of Foul Play.

Special per Deseret Telegraph:

Fillmore, Utah, Feb. 14.—County Attorney Melville of Millard county, received a communication from Sheriff Kelley, who is at Wah Wah Springs, near Frisco, searching for the missing E. W. Penney and son, to the effect that he, Kelley, has found the identical spot where he believes the two men were murdered, but does not describe the place, the evidence being blood stains. There is no trace of the bodies, and the sheriff hardly expects to find them, but is exerting every effort to apprehend the guilty parties.

Deseret Evening News
February 15, 1900

HOLDEN.

Death Summons Mrs. Sarah B. Cherrington to a Well Merited Rest.

Special Correspondence.

Holden, Millard Co., Feb. 12.—Sarah Cherrington, the estimable wife of John Cherrington, died after a life of faithful service on the 9th inst., after a lingering illness of several months. The maiden name of the deceased was Sarah Belcher. She was born in Staffordshire, England, Sept. 10th, 1823, and was in her seventy-fifth year when the summons came. The deceased was united in marriage with John Cherrington in England, May 11th, 1845. Fourteen children have blessed the union, only four of whom survive her. She and her husband embraced the Gospel in 1850, and in 1855, with their five children came to America and settled in the State of Delaware. After a residence of five years in Delaware they emigrated in 1860 to Utah, and for eleven years resided in the eighth ward in Salt Lake City. They removed from that city to Lehi, where they lived four years. Twenty-four years ago they settled in this village.

The funeral of deceased was held in the meeting house on Sunday at 1 o'clock. Appropriate remarks were made by Elders Joshua Greenwood and Alonzo Roblson of Fillmore, after which the remains were followed by a large concourse of friends and relatives to the cemetery and tenderly laid to rest.

LAND ENTRIES.

Original Homestead, Feb. 15.—David Duncan, Meadow, 160 acres, section 24, township 22 south, range 5 west.

Feb. 17.—Jesse H. Giles, Fillmore, 160 acres, sections 4, 5 and 9, township 21 south, range 4 west.

FINAL HOMESTEAD.

Feb. 15.—William H. Statt, Jr., Meadow, 160 acres, sections 27 and 34, township 22 south, range 5 west.

Feb. 19.—Charles H. Pickett, Gunnison, 81.59 acres, sections 14 and 15, township 19 south, range 1 west.

John E. Pace, Richardson, 157.61 acres, section 6, township 25 south, range 23 east.

ORIGINAL DESERT.

Feb. 16.—Edwin S. Crawford, Woodruff, 80 acres, section 15, township 10 north, range 7 east.

Feb. 12.—Jens Nielsen, Huntington, 40 acres, section 12, township 17 south, range 8 east.

WESTERN UNION GETS DESERET TELEGRAPH

The Old Utah System, So Potent in the Civilization of the West, Loses Its Identity.

Absorption Decided Upon After Negotations Extending Over a Very Short Period of Time—Construction of the Old System was Commenced in 1865—First Message Sent to Ogden by President Brigham Young of the Company on December 1st, 1866 — Incorporated January 18, 1867 — List of Names of Officers—Names of Operators at the Stations First Established in Utah—Col. Dickey Left Omaha Today to Complete the Arrangements for the Transfer.

One of Utah's greatest and most potent agencies in the promotion of civilization in this part of the country is about to lose its identity and to be absorbed as an integral part of one of the biggest systems in the world. The foundation for this statement is the fact that the Deseret Telegraph company's system of telegraph lines has been sold to the Western Union Telegraph company. For a short time negotiations for the transfer have been in progress, and today a dispatch from Chicago to the "News" makes the announcement that the deal has been consummated, as follows:

"Col. R. C. Clowry, vice president and general superintendent of the Western Union Telegraph company, today completed the purchase of all the lines of the Deseret Telegraph company which have heretofore belonged to and been operated by the Mormon Church. These lines extend throughout Utah and to all the Mormon settlements in the States of Idaho and Nevada, and their construction by Brigham Young was in advance of the building of railroads and for many years they were the principal means of immediate communication for the Mormon Church and its business connections.

"Col. J. J. Dickey, superintendent of the Third district of the Western Union Telegraph company, with headquarters at Omaha, goes to Salt Lake this afternoon to complete the transfer of the property."

Begotten of necessity and reared in hardship and bloodshed—for the Black Hawk war raged around some of its pitiless poles and wireless poles during the early days of its construction—the old Deseret Telegraph came to be a great factor in the development of the western country and was the means of facilitating the advance of civilization into the wilds and deserts occupied by Indians and wild beasts and fowl.

The construction of the lines of the Deseret Telegraph company was commenced in 1865, under a plan which had been previously formed by President Brigham Young, and on Dec. 1, 1866, the line between Salt Lake and Ogden was opened. The first message was sent at 2 o'clock on the afternoon of that day by President Young to President Lorin Farr and Bishop Chauncey W. West, of Ogden, and the people generally, and was in the nature of a dedication of the system and congratulation of the people upon its completion. On Dec. 5th of the same year communication with Logan was opened and on the 15th Manti was connected up. By January 1867, 500 miles of wire had been strung, and the cost was $150 per mile. At this time the circuit connected Logan in the north with "Dixie" in the south, St. George having the southernmost station.

While the building of the lines was in progress a number of young men were sent from the different towns, which were to be included in the circuit, to Salt Lake City, to be schooled in the operation of the wires. They were sent here at the suggestion of President Young and were taught by Mr. John C. Clowry, who came to Utah in the spring of 1861, soon after the advent here of the Overland telegraph line, of which he was one of the original local operators.

Following is a list of names of the first operators on the Deseret Telegraph company's system:

Joseph Goddard Logan.
Peter F. Madsen, Bingham.
David E. Davis, Ogden.
Morris Wilkinson Salt Lake.
Joseph A. West, Provo.
John D. Stark, Payson.
William C. A. Bryan, Nephi.
Zenos Pratt, Scipio.
Richard S. Horne Fillmore.
Clarence Merrill, Cove Creek.
S. A. Kenner, Beaver.
George A. Pearl, Kanarra.
George H. Tribe, Toquerville.
A. R. Whitehead, Washington.
Robert C. Lund, St. George.
Knud Torgerson, Moroni.
Anthon H. Lund, Mt. Pleasant.
John H. Hougaard, Manti.

On the 9th of January, 1867, the Deseret Telegraph company was incorporated by the following named persons: Brigham Young, Edward Hunter, A. Milton Musser, Edwin D. Woolley, Alonzo H. Raleigh, John Sharp, William Miller, John W. Ross, Andrew J. Moffitt and Robert Gardner. On March 21, 1867, the company was organized with the following officers:

Brigham Young, president.
Daniel H. Wells, vice-president.
William Clayton, secretary.
Geo. Q. Cannon, treasurer.
A. Milton Musser, superintendent and general manager.

These gentlemen were members of the directorate, in company with the following Edward Hunter, Geo. A. Smith, A. O. Smoot, A. H. Raleigh, John Sharp, Joseph A. Young, Erastus Snow and Ezra T. Benson.

Subsequently lines were built from St. George to Pioche, Nevada; from Toquerville to Kanab; from Moroni to Gunnison and to other Sanpete settlements; up the Sevier to Monroe; from Payson to Tintic; from Beaver to the Star mining district; from Salt Lake to Alta and Bingham; from Brigham to Corinne; from Logan to Franklin and thence to Paris, Idaho.

When seen by a representative of this paper today Mr. W. D. Dougall said: "I am surprised at this announcement coming from Chicago. So far as I know, all that can be said truthfully is that negotiations have been pending between the Deseret Telegraph company and the Western Union Telegraph company for some time past, but they have not yet been consummated. We do expect Col. Dickey here this week, and anticipated that in the event the sale was consummated it would be closed up about the first of next month."

Deseret Evening News
February 22, 1900

MILLARD'S DELEGATES.

Republicans at Fillmore Choose Men for State Convention.

[SPECIAL TO THE "NEWS."]

Fillmore, Utah, Feb. 21.—The Republican county convention convened in this city at 10 a. m. After some preliminary matters were attended to the convention adjourned until 2 o'clock p. m., when the following named persons were elected delegates to the State convention. C. W. Watts, W. F. Aldrach, F. T. Slaughter, H. S. Cahoon, E. W. Kelly, Henry Hughes, Andrew Peterson, F. E. Brown, Virgil Kelly, Joseph Averson, T. C. Callister and C. D. Smith. Alternates, George A. Black, J. S. Black, Dr. Stepens, C. W. Aldrach. The delegates are uninstructed.

Deseret Evening News
February 23, 1900

LAND ENTRIES.

Feb. 17.—Jesse H. Giles, Fillmore; 160 acres, sections 4, 5 and 9, township 21 south, range 4 west.

FINAL HOMESTEAD.

Feb. 19.—Charles H. Pickett, Gunnison; 159.61 acres, sections 14 and 15, township 19 south, range 1 west.

John E. Pace, Richardson; 157.61 acres, section 6, township 25 south, range 23 east.

Deseret Evening News
March 6, 1900

FOR PEACE DISTURBANCE.

Peter Huntsman Found Guilty, but Promptly Appeals.

Special per Deseret Telegraph.

Fillmore, Utah, March 6.—Yesterday Peter Huntsman of this place was arrested on the charge of disturbing the peace and arraigned, and tried before Justice Jukes. He was found guilty and fined $20, but perfected an appeal to the district court. The evidence of the prosecution was to the effect that an attempt was made by defendant to enter the residence of Jacob Davis about 11 o'clock p. m.

Deseret Evening News
March 10, 1900

FILLMORE.

Farewell Social—Sunday School Superintendency—Politics.

Special Correspondence.

Fillmore, Millard County, March 9.—County commissioners were in session last Monday and Tuesday. Commissioner Pack was absent owing to sickness of his wife who has been ill for several weeks. He tendered his resignation but no action was taken on the same.

FAREWELL SOCIAL.

Our Mutual missionary, John Hinckley, was tendered a farewell party last Wednesday evening. An appropriate program was rendered at intervals between the dances, and supper was served at private residences.

SUNDAY SCHOOL SUPERINTENDENCY.

John Cooper, who has been superintendent of our Sunday school for several years, has resigned. Daniel Stevens was chosen as his successor. Brother Cooper was always energetic, ready and willing to make any personal sacrifice to promote the interest of the Sabbath school, and the same is now thoroughly organized with an efficient number of industrious teachers.

POLITICS.

Campaign literature is being freely distributed by both parties, but no political speakers have made their appearance yet. The people are studying the new issues and preparing themselves to cast their votes intelligently.

Salt Lake Herald
March 17, 1900

Little Child Burned.

(Special to The Herald.)

Fillmore, Utah, March 16.—While playing around a bonfire this afternoon with a number of playmates, the pretty little 3-year-old baby girl of Mr. and Mrs. Frank Brunson in some way got her clothing afire and was frightfully and doubtless fatally burned before the cries of the other children summoned help.

Burns Proved Fatal.

(Special to The Herald.)

Fillmore, March 17.—The little 3-year-old Brunson child, who was so terribly burned while playing around a bonfire yesterday, died at noon today.

Ninety-six Years Old.

Mrs. Martha Knight of Hooper yesterday celebrated the 96th anniversary of her birthday. The old lady is still strong and vigorous, and is able to read without the aid of glasses. She is much interested in reading the accounts in the daily newspapers of the Boer war. Mrs. Knight is a grandmother of former Sheriff Gilbert R. Belnap. She has lived in the state of Utah for a half century, and was formerly a resident of Fillmore. She is personally acquainted with Judge W. H. King, and takes a great interest in reading the newspaper reports of his campaign speeches. When she read of his nomination she made the remark that she considered him well worthy of the honor that had been conferred upon him. Mrs. Knight has every confidence that she will live to be a centenarian.

Deseret Evening News
March 17, 1900

FILLMORE.

Mild Winter Causes Fear of Drouth —Another Penney Rumor.

Special Correspondence.

Fillmore, Millard County, March 16.—During the past winter very little snow has fallen in the mountains and many of the farmers apprehend a partial, if not a complete drouth. The ground has been dry and dusty most of the winter, and at present does not contain sufficient moisture to cause the seeds to germinate and grow; consequently, many acres which would otherwise be under cultivation will be dry and sterile this season. Only the first-class water right farms will be irrigated unless more moisture falls during the spring months than is usual, and those who depend upon secondary rights will be compelled to seek some other employment in order to procure means to sustain themselves and families. However, there are a few optimists in our community who predict that the coming season will be as productive as is usual and that the harvest will yield sufficient returns for all.

Political issues are being freely discussed on our streets daily; and the great problems which confront the minds of the American people are being investigated by the voting populace of our community; many have thoroughly investigated the intricacies of these political questions, while others can scarcely comprehend their scope.

THINKS HE HAS THE BODIES LOCATED.

Word comes from Deseret, says the Progress, that Sheriff Kelly left there Monday on another search for the missing Penneys. Mr. Kelly thinks he has the bodies located, as reports have come in from sheepmen that a grave has been discovered about six miles west of Blind Springs, in the Sawtooth mountains. The grave is said to be a large one, and it is thought that their outfit might be buried with the bodies.

Salt Lake Herald
March 22, 1900

GLEN MILLER HISSED.

Federal Office Holder Attacked King at His Old Home.

(Special Correspondence.)

Fillmore, March 21.—The first Republican rally of the campaign in this city was held tonight. The drawing cards were Marshal Glen Miller and H. S. Tanner. The old meeting house was crowded, but fully one-half were Democrats. Mr. Miller occupied a full hour in an effort to tear down Democratic principles, but made a flat failure. He spoke of the Hon. William H. King, in a sneering way, going to Cuba, but just then there was a hissing noise and he dropped the subject like one would a hot potato and did not refer to it again.

Mr. Tanner followed in the same lines as the first speaker and worried the people for another hour. All in all, it was rather a chilly reception throughout and the impression is that "Little Glen" and his companion did more harm than good in King's old home.

Salt Lake Herald
March 25, 1900

DUNBAR AT FILLMORE.

Millard County Will Give King a Good Majority.

(Special to The Herald.)

Fillmore, Utah, March 24.—The campaign for Judge King and Democracy was opened tonight in the old ex-capitol. The speaker was Hon. D. C. Dunbar, and he spoke to one of the largest audiences any political speaker has had the pleasure of doing in this city for many years. The stage was neatly decorated with flowers in profusion, which made the platform look very pretty, such a contrast to the cold and chilly stage that Miller and Tanner occupied two nights previously.

When Mr. Dunbar was introduced by Chairman J. E. Ray, he was received with great applause. All listened to his remarks with the closest attention. It was a representative gathering, and a responsive one, and every point made, and there were many, was appreciated. He spoke of the cause leading up to this special election, showed where the responsibility lay, and answered Miller's and Tanner's talk made Wednesday evening. His arguments on the silver question and trusts were clear and interesting, and without a doubt won many doubtful voters over to Democracy.

At the conclusion of his speech, which occupied one hour and thirty-five minutes, three rousing cheers were given for Judge King.

The Democratic Glee club deserves much praise for the fine music it furnished.

Mr. Dunbar spoke at Kanosh last evening to a large house, and tomorrow he goes to Deseret, where he speaks Monday night, and then to Salt Lake.

Upon a conservative estimate Millard county will give King at least 150 majority; his old home, Fillmore, which has always gone Republican from thirty to fifty, will give King a handsome majority.

Deseret Evening News
March 27, 1900

FILLMORE.

Political Rallies — Want to Secure Land for Homes.

Special Correspondence.

Fillmore, Millard Co., March 26.—The political issues of the day are being freely discussed by the voting populace. Glen Miller and H. S. Tanner have been here representing the political faith of the Hon. James T. Hammond; and the Hon. D. C. Dunbar did honor to his party in expounding the principles of Democracy.

J. D. Smith and James McMahon addressed the Saints here Sunday as home missionaries, encouraging and stimulating the people to greater activity and more faithfulness in the performance of their duties.

WANT TO SECURE LAND.

Many of the people of Millard county are anxious to secure land under the Bonneville grant, and are indulging in speculation as to whether or not the Bonneville enterprise will prove a success; they realize that the soil is fertile, and when properly irrigated will produce abundantly; and a portion of the land embraced in the grant is adapted for dry farming and will be settled upon by home seekers as soon as the land is subject to entry. Many expressions are heard to the effect that the people will develop the country as soon as the rights of the Bonneville people are cancelled.

Salt Lake Herald
March 31, 1900

Millard County Prediction.

(Fillmore Progress.)

Our political reporter predicts that King will be elected next Monday by a majority of 2,600; that he will carry Fillmore by a few votes; that Millard county will give him a majority of 150.

Deseret Evening News
March 31, 1900

NOTABLE UTAH WOMEN.

MRS. DELILAH KING OLSON.

MRS. DELILAH KING OLSON was the only daughter of Thomas R. King and Matilda Robison King, who are of English descent, and whose ancestors were among the early settlers of the New England States. Later her grand parents moved to the State of New York, (her parents' native State) and here they accepted "Mormonism" in 1840, and the following year emigrated to Nauvoo. It was during this journey on the Northwestern prairie of the State of Ohio, in an unnamed place, the subject of this sketch was born, hence her early years were one scene of Pioneer life. Arriving in Salt Lake September, 1851, later in the same year, she was one of the Pioneers of Fillmore, Millard county, which has been principally her home and place of development into the actual duties and realities of life. Prosperity attended this little colony. Good schools were established, and the following ten years of her life were spent in the school room. Having acquired quite a liberal education and being a lover of books and a promoter of education, she has been led to follow teaching as an occupation at intervals during life. It has ever been her greatest pleasure to guide the young to higher ideas and loftier ambitions in social life, and she has received many pronounced eulogies for her efforts in this direction. She became the wife of the late Daniel Olson in 1861, and though a devoted wife and mother, has found time to devote to public service, working in the various offices of the Relief Society since its organization, in 1868, in Millard Stake, and is at present its Stake secretary. She was chosen president of the first Primary association in Fillmore in 1880, and later became the Stake president of that association. She has also presided over the Y. L. M. L. A. for the past seventeen years, and is an active worker in the Sunday school.

She served eighteen years on the board of examination of teachers in Millard county; has ever been a strong advocate of woman's suffrage, contending that mind capacity rested upon its development, and that a nation's progress depended largely upon the equality of the sexes in the privileges of its governmental laws, and she took an active part in petitioning the State Convention for its adoption into the State Constitution. She was one of the first women of the State to realize the benefits of the franchise, being elected to the office of county recorder of Millard county, November 7th, 1896, and re-elected in 1898, on the Democratic ticket, to which party she became affiliated and served as vice chairman in the Fillmore precinct.

Deseret Evening News
April 2, 1900

FILLMORE CLOSE.

It is Thought, However, That King Will Carry the City.

Special per Deseret Telegraph.

Fillmore, April 2.—A little more than half of the vote has been cast. It is thought that King has a small majority at present and will probably carry the city, but the election is close.

FOR KING.

Bingham, Bountiful, Kaysville, Centerville, Eureka, Mammoth, Draper, Fillmore, St. George, Nephi, Mt. Pleasant, Parowan, Gunnison, Cedar City, Payson, Beaver, Manti, Moroni.

FILLMORE.

Discouraging Drouth — Sheep Have Done Well on the Range.

Special Correspondence.

Fillmore, Millard County, March 31.— The dryness of the spring and the small amount of snow in the mountains is quite discouraging to the farmers and stockmen of Millard county, and Fillmore takes on her full share of the depression. Still, a fine large brick business house has recently been erected just south of Gabriel Huntsman's hotel, which, together with the recently finished district school house, shows that Fillmore is abreast of the times, especially in its educational efforts.

SHEEP ARE LOOKING WELL.

Thousands of sheep are being driven north to the shearing camps and the sheepmen are jubilant over their prospects in the wool and sheep business generally. The herds are in splendid condition, very little loss of wool from scab is reported. A few cases of disease has appeared among them, which causes their heads and ears to swell, but nothing to excite alarm.

"NEWS" AGENCY.

John Ashman, Esq, is out finishing his spring canvass of Fillmore for the "News," he has occupied the position as agent here for many years past and has succeeded in gaining many new subscribers.

King Carries Millard.

(Special to The Herald.)

Fillmore, April 3.—Eleven precincts out of the thirteen in Millard county gave King 654 votes and Hammond 63. The two precincts yet to hear from are Burbank and Smithville, which will not reach us till Thursday. The vote of these precincts cannot change the result. The Democratic county chairman claims these precincts for King by 10 majority. The Republicans claim that they will get a small majority from them, but give the county to King by 18. There was but 70 per cent of the votes cast in Millard. Hamlin got three votes.

Deseret Evening News
April 13, 1900

FILLMORE.

A Peaceful Temperance Crusade—Interesting Educational Discussion.

Special Correspondence.

Fillmore, Millard Co., April 12.—The recent storm caused much rejoicing in our community; it was certainly very much needed and appreciated.

An effort is being made by the female portion of our city to suppress the sale of intoxicating liquors; the measures adopted are peaceful and appeal to the good judgment of their husbands, brothers and sweethearts. They are petitioning the city council to increase the license and at the same time securing signers to the temperance pledge, trusting thereby to decrease the patronage of the saloons, which, together with an increased license, will render the sale of spirituous liquors an unprofitable business from a financial point of view.

The Educational society meeting next Saturday night promises to be an interesting event. The following question will be debated: "Resolved, that the English Government is Justified in Carrying on War in the Transvaal."

Salt Lake Herald
April 15, 1900

STOLEN SADDLE RECOVERED.—Deputy Sheriff Dowse yesterday recovered from a State street second hand store a side saddle which was stolen from Al Mitchell at the rear of the Board of Trade building a few months ago by "Blinkey" Fillmore, now a fugitive from justice.

Fillmore Progress: Two classes of people in this country need more prosperity—viz: the laborer for daily wages and the farmer. If these prosper, all the rest prosper.

Deseret Evening News
April 18, 1900

FILLMORE.

JOSEPH HOLBROOK

Suddenly Passes Away at His Home After a Brief Illness.

Special Correspondence.

Fillmore, Millard Co., April 17.—Last Friday evening Joseph Holbrook, one of our most honored and respected citizens, was taken ill and within a very short time became unconscious with paralysis of the brain; he expired Sunday at 12 o'clock midnight, and was buried today. Mr. Holbrook has been a very hard working and industrious man and comes from an illustrious family, who are noted for their financial success and business integrity.

The deceased was only 52 years of age, and the community deeply regret his early death and realize that they have lost an exemplary citizen who was always willing to do more than his part to advance the interest of the community in which he resided; his many kind and charitable acts will long be remembered by those who were intimately acquainted with him.

Salt Lake Herald
April 28, 1900

Joshua Greenwood, the Fillmore attorney and politician, is numbered among the guests at the White house. Greenwood says that politics in Millard county will be of the tropical order next fall, judging from present indications. In speaking of the Quay case, he placed himself on record as being in favor of candidates for the United States senate being elected by the direct vote of the people.

"There is a tendency," he said, "towards keeping the senate for the aristocracy to the exclusion of the average man with political aspirations. Man is naturally a tyrant, and it is invariably his disposition, when he gets the upper hand to rule with a mailed fist."

Changing the subject, Greenwood stated that the last election at Fillmore was devoid of interest, and despite the fact that rounders went around in conveyances in a great number of cases they could not bring the voters out to the polls. This state of affairs, however, he predicts will be materially changed when it comes to voting for the president of the United States next November. In conjunction with other pilgrims from the south, he reports heavy storms in Millard county, with attendant jubilation on the part of the farmers and the stockmen of that section.

(Special to The Herald.)

Fillmore, April 27.—Last evening about 2 o'clock Pete Huntsman, a noted man some 60 years of age, walked into Speaksman's saloon. The proprietor, William Speaksman, ordered him out. After a few words he left, but returned within twenty minutes with a shotgun. Entering the saloon he found the proprietor and several men in the billiard room, and when the proprietor started to come from the billiard room to the saloon, Huntsman threw the gun down on him and said: "You — of —, if you stick your head out that door I'll blow the top of your head off."

For five minutes he had the saloon to himself, and the proprietor and eight men huddled up in the billiard room like a pack of scared sheep. A gentleman on entering the saloon found this condition, and after a little talk partly pacified the old man. The imprisoned men were allowed to come forth and the gun was taken from him. Later he was arrested and today faced the charge of attempted murder. After the above facts were brought forth he was held to the district court in the sum of $500, which he has failed to furnish.

Joshua Greenwood of Fillmore, Millard county, was in town yesterday, shaking hands with his many friends. It is given out by some of the gentleman's friends that he will be a candidate this fall for the democratic nomination for the office of district judge in his district.

Deseret Evening News
April 28, 1900

DID THEY KILL PENNEYS?

Officers Have Arrested a Couple Whom They Suspect of the Murder.

Two Gypsies Traced to Arizona—Committed Depredations Along the Route They Followed.

Detective Jos. R. Bush has returned from southeastern Utah, where he has often been engaged in hunts for outlaws. He has been instrumental, with the assistance of Sheriff Coons of Sevier county, Marshal Madsen of Salina,

Sheriff Jensen of Manti, and Sheriff Kelley of Fillmore, in putting under arrest H. Harper and Ida Harper, who are suspected of having murdered the two Penneys last winter. The couple were traced down into Arizona and tally with the description sent to the "News" some time ago from Arizona by a relative of the murdered men. Both appear to be Gypsies and the officers are almost certain that they have found the guilty parties. The suspects were taken to Fillmore by Sheriff Kelley and an investigation of their depredations along the route they took from Utah to Arizona will be thoroughly investigated, as well as will be the suspicion of murder entertained by the officers.

FILLMORE.

Enters a Saloon and With a Gun Holds it Against all Comers.

Special Correspondence.

Fillmore, Millard Co., April 27.—This morning Wm. Speakman appeared before Justice Jukes and swore to a complaint charging Peter Huntsman, of this place, with an assault with a deadly weapon with intent to commit murder. Mr. Huntsman was arrested and brought into court, and requested a change of venue, which was granted upon filing the proper affidavit.

The cause was transferred to Justice Greenwood and a preliminary examination held this afternoon. The evidence introduced by the prosecution established the fact that Mr. Speakman was proprietor of a saloon, and that Huntsman entered last evening about 9 o'clock, and was requested to depart by the proprietor. After some conversation, Huntsman left and soon returned with a shotgun loaded, and warned Mr. Speakman not to make an appearance from the adjoining room or he would blow the top of his head off; some time afterwards parties appeared from the outside, and Huntsman was pacified and the gun taken from him. The evidence of the defense did not rebut this.

He was held to appear for trial at the district court, and his bonds fixed at five hundred dollars.

Salt Lake Herald
April 29, 1900

CAUSES EXCITEMENT.

Kanosh Stirred Up by Report of the Arrest.

(Special to The Herald.)

Fillmore, April 28.—For the past two days there have been persistent rumors to the effect that the supposed murderers of W. Penney and son had been located, that a watch belonging to one of the missing men had been found, and that arrests would likely follow any hour.

The rumor is now verified. A dispatch to Deputy Sheriff John C. Kelley today from Sheriff Virgil Kelly says he will arrive tomorrow with the prisoners.

From other sources your correspondent is informed that these prisoners are the man and woman that the officers have been looking for for the past three months; that their companion escaped arrest, but the officers are hot on his trail.

All is excitement at Kanosh over the reported arrest, and there will be many visitors from that little burg tomorrow to size up the suspects when they arrive.

Deseret Evening News
May 1, 1900

FILLMORE.

Arrival of Suspected Murderers — Accused Will Make No Statement.

Special Correspondence.

Fillmore, Millard County, April 30.— Sheriff Kelly arrived here today about 3 o'clock p. m. with the suspected murderers of the Penneys, William and Iva Harper, husband and wife. He drove immediately to the county court house, and was followed by a large crowd of spectators who appeared anxious to obtain a glimpse of the prisoners and satisfy their curiosity; after resting for a short period of time in the attorney's office they were taken to the Huntsman house for dinner. The man will be confined in the county jail and the woman will be carefully guarded until their preliminary examination can be had, which will occur as soon as the officers can collect the evidence and prepare for the same. The couple do not appear to be very despondent, but declined to make any statement for publication, simply alleging that their side of the story had not been told.

Their wagon, team and other personal effects which were taken from them at the time of their arrest, are expected in hourly.

Deseret Evening News
May 2, 1900

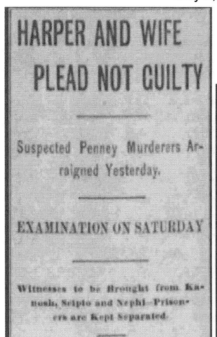

HARPER AND WIFE PLEAD NOT GUILTY

Suspected Penney Murderers Arraigned Yesterday.

EXAMINATION ON SATURDAY

Witnesses to be Brought from Kanosh, Scipio and Nephi—Prisoners are Kept Separated.

[SPECIAL TO THE "NEWS."]

Fillmore, Utah, May 2.—Late yesterday afternoon the suspected murderers of the Penneys were arraigned before Justice Jukes. William R. Harper was charged with murder and Iva Harper, his wife, with being an accessory. The examination will be held Saturday. Subpoenas will be issued for parties at Kanosh, Scipio and Nephi.

Last evening the prisoners were brought into court and charged with the murder of the Penneys. Both pleaded not guilty and apparently not understanding the seriousness of the charge said they wanted no attorney to defend them. The prisoners have been separated with the intention of getting a confession. After separation the woman said, "They are treating us like dogs and I will give the reporter all after the hearing."

Salt Lake Herald
May 7, 1900

Fillmore Will Aid.
(Special to The Herald.)

Fillmore, May 6—The people of this city will aid the sufferers of the Scofield disaster. Mayor E. W. Kelly issued a proclamation today, and appointed the following committee to solicit and receive contributions: T. C. Callister, George C. Velie, James Alex Melville, Joshua Greenwood, I. N. Hinckley, L. W. Gatsford, F. E. Hanson, James A. Kelly, G. Huntsman and the Mesdames Birdie Robison, D. K. Olson and Emily Ray.

Millard County Primaries.
(Special to The Herald.)

Fillmore, May 6.—The Republican primaries to select delegates direct to the state convention were held in most of the towns in this county last evening. Those elected from Fillmore were: E. R. Kelly, F. E. Hanson to state convention, and George Greenway and J. A. Kelly to attend the state league. From Oasis, David Day; Deseret, John R. Bennett; Holden, W. H Hunter; delegates chosen from other towns have not been reported.

Deseret Evening News
May 14, 1900

J. S. GILES ACQUITTED.

Was Innocent of Any Fraudulent Intent, So Says the Jury.

The jury before which J. S. Giles was tried for forging the name of the receiver of the land office to an entry blank, returned a verdict yesterday of not guilty. Giles acknowledged having signed the blank, but explained when he handed it to the applicant that it was no account.

J. S. Giles has resided for over forty years in the city of Fillmore, where no citizen is more highly respected than he, and it is attested in the fact that a score of the most prominent citizens of Fillmore quit their work and came to Salt Lake to testify to his excellent character.

Mr. Giles was defended by Attorney S. A. King, who had partaken of the old man's hospitality from his childhood, and out of his love and respect for him, performed the service of defending him gratuitously.

Salt Lake Herald
May 17, 1900

BIG IRRIGATION CASE.

Suit to Determine Ownership of the Sevier River.

(Special to The Herald.)

Fillmore, May 16.—The trial of the big water suit between the Deseret Irrigation company, plaintiffs, and Samuel McIntyre, defendant, began today before Judge Higgins at this place, in pursuance of a special setting of the case for this time. The suit is brought to adjudicate the water rights of the various towns claimants to the waters of the Sevier river from Sevier county down to and including the town of Deseret. There will be over a hundred witnesses examined in the case and it will perhaps be one of the largest of its kind ever tried in the state.

The attorneys in the case are S. R. Thurman for the plaintiff, and for the various defendants, F. S. Richards, King, Burton & King, Ferguson & Cannon, W. S. Reed, D. D. Houtz, L. H. Erickson and the Cazier Brothers. It is needless to say that some time will be consumed in the trial of the case, although the attorneys seem determined to get down to business and finish the case up with as little delay as possible.

FILLMORE.

Important Irrigation Suit Now in Court.

Special Correspondence.

Fillmore, Millard County May 16.— The district court convened here this morning, Judge E. V. Higgins presiding. There were present besides the local members of the bar, Attorneys D. D. Houtz, W. K. Reid, F. S. Richards, J. M. Cannon, S. A. King, S. R. Thurman, and a large number of witnesses for the various parties concerned.

The case called was the Deseret Irrigation company and Leamington Irrigation company vs Samuel McIntyre et al. Mr. Thurman representing the plaintiffs, briefly outlined the claims of his clients and stated the facts which they expected to substantiate by the evidence. He then called L. R. Cropper for the first witness, who stated that he resided at Deseret and had done so for the past twenty-five years; that a great many acres of land had been brought under cultivation recently, but that less water was required now than formerly to irrigate the land because the land being porous absorbed large quantities until it had been thoroughly saturated, after which very little was required.

F. M. Lyman Jr. was the next witness called; he stated that he was an engineer and had made some measurements for the people of Deseret at the mouth of their canal; the volume of water in and carrying capacity of their canal was then testified to. He had also measured the Wellington canal and gave the dimensions of the same.

John Rytier was then called and testified that he resided at Oasis and that the acreage of land was increased some, but that the quantity of water which reached their canal was less; also, that the reduction of water was not due to natural causes, such as dry seasons. Much documentary evidence was introduced during the day for the purpose of linking together the chain of title.

FILLMORE.

Continuation of Irrigation Litigation in District Court.

Special Correspondence.

Fillmore, Millard Co., May 17.—In the district court today the case of the Deseret Irrigation company et al vs Samuel McIntyre et al was continued; the plaintiffs placed the following witnesses on the stand viz.; William Black, Joshua Bennett, G. W. Cropper, Joseph Damron, and Jacob Hawley, all of Deseret. Their testimony was similar to that of the witnesses who were on the stand yesterday and tended to corroborate what they said.

The parties in Millard county have effected a compromise and will unite in opposition to the parties higher up the river and attempt to prove that parties in Sanpete county have been diverting water that should reach Deseret and Leamington.

Deseret Evening News
May 14, 1900

J. S. GILES ACQUITTED.

Was Innocent of Any Fraudulent Intent, So Says the Jury.

The jury before which J. S. Giles was tried for forging the name of the receiver of the land office to an entry blank, returned a verdict yesterday of not guilty. Giles acknowledged having signed the blank, but explained when he handed it to the applicant that it was no account.

J. S. Giles has resided for over forty years in the city of Fillmore, where no citizen is more highly respected than he, and it is attested in the fact that a score of the most prominent citizens of Fillmore quit their work and came to Salt Lake to testify to his excellent character.

Mr. Giles was defended by Attorney S. A. King, who had partaken of the old man's hospitality from his childhood, and out of his love and respect for him, performed the service of defending him gratuitously.

Deseret Evening News
May 17, 1900

FILLMORE.

Important Irrigation Suit Now in Court.

Special Correspondence.

Fillmore, Millard County May 16.— The district court convened here this morning, Judge E. V. Higgins presiding. There were present besides the local members of the bar, Attorneys D. D. Houtz, W. K. Reid, F. S. Richards, J. M. Cannon, S. A. King, S. R. Thurman and a large number of witnesses for the various parties concerned.

The case called was the Deseret Irrigation company and Leamington Irrigation company vs Samuel McIntyre et al. Mr. Thurman representing the plaintiffs, briefly outlined the claims of his clients and stated the facts which they expected to substantiate by the evidence. He then called L. R. Cropper for the first witness, who stated that he resided at Deseret and had done so for the past twenty-five years; that a great many acres of land had been brought under cultivation recently, but that less water was required now than formerly to irrigate the land because the land being porous absorbed large quantities until it had been thoroughly saturated, after which very little was required.

F. M. Lyman Jr. was the next witness called; he stated that he was an engineer and had made some measurements for the people of Deseret at the mouth of their canal; the volume of water in and carrying capacity of their canal was then testified to. He had also measured the Wellington canal and gave the dimensions of the same.

John Styler was then called and testified that he resided at Oasis and that the acreage of land was increased some, but that the quantity of water which reached their canal was less; also, that the reduction of water was not due to natural causes, such as dry seasons. Much documentary evidence was introduced during the day for the purpose of linking together the chain of title.

Deseret Evening News
May 18, 1900

FILLMORE.

Continuation of Irrigation Litigation in District Court.

Special Correspondence.

Fillmore, Millard Co., May 17.—In the district court today the case of the Deseret Irrigation company et al vs Samuel McIntyre et al was continued; the plaintiffs placed the following witnesses on the stand viz.: William Black, Joshua Bennett, G. W. Cropper, Joseph Damron and Jacob Hawley, all of Deseret. Their testimony was similar to that of the witnesses who were on the stand yesterday and tended to corroborate what they said.

The parties in Millard county have effected a compromise and will unite in opposition to the parties higher up the river and attempt to prove that parties in Sanpete county have been diverting water that should reach Deseret and Leamington.

Salt Lake Herald
May 20, 1900

NICE SUM ADDED TO FUND

SCOFIELD DONATIONS YESTERDAY CAME TO $3,000.

Herald Fund Swelled by the Addition of $256 Received From Outside.

There was almost $3,000 added to the Scofield relief fund yesterday, increasing the grand total to $117,370.25. The Herald fund was swelled by $202, received from the good people of Pleasant Grove, by $43.50 from the good people of Manning, by $10 from A. B. Kirchbaum of Philadelphia, and by $1 from C. H. Morrison of Eureka. This brings The Herald fund up to the splendid figure of $8,131.50. The additions to the general fund were from:

W. F. Colton	$ 1,816 50
Chairman Hammond	263 80
Provo, additional	200 00
Logan concert	76 70
West Jordan	8 10

Money and Food Still Coming.

Chairman Hammond of the state relief committee yesterday received the following amounts remitted by contributors to the Scofield relief fund:

Citizens of Fillmore, through E. W. Kelley	$ 100 80
Citizens of Gunnison, through Laura Christensen	84 00
Citizens of Robinson, through J. B. Roberts	43 50
Citizens of Huntington, through William Howard	35 50
Total	$ 263 80

In addition to the above, N. C. Christensen of Sterling has written that the people of his village have sent to Scofield 600 pounds of flour, eighty bushels of potatoes, a case of eggs and a quarter of beef.

CYRUS SANFORD.

Sketch of the Life Work of a Faithful Citizen of Utah.

Cyrus Sanford was born in Bristol, Addison county, Vermont, December 18, 1813. His father's name was Ira Sanford and his mother's maiden name Margaret Vrandenburg, both of whom were raised in Vermont. He married Sylvia Elmina Stockwell in De Kalb, Lawrence county, October 5, 1836, and was baptized in 1840 by Simeon J. Comfort, and was confirmed by John E. Page and Orson Hyde. He was at Nauvoo when the corner stone of the temple was laid and furnished means to aid in building it, and rendered material aid to the sufferers of Morley settlement when the mob killed Edmund Durfee. He passed through those intense scenes of suffering near Warsaw when the sick had no covering but the canopy of heaven. He aided in moving one of the outer settlements to Nauvoo, and was one who made an agreement with the mob to vacate in the spring. He saw Frank Worl shot at the time of the burning, and was at the trial of Backenstock, sheriff of Hancock county. He left Council Bluffs in the spring of 1850, and on the 14th of June following commenced his journey for the Rocky mountains, with a wife and six children, in William Snow's company, arriving at Salt Lake in the middle of October. After a brief stay there, he located at Hobble creek, afterwards Springville, Utah county, and helped build a fort there against the Indians. He helped to survey the site for Fillmore city. He was appointed by Major Rose, Indian agent, for Springville and Spanish Fork, and was the first district school teacher and superintendent of Sabbath schools in the former, and was elected mayor of Springville city after having previously held the office of justice of the peace for fourteen years, subsequently he was promoted to the office of major of the battalion which went out against the Indian chief Walker. Mr. Sanford was in the companies who fought against the Salt Creek Indians near Goshen. He was president of the Springville co-op for a short time, and was one of its directors for years. Took a mission to the State of Illinois November 15, 1871. Hauled supplies to the hand cart companies, badly freezing his feet. Was ordained a Seventy in Nauvoo about 1845 and a High Priest by Henry Maiben, December 16, 1881.

Mr. Sanford departed this life May 15, 1900, aged 86 years and 5 months, and was the father of 11 children, 71 grand children, 112 great grand children, and 3 great, great grand children. Nine of his children are living and were present at the funeral, together with his two wives Sylvia and Mary. No truer man ever lived, and none was braver. He rests in peace with the high honors of a life devoted to God, to family, to humanity and truth.

CHARLES D. EVANS.

FILLMORE.

The Big Water Suit Still Before the Court.

Special Correspondence.

Fillmore, Millard Co., May 15.—The district court convened again yesterday and the following proceedings in the water case, involving the rights of the parties along the Sevier river, were heard. The Deseret Irrigation company, one of the plaintiff corporations, had concluded the evidence on their part and the Leamington Irrigation company, the other plaintiff corporation, called the following witnesses, to-wit: C. Overson, August Neilson, Amel Johnson, and John Talbot. Their testimony was substantially the same and established the fact that until the last seven or eight years they had had sufficient water to properly irrigate and mature their crops, but that recently there had been a partial failure, owing to a shortage of water which they claimed had been diverted from the river higher up the stream.

The plaintiffs rested their case and Mr. John M. Cannon, representing the Deseret and Salt Lake Agricultural and Manufacturing Canal company, made the opening statement for the defendant corporation, which he represented, briefly outlining the purpose and object of the creation of the corporation and their work in the construction of canals and diversion and storage of the water. The first witness placed on the stand was Chas. Wilkins, an officer of the corporation, who has been connected with the same since its organization. He furnished some data with reference to the dimensions of their reservoirs and canals and the quantity of water they had stored for the last ten years.

Wm. Black testified that all the water which the defendant company had was obtained by reservoiring the same during the winter and early spring months and that recently it had been insufficient to irrigate their land.

Today the court is still busy taking testimony in the big water case. McIntyre has put in his defense and the Wellington Canal company is putting in its testimony at the present time; the probabilities are that the case will continue for two days yet.

A large number of our citizens left for Holden today to attend conference, which will be in session today and to-morrow. Apostle Lyman will be there to give some instructions to the Saints in his usual good-natured manner, which the people appreciate very much.

The regular session of the district court will convene next week with a large calendar of cases; the probabilities are that this coming term will be longer than any preceding for some time past. There will be two criminal cases and considerable civil work to dispose of.

Deseret Evening News
May 22, 1900

MAMMOTH MINE.

Good Ore Body on 1900 — The Reported Purchase of the Control.

President McIntyre of the Mammoth Mining company reached town today, having come from Fillmore, where he has been engaged in a water suit. From Fillmore Mr. McIntyre traveled to Leamington and thence to Mammoth by wagon.

In discussing the condition of the mine today, Mr. McIntyre said it is looking well. The 3 foot stringer of ore that was encountered on the 1900 level has been followed some 30 or 40 feet and has now disclosed a fine ore body, 5 timber sets wide. A high percentage of copper was found in the ore first struck. This has disappeared and a gold and silver ore has taken its place. Some of the ore on the 1900 runs up to 4 ounces in gold, but the bulk of that at present extracted is milling ore. Mr. McIntyre says it is exceptionally good milling ore, and for this reason nearly all of it is being sent through the mill. A sump is being sunk at the 1900, but it is the intention of the management to put a winze down in the vein before continuing any deeper with the shaft.

In about ten days it is expected that connection will be made with the new ore body on the 800 level through Grand Central ground. This will prove a great advantage to the company. The values of the ore on this level are principally in silver and gold, though a body of lead ore was broken into yesterday.

In speaking of the talked of purchase of the Mammoth control, Mr. McIntyre said that Messrs. Farrell and Grant had not shown any great desire for his holdings, though he understood from other parties that they want them. The matter was discussed last fall when Mr. McIntyre offered them at $4 per share. Since that time it is intimated that the control has been offered at a lower price, but at just what figure Mr. McIntyre declined to mention. The gentlemen named have recently secured a great deal of data regarding the mine from whence it is inferred that while nothing has yet been consummated it will probably be done in the near future.

Salt Lake Herald
May 23, 1900

COURT AT FILLMORE.

Big Irrigation Case Still on Trial — Cases Set.

(Special to The Herald.)

Fillmore, May 22.—The trial of the Deseret Irrigation company et al. against Samuel McIntyre et al. is still in progress. The plaintiffs have rested and the defendants' case is well under way. It looks now as if the case would be completed before this week is ended.

Today being the time for the regular May term to begin, Judge Higgins called the calendar and made the following settings of cases.

White Mountain reservoir company vs. James Duncan, set for trial for the 25th instant. White Mountain Reservoir company vs. Fisher et al., set for the 25th. White Mountain Reservoir company vs. Labrum et al., set for the 26th. Maverick W. McDonald vs. Myrtle M. McDonald, set for the 26th. State vs. Peter Huntsman, set for the 29th. The defendant in this case was arraigned upon an information charging him with assault with a deadly weapon and he took the statutory time to plead.

Margret M. Blythe a native of Scotland, was naturalized. A jury was ordered for the 29th instant.

MAMMOTH ORE BODIES.

Connection on 300-level Will Be Made In Ten Days.

President Samuel McIntyre of the Mammoth Mining company returned yesterday morning from Fillmore, where he has been for the past week on legal business.

Speaking of the condition of the mine, Mr. McIntyre says it looks well; in fact, never better. On the 1,900 level, where a three-foot streak of ore was encountered some time ago, the vein has been followed for nearly forty feet, at which point a fine body of ore has been disclosed. The values run largely in silver and gold, with some copper.

It is thought that the connection with the new ore body on the 800 level will be made through the Grand Central ground within the next ten days.

A meeting of the directors will likely be called some day this week, but Mr. McIntyre declined to say whether a dividend could be counted on as a sure thing this month.

Deseret Evening News
May 23, 1900

FILLMORE.

Irrigation Hearing Still in Progress— Cases for Regular Term of Court.

Fillmore City, Utah, May 22—Proceedings in the trial of the water controversy involving the rights of the parties located on the Sevier river are progressing very slowly. Attorney S. A. King, representing the Rabina and Kanosa Canal company, has been putting in his evidence today, and it is thought likely that testimony will be concluded tonight, and that the arguments will be made tomorrow, then the case will be in the hands of the court. The parties whose rights are being litigated appear to take a deep interest in the trial and are seldom found outside the court room during the time court is in session. This has been a very interesting case, and has established the fact that water rights in this county are not yet settled and the future promises to develop further litigation, involving the legal title to water for irrigation.

The regular term of the court will not commence until after the termination of the present suit. The calendar was called this morning, and the cases set for trial at a later date, coming on the latter part of this and first part of next week.

Salt Lake Herald
May 26, 1900

IRRIGATION SUITS.

Testimony in Deseret Case Finshed at Fillmore.

(Special to The Herald.)

Fillmore, Utah, May 2.—The testimony in the case of the Deseret Irrigation company et al. against Samuel McIntyre et al. was finished last night and the arguments in the case will be had at Nephi on June 2.

The cases of the White Mountain Reservoir company against James Duncan et al. and the White Mountain Reservoir company against James Fisher et al., and the case of the White Mountain Reservoir company against George Labrum et al., being common in many of the issues joined, by agreement of the parties, are being tried all together.

The testimony in one case will be to a considerable extent the testimony in the other two, so that the trial of these cases will be very much shortened by the arrangement. This triple trial was begun this morning and the testimony of the plaintiff heard in part.

Deseret Evening News
May 26, 1900

FILLMORE.

Hearing on Irrigation Case Concluded —County School Commencement.

Special Correspondence.

Fillmore, Millard County, May 25.— All the evidence in the big water case that has been pending in our court for the past week has been taken and witnesses and attorneys left town yesterday after a very long siege of hard work in court; the arguments will be made at Nephi some time in the future, but it is not likely that a decision on the matter will be reached by the court for quite a long time to come owing to the complications of the case.

Today the case of the White Mountain Reservoir Co. vs James Duncan, James Fischer et al. was called; Melville & Shepard appeared for the plaintiff and Houtz & Greenwood appeared for the defendants. The case is a question of water rights to determine the ownership of water running down the Meadow creek slough.

SCHOOL COMMENCEMENT.

The first annual commencement exercises of the graduates from Millard County are being held in the new school house today; a very appropriate program has been prepared and instructors from the north have been secured to render some assistance for the entertainment of those who will have the privilege of attending. A large crowd of spectators from the various parts of the county are present for the purpose of enjoying the exercises.

Washington County News
May 26, 1900

LOST—A sack containing clothing, letters, papers, and a day book, between Hebron and the Ranch house on Five-mile flat, east of R. R. grade near Clover Valley. I will reward any person that gives information concerning it or restores it to me, either at Fillmore, Cedar City, or St. George, by express, and I will pay all charges.
JESSE TYE.

Salt Lake Herald
May 27, 1900

WATER SUITS COMPROMISED.

Settlement of White Mountain Reservoir Cases—Divorce Granted.

(Special Correspondence.)

Fillmore, Utah, May 26.—The three water suits of the White Mountain Reservoir company against James Duncan et al., James Fisher, jr., et al. and George H. Labrum et al., the joint trial of which was begun yesterday before the court, were today compromised and a decree entered adjusting their differences.

Catherine Haycock was granted a decree of divorce from Samuel Haycock on the grounds of failure to support and desertion.

In the case of Rebecca Dame against Joseph S. Dame for separate maintenance the court ordered that the defendant pay into court $60 a month temporary alimony and $100 attorney's fee.

Salt Lake Herald
May 30, 1900

MILLARD COUNTY GRADUATES.

Thirty-four Public School Pupils Receive Diplomas.

(Special Correspondence.)

Fillmore, May 26.—The first annual commencement exercises of the public schools of Millard county took place in Fillmore Friday, May 25, and were attended by the usual ceremony. Many teachers and parents were in attendance. Thirty-four students received diplomas, there being seven young ladies to each boy. The stand was beautifully decorated and the graduates occupied one side, and such distinguished educators as Professor J. E. Hickman of the B. Y. A., County Superintendent of Schools T. C. Callister and others were given seats on the other side. A magnificent programme was carried out by classes of the various towns. Professor Hickman's address to the graduates was a masterpiece and well received. In the afternoon an elegant banquet was given by the graduating class of Fillmore.

The names of the graduates follow:

Fillmore—Bertha Starley, Irene Kelly, Chloe Huntsman, Pearl Baldwin, Jessie Mitchell, Marion Owens, Katie Anderson.

Meadow—Mary Adams, Alice Duncan, Martha Fisher, Marinda Bennett.

Kanosh—Florence Barney, Georgiana Bird, Eva Dorrity, Elva Roberts, Susannah Paxton, Emma Rappleye, Isabel Whatcott.

Deseret—Mary A. Cropper, Wilford Warnick.

Oak City—Millie Lyman, Soren J. Rawlinson, Edgar Nielson, Joseph L. Anderson.

Holden—Edith Ashby, Ruby Johnson, Emma Hunter, Francis Nixon, George Stephenson.

Scipio—Blanche Robins, Emma Memmott, Walace Matthews, Bertha Robins, Ellis Thompson.

Salt Lake Herald
May 31, 1900

COURT AT FILLMORE.

Two Divorce and Two Criminal Cases Disposed Of.

(Special to The Herald.)

Fillmore, May 30.—The only business transacted before Judge Higgins yesterday was probate matters.

Today, in the case of the state against Peter Huntsman, who was charged with assault with a deadly weapon with intent to do great bodily harm, the defendant withdrew his former plea of not guilty and entered a plea of guilty of simple assault, which was accepted by the prosecution, and the defendant waiving time for sentence was fined $75. In default of the payment of that amount he is to serve one day for each dollar of said fine, in the county jail.

Lee Baker, who was charged with selling liquor to Indians, was tried by a jury and a verdict of guilty returned. He was fined $50.

John H. Lundahl, a native of Sweden, and John A. Iverson, a native of Norway, were each admitted to citizenship.

The case of Maverick W. McDonald vs. Myrtle M. McDonald was tried and the court refused to grant the divorce, holding that the evidence was not sufficient to establish the charges set out in the complaint. The case was dismissed and it is understood a new action will be filed.

In the case of Sarah R. Dame vs. Joseph S. Dame the plaintiff was granted a divorce on the ground of desertion and failure to support. She was also decreed some real and personal property, amounting to about $1,000, and an additional $1,000 as alimony. The plaintiff was also given the custody of the four minor children and was restored to her maiden name.

Salt Lake Herald
June 4, 1900

IRRIGATION INJUNCTION.

Judge Higgins' Order in the Sevier River Case.

(Special Correspondence.)

Nephi, June 2.—At a special session of court held here today, to hear the arguments in the big water case that was tried at Fillmore, the whole day was consumed, and at 10 o'clock tonight the judge made the following temporary injunction:

"It is hereby ordered that the West View Canal company and the Fayette extension be restrained from using any of the waters of the Sevier river or obstructing the flow thereof; and that the Robins & Kearns Dam & Canal company and the Roberts Bros. and the Dover Canal company, and the Wellington Canal company and the Lemington Irrigation company and Samuel McIntyre and William H. McIntyre be restrained from in any manner interfering with the flow of the water of the Sevier river, excepting to the extent of three-fifths of the amount heretofore and now used by said parties respectively.

"And that this order remain in full force and effect until further ordered by the court."

Salt Lake Herald
June 10, 1900

MADE FARMERS HAPPY.

Good Rain Saved the Crops in Millard County.

(Special to The Herald.)

Fillmore, Utah, June 9.—One of the finest rains that has visited this section for months is pouring down today in large quantities, and is worth many thousands of dollars to the farmers and stock raisers. Only yesterday things looked pretty gloomy in Millard for crops, especially the lucern, for they were burning up, and some farmers were cutting wheat for hay, but all is now changed. The earth is thoroughly soaked, and the storm is not yet over.

Deseret Evening News
June 11, 1900

PETERSON-CUMMINGS NUPTIALS.

Cards are out announcing the wedding of Mr. Fred Cummings to Miss Amanda Peterson, both of Fillmore; the event occurred June 6th, 1900.

Joshua Greenwood has gone to Milford to attend a meeting of the county chairmen of the Fifth judicial district, which has for its object the selection of the time and place for holding the district convention.

DROUTH

The weather is very warm and crops generally are suffering except in some small fields, where the owner had an ample supply of water for irrigation. Unless this drouth is broken soon the harvest next autumn will be much lighter than hoped for.

FILLMORE.

Board of Equalization — Wedding — Drouth Threatens Crops.

Special Correspondence.

Fillmore City, Millard Co., June 7.— The county court met Monday as a board of equalization and will likely continue as such the greater portion of this week, as yet very few people have appeared to have any change made in their assessment or the valuation placed on their property.

Deseret Evening News
June 13, 1900

FILLMORE.

Louis Phillips, Jr., Held for Burglarizing a Saloon.

Special Correspondence.

Fillmore, Millard County, June 12.— County Attorney Melville returned last evening from an official trip to the western part of our county. Louis Phillips, Jr. and Jas. W. Shougard were arrested on a charge of burglarizing a saloon at Deseret. Shougard is a young man from Sevier county and was partially coerced to participate in the crime, and after some consultation with the county attorney and his mother, was induced to relate the whole circumstance and Phillips afterwards acknowledged his guilt. Shougard was discharged and Phillips was held to appear for trial at the next term of the District court and his bond fixed at $500 which had not been furnished last evening. The proprietors of the saloon lost nothing more than perhaps six or seven bottles of whiskey.

Salt Lake Herald
June 17, 1900

MILLARD CONVENTION.

Harry P. Brown Renominated For School Superintendent.

(Special to The Herald.)

Fillmore, Utah, June 16.—The largest non-partisan county convention ever held in Millard county convened here this afternoon for the purpose of placing in nomination a county superintendent of district schools. Every district was represented in full. Two candidates were out for the position, Harry P. Brown of Holden, the present superintendent, and Albert N. Hanson of Fillmore. For weeks the friends of both candidates have been working hard for their respective choice, and both felt confident of victory, but on the first ballot Mr. Brown received the nomination by a majority of ten and was then made the unanimous choice of the convention. The following resolutions were introduced by Alma Greenwood and passed by the convention and all is favorable for Millard county to have a high school established this fall:

"Resolved, That we the delegates to a regularly called convention for the purpose of nominating a person for county superintendent and representing the educational interest of the people of Millard county do declare that,

"First, We favor the establishment and perpetuity of a high school in Millard county.

"Second, That the matter as to where said school should be located be left to the franchise of the people of Millard county.

"Third, That the trustees of the various school districts of Millard county are requested to join in a request to the county superintendent to fix or appoint the 9th day of July, 1900, as the time for the people to vote for or against the institution of said school."

Deseret Evening News
June 19, 1900

FILLMORE.

County School Superintendent Brown Renominated.

Special Correspondence.

Fillmore, Millard Co., Utah, June 18.— The county convention called for the purpose of nominating a county superintendent of schools, met on the 16th, pursuant to call and placed in nomination the present superintendent, Harry P. Brown, who has served in that capacity for five years; as the call was non-partisan, there will not be any other candidate in the field.

SUNDAY SCHOOL CONFERENCE.

Yesterday the best Sunday school conference ever held in our county was closed with many regrets that it did not last longer; every part of the program was carried out successfully and the rendition was far superior to anything witnessed in this county for years. The instructions by W. D. Owen, of the aids to the general board of Sunday schools, were much appreciated and the singing of Geo. D. Pyper was simply grand.

A. A. Hinckley, who has been absent laboring as a missionary for three years in Holland, has returned to his home at Hinckley and paid his parents and many friends residing here a visit.

Salt Lake Herald
June 27, 1900

SMALLPOX AT FILLMORE.

First Case in That City Causes Some Excitement.

(Special to The Herald.)

Fillmore, June 26.—The people here are quite excited over a supposed case of smallpox, the first that has appeared in this city. The man afflicted is John T. Ashman, who but recently returned from Mercur. Dr. Beatty was wired the condition of the patient and pronounced it smallpox. A large number of people have been exposed, as up to yesterday no restrictions had been put upon the man, but now he is isolated and every precaution is being taken by the city officials.

Salt Lake Herald
June 28, 1900

SMALLPOX AT FILLMORE.

Another Case is Reported to Dr. Beatty—Physicians Are Wanted.

A letter was received yesterday by Dr. Beatty from the mayor of Fillmore stating that another case of smallpox had developed in the town. On account of there being no regular physician at the place, fears were entertained for the safety of the people.

The case is that of a young man who lately went to Fillmore from Mercur. A number of people were exposed to the disease after it was fully developed, but every effort is being made to help them all under a strict quarantine to prevent further exposure.

A letter was also received from a resident at Riverton stating that the case of smallpox which was reported from there a few days ago had been neglected and the physician which they asked to be sent down was not sent. The letter said that the neighbors were afraid to go near the patient and that she was suffering from the lack of medical aid.

SMALLPOX SCARE.

Two Suspects From Fillmore Quarantined at Manti.

(Special Correspondence.)

Manti, June 27.—Quite a scare was created here yesterday by a telegram received from Fillmore, stating that a man named John Ashman was on his way to Manti, bringing Mrs. Matheny to her home here by team, and that Ashman had been exposed to smallpox of the worst type. Quarantine Physician Hosford and Marshal Ottosen kept a close watch for the parties and on their arrival last night immediately placed them under quarantine at the home of Mrs. Matheny. Both submitted cheerfully to the action of the officers, but Mr. Ashman insisted that he knew of no smallpox existing in his town, and had not the slightest suspicion of having been exposed to the disease. He was anxious to return home at once, which privilege was granted, and he left here this morning at daybreak. He is an old, gray-haired man. Mrs. Matheny has been quarantined for the regulation time awaiting developments.

Deseret Evening News
June 28, 1900

FILLMORE "SMALLPOX."

Case There Seems to be of the Prevalent Type.

[SPECIAL TO THE "NEWS."]

Fillmore, Utah, June 28.—John T. Ashman came home sick from Mercur, a few days ago, and many were of the opinion that he had "smallpox." Dr. Andrews, from Gunnison, diagnosed the patient this morning and confirmed the opinion. Many have been exposed and new cases will likely develop soon. The local board of health will have all quarantined whom they think likely to spread the disease, but as the patient was up town shaking hands with his friends no doubt some will escape the quarantine regulations.

Salt Lake Herald
June 29, 1900

GENUINE SMALLPOX.

Fourteen Families Are Quarantined at Fillmore.

(Special to The Herald.)

Fillmore, Utah, June 28.—Dr. Andrews of Gunnison arrived here late last night and this morning examined the supposed case of smallpox and pronounced it a genuine case. All that is possible is being done to stop the disease from spreading. As yet no other cases have been reported but fourteen families who are supposed to have been exposed to the disease are now under strict quarantine.

Deseret Evening News
June 30, 1900

FILLMORE.

City in a Fever of Excitement Over "Smallpox."

Special Correspondence.

Fillmore, Millard Co., June 29.—The city is in a fever of excitement since the development of "smallpox" in our midst; no new cases have developed since Dr. Andrews from Gunnison was here yesterday, but fourteen families have been quarantined as a precautionary measure to prevent the spread of the disease.

F. F. Merrill, one member of the board of health, resigned and F. C. Melville was appointed to fill the vacancy; the board is in a good working condition and will do all in his power to prevent any further exposures to contagion.

John Ashman, who left for Manti a few days ago, and whose grandson introduced the disease in our midst, only stayed over night in Manti, as there was fear that he had been exposed to the disease. He arrived home Wednesday night. Mr. Ashman had not been exposed and had not even seen his grandson, and there was no need of the fear he occasioned. Mr. Ashman states that he was treated very kindly by the city marshal at Manti and that he feels grateful to him for his magnanimity and courtesy.

Salt Lake Herald
July 1, 1900

FIFTH DISTRICT NOMINATIONS.

Thomas Marioneaux For Judge and Greenwood For Attorney.

(Special to The Herald.)

Milford, Utah, June 30.—The Democratic convention of the Fifth judicial district met here at 11 o'clock this morning. This district comprises the counties of Juab, Millard, Beaver, Iron and Washington. Of the forty-five delegates elected to the convention, forty were present, and they were representative men of the party in the several counties.

Thomas Marioneaux of Beaver was nominated by acclamation for judge of the district. There were a number of candidates for district attorney, namely: Joshua Greenwood of Fillmore, Frank Holzheimer of Eureka, George R. Lund of St. George and Thomas Adams of Salt Lake City. The contest for this nomination was spirited, and it was only after five ballots that Mr. Greenwood was declared the nominee of the convention.

Mr. Marioneaux is at present the district attorney of this district, having been appointed by Governor Wells a year ago. He is a southerner by birth, 34 years of age. He moved to Beaver City in June, 1898. Prior to that time he practiced with the old firm of Bennett, Marshall & Bradley, and for a time it will be remembered was official reporter of the Third district court. Mr. Marioneaux has demonstrated in the past few years that he is eminently qualified for the high office for which he has been nominated. The selection will prove very satisfactory to the bar of Salt Lake who practice at Nephi, as he is highly esteemed by the lawyers, and among them enjoys a fine reputation. His conduct of the office of district attorney in the past year has placed Mr. Marioneaux beyond question in the front rank of the young lawyers of the state.

Mr. Greenwood, the nominee for district attorney, is about 37 years of age, a good lawyer, a gentleman of fine presence, a staunch Democrat and one of the most polished and forceful speakers in southern Utah. He will make a splendid prosecuting officer.

Frank Holzheimer of Eureka had been a prominent candidate for the judicial nomination, and was expected to make a hard fight in the convention, but he finally concluded that Mr. Marioneaux would be the strongest man and Frank and his friends magnanimously withdrew his name as a candidate for judge. Had this step not been deferred until the last moment, Mr. Holzheimer would doubtless have been nominated for district attorney.

Salt Lake Herald
July 6, 1900

MORE POSTAL CHANGES.

Two Postmasters Appointed—Rural Delivery Extended.

(Special to The Herald.)

Washington, D. C., July 5.—Fourth-class postmasters appointed: Utah—M. M. Fillmore, Burbank, Millard county, vice F. G. Schumacher, resigned.

Idaho—H. E. Richmond, Pearl, Boise county, vice O. C. Wylie, resigned.

Rural free delivery will be established July 16 at Bingham canyon, Salt Lake county, Utah. There will be two carriers; the length of the routes is eighteen miles, and the area covered forty-one square miles; population served being 1,400. Service at Sandy, Salt Lake county, will also be established, with one carrier. The length of the route is twenty-two miles, and the population served 1,666.

Star postal service in Idaho has been established from Concord by Buffalo Hump and Morrer station to Adams, twenty-five miles and back, three times a week.

Star postal service from Rockford to Bell Grove, Ida., has been increased to supply patrons three times a week.

Salt Lake Herald
July 7, 1900

PERSONAL MENTION.

S. W. Kelly, the Fillmore merchant, came up from the south yesterday and registered at the White House.

J. P. Gardner, the clothier and furnisher, leaves for the east this morning on a business and pleasure trip.

Senator J. L. Rawlins returned home yesterday from the Kansas City convention. He is very well pleased with the nominations made by the national convention and with the platform adopted by it. The senator's private secretary, R. B. Thurman, and Mrs. Thurman returned with him.

Washington County News
July 21, 1900

Fillmore is advertising for a doctor.

FILLMORE.

"Smallpox" Situation — Harvest is Light—Will Celebrate the 24th.

Special Correspondence.

Fillmore, Millard Co., Utah, July 11.— John T. Ashman, who has been confined with "smallpox," has nearly recovered from his affliction, but his wife and one child are suffering with the same disease. The local board of health is taking every precaution to prevent the spread of the disease and it is hardly likely that there will be any new case outside of the family.

Harvest is progressing nicely but the yield is very light compared with previous years owing to a scarcity of water for irrigation, but the people are looking for a better season next year and trusting to providence to send them the usual supply of moisture to mature their crops.

Some preparations are being made to hold a grand celebration here on the 24th of this month and the program which was announced for the Fourth and held over on account of smallpox, will be carried out as far as it is appropriate to Pioneer day; no doubt a great effort will be made to have an enjoyable time because there has not been any public gatherings of any kind for the last three weeks.

FILLMORE.

Sports on the 24th—Ice Famine—Political Aspirants.

Special Correspondence.

Fillmore City, Millard County, July 25, —The afternoon sports were the only features of Pioneer day, however, they were very enjoyable, consisting of racing of various kinds for prizes, wrestling and base ball; in the evening the dancing portion of our community attended a hop at the old State House building.

There is an ice famine prevailing here at present; a good quality of ice was stored here in large quantities last winter, but the demand for the same has been in excess of that of ordinary seasons.

Lester O. Cartwright of Springfield, Illinois is here on mining business; he expects to negotiate some sales in the Detroit Mining district in the near future.

We have quite a number of aspirants for office in the political arena from the two leading parties, and there is a probability that others may have an ambition to serve their country in an official capacity before the convention meets.

Deseret Evening News
August 10,1900

FILLMORE.

Millard County Business — Academy League—Politics.

Special Correspondence.

Fillmore City, Millard Co., Aug. 9.—
The county court was in session this
week and fixed the salaries of all county officers for the ensuing two years,
divided Fillmore into two election districts, heard the report of the county
surveyor on a proposed wagon road
from here to Deseret, and attended to
the ordinary monthly business.

ACADEMY LEAGUE

An organization known as the "Academy League" is in a perfect working
condition in this city; all persons who
have attended the B. Y. academy at
Provo are eligible to membership in
the organization, which has for its object the perpetuation of the influence
and patriotism of the academy, and the
extension of social, moral, and intellectual development. The organization
will convene tomorrow evening at the
home of ex-Senator J. V. Robison in a
social capacity.

POLITICS.

The Democrats have decided to hold
their convention for the nomination of
all county officers and election of delegates to the State and senatorial con-

Deseret Evening News
August 25, 1900

FILLMORE.

Smith-Veile Nuptials — Political Pri-
maries—Academy League.

Special Correspondence.

Fillmore, Millard Co., Aug. 24.—J. V.
Robison has returned from his mining
property at Deep Creek.

SMITH-VEILE NUPTIALS.

Cards are out announcing the marriage of Miss Louise Smith and Mr.
Earl Veile; the ceremony will take
place at the home of the bride's father in this city on the 29th inst.

POLITICAL PRIMARIES.

The Republicans of this precinct
held a primary last Wednesday night
and elected ten delegates to the county convention to be held in this city
August 30th, 1900. The Democrats will
hold their primary tomorrow night and
elect twelve delegates to the Democratic convention to be held in this
city on September 1st, 1900.

A number of men with teams have
gone to Wyoming to do railroad work
for a short time to earn money for the
coming winter, as their harvest has
been light compared with previous
years.

Those who attended the Stake conference held at Deseret last week enjoyed a spiritual feast.

Prof. E. S. Hinckley lectured to the
members of the Academy League last
Wednesday evening, and Prof. Newton
Noyes of the Sanpete Stake Academy
will address the same body next Sunday night. The work of the active
members of the league is very much
appreciated and has added much social
enjoyment to the instructive entertainments rendered recently.

Deseret Evening News
September 1, 1900

MILLARD REPUBLICANS.

Personnel of the Ticket Put in the Field at Fillmore.

[SPECIAL TO THE "NEWS."]

Fillmore, Utah, Sept. 1.—The Republicans of Millard county assembled in convention here yesterday and after attending to preliminary matters placed in nomination the following candidates:

Representatives to legislature—E. W. Kelly; attorney, Joshua Bennett; treasurer, Frank Rogers; assessor, F. T. Slaughter; clerk, T. C. Callister; sheriff, Vhasl Kelly; recorder, Mrs. L. E. Robison; commissioners, W. R. Thompson, John E. Hunter, C. W. Watts.

Deseret Evening News
September 13, 1900

FILLMORE.

Schools Will Open Monday Next — Light Fruit Crop.

Special Correspondence.

Fillmore, Millard County, Sept. 12.— A number of the young people of Fillmore leave for Provo to attend school at the Brigham Young academy, among them Mrs. Mary Henry and family, J. Harvey Melville and others.

Emily Frampton, a widow lady, is ill at her home.

John Kelly has received word of the death of Mrs. Quinton Kelly, his son's wife.

Mr. Allen Russel has gone to Springville to attend the funeral of the child of his daughter, Mrs. Mary Crandall.

The fruit crop of Fillmore is very poor this season on account of the drouth.

The district school starts on Monday next. Thomas D. Rees Jr., from Wales, Sanpete county, will be principal.

FILLMORE.

Schools Open With Increased Attendance—Death of Mrs. Frampton.

Special Correspondence.

Fillmore, Millard Co., Sept. 17.—Our public schools opened this morning with the following teachers: Thos. Reese, George Olsen, Grace Cropper, Maud E. Melville, Nellie Holbrook, Ella Bishop. The attendance was much larger than usual, and the citizens of our city are delighted with the bright prospects for the intellectual advancement of their children.

The citizens of our town have been called to mourn the death of one of the most estimable and kindhearted women known in Millard county, Mrs. Emily Frampton, who died yesterday of general debility, aged sixty. She was a native of England. Her work in a Church capacity was always appreciated, as were also the many benevolent acts of kindness which she was constantly bestowing on some one who was in need of the same. She never possessed anything that was too good for her friends, and was continually sacrificing her own comfort and interest for the comfort and interest of her friends.

Her husband died more than six years ago. The funeral services were held in the school house this afternoon, and the body interred in Fillmore cemetery.

FILLMORE'S BIG RALLY.

Messrs. Moyle and Weber Address Democratic Gathering.

(Special to The Herald.)

Fillmore, Oct. 3.—The Democratic campaign opened here tonight at the former capitol with Messrs. Moyle and Weber as the speakers.

The first speaker, Mr. Weber, was received with hearty applause and was listened to by the large audience with close attention. Mr. Weber first paid attention to the free silver question, then he paid his respects to the statements George Sutherland has been making in his campaign speeches. Getting down to the Cuban and the Philippine questions he made the most clear and logic argument the people of this city have ever listened to and it was most convincing to all.

He read in full from "The Herald" of Sunday Governor Wells' speech of July 4, 1898, showing the different policies advocated then and now by the Republicans. Weber was applauded heartily throughout his speech.

J. H. Moyle was the next speaker and introduced "as our next governor." He referred to Governor Wells' and Judge Botkin's speeches and made some telling points on the evils of trusts and combinations, also some good hits on the attitude of the Republican change of front on the silver question. Moyle made many votes for himself and party tonight.

Tomorrow night Judge Botkin and Orice Murdock speak here and on the 10th Thomas Marineaux, nominee for district judge, will hold forth.

The singing by the glee club was much appreciated.

Deseret Evening News
October 5, 1900

¡ORE FROM FILLMORE.

Samples Found Assaying Between $1,500 and $2,000 Per Ton.

A letter from Roy Dame, of Fillmore, conveys the news that Reube Keene has found some very rich ore in the mountains east of that town. Assay returns show values running between $1,500 and $2,000 to the ton. A number of samples of ore were also forwarded to be assayed. Mr. Dame says the Mud Springs district, about twenty miles northeast of Fillmore, is giving promise of big things. The country is staked off and a great number of men are busy prospecting.

Deseret Evening News
October 10, 1900

FILLMORE.

Court Holds Three Sessions — Judge Higgins Turns Out Grist of Business.

Special Correspondence.

Fillmore, Millard Co., Utah Oct. 9.—
The district court convened here this morning at 10 o'clock a. m. with Judge E. V. Higgins presiding. After setting the calendar the case of D. E. Crafts et al vs Ewen Cank et al was called, which was pending on demurrer of one of the defendants, Lloyd Crapper. After examination of the complaint, demurrer was overruled and defendant given twenty days in which to answer.

At 2 p. m.—State of Utah vs Louis Phillips, Jr., was called and defendant arraigned on the charge of burglary, and entered a plea of guilty. The defendant will be sentenced tomorrow.

Night Session—Stewart vs Stewart, an action for divorce, was called and the plaintiff, Victoria Stewart, Virgie Kelly and David Palmer were examined as witnesses, after which a decree of divorce was granted on the grounds of desertion.

Agnes George made application for divorce from her husband, James A. George, which the court granted after hearing the testimony of herself and witnesses. It appeared to the court that defendant had abandoned her and failed to support her.

Court then adjourned until tomorrow.

Salt Lake Herald
October 11, 1900

Phillips Goes to Prison.
(Special to The Herald.)

Fillmore, Oct. 10.—Louis Phillips, Jr., who pleaded guilty to burglarizing a store at Deseret and stealing six bottles of whisky, was sentenced by Judge Higgins to one year in the state prison. The young man has many sympathizing friends and showed a number of circumstances of mitigation of his penalty. The business was very light this term. District Attorney Marioneaux being the only attorney from the outside, the other lawyers preferring to talk politics rather than try law suits. Court adjourned till the next regular term.

MARRIAGE LICENSES.

The following permits to wed were issued last week by the county clerk of Salt Lake county:

Charles M. Foukes, Almy, Wyo.
Edith Bel, Almy, Wyo.
Andrew Tangren, Moab
Anna Somerville, Moab
Thomas Brown, Lajara, Colo.
Frances M. Kelly, Lajara, Colo.
Henry Wynder, Cardston, Canada
Ethel Davies, Cardston, Canada
George F. Sevey, Colonia Juarez, Mex.
Anna C. Heder, Colonia Juarez, Mex.
William J. Mumford, Beaver
Martha Canning, Bingham Junction
Joseph L. Sorenson, Leamington
Annie E. Johnson, Leamington
Leander S. Harris, Harrisville
Eliza A. Barlow, Ogden
James R. Turman, Salem, Ida.
Selma M. Anderson, Salem, Ida.
Elbridge L. Thomas, Salt Lake City
Flora T. Griffin, Salt Lake City
John J. Hutzly, Harrisville
Anna B. Quigley, Harrisville
Joseph Falkner, Eureka
Fretriker Trautwein, Salt Lake City
Wilford N. Ward, Salem, Ida.
Mary E. Jacobs, Island, Ida.
Joseph F. White, Plano, Ida.
Eliza M. Chandler, Plano, Ida.
Niels A. Peterson, Hinckley
Annie S. Walker, Hinckley
James R. Hughes, Samaria, Ida.
Elizabeth Jenkins, Samaria, Ida.
James W. Richards, St. Joseph, Ariz.
Mary Westover, St. Joseph, Ariz.

Robert Roden, jr., Salt Lake City
Pansy M. Yeager, Salt Lake City
William R. Robinson, Marion, Ida.
Viiate Bates, Marion, Ida.
Earl J. Kidd, Marysvale, Ida.
Estella M. McGavin, Marysvale, Ida.
Lars P. Amtoft, Oasis
Christeen Anderson, Oasis
Frank J. Westcott, Park City
Margaret Kearns, Salt Lake City
Jay T. Harris, Salt Lake City
Nellie M. Bransford, Salt Lake City
Don C. Spafford, Annabella
Elizabeth Hickey, Providence
Harvey H. Cluff, Provo
Freda Barnum, Provo
John Roberts, Goshen
Mary Fryer, Goshen
Hyrum A. Green, Garden City
Florence H. Hollingsworth, Salt Lake City
George Poulter, Deseret
Margaret J. Parker, Salt Lake City
Joseph A. Harris, Richfield
Rhoda Shepherd, Beaver
Albert S. Newman, Leorin, Ida.
Julia Anderson, Holliday
John E. Hepworth, Grover
Boletta C. Thomsen, Grover
Stephen M. Bailey, Salt Lake City
Rose Rutherford, Salt Lake City
Junius Romney, Colonia Juarez, Mex.
Gertrude Stowell, Colonia Juarez, Mex.
Peter Q. Barker, Escalante
Johanna Roundy, Escalante
Leo T. Carter, Greenville
Caroline A. Webb, Hinckley
William H. Swift, Salt Lake City
Claudia West, Salt Lake City
William C. Wrest, Salt Lake City
Maud Hider, Ogden
Judson A. Mabey, Bountiful
Ruby P. Pickett, Marion, Ida.

Edwin P. Bullock, Salt Lake City
Katie Buchanan, Salt Lake City
David Adamson, Murray
Edith B. Gibbs, Murray
Joseph Evans, Salt Lake City
Hannah H. Langton, Salt Lake City
Chris E. Christensen, Salt Lake City
Sena Carney, Ogden
William F. Asimus, Richfield
Callie Ottle, Tennessee, Mo.
James T. Atkinson, jr., Woods Cross
Anna M. Rudy, North Point
Frank Movobek, Salt Lake City
Marcia E. Ingersoll, Salt Lake City
John Strom, Bingham
Anna Dalin, Bingham
Henry Bews, Salt Lake City
Rose Roundy, Salt Lake City
Emil Anderson, Murray
Luina Erickson, Murray
Samuel Jones, Evanston, Wyo.
Amelia Peterson, Salt Lake City
Abe Webb, Eureka
Hilda C. Nelson, Eureka
Frank H. Ireland, Salt Lake City
Lillie Rafferty, Salt Lake City
Frank W. Peterson, Mercur
Carolina Johnson, Salt Lake City
Robert V. King, Fillmore
Herma L. Robison, Fillmore

Salt Lake Herald
October 19, 1900

FILLMORE RESIDENTS GAVE SPELLBINDERS MORE THAN THEY HAD BARGAINED FOR

(Special to The Herald.)

Fillmore, Oct. 18.—Governor Wells, C. E. Allen and George Sutherland received quite a reception today, after a hard week's work on the part of all the leading Republicans, with some expense attached. Horsemen were engaged to go out to meet the party, who were escorted to the hall.

Both Republicans and Democrats honored the governor by attending the rally, and he and his associates had a crowded house. Governor Wells, upon being introduced, was heartily applauded. He spoke of his economical government during the past five years, praising himself and party for same; attempted to give a plausible reason for vetoing the eight-hour law and said if the same law ever came before him he would do the same thing over again.

His explanation on his change from silver was rather interesting.

George Sutherland followed the governor and spoke on the silver question.

Sutherland was challenged by State Senator Robison to discuss the silver question before the people of Millard, and in making the challenge Mr. Robison said, "I will give you thirty minutes to my twenty."

Mr. Sutherland refused to accept the challenge, under the plea of "not sufficient time," and refused Robison the courtesy of a few minutes in which to answer him; but the challenge badly rattled the Salt Lake gentleman.

Ex-Congressman Allen followed. His remarks were the most interesting of the three. In reading the platforms of 1896 and 1900 Allen only read part and was called down by a gentleman in the audience, who said Allen was trying to deceive the people. Allen replied hotly and denied the charge. Some very warm words passed back and forth and for a few seconds it looked as though serious trouble would occur, but it was avoided by a little tact.

Throughout the meeting was a warm one, but not a vote-getting one, for there was too much abuse. The music by the glee clubs was the most interesting of the whole show.

Salt Lake Herald
November 2, 1900

SPLENDID MEETING ADDRESSED BY CRANE AND THORSEN.

Former Tells Why He Left the Republican Party and Quotes President Snow.

(Special to The Herald.)

Fillmore, Nov. 1.—Politics are very warm in Millard county these days, and they will continue so till the election is over. A hard and bitter fight is being waged. Charges and counter charges are made and high officials here are getting mixed up in the political struggle. The trouble originated by Bishop Callister's accepting the nomination for county clerk on the Republican ticket. The Democrats claim he did so without a permit from the church authorities, while he and the Republicans say the permit was granted. Things have gone so far that only a church trial can settle matters and this is expected right after election.

The battle of ballots will, as usual, be very close in this county, both parties claim it, but from a conservative canvass the Democrats feel confident of winning by a majority of thirty to sixty.

Tonight Charles Crane and L. C. Thorsen spoke here. One of the largest audiences ever seen in the meeting house greeted them. From appearances the whole town was in attendance. The first speaker was Mr. Crane, and he was heartily received. He said he had a duty to perform and would fill it to the best of his ability. He explained why he left the Republican party. While doing this he was applauded time and again. He said he was a larger sheep owner now than when he belonged to the Republican party. Only last Sunday, he said, President Snow assured him that he (Snow) wanted the people of Utah to vote as their convictions dictated. Mr. Crane said he stood today as formerly, but he would not let Mark Hanna debauch and corrupt him. He spoke on the several issues of the campaign and made one of the most interesting and convincing talks heard in the old ex-capital during this campaign. His talk has turned a number of doubtful voters and the Democrats here tonight are very jubilant.

L. C. Thorsen followed with an interesting talk on the trusts. He said he was certain of being elected but wanted a handsome majority. The meeting throughout was a very interesting one.

Salt Lake Herald
November 4, 1900

BIG MEETING AT FILLMORE.

Crowds Turn Out to Hear Crane and Thoresen.

(Special Correspondence.)

Fillmore, Nov. 1—Charles Crane and wife and I. C. Thoresen arrived here at [...] a. m. and were received by a host of Democrats at the Huntsman house. The reception continued for nearly two hours

and not only Democrats but many Republicans welcomed the visitors, especially Mr. and Mrs. Crane, their former neighbors.

Early in the afternoon people came in from counties and surrounding towns and by [...] the hall was crowded, and standing room at a premium when Messrs. Crane, Thoresen, the speakers, and the committee who escorted them to the hall arrived just before 8 o'clock.

Amos Greenwood acted as chairman. The glee club of some twenty-five members sang a selection.

Mr. Crane was then introduced and spoke upon the issues of the campaign for over an hour, having the undivided attention of the vast audience and receiving hearty applause. Many Republicans came to hear Mr. Crane explain how and why he left the g. o. p., and his explanation upon this subject was complete. He showed that the Republican party had lost him and all other Lincoln Republicans and sold out to Mark Hanna and the money power of the land.

"I stand where I always stood, and shall remain, the constitution and the flag, equality of all men before the law and a government for, by and of the people," said the speaker. "These cardinal principles, my neighbors, friends and former political associates, are worth a thousand times more than a party name, and you should vote them on Nov. 6, which will be done by supporting that great American, William J. Bryan, and the Democratic ticket."

The glee club sang "The Thomas Kearns Silver Cup."

I. C. Thoresen was then introduced and spoke nearly an hour upon the silver question, trusts and their remedy and the political integrity of the people of Utah. He assured the meeting that Utah would give Mr. Bryan a handsome majority and maintain its record in the past on bimetallism and in support of constitutional rights of all people under our flag, made in our territorial days. He described the formation and operation of trusts, explained the amendments to the constitution to be voted for at the coming election, and advised all to vote for the same in the interests of the people of the state.

Mr. Thoresen closed by saying he had heard it predicted that the time would come when the constitution of our country would hang by a thread or be trampled in the dust and this people would be required to "rally to its defense." That time is now, and the "rally" should be on Nov. 6 by voting the Democratic ticket straight.

Deseret Evening News
November 8, 1900

Salt Lake Herald
November 11, 1900

The Fillmore Progress, printed in the heart of Millard county, which went stoutly for sound money on Tuesday, isn't a stickler for gold in exchange for subscriptions. Wheat or cordwood will satisfy the Progress just now.

Deseret Evening News
November 14, 1900

MILLARD COUNTY OFFICERS.

All Republicans Except Attorney
and Surveyor.

Special Correspondence.

Fillmore, Millard Co., Nov. 12.—The county court was in session yesterday and to day making the official canvass of the election and declaration of the county officers elected. The following named persons will serve the people of Millard county in the official capacities named for the next ensuing two years:

For County Commissioners—W. R. Thompson, C. W. Watts, and John E. Hunter.

For County Clerk—T. C. Callister.

For Treasurer—Frank Rogers.

For Recorder—J. E. Robison.

For County Attorney—James Alex. Melville.

For Sheriff—Virgil Kelly.

For Surveyor—Willard Rogers.

For Assessor—F. T. Slaughter.

All the above named officers are Republicans except attorney and surveyor.

The official canvass gives W. H. King 856 votes and Sutherland 852 votes; all the Republican State officers and the Republican presidential electors received a plurality vote ranging from fifty to one hundred votes.

LIVE STOCK NOTES.

Salina, Utah, Press: Neal McMillan, of Salt Lake was in town Thursday. He is preparing to ship 800 cattle to Denver in a few days.

The fat stock show now on at Pittsburg, Pa., is said to be a great success. It continues till Monday night.

Stockmen are preparing for a storm, as the weather signals point that way.

Fillmore, Millard County, Progress: "Joe" Carling has gone in the sheep business on a small scale. Last week and this he and his brother, Abe, purchased about 190 head.

Tooele Transcript: John Erickson of Grantsville has delivered 159 head of cattle to Sol Worthington at Pilots Peak, Tecoma, Nevada.

Clear Lake, Millard County, Review: A sheepman lost about 159 head of sheep from some unknown cause in the cedars east of here. With his consent some young men made a very good thing pelting them.

Salt Lake Herald
November 18, 1900

PRESIDENT PARTRIDGE OF UTAH STAKE
PASSES FROM LIFE TO DEATH

(Special to The Herald.)

Provo, Nov. 17.—President Partridge of the Utah stake passed peacefully away this morning at 4.15 o'clock. He was surrounded by a large number of his family. He passed a comparatively easy night,

but gradually grew worse until the spark of life disappeared.

Funeral services will be held from the stake tabernacle Monday afternoon.

President Edward Partridge was born June 25, 1833, at Independence, Mo. He was the son of Edward Partridge, sr., who was one of the first bishops of the Mormon church and one of the early builders of the church in Illinois and Missouri. It is said that Edward Partridge, sr., was the owner of valuable real estate in Jackson county, Mo., the legal title to which descends to the surviving wife and children of deceased. Mr. Partridge has lived 67 years of great usefulness, both in a church and civil way. He was born into the Mormon church, and when but a young man drove an ox team across the plains, arriving in Utah in the early '50s. Here he

has lived ever since, with the exception of brief periods spent on foreign missions.

Mr. Partridge has lived in different places of the state, notably in Farmington, Salt Lake City, and Fillmore, and held important ecclesiastical and civil positions wherever he has been. He resided in Fillmore for upwards of fifteen years, where he raised the major portion of his large family. He held the position of probate judge in Millard county, was bishop of Fillmore, superintendent of the Fillmore Co-operative Mercantile institution, and was a member of the presidency of the Millard stake of Zion.

Mr. Partridge was also prominently connected with the "united order" movement of the Mormon church in early days. While a young man, only 20 years old, he was sent to the Sandwich Islands, where he filled a creditable mission. After his return he married Sarah Lucretia Clayton and later on took a second wife, Lizzie Buxton, by both of whom he raised families. This second wife died a   years ago, but his first wife survives him.

In the year 1882 he was again sent to the Sandwich Islands with one of his families on a mission, and was made president of the Sandwich Islands mission. He was closely identified with the early development of the sugar industry of the islands. He returned to Utah in 1885 and settled on a farm on Provo bench, and was immediately called to act as counselor to the late President Smoot, whom he succeeded as president of the Utah stake. He has also been a member of the legislature and was one of the members of the first constitutional convention.

Mr. Partridge leaves a wife and a sister, Mrs. Caroline Lyman, who was a wife of the late Apostle Amasa Lyman, now living in Oak City, Millard county, and twelve children, nineteen grand-children and one great-grand child, who are   in different parts of Utah and adjoining states.

President Partridge has always been an industrious,   conservative man, scrupulously religious and a lover of his home, accustomed to the communities in which he has lived, naturally a leader of men and constantly called to the higher councils of his church and country. For   time past he has expressed himself that he was ready to go to the great beyond, and when his last illness came upon him he apparently gave up all hope of surviving.

During the last few years he has suffered much from various ailments, which has caused him to be somewhat despondent at times.

He had a wide acquaintance in Utah and a host of intimate friends are left to mourn his death.

Deseret Evening News
November 27, 1900

FILLMORE.

STAKE CONFERENCE AT KANOSH

Fell a Victim to Typhoid — Precautions to Prevent Its Spread.

Special Correspondence.

Fillmore, Millard County, Nov. 26.— The four-year-old son of John Woolsey's died early this morning with typhoid fever; he has been sick for several weeks and has had the best care a watchful mother and kind friends could give him. Funeral services will be held tomorrow.

Two other children of the same family are down with the same disease but their condition is not thought to be critical; the children are not permitted to attend the schools and every precaution is being taken by the local board of health to prevent the spread of the disease.

A large number of people who reside here are attending conference at Kanosh, which convened yesterday; the remarks made by Apostle Grant were very appropriate and much appreciated. President Hinckley also made his report on the condition of the Stake, as did many of the Bishops on the condition of the wards which was much more pleasing than some had expected; from the reports all the Church organizations are in working condition except the religious class, and many of them are making rapid advancement along the lines indicated by the nature of the work they are performing.

Mr. and Mrs. Alex. Melville returned from Kanosh last evening where they had been summoned to attend the funeral of Mrs. Roberts, a sister of the latter, who died there last Thursday morning of pneumonia.

Salt Lake Herald
December 1, 1900

FILLMORE'S HARD LUCK.

Millard County Afflicted By Drouth and Republican Landslide.

"The storm god certainly has it in for Fillmore," declared Joshua Greenwood, the newly-elected district attorney for the Fifth district. "After the awful drouth of the past two years down in our county, we had to read it before we knew there had been a storm. I never have seen anything just like it. It rained and snowed beautifully north and south of us, but the precipitation seemed to jump right over the Fillmore region, and our country is just as dry as ever.

"And right on that came the Republican landslide. There certainly is an unholy influence at work somewhere."

Mr. Greenwood was one of the Democrats who survived the slide, being the running mate of Judge Marioneaux. His district includes Juab, Millard, Beaver, Iron and Washington counties, and he anticipates being kept busy.

"There is some excitement down that way," continued Mr. Greenwood, "over the recent decision of the supreme court making the filing of information by district attorneys illegal. The impression seems to be that a good many crooks will have to be released, but some lawyers take the stand that the men never have been in jeopardy, since the filings were illegal, and can be tried again. Even then there is much of the evidence that cannot be collected. It is possible that the fellow who killed Policeman Strong in Provo will get away."

Mr. and Mrs. Greenwood are at the White House. They expect to return south today.

Salt Lake Herald
December 14, 1900

Death of "Blinkey" Fillmore.

A. M. Fillmore, commonly known as "Blinkey" Fillmore, a well known character in police circles, died at the county infirmary last night. Yesterday he strolled into the Gospel mission in a sick condition, and as he had no money to pay for medical treatment he was sent to the infirmary, where he died a short time after arriving. He was 42 years of age and has been in Salt Lake for five or six years and was usually engaged in horse trading. It is said he has no relatives here, but leaves a divorced wife in the southern part of the state.

34079431R50301

Made in the USA
San Bernardino, CA
20 May 2016